W9-DDW-541

BK 305.896 I35
IN BLACK AMERICA, 1968: THE YEAR OF AWAKENING
1 1969 11.25 FV
3000 324801 30012
St. Louis Community College

WITHDRAWN

St. Louis Community
College

INTERNATIONAL LIBRARY OF NEGRO LIFE AND HISTORY

INTERNATIONAL LIBRARY OF

IN BLACK AMERICA

1968: The Year of Awakening

Compiled and Edited with an Introduction by

PATRICIA W. ROMERO

PUBLISHERS COMPANY, INC., NEW YORK, WASHINGTON, LONDON

under the auspices of

THE ASSOCIATION FOR THE STUDY OF NEGRO LIFE AND HISTORY

LIBRARY OF CONGRESS CATALOG CARD NO. 69-17399

PRINTED IN THE UNITED STATES OF AMERICA
FIRST EDITION

WORLD-WIDE DISTRIBUTION BY
UNITED PUBLISHING CORPORATION, WASHINGTON, D.C.

 13

To

CHARLES H. WESLEY

Editor-in-Chief, CHARLES H. WESLEY
Research Editor, PATRICIA W. ROMERO
Production Editor, ALLAN S. KULLEN
Art Director, ARCHIE MIDDLETON
Copy Editor, EMILY EVERSHED
Editorial Coordinator, ELIZABETH KRAMER

Preface

THE Association for the Study of Negro Life and History joins with Publishers Company, Inc., in presenting this new series of volumes which treat in detail the cultural and historical backgrounds of Black Americans. This Association, a pioneer in the area of Negro History, was founded on September 9, 1915, by Dr. Carter G. Woodson, who remained its director of research and publications until his death in 1950.

In 1916 Dr. Woodson began publishing the quarterly *Journal of Negro History*. In 1926 Negro History Week was launched, and since that time it has been held annually in February, encompassing the birth dates of Abraham Lincoln and Frederick Douglass. The *Negro History Bulletin* was first published in 1937 to serve both schools and families by making available to them little-known facts about Black life and history.

During its fifty-four years of existence, the Association for the Study of Negro Life and History has supported many publications dealing with the contributions of Negro Americans to the growth and development of this country. Its activities have contributed to the increasing interest in the dissemination of factual studies which are placing the Negro in true perspective in the mainstream of American history.

We gratefully acknowledge the contributions of previous scholars, which have aided us in the preparation of this *International Library of Negro Life and History*. Our grateful acknowledgment is also expressed to Charles W. Lockyer, president of Publishers Company, Inc., whose challenging approach has made possible this library.

Though each of the volumes in this set can stand as an autonomous unit, and although each author has brought his own interpretation to the area with which he is dealing, together these books form a comprehensive picture of the Negro experience in America. The three history volumes give a factual record of a people who were brought from Africa in chains and who today are struggling to cast off the last vestiges of these bonds. The anthologies covering music, art, the theatre and literature provide a detailed account of the Black American's contributions to these fields—including those contributions which are largely forgotten today. Achievement in the sports world is covered in another volume. The volume on the Negro in medicine is a history of the Black American's struggle for equality as a medical practitioner and as a patient. The selected Negro leaders in the biography book represent the contributions and achievements of many times their number. The documentary history sums up the above-mentioned material in the words of men and women who were themselves a part of Black history. Lastly, the year book covers the recent developments in Black America.

CHARLES H. WESLEY

Washington, D.C.

Contributors

J. Erroll Miller is at present serving as visiting professor in the Department of Police Administration at Indiana University, Bloomington, Indiana. He is on leave from Lincoln University in Missouri, where he is professor of government, head of the Department of History and Government and chairman of the Division of the Social Sciences. His articles and book reviews have appeared in *Public Opinion Quarterly*, *Journal of Negro History*, *Mid-West Journal*, *Annals*, *Phylon*, *Journal of Social Science Teachers*, *Quarterly Review of Education among Negroes*, *Negro Educational Review* and *Choice*.

St. Clair Drake is at present professor of anthropology at Roosevelt University in Chicago. He is co-author (with Horace R. Cayton) of *Black Metropolis* (1945). Recently he has published articles in *Negro Americans*, edited by Talcott Parsons and Kenneth Clark (1966); the *New York Times Magazine*'s "Symposium on Violence"; and *Urban Riots: Violence and Social Change*, edited by R. H. Connery (1968). He is working on a book currently titled *Black Diaspora*, a study of the flow of Negroes to the New World and of the Black American's influence on Africa.

Daniel C. Thompson is professor of sociology, chairman of the Division of the Social Sciences and director of research at Dillard University in New Orleans. In addition to many articles and reviews, he has published two books, *The Eighth Generation* (1959) and *The Negro Leadership Class* (1963).

John Ohliger is assistant professor of adult education at Ohio State University. He is editor and chief writer of *Mass Media/Adult Education*, a monthly newsletter of the Mass Media in Adult Education section of the Adult Education Association of the U.S.A., and consulting editor of *Adult Education*.

Prince Wilson is Executive Secretary of the Atlanta University Center Corporation. He has written numerous articles and book reviews for *Phylon* and other journals. He has been consultant to the U.S. Civil Rights Commission, to the Miles College program for curriculum revision and to the Ohio Emancipation Proclamation Centennial Committee, and has been sponsor to the Atlanta program of the Government Affairs Institute.

Edward F. Sweat is professor of history and chairman of the Department of Social Science at Clark College in Atlanta. He has published articles in such journals as *Phylon*, *Negro History Bulletin* and *Journal of Negro History*.

Lyn Shepard is now serving as Congressional correspondent for the *Christian Science Monitor*. Before joining the *Monitor*'s Washington bureau, he reported on the "War on Poverty," from the New York bureau, and on general social welfare trends from the New England bureau. He was also an editorial assistant in their American news department.

James M. Nabrit, III, is associate counsel for the NAACP Legal Defense and Educational Fund, in New York City. He has argued before the U.S.

Supreme Court cases involving such issues as the Constitutionality of loitering laws (*Shuttlesworth* v. *Birmingham*), the right of public housing tenants to a hearing before evictions (*Thorpe* v. *Durham Housing Authority*) and school and park segregation; he has been actively involved in major civil rights cases.

Herbert Hill is national labor director of the NAACP and teaches at the New School for Social Research in New York City. During 1968 Mr. Hill was distinguished professor of American history at San Fernando Valley State College, California. Mr. Hill is the author and editor of several books, and his writings have appeared in many scholarly journals. He is co-editor (with Arthur M. Ross) of *Employment, Race and Poverty* and editor of *Anger and Beyond: The Negro Writer in the United States* (1966).

Edward D. Irons is executive director of the National Bankers Association, an organization for Black-owned banks, and head of the Department of Business Administration at Howard University. He is also consultant-president pro tempore of the New York Urban Coalition Venture Capital Corporation and is a member of the Mayor's Economic Development Advisory Committee, Washington, D.C.

Paget L. Alves, Jr., is a housing and urban development consultant. Before the establishment of his firm, Pat Alves and Associates Corp., he served the National Urban League as associate director of housing, negotiating grants for open occupancy housing, assisting in the development of non-profit corporations to build or rehabilitate housing, and stimulating stronger housing programs.

Charles Prejean is executive director of the Federation of Southern Cooperatives, a central service organization for member grass-roots cooperatives. He and his staff provide forty-five cooperatives representing 15,000 families in eleven states with assistance in training, marketing, financing and organizing. Their activities range from agricultural marketing to handicraft production, from consumer to credit union projects.

Richard Sommerfeld is professor and chairman of the Department of Sociology at Capital University, Columbus, Ohio. He is the author of *Socio-Economic Circumstances of Negroes.*

John Oliver Killens—novelist, screen writer and lecturer—is currently conducting a seminar on Black culture and a writers' workshop as adjunct professor at Columbia University. Before this he was writer-in-residence at Fisk University. His interest in Black literature led him to help found, and to serve ten years as chairman of, the Harlem Writers Guild. Mr. Killens' novels include *Youngblood*, *And Then We Heard the Thunder*, *'Sippi* and *The Slaves*. His articles have appeared in *Ebony*, *Nation*, *Negro Digest* and *African Forum Magazine*. He has published a book of essays, *Black Man's Burden*, and has just completed a novel, *The Cotillion.*

Elton C. Fax has illustrated some twenty-seven books and has exhibited in museums in New York, Baltimore and Washington, D.C. He is the author of *West Africa Vignettes* and is a contributing writer to the *International Library of Negro Life and History* and to *Freedomways* magazine. He is mentioned in *Who's Who in American Art*, *Who's Who in the East* and *The Dictionary of International Biography.*

Orde Coombs and **Barry Beckham** are free-lance writers in New York. Mr. Coombs is co-author of *Eastern Religions in the Electric Age* and is a graduate of Yale. Mr. Beckham, whose first novel will be published by Walker and Company, is a graduate of Brown University.

Lindsay Patterson is editor and compiler of *The Negro in Music and Art*, *Anthology of the American Negro in the Theatre* and *An Introduction to Black Literature in America.* He worked with Langston Hughes on numerous projects, notably the books *Black Magic* and *The Best Short Stories by Negro Writers*, and has contributed articles and short stories to *Freedomways*, *Saturday Review* and the anthology *The Best Short Stories by Negro Writers.* He is now a regular contributor on theatre and films to the *New York Times* and is working on a novel, *Pierian Spring.*

Luther P. Jackson, Jr., is associate professor at the Columbia University Graduate School of Journalism. Previous positions held include the directorship of Communicating Research on the Urban Poor (CROSS-TELL) in Washington, D.C., and associate directorship of public relations for the NAACP. He was formerly a reporter for the *Washington Post* and the Baltimore *Afro-American*.

Ernest Kaiser, a member of the staff of the Schomburg Collection for more than twenty years, is a researcher and bibliographer whose help is acknowledged in many books. He has published critical essays and reviews in *Freedomways*, *Negro Digest*, *Science and Society*, *Journal of Negro Education*, *Phylon* and other magazines. His essays are included in the books *Harlem: A Community in Transition* (1964) and *William Styron's Nat Turner: Ten Black Writers Respond* (1968), both edited by John Henrik Clarke.

Clifton F. Brown is both assistant librarian and a divinity scholar at the School of Religion, Howard University, where he specializes in the area of church history. A member of several academic honor societies, he is the recipient of the Protestant Theological Fellowship for 1969–70.

Theodore D. Harris is a faculty member of the University of Minnesota and is a specialist in both military history and Negro history. He is the editor of *Negro Frontiersman: The Western Memoirs of Henry O. Flipper, First Negro Graduate of West Point* (1963) and is preparing a forthcoming edition of Flipper's autobiography, *The Colored Cadet at West Point*. In addition, he is preparing a publication of the overland army journal of John H. Alexander, the second Negro graduate of West Point.

Herbert M. Morais is currently engaged in research and writing. His first book, *Deism in Eighteenth Century America*, was published in 1934, and his latest, *The History of the Negro in Medicine*, in 1967. His contributions have appeared in collective works such as the *Dictionary of American Biography* and in numerous journals.

Wilhelmena S. Robinson is currently an associate professor of history at Central State University, Wilberforce, Ohio. She is a consultant on the inclusion of the contributions of minority groups in the school curriculum for the Yellow Springs, Ohio, public school system. She is the author of *Historical Negro Biographies*.

Dave Sendler is executive editor of *Pageant* magazine and is currently writing a paperback book, *Football Stars of 1969*. He was a former associate editor of *Sport* magazine, and has written numerous articles on sports and sports figures.

Foreword

TODAY as never before the American public has become conscious of its Black component. This heightened awareness of the presence of the Afro-American has stimulated the quest for accurate information about his activities and attitudes. This inquiry as to the texture of Negro life comes from many quarters, including teachers and their students, public officials, newspaper writers and the mass media in general. Hence the need for reliable data on the contemporary Black American is well served by a year book such as this.

As a reference work this volume, like others of its type, has a wide-ranging scope. Anything less would fail to convey the always complex and often kaleidoscopic pattern of life in America, in whatever section of the country or segment of the population. However, as in any general work dealing with the Black experience in our land, there is no escaping the recurring theme of unusual frustrations to be faced and unusual exertions to be put forth. The achievers, those who overcame, are ever present in these pages, with the full spotlight falling on them in the sections on biographies and personalities of the year.

This work has its share of statistics and listings. But not in every instance do cold facts speak for themselves. Taking this into account, this year book opens with a series of articles which provide analysis and interpretation. Written by authorities, these articles draw their sustenance from the hard data, the most recent and reliable. But they give to it an angle of vision that must command our respect even when we might not concur in all their conclusions.

Among their other features these articles serve as a bridge between the past and the present. The charge is often made that Americans approach their national problems with no sense of history, and hence with a crippling lack of perspective. Certainly this volume is not guilty on that score. Its auspices, no less than its content, are reassuring as to an awareness of the living past.

This annual is the product of an organization founded by the late Carter G. Woodson, the great pioneer in the scientific study of the Black experience in America. Woodson was a past master in every sense of the term, founding the Association for the Study of Negro Life and History and issuing the path-breaking quarterly *The Journal of Negro History*. A man of impressive scholarship, Woodson was a historian's historian. But he did not dwell on the Olympian heights of history. Believing that the past had something to say to the present, he sought to set the record straight in order to bring about a better social order. Hence the organizations he founded, particularly the Associated Publishers, issued a variety of informational materials, including pictures, calendars and posters.

No year book was ever brought out by Woodson—his day, after all, had only twenty-four hours. But such a work would have fitted well into the range of his interests and the scope of his activities.

Woodson's colleague and successor, the truly eminent Charles H. Wesley, has expanded the work of the Association. Among other notable ventures, Dr. Wesley inaugurated and has been editor-in-chief of the *International Library of Negro Life and History*, a comprehensive, ten-volume set of reference books. It is to Dr. Wesley's research editor in this series, Patricia W. Romero, that we owe the present year book.

Mrs. Romero, like Dr. Wesley, not only did editorial work on the ten-volume set, but also contributed substantially to its writing. To this annual, then, Mrs. Romero brings considerable skills as an editor and an author. A student of the career of Carter G. Woodson and an executive in the Association for over five years, Mrs. Romero personifies a point of view and exhibits a technical competence that augur well for the high usefulness of this reference work.

BENJAMIN QUARLES

Baltimore, Maryland

Editor's Note

TO PROPERLY ASSESS the value of and the help from my associate, Elizabeth Kramer, is impossible. She had the often thankless task of being sure all the busy work was taken care of; of sending materials to authors; and of coordinating staff and assignments at the office. To say that I am extremely grateful to her is simply not adequate, but is quite true. Gretchen Fox prepared the Bibliography of books and Harriet Moger compiled the Annotated Bibliography of articles: each of them did an excellent job. For the editorial assistance given to both Mrs. Kramer and myself by Wendy Schempp, Barbara Dwyer, and part-time student workers; for the production work of Allan Kullen and Luther Stovall; for the copy editing by Emily Evershed; and for the cover design by Lloyd McNeill, I am also grateful; I thank everyone for their assistance, knowing that none of this could have come to publication without those above who gave of their services so graciously. For the format, selections and tone of the book I assume full responsibility.

P. W. R.

Table of Contents

Introduction

THE TRAGEDY which found its most poignant expression in 1968 in the violent deaths of Martin Luther King, Jr., and Robert F. Kennedy was ameliorated to some extent by an outstanding development of the year—the awakening of America. Amidst a bloody and riot-torn background in the spring of 1968, America was reminded of the fact that violence was not new to its society; that the Black revolution was predicated upon a conditioning of violent behavior patterns established before the country officially became a nation and which have continued ever since.

Only in 1968 a different mood was present. Blacks reacted violently to the passing of a leader —a nonviolent leader—and much of white America soon awakened to the reality that militant and aggressive men in the persons of Eldridge Cleaver, LeRoi Jones, Nathan Hare and Dick Gregory, among others, were to be formidable foes in the challenge to the status quo.

From the depths of violent reprisal came a series of new awakenings in 1968. These became evident in nearly every aspect of interracial relations and within Black America itself. The most obvious visual sign in Black America of this awakening was the widespread adoption of the Afro hair style by both men and women. Worn previously among pronounced militants and among students, the "Afro" was not conspicuous on the American scene until mid-1968, when it became the norm rather than the exception. Although the Afro was merely a new hair style, its roots went much deeper, reflecting the inner stirrings of the new surge of Black pride.

To look like whites, to emulate their fads and fashions, had become passé. From this growth of racial identity there came a new respect from whites—an awakening, on their part, to Blacks as equals, as a people who no longer pretended to be white or wanted to be white, but found their glory, laud and honor in their own innate beauty —in their Blackness, Brownness or Tanness. White America may not altogether have liked the growing Black awareness and pride which seemed to threaten the psychological grip which it had maintained on the "white" Negro, but it woke to a new regard for the Black man.

The year 1968, if nothing else is to be written about it, WAS the year of the Black *Man*. This emergence of Black masculinity from the depths of American society, where it had been buried for three hundred years, meant the beginning of the end for the stereotype. And with the Black man's assertion of his views and assumption of the dominant role within the group, a further awakening took place in relation to the Black woman.

Two Black women were especially prominent on the national scene in 1968. Mrs. Shirley Chisholm, the first Negro congresswoman ever elected, defeated civil rights leader James Farmer in November of that year. She had run on the Democratic Party ticket in Brooklyn. No statistics are available as to the breakdown of voting patterns, but it can be assumed that Mrs. Chisholm was elected by a matriarchal-middle class coalition which—despite the "year of awakening"—had not yet crumbled. There may also have been some pride on the part of the Black man to know that one of his women would achieve equality in the white-male-dominated Congress. This was a symbolic answer to yesterday's stereotype of the Black woman in relation to the white man.

The other woman who gained national attention in 1968 came to it unwittingly. Mrs. Coretta King was thrust into the limelight through the death of a Black man—her husband. The notice she received revolved around the man by whom she had been widowed. This reversal of the roles of the Black man and Black woman brought with it a profound appreciation of the feminine qualities of the Black woman, which were finally being placed in their right perspective.

However, it was not only Black America which gained a new appreciation of Blackness in 1968. The awakening of American society in general was seen on all fronts. The mass media, despite criticism, began diligently to pursue Black faces, until by the end of the year Blacks were seen in soap operas, newscasts, TV commercials, specials and prime time productions. When we view these new faces, the concept of the Black male as "catching on" is reinforced. The trend in radio and TV circles has been to place more men than women in the prize roles reserved for Black faces.

Hollywood, too, gradually began to broaden its use of Black actors and actresses—again with the stress mostly on the male. The life of photographer Gordon Parks was being planned for filming—the first positive attempt by Hollywood to portray the life of a Negro who had "made it" in the American tradition.

The conservative American business organizations, which had earlier awakened to the reality of the Black dollar, began to perceive the need of the Black masses for jobs and for training as part of the productive economy of the country. The need for skilled workers, in part, forced American big business to enter the Black ghettoes and make an attempt at on-the-job training programs for the unskilled. Whatever the motivation, the process began to be fairly widespread—on the surface, at least—by the end of the year.

But more important to the Black self-image was the growth of Black owned and operated small businesses. The formerly gradual evolving of concerns owned by Blacks met with an unprecedented spurt of growth in new types of businesses opened in 1968. These ran the gamut from Willie Mays' plans for a franchised national chain to the single design shop opened by a man in Washington, D.C. Black America awakened to its own initiative and abilities and had the power of conviction behind it.

Literature and the arts also reflected the year of the Black man. From shows in major art galleries to books selling in the top ten, Black men were noticed: their books were read, their works of art admired; and the results were an inner appreciation and an outward gain in respect. A "new" man had been born—after three hundred years of gestation—and America was in the process of getting to know him.

Unfortunately, not every facet of the awakening was operating to the benefit of the majority of Black people in every way. Perhaps nothing better illustrates this than the assault on Black faculties by the major, white-controlled, universities during 1968. Black students attending "white" colleges (and integrated public schools), presumably in quest of a better education, suddenly found themselves becoming "unculturated." They discovered that their new awareness of themselves was not being shared by administrations who provided no courses with which they could identify in a positive manner. Therefore, a clamor arose for Black studies programs across the nation, from major universities to small colleges.

This played havoc with the Black-oriented faculties in the still largely Negro schools, which are responsible for educating 50 per cent of the Negroes who seek higher education. By skimming off the cream of the Black faculties in these schools, the white schools created a brain-drain which in time could be devastating to the educational processes of the Negro-dominated colleges and universities. The white man, in reacting to the developing Black awareness, reverted to the old practice of filling his needs with no realization of the void he created in the process. This was but one problem arising in 1968, the effects of which will be felt far into the future if more Blacks are not sought for higher education and for graduate schools.

In each of the following articles in this book there is an analytical discussion of what happened in 1968. There are studies devoted to race relations and to political, social, cultural and economic developments. Some of the nation's leading authorities in their fields have contributed to this work—each giving his own interpretation of events as he saw them. But the unifying theme running through these studies is that of the awakening of Black America and the resultant reaction —whether to the left or to the right—of the rest of the country. All of this points to the fact that the problems were not solved by any means, and that the awakening did not signify the dawning of Utopia.

There was still poverty and hunger in the rural South and in the urban ghettoes. There was crime and violence everywhere, with overt acts of hostility committed by Black upon Black; by Black upon white; and, of course, by white upon Black. But Black America was working at the eradication of these evils. There was a new awareness on the part of Black people that they could help solve the problems of hunger and poverty, crime and violence, through group motivation of the Black brother and sister to overcome their psychological dependence on the white power structure.

At the same time, an awakening white America, confused by the new goals of the transitional Black leadership, seemed to be more anxious than ever to preserve its traditional institutions, although it was now making efforts to understand the changes which were occurring all over the nation. Traditionally in this country, when the economic institutions begin to move forward, the rest of the nation follows. Hopefully for all of us, 1968 was the beginning of such a move.

Black awareness really came to life in 1968, and began to filter down to the masses. Black power, Black culture, Black enterprise, Black ideals of beauty—all grew to real significance in 1968. But in none of them was the goal of equality met. The major task—that of attaining this equality—remains as a challenge to Black America, so that 1968 will be remembered not as the year of the "Black Fad" but as the beginning of a Black Reality.

PATRICIA W. ROMERO

Worthington, Ohio
April, 1969

SECTION I

The Reverend Channing Phillips was the first Negro to be nominated for the Presidency by a major political party. He attended the Democratic national convention in Chicago as chairman of the District of Columbia delegation.

The Negro in National Politics in 1968

J. Erroll Miller

THE YEAR 1968 was characterized by events which represented, as Elmo Roper puts it, "a mixture of confusion, apprehension, and hope." The ill-fated and especially unpopular war in Southeast Asia, the uncertainty over the continuing stability of the dollar, the assassinations of Dr. Martin Luther King and Senator Robert Kennedy, and the difficulty of ascertaining the "facts" of, and "what is going to result" from, the multiplicity of student, ideological, and racial protest movements accounted for much of the confusion and the apprehension rampant.

However, all was not frustration, despair and disillusionment. There was much that presaged a better day. President Lyndon Johnson's decision not to seek his party's nomination for the Presidency, and the entrance of Eugene McCarthy and Robert Kennedy into the race, with the ensuing dialogue over desirable methods of terminating the war in Vietnam, brought hope for peace. The rights and general welfare of all citizens—particularly of minorities, the disadvantaged and the unfortunate—were given a new affirmation by the United States Supreme Court's decisions dealing with "fair housing," aid to dependent children, the selection of jurors in cases involving capital punishment, the reclassifying of students who protested against selective service policies, wiretapping, "freedom of choice" in attending public schools, the right of illegitimate children to recover damages for the death of the mother upon whom they depended for support, and the right of a law enforcement officer to "stop and frisk" persons who appear suspicious, and by the agreement to hear arguments to the effect that Congressman Powell had been unconstitutionally denied his seat in the 90th Congress. The passage of the 1968 Civil Rights Act and the enactment of legislation on model cities, rent supplements for the poor, aid to education, methods of improving jury selection and the extension of government support for the economic opportunity programs contributed to the growing atmosphere of hope. For those who were especially apprehensive about "crime in the streets," "law and order," etc., the Omnibus Crime Control and Safe Streets Act of 1968 and the Report of the National Advisory Commission on Civil Disorders offered additional solace.

The temper, aspirations and activities of Negroes in 1968 must be examined within the above-mentioned conceptual framework, as Blacks constitute a significant proportion of this country's population. Negroes, who have become impatient, frustrated and disillusioned with the changes—mainly peripheral—which have been too long and too slow in coming, have begun to use more direct, and perhaps more sophisticated, approaches to extricate themselves from the plight which has forced them to accept a position of accommodation and subordination in the American scheme of things.

The national political scene has been greatly affected by the maturing political awareness, solidarity and aggressiveness—at times even militancy—of Blacks at the state and local levels of political expression—at the grass roots, if you will.

The Civil Rights Acts of 1957, 1960, 1964 and 1968, and the Voting Rights Act of 1965, together with mass demonstrations, the firm commitment of President Johnston to grant Negroes a full role in American society and the various

Supreme Court decisions affecting suffrage and political participation in general, have made it possible for American Blacks to become more effective members of the body politic, as voters, holders of public office, political party committeemen and committeewomen and delegates to party conventions. These opportunities, which had been available for some time to a limited degree on the national level, increased considerably on the state and local levels in 1968. It is in these latter areas that the demand for complete national political recognition and participation must have its genesis. It is there that Presidential electors are chosen, congressmen and senators are nominated and elected and delegates to the party nominating conventions are selected. Failure to become actively involved in those political expressions reduces the probability of getting favorable legislation passed by Congress, of securing appointments or gaining the necessary support for election to government positions, and often of receiving favorable national administrative reactions to important requests for policy changes which affect national and state programs.

Negro Candidates for Elective Offices

Presidency and Vice-Presidency. Excluding the "ceremonial" efforts which were made at the Democratic national convention to nominate the Reverend Channing Phillips for President and Georgia Representative Julian Bond for Vice-President of the United States, no Negro sought either of the major party nominations for those offices.

Three minor parties nominated Negro candidates for these positions in 1968. The Communist Party, which is excluded from the ballot in thirty-seven states, nominated Mrs. Charlene Mitchell for President. The Socialist Workers Party named Paul Boutelle for Vice-President. The newly formed Peace and Freedom Party chose Eldridge Cleaver over Dick Gregory to run at the head of its ticket. Cleaver was given 161½ delegate votes to Gregory's fifty-four. Cleaver was backed by the Freedom and Peace Party in Michigan.

Dick Gregory's candidacy for President was somewhat unique: he ran on the Freedom and Peace Party ticket in New York, where Cleaver was denied a place on the ballot because he was only thirty-three years old—two years below the United States Constitutional minimum age of thirty-five for a President. Gregory was also a candidate in four other states—in New Jersey and Pennsylvania on the Peace and Freedom slate and in Colorado and Virginia on the Freedom and Peace ticket. Since there were few basic philosophical differences between the tenets espoused by the Peace and Freedom Party and those advanced by the Freedom and Peace Party, it was hoped that voters could express their choices for the protest represented by these parties by casting their ballots for the candidate of either of them who appeared on the ballot in that particular state. It should be noted, however, that the Freedom and Peace Party supported Senator Eugene McCarthy in Arizona, although Cleaver's name appeared on the ballot as the Peace and Freedom candidate.

Gregory's targets during the campaign were what he called "moral fallout," the spreading cruelty and corruption, the disrespect for the dignity of any individual of any color, and the political decay that leads to immoral and illegal wars. His campaign appeals included the improvement of the plight of American Indians and the implementing of sanctions against Rhodesia by an "executive order" directing that "nothing except tuna fish, cranberry sauce, cigarettes and color TV sets" be exported there from the United States.

Several interesting developments took place during his campaign. His handbills were confiscated by the United States Secret Service in Nashville and in New York City, where complaints had been made that some of his money-sized handbills were showing up in automatic money-changing machines. The handbills, unlike dollar bills which bear an American eagle and a picture of George Washington, had a dove and a picture of Gregory on them. Protesting that his handbills had been seized because they constituted a threat to the political machine, he warned that his aides in Nashville were going to seek a federal injunction to stop the election on the grounds that his right to distribute campaign literature had been illegally interfered with.

Gregory had two other grievances. He protested strongly the refusal of the federal government to accord him the Secret Service protection which had been provided for the major parties' Presidential candidates. His other complaint involved the government's failure to give him the standard briefing on international affairs. "They gave my spot to Harold Stassen," he said. At the time Gregory was making these protests, two of his supporters filed a $5 million damage suit in a United States District Court against the three major television networks because of their refusal to grant him "equal time" in which to present his views to the American voters. They also asked for an injunction to force the networks to give him "equal time."

To show that he had the courage of his convictions, Gregory participated in a fish-in with some Indians in the Nisqually River as a protest against the alleged breaking of an 1854 treaty which guaranteed the Indians, in return for lands taken from them, that fish and game would belong to them "for as long as the sun shall shine and the grass shall grow and the mountains shall stand." He was given a ninety-day jail sentence for this illegal action. The United States Supreme Court rejected the Indians' claim to the fishing rights and affirmed Gregory's conviction.

Although Gregory and Cleaver directed their appeals for support to the same categories of voters, there were two notable differences. Gregory was the dramatist who used overt acts, within the generally accepted canons of decent language, to deliver his message. On the other hand, Cleaver was the philosopher who, in the opinion of this writer, relied on rationalizations and shockingly vile—at times revolting—language to tell his story. Another difference lay in the scope of the appeals. Gregory's concern transcended racial lines to include all poor people, while Cleaver devoted most of his message to matters which pertained to Black people—especially the undue and illegal actions of policemen (the "pigs") against Negroes and in Black communities.

Eldridge Cleaver, the nominee of the Peace and Freedom Party for President, is better known as the Minister of Information for the Black Panther Party in Oakland, California, and the author of *Soul on Ice*, a best-selling autobiography. Although Cleaver at age thirty-three was too young to fill the office of President even if he were to be elected, he waged a campaign which attracted attention—not because of the number of supporters he was able to win to his side but because of the unusual language which he used to convey his single-minded militancy on social relations in general and on racial relations in particular in this country.

His major attacks were directed against alleged police brutality in Black communities and the exploitation of poor Blacks. The following are examples of his campaign utterances:

> America is up against the wall. This whole apparatus, this capitalistic system and its institutions and police . . . all need to be assigned to the garbage can of history and I don't give a ——— who doesn't like it. . . . The right to revolution can't be taken from the people. . . . We can go nowhere unless we have the right to defend ourselves against the pig cops.

Speaking to a group of lawyers in a California city, he boasted:

> If I could get two machine guns out of this crowd, I wouldn't care if you applauded me or threw glasses at me. I'd get my black ——— out of here. I meant all of my insults to those who won't choose my side—the right side. You people can take your wallets, credit cards, and cut your mother ——— necks.

Cleaver's name appeared on the ballot in only four states: Arizona, Iowa, Michigan and Minnesota. Efforts to get his name on the ballot in Nebraska and New York failed because his petition did not have a sufficient number of valid signatures in the former state and because he was too young to qualify for the office in the latter state. Write-in campaigns were conducted in several states.

The Communist Party candidate, Mrs. Charlene Mitchell, age thirty-eight, who was until recently a resident of Los Angeles, where she was employed as a bookkeeper, moved to New York to join the party staff in midyear. She is a graduate of Herzl Junior College (Chicago). Mrs. Mitchell joined the party when she was sixteen and has been a member of the national committee since 1959. She regards racism as the number one issue in the United States. In addition, she feels that police should be disarmed and should live in the immediate communities in which they work, and that the residents of a community should be active participants in the administration of justice. To her, the recent Soviet action in Czechoslovakia was "regrettable, but necessary." She is unequivocally opposed to the present United States involvement in Vietnam. Her name appeared on the ballot in two states: Minnesota and Washington. Write-in campaigns were conducted in several other states, notably Ohio and California. During the campaign she protested the refusal of the federal government to provide her with the same Secret Service protection and the briefing on international affairs which had been given the major party candidates for the Presidency. Mrs. Mitchell expressed her true feelings regarding her chances for victory when she said, "It's really impossible for any Black person to aspire for the White House."

Paul Boutelle of Newark, age thirty-six, the Socialist Workers Party candidate for Vice-President, appeared on the ballot in twenty-one states. The major policies which this party stressed in 1968 were an immediate peace-in-Vietnam effort and Negro control of Black communities. Mr. Boutelle, who has very strong convictions on the "Black power" movement, in explaining his party's plank on the race issue, told a group of students at Georgia State College that "the Pledge of Allegiance [to the flag] of the United States is a lie. No black man should salute that rotten flag." Speaking of violence, he said: "We do not advocate violence, but we don't condone nonviolence. We advocate social revolution by any means necessary, any means."

He advised the United States to withdraw all of her troops from Vietnam immediately and to let that country "sink or swim." In addition, he urged all Black men to "stay home and fight your enemies here." In his view, no Black man should fight for the United States anywhere in the world.

During the campaign he warned his hearers and readers about the other candidates for President. He characterized George Wallace as an ignorant, frustrated white man, appealing to others like himself. Regarding the two major party candidates he said, "We are not fooled by the Humphreys and the McCarthys and the Nixons and the Muskies and the Agnews either because they all stand for the same rotten capitalistic government."

Congress. The decisions of the United States Supreme Court in the recent reapportionment cases (*Baker* v. *Carr*; *Reynolds* v. *Sims*; *Wesberry* v. *Sanders*) have had a significant impact on the manner in which state legislative bodies are establishing the boundaries of Congressional districts. The compact and contiguous rule has been given a new dimension—one which precludes the creation of districts which differ in size (population-wise) so greatly that voters in some areas are victims of the discount process: that is, their electoral expressions do not carry as much weight in the selection of public officials as do those in other areas which have about the same number of people.

The reapportionment decisions, coupled with the increased and more sophisticated political involvement of Negroes, have forced state legislators to draw Congressional district lines so that Blacks will have a better opportunity to send representatives from their communities to the United States House of Representatives. An overt manifestation of this was seen in 1968 when, for the first time, Negro congressmen were elected in Brooklyn, Cleveland and St. Louis.

In each of these cities both major parties nominated Black candidates in areas which had previously been represented by white congressmen. All three of the seats were won by Democrats. In St. Louis, William L. Clay defeated the Republican candidate Curtis C. Crawford in the newly created First Congressional District. Clay, a former alderman, is a local union official. Crawford, a lawyer, had served as an assistant circuit attorney in St. Louis.

The voters in the Twenty-first Congressional District in Cleveland elected Louis A. Stokes, a lawyer and brother of Mayor Carl Stokes. His opponent was Charles B. Lucas, a real estate broker.

Mrs. Shirley Chisholm, a member of the New York state legislature, defeated James Farmer, who served for many years as director of CORE. Mrs. Chisholm is the first Black woman to win a seat in Congress. On election night (or early the following morning, depending on the state) Vice-President Humphrey, after thanking his supporters and sending a congratulatory message to Mr. Nixon, rushed to the telephone to congratulate her on her victory. He told her: "Shirley, I'm sorry I won't be there to work with you."

The 91st Congress would have nine Negro members in the House of Representatives, all Democrats, and one senator, Edward Brooke of Massachusetts, a Republican. In addition to the three newly elected representatives, John L. Conyers, Jr. (D, Detroit), William L. Dawson (D, Chicago), Charles C. Diggs, Jr. (D, Detroit), Augustus F. Hawkins (D, Los Angeles), Robert N. C. Nix (D, Philadelphia), and Adam Clayton Powell (D, New York), each of whom had been elected to the 90th Congress, were reelected. Powell, because of allegedly improper conduct, was not seated in the 90th Congress. In 1968 he instituted legal action to be seated and to have his seniority rights restored. The United States Supreme Court agreed to review his case. In the meantime, he was reelected to the 91st Congress, which voted to seat him if he would pay a fine of $25,000 and agree to relinquish his seniority rights.

Other Blacks sought Congressional seats but, failing to secure the endorsement of the dominant political party in the district, they were easily defeated. It is not unusual for a minority party to nominate Negroes in districts where they do not have even a faint chance of winning. But when a party feels that it is in a really competitive position, Blacks find it very difficult to win a nomination. However, there are also social and economic protest parties which seek Negroes as candidates in order to dramatize a particular issue. These parties are not even in the game! Illustrative of this were the Congressional contests entered by the Peace and Freedom Party in California in the 1968 elections. In one Congressional district the party's candidate received 2,858 of a total vote of 187,895; in another, it was 5,042 of 181,036; and in a third district, the candidate was able to capture only 2,517 of the 135,797 votes cast.

As long as race continues to be a major determinant in the expression of voting choices, the number of Congressional districts which will elect Negroes will remain small. Despite the paucity of Blacks in Congress, the fact that they are in there—serving on committees, debating and voting on the issues—will contribute to the enactment of legislation which will benefit Negroes. As the number increases, the influence will be greater. Within the next decade or so we can reasonably expect such urban areas as Atlanta, Houston, Pittsburgh and Gary, with their rapidly rising Negro populations, to elect Black congressmen.

National Party Committees

Each political party's national committee, which has at least one man and one woman from each state, makes arrangements for the national convention, conducts the Presidential campaign, raises finances, runs national party affairs between conventions, and advises the President—if he is a member of that party—on many of the major appointments to public office at the national level.

Louis Martin, who at the request of Sargent Shriver left his executive position with the Chicago Sengstacke newspaper chain soon after the 1960 Democratic convention for a one-day emergency discussion on ways to woo the Black vote for John F. Kennedy, has completed eight years as deputy chairman of the Democratic National Committee. In this position "Louie," who is very intelligent, proud, "not hungry" financially, and a master politician, exerted tremendous influence on Presidents Kennedy and Johnson in their racially ameliorative policies and appointments to national governmental positions. Among the approximately five hundred Negroes who were appointed during the Kennedy and the Johnson administrations largely because of his influence, were a cabinet member, several sub-cabinet members, a justice of the United States Supreme Court, several judges on other federal courts, and first-time Black members in such agencies as the Federal Reserve System, the National Labor Relations Board, the Atomic Energy Commission and the Import-Export Bank. It is quite probable, too, that the elevation of Colonel Frederic Ellis Davison to the rank of brigadier general on October 1, 1968, was, as Carl Rowan puts it, "in part because Martin had quietly built up a drumfire of pressure on the Pentagon protesting the fact that Negroes seemed to make the Vietnam casualty lists a lot more easily than they made the promotion lists."

Mr. Martin also has played a major part in the desegregation of the Democratic Party. The party, as a result of the dispute within the Mississippi delegation at the 1964 convention, adopted an effective desegregation rule which had to be applied against the "Regular" Georgia and Mississippi delegations to the 1968 convention. The guiding hand of Mr. Martin was undoubtedly a factor in the settling of that perplexity.

David S. Broder, commenting in the *Washington Post* (December 24, 1968) on Martin's role on the national political scene, said:

> Martin is a publicist, a politician and—if the word can be used without seeming to condemn him—an operator. He has moved quietly among the power centers of Washington, promoting the interests of civil rights, Negroes and the Democratic Party and insisting that the three are inextricably linked. By the nature of his role, it is hard to lay specific achievements directly to Martin's work, but those inside and outside the government who have watched his operation are nearly unanimous in their view that none of the causes to which he devoted himself would have progressed as far as they did in the last eight years without his skillful prodding.

As Mr. Martin left his post with the Democratic National Committee and returned to Chicago to serve as vice-president and editor of Sengstacke Publications, he felt that the battle had been won, and he remarked:

> There is no way now for anybody to turn the clock back, [for] the Black American is in the political process to stay, and he knows that the political ladder will work for him, just as it has worked for so many other groups in our history. There are still battles to be won, but we have turned the corner on that main issue.

Congressman William L. Dawson of Illinois is chairman of the minorities division of the Democratic Party. Clarence L. Townes, Jr., is head of the minorities division of the Republican National Committee. Since his party played a minority role on the national level in 1968, he was not in a position to shape public governmental policies and appointments to the same extent as Louie Martin did for the Democrats.

The increased involvement of Blacks in the intra-party activities at the state and local levels, together with their greater and more sophisticated voting power, have led to their becoming serious contenders for posts on the national committees of the two major parties. Although the national committee members are actually selected in the various states according to their respective laws, each national convention formally elects the members of its national committee.

At the 1968 Democratic convention Julian Bond's group, the Loyal National Democrats of Georgia, challenged the right of William P. Trotter and Marjorie Thurman, the choices of the "Regular Democratic group," to sit as the Georgia representatives on the Democratic National Committee. The Bond group argued that since it constituted one-half of the Georgia delegation, it should be entitled to one of that state's memberships—either that of a committeeman or a committeewoman. Rejecting the request of national committeeman Marshall Brown from Louisiana that the matter be tabled because it had not come through the full convention as required by party rules, the committee created a panel to consider the contention of the Loyal National Democrats of Georgia that a member of their group be given one of the committee posts to which Georgia, like every other state (and some territories), is entitled. Pending the panel's determination of the issue, the two "Regular" designatees were to be seated.

After the meeting, Mrs. Mercedes Wright of Savannah, one of the "Loyalist" hopefuls, remarked: "We've worked for ten years in a community where Black people had lost all hopes. Where we once had 3,500 Negroes registered, we now have 22,000. I would not like to see you repay our efforts by turning us away as if we were nothing."

Mrs. Thurman of Atlanta, the woman nominated by the "Regular" group, admitted that the challenge hurt her, but said that she would abide by whatever decision the ad hoc panel reached on the matter. She told a group of newsmen: "Of course it hurts me. I came up here not as a segregationist, but as one who has worked consistently for human rights."

Appointments to National Governmental Positions

There were more Negroes holding top-level national governmental positions in 1968 than there have been at any other time in American history. Owing to the constant movement "in and out of government," it is not possible to compile a complete list of the persons who were appointed during 1968. However, it can be stated without equivocation that President Johnson appointed more Black people to administrative and judicial positions than has any other President. The year 1968 showed a very pronounced shift from the situation which had existed during the pre-New Deal days, when Negro appointments at the national level consisted chiefly of clerical and custodial positions, and from that of the New Deal era, when the prestigious administrative positions for Blacks were mainly those as "specialists in Negro affairs."

Within the last five years Negroes have been appointed to real policy-making positions, in which they have been able to exert a tremendous influence on the day-to-day operations of government at the national level, which in turn has had a significant impact on activities within the state and local areas. In addition to bringing "a breath of fresh air" to the governmental atmosphere, these individuals have provided inner sanctum voices and/or representation for the previously ignored Blacks. (A representative selection of such appointees appears on pages 383–384.)

Today Blacks also hold prestigious foreign service positions as high as the rank of ambassador, and positions of associate counsel, special deputy undersecretary and special assistant. Negroes also hold important local government posts in the District of Columbia.

The Republican Convention

The pre-convention campaign for the Republican Presidential nomination was Richard Nixon "all the way" except for the short early venture of Governor George Romney into the contest and except for the "last minute" efforts of Governor Nelson Rockefeller to stall the Nixon bandwagon. Nixon's advisers, realizing that the Negro vote could not be deflected from Rockefeller and/or from the Democrats, focused their attention in the North on the so-called white backlash issue of "law and order" and in the Southern and the border states on a watered down "states' rights" appeal. These two approaches were sufficient to enlist the sound backing of Senator Strom Thurmond, whose support was vital if Nixon was going to neutralize candidate George Wallace in the Southern and border states. In following this course of action, Nixon was looking beyond the convention, where he knew that the Negro and the liberal white vote, solidly behind Governor Nelson Rockefeller, would be unable to block his nomination.

While the Governor addressed himself to such pressing issues as Vietnam, social welfare programs and urban problems, Mr. Nixon too often either told each audience what he thought it wanted to hear regarding his position on particular issues or spoke in such platitudes that it was difficult to ascertain his specific stand on the more controversial issues. Here it should be emphasized that, contrary to the allegations of some Negroes, he did not ignore the economic plight of Blacks. Although he did overplay the "law and order" cliché, he did on occasion stress the obligation of America to give Negroes a "fairer break." For example, in a nationwide radio broadcast in March in which he fully endorsed the idea that Blacks must be given the opportunity to acquire economic and political power so that they could begin to "redeem" their self-respect, Mr. Nixon declared:

> The American opportunity is neither [a] black nor a white opportunity . . . if we are to make our nation whole again by making our people one, we must begin with the recognition of a need for greater black opportunity. The only way to set right the power balance in our cities is to put a greater measure of power in the ghetto . . . by this, I speak not of black power as some of the extremists would interpret it—not the power of hate and division, not the power of cynical racism, but the power the people should have over their own destinies, the power to affect their own communities, the power that comes from participation in the political and economic processes of society.

In other radio addresses he advanced three proposals which were aimed at "breaking the dismal cycles of despair and dependency" in the urban slums. His suggestions were: (1) a system of "core city credits"—direct tax credits or accelerated depreciation or both—for businesses which would build new plants or establish branch offices in urban or rural poverty-stricken areas; (2) the making of low-cost capital available to Negro businessmen; (3) the providing of tax incentives for corporations which would train and employ the unskilled and upgrade the skills of those who now stand on the lowest rounds of the employment ladder.

Then, too, Mr. Nixon and his campaigners visited the heavily populated areas in several large cities, where he engaged in direct and mutually informative exchanges with Blacks on such problems as housing, employment, education and law and order. Nixon, according to the national director of the Nixon for President Committee, was convinced that the "next president would be made or broken on the race issue." This issue he placed second in importance only to the international problem.

Despite Mr. Nixon's apparently sincere attempts to establish rapport with Negroes, Blacks continued to distrust him and continued to express a strong preference for the selection of Mr. Rockefeller as the Republican nominee at the Miami convention. Even Black leaders who believed in Mr. Nixon and admired his plans to ameliorate the economic plight of Negroes wearily stated, "We can support Nixon, but we cannot sell him to our people."

Unlike Mr. Nixon, Governor Nelson Rockefeller was respected, trusted and admired by Negroes. Most Negro Republicans and a large number of other Blacks, together with the major Negro weekly newspapers, warned that if Rockefeller were rejected at the convention Black Republican voters would either support the Democratic Presidential nominee or "just sit out the election."

Since the Presidential nominating conventions usually follow the script which has been prepared according to the wishes of the "professionals," Mr. Nixon's nomination on the first ballot was not wholly unexpected. The failure of the "favorite son" arrangement to hold firmly in some state delegations on the first ballot destroyed Governor Rockefeller's plans for a second ballot; thus his "long shot" chance to win the nomination through defection of delegates from Mr. Nixon never reached fruition. Many people have speculated that had Mr. Nixon not won on the first ballot there was a strong possibility that Nelson Rockefeller would have captured the nomination.

The defeat of Nelson Rockefeller was easier for Negroes to digest than was Mr. Nixon's selection of Governor Spiro Agnew of Maryland to be his running mate. Many Negroes regarded his nomination for the Vice-Presidency to be not only a direct slap in the face but also an invitation "to take a walk." To them the selection of Governor Agnew—who was a very vocal and staunch defender of "law and order"—was a concession to the arch-segregationist Nixon adviser, J. Strom Thurmond, and to the reactionary Southern wing of the party.

Senator Edward Brooke, who served as temporary chairman of the convention (the first time since 1884 that a Negro had served in that position), had been regarded by some as a possible Vice-Presidential nominee. He stated that Mr. Nixon had run a national poll on a possible Nixon-Brooke ticket but that Mr. Nixon had not talked with him about the possibility of such a pairing.

The adverse reaction of some Blacks to the Nixon-Agnew ticket was expressed very candidly. One delegate protested: "There is no way in hell I can justify Nixon and Agnew to Negroes." Another warned, "They're telling us flatly that they want the white backlash and that they don't give a damn about us. Trying to fight this thing is like trying to whistle in the wind." Others took a more resigned view. A New York delegate stated: "I'll work for Nixon, but I cannot speak for the Republicans in the Twenty-sixth District in Queens, because there's a strong anti-Nixon feeling there. I'll work for Nixon because we must fight this thing from within the party and not continually run away just because our own advice is not followed."

In addition to the role played by Senator Brooke, there were two other bright spots for Blacks in the 1968 Republican convention at Miami. The number of Negro delegates and alternates had increased from forty-three in 1964 to seventy-eight in 1968. "They ranged from militant Black-power-oriented youngsters to middle-aged men with closely cropped haircuts who objected to being called Black." The Black representation from the South consisted of three delegates and ten alternates.

The Republican national convention, anxious to build a broader base for party support in the South and apparently recognizing the validity of the constant complaints lodged by Negroes against the "racist policies" which were being followed in the selection of delegates in the Southern states, heeded the plea of the National Council of Concerned Afro-American Republicans that prompt action be taken to end the racial and discriminatory practices at the state and local party levels. This group of Concerned Afro-American Republicans, headed by attorney Thurman L. Dodson of the District of Columbia, urged that the party alter its rules so that from the 1972 national convention onward "no delegation will be seated unless there has been free and unrestricted participation of Black Republicans."

This led to the other bright spot in the convention—the adoption of a rule barring racial and religious discrimination in party affairs and authorizing "positive action to achieve the broadest possible participation in party affairs." The exact words were as follows:

> Participation in a Republican primary, caucus, any meeting or convention held for the purpose of selecting delegates to a county, district, state or national convention shall in no way be abridged for reasons of race, religion, color or national origin.
>
> The Republican state committee or governing committee of each state shall take positive action to achieve the broadest possible participation in party affairs.

The newly adopted rules also directed the national committee to appoint a panel to review the implementation of the anti-discrimination resolution and to report its findings prior to the 1972 convention. Although these rules represent a step in the right direction, they lack a clause to ensure compliance.

The credentials committee did not recommend that any action be taken on the complaints which were made against the racially discriminatory methods which the Republican organizations in Louisiana and Florida had followed in selecting their delegations to the convention. A spokesman said the committee would have been glad to act, but the plaintiffs did not appear.

A group of Negro Republicans from those states sought a federal court order to unseat the "lily-white delegations." When they failed to get this, attorney John H. Clay of Philadelphia stated that the case would be appealed on the grounds that "the party practices racial exclusion."

The Democratic Convention

The pre-convention part of the Democratic campaign in the 1968 Presidential contest was highlighted by Senator Eugene McCarthy's "bold" and at first "thought to be lonesome" bid to win enough delegates in the preference primaries to give him a reasonable chance to win his party's Presidential nomination. During the early stages of his campaign he did not have any appreciable degree of opposition, for President Johnson did not run in the primaries and Senator Robert Kennedy was not then an active candidate.

The real fight began when Senator Kennedy entered the race, and when President Johnson made his famous "I will not seek my party's nomination" speech, which removed him from the scene and set the stage for the entrance of Vice-President Hubert Humphrey into the campaign. Here it should be noted that until Johnson's withdrawal, Negroes seemed to have divided their voting preferences between him and the hoped-for candidate, Senator Robert Kennedy. Senator McCarthy's personality, style and program made very little impact on Blacks, except for those who placed themselves in the intellectual-liberal "stop-the-Vietnam-war" category.

Lacking the flamboyancy of Kennedy, Senator McCarthy relied on logical presentations, wit, sincerity and the "bread-and-butter issue" of ending the war in Vietnam. He addressed himself to the issues, and he did not shift his positions in an attempt to tell the audience what he thought they wanted to hear on a particularly controversial subject. Instead, he told it as he saw it, and let the chips fall as they would. Illustrative of his views were the following remarks, which he made at an early summer meeting in Louisville:

> Most of the urban poor in 1968 are Black people—poor because they are powerless, and powerless because they are Black. They are still held in isolation as a colonial people. . . .
>
> Now, in 1968, the Black people are telling us they do not want to assimilate themselves in our cities on other people's terms.

Speaking of the distribution of state and federal funds to the economically disadvantaged, he declared:

> Poverty funds have too often gone to the wrong people. They have been distributed through political middlemen and through the patronage system to organizations which have no connection with the poor people who live in the areas their programs are intended to affect. Some money gets to the poor—but the real power remains in the hands of the establishment and tends to reinforce the status quo.

During his campaign he also advocated termination of the war in Vietnam; a national minimum annual income; adequate health care supported by a federally subsidized insurance program; the amount and kind of education necessary to develop a person's full potential; the erection of 6 million housing units within the next five years—a goal cited by the President's National Advisory Commission on Civil Disorders; and a "massive job creation program" to aid residents of low income areas. Describing some of the features of his job creation program, the senator explained:

> This will involve tax incentives to private enterprise, encouraging them to locate in areas of unemployment.
>
> We must recognize, however, that it will also mean that the government itself must create jobs.
>
> Perhaps, we can develop a program of state, local, and federal public works so that those now unemployed will have jobs that make a real contribution to the community—whether it is building parks or staffing hospitals.

He regarded this as a step to eliminate "the present degrading welfare system" which stifles initiative and encourages people to remain in line to receive handouts from the federal government.

In a Chicago speech McCarthy even spoke of possible cabinet members from the Black community. It caught the imagination of millions and undoubtedly stimulated the thinking of the other aspirants for the Presidency. He mentioned Mrs. Martin Luther King, Jr., for Ambassador to the United Nations, and Congressman John Conyers, Jr., of Detroit, for Secretary of Labor.

The senator's position on the "law and order" issue as well as on "Black power" might, in the judgment of this writer, have been misunderstood by many Negroes. For example, in responding to a question relative to his position on Black power, he stated:

> There has been Irish power and Italian power, and there never has been a group in America who had more reason [than Negroes] to organize themselves to get their rights.
>
> The question becomes one of how you organize and what you do. But there's nothing un-American about it, nothing contrary to the traditions of this country.
>
> So, here we are together with a sense of what America is all about, talking every day about justice and about equality. But in 1968 I think we are prepared to make a significant turnup from the past so that with all the talk about equality and justice and the inalienable rights, we'll prove we desire these things not just for white Americans but for Americans of all colors.

As we reflect on Senator McCarthy's campaign, we could postulate that the assassination of Robert Kennedy had two major effects for the Black community.

First of all, McCarthy appeared to make a more serious effort to address his remarks to Negroes and to express a stronger commitment to matters and programs which were of direct concern to Negroes.

Secondly, with the virtually certain nomination of Richard Nixon and the consequent removal of Nelson Rockefeller from the Presidential race, many Negroes felt that, because of his strong anti-Administration Vietnam policy and his (apparently) firm commitment to support programs to ameliorate the conditions of the economically and politically disadvantaged, McCarthy was the best available candidate for them. Thus many Negro leaders and organizations which had been strong supporters and active campaigners for Senator Kennedy joined the McCarthy forces. However, it is quite probable that more of the Black former Kennedy adherents shifted their allegiance to Vice-President Humphrey, a late entry in the race.

The Kennedy name generated power and made people take another look at things during the 1968 pre-convention activities. Robert Kennedy, who as President Kennedy's Attorney General had done so much which had endeared him to Blacks and to "liberals" in general, procrastinated on openly seeking his party's Presidential nomination until incumbent Johnson announced his decision not to accept renomination. When he did announce his candidacy, Senator Robert Kennedy found it very difficult to reconcile his desire for the post with his expressed belief that he and McCarthy should work together. McCarthy, of course, viewed with disfavor Kennedy's entrance into the race after he, McCarthy, had waged a lonely and difficult campaign to win supporters in the primaries and in the state conventions by offering alternatives to the existing Administration policies. To many, Kennedy's never-expressed desire and intention was for McCarthy to join forces with him on a Kennedy-McCarthy ticket. That Senator McCarthy steadfastly refused to do.

Kennedy, who was surrounded by Negro aides, chief among whom was Earl Graves of New York, drew heavily on the esteem in which his late brother, President John F. Kennedy, was held by Blacks. He buttressed this with the formulation of a program which appealed to the peace-loving, the disadvantaged white and Black, and the members of the New Deal-Fair Deal-New Frontier combine who had not so securely attached themselves to McCarthy that they could not return "home" and help "Bobby" on his way to the White House.

The record is replete with examples of Robert Kennedy's concern and of his accomplishments—direct and indirect—for improving the status of Negroes. In the 1968 campaign he faced the issues without equivocation or straddling. Generally, his list of priorities for public governmental action coincided with those of Negroes. He called for an immediate and an intensive effort to end the war in Vietnam, including returning "the major burden of the war to the South Vietnamese—where it should have been all along; and lessening the cost in American lives and money for as long as the fighting continues on the ground."

When funds are released from that operation, he said, "We must . . . commit ourselves to the proposition that a substantial share will come to the service of our domestic peace"—that is, for use in fighting poverty in the United States. He also urged that funds be diverted from the space program and certain other marginal research and development efforts to a new and more intensified attack on unemployment and urban problems. On one occasion he advised: "We can slow down the race to the moon, if it means the salvation of our nation on this earth. We can postpone work on the supersonic transport, if it means we can safely sit in our cities."

Addressing himself to the "law and order" issue, he declared: "I want to make it clear that we are not going to have riots and disorder in the United States, but we are not going to have injustice either." He promised to provide education and employment to lift the disadvantaged out of their alienation.

His program to provide tax incentives to induce private industry to establish plants and to build homes in the ghetto areas was substantially the same as that proposed by the other major party candidates.

Some people within the Negro community were unhappy with Kennedy because he did not endorse a guaranteed annual wage. Others questioned his integrity after they had read a nationally syndicated column which charged that he had tapped Dr. Martin Luther King, Jr.'s, telephone while he was heading the United States Department of Justice.

The assassination of Robert Kennedy on June 5, 1968, left these questions unanswered: (1) Could he have won his party's Presidential nomination? (2) If he had become the Democratic nominee for President, could the Black vote coupled with the support of the old "New Frontiersmen" have elected him?

In reality, Vice-President Hubert Humphrey, being the heir apparent to the Democratic nomination, was just about "home free" after the assassination of Senator Kennedy. In the event that that tragic action had not occurred, it is quite probable that Mr. Humphrey would have been forced to wage a more intensive campaign for the nomination, particularly in the Negro community.

Hubert Humphrey, like Robert Kennedy, had developed a good image within the Negro community. Throughout his career in public office—as mayor, as United States senator and as Vice-President of the United States—he had championed the causes of the disadvantaged. He had supported liberal and racial ameliorative programs even when his political associates had not been prepared to go as far as he. It was quite ironical in 1968 to hear him castigated as an active participant in a reactionary political establishment.

In several key cities Black leaders and organizations warmly endorsed his candidacy. This was particularly true after the assassination of Senator Kennedy. An example of this transfer of allegiance was the action taken by twenty Los Angeles area Negro Democratic leaders, headed by California Congressman Augustus F. Hawkins. Included in the group were a state senator, state assemblymen, city clerks, city councilmen, a banker, a former White House protocol officer, a newspaper publisher and several educators.

At a press conference the group announced its reasons for supporting Humphrey. After praising his record of "fighting against bigotry and injustice," and warning that the 1968 election "will be of historical significance to the future of the American Black man and other disadvantaged minorities of America," they declared:

> The destiny of the United States and its ability to overcome its serious domestic and international difficulties will depend largely on the President and Congress elected in 1968.
>
> We must meet the threat of the election of an ultra-reactionary or candidate who would abandon federal enforcement of civil rights.

The Negroes, lauding Humphrey's record of fighting for civil rights at a time when this was vital, and emphasizing the special interest of their race in the election, further stated:

> Millions of us have uprooted ourselves in recent years in search of better jobs, greater freedom and wider horizons.
>
> The so-called Negro problem is largely the problem of urban America. Therefore, we hail and endorse Humphrey's "Marshall plan." It will provide coordinated and comprehensive help for rebuilding our cities.

Both Congressman Hawkins and California State Senator Mervyn M. Dymally, who was a member of the group Hawkins described as a "steering committee of the Black community," made additional significant comments regarding their endorsement of Mr. Humphrey. Dymally declared: "The only man we can support as Black men is Humphrey. McCarthy has been most eloquent but has not made a full commitment to the Black community."

Congressman Hawkins, pointing out that "we are not against anyone" and that he had great respect for Senator McCarthy, ventured the opinion that Humphrey "can weld together the very best elements in the South." He thought this was necessary for the success of his party, which, as he saw it, was facing a serious threat in that region from George Wallace.

When we reflect on the campaigns which McCarthy, Kennedy and Humphrey conducted and the position each took on the major issues, it appears that while each of them had "something going for him," each had a different personality and a different manner of saying what he wanted to say. Then, too, aside from their pronouncements on the Vietnam issue, their positions on most of the major problems were not significantly different, especially on those with which Negroes closely identified themselves. Vice-President Humphrey, being the loyal team man that he was, was unable to gain the *active* support of many of those for whom he eloquently spoke because he was so reluctant to move away from the Administration's position on Vietnam. The difficulty which many of his ardent backers faced was put very succinctly by a woman who lamented: "I've known the guy twenty years, and I know the great things he has done, but try to tell that to the man in the street! They only see him as LBJ's puppet."

This sentiment turned out to be one of the most vital factors in the 1968 Presidential election.

At the Democratic convention, which was held in Chicago upon the insistence of Mayor Richard Daley and over the objections of a large number of the party faithful, who feared that demonstrations by dissident groups, including Blacks, would have a disruptive effect on the proceedings, Negroes played a greater role than they had in any previous national nominating convention of a major political party in the United States. There were more Negro delegates and alternates in attendance; names of Blacks were placed in nomination for the top slots on the ticket; three of the most eloquent and inspiring speeches—for Vice-President Humphrey, Senator McCarthy and Senator McGovern—were given by Mayor Carl Stokes of Cleveland, Georgia Assemblyman Julian Bond and Mayor Richard Hatcher of Gary, Indiana, respectively. The convention thwarted the attempts of segregationists in two

Southern states (Mississippi and Georgia) to perpetuate their "closed society" techniques of selecting delegates to the national convention (a practice which had greatly reduced, and often completely eliminated, the opportunities for Blacks to be chosen as delegates from those states). Although these were very significant evidences of vital participation, they did not indicate that the millennium had been reached for Negroes. However, as Bayard Rustin has put it, "it demonstrates how important it is for Negroes to continue to work within, rather than to opt out of, the national political process; for it is only by playing their full part in American politics that they can make their presence felt, their power real, and their needs met."

Over three hundred Negro delegates and alternates attended the 1968 Democratic national convention—close to three times the number participating in the 1964 convention. There were Blacks from thirty-five states, the District of Columbia and the Virgin Islands. The largest number—twenty delegates and fifteen alternates—came from Michigan.

Prior to the determination of the contests in Mississippi and Georgia, the old Confederate states had chosen over one hundred Negroes to sit as delegates or as alternates at the convention. Louisiana, with thirteen (nine delegates and four alternates), topped the list. After the credentials committee had made its report, the convention seated additional Blacks from several of the contested state delegations. Here it is interesting to note that in 1964 these eleven states had sent only seven delegates and seven alternates from their Negro Democratic voters.

Commenting on this tremendous increase, Louis Martin, deputy chairman of the Democratic National Committee, observed:

> Despite some contests which are expected, the reports now show a dramatic breakthrough in Negro representation in Southern delegations. At long last the vast political power of Southern Negroes is beginning to make itself felt in national politics. Of the seven million Blacks who will be registered to vote in November, 3,000,000 of them live in the 11 states of the Old South.

Among the Black delegates attending the Democratic convention was Gail McHenry, a nineteen-year-old girl from Hopkinsville, Kentucky. A merit scholar, Miss McHenry is a sociology major at Indiana University where she is active in campus political activities. She says she is especially interested in "the organization of the Black grass-roots people so that they can really obtain Black power—the economic and political kind." That spring she had participated in the Indiana University Afro-American Student Association's march on the home of that institution's president, protesting the scarcity of Black-oriented subjects, Black faculty members and facilities for Black Greek-letter organizations. That experience she had found quite stimulating. Some of her associates, perceiving her political potential, urged her to seek one of the delegate posts to her party's national convention. She accepted the suggestion and, to her surprise, she won. She attributes her victory to the support which many people gave her because of their appreciation for the work of her father, who had directed the affairs of the state NAACP for many years.

Several representatives from the mass communications media sought interviews with her. Their questions centered around such subjects as the participation of young people in politics, particularly young Black people; the activities of "Yippies"; and the treatment accorded the demonstrators by the law enforcement authorities in Chicago. The general impression was that she handled the questions with the ease of a seasoned interviewee, and at times her answers were very blunt. When one reporter asked her why she had come to the convention, she told him very frankly that she had come "to work with the established political structure and learn certain things so that I'll be ready when a Black Party is organized."

Negroes were involved in several of the contested delegation skirmishes. The much publicized and somewhat bitter but unsuccessful fight which had been waged by Mississippi Blacks to gain seats in the 1964 Democratic national convention "bore fruit" in 1968—not only at the national but also on the state level. For the first time since 1876 Blacks were active participants in the state Democratic convention. In ten of Mississippi's eighty-two counties, at least one Negro was chosen to attend the state convention. There were some forty-two in all. Had not widespread irregularities occurred, there would have been many more Negro delegates. The nefarious techniques included physically barring Negroes from entering precinct meetings; changing the location of the convention from that announced in the newspapers; burning ballots before they were counted; falsely counting ballots; and actually arranging the slate of nominees in such a way that Black delegates selected would be those whom the whites could control. These irregularities provided the basis upon which the Mississippi Voter Registration and Educational League (a biracial coalition composed of the Mississippi Freedom Democratic Party, which had pushed the fight in 1964, the Mississippi AFL-CIO and other civil rights groups) challenged the delegation sent by that state to the Chicago convention.

The credentials committee voted 84 to 10 *not* to seat the "Regular" delegation because it had failed to meet national standards to assure the full participation of Negroes in the political process. Then, by a vote of 85 to 9, it recommended that the "Loyal Democrats" (the challengers) be seated. These actions were in line with what New Jersey Governor Richard Hughes (chairman of an equal rights committee formed after the 1964 convention fight) had stated should be the function of that committee: "to make certain that all delegations to the 1968 Democratic national convention are broadly representative of the Democrats of the state."

A few hours prior to the meeting of the credentials committee, Jack Travis, chairman of the Mississippi Regulars, had attempted to reach a compromise with the challengers. He had offered to give them three additional seats and to reinstate two Negro delegates who had previously resigned from the committee. Although that was the arrangement which they had been willing to accept at the state convention, the dissidents, convinced now that their cause would prevail, rejected this compromise.

Commenting on the victory, Mrs. Fannie Lou Hammer, who had fought so gallantly to have the Mississippi Freedom Democratic Party delegates seated at the 1964 Democratic convention and who carried this year's fight to the credentials committee, was elated but restrained. She made the following remarks:

> In 1964 when we rejected a compromise proposal (similar to that being considered by Georgia), some thought we were naive and others said we did not know what we were doing, but if we had accepted a compromise proposal, we would not have won total victory this time.
>
> I want to make it clear to all that we in the Mississippi Freedom Democratic Party are not fighting for a Black government in Mississippi but rather for a unified one which includes poor whites and Blacks as well.

The Georgia group which challenged the Regular delegation held its own convention prior to the meeting of the Democratic national convention—the Georgia Convention of Loyal National Democrats. At this meeting they formulated and adopted the following statement, which all persons who planned to participate in the selection of the group's slate of delegates to the Democratic national convention had to sign:

> I am a Democrat and registered Georgia voter and intend to support and work for the Presidential-Vice-Presidential nominees of the Democratic Party in 1968.

This statement was obviously directed at the Regulars, who had been hand-picked by Governor Lester Maddox and who had not been and would not be asked to sign such a pledge. Many reasoned that since Maddox (an announced candidate who could not possibly win the Democratic Presidential nomination) would throw his support to George Wallace in November, he would be opposed to his group's signing such a loyalty pledge. The Loyalists reasoned that this could be a basis for refusing to seat them in the Democratic national convention.

The Wallace delegation had a surprising number of Blacks—three delegates and four alternates. The Atlanta branch of the NAACP urged the Negro members to withdraw because they did not constitute a proportionate number of Georgia Democrats and also because the delegation would be bound by the unit rule of the convention. Illustrative of the responses to this suggestion were those of State Senator Leroy Johnson, Assemblyman Richard A. Dent, and William Randall, who headed an all-Negro Democratic Party in Bibb County. Senator Johnson stated: "I do not intend to be stampeded into any action which may be adverse to the Negro; later I will struggle for political participation." He made it clear that in the event that members of the Regular group who were loyal Democrats later found it necessary to leave, they should pick the time which would be most advantageous. Assemblyman Dent, who was the only Negro to vote for Maddox when the Georgia house of representatives was called upon to select a governor in 1967, said that he foresaw nothing which would force him to withdraw from the delegation. Mr. Dent expressed the opinion that Negroes could exert a greater influence by remaining within the delegation than by leaving it.

The Loyal Democrats, headed by State Assemblyman Julian Bond, asked the credentials committee to deny seats to the Maddox (Regular) delegation for the following reasons:

> 1. The Georgia Democratic Party did not abide by the 1964 guidelines regarding the racial composition of state delegations to the national convention. Blacks had been given only token representation.
>
> 2. The method of selecting delegates was undemocratic. Bond, later commenting on this matter, declared: "The procedure for picking delegates is worse in Georgia than in any other state in the union. Negroes in Mississippi suffer from exclusion from the process. In Georgia, two men are the process." The two men were Governor Maddox and Democratic state party chairman James Gray.
>
> 3. There was evidence that members of the Regular delegation were not loyal to the Democratic Party.
>
> 4. Negroes were not permitted to participate freely in the deliberations of the Regular Democratic Party of Georgia.

Then, in support of the request that the Loyal Democrats be recognized and seated as the true delegates from Georgia, Bond pointed out the following:

> 1. Their delegates had been elected in an open convention.
>
> 2. They had signed a pledge to support the Presidential candidate selected by the Democratic national convention.
>
> 3. They had abided by the 1964 guidelines for the selection of delegates.

After a long period of heated debate, the convention adopted the report of the credentials committee that one-half of the delegates in each of the contending groups be seated. This was definitely a victory for the Bond delegation.

Commenting on the outcome, Bond declared, "We're not the party. All we've said is that we represent more real Democrats in Georgia than they do." He also promised to work immediately for the elimination of Rule 55—the party provision which permits Maddox to name the state's delegation to the national convention. He also warned: "If they don't do it, they're not going to send another delegation to a national convention. The credentials committee made that pretty clear this time."

Governor Maddox and James Gray, the chairman of the Georgia state Democratic committee, demonstrating their displeasure over the compromise, promised to do all they could to prevent the Loyalists from performing any party functions—including the placing of Democratic electors on the Presidential ballot in November. Further displaying his determination to be vindictive, the Governor directed Gray to withhold party funds from the "Communist or Communist-duped Bond delegation." Then, after claiming that the members of his delegation who walked out of the convention with him were prodigal sons who "got in there mixing with hogs and slop," and who were now coming home, Maddox collected the certificates of the other members of his group. None of the Black members of his delegation walked out of the convention.

Challenges by delegations from North Carolina, Alabama and Texas were not taken up despite numerous instances in which Blacks had been denied the opportunity to participate in party activities at the state and local levels. Some close observers of the Chicago action have suggested that the power structure refused to go further with the "new breed" in its disruption of the status quo in the South, for a coalition of governors in that section had threatened to derail the "Humphrey Express." Then, too, there was apprehension over the possibility that acting favorably on further challenges could lead to a serious confrontation with the "power boys" who greatly influence the election of representatives and senators who, because of their seniority, control the major Congressional committees. It is also quite possible that the Humphrey-McCarthy struggle for delegates was an important factor in some of the challenges which were made and in the way in which they were settled by the credentials committee.

The decision to outlaw the unit rule in future Democratic national conventions can also be placed on the plus side for Blacks. In the event it is honored, Negro delegate votes can become more effective, for they will not be neutralized by virtue of their being lost in the white majority.

The name of a Black man, the Reverend Channing E. Phillips, was placed in nomination at the 1968 Democratic convention. It was not an accident, for the District of Columbia delegation which he headed had decided to nominate him as a favorite son prior to their going to Chicago. During the convention, the National Committee of Political Inquiry voted to support him on the first ballot.

Phillips was nominated by Philip M. Stern, a white member of the racially mixed District of Columbia delegation, which had fourteen Negroes and nine whites. In a very sincere, informative and timely speech, Stern pointed out the unusual qualifications of his candidate and the strong reasons which justified his selection. He then quoted the following passage from Tennyson as he placed Phillips' name in nomination: "Come, my friends, 'tis not too late to seek a newer world."

Concluding his speech, Stern said:

> It was these words that formed the title of Robert F. Kennedy's last book. We from the District of Columbia pay respect to his memory by proclaiming that it is not too late. And it is in the quest of that newer world that my colleagues and I commend to the Democratic national convention for the Office of the President of the United States, the name of Channing Emory Phillips.

Mayor Richard Hatcher, the first Negro mayor of Gary, Indiana, in his seconding speech, reminded the convention delegates that "We [Negroes] have been struggling in the dark for years, listening to the Democratic Party, crying for help but getting precious little. Now we seek a complete breakthrough. Justice must live or America will die."

Although everyone knew that Phillips could not win the Presidential nomination, his name was presented to show that Negroes are sincere in their determination to enter the mainstream of American life, including the holding of offices for which they are qualified. Many who believed that Dr. Phillips was qualified for the position which he sought did not vote for him, either because of their commitments or because they knew he could not win and they did not want to waste their vote.

Phillips received forty-six and one-half votes from seventeen state delegations and twenty-one of the twenty-three District of Columbia votes—a total of sixty-seven and one-half votes. He appeared to be happy with the amount of support he had received. Accepting many congratulatory messages, he said: "What we have done here tonight puts the party on notice that Black people have now entered politics at the highest level." Although he did not receive votes from a majority of the Black delegates, Dr. Phillips won enough of them to indicate that Negroes are becoming aware of the political potential which they possess.

Assemblyman Julian Bond, who had distinguished himself so well during the floor fight between his Loyalist delegation and the Regular delegation from Georgia, was nominated for the Vice-Presidency. Realizing that he did not possess the Constitutional qualifications for that office (being only twenty-eight years of age), Bond withdrew his name from consideration. The fact that he was nominated and did receive some noticeable support was, at least to some degree, a manifestation of the outstanding impression which he had made on the delegates. Commenting on Bond's poise and coolness under fire, an observer stated, "Julian's the man to watch. He showed a courage and a maturity far beyond his age. He helped to inspire many a Black who had given up and uttered, 'Let Stokely take over.' He won the respect of whites who admired his leadership qualities in an atmosphere of confusion and turmoil."

Humphrey was nominated for the Presidency, as was expected, without difficulty. This was distasteful to the McCarthy and former Kennedy supporters, who regarded him as a "me too" Johnson man—especially on the Vietnam issue. Humphrey's selection of Senator Muskie as a running mate was very popular with Negro and most other Democrats.

The name of Senator George McGovern was also placed in nomination for the Presidency. He, like Senator McCarthy, would have received sizable support from Negroes had he won the nomination.

Participation in the Presidential Election

James Harvey Robinson has observed that: "Political campaigns are emotional orgies which endeavor to distract attention from the real issues involved, and . . . paralyze what slight powers of cerebration man can normally muster."

The Presidential campaigns which were conducted by most parties in the 1968 election would hardly fall within the confines of that description, for, although there were some efforts to distract attention from the real issues, the major party candidates explained their positions on the vital issues: Vietnam, civil disorders, urban problems, civil rights, the military draft, the income surtax and United States Supreme Court decisions.

The emotional orgies were found mainly in the Wallace campaign. He relied on that device to create an atmosphere of fear which he promised to eliminate with his program of "law and order" —designed mainly against Negroes and others who protest against anachronistic practices.

The elections provide an opportunity for voters to express their judgment on the issues and on the candidates. Too often in the United States voters do not utilize this opportunity, and, as a result, they have no choice other than to accept the results which have been determined by others.

Although the struggle for the right to vote in the United States has had a long and difficult history, particularly for Negroes, electoral participation, even at the national level, is far less than it should be. A recent Gallup Poll estimated that 15 million eligible voters did not go to the polls. This means that approximately 60 per cent of our voting age population "bothered" to vote—a smaller percentage than in the two previous Presidential elections.

Realizing the importance of the issues which were to be decided in the 1968 elections, and knowing of the paucity of Black registrants in many areas, Negro leaders conducted voter registration drives throughout the United States. Prior to these efforts, there had been a 12 per cent gap between white and nonwhite registration. Organizations ranging from the NAACP to an "aware" version of the old Blackstone Rangers (the Chicago South Side street gang), the Black P-Stone Organization, participated in the drive to increase the number of Black voters.

In the South, recent Congressional statutes (the Civil Rights Acts of 1957, 1960, 1964 and 1968 and the 1965 Voting Rights Act), together with the United States Supreme Court barrier-removing decisions and the extensive voter registration drives of concerned Southern-based organizations, added approximately a million Black votes to the rolls. The Southern Regional Council estimated that there were about 3,124,000 registered Negro voters in the region for the 1968 elections.

The Negro press and Negro leaders such as Roy Wilkins, Whitney Young and Bayard Rustin pleaded with their followers to exercise their franchise rights in the national election. They emphasized the threat which George Wallace posed to their way of life. Even though Wallace was not given much of a chance to win the Presidency, many feared that he could cause the defection of enough votes to throw the choice of a President into the House of Representatives, where (recalling the 1876 fiasco) many feared that George Wallace would be in a position to drive a hard bargain with Nixon or Humphrey if they needed his support to win the Presidency. In an appeal urging Blacks to vote, the Metropolitan (New York) Union of Black Clergy and Laity of the Episcopal Church, without naming but certainly alluding to Wallace, issued this statement:

> Every Black person and every poor person who fails to vote in reality is casting a vote for the third-party candidate and helping his strategy to control the national election by gaining a decisive percentage of the national vote.

Among other exhortations to vote were those from the Southern Christian Leadership Conference leaders Rev. Walter E. Fauntroy and Rev. Hosea Williams. Williams, a leader of the Poor People's Campaign in the District of Columbia, stated:

> Soul brothers and sisters—Soul Power—Soul Power—Soul Power. I may be Black, but I am somebody.
>
> Friends, our nation is at the brink of disaster. . . . Just as the first Reconstruction, nearly 100 years ago, ended after 14 years, the Pharaohs of today are trying to end our stride toward freedom that was so brilliantly started by the Black Moses of the 20th Century, the late Dr. Martin Luther King, Jr.
>
> Either you vote in the coming election or you do not have the chance again for another 85 years. Just as our forefathers were re-enslaved, my friends, so can we be.
>
> Will we allow men like Strom Thurmond of South Carolina and George Wallace of Alabama to re-enslave us? Well, Vote, Vote, Vote, if only so our children will have the chance to redeem the South of America and make Martin Luther King's dream come true.

Fauntroy, Washington director of the SCLC, pleaded:

> If our slain leader, Dr. Martin Luther King, Jr., were alive today, it would be his voice that you would be hearing instead of mine. I urge you to make your vote count this November for the cause of Brotherhood for which he gave his life.
>
> The clock must not be turned back as a result of his death. They have killed the dreamer, but what shall become of his dream? The answer to that question may well rest with your vote. So as a living tribute to the sainted memory of Dr. Martin Luther King, Jr., register and vote this November for Dr. King, for one America, for the fulfillment of his dream.

On the other hand, Blacks were also advised to refrain from voting for any of the Presidential candidates. Roy Innis, director of CORE, in urging Negroes to register heavily to show their potential but not to vote for any Presidential candidate, declared: "It is really irrelevant which of these guys become President. Black people should refuse once and for all to accept the lesser of two evils."

Some Blacks claimed that the Nixon forces conducted an underground campaign to induce Negroes to stay away from the polls. The theory advanced to support this allegation was that the Republicans reasoned that by keeping Negroes from the polls the Humphrey support would be lessened.

The Post-Convention Presidential Campaign

It was generally believed that Richard Nixon would win the Presidential election in 1968. All of the major political polls predicted a victory for him. Even though Mr. Humphrey had enjoyed a long history as a darling of the liberals, many of them deserted him because he appeared to them to be a symbol of President Johnson's alleged "bull-headedness" on the Vietnam issue. This, coupled with the growing dissatisfaction with the Johnson Administration's policies in general, created a burden which Mr. Humphrey was forced to carry during the campaign.

The effect which George Wallace, the nominee of the American Independent Party, would have on the campaign (and the outcome of the election) was not certain. Many felt that he would attract enough votes from the Democratic candidate in the Southern and border states to prevent Humphrey from carrying those usually Democratic areas. Others advanced the idea that Wallace would have a greater impact on Nixon, for both of them based their campaign appeals to a large extent on the "law and order" issue, one which would appeal strongly to a large number of whites and conceivably to some Blacks, who were disgusted with the increased crime rate among Negroes and with the urban riots, which had involved arson, pilfering, and even some shooting (at passersby as well as at law enforcement officers).

Mr. Nixon, virtually writing off his chances of getting any appreciable support from Negroes, structured his campaign to appeal, or at least be acceptable, to most of the non-Black voters. Perhaps his most objectionable tenets to Negroes were his constant emphasis on "law and order," without mentioning justice; his embracing of Southern segregationists such as Senator Strom Thurmond; and his choosing of Governor Spiro

Agnew as a running mate—a man whom many Negroes regarded as having had an unsatisfactory civil rights record when he was Governor of Maryland.

Richard Nixon made his position on "law and order" crystal clear in a radio interview prior to his nomination when, in response to a question which had been asked regarding his views on the Report of the President's National Advisory Commission on Civil Disorders, he declared:

> One of the major weaknesses of the President's Commission is that it, in effect, blames everybody for the riots except the perpetrators of the riots.
>
> And I think that that deficiency has to be dealt with first. Until we have order we can have no progress.
>
> I believe we've got to make it very clear to potential rioters that in the event something starts next summer the law will move in with adequate force to put down rioting and looting at the first indication of it.

His constant reference to "law and order" was particularly objectionable to Negroes. They regarded it as an attack which was specifically directed at them and also as a bid for white support. Jackie Robinson, who had bolted the Republican Party when Nixon was nominated, declared:

> This means that his energies will be directed against punishing the ghetto. And that can lead to the biggest holocaust this country ever has seen. The ghetto victim is no longer afraid of threats, and Nixon displays his utter ignorance of the fact. Agnew does nothing but parrot him in this position.

When Robinson was asked what he thought about Wilt Chamberlain's backing Nixon, he responded:

> I don't know what are Wilt's motives. It is very hard for me to understand how any Black man can support a party which clearly demonstrates it doesn't want him. But it certainly can't be on the basis of what Wilt thinks is best for the Black man.

A union member commenting on Nixon's reliance on the "law and order" issue expressed the opinion that:

> He needs more than law and order in the U.S. . . . There is more than that going on in the world. If you are going to isolate yourself as a country, that's fine . . . but if you are going to be a part of the world at large, then you will need to extend yourself beyond the urban cities.
>
> Then what can Nixon and Agnew do about stopping the riots? Can't no one man stop this. . . . And it will take more than Agnew and Nixon to do this.

The Negro community also objected to Nixon's views on school desegregation. In a taped interview on a Charlotte, North Carolina, radio station, Nixon said: "It is my view there is too much of a tendency for our courts to use the whole program of what we call school integration for purposes other than education."

Later, replying to a question regarding the "freedom of choice" plan of school desegregation, he stated: "The freedom of choice plan is an extremely controversial issue. I think the use of power on the part of the federal government to carry out what a federal bureau might think is appropriate is very dangerous."

Some Blacks regarded statements such as these as evidence of Mr. Nixon's opposition to school desegregation. The record would show that while he was not the Lyndon Johnson type of desegregationist, Richard Nixon could not be justifiably characterized as a segregationist. His general philosophy, it would appear, was one which was based on judicial self-restraint and on limited federal participation in fields of activity where states had historically "called the shots."

Mr. Spiro Agnew was also an unpopular candidate in the Negro areas. Many Blacks objected to his views on the Poor People's encampment at Resurrection City, as well as to his opposition to the bussing of children to achieve integration of schools, and the practice of civil disobedience against "unjust" laws; then, too, there was his stand on "law and order." Explaining his opposition to civil disobedience, Agnew said he would not practice it even against "unjust" laws because it too often leads to violence. He felt that the use of good public relations know-how to dramatize a problem was legal and much more desirable. He suggested that, if he were a Black man in the United States, he would not attempt to swim in a segregated pool, eat at a segregated lunch counter, or drink water from a "whites only" fountain. He would use public relations to desegregate those facilities—a very interesting but hardly a feasible approach.

He opposed bussing children from one area to another because it placed the youngsters in a strange environment. Such action, he believed, could be harmful to a very sensitive child.

Agnew's civil rights record was not bad, for he had sponsored an open housing ordinance for Baltimore County, and he reaffirmed his support for civil rights during the Presidential campaign. It would appear that much of the opposition by Blacks was caused by his strong objections to civil disobedience and by his advocacy of prompt and vigorous prosecution of rioters.

As the campaign progressed, Nixon and Agnew, although believing that they could win the election without Black support, made a more determined effort to relate to Negroes. A nine-member Committee of Black Americans was formed to advise the national Republican campaign staff on matters affecting Negroes and to work with the minorities division of the Republican National Committee to formulate programs which would develop support for the candidates in the Negro groups. The committee was headed by Earl Kennedy, chairman of the Michigan Republican State Committee and a businessman in Detroit. J. Robert Smith, a Negro newspaper reporter for the *Pasadena Independent Star-News*, was appointed as a press aide to the national committee's communications director.

Senator Edward W. Brooke, one of Mr. Nixon's chief advisers, discussed the "law and order" matter with him and pointed out that it was viewed in some Negro areas as a "code word" for discrimination against Black people. After a frank exchange of views, the Republican Presidential candidate agreed to talk about "law and order with justice." In other conferences, Senator Brooke urged Mr. Nixon to refrain from criticizing specific Supreme Court decisions and to confine any criticism he wished to make to general statements about the court. Brooke was elated at the attention which Nixon gave to these suggestions in his subsequent speeches.

Several nationally known Black leaders endorsed the Nixon-Agnew ticket for various reasons: some because they believed he was the best man, others because of his program, and still others because of their belief in the two-party system. These leaders included the general secretary of the A.M.E. Church; the president of the National Association of Colored Women's Clubs; the Grand Exalted Ruler of the IBPOE of W (the Negro Elks); Wilt Chamberlain (who said he would establish "a hot line" for complaints); Lionel Hampton, who served as chairman of a national action committee which had its headquarters in Harlem; Dr. J. H. Jackson, president of the National Baptist Convention; and Bishop C. Ewbank Tucker of the A.M.E. Zion Church.

The *Atlanta World* was one of the few Negro newspapers which endorsed the Nixon-Agnew ticket in the 1968 election.

The old Roosevelt coalition which has made the Democrats the majority political party in the United States for thirty-five years appeared to be cracking in 1968. Mr. Humphrey found himself under virtually constant pressure from party regulars to take many different steps—resign as Vice-President, disassociate himself from the Johnson Administration so that he would feel free to be his "own man," or speak out unequivocally on the vital issues. However, the options open to him were very greatly restricted. Thus, numerous and complex problems faced the Humphrey-Muskie ticket.

Working men are no longer slavish Democratic supporters because, having found a new affluence under the Democrats, they have an active interest in voting to protect their recently acquired suburban homes, motorboats and second cars. Many of them fear—and perhaps detest—Blacks because of the latter's increasingly militant and disorderly conduct. So, with their promises to maintain law and order, to reduce governmental expenditures on welfare programs, and to slow down the judicial decisions which are making it possible for Negroes to enter the mainstream of American life and share our great abundance, candidates Nixon and Wallace offered alternatives which many of the newly "arrived" whites were expected to accept.

The intellectuals and liberals who had broken with President Johnson's Administration over the Vietnam war, seeing no hope within the Democratic Party now that Senator Robert Kennedy was dead and Senator McCarthy's Presidential bid had failed, would either "sit out" the election or give the Humphrey-Muskie ticket only a trickle of electoral support.

The Southern whites, who backed Humphrey as the Democratic nominee because they were less fond of Robert Kennedy and Eugene McCarthy, now found themselves with two far more palatable alternatives in Nixon and Wallace.

Although Blacks remained the most dependable segment of the old bloc, many of them had become distrustful and impatient with their failure to be given an opportunity to get a "fair piece of the action," and had decided to "pass up" the national election and vote only for state and local candidates.

Despite these difficulties the Humphrey team, with lingering visions of the Truman miracle of 1948, waged one of the greatest uphill struggles in the history of Presidential elections in this country.

Vice-President Humphrey and running mate Senator Muskie reasoned that if they could carry the large urban vote in the states with a large number of electoral votes they would have a fighting chance to win the election. Their campaign plans and pronouncements implemented that belief.

They directed a large part of their efforts toward Negro voters. Vice-President Humphrey's women's advisory committee, which had been appointed toward the latter part of August, included ten Blacks among its sixty distinguished women. Members of this committee prepared position papers in their respective areas of competence, emphasizing issues which were of particular concern to women: the family's role; education; the future of women in various types of occupations, including the professions. Several of the committee members sponsored or led discussions to acquaint women with the issues—and of course with the virtues of Humphrey and Muskie.

Negro leaders in various parts of the country organized drives to win support for the Democratic candidates. Many of them visited several cities to sell the Humphrey-Muskie ticket. Rev. Channing E. Phillips endorsed the ticket, as did many others, among them Charles Evers (the NAACP leader from Mississippi); Jackie Robinson; Mayor Richard G. Hatcher of Gary; Mrs. Martin Luther King; Rev. Ralph Abernathy; Aaron Henry (chairman of the Loyal Democrats of Mississippi); and Julian Bond.

It should be noted, however, that several of the endorsements were made with some reservations or reluctance. Mrs. Martin Luther King endorsed Humphrey because she believed that "an administration headed by him will be more resistant to repressive measures than one headed by his opponents." However, she stated: "I am disappointed that Vice-President Humphrey has not separated himself resolutely from Administration policies on Vietnam and that he has too cautiously confronted racism as a national disaster."

In his personal endorsement of the ticket, Rev. Ralph Abernathy spoke of Muskie as "gifted, experienced and capable." He stated that both Democratic candidates had "the sensitivity and intelligence to work for a new America."

Julian Bond said that he planned to spend so much of his time working for Negro and peace candidates on the local level in all parts of the United States that he wouldn't "have much time left" in which to work for Mr. Humphrey. He had endorsed him previously.

The Humphrey-Muskie team, in an attempt to gain the confidence of those Blacks who were indifferent, opposed, or just slightly inclined to give their support, offered a program which included many proposals designed to meet the most serious problems of the Negro community. Among the proposals were: (1) the assurance that "the federal government would become an employer of the last resort and guarantee a job for everyone seeking work"; (2) the continuation and expansion of the economic opportunity program, including newly established model cities plans; (3) the creation by the federal government of a "Marshall plan" for cities, for rebuilding the slum areas; (4) a new and complete national commitment "to human rights"; (5) an intensive and extensive fight for open occupancy in housing; (6) a pledge to implement the proposals of the "Vice-President's Task Force on Order and Justice," which stressed the need for removing the social and economic causes of crime; (7) the taking of immediate steps to end the Vietnam war as early as possible.

In their speeches both Humphrey and Muskie stressed the failure of Mr. Nixon to propose a program which would meet the major problems that face ghetto residents, and stated that Mr. Nixon was really indifferent to the needs and aspirations of Negroes. Moreover, they warned that Mr. Nixon would greatly curtail or badly cripple the War on Poverty program, against which he directed so much criticism during the campaign.

The Vice-President warned Negroes and whites to beware of Wallace, for he was a divisive force in America—his major objective being to "embitter and divide" the American people. In an address in Charlotte, North Carolina, Humphrey described George Wallace's program of "law and order" as "sheer hypocrisy." He pointed to the low status of law in Alabama during Wallace's time as Governor. In closing his speech, Mr. Humphrey declared: "If in this campaign I make no other contribution to America's national life than to expose the Wallace threat—and its dangers to our Democracy—I will rest content on November 5."

George Wallace, former Governor of Alabama, selected himself to run for President as the representative of a party which he then proceeded to create under the name of the American Independent Party. After many difficulties, the party appeared on the ballot in all fifty of the United States.

Contrary to the expectations of many people, this party was not geared to solicit electoral support only from the South. It was fashioned to gain the backing of various malcontents on the right—people who were disturbed by the urban riots, by the civil disobedience programs and by the Supreme Court decisions ordering the desegregation of housing, government facilities (including schools) and public accommodations. In addition to the above, court orders and Congressional statutes extending voting opportunities for Negroes and giving Blacks equal treatment in the administration of justice (thereby removing some of the major barriers in the path of employment opportunities for racial minorities) contributed to the anxiety of the people who were immediately receptive to the Wallace program, for they visualized it as a response to their cry for law and order as well as a promise to return to the local determination of policies involving school attendance, housing, employment and public accommodations.

Wallace chose General Curtis E. LeMay as his running mate; the latter's campaign chores consisted chiefly of answering questions at meetings, news conferences and fund-raising dinners. On the few occasions on which he did speak out, he usually said something which Wallace later found difficult to reconcile with his own beliefs or pronouncements.

Although Wallace denied that he was a racist, an examination of his speeches and other utterances during the campaign show that some of the statements most pleasing to his followers were those which dealt with topics related in some way to the racist-fascist complex and appeared to underlie a part of his basic philosophy of life. The remarks below are representative of statements which pleased certain of his followers:

> When both national political parties say we've got to remove the causes of rioting, looting and burning, they're saying that these anarchists have a cause. They've got to stop saying there's a cause for the breakdown of law and order. Poverty is not a cause for anarchy. . . .
>
> And I'll tell you this, when I am elected President, the first anarchist that lies in front of my car—it's going to be the last car he ever lays down in front of.

On the other hand, there were times when he stated that:

> I believe that He made all mankind and if you dislike anybody because of race or color you're disliking the handwork of God. . . .
>
> Well, certainly Negroes will be in every administration and should be because Negroes are citizens of this country the same as we are and they will always be in the government.

Very few Blacks endorsed Wallace. A Negro weekly newspaper, the *Butler County Weekly* (Ohio), reportedly owned by whites, made the following statement on the Wallace candidacy:

> George Wallace has proved that he has the courage of his convictions . . . whether you like Mr. Wallace or not [if] you are of his party, you have to admit that he really tells it like it is.

Referring to Wallace's selection of General LeMay as a running mate, the paper said:

> We agree, George Wallace, you have chosen wisely and well. With the help of God and patriotic citizens standing up for America, a team like yours cannot fail.

Commenting on the Wallace candidacy, Senator Edward Brooke observed:

> I do not predict revolution, but when people protest and waste their vote for a man like George Wallace, who cannot govern this country, this could bring about a revolution. It sets the stage for militancy of the extremists on the right and left.

George Wallace forced the major party Presidential candidates to recognize him and to respond to the "law and order" issue. Thus it should be noted that Wallace "shook up" the American political scene in the 1968 Presidential election, and in the process he "succeeded in making race a legitimate issue—and backlash a legitimate recourse."

In January 1968 Dick Gregory wrote President Johnson a letter in which he notified the President that, unless five demands which he listed were met, he would lead demonstrations which would make it possible for the Democratic Party to hold its convention in Chicago only over his (Gregory's) dead body.

Gregory's demands, all relating to Chicago, included: (1) the passing of a stricter fair housing ordinance; (2) the appointment of a Negro to a top-level police job; (3) removal of the law which had restricted demonstrations by Dr. Martin Luther King; (4) increased pay for policemen and firemen; (5) a guarantee to protect a civil rights leader, Rev. Jesse Jackson, who had received several threats on his life.

Gregory's demands were not met, and on August 29, 1968, he led about three thousand persons down Michigan Avenue in the direction of the building in which the convention was being held. When the protesters disobeyed the police order and walked through the barrier, one at a time, Gregory and about 150 others, including two white convention delegates, were arrested.

The advance notice which he had given of his intention to conduct demonstrations exerted an additional influence on the events connected with the convention. Hordes of protesters came to Chicago to express their displeasure over the following: (1) President Johnson's failure to end the Vietnam war; (2) the inevitable steamroller which was going to flatten Senator McCarthy's bid for the Democratic nomination for the Presidency (and hand it to Vice-President Humphrey); (3) the economic plight of ghetto dwellers; (4) the racial bigotry which makes itself felt in all parts of our society. These dissidents encountered considerable difficulty in carrying out their objectives.

Mayor Richard Daley, having been alerted to the probability of widespread demonstrations and to the possibility of disgruntled groups' efforts to disrupt the convention proceedings, had taken just about every conceivable step to prevent the protesters (demonstrators and others) from threatening the smooth operation of the convention. When the inevitable confrontation between the "invaders" and Daley's law men came, it resulted in beaten bodies, insulted and overreacting police, damaged property, angry politicians, a raging mayor and an embarrassed and more divided Democratic Party. Horrifying scenes were indelibly stamped on the memories of millions of people who witnessed the events personally or on television.

Two facets of that hate-action-fear syndrome merit comment here. First of all, Gregory's comments did have an influence on the convention in that the wall of security which Mayor Daley erected to meet Gregory's promised demonstration in all probability prevented the demonstrators from breaking up the convention. It is doubtful that such extensive and intensive security measures would have been taken had it not been for Gregory's remarks.

The other aspect of those events which deserves comment is the actual role which Blacks played in the disorder. With the exception of Gregory and a few others, Negroes were conspicuously absent from the melée. This was to some extent because of lack of identification; that is, many Blacks did not feel that there was any connection between their desires and the activities downtown.

The National Committee of Inquiry

In the spring of 1968, Congressman John Conyers, Jr., of Michigan sent out several thousand letters asking Negroes if they would like to join an organization which "would evaluate Presidential candidates and serve as a vehicle for political information in the Black community." The idea of forming such a committee was conceived by either Bayard Rustin or by Congressman Conyers himself; in either case, it was initially implemented by the efforts of Conyers. Mayor Hatcher of Gary joined the leadership a short time later.

The organization which emerged from this idea, the National Committee of Inquiry, held its first meeting in June 1968 with Conyers serving as temporary chairman. In a press conference following the meeting, he stated that the committee (which had at least two hundred members) would evaluate the Presidential candidates and on the basis of its findings would submit recommendations to Negro voters. Thus, as Conyers very directly put it, the committee would act as a "jury to find the candidate" who most merited the backing of "Black America." "We specifically intend to interview every candidate [even George Wallace]." He promised to release a preliminary report prior to the national conventions of the major parties. The final report would be distributed just prior to the November election.

This is a widely based organization which includes representatives from all areas of the Negro community: educators; state legislators; physicians; mayors; newspaper publishers and editors; Black nationalists (and perhaps some "Uncle Toms"); persons on public assistance; Democrats; Republicans; members of minor political parties; entertainers; political party committeemen; state senators; United States congressmen; and the so-called activist groups. Among the persons listed as members of the executive council in October 1968 were: Harry Belafonte; Mrs. Martin Luther King, Jr.; Rev. Ralph David Abernathy, head of the SCLC; Mayor Richard G. Hatcher of Gary; State Representative Julian Bond of Georgia; Floyd B. McKissick, former national director of CORE; and Lerone Bennett, senior editor of *Ebony*.

The National Committee of Inquiry's roster of area (functional and geographical) chairmen reads like a "Who's Who" in Black America. These chairmen appear to be solidly sold on the need and the potential of the venture. One of them, Sammy A. Rayner, who heads the Illinois chapter, expresses the typical view of these committed leaders:

> This is an attempt to show an organized force in politics which has formerly been essentially white. In politics, we have always been too divided. If we are going to cease to be fragmented, then we must learn how to select a candidate according to our interests and stand behind him. With over twenty-two million Black people in the United States, a show of unity could elect or eliminate any candidate.

Several meetings and strategy sessions were held in Chicago during and after the Democratic national convention, which several of the leaders had attended as delegates. At a meeting on August 26, which attracted over 150 followers, the group reached two major decisions: (1) to support all challenges by Black delegates for convention seats, and (2) to push for a commitment from each of the major Democratic Presidential candidates to support the recommendations of the National Commission on Civil Disorders. In urging support for the first of these, Conyers said: "We should support them all, good or bad. We don't have time to sort them out."

Congressman Conyers, in this writer's opinion, displayed a lack of political maturity as well as of good judgment when he advised the group to support good or bad challenges because there was not time to separate the good from the bad. That could be interpreted to mean: support them because they are Black. This would be an advocacy of racism. Moreover, if decisions were to be made wholly on the basis of race, Negroes would be unable to compete because of their lack of numbers, and, in addition, it would be inconsistent for them to ask others to respond differently in an analogous situation.

At other sessions the committee considered the desirability of drawing up a platform which would include pronouncements on ending the war in Vietnam, developing programs for ghetto dwellers, etc. It also discussed the question of whether to nominate a ticket which would offer the greatest hope for Black people. Failing to agree on the above, the group decided to endorse the Reverend Channing Phillips, the District of Columbia favorite son candidate for President (the first Negro to be accorded such a distinction at a twentieth-century national convention of a major party). It also decided to support demonstrations by the Poor People's Campaign, to comply with its request to seat some of its members in the convention hall and to endorse a resolution calling for granting assistance to the fifty-first state—the state of hunger.

The decision to endorse the candidacy of Phillips was reached only after long and heated discussions. Supporters of Humphrey and McCarthy advised the delegates not to waste their votes on Phillips because he could not win the Presidential nomination. Those favoring Phillips retorted: "He's a brother. Let the world know we are not satisfied. Let the country know the Democrats don't have our vote in the bag."

Some also reasoned that, even if Phillips did not win, placing his name in nomination could offer a rallying point for the uncommitted Black delegates, and perhaps, even more importantly, it would give Philip Stern, a white man in the District of Columbia delegation who had placed Phillips' name in nomination at the convention, "an opportunity to discourse on race relations before a national television audience" in a prime time slot.

The concept of establishing an organization to make objective investigations of candidates for public office and evaluations of needed or impending party or governmental policies of direct concern to a particular segment of our population is a laudable and much needed effort, especially for the Black community. However, in disseminating its findings and recommending that specific action or a particular response pattern be followed, the organization has a moral responsibility to be realistic and also to refrain from committing the same sins as those persons or groups against whom the advisees are being urged to react.

The National Committee of Inquiry, within its brief period of existence, has performed a valuable function for Negroes in that it has brought together persons of all shades of political opinion to evaluate candidates and to discuss issues. It has used the results as bases for recommending to Blacks the best responses they can make in the political spectrum to existing conditions. This is an example of the effective use of power by Negroes. In the opinion of most enlightened people, such collective responses, based on rational judgments of candidates and issues, must be employed by Negroes so that they may rise above the existing "accommodative process" which relegates them to subordinate roles. (As a recent article in *Ebony* has put it, "the Black vote" is at present "captured through gimmickry, promises of high paying jobs, and the spreading of thousands of dollars to 'caress Black opinion.' ") The use of the new sophisticated approach will enable Negroes to escape from this subordinate condition and to attain their rightful position in party politics and in government in the United States.

Voting Choices Expressed by Negroes

Various groups and individuals in the Negro community influenced the voting choices of Blacks in the 1968 national elections. An overwhelming majority of the speeches and the literature urged the election of the Humphrey-Muskie ticket. However, the newly established broad-based Negro leadership group, the National Committee of Inquiry, refused to back any Presidential candidate.

At a closed meeting on October 13 in Gary, the group decided that it would not endorse any of the Presidential candidates because it felt that none of them had spoken effectively to the problems and needs of Black people. Two things which were reportedly crucial in preventing a qualified endorsement for Humphrey were: (1) the statement he had made in a televised speech on the preceding night (October 12) in which he pledged to crack down on rioting, violence and crime; (2) a letter he had written to Mayor Hatcher on September 25 in which he had stated that he did not have time to meet with the committee to discuss issues of interest to Negroes.

In announcing its decision the committee said:

> We have waited so late in the campaign to make our statement because we have hoped to be able to make a specific endorsement of a Presidential candidate.
>
> Unfortunately, the major Presidential candidates have become increasingly responsive to racism, reaction and all those groups in the population beset by an overriding fear of Black people. A stark example of this trend was the Vice-President's nationally televised speech, the very eve of our meeting, when he attempted to gain support from these very groups.

Therefore, it continued, before any candidate could receive the committee's endorsement, he would be required to support justice and security through social ameliorative programs which would deal with the "causes of crime rather than police repression, however much hid under the label of law and order."

At a press conference in Gary the next day, Congressman Conyers expressed the opinion that Mr. Humphrey could still secure the committee's endorsement if he would take a positive stand against continuing the Vietnam war and also make a firm pledge to provide effective assistance for solving such ghetto problems as jobs, housing and education.

Once the committee had decided that it could not endorse any Presidential candidate, however, it advised Negroes to vote only in state and local elections.

Blacks were warned by some that in the event of a Nixon victory "the nation would be rocked by some of the most oppressive and repressive measures ever devised by an American President." One of the few Negro newspapers to endorse Richard Nixon was the *Atlanta World*. In its issue of October 22, it urged Blacks to support Nixon for the following reasons:

> I. During the campaign, Mr. Nixon has made major addresses outlining a program to improve the lot of our people.
>
> II. He has proposed a plan to help our people in the ownership of businesses.
>
> III. To accomplish the goals of restoring human dignity and self reliance, Mr. Nixon has proposed:
>
> 1. The Passage of a Human Investment Act to provide tax incentives to hire and train the unskilled and to improve the skills of those at the bottom of the employment ladder.
> 2. Establishment of a Computer Job Bank to be located in the areas of high employment to bring together the job and the man.
> 3. Creation of a National Student Teacher Corps of high school and college students to tutor core-city children.
> 4. To provide Extended Training Programs in core-city schools to teach basic language and communication skills after school hours and in the summer.
> 5. To Recruit Vietnam Negro Veterans for teacher training.
> 6. To Sponsor a National Home Ownership Foundation to increase mortgage capital in the slums to enable the poor to own their own homes.
>
> This program gives the Black man in the ghetto a piece of the action.
>
> So when we see advertisements aimed to incite fear about Mr. Nixon, we can only conclude somebody is becoming desperate.

There was even support for George Wallace in the Black community. Some Negroes, although not working openly for his election, favored a Wallace victory because they "reasoned" it would demonstrate to American Blacks that they could not get a fair deal under the existing system. His election, the argument continued, would foster a racial revolution because Wallace would be expected to "so polarize race relations in this country that a second civil war would result." One wonders whether the Blacks who advocated this approach had given any thought to the possibility of white racism's winning over the Black extremists!

Perhaps the best objective advice to Negroes on how to express their voting choices was offered by the Metropolitan Chapter (New York) of the Union of Black Clergy and Laity of the Episcopal Church. It prepared the following guidelines which it urged voters to use in formulating their electoral preferences:

> Continue and develop a war on poverty that will not only give jobs to the jobless, but which will seek to remove the causes of poverty.
>
> Provide leadership through a vigorous enforcement of laws designed to protect the civil rights of citizens and to prohibit intimidation or violent action by persons who seek to maintain racism in this country.
>
> Press for a speedy end of all military action by American forces in Vietnam and to work "uncompromisingly" to support and promote independence and peace in that country.
>
> Work for a national system of public welfare geared to provide financial assistance, "meaningful" rehabilitation and to maintain the dignity of persons administering and receiving such services.
>
> Press for strengthening the role of the United Nations in keeping the peace and promoting international cooperation.
>
> Encourage private and public participation in programs to promote economic independence and business enterprise in Black communities.

The impact of the various sources and types of advice on the voter cannot be definitely measured. It depends on what he is seeking and the extent to which he feels the advice will help him to fulfill his needs and aspirations. In the 1968 Presidential election, Negro voters appear to have been greatly influenced by the various endorsements made in behalf of the Humphrey-Muskie ticket, for they gave it close to 90 per cent of their votes.

Although the Nixon-Agnew ticket won the election, it received only a trickle of the Black vote—10 per cent or less. Mr. Wallace and the various splinter and extremist groups garnered only a "trace"—hardly measurable. It is quite apparent from the election returns that, realizing that the three Black Presidential candidates couldn't win, Negroes did not choose to cast their votes for them merely on grounds of race.

Thus an overall view of the choices expressed in the Negro majority areas in the 1968 Presidential election shows that there was "no contest" between candidates Humphrey and Nixon. Another observation which can be made is that the support given Mr. Nixon was much closer to that which Mr. Wallace received than it was to Mr. Humphrey's. (For statistics on voting, see pages 412–414.)

As Blacks review and attempt to interpret the results of the 1968 Presidential election, they may wish to do two things: (1) raise the question: Why was Mr. Humphrey defeated? (2) reexamine the validity of the frequent and threadbare cliché that the Negro vote constitutes "the balance of power in close Presidential elections." The shifting political alignments, the expiration of the Solid South and the increasing extremism (on both the left and the right) should be used as a point of departure for any assertion regarding the potential effect of a loosely connected group of voters. It seems that the 1968 election makes such an approach a *sine qua non* for any prognostications which can claim to be valid.

A plausible answer to the question of Humphrey's defeat appeared in the November 11, 1968, issue of the *Chicago Daily Defender* in an editorial entitled "Black Vote Re-Appraised." It attributed this defeat to: failure of Blacks to vote, a lack of agitation or "sustained" crusade among Black people on behalf of the Vice-President, and the refusal of the National Committee of Inquiry to endorse him. The editorial stated:

> The self-appointed political advisers of the race who met in Gary during the twilight hours of the campaign, did much to dampen enthusiasm and repress active participation among black citizens. Their advice was neither definitive nor politically astute. By telling the people, who had looked to them for direction, to vote for candidates who "show respect for our rights," our political "wise men" were giving what amounted to a counsel of despair.
>
> Such a counsel did not help the Humphrey cause, nor did it help the civil rights cause. When to this irresolution is added the plea to stay away from the polls, the stupidity is compounded beyond remission.
>
> It is one of today's most pungent tragedies that a man like Hubert H. Humphrey, who has done so much for freedom and recognition for American black men, should be caught in the toils of what is certainly a most ungracious and ungrateful resolve in American political history.

The above reasons carry conviction, but it appears that the fundamental reason was that the people just wanted a change. The electoral results clearly indicate that the American people did not vote for Nixon, they voted against the Johnson-Humphrey Administration, and Mr. Nixon happened to have received more votes than had any of the other Presidential candidates. The tendency of the electorate to vote against instead of for something has been a common phenomenon in American political history. The 1968 Presidential election was an example of history's repeating itself.

Aftermath of the Election: Mr. Nixon and the Negro

The Nixon-Agnew ticket won despite the opposition of a large and virtually solid Black vote. Since Mr. Nixon won without Negro support, what he will do to solve the problems of the ghetto is not certain. This is of the greatest concern to the country at this time, for the way in which the new Administration handles it will have a great bearing on the welfare of over 200 million Americans. Equally important will be the frame of reference within which those who are disappointed with the outcome of the 1968 Presidential election will operate.

Mutual trust, patience (but not accommodation), objectivity, realistic appraisal, courage and tact must provide the base upon which an acceptable relationship can be built and maintained between the Nixon Administration and all segments of our society. Name-calling, restlessness, suspicion and prejudice can only lead to increasing frustration, disillusionment and, no doubt, suffering—both physical, if it is generated by rebellion, and psychological, for those who permit themselves to be motivated by vapory idealism.

Members of the Black community have already expressed disappointment with some of Mr. Nixon's appointments. The National Council of Concerned Afro-American Republicans has written him protesting the appointment of Robert Brown to the White House staff and also the reappointment of District of Columbia Mayor Walter Washington. In their letter, they advised Mr. Nixon that: "In making such appointments, the administration should consult with the recognized Black Republican leadership in the various states from which the appointments come." The group also told him that he and his political advisers should appoint Negroes who have supported the Republican Party. This was apparently directed at the reappointment of Mayor Washington.

Mr. Nixon faced a problem in the Washington appointment. It was generally conceded that Washington, a Democrat, had done a good job as mayor of the District of Columbia. It was also common knowledge that a certain Southern member of Congress was using his influence to block Washington's reappointment. If Nixon had not reappointed him, he in all probability would have been accused of bowing to a Southern segregationist. This is not to suggest that Mr. Nixon should not seek the advice of Black Republican leaders; neither is it meant to deny the validity of the claim that Republicans should get the patronage jobs.

The failure of Mr. Nixon to select a Negro for a cabinet position has caused much more discussion and consternation among Blacks. It has been reported that he offered Senator Brooke a spot in the cabinet and that the senator turned it down. Considerable speculation has occurred over whether Brooke refused the position for the reason which he announced: "In my case, I turned it down because I'm happy and could do more in my present position."

That was a polite reason, but one wonders if Brooke's refusal was not due to his distrust of Mr. Nixon or to the belief that he and Mr. Nixon could not see eye to eye on certain basic policies —or to some other unexplained reason (such as the fear of losing face with Negroes if he were to work too closely with Nixon).

Whitney Young was reportedly offered a top-level position in the Nixon Administration, but he also refused to accept it. Young apparently felt that he could make a better contribution toward the solution of urban problems by remaining in his present position as director of the National Urban League. He has been quoted as remarking: "I don't know of any Black man who was asked, who conceivably would have found this [appointment to the cabinet] a promotion in what he is doing, or would conceivably have found this a more responsible assignment at this moment in history."

This question could very well be asked: Did Mr. Nixon offer Brooke and Young positions because he felt certain that they would not leave their present posts? Some maintain that that was his plan. Now he can answer his critics by saying, "I offered cabinet positions to two Blacks, and they refused them."

It would appear that it is much too early to make a valid judgment of Mr. Nixon's attitude toward the appointment of Negroes to top-level positions in his Administration. Certainly his failure to have a Negro cabinet member could hardly be a valid reason to conclude his Administration will not accord due recognition to Black appointments.

In a recent conference with six Negro leaders, Mr. Nixon told them (allegedly promised them) that he "is going to do more for the underprivileged and more for the Negro than any President has ever done."

Added to the anxieties and fears about Mr. Nixon is the feeling that he may hold the opinion that he owes Blacks nothing because they did not support his candidacy in the election and that he would not make any effort to formulate and to implement programs to deal with the problems which are of direct concern to members of that racial group. Many recall the displeasure which he expressed over the poverty program, the withholding of federal funds from racially segregated facilities and the United States Supreme Court decisions which have used the Fourteenth Amendment to expand national protection for constitutional rights in fields where states had acted with relative freedom previously.

Upon the basis of Mr. Nixon's narrow victory and his specific pronouncements since the election, it is logical to assume that he will give Negroes a "fair piece of the action." It would appear that he will make a serious effort to regain the Black vote that supported the Republican Party prior to 1932. To accomplish this objective, he will have to use the power and the prestige of his office to put into operation realistic programs which will meet the problems that face Negroes, especially those in the ghetto areas of our cities. Although Blacks do not seem to have much confidence in Mr. Nixon, they should give him a chance before they conclude that he will be unreceptive to their pleas and unconcerned about their needs. At the end of 1968 this seemed to be a logical approach to the non-extremist sector of the Black community.

Mr. Nixon, recognizing the narrowness of his election victory and looking forward to 1972, will, in the judgment of this writer, work to win the confidence of Blacks so as to provide a broader base for political support. Even more importantly, he will be expected to do so because he knows that a divided America cannot survive.

Postscript

To show their appreciation to President Johnson for the contribution which he and his Administration had made to the improved status of Negroes in the United States, several hundred persons, including close to two hundred of his appointees to governmental positions at the national level, honored him at a farewell reception in the District of Columbia on November 17.

The group presented him with a desk set with the inscription:

> To President Johnson in deep appreciation from the Negro officials you appointed.

Secretary Weaver introduced Justice Thurgood Marshall of the United States Supreme Court, who said: "The people in this room have come for just one purpose—to say thank you, Mr. President." The Justice also told President Johnson: "You didn't wait. You took the bull by the horns. You didn't wait for the times. You made it."

President Johnson, visibly moved by the affair, advised the guests to look forward, not backwards, because there is still a long way to go. He also told them that he was happy that he had made a contribution toward bringing Negroes into the mainstream of the action. Referring specifically to the appointees, he said, "I'm proud to have played a role in matching some of you to these great responsibilities." However, he reminded them that they were the vanguard, and that millions of Blacks who were proud that a Negro American is a Justice of the Supreme Court of the United States still could not get decent jobs. He pledged "to remain joined with [them] in fighting" for all persons to enjoy an equality of opportunity. Closing his remarks, Mr. Johnson said, "So little have I done, so much have I yet to do."

This was a fitting climax for a man whose efforts—through appointments, administrative decisions and legislative programs—were largely responsible for the high status and participation which Negroes enjoyed in the national political scene in 1968.

"Tomorrow will be better" seems to be the conclusion of this touching triptych drawn by a Washington, D.C., elementary school student. The students drew and wrote of their reactions to the death of Dr. Martin Luther King, Jr., and to the subsequent riots, as part of a crash program introduced into the Model School Division's curriculum immediately following the assassination of Dr. King.

The Patterns of Interracial Conflict in 1968

St. Clair Drake

DURING THE SUMMER of 1963 one of the greatest demonstrations of interracial unity on behalf of full equality for Black Americans that the U.S.A. has ever witnessed occurred in Washington, D.C. Over 200,000 people—Black and white—gathered around the Lincoln Memorial and heard Dr. Martin Luther King speak eloquently and passionately of "The Dream" which he hoped would be realized by nonviolent, hate-free, social action. Five years later, in the spring of 1968, his body lay shattered by an assassin's bullet, and the smoke of fires set by angry Black people when they heard of the tragedy billowed over the capital city. In scores of American communities fires burned; white men's stores were broken into; Black youths hurled rocks at passing cars; and here and there, on the streets and in schools and prisons, white men were beaten by Black men, as spontaneous *violent* protests burst forth across the land, between April 4 and April 12, against the murder of the "Black Apostle of Nonviolence."

The year 1968 began with constant discussion by the mass media and in the citadels of "white power" over how to prevent, if possible, or deal with, if it came, a "hot summer" that was feared. There had been such a summer in 1967 in more than 160 cities. Eighty-two persons had died during those disturbances, and at least $69,000,000 worth of property had been destroyed. The President subsequently appointed a National Advisory Commission on Civil Disorders which released its report in March 1968. But the greatly feared 1968 explosion came earlier than expected—in April—in response to the murder of Martin Luther King, and the magnitude of the "disorder" was greater during this period than it had been for the entire year of 1967 (see Table 1 and Chart 1).

The First Three Months of 1968

The Lemberg Center for the Study of Violence at Brandeis University is currently making an exhaustive study of "civil disorders arising from racial tension" and has released detailed analyses for the first three months of 1968 (*Riot Data Review*, No. 1, May 1968) and for the month of April (*Riot Data Review*, No. 2, August 1968); it has also released a preliminary summary of data for the period of May through August. Records exist of "civil disorders with racial 'overtones'" in 283 communities between January 1 and September 1, 1968. However, only forty-one of these communities (15 per cent) were affected by racial conflict during the three months prior to the assassination of Dr. King. In these forty-one communities, fifty-eight civil disorders of this type occurred as compared with four such incidents during the first quarter of 1967. Table 2 gives the names of these forty-one cities and towns classified by geographical region.

For the first three months, according to the Lemberg Center, "the overwhelming number of recorded disorders" had "centered around schools" (thirty-four out of fifty-eight). Seven of these were at colleges or universities.

In nineteen of the communities in Table 2 (Group I), the disturbances early in the year were a prelude to outbursts in April as well as to episodes later in the year. Among these communities were the great metropolitan centers with

TABLE 1

Civil Disorders: 1967, 1968

(From *Riot Data Review*, No. 2, August 1968, Lemberg Center for the Study of Violence)

	Year 1967	April 1968
Number of Disorders	233 (+16E)*	202 (+53E)
Cities	168 (+8E)	172 (+34E)
Cities with More Than One Disorder ("Repeats")	39	22
States	34 (+Wash., D.C.)	36 (+Wash., D.C.)
Arrests	18,800	27,000
Injured	3,400	3,500
Killed	82	43
Property Damage	$69,000,000	$58,000,000
National Guard		
Times used	18	22
Numbers used	27,700	34,900
Federal Troops		
Times used	1	3
Numbers used	4,800	23,700

* E = **equivocal event.** The definition of "civil disorder" implies tension expressed in aggressive behavior by a group motivated by a sense of injustice or feeling of hostility, and with selectivity of targets. When it is not clear that a disturbance meets all of these criteria it is classified as "equivocal."

CHART 1

Civil Disorders Arising in 1967 and 1968 from Racial Tensions: by Month*

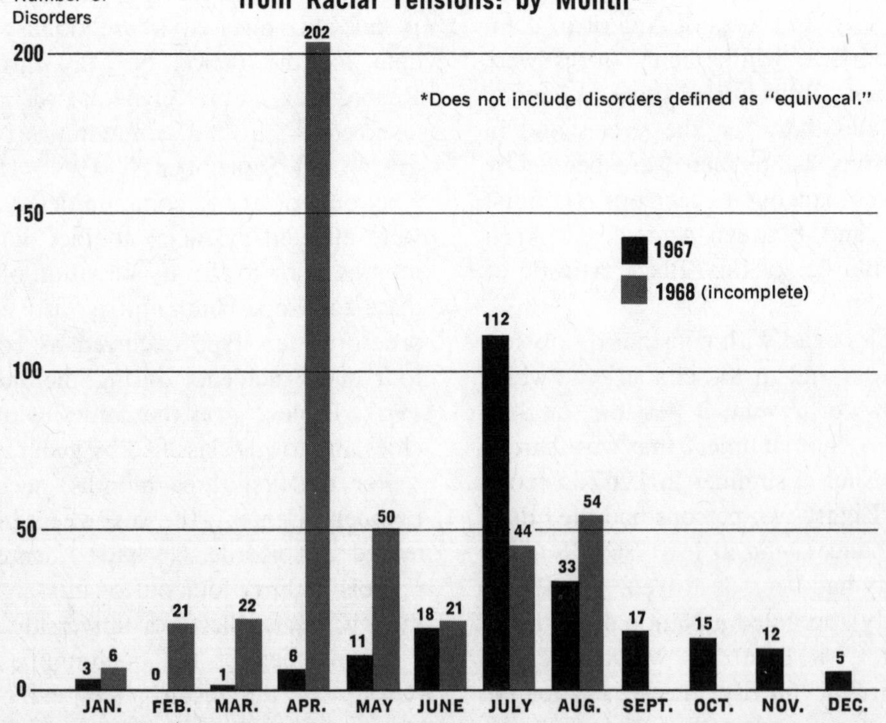

Modified from chart in *Riot Data Review*, No. 2, August 1968, Lemberg Center.

TABLE 2

Cities and Towns Having Civil Disorders with Racial Overtones during the First Three Months of 1968

(Cross tabulated from *Riot Data Review*, Nos. 1 and 2, and *Index of Disorders*, January–August 1968, Lemberg Center)

Periods of Disorders	Northeast	Middle West	Upper South	Lower South	Far West
Group I					
Before April, during April, also May-August	Newark, N.J. New Haven, Conn. New York (Brooklyn) New York (Manhattan) Philadelphia, Pa. Pittsburgh, Pa. Syracuse, N.Y. Wilmington, Del.	Chicago, Ill. Cincinnati, Ohio Milwaukee, Wis. Omaha, Neb.	Baltimore, Md. Durham, N.C. Memphis, Tenn. Washington, D.C.	Columbia, S.C. Gainesville, Fla. Orangeburg, S.C. Tampa, Fla.	None
Group II					
Before and during April, but not after	Carteret, N.J. Mt. Vernon, N.Y. Trenton, N.J.	Dayton, Ohio East St. Louis, Ill.	Nashville, Tenn.	Lorman, Miss.	None
Group III					
Before April, not during April, and after April	Cheyney, Pa. Dover, Del.	Maywood, Ill. Mt. Clemens, Mich.	None	None	Los Angeles, Calif. Seattle, Wash.
Group IV					
Before April only	Hartsdale, N.Y. Lackawanna, N.Y. Linden, N.J. Springfield, Mass.	None	Knoxville, Tenn. Seat Pleasant, Md.	El Dorado, Ark. Social Circle, Ga.	San Diego, Calif.

vast "ghettoes" where Black people are heavily concentrated in their tens of thousands: Manhattan, Brooklyn and Newark in the Greater New York area, and Chicago, Philadelphia, Washington, D.C., and Baltimore. It was in these cities, too, that a "hot summer"—as well as sporadic violence throughout the year—had been considered most likely to occur. In some of these, as well as in other cities, groups of militant Black college students were experimenting with ways of expressing "Black power": At Morgan College in Baltimore; at Howard University in Washington, D.C.; at University of Florida in Gainesville; at South Carolina State and Claflin in Orangeburg; and at North Carolina State in Durham. In Milwaukee an NAACP youth group, under the leadership of a white priest, Father Groppi, was engaged in a prolonged militant attack on residential segregation. That so-called "disturbances" went on in these areas throughout the year was not surprising.

Among the communities in which disorders occurred between January and April were nine in which the only disorders of the year were *prior* to the assassination of Dr. King (Group IV). Four of these were small Northern communities where tensions between Black and white students in integrated high schools erupted in violence. Three were small Southern communities in which school desegregation triggered off conflicts (Seat Pleasant, Maryland; El Dorado, Arkansas; and Social Circle, Georgia). Knoxville, Tennessee's, disorder involved Negro college students. Dr. King's death did not reactivate aggressive action in any of these communities.

In five other communities (Group III) there were disturbances before the assassination but none in response to it, yet more interracial conflict broke out *after* April: in Cheyney and Dover, grievances of Black college students were involved; in Maywood, Illinois, a chronic conflict at an integrated high school continued. Los Angeles was quiet during April, owing to the highly disciplined efforts of Black leaders to "keep it cool." In Lorman, Mississippi, and Nashville, Tennessee (Group II), Black college students who had been fighting their own campus battles also led demonstrations when Dr. King was killed.

Of all the pre-April situations, two were most significant in terms of "things to come"—Nashville and Memphis. A serious disturbance occurred in the former in January, originating in a Black community but soon involving students from two predominantly Negro educational institutions nearby—Fisk University and Tennessee A. and I. State University. During the rioting a policeman was killed, and warrants were issued for the arrest of five young men in their teens from Cincinnati and one from New York. The funeral of the policeman was highly publicized, the victim being called a martyr to the defense of law and order. The Nashville police department said that while the funeral was going on a leaflet was being circulated at the two schools which charged, erroneously, that Fisk co-eds had been taken from their dormitories for questioning, and which was inciting to riot by stating: "We should not let honky cops come into our black community and arrest our fellow students. When the man comes, take off your soft shoes and don't Tom. Arm yourselves and be ready."

This was the voice of a young militant group that had earlier adopted nonviolence as a tactic but by 1968 had abandoned it. The summer of 1964 had been the turning point in race relations for them as well as for many others. By then the Student Nonviolent Coordinating Committee (SNCC), the Congress of Racial Equality (CORE) and the Southern Christian Leadership Conference (SCLC) had broken the back of the caste system in the South so far as public accommodations were concerned, but racism in the North still subjected thousands of ghetto dwellers to police brutality, residential segregation with overcrowding and exorbitant rents, high unemployment rates and massive economic exploitation. In these ghettoes the unemployment rate for Black youth ranged from 25 to 45 per cent! Resentment and alienation among the Black masses had erupted during the summer of 1964 in Harlem, Rochester and Philadelphia—the first storm signals. This was also an election year, and thousands of idealistic students—Black and white—flocked into the South to participate in massive voter registration campaigns. Some of them were murdered there. The militants in SNCC became disillusioned and frustrated when the Democratic national convention refused to seat the Mississippi Democratic Freedom Party delegation, and the first Black Panther Party was born in Lowndes County, Alabama.

By the summer of 1964, too, a dynamic leader who had never accepted the doctrine of nonviolence, Malcolm X—the alter ego of ghetto youth—had become a hero, only to have his life snuffed out early in 1965 by an assassin's bullet. In the summer of 1965 the Watts area of Los Angeles exploded to the cry of "Burn, Baby, Burn!" It was obvious that the ghetto masses were not only impervious to pleas for nonviolence, but were also without national leadership.

Both Martin Luther King and the young SNCC militants turned their eyes northward after 1965, in an effort to give form and direction to these outbursts. By this time, SNCC leaders had shifted to a Malcolm X point of view, and Stokely Carmichael, preaching the need to forget "integration," was calling upon the people of the ghetto to "get yourselves together," and "mobilize your Black Power to T.C.B." (take care of business). King came North in 1966 to organize nonviolent protest on a large scale in Chicago. An outburst of arson and looting broke out while he was trying to channel grievances—a pattern he and others were to face often in the future.

After popularizing the Black power slogan in the summer of 1966, Stokely Carmichael traveled widely abroad; during the fall and winter of 1967 he traveled throughout the United States, counseling armed self-defense, the organization of local Black United Fronts, and a "Third World" perspective that saw uprisings in the ghetto as a form of guerrilla activity against what he defined as American racism and imperialism in Vietnam and Cuba. This is a part of the background of events and ideas against which patterns of interracial conflict in 1968 must be considered.

February is a month during which the minds of Americans are deliberately focused upon race relations by numerous institutions (particularly the Association for the Study of Negro Life and History) and by the mass media. For over forty years Black Americans have celebrated Negro History Week in February, and over a much shorter time a variety of religious and liberal groups have designated this week in February as Brotherhood Week. On January 15, 1968, the *New York Times* carried a story headed: NEGRO HISTORY WEEK STIRS UP SEMANTIC DISPUTE. The paper was acquainting a broader public with the results of a *Jet* magazine poll in which 59 per cent of those questioned said they would prefer the terms Afro-American or Black to Negro. It was reported, too, that a Black militant in Harlem had recently ripped down a *Negro* History Week poster at a public school. *Black* history, *Black* power, *Black* pride, *Black* dignity—these were the new themes. And the day of Malcolm X's assassination, February 21, was assuming the importance of a national holiday for young Blacks. Natural hairdos, dashikis and Swahili became symbols of Afro-American self-definition. Young militants had been developing an ideological stance since 1964 that incorporated more of the philosophy of Malcolm X than of Martin Luther King. Among ghetto youth in school and out, nonviolence was defined as old-fashioned and unworkable, and on college campuses a cult of Franz Fanon and Malcolm X was to the most militant Black students what the cults of Mao, Che Guevara and Castro were to their white counterparts.

Soon after Negro History Week 1968 had ended, J. Edgar Hoover, testifying before a closed session of the House Appropriations Committee, was quoted as having said of urban riots that "tense situations have been further aggravated, with the crowd taking violent action following the exhortations of extremists such as Black Power advocates Stokely Carmichael and H. Rap Brown." These two men *were* heroes to militants in the high schools and colleges, but local leaders emulating their militant rhetoric, rather than these two men themselves, were the initiators of action in the numerous situations in which outbreaks actually occurred. For instance, in Oakland and nearby towns in California, the Black Panther Party for Self-Defense had developed their own para-military organization and only later invited Carmichael to become their prime minister.

During the months of February and March 1968, one focus of conflict was on the Atlantic Seaboard from Washington, D.C., northward, with a scattering of events in inland cities in New York and New England. The majority of these disturbances involved high school students (Springfield, Massachusetts; New Haven, Connecticut; Trenton and Carteret, New Jersey; Mount Vernon, Hartsdale and Lackawanna, New York; Philadelpia; Wilmington, Delaware; and Baltimore). Within this area, too, were: one labor disturbance that took the form of a racial conflict (Newark); teen-age conflicts of out-of-school youth (Brooklyn and New Haven); college campus disturbances at Cheyney, Pennsylvania, and Howard, in Washington—as well as one off-campus Pan-African protest by Howard students that drew police action. Another focus was on the western side of Lake Michigan in the Chicago metropolitan area, where all of the episodes involved high school students—in the central city and in suburban Maywood, as well as in Milwaukee, where the NAACP youth were in action against housing discrimination.

The February and March protest pattern was not confined to the Northern and Eastern states, however. In Orangeburg, South Carolina, on the night of February 5, some students from Negro Claflin University and South Carolina State College tried to end, once and for all, their exclusion from a downtown bowling alley. On presenting themselves at the door, they were told that the right to bowl was reserved for "members only"—that All-Star Bowling Lanes was a private club. Several hundred students returned the next night, and a fight with the police broke out, during which the students shattered the windows of the bowling alley and of several nearby businesses and overturned a number of cars. One policeman was injured. Seventeen Negro students were arrested and charged with trespassing, and seven were hospitalized after a clubbing by the police. By 9:00 P.M. the National Guard was in the streets and the students were back on their campuses.

The next day seventy-five Guardsmen with bayonets were assigned to the bowling alley and the surrounding shopping center. That evening

Federal troops guarding Washington, D.C., after the April riots.

the students did not go downtown but were alleged to have pelted cars passing the two campuses with stones and bottles. About a hundred highway patrolmen, some with riot guns, then cordoned off the campus. What actually went on afterwards is not clear, but the *New York Times* reported that "throughout the evening sounds that appeared to be gunfire were heard." The following day three men students were treated at a local hospital for gunshot wounds. The next day the president of South Carolina State issued a sharp protest against "police brutality," called for an economic boycott of downtown stores instead of demonstrations, and pledged faculty support for such a strategy. He suspended classes so that students could meet among themselves and with city officials. The students asked the mayor to establish a Human Relations Committee and reiterated the demand for a nondiscriminatory policy at the All-Star Bowling Lanes.

The next day students submitted a list of seven grievances to the Orangeburg city council, staged a pray-in and then held a meeting in a ball park near the campus. Someone set fire to a grassy slope on the part of the campus bordering U.S. Highway 601. White firemen and policemen began to advance up the slope, and Associated Press representatives claimed that shots came from among fifty to seventy-five students at the top of the embankment, hitting an officer and provoking other officers to open fire. (It was later claimed that the students had not had guns but had thrown various objects—torches, etc.) By the time the shooting was over, three students had been killed. In addition, some thirty students were wounded, some seriously. Both campuses were then closed and classes were suspended for three weeks. On February 11, eight hundred Orangeburg, South Carolina, Negroes met to call for the lifting of their curfew and the immediate removal of the National Guard from the city, as well as to plan a boycott of local white businesses and to begin a broad civil rights campaign. The state was asked to make restitution to the families of the students who had been killed and to the injured students.

On February 15, two hundred Black students in Durham, North Carolina, marched in sympathy with their fellow students in South Carolina, and on February 21 students at Alcorn College in Mississippi were involved in fighting with police. Southern law enforcement officers, throughout the year, used their guns on students to an extent not found anywhere else in the nation.

While these and other students were engaged in confrontations with police and National Guardsmen, Martin Luther King was traveling about the country trying to mobilize support for a nonviolent anti-poverty march on Washington, D.C., to take place in April and to embrace representatives of all the poor—American Indians, Mexican Americans, Puerto Ricans and "poor whites" as well as Negroes. It was generally believed that the young militants had promised not to embarrass Dr. King with any violence in Washington during the planned April demonstration. Later in February Dr. King, speaking in Atlanta, warned that urban riots might bring in their wake a "right-wing takeover" and stated that every time a riot develops "it helps George Wallace." Muhammad Ali (Cassius Clay) agreed with Dr. King, and in speaking to a California college audience said, "Rioting is like a bull running into a locomotive. Allah fights our battles." In the meantime H. Rap Brown, commenting on events in Orangeburg, had said, "If we are to be murdered for acting peacefully, we might as well be murdered while trying to kill a few white honkies."

But "next summer"—not Martin Luther King's poverty march—was the major preoccupation of public officials. On January 10 Governor Otto Kerner of Illinois and Mayor John Lindsay of New York had announced in a press conference that the report of the President's Advisory Commission on Civil Disorders would be completed by March 1 and had given a preliminary briefing of its contents and its conclusions. The commission chairman, Kerner, warned that the report was "going to be uncomfortable for the people of the United States," and said that "in some places it may even appear abrasive." The *New York Times* reported that he and the vice-chairman, Mayor Lindsay, had "denied persistent reports that the White House had toned down some of the recommendations because they were too expensive or controversial." Yet it was obvious that an attempt was being made to allay Congressional apprehension by stressing the fact that there had been "no effort to persuade the

White House to include funds in the forthcoming budget to pay for programs that the Commission might recommend," and that there was "no intention of requesting X dollars, or anything of that nature for the program." This press conference was the opening move in a program to try to prevent the summer of 1968 from being as hot a one as the summer of 1967.

While the year's first signals of serious disorders to come were flashing from Nashville, the Department of Justice was beginning a three-week series of meetings in Washington with police chiefs and officials from 120 cities to discuss riot prevention and control. These briefing sessions were to be followed by regional conferences in Sacramento; Cleveland; Norman, Oklahoma; Athens, Georgia; and Berkeley Springs, West Virginia. Attorney General Ramsey Clark was optimistic, stating: "We can prevent riots in America this summer and we can control them if they occur, and gain time to eliminate those conditions which have to be eliminated."

In his own department, he was concentrating on programs to raise police morale throughout the country through better pay and better training, and he said that he hoped city officials would realize that "excessive show of force or a show of force too early is itself a provocation." He appealed to law enforcement officers to consider the fact that "one policeman on the beat who cannot control his temper can undo the work of the entire force." At one press conference in January, the Attorney General predicted that *1968 will be the year of the policeman in America. He will have responsibilities that affect the future of America.* He was right, but the stubborn resistance of many policemen to new conceptions of law enforcement meant that few ghetto dwellers changed their definition of them as Enemy No. 1, and before the year was over large segments of the country's college student population were making the same appraisal—abusing the police with the epithet "pigs."

During the rest of January and in early February, President Johnson adopted a two-pronged strategy in his attempt to persuade Congress to legislate favorably on issues affecting Negroes. On the one hand he stressed the "law and order" theme; on the other he appealed for new civil rights and anti-poverty legislation. While the President, his Attorney General, and his Commission on Civil Disorders were trying to educate the public and the government, other agencies were also hard at work on "riot prevention." On January 22–23, Plans for Progress held its fifth annual meeting in Washington, D.C., and a prominent Negro, Hobart Taylor, complimented the 101 member companies for increasing their minority employment and said they were "in the vanguard of the effort to create job opportunities for the teeming hard core of our urban ghettoes." Bayard Rustin of the A. Philip Randolph Institute spoke to the group, pleading with them to recognize that the nation faced a crisis and begging businessmen to take some of the responsibility for seeing "the major social planning job through." According to Rustin, a sense of hopelessness was the prime factor in Black discontent. In addressing another influential group of Americans during the same week, Attorney General Clark had said, "I think we have to plan for the worst and work for the best."

The violence on the Southern college campuses and in Black communities adjacent to them struck some observers as a rehearsal for rebellion—although not in the areas where it had been expected. At the end of the stormy week in Orangeburg, the *New York Times* carried a headline: ARMY STOCKPILING RIOT EQUIPMENT: AIRLIFT TO ANY CITY PLANNED FOR DISORDERS IN SUMMER. The chief of the National Guard and his deputy planned to tour forty states in the spring to check up on preparations, and the Guard's special office for military support to civil authority had 227 full-time operatives scattered throughout the country. The Army had a thirteen-member special civil disturbance board at work on planning, and the Army chief of staff told Congress that seven brigades had been earmarked for civil disturbances. The Army was very proud of SWAT (Special Weapons and Tactics Team), trained to fight snipers, and its weekend courses on riot control at Fort Benning, Georgia. The Department of Justice installed a special computer with data fed in from cities across the nation to "help decide what, if any, Federal response is required to meet trouble this summer."

On March 1 the Associated Press announced that "in city after city across America, the police are stockpiling armored vehicles, helicopters, high-powered rifles," and "sending undercover agents into the slums," as well as "recruiting civilians as ready reserves." Pieces of the new equipment were described in detail, and it was noted that even riot veterans were "awed by some weapons developed in the aftermath of Watts, Newark and Detroit." The police chief in Tampa, Florida, was quoted as saying, as he showed off his arsenal, "We have taken off the kid gloves with these elements that cause riots." Black militants were incensed and were determined to prepare to fight it out if necessary.

Moderates warned that unless the nation gave serious attention to reforms as well as to "law and order," it was headed for disaster. Dr. King saw his poverty crusade as preventive action, as an attempt "to force Congressional action to provide either jobs or income for the poor," and thus to relieve some of the pressures that were leading to violent outbursts. Early in March a distinguished Black social psychologist, Kenneth Clark, speaking before a meeting of the Association of Existential Psychology and Psychiatry in New York, said that it was "continued white violence aimed at keeping the Negro in second place that was responsible for the Negro uprisings." With devastating irony and with references to Vietnam, Dr. Clark reminded white Americans that although maintenance of their superior status was their prime value, "you cannot have superior status if all the people over whom you were superior are dead." At the same time, however, he gave no comfort to the militants who wanted to take on the police-military establishment, stating that these forms of protest were "pathetic" because the numbers and resources of the Negro in the United States were "inadequate to mount the kind of violence that would do anything more than bring about his own destruction." According to Dr. Clark, Vietnam had made Americans—black and White—so callous with regard to violence that more and more people saw it as the only answer to their problems, and that some Negroes reasoned that it is "better to die quickly in a society incapable of bringing about justice instead of stringing the suffering out for a lifetime."

It was hard to convince the students in Orangeburg, however, that the blood there had been spilled in vain. By the time Dr. Clark spoke the students were back in their classrooms, and when twelve students walked down to the All-Star Bowling Lanes they were allowed to bowl! The management was now under a federal court order to cease and desist from discriminating. The Black community was unified behind an effective economic boycott and a biracial committee was meeting regularly to discuss grievances.

During the first week in March, the first serious ghetto outburst of the year occurred in Omaha, Nebraska. At the formative convention of George Wallace's American Independent Party, a group of Negro youths led by two white Catholic priests set off a demonstration in front of the speakers' platform. Between ten and fifteen persons were injured in the melée that broke out, and one youth and the two priests were arrested. Later in the evening an alleged Negro prowler was shot and killed by a guard, and shortly after, rioting and looting spread through the Black community. After this incident the local Urban League called upon the Department of Justice to investigate "white racism" in Omaha.

Throughout March the media were involved in constant discussion of the report of the President's Commission on Civil Disorders, which had been released in book form on March 3. In mid-March, the Senate permanent subcommittee on investigations, after having investigated rioting in Nashville, Houston and Plainfield, New Jersey, opened hearings on the causes of the Detroit disturbances during 1967. Senator John L. McClellan (D, Arkansas)—the chairman—and Senator Carl T. Curtis (R, Nebraska) seemed convinced that a national conspiracy was at work and were for firmer measures to put down disorders. But the first witness, Governor George Romney of Michigan, stressed the point that "we cannot expect to have law and order without justice." He and the Michigan state police director were skeptical of conspiracy theories. Romney recommended passage of a federal open housing law and called on the government "to invest more in people and less in space," but he cautioned against regarding increased spending as a panacea. Self-help by Negroes and greater respect for Negro individuals by white people were absolutely necessary. The Arkansas senator could not agree with him. Four days after Governor

Romney's testimony, President Johnson finally spoke out on the report of his National Advisory Commission on Civil Disorders. Harold Gal of the *New York Times* described his remarks as "long, rambling and somewhat defensive." It was an election year, and "law and order," not prescriptions for reform, was the popular theme. The President was treading warily.

Throughout the month, while the commission report was being debated, Dr. Martin Luther King had continued his effort to organize an interracial, interethnic, poor people's march to Washington, D.C. Meanwhile, a group of sanitation workers in Memphis, nearly all of whom were Negro, were on strike for union recognition, wage contracts, establishment of grievance machinery, and a payroll checkoff of dues. The mayor declared the strike illegal. The strikers began to engage in a series of demonstrations in the streets. The city government was adamant in its refusal to deal with the union. As the Lemberg Center reports in *Riot Data Review*, during the fourth week of the strike:

> . . . there were incidents of firebombings, bottle-throwing, garbage set afire and stoning of stores and police cars in black neighborhoods. Incidents took place as orderly meetings were conducted in black churches to organize a boycott of downtown stores. Sit-in held at City Hall. Police used nightsticks and antiriot gas in a Main St. clash with black marchers.

As the strike continued, some of Dr. King's followers in Memphis felt that his presence might help reduce the level of violence; also, the sanitation workers were anxious for his support. Advisers at the national level in the SCLC saw an expression of solidarity with these workers as being in line with preparations for the antipoverty march. Dr. King arrived and a march was planned on March 28. The Lemberg Center reports:

> . . . two hours prior to the march, 250 black students outside Hamilton High School tried to keep other students from entering and urged them to join the march. Students threw rocks and bottles at policemen who then donned gas masks. Groups dispersed and no gas was used. Shortly after 11:00 A.M. black youths who had refused to join the march [reputedly members of a gang called the Invaders] broke store windows along the march route. At 11:40 A.M. young blacks threw missiles at advancing policemen, who cleared the street, using fists, clubs, tear gas and Mace. Several instances of looting, numerous small fires . . . [and] reported cases of sniping followed.

The marchers took refuge in a church. Dr. King was whisked away uninjured. When he left he pledged to return (which he did) to demonstrate that a nonviolent protest could be successful. In the meantime, the Governor sent in state troopers and the National Guard. One boy had been killed on March 28 for alleged looting, and the casualties for the month in addition to this death were sixty-two injured. Over four hundred people were arrested, and property damage was estimated at $500,000. On April 3 the National Guard and the troopers were withdrawn, and a federal district judge issued a temporary restraining order to Dr. King against organizing a "massive demonstration." Speaking to two thousand persons in a Memphis church that night, Dr. King referred to the order as "a basic denial of the First Amendment privileges," and said that he would ignore it if he could not get it lifted. As he closed his speech, he said: "Well, I don't know what will happen now. We've got some difficult days ahead. But it really doesn't matter with me now. Because I've been to the mountain top. I won't mind."

This was his last speech. The next day (April 4), at about 6:00 P.M., as he stood on the balcony of his hotel room, Dr. King was shot. He was dead by 7:05 P.M.

Reactions to the Assassination

That widespread violence erupted immediately after the death of Dr. King was an ironic tragedy. Certainly it was a type of response completely alien to his philosophy. But the Black masses, however much they may have respected and admired Dr. King for his courage and his achievements, had never made a commitment to the philosophy of nonviolence.

The events of the summer of 1967 set the pattern for the response to Dr. King's death. Between April 4 and 6, 1968, two persons were killed in Memphis, thirty were injured and 262 were arrested. The Lemberg Center summarized the reaction in Memphis as follows:

Dr. King was hit in the jaw and neck by a rifle bullet at 6:01 local time. He died an hour later at 7:05. Soon after, sporadic violence began in the black section of Memphis in the form of sniper fire, the throwing of bricks and bottles at policemen and the firebombing and looting of stores. Mayor Loeb reinstated a curfew minutes after hearing news of the assassination while on his way to a speaking engagement at the University of Mississippi. The night's violence ended shortly after midnight. On Fri., Atty. Gen. Ramsey Clark met with black and white leaders in Memphis in an effort to stabilize the city, as an uneasy calm was broken by occasional window-breaking and looting. Some 400 National Guardsmen kept generally out of sight, but individual units dispatched to scenes of incidents as they were reported. Middle-aged blacks, mostly ministers, walked the streets and urged youths to avert further violence. One black fatally shot by police during a gunfight after he was allegedly caught looting. Sporadic acts of looting and arson continued Sat. but were less frequent as only 4 people were arrested. 229 fires, 17 listed as major, reported in the three-day period.

The reaction in Washington, D.C., stunned the nation. Looting and arson accounted for over $20,000,000 in property damage; eleven persons were killed, 1,113 injured and 8,236 arrested over a six-day period. The Lemberg Center gives this report:

Dr. King's death reported at 8:19 P.M. Thurs. Minutes later, a crowd gathered in the area of 14th and U Streets, scene of a disturbance on April 2. Stokely Carmichael arrived at 9:06 P.M. For the next hour he led crowds of up to 200 people around the area telling store owners to close in respect for Dr. King. By 10:00 people began ignoring his advice to "go home! This is not the time, brothers! . . . If you don't have a gun, go home!" Window-breaking and fires continued until after 1 A.M. Early Fri. morning, the entire 2,800-man police force mobilized and 6,721 Federal and National Guard troops entered the city as widespread looting and arson occurred in the Near Northwest section. Police used tear gas to disperse groups of 200 to 300. Mayor Walter Washington imposed a 13-hour curfew. There were several reports of sniping. Relative calm observed Sun. (4/7) as 1,874 additional troops were present. 2,094 troops added Tues. bringing the total to 15,246. Total of 711 fires reported, 645 buildings damaged or destroyed, encompassing 283 housing units and 8 public and institutional establishments.

In nearby Baltimore $14,000,000 worth of property was destroyed; six persons were killed, 900 injured and 5,800 arrested. The Lemberg summary continues:

At about 4:30 P.M. Sat. [April 6] police dispersed a crowd numbering 200 black youths. Activation of the National Guard began at about 6 P.M. The first major fire set at 6:15 at a furniture store. At 7:30 some 400 state troopers ordered into East Baltimore, where rock-throwing and window-breaking were widespread. Federal troops use CS gas on 2 occasions to prevent crowds from looting. Gov. Spiro T. Agnew imposed a curfew. Incidents Sun. most frequent between 5 P.M. and 11:15 P.M. at which time 5,900 National Guard troops moved into East Baltimore to assist 1,200–1,500 city and 400–500 state policemen. Widespread looting and fires reported. Firemen shot at as they responded to calls. On Mon. (4/8) groups of whites and blacks confronted each other in the streets, but no major violence resulted. Tues. incidents confined to scattered fires and sniping at policemen. In all, 883 white-owned and 74 black-owned businesses burned, looted or damaged. A total of 11,000 Federal and National Guard troops in the city.

In Chicago, high school students began a series of protests; then the poverty-stricken overcrowded West Side, which had rioted in 1966, exploded again:

Tensions high *prior* to Dr. King's murder. On Thurs. afternoon, all white public aid case workers ordered out of the West Side due to reports of impending trouble. At the same time, black students at 5 or more high schools planned to stage walkouts protesting local conditions. On April 5, approximately 80 inner city schools in predominantly black areas closed . . . during the day due to student walkouts, school disturbances and neighborhood tensions. Many students marched from school to school seeking a way to memorialize Dr. King. In some areas, students clashed with police. That afternoon, groups of youngsters, mainly of high school age, marched toward the Loop. 6,700 Guardsmen arrived later in the day. Leaves cancelled for the city's 11,500 policemen. On April 6, looting and violence spread from the West to the

South and Near North Sides. The Guard Commander authorized use of tear gas but no evidence it was actually used. Mayor imposed a curfew and banned the sale of guns, ammunition and flammables in portable containers. 5,000 Federal troops arrived on April 6. Police activity along with looting, firebombing and sniping heaviest between April 5 and 7. Scattered incidents occurred between April 7 and 11. Federal and National Guard troops left during the following two days. Virtually all businesses attacked were white-owned; most were in black neighborhoods. Several teenage gangs, including the West Side Vice Lords and the Woodlawn Blackstone Rangers, praised in quieting violence in their neighborhoods.

Over an eight-day period, nine persons were killed, five hundred injured and 2,931 arrested. Property damage amounted to $11,000,000.

Almost two-thirds of the deaths and nearly 85 per cent of the property damage occurred in three cities—Washington, D.C., Chicago and Baltimore, while over two-thirds of the federal and National Guard forces used were deployed in these three cities (see Table 3).

Rioting in New York City lasted only three days, and there was a concerted successful effort to "quiet" Harlem. The Lemberg report continues:

Hours after Dr. King's death, looting, window-breaking and suspected arson occurred in Harlem. Hundreds of stores looted, and two multi-alarm fires and several smaller ones reported. Mayor Lindsay made 2 tours of the area. Near Times Square, black youths who had been watching a march from a city housing project smashed the windows of a shoe store and fled with some merchandise. Between midnight and 7 A.M. Fri. there was extensive looting of black- and white-owned stores. No sniping reported. By Fri. morning hundreds of young blacks, including members of Harlem CORE, worked to stop the disorder by persuasion. By Sat. morning, calm restored. On April 15 group of 70 black and Puerto Rican small businessmen, many of whom sustained losses from the disorder, charged Mayor Lindsay and the police with playing down the damage and exhibiting "an attitude of appeasement" toward rioters.

In Newark, New Jersey, with its recent history of riots, the immediate reaction was comparatively restrained but before the month was over there was a serious flareup. There were no casualties, but $1.5 million in property damage was done:

On nights of April 4 and 5 disorder confined to sporadic looting, broken store windows, isolated gatherings of black youths and several small fires of suspicious origin. On April 9 a series of 392 fires began at 2:30 P.M. in the Central Ward as funeral services for Dr. King were in progress in Atlanta. Most of the 20 major blazes, the looting of over 50 stores, and the smashing of 300 windows, took place between 10 P.M. and midnight. The following day Mayor Addonizio charged that the Tues. fires might have been set by "white militants." Sporadic looting and 58 fires reported April 10. No further incidents until April 20, when

TABLE 3

Comparison of Totals for Three Cities Having Civil Disorders Following the Assassination of Dr. King

(Total figures are for April 1968)

(From *Riot Data Review*, No. 2, Lemberg Center)

City	Dates of Disorders	Arrests	Injured	Killed	Property Damage	All Troops
Chicago	Apr. 4–11	2,931	500	9	$11,000,000	11,700
Washington	Apr. 4–9	8,236	1,113	11	24,000,000	15,100
Baltimore	Apr. 6–9	5,800	900	6	14,000,000	11,000
1. Totals: 3 cities		16,967	2,513	26	$49,000,000	37,800
2. Total for all areas		27,000	3,500	43	$58,000,000	58,600
3. Per cent of nation-wide total figures for April held by all 3 cities		62.8	71.2	60	84.5	64.7

CHART 2

Number of Disorders Beginning on Each Day: April 1–12, 1968

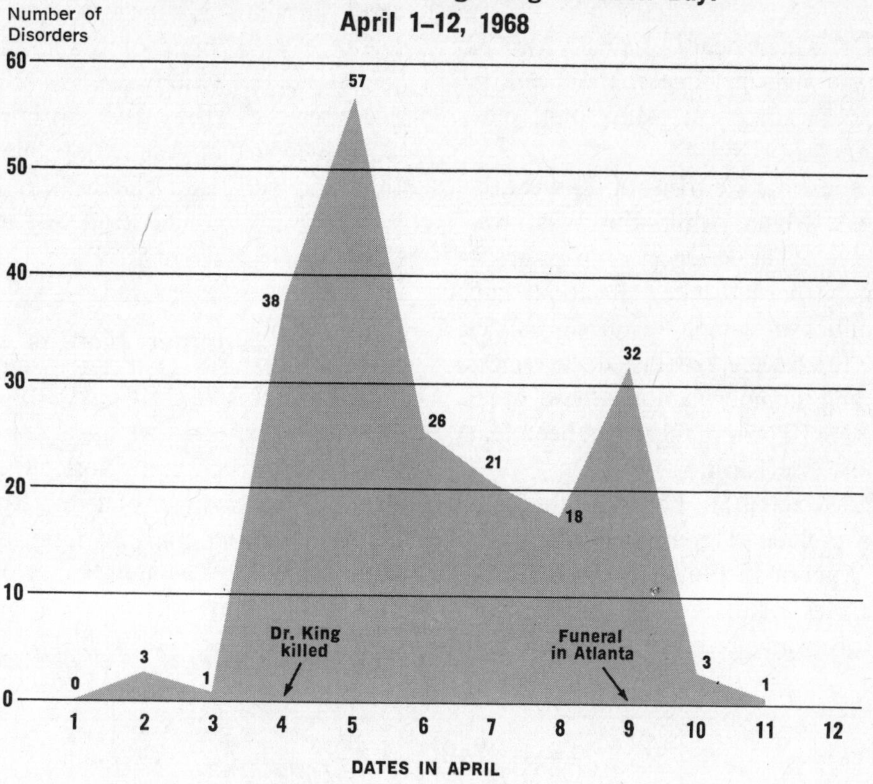

Number of Disorders

Dr. King killed

Funeral in Atlanta

DATES IN APRIL

From *Riot Data Review*, No. 2, August 1968, Lemberg Center.

> fires destroyed 34 buildings on 5 Central Ward streets leaving more than 500 persons homeless.

For the month of April, 202 disorders, distributed throughout the nation, appear in the Lemberg count. At least 180 were directly associated with Dr. King's death. The relation between the disorders appearing in the first half of April and Dr. King's assassination appears clearly in Chart 2.

The National Guard and federal troops were used more times and in greater numbers in April 1968 than during all of 1967. (They were used only twice in 1968 *prior* to April: six hundred in Orangeburg and four thousand in Memphis.) During the period immediately following Dr. King's assassination, 34,920 National Guardsmen and 23,700 federal troops were stationed in twenty-two cities. Despite this massing of forces, the number of persons killed was smaller than in the previous year: forty-three in twelve localities as against eighty-two in thirteen localities during 1967 (see Table 1).

Casualties were kept low by deliberate decision, in most cities, not to fire upon people caught in the act of looting. On April 15 Mayor Daley of Chicago expressed his disagreement with such a policy, and on April 18 the Attorney General publicly rebuked him. For the rest of the year there was considerable controversy over this question.

The results, then, of the Lemberg Center's report showed the following facts about the April disorders:

> 1. Almost as many disorders in the month of April this year were recorded as were recorded for the entire year 1967. . . .
>
> 2. More cities and more states were recorded as having experienced disorders in April 1968 than in the entire year 1967.
>
> 3. More arrests and more injuries were recorded during disorders in April 1968 than for the entire year 1967.
>
> 4. Only slightly less property damage was recorded in April 1968 than for the entire year 1967.

The Post-Assassination Period: May and June

Anger over Dr. King's death gradually cooled after April. There were fifty-one communities in which disorders occurred in May, but only twenty-one in June (see Table 4).

During May and June the focus of the disturbances was in the North, while the West was virtually uninvolved. The sharpest drop in activity occurred in the border states. In about half of the communities in which disturbances occurred in May, these were the last disturbances for the spring and summer; among these areas was Washington, D.C., where there had been fear of a "hot summer" (see Table 5).

In Boston and Manhattan, however, the May episodes were a prelude to continued conflict in June, July and August. In Philadelphia, Chicago and Gary there was a lull in June with an upsurge in July; in Newark, N.J., a lull in June and July, with an outburst in August; in Baltimore, quiet in July only; and in Brooklyn, Memphis and Louisville, only in June.

There were fifteen cities in which May was "cool" but in which flareups occurred in June; the largest of these was Pittsburgh, where violence recurred in August. Mobile had trouble in June and July, and Natchez in June only. One Western city was involved in June—Richmond, California (see Table 6).

The Summer Months of 1968

The months of July and August did bring a "hot summer," as had been feared, but neither property destruction nor loss of life was so extensive as in the summer of 1967. Nor was the number of cities involved so large as in April and May of 1968. The number in June was about half that of May; then it rose sharply in July and again in August (see Table 4). Cities that had

TABLE 4

Number of Communities Having Disorders, May–August 1968

(By month and region)

	May	June	July	August	Total
North	23	7	10	15	55
Midwest	10	6	18	23	57
West	1	2	9	3	15
Border	9	2	5	8	24
South	8	4	5	11	28
Total	51	21	47	60	179

TABLE 5

Communities Having Disturbances in May 1968 and After

1. **May, June, July and August:** Boston, Mass.; New York (Manhattan)
2. **May, June and August:** Baltimore, Md.
3. **May, July and August:** Brooklyn, N.Y.; Chicago, Ill.; Louisville, Ky.; Memphis, Tenn.
4. **May and June:** Camden, N.J.; Lancaster, Pa.; Milwaukee, Wis.
5. **May and July:** New Bedford, Mass.; Gary, Ind.; Minneapolis, Minn.; Paterson, N.J.; Philadelphia, Pa.; Somerville, N.J.
6. **May and August:** Alexandria, Va.; Madison, Wis.; Newark, Del.; Newark, N.J.; Salisbury, Md.; Tampa, Fla.
7. **May only:** Ann Arbor, Mich.; Banning, Calif.; Battle Creek, Mich.; Bristol Township, Pa.; Carbondale, Ill.; Charlottesville, Va.; Cheyney, Pa.; Columbia, S.C.; Coral Gables, Fla.; Dearborn, Mich.; Dover, Del.; Elizabeth, N.J.; Evanston, Ill.; Fayetteville, Ark.; Fruitland, Md.; Gaffney, S.C.; Hillsboro, N.C.; Jamaica, N.Y.; Jefferson City, Mo.; Jersey City, N.J.; Long Island City, N.Y.; New Britain, Conn.; Newburgh, N.Y.; New Haven, Conn.; Oxford, Pa.; Stamford, Conn.; Washington, D.C.; Wilkinsburg, Pa.; Yonkers, N.Y.

TABLE 6

Cities Having No Disorders in May 1968 but with Disorders in June and After

1. **June and July:** Mobile, Ala.; South Bend, Ind.
2. **June and August:** Pittsburgh, Pa.
3. **June only:** Altamonte Springs, Fla.; Darby, Pa.; Denver, Colo.; Durham, N.C.; Flint, Mich.; Franklin, Tenn.; Massillon, Ohio; Natchez, Miss.; Paulsboro, N.J.; Richmond, Calif.; Topeka, Kan.; Wilberforce, Ohio.

TABLE 7

Cities Having No Disorders in May or June 1968 but with Disorders in July and August

1. **July and August:** Akron, Ohio; Cincinnati, Ohio; Cleveland, Ohio; Gainesville, Fla.; Grand Rapids, Mich.; Jackson, Mich.; Kansas City, Kan.; Los Angeles, Calif.; Wilmington, Del; York, Pa.
2. **July only:** Benton Harbor, Mich.; Bronx, N.Y.; Dade City, Fla.; Erie, Pa.; Goldsboro, N.C.; Hanford, Calif.; Jefferson, Ind.; Kalamazoo, Mich.; Maywood, Ill.; Midland, Tex.; Muncie, Ind.; Omaha, Neb.; Pacifica, Calif.; Pasco, Wash.; Peoria, Ill.; Pittsburg, Calif.; St. Louis, Mo.; San Francisco, Calif.; Seattle, Wash.; Stockton, Calif.; Weirton, W. Va.; Whitewater, Wis.

had no disorders in May or June were now the scene of summer riots: small Western towns not previously rent by such conflicts, as well as such cities as Los Angeles and San Francisco, which had been relatively quiet earlier in the year; and several large Middle West communities.

One previously quiet Midwestern industrial city had its complacency shattered by a conventional-type ghetto riot in mid-July—Akron, Ohio. For three years Negro leaders and an interracial ministerial group had been pleading, without success, for the city administration to institute a riot prevention program (to include Black militants, among others). The small but clearly defined ghetto had all the grievances of similar communities elsewhere, and after the assassination of Martin Luther King, an SCLC leader, Albert Cox, opened an office for the Midwest Caravan of the Poor People's March. During the week of July 20 a fight broke out between two ghetto gangs. It involved between five hundred and a thousand individuals, and it quickly turned into burning and looting directed at white stores. Before it was over a fifteen-year-old youth had been wounded by a policeman's shotgun blast; forty-two arrests had been made; scores of people were injured; and the National Guard had been called in to restore order. Early in the disturbance Cox, at the request of high police officials, had waded into the crowd to try to restore order. He was beaten and sprayed with Mace by a nervous young policeman. A police officer called this a "tragic mistake." The SCLC leader commented: "All they saw was a Black face and they just lashed out at it." The Urban League director said, "Akron has been warned that it was sitting on a powder keg, but we're still apathetic."

In Cleveland, forty-two miles from Akron, the years of apathy had been overcome. A Black mayor, Carl Stokes, was in office. The ghetto had coined a slogan in 1967: "Keep it cool for Carl," and his influence had helped to snuff out incipient rioting after Dr. King's assassination. Soon after the Akron fracas, however, Cleveland saw a disturbance that was very different from the usual riot. It was a type that had been expected to occur someday, somewhere.

During his first year in office Stokes had tried to keep the channels of communication open with Black militants as well as with moderates and to see that some of the militant organizations shared in the anti-poverty money being spent. The leader of one small group, Fred Ahmed Evans of the Black Nationalists of New Libya, had received public assistance for some of his projects.

On July 21 Mayor Stokes, while participating in a panel discussion in Washington, was informed by his office that the Cleveland police had evidence that armed "uprisings" by Black militants were scheduled for the next morning in Cleveland, Detroit, Chicago and Pittsburgh. Events moved quickly. At a meeting with the Mayor's aides, police officials accused Fred Ahmed Evans and his followers of assembling weapons which would probably be used in the planned "uprising." A delegation headed by George Forbes, a Negro councilman, was sent to Ahmed's home to "touch bases with the brother." When the Black delegation arrived, Ahmed ventilated some of his grievances. He had been evicted from his original headquarters and now, having renovated a storefront at his own expense, he had received a notice to vacate the premises. He was reported as saying: "You know, Black folks got a right to have a piece of the earth. I'm not going to be shoved off this earth." He then asked Councilman George Forbes to "get these damn cops out of here," promising, "George, I'll be cool."

The police were not removed, however, and Ahmed's men decided to do battle with them. Violence precipitated by snipers set off a more general attack by ghetto dwellers involving some looting. Mayor Stokes decided to withdraw all white police from the area on the first night, an action which drew much criticism from some circles. The next day, however, the National Guard moved in to restore order, and the episode was over. The first large-scale episode triggered off by a small group of organized snipers had taken place in a Black community. This was the basic significance of the Cleveland incident. No "uprisings" occurred in other cities.

During the week of July 28 to August 3, there was widespread fear that a wave of summer riots had begun. An episode in Pittsburg, California, combined the conventional riot pattern with the new "guerrilla tactics." A crowd of between seventy-five and a hundred persons had gathered to try to prevent an arrest. Members of the crowd hurled bottles at the police car. A call for assistance brought other police cars to the scene, at which point snipers hidden behind bushes and buildings opened fire. The police did not return the fire, but arrested fifteen individuals.

The night before this episode, in San Francisco, snipers had fired on a police car carrying two members of the San Francisco Crime Commission who had come to inspect a public housing project that had been firebombed. At about this time, too, fires were set on three successive nights in Goldsboro, North Carolina. A serious incident also occurred in Gary, Indiana, another city with a Black mayor. One thing became clear from the experiences of Washington, Cleveland and Gary: that the presence of a Black mayor was no guarantee of a riot-free ghetto.

On July 31 a *Chicago Defender* headline proclaimed that: VIOLENCE FLARES ANEW IN STEEL CITY'S STREETS, " . . . as scattered incidents of firebombing occurred in an area approximately forty blocks from where sniping . . . and wholesale looting had occurred last weekend." The precipitating incident seemed to have been resentment over the arrest of two members of a motorcycle gang on a rape charge.

The next week the press was referring to "guerrilla warfare" in Chicago, as about a hundred Black young people looted an A. and P. store being boycotted by Operation Breadbasket; and in nearby Maywood some three hundred Black NAACP youth tried to force their way into a meeting of the village board to present grievances. In northern California the Black Panther Party for Self-Defense was warning the ghetto to avoid mass confrontation with the police ("the pigs") and to leave the fighting to well-disciplined "vanguard" groups.

New York, Baltimore and Newark, as well as Boston and Memphis, were the scenes of disorders in August, as they had been in earlier months. Thirty-six communities had their first disturbances of the May–August period. Nineteen of these had not been affected during the pre-May period (* in Table 8).

Mayor Richard J. Daley's eleven-member Chicago Riot Study Committee handed in a 165-page report early in August, having found "an alarming hatred for whites," and a widespread feeling that "the entire existing political-economic-educational structure . . . is anti-Black." This report was emphatic, however, in its conclusion that there was no "evidence of any plans of violence or disorder, organized from within or without the city by any persons, group, or groups constituting a conspiracy." Regarding possible "conspiracies" for disturbances in August, a prediction appeared in an article by Richard E. Rubinstein and Stephan Kaplan in the April 1968 *New Republic* ("Black and Blue in Chicago"), which cited Charles Hamilton and Stokely Carmichael's book *Black Power* (1967) to back up a statement that "the most militant black organizations are not terribly interested in

TABLE 8

Cities Having Disorders in August 1968, but Not in May–July

*Bedminster, N.J.	Chicago Heights, Ill.	*Charleston, W. Va.
*Fostoria, Ohio	*Evansville, Ind.	Charlotte, N.C.
Hartford, Conn.	*Fort Wayne, Ind.	East Point, Ga.
*Lima, Ohio	*Harvey-Dixmoor, Ill.	*Fort Hood, Tex.
*Middletown, Conn.	Inkster, Mich.	Little Rock, Ark.
Providence, R.I.	Lansing, Mich.	Miami, Fla.
Queens, N.Y.	*Muskegon, Mich.	N. Little Rock, Ark.
Rahway, N.J.	*Racine, Wis.	*Owensboro, Ky.
*Springfield, Ohio	*Saginaw, Mich.	*Riverside, Calif.
Syracuse, N.Y.	*St. Paul, Minn.	*St. Petersburg, Fla.
*Waltham, Mass.	Waterloo, Iowa	Seaside, Calif.
	Wichita, Kan.	Zebulon, Ga.
	*Ypsilanti, Mich.	

plans for August demonstrations. Black guerrillas *might*, of course, try to take advantage of the confusion—if, for example, white troops . . . are stationed in ghetto streets."

One serious riot during the first half of August was that at the Republican national convention in Miami. Rev. Ralph Abernathy of the SCLC helped to quiet the rioters. Other Southern cities also had disturbances, but relatively minor ones, such as: fourteen cases of arson in Mobile, which the police blamed on a recent visit by Stokely Carmichael; a sharp battle in St. Petersburg, Florida; and three nights of fighting in Goldsboro, North Carolina.

The most ominous outbursts occurred in San Francisco and in a nearby town, Pittsburg, California, and in Los Angeles at the conclusion of the annual Watts community festival. There was skirmishing along the boundary between Dixmoor and Harvey, Illinois, near Chicago, and in Inkster, a suburb of Detroit. But the big ghettoes were relatively quiet.

Memphis had a scare during the third week in August when a group of four or five Black youths (allegedly members of the Invaders) had a "shoot-out" with the police and when several other youths were arrested for pointing guns at two white men. At that time, too, "disturbances" took place in Ypsilanti, Michigan, Evansville, Indiana, and Wichita, Kansas, as well as in Providence, Rhode Island (somewhat earlier). In none of these cases was there loss of life or extensive property damage. Even flareups in Cleveland and in Pittsburgh, Pennsylvania, did not assume serious proportions. August had ended, and all in all Black people had not made the summer exceptionally "hot." They had "done their thing" in April, when they had let America know how they felt about the murder of Martin Luther King. The summer confrontation that really shook the nation was the battle between white students and the Chicago police during the Democratic national convention—not a ghetto explosion. It was a reminder, however, that many white students—as well as Black—were insisting upon thoroughgoing social change.

The Last Four Months of 1968

Past experience had led to the expectation of greatly diminished ghetto rioting in the fall and winter, and outbreaks of the conventional type *were* few at this time in 1968. During the first two weeks in September, however, a group of young people in a Syracuse housing project turned it into a virtual fortress from which they stoned the cars of passing white motorists and sallied forth to attack white pedestrians for three nights. The chief of police decided to "saturate the area." This increased the tension still more. The nature of the precipitating incident is not clear, but one mother of five said: "Black kids are simply showing that they are tired of white promises and white abuses. They're showing that we can have a long hot winter as well as a long hot summer." The chief of police, after talking with some of the young people, commented: "No one speaks for these kids and no one controls them—not the neighborhood organizations, not their parents, not even their own clubs. We accomplished nothing."

Tension had been mounting throughout the year at Trenton (New Jersey) High School where the proportion of Black students had risen to 55 per cent. (In fact, the increase in Negro students throughout the city had led to the appointment of a Black superintendent of schools in September.) Before the month was out, fighting between Black and white students at Trenton High led first to a tripling of the security force and then to the closing of the school. After this, some of the Black students began stoning cars of white people passing through a predominantly Negro area. On September 28, the mayor imposed a curfew.

On the same day, in Aurora, Illinois, and on Chicago's North Side, Negro teen-agers became involved in rock-throwing episodes that drew police action. In Sarasota, Florida, according to the *New York Times*, "the police broke up a milling crowd of 300 rock-hurling Negroes with tear gas barrages," and "several shots were fired in the melée but it was not immediately known who fired them." A Negro night-spot had been teargassed the night before, and the community had retaliated by stoning cars having white occupants. As the month ended, Chicago North Side disturbances were centered around one particular high school.

On October 4 the *New York Times* reported that the Attorney General was pleased with the "clear and significant decline" of riots and disorders during the summer of 1968, and that he attributed it to "police trained to neither overact nor underact." Before a week had passed, however, the city manager of Peekskill, New York, declared a state of emergency and instituted a curfew after small groups of Negro young people had smashed windows in twenty-five downtown stores and in the city hall. (There was no looting.) They were protesting the shooting down on the streets of a young Negro by a white bartender, and they were rebelling against moderate Negro leaders who wanted to organize a more sedate form of protest.

In Pittsburgh in the second week of October, when a white grocer was killed by two young Negroes and whites retaliated with a bomb and gunfire, ghetto dwellers spoke of organizing vigilante groups. Even more significant and serious than these disturbances, however, were those involving educational institutions. Throughout the week the police arrested Blacks for possession of fire bombs and other weapons, and on other charges. Two white youths were also arrested in the Negro section. Rioting broke out in Buffalo, New York, on October 17 after a peaceful rally for Presidential candidate Dick Gregory and lasted several days. Negro leaders charged police brutality.

The Lemberg Center *Riot Data Review*, No. 2 (published in the summer of 1968), commenting on trends in civil disorders, noted that:

> There were 44 disorders involving schools recorded for the first three months of this year. The figures break down as follows: 5 in January, 19 in February and 20 in March. . . .
>
> Our conclusions regarding schools are, therefore, consistent with our findings for the total number of disorders. The assassination of Dr. King precipitated an unusual number of "school disorders" for the month of April [89]. At the same time, a continuation of the rate of civil disorders involving schools was uncovered *irrespective* of the King tragedy [20 out of 89 that would probably have occurred even if the assassination had not taken place], which served to intensify the trend.
>
> Unrest in the schools appears to be a general and long-range phenomenon, the sources of which must be sought for in any or all of the following areas: the search for excitement and action by youth, specific grievances directed at the quality of education and school facilities and rising antagonism between white and black students.

The analysts went on to say: ". . . we can predict that schools, everywhere, at both the college and pre-college level, will be sites of disorders when they reopen in the fall." The prediction was borne out during the last four months of 1968.

Two conflicts held the news spotlight during the fall and winter: the struggle between the Ocean Hill-Brownsville community school board in Brooklyn, New York, and the teachers' union which opposed the methods by which Black control was being established in this decentralized school district; and the prolonged conflict at San Francisco State College, where the Black Students Union, in alliance with the Third World Liberation Front, was locked in battle with the college administration over a demand for an autonomous Black studies department. Both conflicts were extreme examples of types of situations which triggered off civil disorders throughout the country. These disorders involved a thrust toward a greater measure of "Black power." There was a shift in setting from the ghetto streets, with their unorganized crowd behavior, to college campuses and high school corridors, where organized groups of Black people were involved in confrontations with governmental officials who sometimes invoked "police power" to maintain "law and order."

The *Riot Data Review* suggested in August that:

> In this summer's interlude, it would be highly advisable for school superintendents and members of school boards to hold conferences in which experiences with tense interracial situations were shared and solutions, not relying upon last resort repression imposed by law enforcement agencies, were discussed. Law enforcement, of course, is important. But it is not the permanent nor the final solution and in many instances is provocative of further disorder.

Few such preventive measures were taken, and a type of disturbance that had been endemic earlier in the year continued after the summer was over. The following are some of the more dramatic of the earlier cases:

MILWAUKEE, FEBRUARY 6

> Students at North Division High School (99% black) involved in a disturbance as at least two fires are set in rest rooms, file cabinets are toppled, window shades and bulletin boards are torn and a number of windows are broken. A police officer hit in the head by a rock. The disturbance apparently stemmed from student grievances centering around [the desire for] greater emphasis on Afro-American history.

LACKAWANNA, NEW YORK, FEBRUARY 9

> Lackawanna Senior High School closed on Friday afternoon following fist fights between whites and blacks. Police called in from Lackawanna and Buffalo to quell the disturbance. The tensions may have increased because of Negro History Week beginning next Monday and complete lack of black teachers employed by the school (11% of the students are black). Up to 350 of the school's 1,090 students involved in the incident.

CHICAGO, FEBRUARY 21

> Disturbance occurs after black students attempt to hold memorial programs for Malcolm X. At Calumet High, a school dropout tries to address a group of students from atop a lunchroom table, urging them to leave school. Students throw plates at policemen sent to maintain order. As classes end at 12:50 P.M., about 200 Calumet students begin marching toward St. Leo High School but are dispersed by police. A brick is thrown through a window of St. Leo High School by an unidentified passerby.

During 1967 there had been a progressive decline in civil disorders after August, the number dropping to five cases by December. Similar de-escalation was expected for 1968, and it did take place. A contributing factor was the Presidential election campaign which siphoned off some potential discontent. Offsetting this factor, however, was the commotion frequently caused when George Wallace appeared in Northern and Western communities and in which young Black people sometimes took an active part. There was an extension, too, of the Black Panther organization to Middle Western and Eastern Seaboard cities as well as to some college campuses, although, on the whole, direct confrontation with the police within ghettoes was avoided by the Panthers.

There seemed to be emerging within Negro communities a drive toward guiding aggression into constructive channels and away from expressing itself in sporadic outbursts, and some of the most militant Black nationalist groups were cooperating, through Black caucuses and Black united fronts in this activity.

There was also a tendency to pinpoint the police rather than the white merchant as the main enemy. In militant circles there was fear that "law and order" might be given priority over social reform, with attempts being made to round up the more militant—and violent—Black leaders, and to incarcerate them as part of a general riot-prevention plan.

As far as Black student unrest was concerned, however, there was a growing feeling that it must be seen in perspective, as a special part of the world-wide student demand for greater participation in the educational process.

Banner-carrying members of the militant Black Panther Party march along 42nd Street in New York, en route to a scheduled news conference at United Nations Plaza. The July 22 conference was called to protest the murder trial of Black Panther defense minister Huey P. Newton in Oakland, California.

The Civil Rights Movement—1968

Daniel C. Thompson

Introduction

THE UNFOLDING of American history, as seen from the vantage point of 1968, emphasizes the important fact that civil rights organizations are inherent and indispensable to the democratic process, to which this nation is heavily committed. They are necessary to the continuous extension of democracy to an increasing number of relatively powerless groups.

From the very beginning the civil rights movement in the United States has been primarily identified with Black Americans' struggle for equality of citizenship. This is so because civil rights organizations designed specifically "for the Advancement of Colored People" have, in a much broader sense, championed basic issues which have helped to clarify the essential legal and moral principles upon which this nation was founded and for which it has continued to sacrifice, especially during times of war. Thus practically all civil gains achieved by Black Americans have been in actual fact gains for all Americans, regardless of race. The civil rights movement is actually much broader in scope and function than are the total activities and membership of the designated civil rights organizations. From time to time all institutions, agencies and organizations in American society are expected to make some direct or indirect contribution in support of individual integrity and citizenship rights. This is especially true of Black American organizations. Indeed, to a large extent Negro Americans tend to measure the effectiveness of their organizations in terms of their support of "civil rights" activities, programs and ideologies.

For the most part the civil rights contributions made by non-civil-rights organizations such as the church, the schools, business, and civic and social clubs stem from what might be called "enlightened self-interest" and are only indirectly related to the Black American's struggle for equality. As a rule their civil rights activities and contributions are secondary to their traditional programs and activities. Their efforts, though very important, would not be sufficient to initiate and sustain a viable civil rights movement such as is essential in this society, which is characterized by powerful special interest groups who are in relentless competition for success and survival. In such a social context any weak or disesteemed minority group is very likely to be overlooked altogether, deliberately exploited by one or more of the competing power forces, or even persecuted when deemed expedient. Consequently, Black Americans, who have been more or less relegated to the status of despised foreigners in this nation, have had the most constantly negative experiences with established power groups. Therefore, in order to survive they have had to invent organizations, social strategies and a wide variety of leadership patterns designed to bring effective social pressure to bear upon established institutions and power groups with whom they have had to live and do business. For a relatively weak minority group to exert effective social pressure on a major power group—such as a political party, large business enterprise or school system—its activities must be calculated to compromise or undermine the competitive potentials of that group in relation to other major power groups. This, precisely, has been the grand strategy of civil rights organizations.

Traditionally each civil rights organization has focused mainly upon some central social issue directly related to the citizenship status of Black Americans while giving secondary attention to other problems of citizenship; and the organizations differ in the primary issues they espouse. There are times, however, when the ideologies, major programs and central issues championed by the several organizations draw close together and even overlap. This consensus usually occurs during times of more than ordinary interracial crises, when some one or two issues of Black citizenship become dominant. This has been the case a number of times since the school desegregation crisis began during the middle 1950's. Time and again, in one community after another, crises over such issues as school desegregation, the use of public facilities and accommodations, voter registration, open housing and better employment have brought all civil rights organizations together to attack a key problem.

Such cooperation became a familiar pattern during the late 1950's and early 1960's. At times an accepted minor program of one organization became a major program for all. The 1963 massive March on Washington and the epic march from Selma to Montgomery, in which many thousands of people, representing all races, social classes and religious groups in this nation, participated, were planned and executed jointly by all major civil rights organizations. These marches dramatized the unity the organizations had come to feel was necessary in order to exert effective pressure upon a powerful, reluctant Congress.

During 1968 each of the civil rights organizations made a strong bid to reestablish its self-identity. Some attempted to do this in a constructive manner by reaffirming and extending their commitments to traditional programs of action. Others did it by denouncing other civil rights organizations and bitterly criticizing established civil rights leaders. The fact is, except for a few public demonstrations sponsored jointly by all of the better-known organizations, during 1968 *conflict* within the ranks of the civil rights movement was much more characteristic than *cooperation*.

Some Major Characteristics of the Civil Rights Movement in 1968

During 1968 a fundamental change in the stance of the civil rights movement became increasingly pronounced. Whereas in the past most of the energy and resources of civil rights organizations had been directed toward activities calculated to *remove* legal, extra-legal and customary barriers to equal citizenship for Black Americans, *in 1968 the programs and resources of civil rights organizations were primarily directed toward implementing certain basic citizenship rights.* An analysis of the many ideological pronouncements by top civil rights leaders and key resolutions accepted or endorsed by both the more established and the new civil rights organizations indicates that the primary concern in 1968 was with "human rights" rather than with the narrower, legalistic conception of "civil rights." Therefore, there was an abrupt, dramatic end to the determined patience Black Americans had developed during the long period of slavery and had somehow managed to keep during the more than fifty years of meticulous civil rights litigation. In 1968 Black Americans showed little willingness to wait patiently for their personal and civil rights to be decided by reluctant courts whose practice had been to make one narrow "civil rights" decision after another. Furthermore, even after limited court orders regarding the civil rights of Black Americans were handed down, white power groups had invariably resorted to every possible subterfuge to evade such orders.

And so in 1968 the general mood of the civil rights movement was significantly different from what it had ever been before. This mood is best characterized by the angry impatience of Black youth in the ugly, disesteemed ghettoes of large, poorly governed cities outside the South. These youths scornfully reject the generally slow, painfully logical, red-tape-ridden decision-making process employed by the Establishment in response to demands for needed changes. As a rule this impatient Black youth in 1968 tended to ignore so-called "traditional channels and constituted authority" as they demanded revolutionary changes in the status of Black Americans—"NOW!"

The new attitude in the civil rights movement may be understood in terms of several basic trends that emerged or became more pronounced during 1968. Among these was the tendency for *the main focus of interest and activity of civil rights organizations to shift away from racial segregation in the South toward the plight of the poor in the Black ghettoes of the North.* This change in general direction was due, of course, to a number of complex things. Fundamentally, however, it was a response to bitter criticism on the part of many Black Americans that the intense, bloody decade or more of civil rights struggle, which began with the historic Montgomery bus boycott in December 1955, had achieved some significant, though limited, gains for the Black middle class but had brought no noticeable benefits to the poor in the Black ghettoes.

Civil rights organizations differed in the degree to which they responded to the criticism that they were middle-class-oriented. Yet civil rights leaders were disturbed and made some deliberate attempts to make their organizations more relevant to the problems of the urban poor.

The persistent demand for involvement in the economic problems of the Black ghettoes of the North was particularly challenging to the Southern Christian Leadership Conference. This organization had been founded by the great charismatic leader Dr. Martin Luther King, Jr., as a direct response to racial segregation in the South. Not only did this organization set the style of Black protest for more than a decade, but its leader, Dr. King, became the most widely accepted symbol of the civil rights movement. And it was largely owing to the astute leadership of Dr. King that the SCLC made such Southern cities as Montgomery; Birmingham; Selma, Alabama; Albany, Georgia; and Philadelphia, Mississippi, historic names in the Negro American's struggle to achieve individual dignity and equal rights.

Because the SCLC is so indigenous to the problems of Southern segregation it came in for much criticism during the first months of 1968. Some insisted that its nonviolent methods could not be effectively applied in Northern cities. They even said that its most tangible achievements had been in the area of legal segregation, not in those of economic discrimination, poor housing and inferior schools, which are the most pressing problems in Northern slums.

The SCLC sponsored programs in 1968 designed to assist the poor in both the North and the South. Perhaps its most effective Northern program was Operation Breadbasket, directed by Rev. Jesse L. Jackson in Chicago. This program is the economic arm of the SCLC, and the organization is planning to extend to other cities, North and South. Within the framework of this program the SCLC employs various techniques to increase the economic power of the urban poor. These include demonstrations, picketing, Black boycotts and the promotion of businesses owned and operated by Black people.

Nothing dramatized the SCLC's concern with the plight of the poor as much as did its Poor People's Campaign. In the course of organizing the march on Washington, D.C., and planning Resurrection City, SCLC leaders held mass meetings in many communities throughout the nation. Activities centering around the Poor People's Campaign had at least one major consequence: they committed the organization to programs intended to help alleviate the problems of the poor. These programs took priority over its original campaign against racial segregation per se.

From a pragmatic point of view the Poor People's Campaign—especially the disarray and confusion that characterized Resurrection City—was somewhat less than successful. In fact, very few concrete improvements in the condition of the poor resulted from it. The things that were accomplished might have resulted from a much less expensive program of action. However, in the strict tradition of the SCLC the campaign was successful. It called direct world-wide attention to the condition of the poor in this nation, and indirectly it was an indictment of the capitalistic system, American style. As Warren Prichard has pointed out, the campaign "was the hardest indictment of the nation . . . perhaps the clearest measure of response [from official Washington] to the Campaign was that the poor finally had to settle for hunger as their issue of confrontation, and it was a condemnable nation, rendering its verdict in superabundance, that denied them victory" ("The Poor People's Campaign," *New South*, XXIII [Fall 1968]). This is the nation that pays about 92,720 wealthy farmers over $3 billion a year *not* to raise crops, and then appropriates a mere $2 billion or less for its total antipoverty (OEO) program. Thus Senator James Eastland, as a member of the agricultural subcommittee and the very powerful Senate Appropriations Committee, receives $13,160 per month as a federal subsidy payment while a welfare recipient on his land receives less than $35 per month. Therefore, Rev. Ralph D. Abernathy, the successor to Dr. King, was correct in pointing out that the Poor People's Campaign made "an indelible impression on America's mind," that it was "the most stupendous feat," and that "it made America see its poor." It did, undoubtedly, make SCLC a genuine poor people's movement.

Another way in which the SCLC identified with the poor was in its work with and support of garbage workers. It was indeed significant that this was Dr. King's last personal campaign. He was in Memphis in support of garbage workers who were striking for union recognition and increased wages when he was assassinated on April 4, 1968. Since then, SCLC has dedicated itself to the struggle of "civil servants in the South who demand dignified living wages though the jobs they perform are menial."

The Student Nonviolent Coordinating Committee was founded in April 1960. It began as a sort of community action arm of the SCLC. One of its most influential founders was Ella Baker, who was the executive secretary of SCLC. The original purpose of SNCC was to coordinate the abundance of restless energy of college students who were anxious to aid the Black poor in the rural South. Thus it began almost immediately to address itself to such problems as political disfranchisement, illiteracy, poor health conditions and almost total lack of community organization. Therefore, whereas the SCLC, like the other more established civil rights organizations, was primarily identified with the Black middle class and gave sanction and support to middle class values and ways, SNCC was identified with the Black working class. And where the public pronouncements, mass meetings, demonstrations, and even mode of dress and speech of other civil rights participants usually conformed to "middle class" patterns, the personal behavior, dress and methods of action of SNCC gave sanction to the way of life of the Black working class.

The exuberance, idealism and courage displayed by the SNCC workers inspired college students from all over the nation to "join the cause." They literally "invaded" certain rural counties in the South. They dressed in rough working clothes, lived among working-class people and adopted as best they could the ways of life of the rural poor. Their reckless behavior in defense of the rights of the poor singled them out as the most militant of the civil rights groups. Their individual behavior and the programs they initiated were direct condemnations of the so-called "place" assigned Blacks in the social systems of the South. In every way they insisted that Black people should be accorded equal dignity and equal power. Among their most significant programs was that on political organization. The leaders of SNCC founded the Mississippi Freedom Democratic Party, which has had increasing influence upon the political structure of Mississippi, and they also engaged in some meaningful grass-roots political action in Alabama.

In essence, SNCC was founded to extend the philosophy and strategy of nonviolence as enunciated by Dr. King. Yet from the beginning it was much more "militant" than SCLC. Like SCLC, it was indigenous to the South and peculiarly designed to tackle hard-core legal and traditional racial segregation as it exists in the rural counties. Because it was designed so specifically to combat Southern segregation, it has not been able to transfer its original effectiveness to the solution of the problems in the Black ghettoes of the North, where racial discrimination is somewhat more subtle and complex. Consequently, during 1968 SNCC did not respond adequately to the demands of the Black ghetto. It did not sponsor any really viable urban programs. As a result it experienced a rapid decline in membership and prestige. Actually, its membership has just about disappeared. Some estimate that there are only from fifty to a hundred "card-carrying" active members in the entire SNCC operation. By the end of 1968 it appeared to be little more than a loosely organized "paper organization," composed of militant leaders who constantly struggle among themselves for whatever power and prestige the organization still has left. It has failed to make the necessary adaptation to the problems of the ghetto.

During 1968, SNCC's top leaders received constant and wide publicity. Although their action programs were on the wane, these leaders themselves were not. They constituted something like a cadre of itinerant "preachers" of violence. They traveled widely from one college campus to another exhorting students to rebel against *the* "Establishment." More often than not, *the* "Establishment" turned out to be the particular colleges, usually Black colleges, in which the students were enrolled. Little was done to change or pressure the local white power structure which maintained racial segregation and discrimination. Indeed, most of the SNCC itinerant speakers seemed very poorly briefed on the community context in which the colleges are located.

Stokely Carmichael was the undisputed chief among the SNCC spokesmen during the first months of 1968. And while the leaders of other established civil rights organizations were attempting to make their organizations more relevant to the problem of poverty and its related ills, Carmichael moved rapidly throughout this country and abroad behaving as an individual "missionary" of the ideology of Black power. Carmichael was propelled into international prominence. He became the very symbol of the philosophy of the violent resistance he preached. Black youth in urban ghettoes throughout the nation dubbed him their hero. More and more, in one situation after another—including among some winners in the 1968 Olympics—Black youth stood with upraised clenched fists in the "Black power salute" made famous by Carmichael.

And so while the influence and popularity of Carmichael soared, that of the organization that sponsored him, SNCC, drastically declined. This may be, in fact, the underlying reason for the dramatic split between Carmichael and SNCC: he, not his organization or its programs, made the transition from the central problem of segregation as it exists in the rural South to an active concern with the problems of the powerless Black ghettoes of the North; he, not the organization, became "relevant" to the hordes of unemployed, restless, insecure Black youth who have just about lost faith in the workability of the American social system.

In the mid-1960's, the Black Panther Party was formed in Oakland, California, by Huey P. Newton. This organization was immediately relevant to the problems of the disesteemed, disinherited, angry youth of the Black ghetto. Its moving spirit and organizer was a typical representative of that environment and circumstance. It is natural, therefore, that this group has developed rapidly since its founding. Its major appeal is to the thousands of rootless Black young people in the big city slums. As Professor Kenneth B. Clark so eloquently points out in his study of Harlem (*Dark Ghetto* [New York, 1965]), the Black ghetto is virtually powerless. The police, who symbolize just about the only tangible power the Black poor directly experience, have emerged, predictably, as the archenemy of the unemployed, undisciplined ghetto youth. They regard the police as foreigners would an "army of occupation" whose designated purpose is to force natives to obey foreign laws. Consequently, the Panthers were in the news more than were the participants of any other civil rights organization. Most of that news was about their repeated conflicts with the police and the courts. Perhaps the arrest and trial of its founder, Huey Newton, and the circumstances surrounding this, did more than anything else to make the Black Panther Party the most rapidly growing "civil rights" organization in 1968.

Unlike SNCC and the other long-established civil rights groups, the Panther Party has never been dedicated to nonviolence. From its beginnings to the present, it has been the most ultra-militant, even militaristic, Black organization. It insists vehemently upon the fundamental right of self-defense, "in any way deemed necessary." Up to the present, most of its "defense" efforts have been directed at the police.

After Newton was jailed and later imprisoned for from two to fifteen years for his involvement in the slaying of a policeman, Eldridge Cleaver became the charismatic symbol of the Panthers. As their minister of information, he was their chief spokesman in 1968. This was augmented by the fact that the Peace and Freedom Party nominated him as its Presidential candidate.

William Hedgepeth, in his article "The Radicals," in *Look* (January 7, 1969), gave a most perspicacious description of Cleaver. He described him as "the ultimate in pantherdom . . . author, editor, agitator, self-educated ex-convict, parole breaker and 'the hottest piece of radical merchandise on the market.'" Hedgepeth portrayed him in these words: "Leroy Eldridge Cleaver stands lean, mean, tall, bearded and black-jacketed." From his Panther base in Oakland, Cleaver prowled widely and lectured to large audiences, especially students, on the evils and corruption of American society, advocating that Black and white youth join forces to overthrow the status quo. He is quoted by Hedgepeth as saying that "white people in this country have been sold a bill of goods. . . . And even white people are now become victims of pig power. . . . We need a coalition of White Power and every other hue of power in order to rebuke the pigs and bring them back in their place."

Thus, whereas in the past nearly all civil rights leaders advocated equality for Blacks within the frameworks of institutional structures, the Panthers take every opportunity to disavow established authority, to eschew traditional channels of operation and to reject deeply ingrained "middle class values." They are avowedly committed to revolution. This spirit is echoed by the Panther Party's militant chairman, Bobby Seale, who admonished the Panthers to carry arms in order to "protect" Black communities from white police.

The Congress of Racial Equality (CORE) was founded in Chicago in 1942. During its first decade or so CORE was a rather small organization of dedicated people who were willing to undertake direct confrontation with legal and de facto segregation. The organization tested certain specific Jim Crow practices in Northern communities in restaurants, in transportation and in such facilities as the Palisades Amusement Park (New Jersey) pool. Its method was nonviolent and its major technique was direct confrontation. For instance, the sit-in technique, which has been used so widely and effectively since the Montgomery bus boycott of 1955–56, was first used by CORE.

After the 1954 Supreme Court decision against segregation in public education, CORE extended its operations to a large number of communities in the South and for some years established itself as the most militant civil rights organization.

CORE, like SCLC, is well suited to champion the cause of segregation, although it, too, has had some difficulty in adjusting to the *new* civil rights interest—poverty and related problems in the urban ghettoes. There were times during 1968 when the organization seemed to founder, somewhat like SNCC, while its top leaders—such as Floyd B. McKissick, Roy Innis, Danny Gant, Robert C. Carson, Sol Herbert, Wilfred Ussery and a few others—rose to national stature or enhanced their national image. However, it did come up with several significant programs designed to help alleviate some of the problems of the ghetto.

Attempts to deal with ghetto problems range from the boycotting of industries which discriminate against Blacks in their hiring policies to the championing of "Black capitalism." Among other things, CORE instituted in 1968 what it hoped would be a general boycott of all General Electric Company products throughout the country, because an investigation conducted by CORE showed that Black workers were "discriminated against daily." Also, during 1968 CORE began to push for the growth of Black capitalism, with Negroes owning and operating businesses in their communities. CORE announced plans to raise $10 million from already established businesses for that purpose. It set up an organization to spearhead its Black capitalism project. This organization, CORE Enterprise Corporation (CORE NCO), plans to open offices in several large cities outside the South.

The year 1968 was a stormy one for the National Association for the Advancement of Colored People. However, it managed to remain in the forefront of the civil rights movement. Thus Roy Wilkins, its executive director, could report that the 1,700 units of the NAACP increased their membership by 21,540 over 1967 to a total of 448,974 (*Annual Report* for 1968). This makes the NAACP by far the largest of the civil rights organizations. The work of the NAACP "is spread into fifty states and is tailored in emphasis and timing to meet the needs of localities, states or regions."

During 1968, as in the past, the NAACP, working through its many chapters, did in fact carry on a varied national program of activities. It continued with its well-structured program of legal action and used a wide range of pressures to achieve changes which would advance the status of Black Americans on several fronts: justice, employment, voter registration, police action, housing, education and health. It exerted wide influence in the designing of legislation at all levels of government. It also cooperated on various occasions with other civil rights organizations.

Despite the "good works" of the NAACP, it came in for much criticism during 1968. Generally this had to do with the "old stance" of the organization. Some contended that it was still too involved in the problems of racism and segregation as they exist in the South, and had not become as involved as it should in helping to solve the problem of poverty as it exists in the Northern ghettoes. For example, some condemned the NAACP because it did not give substantial support to the Poor People's Campaign. The critics concluded that the NAACP is a conservative middle-class-oriented organization, too willing to compromise on basic civil rights issues, and that it has no genuine concern for the Black masses. Many young "militants" claimed that the slow, tedious, legalistic methods characteristic of the NAACP have not been really effective in helping the poor solve the multitude of problems they face daily in big city slums.

The NAACP has attempted to respond positively to criticism leveled by the "Young Turks." It has renewed its efforts to become relevant to the Black ghetto. It now has in its membership about sixty thousand young people, many of whom are involved in "youth projects" in Black neighborhoods. They serve, so to speak, as "watchdogs" on the racial front. The NAACP also initiated a program to assist migrant workers, assisted on the food stamp program and worked closely with farmers' organizations. Roy Wilkins "reported" that the NAACP's Mississippi Emergency Relief Fund "is the only effort by any civil rights organization to do something on the spot to relieve malnutrition and hunger."

Before the end of 1968, Roy Wilkins announced that the NAACP will be going directly into the slums to train young, militant, leaders and will try to harness the energies and talents of young Black activists. Wilkins concluded: "I am by no means satisfied or pleased with the old ideas. Especially do I want to forget those who urge patience. We could wait out several lifetimes and not get anything done. . . . We are beginning a new thrust of additional services to the urban ghetto and an appeal to the young people." Also, in his *Annual Report* for 1968, Roy Wilkins, speaking specifically in answer to those who had criticized the NAACP for being outdated and moribund, stated:

> It has been the fashion, now, for the past three years (and particularly since the assassination of Dr. Martin Luther King last April) to predict the death of the Civil Rights Movement.
>
> The soothsayers and trend-spotters of both races, those of the curbstone variety and those of the Deep Thinker crowd, have outdone each other in forecasting the end.
>
> It is really not fair to disappoint these avid death-wishers, but the truth is that—as of this year—the Civil Rights Movement is very much alive.

The Urban League, from its founding in 1910, has always been aware of the problems of the Black ghetto. During 1968 it was the most affluent of the civil rights organizations. Working through its ninety or so affiliates, it carried on many programs designed to raise the general status of the urban Negro. There were programs concerned with the following: the strengthening of family life; consumer education; the development of informed, responsible leadership; on-the-job training, especially through the Urban League Labor Education Advancement Program (LEAP); summer fellowship programs for students who would become administrators in industrial firms; scholarship programs; housing improvement; career fairs; and the expansion of Black capitalism. There were also more limited programs sponsored by individual affiliates. The fact is, the Urban League itself has become a significant employer. Its proposed 1969 budget is $6,100,000.

Although the Urban League has always concerned itself with the Black poor in large Northern cities, it, too, was severely criticized by Black militant leaders. Its executive director, Whitney M. Young, Jr., like Roy Wilkins, was labeled a "Super Tom," and the organization was accused of not being sufficiently relevant to the problem of poverty in the Black ghetto. Some said that throughout the years the Urban League had focused upon getting "merit employment" for middle class Blacks while ignoring the worsening plight of poorer Blacks.

The main criticism leveled at the League, however, was not that it lacked promising projects but that its methods of dealing with the white power structure and the Black masses were unsatisfactory. Essentially, the Urban League's leaders, especially its top executives, have always functioned as "power brokers." They have assumed the role of interpreting what the Black community has wanted and then have negotiated with the white power structure for these things. Militant Black leaders criticized this method on two counts. First, they insisted that the middle class Black leaders of the Urban League have generally been too far removed from the Black poor to know what the latter really want. Secondly, they felt that the League has been too ready to compromise. Some felt that the League's practice of dealing primarily with top echelon leaders in government and industry has led it to adopt a sort of "master" attitude with regard to the Black masses—a proclivity to insist that Blacks adopt white attitudes and manners before they are accorded the civil and social benefits of a white-dominated society.

In answer to these criticisms the Urban League has come up with a proposal, an initial $2,000,000 a year Ghetto Thrust Program, to begin in 1969. The central purpose of this program is to make the Urban League a "power convener" rather than a "power broker." This means that it will spend much more time organizing the Black masses to speak and act for themselves, instead of acting in their behalf. It means that a key program will be the training of indigenous Black leaders who are prepared to understand and interpret the needs of the Black poor. On this point Whitney Young averred: "At one time the establishment would only talk with selected Negro leadership such as the Urban League. Now we no longer need to be the power broker. Our role now is to be the convener—to arrange those confrontations between Black and white America." He continued: "The power structure is ready to talk to Black people directly but they don't know in many cases whom to talk to. We intend to have meaningful confrontations instead of shouting matches."

Important in the League's new Ghetto Thrust is the joint involvement of both middle class and unemployed Blacks in the solution of ghetto problems. This means that the League plans to continue its top level negotiations to expand job opportunities, to improve housing conditions and to shape economic policy in both the private and public sectors. The leadership will still press for new laws and are still "gung-ho on getting a domestic Marshall plan in this country."

The Urban League has chosen as leader of this program one of its most knowledgeable and successful urban developers, Sterling Tucker, director of the Washington Urban League. He will head a staff of young executives who will design new programs and extend and improve old ones in efforts to make the League more relevant to the ghetto. Director Young is convinced that "nobody who represents the enemy is remotely concerned about our lung power, soul power, fire power, but about our political power, ballot power and economic power which is possible if we are organized." This he sees as the ultimate goal of the Urban League's new Ghetto Thrust.

A second major trend in the civil rights movement in 1968 was the proliferation of "civil rights" organizations. Some new organization dedicated to the improvement of the status of Black Americans sprang up almost daily. Many minor organizations already on the scene increased in prominence during the year. Also, each of the established organizations set up affiliated special-interest organizations.

The new or newly strengthened civil rights organizations ranged all the way from the ultra-militant Revolutionary Action Movement (RAM) and the Black Muslims to the business-oriented National Urban Coalition (founded in 1967)—which continued to spread to large cities—and included the ultra-race-conscious Black United Front. All of the many new or newly invigorated organizations had at least one thing in common—their leaders and founders were dissatisfied with the pace and accomplishments of the established organizations. In a sense, therefore, they were opposed to the racial policies and practices of the "Establishment" and sought to institute a more democratic status quo.

It is, of course, true that some of the new organizations were founded by ambitious opportunists who wanted to fill what they regarded as a power vacuum in the civil rights movement. Yet these organizations swelled the ranks of the civil rights movement with many individuals who sought to make definite, concrete, contributions to the advancement of Black Americans. And while some of these new leaders and organizations did stir up bickering and conflicts within the civil rights movement, to the extent that some observers felt that the movement for equal citizenship might be dying, the net result was that never before did Black Americans achieve more concrete gains in the pursuit of equality than in 1968.

Black Americans made significant advances on several fronts, for example, in moving away from employment in menial jobs, and in achieving much wider political participation and office-holding. This suggests that there was an emergence of a new kind of white "liberal" in both the public and private sectors of American life. There were more public funds available in support of do-it-yourself projects initiated and controlled by the Black community. Several private industries and foundations manifested greater willingness than before to support projects designed and run by Black individuals and groups. Unlike the traditional white "liberals" who had supported programs for the Black community only when they could exert some significant degree of control, the new liberal seemed willing to allow the Black organizations and enterprises that they supported to "do their own thing."

There was a resurgence of Black pride during 1968. Civil rights organizations sponsored many different kinds of projects intended to develop this.

Perhaps the most effective manifestation of such pride was the fact that Black students throughout the nation demanded that the schools and colleges they attended set up courses in Black history and culture. Many Negroes organized exhibits on Afro-American art and set up "community schools" to teach Black history and culture to non-college youth. Actually, so much emphasis was placed upon "Black" as beautiful and honorable that some feared that Black Americans were borrowing pages from the dishonorable lexicon of the white supremacists. Some Black leaders felt called upon to warn against substituting the theory of Black Supremacy for the discredited theory of White Supremacy.

In summary, we may say that during 1968 the civil rights movement shifted its major sphere of activity and focus from racial segregation in the South to poverty and related social ills in urban ghettoes. Many small organizations were founded which focused upon a variety of barriers which need to be removed before Black people can hope to enjoy first-class citizenship. This new urban ghetto "thrust" led to new "shrines" that symbolize the Black American's struggle for equality. The new "shrines" are such Northern cities as Newark, Cleveland, Detroit and Baltimore. A new type of white liberal seems to be emerging in connection with the new stance of the civil rights movement. Finally, there was a tremendous manifestation of race pride among Black Americans. The concept "Black" was transformed from a badge of inferiority and disesteem to one of beauty and honor.

South Carolina highway patrolmen stand guard over two students wounded during disturbances at South Carolina State College, in Orangeburg.

Blatant Discrimination

John Ohliger

DESPITE PROGRESS made during the year, 1968 was still a period of a good deal of blatant discrimination. Incidents of violence or threats of violence continued; the most obvious discriminatory patterns remained in the areas of employment, political life and private clubs.

General Background

Generally speaking, the most hopeful sign was the calling of a conference by the National Association for the Advancement of Colored People to plan the final legal assault on American racial discrimination. The conference was held in New York's Warwick Hotel from November 20 to 22. It commemorated the centennial of the addition of the Fourteenth Amendment to the United States Constitution. The stated goal of the conference was to plan a five-to-ten-year legal program which would end discrimination entirely. Six sessions were held in which new techniques were discussed by fifty of the country's foremost legal scholars and practicing attorneys. Papers were presented and commentaries offered on the legal and legislative strategies for wiping out discrimination in housing, employment and education. The use of federal aid and state action was also examined. Among the participants were Roy Wilkins, executive director, NAACP; Robert L. Carter, general counsel, NAACP; Lloyd Cutler, executive director, President's Commission on the Causes and Prevention of Violence; Professor Louis Jaffe, Harvard Law School; Professor Charles Black, Yale Law School; C. Clyde Ferguson, Dean, Howard University Law School; Burke Marshall and Louis Oberdorfer, former U.S. assistant attorney generals; Charles Waugh, president, National Bar Association; Franklin Williams, former U.S. ambassador to the United Nations; Derrick Bell, director, Western Center on Law and Poverty; and Richard Sobol, Lawyers' Constitutional Defense Committee in New Orleans. Judge J. Skelly Wright, Court of Appeals, District of Columbia Circuit, was the principal speaker at this historic conference.

A look at various localities in both the South and the North reveals the progess made and the distance yet to be traveled in destroying Jim Crow. Houston, Texas, is the seventh most populous city in the United States. Recently Arnold Rosenzweig visited Houston, after a seven-year absence, for the *Chicago Daily Defender*. Rosenzweig found a city that had "remarkably changed in some ways and remained the same in others." Seven years ago the University of Houston and Rice University were lily-white. Now both universities have been integrated. Black athletes take a prominent place. Close to a fifth of Houston's bus drivers are now Black, where none were in 1961. The fire department has moved from virtually all white to a position of substantial integration. Segregation of such public facilities as hospitals, theatres, hotels, public libraries, water fountains, rest rooms, lunch counters and buses is now, by and large, a thing of the past. Job opportunities have improved somewhat for Black people. Both city and county offices now have integrated staffs, and there is a local Black judge.

On the other hand, much still remains to be done. The local police department is 99 per cent white, though 22 per cent of the city is Black. Welfare facilities and provisions are inadequate.

Complaints about second-class service continue to be made against Jefferson Davis Hospital, 70 per cent of whose patients are Black. And Rosenzweig concludes that the Houston city administration, while making some token concessions to Negro demands, is not committed to racial advancement in the way officials of Northern cities at least say they are.

Meanwhile, in the North problems abound. Take Irasburg, Vermont, a town of eight hundred near the Canadian border. According to the 1960 census, Vermont has only about five hundred Black persons in a population of nearly four hundred thousand. There were none in Irasburg until July 1968, when Rev. David Johnson moved there with his wife and four children from Seaside, California. Mrs. Barbara Lawrence, a divorced white mother of two who had accompanied the Johnson family from California, stayed as a house guest. Sixteen days after the Johnsons moved in, an automobile drove by and one of its occupants sprayed the house with five blasts from a shotgun. Johnson returned the fire, shooting a dozen times with a Luger. After the shooting, Vermont's Democratic Governor Philip Hoff said, "This fully demonstrates there is a white racism in Vermont." Three weeks later, Rev. Johnson was brought into court and charged with adultery with his house guest, Mrs. Lawrence. It was the first time in twelve years that the adultery statute had been used in the county. Johnson pleaded not guilty and was released on bail. At first Mrs. Lawrence pleaded not guilty but then she changed her plea to "no contest," was fined $125, placed on probation and allowed to return to California. The president of the Vermont chapter of the NAACP commented, after it was all over, that "now maybe Vermonters can understand what Black people are always complaining about as far as dispensation of justice is concerned."

The role of literature in keeping alive the fires of discrimination or in combating them is a little-explored area. One leaflet that appeared in 1968 was signed "Voice of the White People." It was titled *What To Do If a Nigger Comes into Your Neighborhood: Or How To Kill a Nigger and Not Get Caught.* Among other things it stated:

> Let's say a nigger comes walking down a street in a white neighborhood and I don't care if he or she is waiting for a bus or just shopping we have to keep them out of the neighborhood and make sure they know we don't want them around again and if we have to kill them there's nothing wrong with that. Just remember a dead nigger is a good nigger and they all should be good and dead.

On the other side is the book *We Charge Genocide,* which reached its ninth edition in 1968. The 240-page book was written in 1951, as a petition to the United Nations, by William L. Patterson and others. It names five thousand Black victims reported to have died at the hands of white men since 1900. Sometimes called the Bible of the Black militants, it is reputed to be much more popular in Asia, Africa and Europe than in the United States.

Violence

The year 1968 was one of much violence and many threats of violence. The assassinations of Dr. Martin Luther King, Jr., and Senator Robert F. Kennedy were the most dramatic and widely publicized manifestations of this violence. There were other examples as well, however, not the least of which was the violence perpetrated by law enforcement officials during demonstrations. On February 8, three Negro youths were shot to death and at least thirty-four persons were injured when state police opened fire on students at predominantly Negro South Carolina State College in Orangeburg, South Carolina. The deaths were the climax of racial differences that had begun on February 5 with student protests against the segregation of a local bowling alley. In the course of these events the National Guard had been mobilized and the college closed for two weeks. The three deaths took place late on February 8 in what was at first reported as an exchange of gunfire between police and students. According to an original report, Negroes had opened fire on police and firemen who were trying to put out a grass fire. In later reports the facts came to light, however. The students had not opened fire and apparently had not even been armed. What had happened was that a state policeman had been knocked down by a piece of lumber thrown by a student; other police thought he had been shot and opened fire. The Southern Regional Council has issued a report titled *Events at Orangeburg*. The report says that the shootings show the dangers of "get tough" police tactics. It goes on to say:

> The events also would at least suggest the implications of forces in motion not just in Orangeburg but across America in 1967-68, including Black Power and white overreaction to its emotional mood, the tendency to violence by Negroes dismayed by the failure of nonviolent and other peaceful protest against social injustice and inequity still enduring, the national tendency nearing public policy to a fear of riots amounting to phobia and a response to Negro unrest with massive police and military force. Although the governor of South Carolina had said that the police shot only after they thought they had been fired on, no one has been able to find any weapons that the students might have used. No one . . . saw any students with guns.

The report also asks why police had not used "less lethal methods of riot control, such as tear gas or Mace," and why students had not been warned before the shooting. By the end of the year the Governor of the state had still refused to appoint a committee to investigate the shootings.

On February 20 state policemen fired tear gas into a group of two hundred demonstrators at the predominantly Negro Alcorn Agricultural and Mechanical College in Lorman, Mississippi. The demonstrators were protesting the dismissal of three students who had handed out campaign literature for a Congressional candidate. The president of Alcorn said the students had been dismissed after they had cursed him when he accused them of being drunk. A second incident occurred shortly before dawn on February 21, when students threw bottles and bricks at state policemen. Six persons were injured; three were hospitalized.

In New York on September 4 more than two hundred off-duty policemen, many wearing "Wallace for President" buttons, attacked a group of Negroes with rubber truncheons at the Brooklyn Criminal Courts building and prevented them from attending a hearing for three members of the Black Panthers. The policemen, members of an unofficial organization known as the Law Enforcement Group, moved quickly on twelve Negroes when they emerged from elevators on the sixth floor where the hearing was to be held. The Negroes were identified as members of the Black Panthers. One of the Negroes, and a white girl who had accompanied them, received head injuries and were bleeding profusely.

In Atlanta in mid-October representatives of six local civil rights groups issued a statement to protest the manner in which recent police raids had been conducted on Negro businesses. The statement said in part:

> On Friday, October 4th, Georgia's Governor Lester Maddox took what may be the first step toward the establishing of a true police state as he directed a gestapo-like attack on the major Black business district of Atlanta under the guise of "Law and Order." An estimated 150 Georgia Bureau of Investigation Agents and state troopers "swooped down" on Auburn Avenue (advance notice having been given to the white press, radio, television and newspapers) to raid several business places suspected of being "fronts" for lottery operators and "havens" for lottery "kingpins." A number of persons, men and young women, employed in surrounding business[es] were harassed and abused by tough-talking state troopers as if they were convicted felons resisting arrest. Young black ladies, guilty of nothing more than eating lunch in a public restaurant licensed to do business by the city of Atlanta, were manhandled, had their purses forcibly taken from their hands, emptied of contents by troopers, finding nothing but the usual feminine necessities; the empty purses were thrown back to the ladies to be refilled with their personal belongings. At other places, homes, and business[es] doors were wantonly "chopped" open with axes, "bludgeoned" open by sledge hammers. Doors that could have been opened by employees or occupants to the lawmen, simply by them announcing their presence.

Three Negro deaths in 1968—two murders and one "apparent suicide"—remain unsolved. On Easter Sunday in Philadelphia the body of a local taxicab driver, George Connelly, was found tied to a tree. He had been methodically hacked to death. Connelly's close relatives termed it a lynching—as did a number of local persons, who called civil rights groups to find out what action had been taken. Robbery was ruled out when police found Connelly's wallet in his pocket and his wristwatch on his arm. Connelly was characterized by his fellow employees as a "good, quiet and square guy who neither smoked nor drank."

On September 21, in Prichard, Alabama, a suburb of Mobile, the body of dock worker E. C. DeLoach was found hanging by its heels from the roof of a formerly all-Negro school which had been ordered closed by federal authorities. Police said that the murder had occurred entirely within the Negro community and that investigation of the "apparent lynching" tended to show that "Negroes had killed DeLoach and hung him from the school house." However, Prichard had had seven fire bombings three weeks before the death of DeLoach, and there had been at least one serious clash between white persons and a Negro at one of the formerly all-white integrated schools.

The attorney general of Connecticut has ordered an investigation into the death of Charles Richardson of Groton. Richardson was discovered dead in a parked car late in September. A medical examiner indicated, after a preliminary investigation, that Richardson had died of carbon monoxide poisoning. Police called the death "apparent suicide." Shortly before his death Richardson had pressed charges with the state Commission on Human Rights and Opportunities, claiming that the city of Groton and the Pioneer Hose Company had discriminated against him because he was a Negro by refusing to permit him to join the volunteer fire company.

Attempts by Negroes to move into previously white areas also resulted in violence in 1968. In Chicago Charles Bolton, a Vietnam veteran, was forced to move out of his newly purchased home because of white harassment. Obscenities were smeared on the back wall of the house and on the garage. A Nazi swastika was painted on one living room window. Fire trucks were sent to the home. Threatening telephone calls were received. The veteran said he had been assured by the agent from whom he had purchased the home that there would be no trouble, because there was another Black family on the next block.

Also in Chicago, Arthur Tyler charged that the Ku Klux Klan had burned crosses on the lawn of his newly purchased home twice in one week. Just before Tyler, his wife and their seven children had moved into the home, five windows had been smashed. Tyler told reporters: "I'm not going to pack up and run just because of that, but I am going to buy me some guns and ammunition for my protection. This neighborhood is all-white, for the most part, and now I know what I have to deal with."

In Carthage, Mississippi, a house being built for a Negro family near a rural white neighborhood was heavily damaged by an explosion. The family had not yet moved in and no one was injured.

There were a number of incidents in which Negro youths were beaten up by white persons. In Cleveland, two thirteen-year-old boys were severely injured when beaten up by older teen-age whites in a predominantly white area in which the young Negroes lived. One boy was beaten with a tow chain. The other boy had his face stomped on; this resulted in a broken jaw, which had to be wired. The father of one of the boys says he feels that the police have given him the runaround on the case. He added, "A squad car passed my boy walking along the street Sunday afternoon with his mouth bleeding and they refused to stop and investigate or assist him."

In Altamonte Springs, Florida, the sheriff reported that a young Negro was taken for a terror ride and "beaten to an unrecognizable pulp" by a group of whites who mistakenly believed he had had sexual relations with a teen-age white girl. The sheriff said that McNeil Simmons, eighteen, had suffered multiple compound skull fractures as well as other injuries in the June 15 beating. He added that the young man had apparently been beaten with a machete and that four hundred stitches were required to close his wounds.

As in years past, civil rights leaders and those sympathetic to civil rights were the subject of violence and intimidation. In Oakland, California, the law offices of Donald C. Warden, founder of the Afro-American Association, were shattered by an explosion. No one was injured, but there was extensive damage to nearby structures. A police officer on the scene stated that he believed the blast was from dynamite with a fuse. Warden commented: "This is very unfortunate, but I have no idea who might have done it. I have received no threats. At any rate, this is not going to alter my beliefs, my opinions, or my activities in any way."

In the community of North East, Maryland, a

white man was arrested and charged with assault with intent to murder the county chairman of the NAACP. The white man had been picked up at the home of the NAACP leader. He was also charged with carrying a concealed weapon and having dynamite in his possession. The rights leader's home had been under surveillance because of an earlier bomb threat.

South Hill, Virginia, is a town of about 4,500 near the North Carolina border. Clergymen in the town who have taken moderate positions on civil rights have been the recipients of anonymous threatening notes and phone calls. The office of one of these ministers was damaged. Later this same minister had part of his church and his home burned. Others in the town also suffered. Three grocery stores that closed in observance of the funeral of Dr. Martin Luther King were fired upon. The home of a Negro family, with two people asleep upstairs, was set afire.

The year also saw the clearing up of several incidents of violence that had occurred earlier. In January 1968 Mississippi authorities arrested eleven men on murder and arson charges in the fire bomb death of civil rights leader Vernon Dahmer. Dahmer, a voter registration leader, had been killed in January 1966. One of those arrested had just been presented with a distinguished service award by the local Junior Chamber of Commerce.

Also in Mississippi, ten men were indicted by a Jackson grand jury on April 10. The indictments charged the ten with bombing a real estate office in Jackson on the night of March 7, 1967, after rumors had been circulated that the real estate operator had sold homes in a white neighborhood to Negroes. One of those indicted was an attorney; another was a state official of the Ku Klux Klan. The incident was the first of a dozen bombings of Jewish synagogues and of the homes and places of business of white liberals in the state.

Mississippi was also the scene, in November, of a judgment of over a million dollars in damages against the White Knights of the Ku Klux Klan and three of its members. The successful federal civil suit had been filed under a Reconstruction era law involving conspiracy to deprive a citizen of his civil rights. The citizen in this case was an aged Negro who had been killed by the three men in June 1966. Earlier trials of the men had not resulted in a conviction. The *New York Times* commented that "Klan observers in Mississippi saw the civil action taken against the three men and the White Knights as a possible new tactic to be used in cases where Mississippi justice had failed to provide satisfaction in the criminal processes."

Finally, on the issue of violence, the continuing danger from the Ku Klux Klan was underlined in a federal court hearing which cleared up the lynching of two Negroes forty years ago. G. T. Miller, a feed mill operator, came into court to complain that the Klan had been intimidating him in recent months because he had refused to fire a Negro employee who permitted his children to be transferred to a previously all-white school under a "freedom of choice" plan. Miller contended on the stand that such Klan threats should be taken very seriously—even today. He stated that as a Klan member who had taken part in lynchings forty years earlier he knew at first hand what he was talking about. At this point he was asked: "Did you ever shoot a Negro?"

"I did," Miller answered.

"How many?"

"A couple," Miller replied.

The judge then leaned over the bench and asked, "Were you tried and acquitted?"

"Yes, sir," said Miller.

"By an all-white jury?" the judge continued.

"Yes, sir," Miller repeated.

Miller then went on to say that in the 1920's he had been a member of the Klan and had committed these murders, but that now he knew that such injustices toward Negroes and others were wrong.

Employment

A review of the employment picture for the year reveals many examples of blatant discrimination but also shows some progress toward wiping out such practices. In mid-January the Anti-Defamation League of B'nai B'rith released the results of a survey which showed that nearly 90 per cent of about four hundred private employment agencies checked in six major American cities disregarded federal, state and local antidiscrimination laws. These agencies accepted orders calling for a "white gentile" or a "white

Protestant" secretary. The survey was taken in New York City, Los Angeles, Phoenix, Atlanta, Chicago and Miami.

On April 15 the Illinois Central Railroad was charged in court with employment practices which discriminated against Negroes as regards promotions, time clocks, and such things as rest rooms and locker facilities. A suit filed by a carman helper in Memphis was a class action on behalf of all Negroes employed in Tennessee by the railroad.

An important 1968 decision was that handed down by an Ohio judge who ruled that all-white Local 212 of the International Brotherhood of Electrical Workers must admit (without examination), and place on their referral list, a qualified Negro electrician who had previously been refused membership.

In late September, a Negro guard at Stateville Penitentiary in Joliet, Illinois, accused prison officials of discrimination when they refused to assign him to a "choice" job that at that time was held only by whites. Willie Cavitt said that he was told by the chief guard: "The position is for whites only, and Negroes should stay in their place. I don't approve of Negroes working there." After his complaint, Cavitt added, Negro guards were assigned to this post. "But even this is only tokenism," Cavitt maintained. "There is not one black captain at Stateville. Of some 500 guards only 35 are Negroes. And yet the inmates are almost 75 per cent black." The warden of the prison denied Cavitt's charges, saying, "We don't assign men on the basis of color. We do it because a man's performance warrants it."

In mid-November two Black caseworkers in Chicago's Circuit Court Social Service Department filed a complaint with the Fair Employment Practices Commission charging that they had been "wantonly" fired because of racial discrimination. This was the second time in two years that such charges had been filed. The supervisor involved in both cases declined to comment.

Early in December the Justice Department filed a civil suit against the Ohio Bureau of Employment Services charging discrimination in job placement. This was the first time the Justice Department had sued a state employment service for racial discrimination. The charges were filed under the provisions of the Civil Rights Act of 1964, which forbids discrimination by employment agencies and state agencies that receive federal funds. The suit accused the Ohio bureau of failing to refer qualified Negroes to jobs or apprentice openings on the same basis as white persons and failing to assign Negro applicants job classifications commensurate with their education, training and experience. It also charged the bureau with failing to circulate job orders to those of its offices with chiefly Negro applicants, and with handling job orders of employers when it knew, or had reason to believe, that these employers had discriminatory policies.

In mid-October a special committee of the Washington, D.C., Council on Human Relations made a unique recommendation. The committee had been investigating charges of discrimination in promotion practices in the division of housing of the local Department of Licenses and Inspections. Although the committee found that the situation had improved considerably since the charges were made, it called for monetary compensation for those discriminated against in the past. The committee's chairman said that this recommendation was made because of "what have been years of deprivation and discrimination" which have done "almost irreparable damage to several workers in the department," damage that "a promotion to a higher position [alone] would not make up for."

Finally, there is the question of the effect on employment practices of the new styles promoted by Black power advocates. Negro columnist William Raspberry, writing in the *Washington Post*, has stated: "It is well known that some Negro women—including some teachers—who would like to experiment with the Afro [natural hair] style fear to do so for fear of jeopardizing relationships with their supervisors and co-workers. Other women who affect the style are convinced that their naturals have kept them out of jobs they might otherwise have had. Most haven't complained because they know they can't prove their suspicions."

Political Life

In politics the year started out on an auspicious note. A spokesman for the new Governor of Mississippi announced in mid-January that the plans of a militant segregationist group to place a white supremacy float in Mississippi's inaugural parade had been thwarted. The spokesman said: "It's been put to a stop. They won't put their float in the parade." He was referring to a float which had been prepared by an organization known as Americans for the Preservation of the White Race, a group closely identified with the Ku Klux Klan. The float portrayed a federal judge handing out unjust sentences. Also, the *New York Times* reported that for the first time in the history of inaugural parades in Mississippi, Negroes rode in open automobiles as distinguished guests.

An inaugural affair in Virginia in February had a less pleasant outcome. Every two years when the Virginia general assembly meets, Richmond's Commonwealth Club is the scene of a party for legislators and other officials. This year invitations to the party went to 139 of the assembly's 140 members—but not to Dr. William Reid. Dr. Reid, a surgeon, is the first Negro elected to the Virginia assembly in this century. Some of his colleagues in the assembly were indignant and refused to attend the party. And participants in the Richmond Catholic Adult Education Program dispatched letters of protest to the Governor and to area legislators.

In May the U.S. Civil Rights Commission issued a 256-page study of the impact of the Voting Rights Act of 1965, called *Political Participation.* The study concluded that Southern Negroes have made strong gains since 1965 in terms of numerical voting participation, but that subtle new forms of discrimination now threaten their gains. The study concluded that despite the rise in registration some newly registered Negroes were being effectively disfranchised by exclusion from full participation in party affairs. The commission called upon the national parties to pass new rules requiring state and local units to encourage equal participation by Negro voters.

The report also documented numerous instances in which Negro votes had been diluted by such devices as gerrymandering, the merging of Negro districts into large units with white majorities, the changing of elected posts to appointive ones, and the abolition of offices sought by Negroes. Another tactic mentioned was that of withholding information about political affairs from potential Negro candidates. In other instances the terms of white incumbents have been extended, filing fees have been raised, extra qualification requirements have been added and nominating petitions for Negroes have not been certified.

The commission made four recommendations for the protection of Negro voting power in the South:

1. The Attorney General should assign federal examiners to register Negroes where Negro registration is still low. There are 185 counties in which less than half of the voting age Negroes are registered.
2. The Attorney General should employ lawsuits and informal persuasion to prevent the use of discrimination, coercion and devices by Southern officials and party leaders to discourage Negro participation.
3. The Voting Rights Act should be amended, if necessary, to extend the present bar against the use of voter registration tests in the South. Under the present law these were suspended, but after August 6, 1970, local officials can ask the courts to reinstate the tests.
4. Congress should make antipoverty funds and other federal reserves available to conduct voter registration drives and educational campaigns.

In late October the *Afro-American* reported that Roy F. Richards, the white supremacist leader who had been trying to oust Cleveland's Negro Mayor Carl Stokes, was running into difficulties. Richards was unable to find a lawyer who would take up his case in court, two judges had disqualified themselves from the case, and he feared what he called "threats" by Black nationalist groups. Richards has been trying to get Mayor Stokes removed by charging him with misfeasance and malfeasance in office. Richards has tried to get the suit shifted to an adjoining county because he contends that "an atmosphere of personal fear and anarchy" instituted by Black nationalists makes an impartial hearing impossible.

Private Clubs

Discrimination in private clubs and resorts has always been slow to yield to legislation and public opinion. The pattern held in 1968. In March the wife of Carl Rowan, noted Negro newspaper columnist and former head of the U.S. Information Agency, was the center of a dispute involving three country clubs in the Washington, D.C., area. The clubs dropped out of the local country club tennis league after Mrs. Rowan became a member of her club's team. Officials of the three clubs denied that Mrs. Rowan's joining the team had anything to do with their dropping from the league. But Mrs. Rowan commented: "The clubs only stopped playing when I joined the team." Sydney Howe, president of the Suburban Maryland Fair Housing Association, admonished one of the clubs in a letter, saying that "current reports of discrimination by the Chevy Chase Club are . . . damaging to the image of Montgomery County as a progressive community. . . . If a constitutional change within your corporation is necessary to end control by what one may hope is a misguided minority, so be it. It is simply too late in our nation's and our world's crisis to tolerate a 'freedom' to discriminate which menaces the peace and freedom of us all."

Over a hundred years ago the state of Minnesota passed a law making it illegal for any resort to discriminate in admitting guests. There have been no prosecutions in the law's history. In July 1968 Frank Kent, the state human rights commissioner, announced that his department had conducted a survey of a hundred resorts in Minnesota, which revealed that one-fourth of them discriminated against Negroes and other minorities. The survey had been made by telephone, and the callers had identified themselves as Negroes. At that point some resorts would give such replies as, "You could hurt us financially," or, "You could go somewhere else, and here is the name of a resort that caters to colored people; and you would be happier with people of your own kind." The human rights commissioner said that he was pleased to hear that many resorts made it clear that they welcomed Negro guests. The statement of one owner, that "we have to get with these things and I would love to have you," was typical.

In November a community swimming club near Washington, D.C., voted to continue a policy of excluding Negro guests despite a complaint by a member—a complaint now being investigated by the local Human Relations Council. The club is in an area which has a local ordinance banning discrimination in places of public accommodation. The county attorney believes community swimming clubs' pools come under the terms of the ordinance.

The first indications of the attitudes of the new Nixon administration appointees became apparent in December. William P. Rogers, Nixon's choice for Secretary of State, signed a petition against the segregation policy of a Bethesda, Maryland, country club to which he belongs. However, Melvin R. Laird, Defense Secretary designate, who belongs to the same club, did not sign the petition. An aide said that Laird is "just not a petition-signer" and that "the petition was never really presented to him," and also stated that Laird "is clearly on record for civil rights. He would support allowing Negroes to become members of this club or any club, and would certainly support allowing Negroes in as guests."

The year ended on a possibly hopeful note. The Supreme Court announced on December 9 that it would hear the appeal of two Negroes from Little Rock, Arkansas, who were denied membership in a club of some hundred thousand white members who use the facilities of a lake and picnic area. The Civil Rights Act of 1964 prohibits places of public accommodation from discriminating against Negroes. To come under this classification an establishment must have activities which affect interstate commerce, or its patrons or the sources of its entertainment must cross state lines. The Negroes who sued argued that the club's snack bar and amusement facilities made the establishment a place of public accommodation. They lost in the trial court and in the United States Court of Appeals for the Eighth Circuit. In the latter, a three-judge panel ruled two to one that the club's clientele was local and that its activities did not affect interstate commerce. In their appeal to the Supreme Court, the Negroes argued that "a significant number of people know that [the club] is in fact open to the white public in general and that a nominal membership fee of twenty-five cents is charged simply to exclude undesirables, including Negroes." The Supreme Court will hear the case sometime in 1969.

Other Areas

Four other objects of concern are: (1) the prices charged to ghetto residents; (2) the discriminatory burial practices of cemeteries; (3) discrimination in education; (4) discrimination in social welfare.

In May, Ester Saverson, the first Negro elected city councilman in East St. Louis, Illinois, was buried. The local undertaker had tried to have him buried in a cemetery whose officers had said, "We only bury Caucasians." In Illinois it is illegal to operate a segregated cemetery. A complaint has been filed.

In October a group of Atlanta area clergymen, after conducting an investigation of food stores, concluded that ghetto dwellers are charged higher prices than those in suburban stores and receive inferior quality products. A spokesman for the group said: "We found in almost every instance that prices were higher in the deprived area stores, even on brand-name items." He described the vegetables and produce found in some of the inner city stores as unmarketable in suburban stores. He added, "Some of the produce in the inner city stores appeared to be extremely old and deteriorated and it was evident in most instances that meat products would not have been placed in suburban stores." He said that, from his own investigations, some of the meats found in the stores were badly discolored and in one instance the pork chops were turning green. If conditions are not improved, the clergyman said, they will organize boycotts of offending stores, set up tent markets beside the stores and bus customers to suburban stores for shopping.

In mid-December the San Francisco Bay Area Association of Black Social Workers charged that the local United Crusade [United Appeal] is shortchanging Negroes in the distribution of funds. The president of the association stated that agencies primarily serving white people received over $12 million last year from the Crusade, while agencies dealing primarily with Negroes got less than $250,000. A spokesman for the United Crusade has denied the charges.

As the year drew to a close, two Negro girls in southern Georgia who had been among the first to integrate local schools were judged delinquent in a private hearing. The girls, sisters aged eleven and fourteen, were first arrested and held in a detention center after a school incident in which it was alleged that one girl used profanity and the other engaged in "disorderly conduct." Following the private hearing, the older girl was committed to a state training school and the younger was placed on probation. No explanation has been forthcoming as to why the girls were not reprimanded, suspended or expelled from the school, rather than arrested and detained with a formal complaint. The girls' parents are leaders in local desegregation activities. The parents had never been approached by the school authorities about any disciplinary problems with regard to their children.

That was 1968—a year of many instances of blatant discrimination, but a year of some progress as well.

Students occupying the administration building at Howard University in Washington, D.C., in March 1968.

Some Aspects of the Education of Black Americans, 1968

Prince E. Wilson

I. Ideas, Money and People

Ideas

MANY SIGNS suggested that 1968 was a crucial year in education for Black Americans. A number of Black people (temporarily and for strategic purposes) abandoned the technique of integration and substituted Black awareness and solidarity as the new order of things. Negroes from coast to coast (with some notable exceptions in the South) sought equality and excellence in their schools and in their values by an appeal to Black awareness or "Black pride." They had been driven to believe that the values of the "white society" do not support Black dignity or Black values. For many, integration had been tried and found wanting. Dr. Alvin Poussaint, assistant professor of psychiatry at Tufts University, pointed out that "integration has taken place almost entirely on white terms," and spoke of the necessity for Blacks to build a positive self-image that would "lead Afro-Americans to greater growth, power and achievement." American school curricula, he contended, either knowingly or unknowingly, teach white racism:

> The styles of life and language in books meant to teach spelling, reading and history were white models that were often divorced from the realities of life of the black child. How could he feel that he was a worthwhile human being if he was not white, and living in a clean suburban house like Dick and Jane? Negro models . . . are seldom presented for the black youngster to emulate. In fact, if he took the textbooks seriously, he might feel that black people don't even exist: a complete negation of the black man's sense of self.

There was also research evidence that supported the idea that "white-oriented" teachers were knowingly or unknowingly responsible for the failure of Negro children to achieve excellence in academic performance. Yeshiva University's Dr. Doxey Wilkerson reported that the "evidence mounts to prove that the 'cultural deprivation' hypothesis, which explains Black children's low level academic performance by their low level—by middle class white standards—cultural environment, is bankrupt." Stokely Carmichael cried: "We are not so concerned about going to a white school—we want a good school."

Bishop College president, Milton T. Curry, told a session of the National Education Association's meeting in Dallas, Texas, that desegregation had led mainly to removal of Negro leadership from the schools. The best Negro teachers were taken to suburban white schools, but the same was not the case when white teachers were sent to Black schools. When "integration" came, he pointed out, Negro principals became "vice-principals and handled the bookwork" while white principals moved ahead. If Texas lawmakers decided, he said, to spend in the next decade the difference in funds used for Negro and white schools since the 1880's, "then the Negro child would go to school from eight to five, six days a week for twelve months." There was reason to know that racial desegregation in the nation's schools too often meant upgrading for more whites in the schools and the elimination or downgrading of the Blacks—principals, counselors, coaches, teachers and students—even when reasons other than race demanded otherwise. The NEA tried to resist this assault.

"Today's Black students," said Fairleigh Dickinson University's Robert S. Browne, "are in a race to build a sense of Black community before a racial Armageddon overtakes them. This sense of urgency must be grasped if one is to understand the powerful forces which are motivating them."

It was apparent that Negro Americans had come in part to believe that America's schools and colleges had always been "politicized" and that it was incumbent on them to make the politicizing serve the needs of Black as well as white people. James Baldwin stated that Negro children grew up with a "feeling of no past, no present, and no future." One reaction to all of this was a call for "Black studies" and "Black universities." In some respects this was seen as the academic aspect of Black power.

Demands for Black studies produced Black textbooks. Two years ago an official of the NAACP listed 175 textbooks with "integrated" pictures. By 1968, more than four times that number were reported to be on the market, and the number continued to grow. Perhaps the most famous of the new high school texts which sought to give the Black man his proper place in American history was *Land of the Free*, by University of Chicago's John Hope Franklin, Howard's Ernest R. May and UCLA's John W. Caughey. It was also the most controversial of the 334 texts under criticism. Many white critics viewed with alarm the trend of Black studies authors to write in complimentary terms of historic Black Americans. They did not make the same criticisms of textbooks such as *Cavalier Commonwealth* (adopted by the Virginia state board of education for use in Virginia schools until 1970), which ignored the closing of the Prince Edward County schools from 1959 to 1963 and made no mention of such terms as "massive resistance" or "interposition," which characterized the state's anti-integration educational policy during that period.

The need for more intensified efforts to incorporate Black awareness into the nation's textbooks was repeatedly revealed. A report from the Michigan state board of education was one example: the twelve widely read American history textbooks which they studied were described by the Michigan group as "seriously deficient" in the treatment of Negroes. In another vein William Katz, white author of several books on Negro history, pointed out the need for white Americans as well as Black to know Negro history:

> If we are to find the intellectual tools to solve our major racial crisis, if we are to move finally toward that brotherhood we have long talked about, then a study of the Negro's past and its relevance to American history can throw light on one path toward this goal.

The Association for the Study of Negro Life and History, at its meeting in New York City in December 1968, presented the biggest display of books on the Black man in its fifty-three years of existence. The nation's Congress moved toward recognition of the problem as New York's Representative James H. Scheuer (D) experienced success in pushing a bill to establish a National Commission on Negro History and Culture. Many educators reported that the use of Black awareness educational materials was motivating Black pupils to significantly higher levels of performance in their classes. The American Textbook Institute's Dr. Austin I. McCaffrey said that the nation was now going through "its second textbook revolution in ten years." The first began with Sputnik, which set off a vast revision of scientific textbooks. The second, which might be said to have begun with the 1954 school desegregation decision of the U.S. Supreme Court, is producing a whole host of new or revised textbooks. This second revolution was given new impetus by the demands for Black studies in the schools, colleges and universities by Black student militants in 1967–68.

Because of the persistent demand of militant Negro students in 1968, many colleges and universities (including some of the Big Ten) established Black studies programs on their campuses. Scarritt College established an Associate of Arts (A.A.) degree in Black studies. The question of control and structure of these programs gripped San Francisco State College through the year's closing. In an effort to solve some of the problems associated with the issue, some four hundred administrators, students and faculty members from colleges throughout the country gathered in December 1968 at the Atlanta University Center. One participant described the conference as "an open-minded and open-ended discussion of African and African-American studies programs." Sponsored by the six Negro colleges of the Atlanta University Center and underwritten by the Southern Education Foundation and forty-nine institutions of higher learning, the conference dealt with such problems as: Who should teach Black studies courses—Black or white professors? Because of the shortage of competent teachers in the field, Clark College president, Vivian W. Henderson, suggested setting up "administrative consortia" among institutions teaching Black studies. These units, he said, would share library facilities, conduct joint seminars and work out short-term teacher-exchange programs. Suggestions for sensitivity training programs for white teachers of Black studies came from several parts of the country. There were predictions that several new major works in Black studies by Black authors would be forthcoming because of the new emphasis on Black curricula. The federal government also lent its support to the movement. The National Endowment for the Humanities, for example, awarded $70,000 to summer workshops on Negro history and culture. Congressman James Scheuer said that it is probably more important "to reach the suburban white than the ghetto Negro" with a true and integrated record of American history. NAACP executive director Roy Wilkins told a Berkeley, California, audience that the National Advisory Commission on Civil Disorders had made it clear that the reeducation of white America is our great national need.

One analysis of the states which officially teach Black history or Black studies in the public schools listed twenty-three by 1968. Some element of obligation was found in at least five of these states: California required the teaching of the role of minorities in American history courses; Florida required that social studies books approved by the state be "fully integrated"; the state textbook commission in Indiana demanded that texts submitted for adoption "accurately depict the multi-ethnic society" in the nation; Kentucky required that minority contributions be included in high school American history courses; New Jersey, too, demanded that its schools give attention to the role of the American Negro. Some states had no requirement and often no known effort under way.

In a special report released in 1968, the Southern Regional Education Board urged Negro colleges to make immediate curriculum changes in order to give their students a "broader range of career opportunities." The report, *New Careers and Curriculum Change*, suggested revisions in sciences (mathematics and new scientific instruments); social and behavioral sciences (including Negro history, the economics of discrimination, urban sociology, process of political action, and "other matters of special interest to Negro students"); humanities (including material on Negro culture); social welfare; business (with on-the-job internships for faculty and students). It also recommended that the colleges support "free colleges" which permit students to establish non-credit courses in areas of their own choice.

Militant Black students at the colleges and in the public schools resorted to abrasive demands and sometimes violence to achieve their objectives. Since only 50 per cent of the total Negro college population were attending Black colleges in 1968, these demands were made on both Black and white campuses. These students or their successors turned away from the civil rights movement which they had started. In 1965–66 these students had protested the paternalism and conservatism of many Negro college administrations. They often viewed this as an attack on white politicians, legislatures and boards of trustees which stood behind the Black administrators. In 1967 they adopted the tactics of violence which had been developed in the ghetto riots of 1964 and afterwards. They also turned to the image of Malcolm X, and considered his death to be a grave tragedy in the Black world. Their organizations assumed many names: Afro-American Student Association; Black Students Union; Afro-American Society; Sisters in Blackness; Black Pride, etc. It was rumored that an underground national unification was achieved in late 1968. These groups generated magazines, pamphlets, newsletters and other literature (as did their public school counterparts). Some titles included: *Soulbook, Umbra, Black Dialogue* and *The Black Student*. It was predicted that the numbers of their associations and their memberships would grow. They tended to be the most aggressive and violent of the student groups causing campus disruption in the nation in 1968.

Their fellow white disrupters more often than not played a supportive role to these Black groups.

Federal, state and local programs related to the education of Black people grew apace in 1968. Early in the year, President Lyndon Johnson called on Congress to declare a "fifth freedom—freedom from ignorance." He proposed as a new goal of American higher education that "in America there must be no economic or racial barrier to higher education; that every qualified young person must have all the education he wants and can absorb." Harold Howe, the U.S. Education Commissioner, called Johnson's proposals "the largest package of higher education legislation ever considered by any Congress." These proposals included the provisions for Head Start, Upward Bound, the Teacher Corps, a new stay-in-school program for potential high school dropouts, adult basic education classes and a Partnership for Learning and Earning program; the Education Opportunity Act of 1968; new programs for tutoring, counseling and special services to the neediest students; and the Networks for Knowledge Act of 1968, to encourage pooling of facilities, faculties, television services, etc., among the nation's colleges and universities. The Department of Health, Education and Welfare announced plans to eliminate segregation in the Northern states in support of the Presidential and national pressures.

Hundreds of programs—and problems—developed around the country in continued response to federal leadership in education for the poor and thus for the Black American. The nation's first undergraduate Teacher Corps program was established at the University of the Pacific. New York City's Youth Corps head was briefly suspended from his post for participation in a demonstration. Charges of fraud and improper use of federal funds to support Black power groups were continually brought during the year. Upward Bound programs on many campuses sometimes caused trouble as ghetto youth confronted middle class white Americans. Some Upward Bound youngsters began to demand that college administrations respect their adulthood and their dignity. (More than 90 per cent of the Upward Bound students on many campuses were Negroes.)

Local groups provided various educational programs for Negroes who had dropped out of school and were probably too old to return. Washington, D.C.'s, Youth Pride Economic Enterprises provided training and work experience for young dropouts. Atlanta's Manpower Development Center did likewise with money from the Office of Economic Opportunity. Summer institutes for training teachers for the slums in New York City came under attack for lack of innovation and creativity, but continued to serve.

New programs sponsored by industry and business appeared on the scene, as they had in preceding years. The Olin Mathieson Corporation awarded the Atlanta University Center $250,000 in support of a program to produce Black engineers. The Atlanta-based Citizens and Southern Bank also gave the University Center $250,000, to support a professorial chair in banking and finance. Plans for Progress made definite headway in helping industry across a broad spectrum to plan increased financial support for Negro colleges and universities. Perhaps one of the most important continuing programs of cooperation between industry and higher education was the Cooperative Education Program. In this program, students alternated semesters of job experience with semesters of study and thus earned money to support their education while gaining valuable on-the-job training. Some industries such as Chrysler Motor Company began to "adopt" high schools. The plan called for the company to give advice on adapting high school courses such as physics, chemistry and mathematics to the needs of industry, and to provide extensive plans for student counseling. Chrysler also joined with Atlanta's SCLC to bring automotive training and dealerships to Atlanta's Negro community. Western Electric sponsored a class in machine operation in Cicero, Illinois, and scores of other business and industrial groups contributed to the movement.

Programs to teach the ghetto Black man abounded in 1968. They proliferated to such an extent that classification is almost impossible. The New York Urban League, for example, opened Harlem Prep in 1967, which by 1968 was given a state charter to issue diplomas. It sought to take intelligent high school dropouts and boost them into colleges. New York's College Bound Corporation was given more than $3 million to perform a similar task in the city. Project Breakthrough and Harlem Teams for Self-Help, Inc., were similar projects. New York's Harlem Training Center sought ways permanently to increase the intelligence of slum children by beginning their formal education at the age of two years. (Head Start programs do not accept them below four years normally.) Philadelphia's Temple University sought to develop Black leadership potential among Negro high school students through an autumn conference at the university. The University of Chicago adopted four public schools. Detroit's Institute of Technology considered developing a one-hundred-square-block community in the heart of the city for Black Americans. The Ford Foundation's Educational Facilities Laboratory urged colleges to "build neighborhoods, not campuses," and to avoid the traditional "island approach to campus planning." The University of California at Davis joined with the Black Student Union to offer classes in mathematics, English and social sciences to ghetto youth, with the idea that if they persisted for at least one year they would be admitted to the university. Cleveland, Ohio, operated a special public service radio program urging those having difficulty completing their education to dial "Drop-Outs Anonymous," where they could talk directly with members of a team of professional counselors. College students in the Atlanta University Center carried out special programs of tutoring for the ghetto youngsters. The Urban League's "street academies," now in their third year, continued to lure high school dropouts to education.

Miami, Florida, initiated an expensive laboratory school for disadvantaged youngsters with a half-million dollars of federal support. Students were divided into four separate groups, each with an instructional center equipped for the total educational needs of the group. Each instructional "pod"—a 4,200-square-foot room—was assigned three certified teachers, a teacher aide, and a Teacher Corps intern. These air-conditioned pods housed seventy-five students or less in a setting that contained all the comforts of a middle class home—including bathtub, shower, living room, dining room, kitchen, window drapes, carpets, full-length mirrors, etc. The basic premise was that most disadvantaged children fail to achieve because of inadequate nutrition, poor health, shattered families. Thus, the "Centerette," as it was called, regularly scheduled its students for medical and dental care in its clinics and provided an individual program of instruction for each student. Data on pupil and teacher performance were fed into a computer to keep track of each student's intellectual and emotional development, changes in his learning style, and the appropriate teaching methods to match these changes.

An added dimension of the educational picture was the program of several white universities and colleges to seek out and admit more "high risk" Black students. Frequently this was the result of pressure from the Black militants on campus. A study released by the Southern Education Foundation in Atlanta pointed out that Negro colleges had always taken high risk students in large numbers.

A 20 per cent increase was noted, during 1968, of low income level students in the nation's colleges. The Rockefeller Foundation had helped several colleges finance recruitment of high achievers from minority groups and low income families. In 1968 most white institutions engaging in the high risk endeavor were not Southern. Only seven white institutions were found in the South. For most Negro students admitted to white colleges as high risks, the ideas of Black power and white help were often in conflict. Neither absorption into the prevailing middle class culture nor withdrawal into a separate Black society seemed fully acceptable or even fully possible, said the reporters.

The Southern Association of Colleges and Schools operated two programs—Project Opportunity and the College Preparatory Center—aimed at identifying and assisting disadvantaged youngsters with college potential. Project Opportunity, funded by the Ford Foundation, involved sixteen colleges and eleven high schools in eight Southern states. The College Preparatory Center, funded by the Office of Economic Opportunity, involved three small, church-related junior colleges in South Carolina in a program of remedial and financial assistance for prospective students.

The Southern Education Foundation report on the subject concluded that a growing number of white colleges sought the bright and able but poverty-stricken student, but "those whose past performance has been blunted by discrimination and poverty represent a risk that very few colleges are willing to take. . . . Higher education for high risk students—in spite of the precedents which athletes, foreign students and war veterans established—is still largely an unexplored territory for racial minorities and the poor."

New programs in Black colleges continued to involve high risk students, however. One of the appealing efforts was in the area of cooperative education projects (see above). Such institutions as Wilberforce University in Ohio, which had led in the field, were joined by Virginia State College, Hampton Institute and others. Clark College in Atlanta, aided by federal funds, joined with a dozen other institutions in an effort to upgrade the effect of college instruction on low achievers. Benedict College in South Carolina and Virginia Union University in Richmond were among other Black colleges which offered special remedial work for low achievers. Fayetteville State College in North Carolina built a new accelerated learning laboratory with "catch-up" funds provided by the state for Negro institutions. This was designed to provide students with access to materials that would broaden their scope and prepare them for advanced studies. The laboratory was equipped to help students identify their weaknesses and remedy their deficiencies, giving them opportunities to use programmed instructional materials, training to increase their reading skills, and help to broaden their analytical ability.

Bennett College in North Carolina offered a degree program in medical technology under approval of the Registry of Medical Technology of the American Society of Clinical Pathologists. Bennett also entered into inter-institutional cooperation with Guilford and Greensboro colleges in the area, and held membership in the Piedmont University Center in the state. Meharry Medical College offered the Master of Medical Science degree, which is designed primarily to aid students with high aptitudes but weak educational backgrounds who wish to enter medical or dental schools. Hampton Institute conducted a massive Centennial Curriculum Self-Study to determine its new academic directions.

There was no doubt that the area of education for Black Americans was replete with ideas and programs. There was some increasing evidence that small gains were being registered in the achievement levels of Black youth because of these programs. But funding for Black education remained extremely slight.

Money

Despite sharply increased attention to the situation, the moneys devoted to the solution of the problems of education of Black Americans remained extremely small and inadequate. With estimated annual budgets of about $150 million, about 120 Black colleges sought to educate some 150,000 of the 300,000 Black students in American colleges. Thus, an allocation of about $1,000 per year was made to house, feed, entertain and educate each student who came onto the Black campus. It is estimated that private Black colleges get 50 per cent of their income from student tuition and 25 per cent from endowment earnings, earnings of auxiliary enterprises and federal grants. The remaining 25 per cent comes from private gifts and grants, especially from churches.

Specific data on Black college budgets were unavailable, but it was clear that the federal government was the largest source of grants or loans to these institutions. Federal spending for all education in fiscal 1968 was about $4.5 billion. Reductions were anticipated for fiscal 1969 in college construction and in the purchase of textbooks and equipment, but increases were predicted in aid to the underprivileged and for teacher training. Of the $32 million granted under Title III of the Higher Education Act of 1965, the larger share went to Black colleges because more of them met the requirement of being "developing institutions." It was estimated that larger percentages of funds under the Elementary and Secondary Education Act went to the poor and thus to Black public schools, although considerable sums went to such wealthy white suburban areas as Scarsdale, New York, Winnetka, Illinois, Shaker Heights, Ohio, and Newton and Wellesley, Massachusetts. Massachusetts' Black Senator Edward Brooke proposed an amendment to cut off such funds to schools with less than 10 per cent of their students from poor families.

Of the $300 million donated by industry to higher education in 1967, only 6 per cent or less than $18 million trickled down to almost 120 Negro colleges—an average of $150,000 per institution—according to Knoxville College's president, Robert L. Owens, III. This was reported to be much too high an estimate by other educators. Data on contributions from industry and from foundations are scattered and incomplete.

The nation's biggest foundation, the Ford Foundation, continued to show some interest in the education of Black Americans. In February 1968 the foundation announced a grant of $3 million to help strengthen three predominantly Negro colleges: Shaw University and Hampton and Tuskegee Institutes. To Tuskegee went $1.1 million for its general development over the next three years. Hampton Institute got $875,000 for the same general purpose. Other smaller grants were given to improve the business administration practices of other Black colleges. Ford Foundation officials reported that these grants brought to a level of more than $28 million aid given by them to Negro higher education in the last five years. During the summer of 1968, Ford announced another series of grants to both white and Negro colleges for the purpose of strengthening their fund-raising, student relations, business procedures, library services and administration. It also gave $10 million to Columbia University for new efforts in urban and minority affairs and $1 million for doctoral fellowships for Black graduate students.

Such national foundations as the Rockefeller Foundation, the Carnegie Foundation, the Sloan Foundation and the Phelps-Stokes Fund continued their long-time interest in Negro education. The Rockefeller Foundation, for example, continued to develop its Toward Equal Opportunity Program, which focuses chiefly on strengthening higher educational opportunities for minority groups, primarily Negroes. It supported visiting professors programs in the Atlanta University Center as well. The Sloan Foundation and the Phelps-Stokes Fund contributed moneys to the Cooperative College Development Program to aid Black colleges in improving development offices for fund-raising purposes.

Thirty-six Negro institutions collectively sought money from corporations and philanthropists under the umbrella of the United Negro College Fund (UNCF). With a total enrollment of 42,000, these private schools sought a total of $6.5 million. It was estimated that Negroes contributed about $700,000 during 1967 to the annual UNCF drive. George Champion, president of Chase Manhattan Bank, led the campaign in 1968–69 under the guidance of the UNCF president, Stephen J. Wright. Joining the UNCF board for the first time were Time, Inc.'s, Andrew Heiskell, Johnson Publications' John H. Johnson, Polaroid Corporation's Peter Wensberg and National Educational Television's John F. White. Now in its twenty-fifth year, the fund has raised about 40 per cent of its moneys from corporations. It raised $4.6 million in 1967.

Interesting new financial support developed in the South in 1968. Under the leadership of its president, Mills B. Lane, Jr., the Citizens and Southern Bank contributed $250,000 to establishing a chair in banking and finance in the Atlanta University Center. This was the largest single grant in the history of Southern philanthropy to Black institutions. Following close on the heels of this came the $10 million grant by the Calloway Foundation to thirty-eight white and Black colleges in Georgia. At least eight Negro institutions in the state shared benefits from this grant to establish professorial chairs. Rich's, Inc., was reported to have made a $50,000 grant to Negro colleges in Atlanta as well. Other less publicized and smaller grants were made to various Black institutions in the South and Midwest. However, throughout 1968, as before, money remained a more serious problem for Black colleges than for white institutions.

People

At least seven predominantly Negro colleges gained new presidents during 1968. Texas Southern University in Houston named Granville M. Sawyer its new chief executive, after a search during several months of student disruptions and problems. Dr. Sawyer had been assistant to the president of Tennessee A. and I. University. He holds a Doctorate from the University of Southern California and a B.A. degree from Tennessee A. and I.

Two of the Atlanta University Center institutions appointed new presidents in 1968. Dr. Oswald P. Bronson was named to the chair of the

Interdenominational Theological Center. He holds a B.S. degree from Bethune-Cookman College, a B.D. from Gammon Theological Seminary and a Ph.D. from Northwestern University. Atlanta University's board of trustees named Dr. Thomas D. Jarrett as its seventh president in 1968. He holds a B.A. from Knoxville College, an M.A. from Fisk University and a Ph.D. from the University of Chicago; he moved into the presidency from the university's School of Arts and Sciences, in which he had served as dean for eight years.

The state board of education chose Dr. Andrew P. Torrence, vice-president of Tuskegee Institute, to be the new president of Tennessee State University. He succeeded Dr. Walter S. Davis and became the third president in the institution's history. The new president took his M.S. and Ph.D. degrees at the University of Wisconsin, where he later served as a visiting professor. Following major student demonstrations on the campus, Dr. Wade Wilson was named president to succeed Dr. Leroy B. Allen at Cheyney State College in Pennsylvania. Dr. Wilson had been director of development at Cheyney prior to this appointment. He took his B.S. degree at Cheyney, his M.Ed. at Pennsylvania State University and his Ed.D. at New York University. Dr. M. Maceo Nance, Jr., was named president of South Carolina State College after serving as acting president of the college for several months. Ohio's Central State University chose Howard University physicist Herman R. Branson as its new president. Nationally famed Dr. Branson received his B.S. degree from Virginia State College and his Ph.D. in physics from the University of Cincinnati.

Xavier University in New Orleans named its first Black president, attorney Norman C. Francis. He is the first layman to head this Catholic college which has a predominantly Negro student body.

Predominantly white educational institutions named a few Black men and women as their leaders in 1968. Perhaps the most outstanding educational appointment was the naming of Mrs. Elizabeth D. Koontz to be the first Negro president of the million-member, 106-year-old National Education Association. Mrs. Koontz, chosen in 1964 by the members, was installed four years later (according to tradition), in 1968, at the Dallas meeting of that leading body of educators. After serving in the association for fifteen years and giving attention to its Classroom Teachers group, she urged complete integration of education not only by races but by economic levels. The group has taken the lead in seeking to desegregate the nation's teachers associations and to protect Negro teachers and administrators in their jobs. She took her Bachelor's degree at Livingstone College in North Carolina and her Master's degree at Atlanta University, and did additional graduate work at Columbia and Indiana Universities. The Distinguished Service Award was presented to her by the Association for the Study of Negro Life and History at its fifty-third annual meeting in New York City in 1968.

For the first time in the history of the New York City public school system, a Negro was named principal (of Boys' High in Bedford-Stuyvesant). Previously, Dr. Norvel Clark had spent ten years teaching in the New York public schools and ten years administering the Police Athletic League centers in the Bedford-Stuyvesant district of Brooklyn. He holds a Bachelor's degree from Morehouse College in Atlanta, an M.A. from Columbia University and a Ph.D. from New York University.

Los Angeles named its first Negro head of the board of education in its 115-year history. The Reverend James E. Jones was elected president of the board in June 1968 by an official unanimous vote.

An increasing and unrecorded number of white universities have appointed Black educators to serve their Black student groups on campus. Andrew Billingsley (author of *Black Families in White America*) was made assistant chancellor of academic affairs at the University of California's Berkeley campus. A former Peace Corps executive and ex-president of at least two Negro colleges, Dr. Samuel D. Proctor served as dean of special projects for the University of Wisconsin. Proctor is the author of *The Young Negro in America* and served as an official in the Institute for Services to Education, which developed ideas for educational programs for the disadvantaged. Princeton University named Dr. Carl A. Fields as the first Negro dean in its 221-

year history. Columbia University appointed Franklin H. Williams as its Negro director for the university's Center on Urban and Minority Affairs. Several scores of white institutions chose Blacks to serve in the capacity of supervisor for their increasingly large numbers of Black students, many of whom were leading student disruptive actions on the campuses of the nation. Black students, however, did not automatically give them their loyalties.

At least two white institutions named a Negro as president. Connecticut named Dr. Arthur Banks as president of one of its junior colleges, and Dr. James Colston was named president of Brooklyn Community College in New York.

Whether the trend to appoint Negroes to administrative posts in predominantly white institutions would continue was not clear at the end of 1968. It seemed safe to hazard the guess that the trickle would not soon become a flood. Black awareness had not yet produced significant Black power in white educational institutions, although it had removed some Blacks in Black institutions.

Perhaps the most important development of all in the education of Black Americans in 1968, however, was the fact that a shift occurred from integration to Black awareness. In effect, Black awareness was another expression of the idea of Black power in the education of Black Americans. Experimentation with this idea and its refinements produced ferment, confrontation and violence in the nation's schools, colleges and universities. The assassination of Martin Luther King, Jr., in April 1968, to a large extent marked the watershed between integration and Black awareness in the nation's education. The future of the experiment was still in doubt, although significant battles had been won, as 1968 drew to a close.

II. Integration and the Law

Fourteen years after the famous Brown decision of 1954, which ruled segregated education to be illegal, integration was yet to be attained in any serious degree in the public schools or in the public mind. Tokenism or less was still the objective of millions. Others this year for the first time, including large numbers of articulate Blacks, were of the opinion that integration was unrealistic in fact and perhaps undesirable at this historic moment. Militant Blacks began to express the thought that Negroes should withdraw to themselves in order to seek their strength and dignity —and only after doing that should they be willing to negotiate the terms of any integration. Some of the ultra-militant rejected even this approach to integration and turned their eyes to Africa or the Third World—rejecting completely the white world as rotten and corrupt beyond repair.

The facts of integration in the public schools were more difficult to determine than ever in 1968. The Southern Education Reporting Service complained in a public report over federal delays in releasing data. In 1967–68 the U.S. Department of Health, Education and Welfare (HEW) defined a desegregated school as one "attended by minority group children in which at least 50 per cent of the students are white." The preceding year, such a system was defined as one with as much as 5 per cent of the student enrollment white. This is interpreted as a numbers game by some. With one exception (the NAACP), none of the major civil rights organizations in the last three years mounted a major program of school desegregation in the South. According to HEW figures, the percentage of Blacks attending racially mixed Southern public schools in 1967–68 was 14; in 1968–69, it had risen by 6.4 per cent to about 20 per cent. The range in the South was from Texas (with 38.9 per cent in the fall of 1968) to Mississippi (with about 6.1 per cent) and Alabama (with about 7.4 per cent).

When viewed nationally, however, the racial imbalance in the public schools was worsening as the school populations grew larger and polarization of the races in the cities carried the whites to the suburbs and left the Blacks in the center cities. Massachusetts, the only state in the nation with a Racial Imbalance Law (adopted in 1965), reported that racial imbalance had spread to more schools this year than ever before in that state. Similar reports came from many urban centers throughout the nation. A *New York Times* editorial pointed up increased segregation in the schools of the nation's largest city a few days before the assassination of Martin Luther King, Jr. The New York State board of regents pointed to the increasing racial imbalance in the state schools in a report released by its commissioner of education, Dr. James E. Allen, Jr. Commissioner Allen called on the local school boards to find ways to reverse the trend and develop more integration of the schools. Detroit reported failure of its large-scale efforts to maintain racial balance in three selected neighborhoods by improving the public schools. Whites continued to leave the center city as they resisted integration. U.S. Commissioner of Education, Harold Howe, II, stated:

> It is a sorry thing to have to acknowledge that much of the desegregation that has taken place has occurred because thousands of Negro students and their parents have been steadfast in the face of pressures of the cruelest sort.

Black Americans in 1968, however, were to tire of their failing efforts to integrate and would turn increasingly to separatism and Black nationalism. Some white Americans have to bear a large share of the responsibility for this. Proposals in 1967 for widespread bussing of students, moving of city students to the suburbs, building of school parks, compensatory education programs such as Head Start, elimination of track levels, etc., did not significantly alter the degree of polarization of American society between Black and white. The director of the Office of Civil Rights in HEW reported that the rate of school desegregation in the South, after doubling in both 1965 and 1966, had advanced more slowly in 1967. Most of the gain HEW director Peter Libassi attributed to the freedom of choice plan, admitting that this plan was limited by harassment of Negroes, Negroes' fears that they would (they did) lose their positions, and academic problems faced by transferring Black pupils. President Emeritus Benjamin E. Mays of Morehouse College in the Atlanta University Center noted: "At the current rate, it would take about 100 years to complete the job [of desegregation]."

The courts in the nation, on the other hand, continued to interpret the laws regarding segregation in the public schools so as to achieve desegregation. In February the Detroit school board instituted an important suit against the state of Michigan in an effort to force the state to allocate more money to the slum area schools than to the middle and upper-class schools on the basis that it costs more to provide equal educational opportunities for deprived children. New Yorkers took steps to file a federal court suit, similar to one in Newark, New Jersey, designed to make Black public schools at least "equal" through means other than integration, which was viewed as a practical impossibility.

In its first school desegregation action in the North, the Department of Justice filed suit against Cook County, Illinois, for discrimination in faculty and staff assignments. The second such case in the North was filed against the Indianapolis public schools. The first case in the Far West involved the Pasadena, California, school system.

A milestone in federal court decisions came on May 27, 1968, when the United States Supreme Court ruled unanimously that freedom of choice desegregation plans are inadequate if they do not in fact put an end to segregation. The Court declared that "delays are no longer tolerable," although it did not declare freedom of choice plans inherently unconstitutional. (Nine out of every ten Southern communities in 1968 used the plan, which permitted children of all races to pick their own schools.) The Court also restricted this ruling to Southern and border states which had legally sanctioned dual systems in 1954 when the first desegregation ruling was made. Appeals which led to the May 27 decision were brought by Negro parents in New Kent County, Virginia; Gould, Arkansas; and Jackson, Tennessee. Jack Greenberg of the NAACP had argued the cases before the Court for the Gould Negroes; Samuel Tucker of Richmond, Virginia, had argued the case for the New Kent appellants; and James M. Nabrit, III, of New York, for the Jackson, Tennessee, appellants.

On Friday, May 31, the Fourth Circuit Court of Appeals in a Norfolk, Virginia, case warned that geographical zoning or "neighborhood schools" which did not lead to an end of segregation were suspect to the court. This Norfolk case suggested that the courts were now looking at the actual results of the plan rather than at its theory for desegregation.

A similar look at the results of desegregation plans was taken by the courts on the level of higher education. The Department of Justice filed suit in July against the state of Tennessee for its plans to build an extension to the Nashville Extension Center of the University of Tennessee (predominantly white), thus in effect guaranteeing that the Tennessee A. and I. State University would remain predominantly Black.

A fourth milestone was the September 24 ruling of the United States Fifth Circuit Court that all Southern schools that have only Black students must be integrated or abandoned by September of 1969.

Several groups of whites, both North and South, took various steps to resist the new federal interpretations of the law. The NAACP Legal Defense Fund, however, filed thirteen appeals to implement these decisions in Louisiana and Mississippi. Blacks and whites in Mobile, Alabama, on the other hand, found their desires to follow the new law being subverted by more powerful whites. The United States Fifth Circuit Court of Appeals in August ordered a close study of the effects of forty-two plans submitted in Louisiana, Texas, Mississippi and Georgia before it would approve them, and ordered new plans to be filed by November 28 where the evidence suggested that no real integration would result from the old plans. On August 28, a two-judge panel ruled that Alabama must desegregate its school faculties, with at least one out of every six teachers in a school being of a different race. It also ordered the closing or partial closing of 146 Negro schools by the fall of 1969.

There was intense and bitter white reaction in the South against these renewed legal integration efforts. Perhaps the most serious potential challenge to the federal court rulings came in the United States Congress. Representative Jamie L. Whitten (D) of Mississippi sponsored an anti-integration "rider" to the $18.4 billion HEW money bill that would bar the use of the withholding of federal funds to force the bussing of students, to close a school or to force any student to attend a particular school against his parents' will. Had it passed, it would very likely have killed desegregation efforts, at least in the South. President Lyndon B. Johnson reportedly threatened a veto, and the House of Representatives reversed its June 1968 support of the provision and voted to drop it on October 3, 1968. In the interim, Presidential candidate Richard Nixon at first opposed the withholding of federal funds for this purpose, but changed his opinion after conferring with civil rights advisers.

III. Black Awareness and the Public Schools

"Pessimism" was the word used by the dean of Harvard University's Graduate School of Education to describe public opinion about public schools in the nation as 1968 dawned. Dean Theodore Sizer pointed out that: (1) the vaunted federal aid to education amounted actually to only $92 per capita per annum; (2) rebellion by the ghetto poor was driving Washington officialdom to thoughts of a police state, not a welfare state; (3) college professors had no easy solutions to the problems of ghetto education; (4) the Negro community felt cheated by the failures in public school education; (5) technologists had not solved the problems of packaging an education in computers and teaching machines. Dean Sizer's comments follow many critical books on the urban school scene: Herbert Kohl's *Thirty-six Children*; Jonathan Kozol's *Death at an Early Age*; Nat Hentoff's *Our Children Are Dying*; and John Holt's *Why Children Fail* and *How Children Learn*. All of these books spotlighted defects in the ghetto schools, and all these authors seemed to agree that racial and class prejudice was no less pronounced in our school systems than elsewhere in our society.

The question was how to translate criticism into action. That is why Black awareness advocates created a new facet in the picture of American society in 1968. The year saw so much disruption, dissension and discord that Brandeis University's Lemberg Center for the Study of Violence predicted in October that the summer rebellions were to become winter rebellions in the schools and would continue for another fifty years!

The most hopeful sign that the Brandeis experts might be wrong came in the Far West, in Berkeley, California. There "the first complete racial integration of schools in an American community of over 100,000 was achieved." (On September 9, 1968, some 3,500 students were transported to schools throughout the community to achieve a racial balance accurately reflecting school enrollment figures—50 per cent white, 41 per cent Black and 9 per cent Oriental and others.) Superintendent of schools Neil V. Sullivan called the day ". . . a great one for Berkeley and for the United States." The decision to integrate the university community's fourteen elementary schools was made in 1967 after several years of study, and the program was generally well received by both parents and teachers, according to reports.

New York

Generally speaking, however, the Brandeis report was borne out by the events in many of the nation's public schools, from Massachusetts to Florida to California. The worst and most intense of the agonies perhaps were experienced in the fires of the Ocean Hill-Brownsville rebellions in New York.

A relatively unknown woman (Brooklyn's Mrs. Evelyn Sistrunk) pinpointed a key issue in the 1968 school crises in New York City. Smiling shyly, she told a *New York Times* reporter:

> I might be speaking out of turn, but you know that black people must get together and do something for one another because white people don't really care about us.

This conviction, exacerbated by unknown thousands of racial incidents, led New York's Negroes to demand "community control" of their neighborhood schools. Community control came to involve many of America's deepest passions and issues: (1) a crash in Black expectations of true integration following the civil rights efforts; (2) the belief that desegregation laws were being twisted by whites both to support white supremacy and to rob Blacks of many gains in public school systems which they had made before the civil rights movement; (3) the continuing failure of large metropolitan areas to solve their urban problems generally; (4) the growing militancy of Black power advocates; (5) the role of a major foundation as an agent of social change; (6) anti-Semitism; (7) trade union establishmentarianism; (8) legislative frustrations on local and state levels.

That the Black community became the battleground becomes more understandable when it is known that there are only 6,500 Negroes in the New York City public school staff of 60,000, while more than 50 per cent of the 1.1 million student population is Black. New York officials appointed the first Negro high school principal in the history of the city in late summer of 1968. The first Negro in the city's history to become a member of the 184-year-old board of regents is famed psychologist Kenneth Clark—very recently named.

Charges of "teacher brutality" to Negro and Puerto Rican children were made at the end of 1967 and early in 1968 by CORE. Teachers allegedly beat Black boys and girls repeatedly. One boy was hospitalized, one girl was apparently knocked through a pane of glass, and another youth had a teacher pour gasoline on his hands. Apparently, none of these teachers lost his job. (The records showed that tenured teachers were not likely to be dismissed at all. A five-year survey showed that only twelve such teachers out of a total teaching staff of 60,000 had been removed for reasons other than retirement or resignation.) Negro parents despaired of influencing a white board of education under a centralized system. "The roots of the controversy," said one reporter, "are embedded in the low academic achievement of many poor children, particularly those of minority groups."

A New York psychologist summed up one problem of the schools in this fashion:

> American public schools have become significant instruments in the blocking of economic mobility and in the intensification of class distinctions, rather than fulfilling their historic function of facilitating such mobility. In effect, the public schools have become captives of a middle class who have failed to use them to aid others to move into the middle class. It might even be possible to interpret the role of the controlling middle class as that of using the public schools to block further mobility.

Dr. James B. Conant's 1961 edition of *Slums and Suburbs* warned of the "social dynamite" being created in the nation's urban streets. Countless experts continued to show that schools for Blacks in America were not educating their pupils as well as schools for whites were. The first city-wide boycott of New York schools occurred in 1964, when Negroes demanded integration in an erroneous hope that this would make their schooling equal to that of whites.

Black people of Harlem first raised the issue of community control in 1966, when they demanded that the city's board of education either integrate the student body and faculty and provide sufficient experienced teachers, or arrange for community control of a proposed windowless, air-conditioned Intermediate School 201. When they found that more state aid would come to the city if the system were divided into districts based on the city's five boroughs, the board of education endorsed the principle of decentralization. Under a grant from the Ford Foundation a plan was released in the winter of 1967 by a panel appointed by Mayor John Lindsay and headed by the Ford Foundation's McGeorge Bundy. The plan called for the creation of up to sixty semi-independent school districts, each with an eleven-man governing board (five appointed by the mayor and six elected by the community). Under heavy pressure from the teachers' union (United Federation of Teachers, or UFT) and the city's Central Labor Council, the state legislature rejected the plan and directed the state board of regents and the city board of education to arrange a more limited temporary decentralization plan.

The temporary plan provided for three demonstration districts: Intermediate School 201 (with five member schools) in Harlem; Ocean Hill-Brownsville (with eight schools), near Bedford-Stuyvesant, in Brooklyn; Two Bridges district in Lower East Side Manhattan. District or local governing boards were to have wide powers over the selection of personnel, allocation of budget funds, adaptation of the curriculum, and deployment of staff. The city board of education would retain substantial powers over the curriculum, would protect teachers' rights, would continue system-wide collective bargaining with the union and would allocate budgets to the local districts. That these generalized and overlapping areas of control were never detailed added to the confusion and helped to precipitate the crises when variously interpreted.

Initial trouble developed in the fall of 1967 in school district IS 201 over the efforts of the local board to have a white principal transferred and replaced by a Black one. The efforts continued into January 1968, and the situation was further exacerbated by an attack on a white principal in the Brooklyn Ocean Hill area. Black parents and residents defended the attack as "the only means left open to protect our youth." Superintendent Bernard E. Donovan's proposal to send armed guards to the schools met with community threats of violence against the guards. The African-American Teachers Association (AATA) blamed the violence in the schools on the board of education and on the UFT.

The ugly issue of anti-Semitism was apparent by late January 1968 in a charge of racism and anti-Semitism made by the New York Board of Rabbis, who criticized the decentralization plan as a "potential breeder of local apartheid." Rabbi Gilbert Klaperman said it was ironic that Jewish people should "now be singled out by these [Black] extremists in their blind hatred of the white community." Ocean Hill-Brownsville at one time had been a Jewish ghetto and now was predominantly Black and Puerto Rican. A Negro teacher distributed circulars in the fall of 1968 which were violently anti-Semitic, but the Urban League's Whitney Young accused UFT President Albert Shanker (fifty-year-old son of a Polish rabbi) of raising the issue in order to get control of the schools for the union. Although the anti-Semitic aspects of the situation continued through most of the year, both the local board president and an official of the American Jewish Committee agreed that the issue had been introduced in order to manipulate Negro and Jewish communities for the purposes of those who initiated it.

Ocean Hill-Brownsville forged its way to the front with the early development of crises. Charges of "teacher brutality" were formally made by February 1. Bedlam developed among the eighth-graders in one of the junior high schools (258) as the demands for the ousting of a white principal grew louder. Peace returned only temporarily with the appearance of six policemen. Negro parents in PS 96—not in the demonstration school group—also pressured for the removal of a white principal within the week. Among the charges they leveled against him were racism and neglect of academic programs in favor of cultural exercises. A member of the Ocean Hill governing board allegedly slapped the face of an assistant principal in PS 96 who blocked her entrance to the school.

Harlem's IS 201 district suffered similar violence. An exodus of pupils who had been harassed, assaulted or robbed was reported in early February of 1968. A dramatic crisis arose on February 21 when a Malcolm X memorial program was held at IS 201. During the program, co-sponsored by the local governing board and the AATA, ex-teacher and member of the Black militant group RAM, Herman B. Ferguson, exhorted the Negroes to get guns for "self-defense" and to practice using them so that when the "hunting season" began they would be ready. Ferguson had been suspended in the summer of 1967 for an alleged conspiracy to murder moderate Negro leaders Whitney Young and Roy Wilkins. Other attacks were leveled against white Americans during the four-hour program by such famous Negroes as James Baldwin and LeRoi Jones. Superintendent Donovan decried these developments and indicated that the schools "cannot become the vehicles of political power, racism, or ideological struggles." It was obvious that many Negroes felt that they had already become just that. The local governing board, however, went on record as opposing these statements. Several non-tenure teachers who went to the program were disciplined, and some were released for that reason. The dismissal of John Hatchett was most notorious.

The conflict between the local boards and the centralized board of education came to light as the turmoil around Ferguson boiled. Superintendent Donovan ordered the local governors to refrain from interfering with the operation of IS 201 until an administrator had been selected and the governing board was officially recognized by the city board.

Meanwhile, in a report highly critical of the physical facilities of one of the Ocean Hill schools, the principal complained of dead rats in the building and of most of the equipment being sent to the "rich schools." By April (before the assassination of Dr. Martin Luther King, Jr.) the local governors had apparently resolved on confrontation to force the board of education to transfer control to the local districts. April 9 was set as the deadline, and boycotts were threatened. The vice-chairman of the Ocean Hill-Brownsville district correctly predicted that the situation resulting from a boycott "might just be a disaster over here and this might not be a place for anybody to come to." Six thousand pupils were kept out of classes on April 10 as the city board claimed that it had no authority to grant the demands of the Brooklyn unit in Ocean Hill-Brownsville. Although Superintendent Donovan blamed the boycott on the local governors, the parents insisted that it was they who were sponsoring the boycott in support of the local board. United States Commissioner Harold Howe symbolically supported the demands for local control when he stated: "It is understandable that a black group may want to set aside the need for keeping an integrated society on the agenda." At the same time the New York State commissioner for education was calling for improvement in the teaching of the contributions of Negroes to American life and history.

The assassination of Martin Luther King, Jr., on April 4, led to increased racial tensions and exacerbated feelings in the demonstration districts. An interracial fight occurred between two teachers in the area. The board of education soon thereafter appointed Rhody A. McCoy as administrator of the Ocean Hill-Brownsville district. McCoy's forte was reported to be community education. He envisioned a system in which parents, neighbors, teachers, pupils—all were involved. He especially wanted teachers immersed in the local situation—living in the slums, becoming part of the community. Better still, he would train local community people who do relate to slum children to become teachers. McCoy's selection of teachers for the area proved to be on grounds other than race—most of them were white.

On May 9 the confrontation escalated. Administrator McCoy and his district board sent letters to thirteen teachers and six administrators terminating their employment in the district schools. McCoy said they were released because "the community lost confidence in them" and because they were suspected of trying to sabotage the demonstration project. They were not fired but were told to report to the city board for reassignment. The city board sent telegrams telling them to ignore the dismissal notices and return to their posts. President Shanker of the UFT said he would ask Mayor Lindsay to provide escorts if the teachers were threatened. A local board member expressed the view that charges of violating state laws in this action were not valid because "the people in the street considered these laws written to protect the moneyed white power structure of this city." Representing the city administrators, the Council of School Supervisors demanded the immediate removal of Rhody McCoy for dismissing the six administrators. The community groups made plans to prevent the return of the transferred personnel to their classrooms.

The plans materialized. On May 14, defiant Black parents and their supporters took over Junior High School 271 in the Ocean Hill district and prevented the return of some of the teachers. Two hundred policemen patrolled the area and eighty-five teachers followed UFT advice and remained out of the area in support of the dismissed teachers. Mayor Lindsay declared his support for the teachers, while he reminded the public of the conditions that had led to the confrontation. He also pointed to the city board's failure to define the powers of the local district board. These allegations were vehemently denied by the city board, which insisted that the powers had been defined in guidelines laid down on December 12, 1967, but that the local board was unwilling to accept these definitions.

The state capitol at Albany saw legislative frustration emasculate efforts to provide the strong local district controls which had been recommended in a bill by the board of regents. Negro regent Kenneth Clark threatened resignation over the lobbying that was destined to result in a watered-down version of the original bill. State Senator John J. Marchi proposed simply to direct the board of education to restudy the matter and report a year later on a new plan. The regents and Commissioner Allen firmly opposed retention of the current board of five members because of the view that the board was definitely opposed to any substantial decentralization. After what was described as "vicious" lobbying by the UFT, Governor Nelson Rockefeller's administration developed and pushed through successfully a compromise plan that kept the old city board but enlarged it by adding five new members who were expected to be more amenable to decentralization. This enlarged board was to decentralize the city system by July 1, 1969. Up to thirty districts could be created, with the power to hire and dismiss teachers within the limits of the laws and regulations on tenure.

Faced with the fact that the parents' boycott had practically emptied five of the Ocean Hill schools, superintendent Donovan ordered the remaining three closed on Thursday, May 16, with the directive that all eight would open on the following Monday, May 20. The Reverend Milton A. Galamison, who had led two massive citywide school boycotts in 1964, announced plans for a limited boycott in support of the Brooklyn district parents. Over the weekend, negotiations produced a local compromise which saw Rhody A. McCoy formally request transfer of the dismissed teachers and administrators and superintendent Donovan order them to report for hearings on the basis of that request.

Lobbying in Albany, Albert Shanker issued a counter-order and told the "illegally fired teachers" to report to work until specific charges were brought against them. Superintendent Donovan, however, upheld the suspension of seven of the original nineteen and confirmed the authority of McCoy to transfer teaching and supervisory personnel. President Shanker had initiated a three-day teacher walkout in protest of this action by the city board and threatened to continue it if necessary. The school season closed with the issues still unresolved.

Despite the threats of Dr. Kenneth Clark to mobilize slum communities against the watered-down version of the regents' bill for community control and decentralization, Governor Rockefeller signed the bill into law and the new members were added to the old city board. Among those sworn into office on July 24 were the Reverend Milton A. Galamison and Ernest R. Minott (Negroes), Hector Vazquez (Puerto Rican) and William Haddad (white). Immediately it became apparent that the old members were in some conflict with the new ones.

September saw the reopening of school and the reopening of the controversy. Albert Shanker issued immediate plans for a strike of New York's nine hundred city schools, despite the illegality of such action. Rhody McCoy announced the hiring of 350 new teachers to replace those that might strike in the Ocean Hill district. Mayor Lindsay sought to get the two groups to compromise, but failed. A decentralization compromise had been voted during the first week of September giving thirty-three community school boards power to run schools (but not to fire teachers), with the superintendent having a veto over local actions.

Shanker moved inexorably toward a general city-wide strike of teachers. Efforts of state commissioner of education James Allen were of no avail. A two-day strike on September 9 and 10 ended with an agreement which permitted the teachers to return to their classes, but angry demonstrators prohibited their reentry. Rhody McCoy and newly elected local board chairman Rev. C. Herbert Oliver pointed out that they would no longer stand as buffers between the community and the central board and that the community would control its schools in the face of a city-wide strike called by the UFT. Union leader Shanker stated that "McCoy and the governing board must be removed and we must get complete protection for the teachers before we go back." In the meantime, members of the Black Panther group stationed themselves near one of the controversial schools. Sporadic fights, helmeted police, bomb scares and false fire alarms contributed to the disruption of New York City's schools during these early days of reopening.

Brooklyn's Ocean Hill-Brownsville school district had in early September 1968 come under the legal authority of an eighteen-member board. Seven parent representatives were elected by popular vote. The parents then chose five community representatives (Rev. C. Herbert Oliver, Assemblyman Wright, two local white clergymen and a professor of education from Brooklyn College). Four teachers and two supervisory board members were elected by other teachers and supervisors in the district.

Among the eight principals appointed by this local board, one was a Jew, one a Chinese American (the first in New York), one an Italian, and four were Negroes—hardly an extreme Black nationalist group. More than 50 per cent of the new teachers appointed by McCoy were white. Charges of Black power in action were true mainly in that Black people were exercising power in selecting white people of their choice as well as selecting Negroes. "Law and order" in Ocean Hill were technically on the side of Black people. Their schools remained open despite the UFT city-wide teachers' strike. Rival National Education Association's president, Elizabeth D. Koontz (the first Black to head that group), avoided open conflict with the PFT but called for a return to the individual school and an end to centralized bureaucracy.

Ignoring a court injunction and the threat of being jailed, the UFT leader continued the strike. Efforts of the board of education to reopen the schools on September 25 failed. Violence erupted at Junior High School 271 in the Ocean Hill-Brownsville district on October 1, when an open attack was made on the large number of police stationed at the school. More than a thousand of "New York's finest" were reported present. Violence erupted again as two hundred students and their supporters battled police with rocks and bottles on the Lower East Side and at Junior High School 271. The controversy threatened to spread throughout the entire school system. On October 4 the union leader advocated another strike call, because the board of education had failed to enforce compliance with an agreement that had ended the previous three-week "walkout" —an agreement requiring McCoy to reinstate 110 teachers he did not want.

Rhody McCoy's local board enjoyed "legality" only a short time. Faced with the new teachers' strike and with McCoy's insistence on the release of the 110 teachers in the Ocean Hill district, the city board, on Sunday night, October 6, suspended the local board for thirty days and ordered Donovan to take charge of the eight schools. McCoy announced that he was under the authority of the local board and would follow their orders and release eighty-three of the 110 controversial teachers. Massive police forces were called out again, and union president Shanker decided to delay the strike until the future of McCoy was clear. On October 8 the board dismissed McCoy and the principals of the eight schools. Donovan sought to confer with the UFT teachers and the local board teachers on October 10 and 11, but he gave up when the union leader insisted on being present. These efforts failing and Mayor Lindsay's appeal to the UFT not to strike going unheeded, Shanker successfully called for a strike vote.

New York City officials sought continuously to find ways to end the strike. Unionist Shanker was equally adamant. He rejected Mayor Lindsay's compromise efforts and insisted on the return of the eighty-three teachers, the dismissal of Rhody

McCoy and the closing of JHS 271, where most of the disturbances against union teachers had developed.

Again the city failed and the state legislature was called upon to resolve the crisis. A special session of the joint legislative committee on the education law was called on November 10, while Mayor Lindsay met with officials of the teachers' union and the board of education. Lindsay and Shanker succeeded only in moving further apart.

Violence continued to erupt in Ocean Hill-Brownsville schools. Significant development of high school student power was observed. Student representatives from some seventy New York high schools attended a strategy session at the Granada Hotel on Saturday night, November 30. A Black student group, the High School Coalition, secured an office with the Harlem Committee for Self-Defense while the African-American Students Association and the City-Wide Student Strike Committee used an office of the African-American Teachers Association in Brooklyn.

Not only did trouble escalate the growth of student organizations, but it now spread to a second local district in early December of 1968. Harlem's IS 201 district erupted into violence when union teachers were blocked by Negro parents as the former sought to enter PS 39 in the IS 201 complex. The teachers were promised police protection as parents planned further resistance.

Rhody McCoy's troubles continued briefly. He was arrested and charged with criminal trespass on Wednesday, December 11, when he sought to open Junior High School 271, which had been closed by state orders on December 3. The state of New York had appointed Dr. William D. Firman as trustee for the decentralized Ocean Hill-Brownsville district upon the suspension of McCoy. Dr. Firman ordered McCoy's arrest. Parents kept their children out of the schools in support of McCoy, while the assistants in McCoy's office were forced to leave by December 13. Whitney Young and Kenneth Clark publicly called on the state to recall Firman at the same time that the city board announced its plans to decentralize the New York City school system by 1970.

December 16 saw the harried administrator McCoy returned to power. The arrangement which provided for his return had been worked out in several meetings. A key meeting was held in the offices of the Metropolitan Applied Research Center (headed by Kenneth Clark). Upon the report that Dr. Firman had developed influenza, the new acting trustee, Wilbur R. Nordos of the state department of education, announced the return of the embattled Black administrator. Two days later, Junior High School 271, which had been closed for two weeks, reopened in Ocean Hill-Brownsville. As the year ended, the schools were apparently returning to some normal operations, and the city took legal action against the illegal strike called by Shanker's UFT. The future was not yet entirely clear with regard to the ultimate resolution of this sticky question of community control.

The future of community control is still in doubt, although it was observed in several of the nation's largest cities in 1968.

The South

In the South the traditional hostilities to desegregation continued.

Atlanta, liberal metropolis of the South, witnessed the failure of the two professional organizations of public school teachers to achieve unification despite efforts of the National Education Association. Black leaders of education blasted HEW officials for not developing "reciprocal integration," which would permit the placing of white students in previously Black schools as well as the reverse. Dr. H. E. Tate, executive secretary of the Black teachers' group (Georgia Teachers and Education Association), pointed out that the Negro "has been given the entire burden of desegregation," and insisted that too many systems still discriminated against Negro teachers; they desegregated their schools, but then demoted or fired Negro teachers and principals. Too often desegregation was turned into denigration for Blacks. Paul Rilling, regional civil rights director of HEW, observed that he had no authority to accomplish the ends demanded by Dr. Tate.

Black and white Atlantans called upon the school board and the superintendent to provide for accelerated desegregation of the schools and to correct the serious racial inequities. Graduates from Black schools were two to four years behind graduates of white schools in achievement tests, while book collections in white schools were 600 per cent superior to those in predominantly Black schools. The group called Better Schools, Atlanta, with an integrated membership and led by Robert F. Tuve, reported that 92.3 per cent of Negro elementary school pupils in the city attend all-Black schools. The school board responded at first by having detectives or investigators check on the backgrounds of the members of the organization. Failing to frighten off the group, the school board then scheduled a meeting to explain its position in the matter. Speaking to the Atlanta Jaycees, superintendent John Letson stated in effect that the white residents' flight from the city made it almost impossible to achieve desegregation as the Black population increased. This did not, however, explain the inequities in fund distribution or book collections in Black schools. Atlanta Black people, led by such men as Dr. Otis Smith and Dr. Samuel Williams, were not satisfied with the explanations.

Miami, Florida, reputedly another "liberal" center in the South, had its racial problems in high schools. Black students boycotted the South Dade High School in protest of use by the athletic teams of Confederate symbols and songs. The local authorities reacted by temporarily transferring the Black students from the high school. Consequently, Negro parents requested federal authorities to withhold $4 million in aid to Dade County for its racist practices.

Reactions in South Carolina varied from unity meetings by grass-roots-level Blacks in Frogmore, South Carolina, to a boycott of white schools by white students after a desegregation order was enacted. The two local schools were then closed. In Cheraw, South Carolina, all of the Black students boycotted the Robert Small Elementary School following the decision of the school board to drop plans for pairing Negro and white schools. Despite these isolated cases, in 1968 federal court rulings had increased the number of desegregated classes in the state.

Boycotts against the school systems in Social Circle and Waycross, Georgia, took different forms but sought the same basic objective—desegregation and equity in the education of Blacks. More lasting and serious trouble brewed in Sylvester, Georgia, where two Negro girls were jailed following a fight on a Worth County school bus. In Jeffersonville, Georgia, the Southern Christian Leadership Conference (SCLC) and the NAACP joined hands with local leaders to agitate for an abandonment of the freedom of choice plan used in the Twiggs County schools and for improvement of conditions in the Black schools. Racism was likewise protested by Blacks in De Kalb County and in Buford, Georgia. Four Georgia counties and scores of thousands of whites were reported to be awaiting the inauguration of newly elected President Richard M. Nixon in the belief that he would not cut off federal funds to non-desegregating school systems. A short boycott of a white woman principal appointed to a predominantly Black school was mounted by Black parents in Zebulon, Georgia. They were supported by the SCLC and the Black Georgia Teachers and Education Association.

A new dimension of Black awareness in public schools developed in Swanquarter, North Carolina, in November 1968. When local Negroes realized that the result of a desegregation order's enforcement would lead to the closing of the Black schools in the town, they mounted a boycott that led to violence, arrests and serious injuries to Black students. When twenty Negro children marched into a room of the Hyde County courthouse, the police hurled smoke grenades into the room and slammed the door shut. A seventeen-year-old girl leaped from a second floor window and was hospitalized with a fractured pelvis. Meanwhile, the county threatened to cut off welfare payments to parents of children boycotting the schools. It was difficult for the local whites to understand that the Blacks feared that they would be used as "guinea pigs to foster white supremacy disguised as integration."

In the nation's capital 93.6 per cent of the school enrollment was Black. The first school board election in the city's history was made possible by an election law passed in April 1968 by Congress. The issue at stake was how to achieve quality education for poor Black students without discouraging white and upper and middle class Negro students from staying in the public schools. Community control was not an issue in the elections, as was true in other major cities of the nation.

As one left the deep South, Black dignity and equality remained the objectives, but 1968 saw more Blacks decide that separatism was the avenue or way—not integration. This switch in tactics puzzled most whites and many Blacks across the nation during the whole of 1968. Perhaps this confusion added a new dimension to police barbarity. Reactions to the new separatist dimensions of Black awareness were varied, sometimes violent, and especially puzzling to those unaccustomed to high school pupils acting as agents of social change.

The Northeast

New dimensions of the struggle over Black awareness in public schools appeared in the ferment in Northern schools. New York State witnessed concern and action in several of its larger cities. Negroes in Buffalo pressed for an end to racial imbalance in the schools and showed signs of increasing bitterness over the failure of the board to follow the orders of state education commissioner James E. Allen, Jr., to submit a plan for school integration. Mount Vernon, New York, adopted a plan to correct its racial imbalance, which called for a continuation of neighborhood schools up to the fourth grade, a new centrally located middle school for two grades, another centrally located school for the next two grades, and a four-year high school. Thus the last eight grades would be totally desegregated.

Trouble flared at Syracuse, New York, over alleged efforts of Jewish students to keep Negro youths out of a public Jewish fraternity dance. A melée ensued the following day, and the principal of the school was struck on the head by a chair. Subsequent discussions by parents, school officials and students saw both Negro and white student leaders agreeing that both races were responsible for the disorders. Mount Vernon saw hundreds of Negro students demonstrate against inadequate bus service and demand the teaching of Negro history, better counseling and more vigilance against the use of dope by students. In Yonkers, four hundred Negro and Puerto Rican students left their classes to protest for greater recognition of their cultures and contributions.

Major problems in Connecticut developed in New Haven. Violence erupted there early in the year. Sporadic fighting and property damage brought the police to a racially tense Hill House High School where Black students accused their teachers of racial discrimination. Black and white youth fought in the cafeteria in Lee High School. Mayor Richard Lee offered "police patrols on a saturation basis" to continue until the violence and tension were relieved. At the year's end the state board of education in Hartford voted unanimously to attempt a frontal assault on racial imbalance in the state's public schools, and drafted a bill that would give it power to withhold state aid from towns that were found to have de facto segregation. The board chairman expressed the opinion that "segregation hurts both the Black and white children."

Massachusetts in early 1968 was the only state in the nation with a law against racial imbalance in the public schools. Boston, however, experienced considerable racial problems over community control of the schools. Jonathan Kozol brought unwanted national fame to Boston by reading a poem by a Black writer (Langston Hughes) entitled "Ballad of the Landlord." He was dismissed, and wrote the book *Death at an Early Age*, which leveled charges of vicious racism at white teachers in his school.

Boston's school problems continued into the fall of 1968. Black parents took their own action in early September and decided to install their own principal and teachers in one of the elementary schools. Pupils were withdrawn when the police blocked the entry of the community's chosen principal. Some white teachers escorted 150 Black children out of the school to a community-controlled school in another section of the town. The latter school was dubbed a "liberation school" and a boycott was mounted against the regular school.

Racial tension increased in Boston when an assistant superintendent of city schools overruled a headmaster's permission for Black students to wear African style clothing and to cut their hair in an "Afro" style. Twenty white students burned their neckties in support of a Black boycott. The headmaster's recognition of a Black student union was also overruled by the superintendent. The difficulties spilled over into street violence in the Black section of Boston (Roxbury) on September 25. Sporadic rock throwing, window smashing and fire bombing forced the police to seal off the low income area in which the trouble had developed. Black militants demanded decentralization of school control. A biracial committee was set up by the mayor, while the National Guard was alerted. Militant Blacks held a rally in the city's Franklin Park and stressed Black nationalism and self-determination. Following the rally, a three-minute battle between Roxbury Blacks and police ensued. At Boston Latin School the headmaster, reflecting 333 years of tradition, adamantly refused to permit African dress. In early October the student body voted 1,003 to 970 against changing the dress code, which required the wearing of ties and, by implication, prohibited the wearing of African garb (dashikis). The American Civil Liberties Union issued a statement that students should have the right to choose their own dress, hold meetings and invite speakers of their own choice.

Rioting also closed the Martin Luther King, Jr., School on December 6. Deepening racial friction between Black ghetto residents and school board officials led to a series of violent episodes among students of the sixth, seventh and eighth grades. Black parents insisted upon the right to be consulted in the naming of a new principal in the school—a right which the board ignored. The year ended in Boston with the situation still unresolved over community control of the Black schools. A Harvard-Boston University study indicated that the Black parents had as their greatest concern the provision of a high quality education for their children. Integration or segregation was not the issue with them except as it related to a quality education.

Cities in New Jersey also experienced trouble in the public schools over race and Black awareness. In one of its first major crackdowns north of the Mason-Dixon line, the federal government ordered Union, New Jersey, to comply with the 1964 Civil Rights Act and draw up a plan to end segregated schools there. Montclair, New Jersey, mostly white, had a Black mayor. Racial antagonism rose to the surface there in the fall of 1968 with a series of fist fights and scuffles in the high school. Some observers traced the flare-up to the formation of a Black student union in the spring of 1968. Black students sought unsuccessfully to keep white students from membership in it.

In East Orange, where the school enrollment was 80 per cent Negro, a Negro was named superintendent of schools.

In August 1968 Newark's board of education voted to name ten Negroes to administrative posts and to partly decentralize the school system. Plans had been worked out for this with the Newark Teachers Association. The written and oral tests for administrative posts were replaced by a system of committee screening. It was expected that this new plan would provide more Black principals and vice-principals for the Newark schools. This significant action followed on continuous and violent fighting by Black and white youths in the city schools. LeRoi Jones was regarded as the Black power strategist in the city.

In Trenton, New Jersey, Black students staged a walkout as a means of pressing their demands for the inclusion of Afro-American history in the school curriculum and for more Negro guidance counselors in the schools. Compromises were finally reached. This action had been preceded by frequent fights between Negro and white students and, at times, the intervention of helmeted police on the school grounds.

Camden's troubles centered around reactions to a group of Black students who forced the closing of classes during their demonstrations for more Black awareness courses and for the appointment of a Negro principal and Negro athletic coaches. Failure of the city to provide satisfactory housing for a Negro family that had had its slum dwelling burned was a complicating factor in the demands of the local Black People's Unity Movement, which aided the school disruption. (New Jersey was one of the few states requiring its public schools to give attention to Blacks in its curriculum in 1968. Others included California, Indiana, Florida and Kentucky. California had led the way three years earlier.)

Nor did Pennsylvania escape the Black awareness movement. In Pittsburgh, school officials bowed to demands of Black pupils for the teaching of Negro history, art, literature and music in the public schools; for improvement of the pupil-counselor ratio; for better food; for improved sanitary conditions in the rest rooms; for cessation of "brainwashing" of Black pupils by the white teachers; and for a promise to exercise no reprisals against those student demonstrators who had forced the adoption of these demands. By "brainwashing" the students had referred to efforts by white counselors and teachers to encourage Black students to attend technical schools rather than colleges.

Philadelphia witnessed an acceleration of its racial tensions as the year ended, with police forces doubled to provide order inside the city's twenty-two high schools. Blacks students called for expulsion of white teachers at two Negro high schools, staged sit-ins and fist fights with white students, and demanded change of the name of the Benjamin Franklin High School to "Malcolm X High School." Whites staged a sit-in at Bok Vocational High School in protest against actions of Black students.

The Midwest

Black parents in Indianapolis brought a desegregation suit against the school system. As a result, the school officials agreed to assign at least one Black teacher to each of its 110 elementary schools and more white teachers to sixteen predominantly Black schools. The state moved to require multi-ethnic considerations in the textbooks and curricula.

In Detroit's school system 60 per cent of the pupils were Negro. Continuing progress was made in placing more Negroes in the schools as principals and administrators. Thirty-one principals in 259 schools in 1968 were Black—this was an increase over the nineteen principals in the fall of 1967. Negro assistant principals were increased from thirty-nine to fifty-nine, and counselors, from 105 to 140. Detroit seemed on the way to escaping the thrust for community control by increasing its ratio of Black administrators in the regular framework of the school system. This acceleration came after an epidemic of small fires, sit-ins, school closings and walkouts, as well as false alarms, in the public schools of the city. And in February the Black nationalist Malcolm X Society had met in the city to plan a separate Black nation in five Southern states. Detroit's superintendent of schools, Dr. Norman Drachler, stated his belief that "a better balance of Black and white administrators is educationally sound." Blacks wondered why it had taken so long to reach that conclusion.

Grand Rapids, Michigan, officials faced violence as Negro students demanded more Black staff members and a Negro history course, and complained about overcrowding on school buses. As the calendar year came to an end, police were forced to use clubs and chemical sprays to quell a riot between Black and white students on school grounds.

Chicago's Black awareness and student power problems meshed with demands for community control. Negro students organized various groups to push their demands: the New Breed (at Harrison High School, where most of the disruption occurred) and the Black Students for Defense were among the more tightly organized groups. They were supported by Latin American students in the schools, by adult groups such as the Woodlawn Organization and Operation Breadbasket (which had been organized by Dr. Martin Luther King, Jr.), by Northwestern University's Afro-American Student Association, by Black school principals and by Black teachers' organizations such as the Black Teachers Caucus and the Teachers for Quality Education.

Action began early in the year. At the Carter H. Harrison High School in February, the New Breed led a group of five hundred students in a walkout, demanding Black teachers for the Afro-American history course which their pressure the preceding spring had brought about. Part of the reason for the controversy was that none of the U.S. history texts in use in the Chicago public schools included information on Black people in America. The board of education placed *Land of the Free*, a famous new text which does include such information, on the approved reading list, but categorized it as "ancient world history." Some Blacks concluded that "someone doesn't want us to know the book is available, since the book is really a U.S. history text and is a 'balanced' one."

School opened in the fall in Chicago against a background of racist charges—as seen in the first school desegregation suit in the North, filed by the federal government against Cook County, Illinois. Fist fights between Black and white students further exacerbated the racist picture. Harrison High School was the scene of the first organized activism in October. The New Breed and Puerto Rican students walked out of the school demanding more Negro teachers and an expansion of the Afro-American history course from one semester to one year. The walkout spread rapidly to six other schools, and the original complaints were escalated to include demands for more Negro administrators and a greater voice for Negroes in school affairs—just short of community control. Black students held an outdoor press conference at 112th and Halsted Streets, adding demands for Black cheer leaders, equal opportunity for Blacks in school activities, and the appointment of Black disciplinary teachers.

On "Liberation Monday," October 14, some thirty-five thousand Black high school students staged a one-day walkout and boycott of some twenty-five Chicago public schools, insisting on more Black awareness in the schools. Among the new demands were holidays for Black heroes, more technical and vocational training and more required homework. Rumors were spread that the college-centered Afro-American Student Association was providing national coordination for a plan to paralyze the school systems in the major cities of the nation. Minor incidents of violence and arrests occurred.

School superintendent James F. Redmond threatened legal action against disrupting students. Twenty thousand students ignored the threats and planned their second "Liberation Monday." They recruited elementary school student support and were joined by Latin American students and an estimated five hundred Black teachers who were members of the Black Teachers Caucus as well as the Chicago area PTA, although some teachers issued a minority dissenting statement. Plans for "freedom schools" and further demonstrations were discussed as the adult community moved to support the students.

Facing an absentee rate of 24 per cent of the total public school enrollment on this second "Liberation Monday," and growing adult support, superintendent Redmond announced his plan to immediately recommend to the board the appointment of seven Negroes as assistant principals of schools with substantial Black enrollment. Pressure from Black students and Black teachers continued. On November 13 the Chicago school board named the first Black deputy superintendent in its history. This was Manford Byrd, Jr., fourteen-year veteran of the Chicago school system. Superintendent Redmond said that he had conducted a nineteen-month nationwide search before deciding on this man as his appointee.

The year's end in Chicago saw a growing interest in the problem of community control of schools. At an Urban League seminar on the issue were such leaders as Philip Hauser, University of Chicago sociologist; Albert Briggs, principal of the Dunbar High School; Rev. Arthur Brazier, president of the Woodlawn Organization; and Warner Saunders, director of the Better Boys Foundation. Rev. Brazier denounced the school system for failing to educate children in Black ghettoes, and called for community control of the educational system.

Cook County, Illinois, meanwhile, lost its fight against the desegregation order of the United States Court of Appeals. Suburban Cook County Elementary School District 151 was found guilty of administrative practices of racial discrimination.

The Far West

In contrast to the achievement of school desegregation in Berkeley, there was trouble in Oakland, California, where the Black Student Union led disruptive activities for the usual Black awareness demands: Black curricula; more Black teachers; a firm commitment from teachers to respect students; removal of private police from schools. City school superintendent Stuart Phillips indicated support for a Black curriculum but pointed to the scarcity of Black teachers in the school system as a personnel problem.

Violence erupted within two weeks of the students' presentation of their demands to the school board. A small number of Black students went on a rampage at the Technical High School, beating students and teachers alike and forcing cancellation of classes. The principal closed the school early in the afternoon. The violence had apparently been triggered by the arrest of fifteen Black youths on charges of truancy.

Bowing to the militant Black demands, the Oakland board of education replaced a white principal with a Negro (Louis K. Jones) at the McClymonds High School on December 8. The school's Black Student Union had demanded an all-Black administration and counseling staff. Two days later, Black students from the Technical High School presented the board with demands for a relaxed code of dress, improved food in the cafeteria and the dismissal of a substitute teacher. They also insisted that the United States Constitution protected their right to sit-in, although the board had held that they had no such right.

The Black Student Association in San Francisco's Woodrow Wilson High School also pressured for more Black awareness in the school system. The regular student government association and the Black Student Association planned and carried out a discussion session with some four hundred adults over the issue of the racial gap in the local schools. Mayor Alioto's Negro assistant (Joe Johnson) supported their conclusion that riots had achieved much for Black dignity, but cautioned the students not to "toy with anarchy—when you take over, if you don't believe in the rules, who's going to obey you?"

There were continuous indications that Black college and high school students were interacting and mutually supportive in California as elsewhere.

IV. Black Awareness and Higher Education

In 1968 approximately 120 institutions of higher learning were variously referred to as "Negro," "predominantly Negro" or "Black" colleges and universities. Located in the South (except for four institutions), these institutions run the gamut from the small, unaccredited junior college to the full-fledged university such as Howard or the "consortium" known as the Atlanta University Center. With the exception of Cheyney State College and Lincoln University in Pennsylvania, all of these institutions were founded during the last 104 years. During the first twenty years after the Civil War, private colleges were founded by Northerners and were church related. Negro churches dominated the second period, from 1885 to 1916, in forming these colleges, although the Southern states also began to make commitments to college education for Black Americans during the same period. The passage of the second Morrill Act in 1890 stimulated the support for so-called "land grant" colleges for the Negro. In 1938 the famous ruling of the United States Supreme Court in the case of *Gaines* v. *Canada ex rel. State of Missouri* was the first of a series of decisions the effect of which was to open more widely the doors of white colleges and universities to Black Americans.

Problems which developed on Black campuses in 1968 were also found on predominantly white campuses. Various solutions to these problems were pressed by Black students, sometimes with the support of white sympathizers (both faculty and student). Almost always these suggested solutions were pushed with great vigor and frequently with harshness, abrasiveness and even violence. Institutionalized college authority in 1968 witnessed intensive action and ferment designed, among other things, to achieve a greater relevance of curricula, to gain increased student power in the governance of these institutions, and to establish significant influence of the Black American community in this nation.

Activism in Black Colleges and Universities

The owners of All-Star Bowling Lanes in Orangeburg, South Carolina, refused to open their doors to Black people. Students in the town, mainly at Claflin University and South Carolina State College, began a demonstration on Monday, February 5, that lasted three nights and resulted in the shooting by police forces of some thirty-four Blacks. At least sixteen were struck from the rear—two were struck in the soles of their feet as they either lay down or tried to run away. Three youngsters (including a high school boy) were killed. The National Guard was called and classes were suspended. A boycott or "non-buying quarantine" was initiated by the Black population. Black students across the South demonstrated. Marches were staged in Petersburg, Virginia, and in Durham, Greensboro, Chapel Hill (including white students) and Raleigh, North Carolina. Upon request of their students, the six presidents of the Atlanta University Center institutions issued a public letter to President Lyndon Johnson and the United States Attorney General calling on them to take action against persons who randomly shoot Black college students. The demands of the Orangeburg students for South Carolina Governor McNair to take action against those who shot the students in the back brought only a grand jury refusal (November 25) to indict "nine unnamed highway patrolmen."

Orangeburg was perhaps the last of the college-level riots for the older "civil rights and integration" efforts. "Black awareness" efforts dominated the scene for the rest of the year. Howard University's student leader Anthony Gittens bemoaned the failure of his institution to produce the "kind of black leaders it should have, [or] there wouldn't have been an Orangeburg." On February 23 he called for the resignations of the president (James Nabrit), the vice-president (Stanton Wormley) and the liberal arts dean (Frank Snowden) as a first step to making Howard a "Black university." The demands escalated into action that forced officials to close the institution as hundreds of students took over the administration building, beginning Tuesday, March 19. The mass sit-in resulted from university action against two dozen students of the sixty involved in disrupting Charter Day ceremonies on the campus on March 1. The administration took no immediate steps forcibly to evict the dissident students, although the latter expected to be arrested. The students demanded amnesty for the group of Charter Day student disrupters, the establishment of a "Black Awareness Institute," and the teaching of more Negro history and culture courses. They were reportedly supported by Black students from Central State University (Wilberforce, Ohio), and by some of Howard's white students.

With parental pressure on the one hand and a university compromise agreement on the other, the students ended their protest after four days of occupying the administration building. Involved in the negotiations were Mayor Walter Washington, Dr. Percy Julian, Jr., Judge Myles Page, and prominent psychologist Kenneth B. Clark—all famous Black leaders. A compromise promised the establishment of a judicial tribunal in which students would have the major responsibility to determine charges to be lodged against the thirty-nine students accused of misconduct. The student occupation of the administration building resembled the 1964 sit-in at Sproul Hall on the Berkeley campus of the University of California. More than two thousand of Howard's 8,200 students actively participated in the demonstrations.

(The mood spread quickly to other Negro campuses. Within a very short time protests erupted at Tuskegee Institute [Alabama], Fisk University [Nashville], Virginia State College [Petersburg], Delaware State College [Dover] and Bowie State College [Maryland]. Carloads of Howard students traveled to Maryland to support the Bowie students.)

On May 18 the Howard board of trustees approved: (1) a procedure to receive student reactions and recommendations about curricula; (2) lodging of disciplinary authority in the faculties and student bodies of the various schools and colleges; (3) students' handling of dormitory rules infractions in the residence halls; (4) a new board of educational development to permit experimental courses, programs and projects; (5) holding of 50 per cent of the seats by students on school and college judiciary committees; (6) permission of alcohol in residence halls; (7) abolition of compulsory ROTC; (8) abolition of freshman assembly; (9) elimination of curfew for senior women and liberalization of curfew for others; (10) membership of students on almost every major committee dealing with student affairs—including the registration committee, the calendar committee and the publication board; (11) freedom of student groups to invite any speaker of their choice; (12) removal of student press censorship by the university; (13) abolition of the requirement of faculty advisers for student organizations; (14) provisions for additional study of Afro-American history and culture, etc. For the first time in Howard's history, students and faculty met with the board of trustees. Student body president Q. T. Jackson demanded further movement toward Black awareness in the September opening ceremonies at the university. A five-day "Towards a Black University" conference was held in November, featuring speeches by Stokely Carmichael (former head of SNCC), Ron Karenga (founder of Los Angeles-based Black nationalist organization "US") and Harold Cruse (author of *The Crisis of the Negro Intellectual*). San Francisco State College's Professor Nathan Hare allegedly boycotted the conference for its not being sufficiently activist.

The Black awareness movement erupted on many other Black campuses, together with associated secondary issues. Eighteen miles northeast of Washington, D.C., Bowie State College students temporarily shut down 90 per cent of the classes at the end of March, with complaints about the operation of their institution. In early April, Kentucky State College began spring vacation a week early in an effort to end student violence that had erupted.

The confrontation at Tuskegee Institute, beginning April 6, was highly dramatic. Some 250 irate students padlocked their twelve trustees and president in famed Dorothy Hall. A piece of concrete had been hurled through the president's home earlier in the year. Students presented eleven grievances including the demand for a greater voice in policy making and the abolition of compulsory ROTC. The South's only Black sheriff, Macon County's Lucius Amerson, requested help from the National Guard, but by the time the Guard had arrived the trustees had been released.

The trustees reacted quickly. They immediately closed the school and informed all students who wished to be readmitted that they must fill out new admission forms and sign agreements to abide by campus discipline. This was an unusual tactic in dealing with student unrest and was carefully scrutinized by beleaguered college administrators. A student-faculty committee was appointed later to explore the "Black university" concept. Its recommendations recognized the Institute's current offerings in Negro studies but called for increased opportunities. Dr. Preston Valien, a Black United States deputy associate commissioner for higher education, called on Howard, Tuskegee, Fisk and the Atlanta University Center to join their library holdings and develop a program in Afro-American studies or in studies of the nonwhite world.

Immediately following the April assassination of Dr. Martin Luther King, Jr., students of the Atlanta University Center called upon their six presidents to establish a Black studies curriculum. After two meetings with the students, the officials financed a "summer task force" of students and faculty members to study the current offerings and make recommendations. Wesleyan College officials sent two students and two faculty members to Atlanta to join the task force. A resulting report was studied by various curricula committees and by the Atlanta University Center senate as well as by the council of presidents, after which agreement was reached to appoint a director of Afro-American studies for the Center. Meanwhile, Morehouse College made provisions for a minor in Afro-American studies and Atlanta University took steps to establish a Master's degree program in the field. The Interdenominational Theological Center expanded its offerings, as did Clark, Morris Brown and Spelman Colleges. Atlanta college students' confrontations were in the main nonviolent, but they were threatening and abrasive as students in the Center demanded and secured an end to curfews, compulsory class attendance, and modes of dress as determined by college officials. Black awareness characterized some anti-white attitudes. College officials hastened to explain that they could not operate a racially exclusive institution, when two students ejected a white professor from the classroom for alleged "racist behavior."

Black student activists grew more violent in West Virginia. Bombing of a new building at Bluefield State College on November 21 by a Black student leader resulted in $80,000 damage to the building and in the closing of all dormitories indefinitely. These dormitories had housed mainly Black students. The college reopened December 2 as a commuter college. For most of its seventy-three-year history it had been a Negro institution; in recent years white students had become the majority, and in 1968 the college had its first white president.

Violence also plagued Cheyney State College, in Pennsylvania, as militants disrupted administrative offices and classrooms.

Black awareness in other Black colleges produced gains in student power as it had at Howard, Tuskegee, Atlanta University Center and other institutions. In at least one example (Bluefield) no immediate gain was apparent. Black awareness was obviously another facet of Black power, with educational overtones.

Black Power at "White Universities"

As in the Black colleges in early 1968, the first 1968 activism in "predominantly white" colleges and universities had elements of the pre-1968 civil rights struggle. Shortly after the assassination of Dr. Martin Luther King, Jr., Black and white students and faculty at Colgate University (Hamilton, New York) joined forces to end discriminatory fraternity housing. A white junior praised the "integrated Black-led militancy without violence." As at Howard, the protesters occupied the university administration building.

Confrontation at Columbia University became highly dramatic and violent and was characterized by problems concerning the method of governance of the university, demands of Black students to lead movements, and efforts by neighboring community groups and individuals to have an influence in university policy. (Community control or power in New York City was also an issue in the public schools, as mentioned earlier.)

On April 23 dozens of Black and white students seized Hamilton Hall. Within a short time, five buildings were occupied by student protesters. Among the demands were: more courses in Negro and Puerto Rican culture; faculty jobs for minority group members; a restructuring of the authority at Columbia, with especial emphasis on the powers of the trustee board; student participation in determining curriculum, instruction and faculty personnel. The most dramatic issue involved a campus-community campaign led by students and various Black civic organizations to stop permanently the proposed construction of a college gymnasium in Morningside Park, which borders on Harlem.

Harlem citizens staged intermittent street marches and rallies for at least three days before the student action began. Among the interested community leaders were Charles King, director of the anti-poverty agency HARYOU; Omar Ahmed of the United Black Front; Carlos Aponte of the Peace and Freedom Party; John Shabazz, alleged member of the Revolutionary Action Movement (RAM), who was arrested in an alleged plot to kill civil rights leaders Roy Wilkins and Whitney Young; Charles 37X Kenyatta of the Mau Mau Society; and Edward Davis, longtime Harlem street-corner speaker.

The Students Caucus Coordinating Committee (of eight student groups) directed class boycotts and demonstrations—which erupted into violence involving alleged police brutality; small fires in campus buildings; marches through Harlem led by the university's Student Afro-American Society and the Harlem chapter of CORE. Support for the movement came from Columbia University faculty members; students from the State University of New York, in Stony Brook, who staged a sit-in; from Black and white students and faculty members who started a "sleep-in" at the Nassau Community College in Hempstead and made demands of their own in the process. By early June, after considerable disruption, the students and the Harlem Black leaders expressed the opinion that their major objectives were being achieved and that a new and harmonious working relationship between the community and the university was emerging from the student rebellion. Thus campus-style and community-style Black power were successfully wed at Columbia University. Faculty power also benefited.

New York University witnessed a similar dramatic and effective series of confrontations, beginning shortly after the assassination of Martin Luther King, Jr., and continuing into November and December. Apparently spearheaded by the NYU Black and Allied Students Association and supported by Black and white students and faculty, a day-long symposium to explore means to expunge racism from the campus resulted in demands being submitted to the administration. These were the teaching of basic survey courses in African history, Afro-American history and the art, music and literature of the Black people; and the establishment of a Dr. Martin Luther King, Jr., Institute of Black Studies. During this symposium classes were suspended at all fifteen schools of NYU; twelve workshops met to draw up further plans for such a program.

The university officials quickly agreed to the demands and established a $1 million scholarship fund for Negro students, naming the fund after Dr. King. After one day's consultation, President James M. Hester announced the decision of the NYU faculty senate to support greater efforts on behalf of Negro students and give more attention to Negro affairs. The university pledged an increase in recruiting Afro-American, Puerto Rican, Mexican-American and American Indian students; more Black educators and administrators at the university; the establishment of an institute to increase university research and instruction in Afro-American areas; and the strengthening of existing remedial programs for incoming Black students. "We are really going to pour it on," said the dean of admissions, "and it will be interesting to see how many we can attract." President Hester viewed the special admissions effort and the scholarships as "the institution of discrimination in favor of Black Americans." The order was given to recruit more Black students, Black faculty members and Black administrators for new courses in Black awareness.

The aftermath of seeking Black administrators and Black faculty led to the second stage of problems for the university. John F. Hatchett, a young sociology graduate of Wayne State University (Detroit) and Boston University's Theological School, and a former college professor, was dismissed from New York's Public School 68 where he had been serving as a substitute teacher. His dismissal resulted from his taking his students to a Malcolm X memorial program, contrary to orders which he stated that he had never received. On July 24, New York University announced his employment as director of the newly created Martin Luther King, Jr., Afro-American Student Center.

Immediately the university was engulfed by protests about an alleged anti-Semitic article which Hatchett had written. The university's preliminary investigation of its new director had not turned up this matter. The article had appeared in the November–December 1967 issue of the *African American Teachers Forum*, under the title "The Phenomenon of the Anti-Black Jews and the Black Anglo-Saxons."

A number of Jewish organizations called for Hatchett's dismissal. One of the strongest criticisms came from the Anti-Defamation League which criticized the employment of Hatchett as an affront not only to Jews but to the memory of Dr. King. Similar appeals were made by the Jewish Labor Committee, the American Jewish Committee, the American Jewish Congress and the Jewish War Veterans of New York. (Criticism of Hatchett's diatribe against "Black Anglo-Saxons," if any, was not highlighted by the news media. Indeed, a *New York Times* editorial of July 31 showed concern only over respect for "non-Black" members of the academic community.) Fifteen Jewish demonstrators picketed NYU on August 5, carrying placards reading "No Nazis at NYU," and urging the dismissal of Hatchett.

Defense for the new Black director came from several sources. The author himself declared, "I have never been, am not, and never will be an anti-Semite. . . . What I am against is the systematic exploitation of Black people in the city's schools." Two trustees of the university came out in support of his employment. The director of Harlem's chapter of CORE supported Hatchett's statements criticizing the public schools of New York City. The New York Civil Liberties Union charged that his firing would be a violation of academic freedom. By early August, fifteen of the sixteen members of the university's student presidents' conference urged that he be retained in order to forestall a destructive breakdown in relations between Jewish and Black students on the campus. Most of these student leaders were white and several were Jewish.

Chancellor Allan Cartter wrestled with the problem from the time of the announcement of the appointment on July 24 until August 1, when President Hester returned from a ten-day vacation. President Hester sought the advice of federal district Judge Constance Baker Motley, a Black woman of considerable distinction in the civil rights movement, and of former Supreme Court Justice Arthur Goldberg, a Jewish statesman and former ambassador to the United Nations. The Black Allied Student Association's vice-president publicly assailed Hatchett's opponents for ignoring the importance of the new administrative position created by the university and "overemphasizing" the importance of Hatchett's article. The university had decided by August 10 to retain Hatchett, to establish a board for the Afro-American Student Center under the chairmanship of Judge Motley, and to seek to avoid the kind of chaos that had almost wrecked Columbia University in the spring. The Commission on Social Action of the Union of American Hebrew Congregations, which represents all Reform Jewish congregations in the Western Hemisphere, was angered by what it called President Hester's effort to serve as an apologist for director Hatchett. The Far Rockaway Jewish Community Council announced plans to seek 100,000 signatures protesting the university's decision to retain Mr. Hatchett.

Events took a new and fateful turn for Hatchett, which had its beginnings in the Presidential election campaign. On October 8, the Black student leader stated that Presidential candidates Richard M. Nixon and Hubert Humphrey, and New York teachers' union leader Albert Shanker, "all have something in common—they are racist bastards." This statement was made before seven hundred students in the Gould Library Chapel on the university's Bronx campus. He further asserted that racism permeated the nation. "I'm suggesting . . . that no white person in America is free of racism. I am opting for a psychological separation from the decadence that runs through it all. . . . The educational bureaucracies of this country have become guardians of the status quo. But black students doing their thing on campuses are turning the whole educational system upside down. So, brothers and sisters, keep on turning."

The university officials quickly decided to fire the controversial director. Within forty-eight hours of his speech, Hatchett was informed of his dismissal. Following student protests, which led to their occupying two buildings on the Bronx campus, the administration compromised with an offer that he could be an adviser to Negro students at the school, using his year's severance pay as salary. A rebellion at the Bronx campus was led by sixty-five white students, some of whom were connected with the nationally famous Students for a Democratic Society (SDS), who occupied the Gould Library. In the meantime, forty Black students, under the banners of a group called Katara, occupied the Gould Student Center. Other students conducted a strike at the Washington Square campus. Police were summoned to both campuses. President Hester, Chancellor Cartter and Winston Duckett (president of the Black Allied Students Association) negotiated a compromise that led to evacuation of the buildings after seven hours. President Hester (at forty-two the youngest president in NYU history) continued his practice of "defusing" student dissidence by discussion and compromise. Several radical students at the university noted that this made difficult the creation of "anti-administration" on the campus.

Opposition to Hatchett's dismissal continued. Hatchett himself refused to accept any compromise short of complete reinstatement. Radical white and Black student groups organized to hold a strike. On October 14 two small bombs were exploded, fire hoses and telephone lines were cut, locks were damaged and toilets were plugged. Two hundred students picketed noisily but without violence. The SDS called for the dismissal of President Hester and for greater student representation in university government. Hester replied that he had defended Hatchett vigorously against charges of anti-Semitism but that the latter's method of expressing Black identity was divisive in the university and he could not be rehired. White students who supported the protest indicated a disagreement with Hatchett's opinions but held that they were concerned over Black student control of their own destinies.

Students were unable to mount a successful strike, however, amid these circumstances. They changed tactics and sought to occupy the president's office. A "fruitless exchange" of conversation developed. Students talked of a series of "hit and run" disruptive actions. The objectives shifted from support of Hatchett's reinstatement to a demand for more student power in formulating university policy. By October 19, after a largely ineffectual week-long boycott of classes, the "radical coalition" of student leaders declared an end to the boycott. Black students did not join the coalition, thus apparently underlining a division between white and Black students.

President Hester continued to negotiate with the Black students and agreed to create an independent board of Black students and faculty members to operate the Martin Luther King, Jr., Afro-American Student Center beginning in September 1969. The board would assume complete fiscal responsibility for the center. John Hatchett declined the offer of the job of director, made once again, this time by the newly created autonomous body of Blacks. An anonymous donor made a gift to cover the cost of the center's operation. Thus the student disruption came to an end. Violence at NYU had been minimal compared to that at Columbia.

Less dramatic confrontations in New York City and State occurred at such places as Fordham University, in the Bronx, where Black students demanded an institute of Black studies, a goal of 20 per cent nonwhite enrollment, a pass-fail grading system for Negroes during their first two years and use of university buildings to establish a dialogue with the surrounding Black community. Confrontations occurred at Brooklyn College and at Hunter College, while at Farmingdale State University CORE ran a program for developing Black leadership.

Following Black student activism at Cornell University, the administration worked out what they called "the first Afro-American studies program adopted by a major university in the nation." In response to the assassination of Dr. Martin Luther King, Jr., the Black students ran summer workshops, made the rounds of foundations and consulted college officials and Black scholars around the clock. By August they presented Cornell President James Perkins with a detailed plan for Afro-American studies. The university quickly endorsed the program and in late October named a seventeen-member committee (which included a Black administrator and eight Black students) to organize it. Half the income from a $1 million grant to Cornell was assigned to Afro-American studies.

In New York State perhaps Columbia University had the most violent confrontation; NYU the most dramatic meeting of a young, intransigent Black with a young, more tractable white administrator; and Cornell the most productive confrontation, in its early establishment of an Afro-American studies program under Black leadership.

Around the Middle Atlantic states activism and Black awareness grew at Fairleigh Dickinson University (Rutherford, New Jersey); the Newark and New Brunswick campuses of Rutgers University; Lafayette College (Easton, Pennsylvania); and Pennsylvania State University.

The Ivy League and conservative New England also faced the challenge of the new Black awareness on campus in 1968. As in New York, the assassination of Martin Luther King, Jr., in April was frequently a catalyst. Harvard, Yale, Princeton, Dartmouth, Williams, Amherst and Brown—long viewed as bastions of WASPS and the white Establishment, made adjustments to the new Black demands.

In June 1968 Harvard University announced its plans to offer in September a new full-year course in the "Afro-American experience" and to consider a degree-granting program in Afro-American studies at a later date.

In mid-December of 1968 Yale University became the "first major American university to offer a degree in Black culture." Unlike the situation in many other institutions of higher learning, the Yale development resulted from Black activism initiated before the King assassination. The Black Student Alliance (formed in 1964 at Yale) had conducted a short boycott of classes designed to express their feelings of alienation from Yale and their anger over treatment of Black people in the city of New Haven by Yale and New Haven officials. They had also initiated a court suit against harassment of Blacks in the city. On March 12, 1968, a group of outstanding Negro intellectuals joined in conference at Yale with a hundred representatives of some thirty-five colleges and universities and seven major Eastern school systems. Passionate demands for the development and adoption of courses on the "Black experience" were voiced. No major exception to this plea was voiced by the predominantly white audience. At the luncheon on the second day of the conference, announcement was made of a recommendation by a joint committee of Yale faculty members and Black Student Alliance members that a divisional major be offered at Yale College in Afro-American studies. The Ford Foundation's president, McGeorge Bundy, in attendance at the conference, joked about Yale inviting people to come to "discuss something which Yale has already decided." Bundy supported the idea, but cautioned that the study of the Black experience might not always be happy and joyous and that it revealed much that was painful for the Black as well as the white man.

Among those Black intellectuals attending the conference were: Ron Karenga, community organizer in Los Angeles; Harold Cruse, author of *The Crisis of the Negro Intellectual*; Nathan Hare, professor of sociology at San Francisco State College and author of *The Black Anglo-Saxon*; Alvin Poussaint, assistant professor of psychology at Tufts University School of Medicine; Boniface Obichere, professor of African history at the University of Southern California; Martin Kilson, Jr., assistant professor of government at Harvard. Professor Cruse emphasized that "the new black cultural nationalism understands its own limits and seeks not to replace one particularism with another but to counterbalance the exclusivity of the dominant culture."

On December 12 the Yale faculty approved a broad new program in Afro-American studies that made the institution one of the few in the country in which an undergraduate could major in Negro culture. The program was one of the first significant changes in the history of Yale in which undergraduates played a major role. The university was already offering forty-five courses related to Afro-American culture in the departments of anthropology, economics, history, English, history of art and music, political science and American history. The faculty report stated that "the experience of the black people in the world is not merely a suitable object for a serious academic study and teaching, but one too relevant, vital, important and rich in content to ignore."

Professor Robert A. Dahl, chairman of the faculty-student committee, acknowledged that such a major was a demand of Black militants elsewhere, but he insisted that the decision at Yale was educationally sound and indicated that he had had no embarrassment over student pressures. President Kingman Brewster, Jr., had formed the special committee to study the program nine months before the decision was announced.

Other New England institutions were pressed forward. Black students at Princeton University held a three-day conference on Black awareness within a week of the King assassination. (Only fifty-nine Black students were found on the campus and were organized as the Association of Black Collegians.) Within less than a month, the university set up a student-faculty committee to devise ways to integrate material on the American Negro and on African history and culture into the curriculum. All four of the students on the committee were Negroes.

April was a natal month for other Black awareness efforts in the area. On April 12 Tufts University officials bowed to student demands for more Black students on campus. On April 15 the board of trustees approved lowering admission requirements for Black students from slum areas and providing a tutorial program for their academic aid. On April 18 the University of Connecticut agreed to grant paid leaves of absence to faculty members who participated in full-time civil rights work. On April 22 Trinity College students, requesting Black scholarships and led by sixteen Negro students, locked up the trustees in the administration building for a short time.

The Black awareness rebellion continued into the fall and winter months in the Northeast as elsewhere. Following the alleged beating of a Black visitor and a white student by unidentified white students, University of Massachusetts officials faced demands for disarming campus police, adding fifteen Black police to the force, recruiting out-of-state Black students and apologizing publicly for the violent incident.

Mount Holyoke approved a proposal of the Afro-American Society to increase Black enrollment on the campus, and decided to establish a Negro cultural center for both white and Black students. Negro students at Radcliffe College sat in and demanded increased Black enrollment and a change in admissions policy. President Mary I. Bunting immediately expressed sympathy with the movement. Brown University announced that it would devote $1.1 million over three years to improve the lot of Negroes there.

Success crowned many, if not most, of the efforts of Black students in the Northeast. The *New York Times* inquiry in April and May of 1968 revealed that recruiting efforts in the East were (1) achieving noticeable increases in Black enrollment acceptances and (2) often being conducted by Blacks where formerly only whites had served. The nationwide survey made by the Southern Education Foundation and the Southern Education Report indicated that significant enrollment increases came to colleges that made special efforts to overcome defective educational preparation through special tutoring and seminars.

Except for Northwestern University, the Midwestern institutions of higher learning waited until the fall and winter months to experience Black awareness. In early May of 1968, sponsored by the Afro-American Student Union and a group called "For Members Only," and aided by a community group called Evanston Support Committee Coordinated, 105 of the 124 Black students in Northwestern occupied the finance building, promising not to damage the building or its contents (including a computer, other business machines, and important records) as long as no attempt was made to remove them. In a support movement, twenty white students occupied the office of the dean of students. Demands included increased Black scholarships, and Black awareness courses taught by professors approved by Negro students. An item that gained national prominence was the demand for separate living units for Black students. After a thirty-six-hour occupation, the Black students walked out of the finance building with a long list of administrative concessions including greater Negro enrollment and segregated housing. The university promised to seek at least 50 per cent of its new Black enrollment increase from inner city or ghetto school systems.

Among the major items of agreement were: appointment of a committee on human relations; formation of a Black student advisory committee on admissions; acquisition of three guest lecturers in Afro-American studies for 1968–69; formation of a Black student advisory committee on financial aid; acquisition of Black student housing; appointment of a Black student counselor; provision of activity space for the Black student organization For Members Only; and formation of a university committee on discrimination in housing.

The results of the sit-in materialized in the fall of 1968 at Northwestern. The student spokesman for the Black Student Alliance, John Turner, declared the agreements "probably the most sophisticated and productive agreements to come between students and administration in recent times." The controversial segregated housing agreement allowed a group of Blacks to arrange to live together. Three rooms in a university-owned house were set aside for use by the organization For Members Only. Three Blacks were appointed to the faculty in the fall of 1968 to strengthen the Afro-American studies program, particularly in literature and history. (Northwestern has had an internationally famous program in African studies for twenty years.) The Black Student Alliance leader congratulated the university on its "maximum amount of creativity and a minimum of strife and tension" (although one Black student at the December 1968 meeting of the Association for the Study of Negro Life and History in New York City commented that all of these achievements still left things relatively unchanged).

At Kent State University in Ohio, the Black United Students joined with white SDS students and, supported by a reported seventy-five professors, staged a walkout in protest of the charge of creating a civil disturbance made against students who had demonstrated against recruiters for the Oakland, California, police department. Negro and white students joined in giving the famed Black power salute as they rallied to support the departure of the Black United Students to establish their own university in exile at the Centenary Methodist Church in Akron, Ohio. Some white anti-pickets counter-demonstrated, and a brief struggle ensued. Reports that an "administration spy" had made pictures of the demonstrators in order to support disciplinary action intensified the feelings of the Black students who seemed to have been singled out by the picture-taker. The administration, under these pressures, agreed to a study of the situation with the idea of modifying the charges against the students. The university decided not to press legal charges.

Other Ohio institutions reacted to the push for Black awareness. Ohio University at Athens instituted new Black emphasis in established courses. Central State University, Ohio State University, the University of Dayton and Wilberforce University formed a consortium to offer Black awareness courses in the Miami Valley in Ohio. Seventeen instructors from four universities were scheduled to offer thirty-three courses. A Filipino, an African and an Arab were to be among the teachers.

Northern Michigan University coped successfully with demands that its security police cease discriminatory practices against Black students. Illinois State University in Normal, Illinois, had such a large enrollment in its Black history course that arrangements were made to have the lectures telecast on campus closed-circuit TV. The Urbana campus of the University of Illinois experienced a "furniture-smashing fracas" by its Black students who were dissatisfied over the amount of aid given to the students recruited for the school by the Black Student Association. The students who had destroyed property were taken into custody and charged in civil court with mob action after refusing to leave the Illinois Union building. A university subcommittee ruled in mid-December that the 213 Negro freshmen involved in the September 9 and 10 "sit-in" would receive reprimands of record, not to be included in their official transcripts. None were dismissed from the university. The Black students had the support of Black militants from the twin cities of Urbana and Champaign. This incident, more clearly than most, pitted Black ghetto residents against university officials, since this had been a special project to get ghetto dwellers into the university.

One hundred and twenty students comprised the Black enrollment of Wisconsin State University in Oshkosh. On November 21 these Negroes and a small number of whites went on a rampage through the administration building and occuped the president's office. They ransacked offices, ripped down paintings, upset furniture, smashed typewriters, broke windows and scattered financial records. Police were called and the students were arrested and taken to the county courthouse under charges of disorderly conduct, unlawful assembly and criminal destruction of property. No violence was reported during the clearing of the building by the police. On the following day, ninety-one students (mostly Black) were suspended and threatened with expulsion for their conduct.

The Oshkosh Black students who were demanding Black culture courses, Afro-American language courses and a Black student union, had become tired of waiting for the administration to meet their demands. On December 20, the state university board of regents expelled ninety students (practically the entire Negro enrollment of Wisconsin State at Oshkosh).

At Washington University in St. Louis a student protest was triggered by the alleged abrasive behavior of security guards. The local Association of Black Collegians mounted a nine-day occupation of the basement accounting offices of the administration building, where they barricaded themselves in. White supporters took up residence in the second-floor office of the university chancellor. Requests by Blacks for the white students to leave were refused. The students and the administration finally compromised, and the students walked out peaceably. The Black students said their demonstration was meant to call attention to a general condition of insensitivity to Negoes at the university.

In the fall and winter months Black awareness moved to the nation's West Coast on new levels of violence and disruption. The two centers of most of the violence were San Francisco State College and the Berkeley campus of the University of California. A nonviolent "first," however, was achieved at Laney College in Oakland, California, with the creation of a department of Black studies on November 27, 1968. This action followed a student-faculty workshop at the two-year college in December 1967. The new department was authorized to award the Associate of Arts (A.A.) degree with fully accredited transfer status to the California State Colleges or the University of California system.

Trouble at San Francisco State began in September and lasted throughout the rest of the calendar year. The initial action centered around the suspension of the Black Panther minister of education, twenty-two-year-old George M. Murray, who had been hired as part-time English instructor to work with four hundred disadvantaged students admitted to San Francisco State that fall in an experiment to help raise their educational level. In September the college trustees requested that he be suspended, saying that he had reportedly urged Negro students to bring guns to the campus. President Robert R. Smith refused the trustees' request initially and was then ordered to comply by Chancellor Glenn S. Dumke on October 31, who suspended him with pay.

Black Student Union activists, together with Murray, had been planning to strike before Dumke's order. The strike was to protest lack of full departmental status for the new Black studies program at the college, to demand replacing a financial aid coordinator with a Negro administrator, and to seek removal of restrictions on admission of any Black student seeking to enter the college by the fall of 1969.

Instructor Murray's suspension catalyzed the activists and added to their list of demands the lifting of the suspension. Action began with a press conference from which all whites except newsmen were barred. Professor Nathan Hare, chairman of the Black studies department, characterized his department as "a paper department.

. . . I read about it in the paper . . ." and nothing more. At the news conference the Black Student Union announced their plans for a strike and were joined by white militant students under the SDS agreement. Equally important was the vote of the college chapter of the American Federation of Teachers to support the proposed strike. These professors also called for the resignation of Chancellor Dumke for his interference in academic affairs, although the school's academic senate voted against the strike twenty-four to eight.

Efforts to raise a strike were begun on November 6. Stokely Carmichael spoke to the college audience in a packed main auditorium and called on the students to make substantive changes in the power structure of the nation. Scuffles between strikers and non-strikers were reported and some arrests were made, but classes continued. The strike escalated upon vote of the faculty to support the strike and to suspend instruction. The faculty decision was influenced by alleged police brutality against the students at the November 6 news conference. On November 13, after a week of violence on the campus—hit and run raids on campus buildings, ransacking of labs, fires, fights with police, etc.—Dr. Smith indefinitely closed the eighteen-thousand-member campus. "We will keep the campus closed until we can rationally open it," he said.

Governor Ronald Reagan expressed horror at the closing down of the college and proclaimed that the California colleges would stay open as long as he was governor. Faculty meetings on the campus voted to call upon the chancellor to recall his order to President Smith to suspend Mr. Murray. Student confrontation had now reached the level of confrontation between politicans and academicians over the control of academic policies. Yet eight hundred Black students were demanding autonomy on an eighteen-thousand-student campus.

President Smith sought to reopen the college within a week. The faculty voted against reopening classes and continued the discussion of the issues by closed-circuit TV relays to several sites on campus. The BSU called for a boycott of this "crisis convocation" on campus unless all classes ceased operating. The Third World group (an umbrella organization of minority ethnic campus groups—Mexican Americans, Filipinos, etc.) supported BSU demands, and President Smith's efforts thus met with failure. He was replaced by world-famed semanticist H. I. Hayakawa, who became acting president on November 28. Thus Black awareness at San Francisco State had brought about the resignation of two presidents (John Summerskill in 1967 and Smith in 1968).

Savage violence again returned to the campus during the last days of November and in early December. On December 3, for example, four hundred club-swinging police fought four thousand student demonstrators in the worst disorder in the campus' history. Black community leaders now entered the fray openly. Assemblyman Willie Brown, Rev. Cecil Williams, Urban League director Percy Steele, Black newspaper publisher Dr. Carleton Goodlett and Terry D. Francois (the only Black members of the San Francisco board of supervisors) came to the campus and expressed plans to support the student movement.

Acting President Hayakawa adopted a policy relying heavily on the use of police authority and force. He was quoted as saying, "If there's no reduction of tension there will be no reduction of police force." The community Black leaders became disillusioned with Hayakawa, and Dr. Goodlett demanded his resignation less than a week after he took office. The BSU and Third World demands were restated and clarified: the establishment of schools of ethnic studies with students having control of hiring and firing of faculty, control of administration and control of curricula in these schools; appropriation of fifty faculty positions for these schools; admission of all nonwhite students who apply; and the retention of Black Panther Murray. The legally constituted student government on campus demanded Hayakawa's resignation after the vicious police attack on December 3. BUS chairman Ben Stewart announced plans to spread the revolutionary message of San Francisco State to "all colleges, high schools, and junior high schools." Although eight Black Baptist ministers sought to end the violence, they called on the college to set up a "real department of Black studies."

On Friday, December 6, Dr. Hayakawa announced that a Black studies department would be established the second semester of the next calendar year, and also made concessions to other student demands. The student leaders rejected his offer and established new "pre-conditions to negotiation," including removal of police from campus and amnesty for arrested students. The calendar year came to a close with no end in sight for the disruption at San Francisco State College. The Black student movement, supported by Black community leaders, white militant students and white teacher unionists, came into head-on conflict with state politicians and a police-aided university administration which sought to end disruption before being willing to negotiate. The new year was bound to bring a continuation of the troubles at San Francisco State for Acting President Hayakawa.

Trouble at the University of California's Berkeley campus centered around the Black Panther minister of information, Eldridge Cleaver. Cleaver, author of *Soul on Ice*, had gained fame for his attacks on Governor Ronald Reagan and on Dr. Max Rafferty, California superintendent of public instruction, as well as for his frequent use of obscenities in his speeches and for his prison terms for drug violations and felonious assault. Dr. Rafferty was the Republican candidate for the Senate.

In the spring of 1968, the University of California's new president, Dr. Charles J. Hitch, initiated a new program to gear the resources of that institution to urban and ghetto problems. His first steps were to provide a million dollar scholarship fund for disadvantaged students (mostly Black); to provide special teacher training to improve elementary and high school education; to augment the Black enrollment in graduate school; and to upgrade job opportunities for minority groups on the university campus and in placement work.

The Berkeley administration invited Cleaver to give ten lectures in an experimental course called "Dehumanization and Regeneration in the American Social Order," also described as a course in social analysis, or racism. Against the wishes of Governor Reagan, the board of regents, which controls the state's university (not college) system, voted ten to eight to limit to one the number of lectures that could be given in a credit course by academically unaccredited lecturers (such as Cleaver). Rafferty and Reagan were greatly displeased by this compromise and publicly denounced it. Rafferty even threatened the public school administrators who might allow their students to go to a Cleaver address.

Faculty and student reaction on the university campus at Berkeley was quick, although not so violent as was anticipated. Student leaders demanded that the regents' rule be rescinded. A mass meeting of some two thousand students demanded approval of all experimental classes, including Cleaver's. In a thousand-member meeting, members of the faculty charged the board of regents with violating their academic freedom and autonomy, but decided to avoid a direct confrontation and to set up steps for further negotiations with the regents. In the meantime, the faculty urged the course sponsors to proceed with the course either on or off campus and directed the faculty committee on courses to assure course and credit status to the institution's program of experimental studies. The president of the Berkeley Associated Students was quoted as saying that "the breadth and depth of anger of the students [over the regents' action] exceeds anything I've seen in my five years on this campus."

While awaiting negotiations with the regents, Berkeley Chancellor Roger W. Heyns offered a lecture hall for the controversial course Social Analysis 139X, with the understanding that it was temporarily a student-sponsored, non-credit course. The students accepted his offer and called off a scheduled mass meeting, although Black students demanded a waiver of fees for the course under this arrangement.

Efforts to mount a significant student boycott of classes failed, as Cleaver proceeded to give five lectures, instead of one, on the course while awaiting a meeting of the faculty representatives with representatives of the regents. During this period, forty-nine students were arrested for barricading a building on the campus. The university gave them only "interim suspensions," however, which allowed them to continue their academic work but prohibited their extracurricular activities.

Upon reconsideration of the issue and in the light of faculty demands, the board of regents decided on November 22 to give authority over such lecturers as Cleaver to the president of the university system (in this case, Dr. Charles J. Hitch). President Hitch termed the decision an "interim solution" and predicted more discussion in March 1969, when the regents would next meet. Governor Reagan—who had recently been jostled by students at a public meeting—seemed satisfied with the decision.

Politicians had run headlong into confrontation with academicians over a matter of academic freedom related to Black awareness. Academic freedom seemed to be preserved. Cleaver pinpointed an issue by saying that "the important thing developing today in this country is the issue of community control. . . . [The educational process is the] total property of the community, which has the fundamental authority and power, and it cannot be taken away from them. A struggle over the relationships of power is going on. . . . Who controls the educational system reflects who actually controls the community. . . . The real revolution is finding out where you are at, what you are up against, and then getting started."

Berkeley Chancellor Heyns, in the meantime, responded positively to a proposal which had been made during the spring by Black students. Machinery of the university ground out a new degree-granting department of Afro-American studies within the framework of the university. Dr. Andrew Billingsley, an associate professor of social welfare, was appointed as the chancellor's assistant in working with students, department heads and faculty to develop the new program. The new department would offer a Bachelor of Arts degree in Afro-American studies. Students taking the degree would be required to emphasize a political, economic or sociological point of view and would do half of their work in other departments. At Berkeley a forward-looking group of Black students, a creative and flexible university chancellor, a faculty firm in defense of academic freedom, combined to develop a new academic program and to resist political encroachment. Whether community control was developed is highly dubious. The contrast of events at Berkeley with those at San Francisco State seemed to be merely a prologue.

* * * * * *

Anno Domini 1968 marked a milestone in American history. April 4 was probably a turning point for millions of Americans. The assassination of the Black leader who sought an integrated America through nonviolent means bore disturbing signs that it was also the assassination of nonviolence and integration as ideals in the fabric of American life. In a larger sense, however, the killing of Dr. Martin Luther King, Jr., accelerated a movement which had started at least four years before, if not four centuries before. America's unwillingness to develop an integrated, color blind social fabric despite centuries of peaceful and persuasive efforts by Negroes and whites of good will had created a viciously demeaning dual society in the nation. Black Americans chose the halls of academe as the battle ground for 1968. What the future held was not yet clear.

Carl B. Stokes, mayor of Cleveland, Ohio; Walter Washington, mayor of the District of Columbia; and Richard G. Hatcher, mayor of Gary, Indiana, chat with former secretary of HUD, Robert Weaver (left).

State and Local Politics in 1968

Edward F. Sweat

MORE AND MORE Blacks in 1968 came to believe that political involvement was vital for Negro progress. Throughout the nation Negroes went to the polls in large numbers, frequently voting for Black candidates for state and local offices. The trek of Southern Negroes out of the wilderness of political oblivion to which they had been relegated by post-Reconstruction disfranchisement, commanded national attention and elicited both respect and apprehension from residents of the region. Events of this year support the assertion that Black voters and candidates have reached a stage of political maturity missing in years past. The increase in numbers of Black voters and candidates is evidence not only of expanded opportunity to vote, but also of confidence in the efficacy of the political process in solving human concerns and basic social needs. There was in 1968 a growing belief that if the slogan "Black power" was going to be translated into a constructive program of action, its most practical application would be made in the political arena.

Without question the Southern Black's quest for political power was given impetus by the 1965 Voting Rights Act. The movement made headway shortly after the act's passage, gained momentum in the next two years and reached full tide in the election year of 1968. Attempts in the South to sabotage the movement, although not unexpected, alerted Negroes of the need to guard their recently won gains.

While the nation's Black people showed interest in the campaign for the Presidency, direct involvement in state and local politics was a more intimate and urgent matter for them. They realized that it is on this grass-roots level that elected officials are under more constant surveillance, are more immediately responsive to their constituents' needs and are under greater pressure to produce results.

A brief survey of the background will furnish a perspective for an understanding of the Black man in state and local politics today. Properly, this survey begins in the post-Civil War period with focus on the South. It was in the South that Black political involvement was to be found, where post-Reconstruction losses were so visible, and where today events are so highly charged and recent gains so noticeable. The brief period after the war, during which Black men voted and held public elective office, came to an end with the "redemption" by local conservative whites of their states from "radical white-Negro" control. The "use of the ballot by Negroes in the elections of 1868 and 1872 had aroused the planters and political leaders in Southern cities to an incredible pitch of fury." [1] To all intents and purposes, the compromise which resulted from the disputed Presidential election of 1876 marked the end of Black political power in the South. White supremacists took steps to consolidate their control of the political process. Devices and stratagems employed to deprive Blacks of the franchise are too well known to need recounting here.[2] The "white primary," which denied Negroes both party membership and a voice in the selection of the dominant Democratic Party candidates, was the last barrier erected. In this entire disfranchisement movement the Fifteenth Amendment was simply ignored or merely circumvented. Political disfranchisement, accompanied by the rise of Jim-Crowism, led conservative Negroes to turn to other means of escape from their nadir of despair.

In the North, as well as in the South, Black people were largely isolated from the main current of American society. There, too, Negroes depended on their own people in maintaining a viable social life. Violence against Blacks in the North often took the form of race riots, a type of hostility which continued after World War I. The World War II years witnessed the migration of large numbers of Blacks from the South to other regions of the country. By and large, these migrants found their way into urban ghettoes, thereby perpetuating the largely separate Negro existence found in the United States. In the years following World War II, the federal government became more actively engaged in civil rights. Negroes became less reconciled to depressed conditions and more militant in demanding all the rights of full citizenship. Suggestive of the new mood was the passage of the amendment outlawing the poll tax as a condition for voting. Significant for the future was the adoption of the Civil Rights Acts of 1957 and 1960, both of which focused on the right to vote. This legislation culminated with the passing of the Voting Rights Act of 1965, which "provided for direct Federal action to enable Negroes to register and vote without reliance upon often protracted litigation required by previous legislation." [3]

A comparison of figures shows that there has been a noticeable increase in Black registration in the six selected states listed in the table below. The figures were compiled by the Southern Regional Council's Voter Education Project (VEP). This project supports voter registration, citizenship education and leadership training in eleven Southern states. It endorses no parties or candidates. Figures for the years 1962 and 1966 are from *VEP News*, April 1968; for the year 1968, from *VEP News*, September 1968.

The figures below speak for themselves. There is little doubt that gains shown can be attributed largely to the effects of the Voting Rights Act. Certainly the assignment of federal examiners to a number of counties in states covered by the act had a salutary effect. A study made by the VEP in 1966 indicated that Black registration tended to be higher in counties to which federal examiners had been assigned. According to the Civil Rights Commission, as of late 1967 such examiners had been sent to fifty-eight counties in states of the South.[4]

TABLE 1

Southern Negro Voter Registration in the 1960's

State	1962	1966	Fall, 1968	Per cent Negro voting age population registered
Alabama	68,317	250,000	273,000	56.7
Arkansas	68,970	115,000	130,000	67.5
Georgia	175,573	300,000	344,000	56.1
Mississippi	23,920	175,000	251,000	55.3
Texas	242,000	400,000	540,000	83.1
Virginia	110,113	250,000	255,000	58.4

Another important factor in the adding of eligible Blacks to the voting rolls has been the professional assistance, support and encouragement given by such organizations as the VEP. This project has gone far in facilitating registration among Negroes in the South. Workshop sessions such as those in Louisiana and Mississippi, for example, helped to stimulate interest in registration. Enlarged Black voting lists have resulted in the election of Negroes to local and state offices all over the South. In 1965 there were only seventy elected Black officials in the South; at the end of 1968 there were approximately 385.

Another factor which accounts for the upsurge in voting has been the more aggressive attitude of Blacks themselves. The accommodating type, so often personified by the earlier Black spokesman whose influence depended upon the good will of the white power structure and whose sub rosa activities took the place of legitimate political power, is being replaced by more demanding elected officials. Prospective Negro officeholders know that their chances of being elected depend on their getting their Black brothers and sisters registered and out to the polls on election day. Realistic Negro voters recognize that it is to their advantage to have another Negro representing them at city hall, on boards of education, as law enforcement agents and as members of state legislatures.

Negroes in both North and South have achieved a kind of political Black power hitherto denied them. But as more and more Black men and women have been elected to public office, the focus has had to shift from the acquisition of power to the responsible use of it. This is apparent in such cities as Cleveland, Gary and Washington, D.C., where Black men have become the leaders of their municipal governments. In the smaller municipalities and at the state level, too, Negroes have had to become more intimately acquainted with lawmaking, administration, tax problems, social needs and all the other concerns of office. At the same time they have had to remain cognizant of ever-present racism. Talking to local and state elected officials makes one realize that there is present this awareness of the ubiquitous character of racial antipathy. These officials, and other knowledgeable people, know that "registering and voting still expose black people to threats and reprisals, physical and economic, in much of the South." [5]

In some localities Black poll watchers have been excluded while frauds have been perpetrated against Black candidates. On a less crude level, certain obstacles have been erected to retard Black participation in the political process. Changing to "at-large" elections, redrawing election district lines, or refusing to redraw ward lines, dilute the Negro vote and diminish his political influence. "Extending the incumbent's term, abolishing the office, raising filing fees, withholding information" [6] are other devices used against Black people. City council or aldermanic board representation on the basis of existing apportionment plans has come under fire in such cities as Atlanta, Chicago and New York.

Negroes feel that under present setups Black representation is deliberately kept to a minimum. They propose new alignments drawn in such manner as to ensure equitable representation on local governing boards. In Chicago it took a federal district court to compel redistricting on the one man, one vote, principle, which could result in a significant increase in Black representation on the city council. The present council has ten Negroes, who comprise 20 per cent of the body's membership. Chicago has over a million Negroes who make up about 30 per cent of the city's population.

Another concern of Blacks who live in large urban centers is the result of a long-time historic process. Negro migrants have traditionally gone into segregated sections of big cities; because they were crowded into compact neighborhoods, their voting power was isolated. This happened in Milwaukee, where about ninety thousand Negroes until fairly recently had only one Negro representative on the city council of nineteen members. This was of strategic importance, for whether or not Mrs. Vel Phillips, the Negro alderwoman, received the votes of all Black people, she was indeed the spokesman for *all* disadvantaged Blacks of Milwaukee. That the odds were against her has been seen in her several unsuccessful attempts to persuade the council to pass meaningful open housing legislation. The recent election of attorney Orville E. Pitts to the council has added one other Negro to that body.

Whether or not Black elected local officials can operate more effectively in areas of social blight than could their white predecessors is for the future to decide. What is known now is that these officeholders are under a great deal of pressure to get things done, to effect changes, to achieve almost magical results in long-time problem areas such as inadequate housing and recreation facilities. This is true both North and South. These Black officials have no illusions at this point; many have brought to their jobs imagination, skill and the willingness to experiment with new approaches, while retaining the more valuable aspects of earlier programs. The following vignettes illustrate the above.

To say that Richard G. Hatcher became mayor of Gary, Indiana, under adverse conditions is to understate the case. Former president of the Gary city council, he not only failed to receive support from his fellow party members of the powerful Lake County Democratic Committee, but he was actively opposed by the committee and its leader. During the campaign he was labeled by the chairman a "Stokely Carmichael-Rap Brown Black power" extremist controlled by "left-wing" groups. Fearful of taking any chance at losing the mayoral election, the machine resorted to chicanery.

When the Justice Department discovered a "vote fraud scheme" in the organization and secured a federal court injunction to ensure a fair election, the scheme collapsed and a Black man became the mayor of one of America's big cities. It is of interest to note that Mayor Hatcher's margin of victory was 1,389 votes, made possible by solid Negro support. Negroes at this time were some 55 per cent of Gary's population of 178,000. The problems facing a newly elected official coming out of a bitter and heated campaign are compounded for Mr. Hatcher. It is too much to expect that the racial animosity which characterized the mayoralty campaign has completely subsided. It appears symbolic that the oath of office was administered to the new mayor by federal district Judge James B. Parsons of Chicago, also a Negro.

What about the future for this key elected Negro official? Perhaps one can judge his ideological bent from what he himself has said. Speaking to an NAACP Legal Defense and Educational Fund celebration of the fourteenth anniversary of the Supreme Court's 1954 school decision, he asserted that the "logic of Black power was irrefutable." At the same time he pointed to weaknesses in "liberalism," which in his opinion had been "condescending" to Negroes. In a speech delivered at Clark College in Atlanta, on the occasion of a late 1968 conference of Black elected officials, he pledged support for all forms of Black power that "will help America define itself." Mr. Hatcher declared that a Black pride and consciousness are essential in "ending the strangeness Black people feel in America," but he also realized that Black power "can't cure poverty and the other problems plaguing Negroes." His conclusion was that political power in the hands of Blacks, despite its limitations, can help prevent the exploitation of Negro people in this country.

In one vital respect the victory of Carl B. Stokes in Cleveland was similar to that of Mayor Hatcher in Gary. Both men got substantial Negro support: 96 per cent of Cleveland's Black vote in the 1967 mayoralty election went to Stokes. Both got some white votes: about 12 per cent went to Hatcher and something less than 20 per cent to Stokes.

Stokes' political training had included service in the Ohio legislature, where he had earned the respect of his peers and of newsmen. Failure to gain the mayor's office in 1965 proved to be only a temporary setback, for in 1967 he became the first Negro to be elected mayor of a major American city. At the end of his first year in office the staff of the influential *Cleveland Plain Dealer* presented on November 11, 1968, an "account" of that year with an "appraisal of his performance." The paper's staff described him as "probably the most important Negro in the Democratic Party today," referring, among other things, to his being chosen to give a seconding speech for the Presidential nomination of Hubert Humphrey. Mr. Stokes was awarded "high passing grades in all municipal subjects except police-City Hall relations." That these became strained as a result of practical and knowledgeable actions taken by him in the Glenville section of Cleveland in an effort to maintain calm after Dr. Martin Luther King's assassination, is widely known. If indeed his actions then limited his ability to govern, "most politicians do not think [they were] damaging enough to defeat him." This young, aggressive Negro mayor has evidenced a deep commitment to community involvement in city programs and projects—a commitment which led to the birth of his community action program called "Cleveland: Now." This imaginative project has gained financial support from Clevelanders, to "augment city programs in housing, recreation, health and welfare." It "brings together both public and private sectors in an onslaught on the city's problems." He has been successful in obtaining federal urban renewal funds, which had been cut off under the administration of the former mayor. The Stokes administration has been able to secure from the United States Department of Housing and Urban Development a model cities planning grant—a grant which earlier the department had withdrawn.

To counteract allegations of interference by his administration in police affairs, Stokes appointed a new police chief who was given complete authority in running his department. In addition, a $17 million building and modernization is now being implemented; also, the city has undertaken to pay tuition expenses of any policeman who wants to attend college. In an effort to bring the "government closer to the people, making it more responsive to their needs," Mayor Stokes inaugurated a series of "town hall meetings" which were conducted throughout the city. In these meetings citizens were given a firsthand opportunity to complain and question the mayor and members of his cabinet, with the officials "explaining programs, answering questions and fielding complaints."

Although Washington, D.C., "Mayor" Walter E. Washington is in reality a commissioner appointed by the President, he is the Negro head of government of one of this nation's key cities. How this urban community goes about solving its multi-faceted problems is of interest to Black people all over America—moderates and militants alike. Mayor Washington presides over the affairs of a city whose Black population in 1965 was estimated to be over 60 per cent of the total. He has implemented in Washington a program designed to get city hall closer to the people. In one section a staffed "community facility center" was established to offer coordinated services to those who need assistance from several agencies at a time. Basic to this center was the attempt to "centralize the availability of public services to the community and bring them to the doorsteps of the people who need them so urgently." [7]

The important point to consider is that these Black officials have exhibited a sympathetic awareness of the concerns of blighted urban areas and are intelligently and aggressively placing in operation innovative programs aimed at both amelioration and correction. In the process they have revealed a capacity to govern and to administer the highly complex public affairs of modern American cities. That they realistically draw upon the resources of their total communities, Black as well as white, is an excellent augury for fruitful and efficient administrations.

These Negro mayors are the best-known leaders. There are others, a sizable number of whom are found in the South—generally in small towns. They preside over towns in Alabama, Arkansas, Louisiana, Mississippi, South Carolina and other states. Certainly their problems are not as awesome as those of big-city mayors; nevertheless they must handle the reins of power. Basic human concerns and needs for public services are by and large similar to those in large cities.

One method by which more Blacks can become mayors is illustrated in the history of the fledgling town of Roosevelt City, Alabama. This is the concept—not by any means novel—of incorporating new all-Black municipalities, particularly erstwhile suburban areas of certain large urban complexes. Duane Riner, writing in the *Atlanta Journal and Constitution* on December 8, 1968, gave the following example: Roosevelt City was formerly a suburb of Birmingham, "recognized by the white power structure only as 'niggertown' . . . living within the shadow of white opulence but denied an opportunity to share the benefits." A group of Blacks led by a Birmingham Negro attorney was successful in converting it into a municipality empowered to tax, and able to share in state and federal largess. The first major accomplishment of the administration of Mayor Freddie C. Rogers was the securing of street lights for this town of approximately five thousand residents.

There are, on the other hand, those Negroes who view the tactic of creating all-Black towns as an undesirable move in the direction of Black separatism, and they therefore oppose it. John McCown, recently elected county commissioner of Hancock County, Georgia, is one such opponent. This Negro official in a county in which Blacks outnumber whites made it clear that (to quote Riner) "in Hancock County we're not interested in the least in any all-black community." Municipal Judge Orzell Billingsley, Jr., referred to as "the father of Roosevelt City," contended (according to Riner): "The only way it amounts to separatism is that we were separated from the white communities, and now we are organizing." It remains to be seen whether or not this "new" impulse will become a force of major proportions.

Negroes have become mayors of predominantly white towns in at least two states. Matthew G. Carter, a member of the town commission, became in 1968 the first Negro mayor of Montclair, New Jersey—a "generally well-to-do suburban town" of forty-three thousand residents, of whom only about 25 per cent are Black. The mayor himself understood that "the selection of a Negro mayor by a predominantly white community, while no longer unique, is still remarkable. . . ." In Springfield, Ohio, which operates under the commission form of government, Robert C. Henry, a Negro, served as mayor. Mr. Henry became mayor of this city of over eighty thousand people in 1965. Under this plan the candidate for commissioner who receives the most votes automatically becomes mayor. The

Representative Joe Kershaw (right) of the Florida house of representatives is sworn into office. He is the first Negro to sit in this house in Florida in over ninety-six years.

Black population of Springfield is estimated to be around five thousand. If the figures are accurate, the accession of Mr. Henry to the post of mayor reflected a fair amount of popularity with white voters.

Negroes flexed their political muscles in the year 1968 more than they had done in the recent past; indeed, the evidence shows more than *ever* before. Where Blacks have been defeated for public office—and a number of Black candidates were unsuccessful—they are biding their time and preparing for the next elections. In the meantime, they serve as critics of incumbent administrations. The fact that they are learning the historic political role of the "outs" will most certainly have a beneficial effect on the policies and proposed programs of local and state power structures. An entrenched white power elite has to be ever mindful of the possibility of Black candidates running for offices traditionally the exclusive preserve of whites. Already Negroes of Dallas, Texas, are giving consideration to possible Black candidates for the office of mayor in 1969, while a Black civic leader in Pittsburgh has warned the incumbent that his group will look for a candidate for mayor if certain changes are not made quickly. In Newark, New Jersey, the mayor's office is a specific target of the Black community. Negroes in this city, whose population is over 50 per cent Black, have organized to elect a mayor in 1970. They are heartened by the fact that a Black man ran well in the 1966 mayoral election.

For the Black American the year 1968 was one of political significance, fraught with opportunity to translate the slogan "Black power" into political reality. As early as 1966 Negroes had been elected to state and local offices in fairly substantial numbers in the South as well as in other states. Statistics compiled by the VEP in that year attest to the fact that twenty Blacks were elected to state legislatures of three Southern states—the largest number in Georgia, followed by Tennessee and Texas. On the county level, Blacks won a number of elective offices. One of the more highly publicized victories was that of Lucius Amerson of Tuskegee, who became sheriff of Macon County, Alabama. In Mississippi, a Negro was seated on the Jefferson County school board, becoming the first Black elected to a county office in that state since Reconstruction.

It is more difficult to obtain with complete accuracy the numbers of Black elected officials found outside the South. Files of the VEP are accurate and are kept up to date; but they cover only the states of the former Confederacy. A "Roster of Negro Elected Officials" was published in the Spring 1968 edition of the *Civil Rights Digest*; it listed such officials for twenty-two other states. In each of the states surveyed there was at least one Negro in either the state senate or the lower house. As would be expected, such states as California, Illinois, Maryland, Michigan, Missouri, New York and Pennsylvania had the largest Black representation. These were also the states with substantial numbers of Blacks holding seats on city councils.

In February 1968 the VEP released figures showing "the number of elected Negro officials in the South" as of that date: the total was 248 and included eighty-one city councilmen, fifty-nine school board members, twenty-five county commissioners, twenty-one justices of the peace, fourteen constables and fourteen magistrates.

On the eve of the November election, more than 250 Negroes in the South were seeking office. In Georgia alone there were thirty-one Black candidates, of whom twenty-three were seeking seats in the general assembly. Mississippi furnished the largest number of candidates, with a total of seventy-three in twenty-two counties vying for such offices as membership on county school boards and election commission posts. All told, fifty-one Blacks sought seats in their general assemblies. Smaller numbers ran for the offices of justice of the peace, of coroner and of constable, or for membership on boards of revenue, and city council seats.

Commanding widespread interest were the successful attempts of Negroes to win seats in legislative bodies which had had no Black members since Reconstruction. Robert Clark became the first Negro elected to the Mississippi lower house in seventy-four years. An interesting point was that after the swearing-in ceremonies Clark was given a seat by himself at the front of the chamber. In November Joe Kershaw, Florida's first Black member of its house of representatives in ninety-six years, was given the oath of office along with two white freshman lawmakers. The North Carolina legislature, which had been all-white for the past seventy years, witnessed the seating of Henry Frye, a Negro lawyer of Greensboro elected as a representative from Guilford County. And, as reported in the Washington *Afro-American* of January 23, 1968, "The Sky Didn't Fall" when Dr. William F. Reid became the first Negro to win election to the Virginia house of delegates since 1891. Among the four new members elected to the Georgia house was James Dean, who became the first Negro to win election to the state's general assembly from De Kalb County. An encouraging omen for the future can be detected in these statistics: Of the approximately one hundred Black men and women who won office in the South in November, roughly eighty had not held an elective public office before. The election brought to 385 the number of Black elected officials in the region.

Mention has been made of the difficulty of compiling an accurate list of Black elected local and state officials for the entire country. On the basis of information compiled and made available by the Democratic National Committee, it is possible to estimate rather accurately the number holding membership on city councils or boards of aldermen, as well as those holding seats in state legislatures *who are members of that party*.[8] Table 2 indicates numbers of city councilmen and state legislators in twenty-three states outside the South, and Table 3 shows the breakdown for the same offices in the former Confederate states, as compiled by the VEP.

A glance at these tables reveals two things of some significance. In the South, only the three states of Alabama, Arkansas and South Carolina are without Black lawmakers in their general assemblies. The figures also suggest that up to this point it has been relatively less difficult to win seats in the lower houses than in the upper. To hazard an opinion as to how long this state of affairs will continue would be a matter of conjecture.

These are sensitive and key offices; in some cases, especially in the state legislative bodies, the full impact of Negroes on the policy and law-making process will not be felt immediately. But

TABLE 2

Black City Councilmen and State Legislators

State	City Council	Lower House	Senate
Arizona	—	2	1
California	15	5	1
Colorado	—	2	1
Connecticut	12	—	—
Delaware	3	—	—
Illinois	13	9	1
Indiana	9	—	—
Iowa	—	1	—
Kentucky	1	—	—
Maryland	5	—	—
Massachusetts	1	2	—
Michigan	3	10	—
Missouri	9	7	2
Nebraska	—	—	1
New Jersey	13	—	—
New Mexico	2	—	—
New York	3	10	3
Ohio	13	9	2
Oklahoma	—	4	—
Pennsylvania	5	7	2
Rhode Island	—	1	—
Washington	—	1	—
Wisconsin	2	1	—

TABLE 3

Black City Councilmen and Black Legislators in the South

State	City Council	Lower House	Senate
Alabama	29	—	—
Arkansas	11	—	—
Florida	8	1	—
Georgia	6	12	2
Louisiana	14	1	—
Mississippi	6	1	—
North Carolina	9	1	—
South Carolina	16	—	—
Tennessee	7	6	2
Texas	8	2	1
Virginia	18	1	—

to quote Curtis M. Graves, one of the two Black Texas state representatives, Negroes are now in a position "to lift up the lid and see what's cooking." Black legislators may not be able to "pass anything," yet they can exert pressure out of proportion to their numerical strength to get things done of benefit to all the people. Representative Graves touched on a problem peculiar to himself and to other Black legislators when he eloquently described himself as a "spokesman" for Negroes all over Texas, rather than for only those of his Houston district.

It can be expected that an enormous amount of pressure will be brought to bear on these officials. Whether the possibilities are realistic or not, their constituencies want action, and in a hurry. Vernon E. Jordan, Jr., the articulate and perceptive director of the Voter Education Project, put it this way in *VEP News* in November 1968: "Black voters often feel that black officeholders should produce almost instantly all those benefits and services that had been denied down through the years by callous white officials." His realistic conclusion was that "usually—almost always—this is impossible." Augmenting the difficulties already listed are others. Newly elected Black officials are the cynosure of all eyes—some friendly, some hostile. "Often the Negro officeholder will be measured by yardsticks far more exacting than those applied to his white predecessors." (Representative Julian Bond has pointed out that as a Black legislator in the Georgia assembly he devoted a sizable amount of time doing the work of an alderman in a Northern city.) One last observation made by Mr. Jordan bears repeating. Because of years of exclusion from the political process in the South, many Black officials carry "a heavy burden of political inexperience."

Along with the political gains were losses suffered by Black candidates. In the South alone nearly three hundred Blacks were defeated by white opponents. In Tuskegee, Alabama, the white incumbent mayor won reelection over a Negro challenger, while the Negro mayor of Flint, Michigan, decided not to seek a second term. In the states of North Carolina and Washington, Negroes added an exciting dimension to gubernatorial campaigns, but were unsuccessful in winning their races. Arthur A. Fletcher, although nominated in the Republican primary for lieutenant governor of Washington, lost in his bid for election to that office. In North Carolina, Dr. Reginald Hawkins attracted a good deal of attention during his gubernatorial campaign—but not enough votes. It should be pointed out that in a number of races Negro incumbents were opposed by other Negroes, as was the case in Memphis, where two Blacks were ousted from the state legislature by Black competitors.

To what extent Black militants believed that grievances could be best redressed through recourse to the political process cannot accurately be measured. It is significant that SNCC and Black Panther leaders both appeared to want to build "a Black political party," but there seemed to be some disagreement as to the ideology of such a party. SNCC leaders were said to favor one that was opposed to racism, capitalism, imperialism and opportunism. The Black Panthers held out for a "Black revolutionary program" which is sufficiently elastic to defy meaningful analysis. It seems of more practical significance that in 1968 LeRoi Jones, the outspoken Black poet and playwright of Newark, New Jersey, concluded that "the city is ours anyway, that we can take it with ballots." A Negro group, the United Brothers of Newark, headed by Jones, issued a call for a "Black convention to pick candidates for every city office." A convention, whose membership included Newark's Black incumbent councilman, was held in June. But a contributing factor to the defeat of the group's candidates for council seats was the fact that although Blacks form a majority of the city's population, the electorate represents only about 24 per cent of the total population. Another factor was lack of complete unity within the Black community.

If, as one Black legislator has asserted, "politics is no more and no less" for Blacks than an opportunity "of having something to say about what is being done" to Negroes in America, then the problem of strategy becomes of prime importance. Representative Bond argues that Negroes must "be strong, well-organized and politically independent," and never "too closely aligned with one faction or another," or "too predictable." Dr. Vivian Henderson, president of Clark College and an astute observer of the contemporary political scene, feels that Black candidates must run *on issues* rather than *as personalities*. The Negro officeholder has certain choices open to him: he can attempt coalition with his white colleagues, or he can depend upon confrontation as a means of gaining benefits for his constituents. Henderson has suggested to Southern Black elected officials that there is a need "to re-examine the strategy of racial blocs," and to be wary of relying upon "racial solidarity alone to accomplish desired goals." He has also stated that Black officials have not reached the point where they can "abandon racial consciousness under the façade of color blindness."

Two disparate but highly regarded tacticians have recently addressed themselves to the general area of strategy. Dr. Kenneth Clark, head of the Metropolitan Applied Research Center, warned against stressing the race issue to such a degree that the white vote would be lost to the "racism inherent in America." In his opinion (expressed in the *Civil Rights Digest* [Spring 1968]) the "nihilistic brand of Black power" was "unquestionably a liability for the serious Negro politician," but he advised Black officials to "seek to discipline the constructive emotional and practical potentials of this movement." Mr. Bayard Rustin, executive director of the A. Philip Randolph Institute, stressed the desirability of alliances, described by him as "scratching one another's backs" in practical politics. He emphasized the fact that the civil rights struggle was no longer in the era of demonstrations and ideological absolutes, but was now a matter of practical politics.

The facet of broad strategy chosen by Negro elected officials will, in all likelihood, be determined by the exigencies of their own peculiar local conditions, as well as by their ability to manipulate the existing power structure. The most fruitful approach at the moment would seem to be a judicious mixture of alliances combined with confrontation—both securely anchored in a Black voting power base. It is of more than passing interest that the two Black members of the Georgia senate were recently elected, in caucus, chairman and secretary respectively of their county's delegation. Senator Leroy Johnson, the chairman, observed that he was "looking forward to two years of . . . progressive action" from the delegation.

It is increasingly apparent that the more active and more sophisticated Black voters become the less likely they will be to vote simply for the charismatic personality or for a particular political party. Given proper civic training, they will vote as the issues dictate and for projected programs which direct themselves to felt needs. A good deal of evidence to support this is already available. This means, among other things, that some Blacks who are opposed by whites will lose the Negro vote unless they can persuade voters that their programs are relevant to pressing problems and human needs.

Most Negroes seem content to remain within the fold of the two-party system. Most Southern Black elected officials will still give allegiance to the Democratic Party; some will stay in, but with help from white liberals will attempt to force a basic realignment through gaining control and ousting the conservative forces. In a letter to this author, in December 1968, Mayor Carl B. Stokes wrote that it seemed truer in 1968 than ever before that Negroes were "using the political processes now in the same way that European nationality groups like the Irish and Polish used earlier to gain acceptance into the mainstream of American life." Few would argue that the political process represents a panacea, but there is a strong feeling that Black elected officials are in a position to make sure that more benefits will accrue to the Negro community. These officials, more sensitive to Black-oriented problems, will not only "see what's cooking," but will add new ingredients to the contents of the political cauldron and, in some cases, effect needed changes.

Attention has been called to certain problems which are peculiar to the Black official on the state and local level. Help which is expert, consistent and well organized is available to these officeholders, particularly in the South. Reference has been made to the Southern Regional Council's Voter Education Project and its raison d'être. The Southwide Conference of Black Elected Officials, sponsored by the VEP in Atlanta, December 11–14, 1968, was its most ambitious attempt to give practical assistance to the region's officials. To publisher Ralph McGill this meeting was a reflection of Southerners at their best: "There newly elected black men—most of them recall being denied the ballot—come from many segregated backgrounds. They lack political education and sophistication," and "a few will be subjected to sabotage through noncooperation and opposition." [9] Some of these officials were erudite, professionals in their fields of endeavor, school people, but they all had one thing in common. They had gathered for a period of "political schooling" which was dispensed through general sessions and in area workshops.

What the VEP has done and is doing in the South has not been duplicated in other sections of the country. However, a new program, national in scope and designed to help newly elected Black officials, is in the inaugural stage. The Scholarship, Education and Defense Fund for

Racial Equality has given limited assistance in this area before, but not in a comprehensive and systematic manner. Now SEDFRE is inaugurating a privately funded technical assistance program for newly elected public officials, with its headquarters in New York City. James Felder, talented young lawyer and former South Carolina director of VEP, has been selected to direct this program.

It is all to the good that professional or technical assistance is available to Black local and state officeholders. "Increased Negro political participation" is not the same as saying that all Negroes are eligible to vote. Earlier, attention was focused on obstacles placed in the path of prospective Black voters and possible Black candidates, especially in certain sections of the South. But although dramatic gains have been made since the passage of the Voting Rights Act, Negroes still must remain on guard lest these advances in the political arena be nullified through sophistry, subterfuge or even physical violence. In the Northern urban areas, voter registration drives sponsored by civic organizations, institutions and ad hoc groups should be held whenever the books are open. If urban Black majorities are urban voteless majorities—or if they hold the balance of power in their communities without access to the ballot box—they are powerless and will remain so.

Reference Notes

[1] Ralph McGill, "Story from a Cornerstone," *Atlanta Constitution* (December 5, 1968).

[2] An excellent brief but detailed and well-documented summary of the political history of this period is found in: United States Commission on Civil Rights, *Political Participation: A Study of Participation by Negroes in the Electoral and Political Process in Ten Southern States since Passage of the Voting Rights Act of 1965* (Washington, 1968), pp. 1–10.

[3] *Ibid.*, p. 7.

[4] *Ibid.*, p. 12.

[5] Vernon E. Jordan, Jr., "Voting Rights Act Hasn't Solved All Problems," *VEP News* (October 1968).

[6] Joseph H. Rauh, Jr., "Political Participation," *Civil Rights Digest* (Summer 1968), p. 9.

[7] *Afro-American* [Washington, D.C.] (December 12, 1968).

[8] The investigator tried on more than one occasion to obtain such information from the Republican National Committee, but to no avail. An example of error in the compilations is found in the figures for Ohio. Other sources show that a total of three Negroes won seats in the state senate, one of whom is a Republican, while ten hold membership in the Ohio lower house, nine Democrats and one Republican (*Cleveland Call and Post*, November 16, 1968).

[9] Ralph McGill, in *Atlanta Constitution* (December 12, 1968).

Members of Resurrection City march near the Washington Monument during the Poor People's Campaign in the nation's capital in 1968.

A "New Order" Is Born

Lyn Shepard

HIGH ABOVE the Senate's west entrance a plaque bearing the Latin inscription *Novus Ordo Seclorum* greets Capitol visitors. Never before perhaps has that phrase—"A new order of the ages is born"—meant more to Congress and the nation than during the strife-torn spring of 1968. For within rapid succession during this period:

1. Congress passed a controversial open housing section (barring racial bias in the sale or rental of about 80 per cent of the housing market by 1970) as part of the Civil Rights Act of 1968. The statute was probably the last federal "rights" law of its kind.
2. Dr. Martin Luther King, Jr., was killed by a sniper's bullet while conferring with aides on the balcony of a Memphis motel. At the time, he was mapping plans for a national "Poor People's March on Washington." His assassination set off a series of fiery disorders in Black slums across the nation.
3. Dr. King's successor, Rev. Ralph David Abernathy, oversaw construction of a "Resurrection City" campsite on Washington's rain-soaked Southwest Mall. He and other leaders—Black, Indian and Mexican-American—then staged direct action confrontations with Congress and federal agencies on behalf of the poor.
4. A massive housing bill cleared Congress, which met one of the Abernathy group's three basic demands. It granted \$5.3 billion over three years to build more than 1.7 million new or remodeled housing units. And it encouraged home ownership as one means of overcoming poverty.

As a lobbying effort, the Poor People's Campaign proved one of history's most dramatic displays of pressure tactics on Washington policy makers. But at best—owing largely to adverse publicity and dissension within its own leadership ranks—it achieved only a portion of what it set out to.

To trace the widespread unrest which led to Dr. King's planned march, one must go back at least to the closing days of the 90th Congress' first session, in December 1967. The near despair of liberal civil rights spokesmen at that time was due to a hardening of House sentiment against "rewarding the rioters" with a crash program for the cities.

"No Game, Rain"

The disgust of the liberals had been summed up succinctly by veteran Washington lawyer Joseph L. Rauh, Jr., a leading civil rights lobbyist within the Democratic Party structure. He dismissed the record of Congress as "No game, rain," when this newsman visited his office in late 1967.

"As liberals," he explained, "we're concerned not that things are going backward, but that they're standing still . . . I wouldn't say that Congress hasn't done anything. It may have passed some important education and social security legislation. But not much else.

"On civil rights," Mr. Rauh went on, "Congress is entitled to a goose egg. It deserves a minus goose egg on its antiriot bill. I see the President is still signing bills in the Rose Garden, but what's in them? It's been a pretty shallow Congress."

Though Postmaster General Lawrence F. O'Brien, who headed the White House Congressional liaison team, found a few more encouraging trends to point to, he, too, saw Congress' overall performance as less than praiseworthy. The reason, he contended, was the loss of forty-seven Democratic House seats in the 1966 election.

"The story then [after the election]," Mr. O'Brien recalled, "was that the Democrats might as well fold up their tents. The President could not go forward with any new programs. He would need to use a low-key approach with the 90th Congress. Well, that hasn't worked out. What has happened?

"In urban America, we found ourselves in a major struggle to see these programs survive. It would have been a severe setback to have them eliminated." The programs somehow remained intact. Yet the price of survival was that they suffered gravely in the funding process.

Of the model cities and rent supplement programs being tested by the Department of Housing and Urban Development, Mr. O'Brien noted: "They were hanging by a thread, but at least we were able to salvage them. They are still the law of the land, though woefully funded." And of the war on poverty he said: "The Office of Economic Opportunity was supposed to be decimated by Republican actions on the Hill, fragmented into other departments. Yet it survived with its structure intact and with appropriations about what they are now." The Postmaster General found this unexpected victory "nothing short of remarkable."

But Mr. Rauh, in keeping with his gloomy appraisal, saw little to cheer about. "What they call 'the great antipoverty victory,' " he said ruefully, "brought a $465 million cut in funds. A few more victories like that and we'll be undone."

"Open Housing" Filibuster

It was in this atmosphere that the Senate opened its 1968 session, with civil rights at the top of its agenda. Mississippi's arch-foe of racial integration, Senator James O. Eastland (D), had hinted late in 1967 that he would move to amend a milder rights package proposed by Senator Philip Hart (D) of Michigan with a surprise "rider" of his own.

"I know the fatal medicine that can't be swallowed by the Northern liberals—and that's open housing," Senator Eastland had declared. He reasoned that no bill with an open housing section could pass the Senate in 1968—much less the more conservative House of Representatives. And his aides predicted: "We'll fight it [the Hart bill] with everything we've got."

The Hart measure struck most Senate observers as a fairly tame bill. Among other features, it guaranteed federal protection of civil rights workers from racial violence. It borrowed the language of a bill passed by the House in 1967 which had rested its case on the "equal protection" clause of the Fourteenth Amendment to the Constitution.

While Senator Eastland was threatening to scuttle this bill with his "open housing" amendment, two Northern senators, Edward W. Brooke (R) of Massachusetts and Walter F. Mondale (D) of Minnesota, were preparing a similar amendment in earnest. These plans worried Democratic Majority Leader Mike Mansfield and Senator Hart. Both remembered that such a proviso had doomed a 1966 civil rights package when Minority Leader Everett M. Dirksen (R) of Illinois had cooperated with a Southern filibuster. Sensing that the nation's mood had turned sour on civil rights, Senators Mansfield and Hart feared that the 1966 story would be repeated.

But the Leadership Conference on Civil Rights insisted that the open housing amendment be tacked onto the Hart bill when it emerged from the Senate Judiciary Committee in January. The amendment's chief lobbyist, Clarence M. Mitchell, Jr., eventually prevailed on Senator Hart to accept the Brooke-Mondale version as part of his bill. Mr. Mitchell, the Washington director of the NAACP, then worked diligently to line up support for ending the ensuing filibuster.

The Brooke-Mondale amendment was first proposed on February 6, and immediately became the focal issue of debate. By February 20, when the Senate's only Black member, Edward

Brooke, took the floor, the first of several efforts to end debate was under way. The Massachusetts Republican said that he and Senator Mondale hoped, by modifying their bill, to round up enough support to close debate.

"We are not merely interested in an issue and in achieving some psychological victory," he told the Senate, "but we are also interested in obtaining legislation that will help our country." On the first roll call, Brooke and Mondale gained a 55–37 majority but fell short of the two-thirds margin needed to choke off the filibuster. The liberal coalition tried again on February 26. This time the vote on a motion to end debate showed the opposition slipping by only one vote (56-36). But the surprising Republican support for cloture (nineteen for, seventeen against) prompted Senator Mondale to kill his pending measure in the hope that a compromise could be fashioned.

The Dirksen Turnabout

The key to a compromise seemed to lie with the tousle-haired Republican leader Everett McKinley Dirksen. His 1966 stand against open housing ("If ever there was a can of worms . . . this is it.") had ensured its defeat at that time. And he had been adamant about it. He had recalled his secret meeting with then Attorney General Nicholas de B. Katzenbach, at which he had declared his opposition: "We sat in my bedroom for two hours, and I said: 'Nick, we can't take it.' And we can't." He had further warned the liberals: "If there were any doubting Thomases who thought I would beat a miserable retreat, they'd better get it out of their minds." The senator had decried what he viewed as a perilous shift from "rights" legislation in the public domain to that in the private area.

"They'll embrace all of it if they have their way," he predicted, with a sweep of his hand. "And this will be the forerunner . . . and it will extend. And it will extend. And it will extend."

At the outset of 1968 debate Senator Dirksen renewed his earlier stand. Yet he added that a "moderate, equitable and enforceable" civil rights protection bill might win his vote. After the second cloture defeat, the Illinois GOP leader shocked conservatives by going even further. He ordered his staff to draft a compromise bill with an open housing section covering all but owner-occupied single-family dwellings that were sold or rented privately (instead of through a real-estate broker).

Why had the senator now executed an about-face? Some press observers reasoned that he had been forced to shift after Senator Brooke had succeeded in winning over a majority of Republican members. A shrewd, pragmatic politician, Senator Dirksen surely found it easier to support open housing after the February 26 vote. But the real answer may well lie in the reply of the senator's top legislative aide, whom I managed to buttonhole in Washington's Union Station the day Dirksen's decision was announced.

"It was the visit not long ago by a group of Negro veterans just back from Vietnam that changed him, I think," the aide said. "Some were amputees. I guess all of them had been wounded. They asked him whether this was what they had fought for—to be denied a decent place to live because of their skin color. As you know, he's a pretty patriotic fellow, and I think they got to him." The aide noted that within a short time the senator and his staff were working feverishly to paste together the compromise Senators Brooke and Mondale had hoped for. Mondale called the Dirksen version "a miracle" that could not have been expected a week earlier.

But when the Senate tried to close debate for a third time on March 1, the 59–35 majority again lacked a two-thirds mandate. Only two Republicans besides Dirksen (Senators Len Jordan of Idaho and Howard H. Baker, Jr., of Tennessee, Dirksen's son-in-law) switched their votes. At this point, with victory in sight, the Johnson Administration supplied the extra pressure on wavering members to assure the exact margin needed for cloture (65–32) on March 4. Five senators changed their votes, so that by March 11 the amended bill could be sent to the House.

The House Battle

During Senate debate, the overconfident opposition to open housing had been caught napping. It responded in panic when the measure cleared the upper chamber and moved to the House. Three right-wing groups—the Liberty Lobby, the Emergency Committee against Forced Housing and the Emergency Committee of One Million To Save Our Homes—conducted what Representative James G. O'Hara (D) of Michigan called a mail campaign of "hate, fear, racism and outright lies." The other major opposition lobby, the National Association of Real Estate Boards, mounted a less virulent attack. It called the antibias proviso "an immoral doctrine because it seeks to reshape human society by invoking the coercive power of the state." NAREB mailed about five thousand copies of this tract, including a distribution to some twenty influential House members.

But the propaganda sent out by the three rightist groups backfired, offsetting whatever gains NAREB had managed to make. The letter of the Emergency Committee of One Million To Save Our Homes, for instance, warned that House passage would mean that "LBJ's bureaucrats will be swarming over every neighborhood in the United States—setting up Negro-White quotas, forcing homeowners to sell their property, and encouraging vicious gangs of rioters and looters to destroy neighborhoods which dare resist."

The House ignored this admonition. After there had been an early impasse in the House Rules Committee, that panel agreed to bring the Senate bill to the floor for a vote, thereby avoiding the quicksand of a Senate-House conference. On April 10—six days after Dr. King's assassination in Memphis—the House voted 250–172 to accept the Senate version without amendment. An earlier 229–195 vote had proved the most crucial ballot in permitting the final roll call. The tragedy in Memphis apparently made the difference. The next day President Johnson signed the bill into law.

Antiriot Action

The Senate, before passing the civil rights bill, had paired with it a pending measure to punish riot provocateurs. The original version offered by Senators Strom Thurmond (R) of South Carolina and Frank Lausche (D) of Ohio had made it a federal crime to undertake interstate travel or to use the mail, telephone, radio or television (all interstate facilities) with intent to incite a riot, organize one or take part in one. The Thurmond-Lausche bill noted, to the distress of Senate liberals, that if a person engaged in such a disturbance up to fifteen days after interstate travel or use of interstate facilities, that person could be charged with having committed a federal crime. Senators Thurmond and Lausche defined a riot as a public disturbance involving violence or a threat of violence when three or more persons were assembled, thus creating danger of injury to persons or property.

Vice-President Hubert Humphrey, presiding over the Senate on March 5, ruled the Lausche-Thurmond amendment non-germane. But Senate moderates, conceding the temper of the times, supported a more tightly-worded substitute drafted by Senator John Sherman Cooper (R) of Kentucky and others. Cooper argued that the Senate could not "lay out, in a statute, facts upon the basis of which a court will have to say a defendant is guilty." Senator Lausche countered that the Cooper version made it necessary "to prove what was in that traveler's mind when he crossed the state line and that is the hardest thing in the world to do." The Cooper wording also redefined a riot as "tumultuous and violent conduct," by an assemblage of at least twenty persons, that posed "grave danger" to other persons or property.

Like the Lausche-Thurmond proviso, the moderates' substitute set maximum penalties of five years imprisonment and/or $10,000 in fines. While this second version required that the accused should have crossed a state line with intent to incite a riot, it dropped mention of interstate facilities. And it specified that violence must actually have occurred before a suspect could be prosecuted.

The Senate also linked two proposals by Senator Russell B. Long (D) of Louisiana to its antiriot package. The first applied criminal penalties to those teaching others how to use firearms or demolitions in civil disorders. It also covered those who manufactured or transported guns or explosive devices knowing or intending that they be used in civil disorders. The other Long measure punished those who tried to interfere with police or firemen during a civil disorder.

The House accepted the antiriot bill as companion legislation to the civil rights bill. But while President Johnson signed the bill, Attorney General Ramsey Clark and the Justice Department refused to prosecute suspects under its provisions in 1968.

Rallying the Poor

Dr. Martin Luther King, Jr., conceived the idea of the Poor People's Campaign late in 1967. It had been planned for April 1968 by the Southern Christian Leadership Conference. The King assassination on April 4 jolted that timetable, but Rev. Ralph D. Abernathy and his aides were ready to move on Washington from poverty centers across the nation by mid-May. They planned to camp on federal property, which they tentatively renamed "the City of Hope," and to stage nonviolent demonstrations from there before Congress and federal agencies.

The campaign's national coordinator, Rev. Bernard Lafayette, told *Congressional Quarterly* that the SCLC intended "not to antagonize, not to desecrate, but to educate—to show the nation that something has got to be done right now to root out poverty." The marchers would not only lobby Congress, he said, but would "mobilize the American people" by exposing "the horrible conditions in which people live all over the country." If need be, the SCLC would resort to the tactics of civil disobedience.

"Take a traffic light," Lafayette said, borrowing an adage he attributed to Dr. King. "When the light is red, emergency vehicles such as ambulances go through without breaking the law. When we come before Congress we hope the light is green. But if the light is red, then we will have to go through some red lights."

Rev. Ralph Abernathy, SCLC's new leader, spelled out the campaign's basic demands on April 30, when he testified before the Senate subcommittee on manpower. These included "thousands of new units" of low income housing, more generous funding of model cities and rent-supplement programs, repeal of harsh welfare guidelines imposed by 1967 social security amendments, a free food stamp program, a larger school lunch program, collective bargaining rights for farm workers, and a crash food program for 256 counties pinpointed as hunger areas by a citizens' inquiry.

The burly Alabama clergyman also urged Congress to approve Senator Joseph Clark's bill to make the government the "employer of last resort," if necessary. This plan would create one million jobs in 1968 and another million during the next four years. This multi-billion dollar program had also been advanced by the leading Negro spokesman in the House, Representative John Conyers (D) of Michigan, and a group of liberal colleagues.

Another long-time civil rights strategist, Bayard Rustin, saw the Clark bill and other goals of Resurrection City (as the campsite had been renamed) as realistic demands on Congress. "The day-dreamers and utopians are not those of us who have been preparing massive Freedom Budgets and similar ideas," Rustin asserted. "They are the smugly 'practical' and myopic Philistines in Congress, the state legislatures and the city halls who thought they could sit it out. . . . The very practical choice before them and the American people is whether we shall have an authentic democratic social revolution or more tragic and futile riots that tear our nation to shreds."

Reaction in Congress

Despite steady rainfall during the first weeks of the plywood-and-plastic settlement's activity, Mr. Abernathy and the three to five thousand residents of Resurrection City refused to turn back empty-handed. They found Congress part friend, part foe. Black members such as Senator Brooke and Representative Charles C. Diggs, Jr., (D) of Michigan helped set up a liaison group of sympathetic legislators. As Diggs observed in mid-May, the 90th Congress had reversed the progressive record of the 89th Congress. The Abernathy group, he said, wanted "to arrest this trend and turn it around. . . .

"All we can do," the Detroit congressman told the press, "is show some concern with the objectives [of the campaign] and keep moving in that direction." A bi-partisan Senate-House unit, led by Senator Brooke, was formed to keep contact with campaign leaders. But other lawmakers revealed their hostility at the outset. Senate Majority Whip Russell B. Long (D) of Louisiana, for instance, referred to the demonstrators as "disciples of lawlessness and civil disorder." He said he would call for the censure of any member of Congress who favored "bending the knee" to pressure from the marchers.

Another Southern conservative, Senator John L. McClellan (D) of Arkansas, said his subcommittee had received sworn information "from within the militant movement itself" that Black radicals planned to oust Mr. Abernathy and take over his campaign once it reached Washington. Such a coup never took place. However, during the weeks in which the Poor People's Campaign remained in Resurrection City several flareups occurred, including a leadership rift between Abernathy and the fiery Mexican-American spokesman Reies Tijerino.

By late June the campaign's demands had been partially met, and many voices in Congress suggested that the time to vacate Resurrection City was near. Some congressmen, such as Representative William L. St. Onge (D) of Connecticut, advised a strategic retreat in order to ensure that the marchers' earlier gains would not be wiped out by misadventure. "The poor have presented their case," St. Onge said, "and Congress got the message. Now they should break camp and return home. If they stay, some incidents [such as an earlier tear-gas scuffle with police] may come up which would only hurt their cause." Others in the House echoed the remarks of Representative Clarence D. Long (D) of Maryland. "I wish they'd never come," he declared. "This business of petitioning one minute and threatening the next has made it terribly hard for the average person to distinguish between the people of Resurrection City and the rioters."

Such comments obviously disturbed a group of SCLC officials when they met privately on June 27 with a delegation of Negro congressmen. Among the lawmakers were Representatives Conyers and Diggs of Detroit, Representative Robert N. C. Nix (D) of Philadelphia, and Representative Augustus Hawkins (D) of Los Angeles. At the time Rev. Ralph Abernathy was serving a twenty-day jail sentence on a conviction of illegal assembly, and Rev. Andrew Young was directing the campaign in his absence. After the meeting had ended none of its participants would discuss what had transpired. The previous day, though, the Associated Press had quoted Nix as saying that the marchers should leave Washington, since "solid accomplishments" had been made. The Philadelphia Negro suggested that a legislative "task force" remain in Washington to push the campaign's long-range demands on Congress.

Another sympathetic House member, Representative Alphonzo Bell (R) of California, hinted at one of the major campaign problems—its timing. He feared that the excitable House could be goaded into cutting existing aid programs for the poor if the SCLC lost control of Resurrection City.

"We've spent in excess of $23 billion a year in aid for the poor," he reminded this reporter. "We passed a minimum-wage law and a number of education bills. But to ask us to pass this program overnight when we're fighting a war is just not realistic. I'm the last person in the world to say 'let them eat cake,' but their timing is very bad."

The Poor Depart

Finally, late in June, the Poor People's Campaign was forced to leave Resurrection City, and the caravans of marchers, led by two mules named Stennis and Eastland, headed back to the South. Though the lobbying effort fell short of its leaders' expectations, it also left Washington with a far clearer impression of the plight of the poor.

Writing in the *Afro-American*, Bayard Rustin had this to say:

> A great deal was made in the press and in the Congress of the thefts, beatings, shootings, and other activities alleged to have taken place at Resurrection City. Strangely, this is precisely one of the justifications for the existence of Resurrection City and for the Poor People's Campaign. Both dramatized before the very eyes of Congress and the nation what actually happens among people who are grounded in poverty—the acts of violence which frustration, deprivation and desperation drive them to commit. . . .
>
> The Congressmen, therefore, missed a great opportunity. Rather than throwing up their hands, condemning the conditions that existed in Resurrection City, demanding that the poor be chased out, and that the city be torn down, Congressmen should have used the opportunity to commit themselves to the spending of billions of dollars to destroy the real ghettoes, build more decent communities, and eradicate poverty.

Looking back on the actual achievements of the campaign, by far the most dramatic—passage of the omnibus housing bill—would probably have occurred even without the poor people's lobbying effort.

That measure was fashioned largely by a skilled Southern compromiser, Senator John Sparkman (D) of Alabama. The new housing law includes a provision directing the Federal Housing Administration to relax its "economic soundness" requirements for mortgage insurance to potential home owners in America's inner cities.

"We feel it's time for Uncle Sam to take the risk," one Senate source explains. "This formula is like a soft-loan procedure. FHA used to have to be assured that it could recoup any losses. We let them waive that guideline to qualify an 'acceptable risk' for a loan."

The housing statute added an amendment ensuring that the poor would be employed in the construction of low income housing—a move hailed by the Poor People's Campaign. The Johnson Administration had not sought this wording. On the other hand, the SCLC demand for an emergency job program won neither White House nor Congressional support. Congress merely renewed existing manpower programs and added funds for the JOBS program, a private subsidy training program supported by the Administration.

Another priority demand—that Congress repeal the freeze on the number of recipients of Aid to Families with Dependent Children (AFDC) and provide a mandatory work-training program for recipients—met with resistance. Congress agreed only to delay the freeze for one more year.

The Poor People's Campaign had called for higher appropriations for several programs overseen by the Department of Agriculture: school lunches, food stamps, the special milk program and the commodity distribution program. Rev. Bernard Lafayette noted that Congress granted almost $10 million above the fiscal 1968 funds for a restructured school lunch program. But, as the SCLC aide said, the lawmakers "could have gone a lot further," notably in providing free food stamps to the needy.

Congress also earmarked $1.9 billion for the antipoverty program (request: $2.2 billion) and $1.1 billion for poverty area schools (request: $1.2 billion). Mr. Lafayette found the Department of Agriculture most receptive to the marchers' demands. It had been singled out by pickets protesting its administration of its various food-aid programs. Here the most visible gains occurred. And, as the SCLC spokesman observed: "Food is more crucial to poor people than anything else."

Other Antipoverty Gains

Though the Poor People's Campaign overlooked it, the campaign's lobbying pressure may also have prompted a call by liberal House Republicans for a $40 billion crash program to aid inner city schooling. That program, which GOP congressmen, led by Representative Alphonzo Bell of California, intend to press for in 1969, would be phased over five years. The National Advisory Commission on Civil Disorders also helped inspire the Republican bill.

"It showed that all problems of poverty resulted from lack of education," Bell pointed out. "There is where the bat meets the ball. You get good jobs, good homes, all the good things the poor don't get if you have a good education."

Another hopeful sign for poor families appeared with the passage of the Federal Highway Act of 1968. That bill was enacted with a reform proviso governing the relocation aid given families displaced by urban freeways. The new law requires the states to ensure that an adequate supply of comparable replacement housing exists near a freeway corridor before the Secretary of Transportation approves a freeway project. In many Negro areas where freeways are planned (the proposed Century-Imperial Freeway in the Watts district of Los Angeles is one example), the "fair market" price falls far short of the cost of relocating a family. Under the new formula, the government agrees to pay the added cost up to $5,000. The highway statute stipulates that the replacement housing must be "decent, safe and sanitary"—a phrase defined in minute detail by the Federal Highway Administration.

Black History Commission

Congress failed to complete action in 1968 on a proposed Commission on Negro History and

Culture, although the House cleared the bill by a 262–45 vote in September. Only the rush toward adjournment kept the Senate from acting favorably on it. This proposal, sponsored by Representative James Scheuer (D) of New York and Senator Hugh Scott (R) of Pennsylvania, would create an eleven-member federal study group of experts on Negro history and culture. The group would spend one year examining all proposals "to create a better understanding and knowledge of Negro history and culture" and would report to the President and Congress on the means it deemed best to carry this out. After hearing expert testimony in 1968, Scheuer and Scott decided to refile the bill, renaming the study group the Commission on Afro-American History and Culture. Its sponsors expected Congress to act promptly on the bill in 1969.

The 91st Congress: A Preview

The experts who reviewed the 1968 election returns found themselves in rare agreement on their meaning for the 91st Congress. Republicans gained a few seats in both Senate and House, but far fewer than expected. Their gains also proved far short of the margin needed to take control of either house. This outcome would make President Richard M. Nixon the first White House occupant since Zachary Taylor to enter office with both houses of Congress in opposition hands.

The November election appeared remarkable for House incumbents especially. The national unrest that typified 1968 seemed to threaten the "ins" of both parties. Yet all but a handful who had sought reelection returned victorious. The House outlook is thus one of continued retreat from the activist liberalism which marked the 89th Congress (1965–66). Once again a coalition of Southern Democrats and conservative Republicans will hold the balance of power. This "economy bloc" (as it became known in 1967) will again seek to halt federal spending on the home front despite pressure from urban members in both parties.

While no marked shift in voting sentiment seems likely in the new Congress, one added factor should be noted. Retirements, defeat and death removed roughly nine hundred years of accumulated seniority from Congress in 1969—an amazingly high figure considering the slight House turnover. For those critical of Congress' archaic seniority system, this seemed an encouraging sign for the future.

Negro-vote strategists such as Louis Martin, a deputy chairman of the Democratic National Committee, also took heart in Black registration gains in the South since the Voting Rights Act of 1965 took effect. Figures compiled by the Southern Regional Council, for instance, show that Negroes now account for nearly 25 per cent of South Carolina's electorate, 21 per cent of Louisiana's, and almost 20 per cent of Alabama's. Georgia, Arkansas, North Carolina and Virginia also top the 15 per cent level.

Starting in 1969, Martin predicts, a reshuffling of power will occur below the Mason-Dixon line at the Congressional level. The Democratic official declares: "It means the end of the reactionary bloc in Congress." He points out that in some eighty-five House districts in the South, Negroes now represent at least 20 per cent of the electorate. In twenty-six of these districts the Black voter ratio is 35 per cent or higher.

"This is the real drama in the South," Martin says. "We're going to cut off the Southern route for people like Richard Nixon. Lyndon Johnson said when he signed the Voting Rights Act that it would 'open the door.' And now we've got to get the Negro to walk through it."

During the 1968 campaign Martin displayed two posters prominently in his minorities division office. One suggested the problem his party faced in large Northern cities. It depicted three gangster-type caricatures resembling President Johnson, Vice-President Humphrey and Chicago Mayor Richard J. Daley—and the caption: "You white goats won't get our votes." Martin countered this poster with one of his own: a handsome young Black couple with the superimposed legend "Voting is beautiful. Be beautiful—Vote." Below this, of course, appeared the Democratic ticket names "Humphrey-Muskie." Martin's organizing efforts, the disinterest shown by Mr. Nixon in wooing the Negro vote, and the racist appeal of George Wallace's campaign all combined to bring a solid Black majority into the Democratic column in 1968. It came surprisingly close to denying the Republican victor an electoral mandate.

New Black Spokesmen in Congress

At the Congressional level, a new trend developed during the 1968 elections—one favoring Negro candidates in inner city House districts. It brought three more Black congressmen to join the five incumbents. In addition, exiled Representative Adam Clayton Powell (D) of New York, former chairman of the House Committee on Education and Labor, returned to raise the Black bloc's membership to nine.

When the new House met on January 3, 1969, Powell was again challenged before swearing-in ceremonies. During the next five hours the congressmen debated his right to be seated with or without penalties. "He who is without sin in this chamber, let him cast the first stone," suggested Representative Emanuel Celler (D) of New York, leader of the pro-Powell forces. But when the venerable Brooklyn lawyer moved to seat Powell without some form of punishment, the House voted his resolution down by a margin of nearly three to one. Eventually a compromise, agreed to by Powell, was proposed by Representative Clark MacGregor (R) of Minnesota and carried over the protests of the implacable anti-Powell bloc. It seated Powell, reaffirmed his loss of seniority and fined him $25,000 (to be deducted in monthly payments from his House salary). The fine was imposed in order to restore $40,000 in public funds which Powell allegedly misspent before his ouster in 1967.

Since House Democrats had stripped him of his seniority in their 1966 caucus, before the entire House had refused to seat him for the 90th Congress, the Harlem clergyman began his thirteenth House term with only freshman status. Thus Representative William Dawson, aging Democratic baron of Chicago's Black South Side ghetto, remained the most powerful Negro House member. Dawson, chairman of the House Committee on Government Operations, begins his fourteenth term in January 1969.

Several other Black incumbents gained new stature, however, because of changes in the House hierarchy. Representative Charles C. Diggs, Jr., (D) of Michigan, for example, took over the chairmanship of the Foreign Affairs subcommittee on Africa when its most senior Democrat lost a party primary. Diggs starts his eighth term in 1969. Representative John Conyers, Jr., another Detroit Democrat, also moved up five party notches on the House Judiciary Committee owing to retirements and election casualties. And Representative Robert N. C. Nix (D) of Pennsylvania, chairman of the postal operations subcommittee, moved up to third-ranking status on Diggs' panel on Africa.

The three new Negro members—Representatives Shirley Chisholm (D) of New York, William Clay (D) of Missouri and Louis Stokes (D) of Ohio—all owed their victories to reapportioned House districts within their states. Each defeated a Black Republican after winning a free-for-all party primary. In the only contest in which a Democratic win had not been a foregone conclusion, "Fighting Shirley" Chisholm, a state assemblywoman, bested James Farmer, one-time chairman of CORE, who had won both the Republican and Liberal Party endorsements. Mrs. Chisholm, who will represent Brooklyn's Bedford-Stuyvesant area, thus became the first Black woman to sit in Congress.

Louis Stokes, older brother of Cleveland Mayor Carl Stokes, will speak for that city's restive Hough district—an electorate formerly divided between two white congressmen. William Clay, a Steamfitters Union official in his mid-thirties, inherits a newly mapped, largely Negro district. This militant civil rights spokesman replaces Representative Frank Karsten, a white Democrat who chose to retire rather than fight for the new seat.

When *Tuesday* magazine contacted Louis Martin after the 1968 election, he forecast that the Chisholm, Clay and Stokes triumphs were only the beginning of a trend toward Black spokesmen for the inner cities. He said he expects four more Negro members in the House by 1970 and as many as twenty-five more by 1974. His short-range target districts are in Baltimore, Chicago, Gary, Los Angeles, Newark, New York, Oakland and Philadelphia. Over the long haul, though, Martin foresees greater inroads in the South—some of them in Atlanta, Memphis, New Orleans and Richmond.

WHY DO I HAVE TO BE YOUR HANG-UP?
INJUSTICE
RACISTS

The Law—1968

James M. Nabrit, III

IN 1968, more often than ever before, Black Americans turned to courts across the country to assert their rights and to complain of violations of their civil rights. No precise count of such cases can be made, but the trend is unmistakable. There are more civil rights laws, more lawyers, and more ordinary people who believe that the law may do them some good in dealing with their problems. Indeed, the vast increase in the number of cases in which Negro citizens go to court to complain about racial discrimination is a sort of quiet revolution which has crept up on us during the last decade.

So much of this has come to be taken for granted that it is not easy to recall how truly dismal the American legal system was for Black people twenty or even ten years ago. You understand the main point about that era if you know that through one region of the country a white man could kill a Black man and in actual fact the "law" would do nothing about it. There were no Black jurors or judges or prosecutors or elected officials of any kind in the same vast region. Twenty years ago, you should recall that more than half the states had some sort of segregation laws, that some states had elaborate codes requiring segregation from the cradle to the grave, and that all of this was thought to be perfectly "legal" and "Constitutional." Remember, too, that Southern Negroes could not vote in elections, that lynching was a problem of great magnitude and that Negro schools, hospitals, parks and any other facilities you can think of were separate and unequal.

It is surely an understatement to say that we are not yet over all these problems and conditions. But it is also clear that we have come a long distance. It is just as much an error to fail to recognize real gains as it is to confuse the merely symbolic victories with practical progress.

On the level of legal theory, there is no question but that we have come far from a system in which the laws approved and required discrimination to a system in which the laws condemn and punish discrimination. Black schoolboys of my generation never had the foggiest notion that there was anything "illegal" about segregation or discrimination. Today, every student of high school civics ought to know that our law forbids any racial segregation or discrimination by federal, state or local governments and many forms of discrimination by private people as well. Increasingly the message is getting across, and the time is fast coming when schoolboys will also know that anyone who discriminates racially is likely to find himself actually in court trying to explain his conduct.

The progress must not be exaggerated or overstated. But anyone who is skeptical of this legal progress should read the monthly log of cases during 1968 which constitutes the second section of this article. For a start, consider one or two striking cases. On the next to last day of 1967 the highest court of Texas ruled that a Negro whose dinner plate was snatched from his hands by a discriminatory restaurant manager could get money damages for the mental anguish he suffered even though there was no physical injury. To be sure, our legal history has not often reflected much of this kind of solicitude for Negroes' feelings. But consider next the Mississippi jury which in November awarded more than a million dollars in damages against Klansmen who murdered an elderly Negro. Or consider the fact that in March a Black sheriff arrested the white police chief of Notasulga, Alabama, for police brutality. These scattered episodes, mentioned for their novelty, nevertheless reflect the fact that change is afoot in the law of the land.

The year was not without its legal absurdities, of course. A part of the early civil rights legal lore that I learned from a distinguished—but, for these purposes, nameless—lawyer friend was the legend of the Negro youth, arrested for merely leering at a white girl, who was charged with the newly invented crime of "highway looking and attempting to want." Sadly life follows humor. In a little-known Mississippi case, a Negro youth was sentenced to six months' imprisonment for shouting to a fifteen-year-old white girl who was at a picnic in a federal reservation: "Come here baby and let me sock it to you." As 1968 ended the Department of Justice asked the United States Supreme Court (believe it or not, it reached that level) to drop charges. The absurdity of such a case in our highest court cannot escape anyone who knows that the phrase "sock it to me" was uttered on a nationwide television comedy program by countless people, including Richard M. Nixon during his campaign. One can only wonder in 1969 whether the incoming Attorney General will exercise the same kind of judgment to bring cases such as the "sock it to me" one to an end. But remember, too, that Emmett Till was lynched for a "wolf whistle" at a Mississippi white girl not so many years ago. So times have changed.

But the really meaningful developments in civil rights law are often hidden away in duller, less understandable legal battles. It ought to be pointed out that the popular rhetoric about civil rights campaigns having moved "from the courts to the streets" is all wrong. It hasn't happened. To be sure, there has been a great deal of civil rights campaigning in the streets and elsewhere, and it has played a major role in the rights struggle since 1960. But none of this has stopped or even slowed the pace in the courts, where civil rights battles have increased tremendously during the same period. Civil rights cases in the courts have indeed become a kind of permanent part of our national scene. It is now a commonplace and routine public event when Black people go to court to complain of discrimination. And this change in the actual use of the courts is as important as the great theoretical changes in the substance of the laws. The theory changes would be virtually meaningless without citizens who will go to the courts to assert their rights and civil rights lawyers who will represent them.

For nearly thirty years the majority of civil rights cases in the country have been handled by the NAACP Legal Defense and Educational Fund, Inc. (LDF) and its staff lawyers and cooperating lawyers. This was true a decade ago when the LDF legal staff consisted of Thurgood Marshall and five assistants; it was still true in 1968 when the LDF had twenty-five full-time staff lawyers and several hundred cooperating lawyers on call for occasional work. In 1958 Thurgood Marshall spent about $295,000 which was contributed by the public to support the program. Ten years later his successor Jack Greenberg spent over $2.8 million, given by the public for the LDF's diversified legal program.

In 1958 the LDF had a near-monopoly on civil rights cases. While LDF is still the largest such organization, there were numerous other groups with civil rights law programs in 1968, for example, the national office of the NAACP (until the widely publicized mass staff resignations), the Lawyers Constitutional Defense Committee (LCDC), the Lawyers Committee for Civil Rights under Law, the American Civil Liberties Union (ACLU) and others. A major factor, too, in 1968, was the U.S. Department of Justice, which was engaged in protecting civil rights by filing cases authorized by the civil rights laws that were passed in recent years. A decade earlier such federal government civil rights involvement was very slight.

A review of 1968 leaves this observer with the strong impression that the year produced numerous events of general interest and importance, but that there was no single historic change which profoundly altered the legal status of Negroes. There was one development of enormous promise, but it is too soon to know if it will have lasting significance. I refer to the fact that 1968 was the first year in which no person in the United States was killed under a death sentence issued by a court. Over the years, Black people have suffered disproportionately from the death penalty. Since 1930, exactly 2,066 Negroes have been put to death under rulings of state and federal courts. Negroes constituted 53.5 per cent of the total of 3,859 prisoners executed. The death penalty has reflected a sanctioning of violence by society. Its use in such a high ratio against Black men is one reflection of the deep racism in our land.

Courts are still handing out frequent death sentences. In 1967 an average of one Black man was added to a prison death row every eight days. At the start of 1968, 435 men were on death row and 238 of the condemned were Negroes. Many new prisoners were given capital sentences during 1968. But, increasingly, the executions are not being carried out. There was but one execution in 1966 and there were two in 1967. These figures compare with a yearly average of 166 executions from 1930 to 1939, 128 from 1940 to 1949, and 72 from 1950 to 1959.

Many factors may explain the trend against actual use of the death penalty. For one thing, public opinion is more and more against capital punishment. But the first really drastic reduction in executions followed swiftly upon a 1963 Supreme Court decision (*Fay* v. *Noia*) liberalizing the federal writ of habeas corpus as a way of reviewing state court actions. There have been no executions at all since June 2, 1967. It was in that month that the NAACP Legal Defense and Educational Fund expanded a campaign against racial discrimination in death sentences for rape into its present nationwide campaign to prevent executions of all prisoners, Black and white. The Legal Defense Fund team fighting the death penalty, which has been led by Professor Anthony G. Amsterdam of the University of Pennsylvania School of Law, has been representing almost half of the four-hundred-plus death row prisoners in the United States.

During 1968 the Supreme Court made it more difficult for prosecutors to obtain death verdicts by ruling that jurors opposed to the death penalty could no longer be automatically excluded from capital cases. The "death-stacked" jury has been thought by many lawyers to produce a significant bias resulting in many more death penalties than would be approved by a true cross section of society. Late in 1968 the Supreme Court announced that it would review several claims being raised in the Legal Defense Fund national campaign, including arguments that the death penalty is forbidden by the Constitutional ban on "cruel and unusual" punishment. The Court also agreed to hear LDF arguments that it is unconstitutional to leave the life or death decision to juries which are given detailed instructions by judges on all sorts of legal issues but are given no instructions or standards to use in deciding whether to impose death or some lesser penalty. The Court will also review an LDF claim that capital trials are rendered unfair by the commonly used procedure in which the defendant's guilt or innocence and the degree of punishment are determined simultaneously by a single jury.

It is far too early to tell whether the LDF campaign will really lead to the abolition of the death penalty. No state legislatures have acted to abolish capital punishment since 1965, but the American Civil Liberties Union and others are continuing legislative campaigns. At present the death penalty is outlawed in nine states and almost totally abolished in another four. If the death penalty can be banned, it will be an event of enormous social psychological significance. The significance for Black people will be particularly pointed. Abolition of capital punishment will carry the general message that the legal system really does respect life and condemn violence. And abolition will convey to Black people the unmistakable message that the legal system does respect their right to life. It is not too much to hope that the impact of abolition may equal or surpass the impact of the end of lynchings as a major social phenomenon. For, as Dr. Martin Luther King, Jr., has said to us, the process of liberating Negroes from a psychology of fear is of the utmost importance.

The year brought numerous confrontations between Black militants and the law. There were highly publicized criminal prosecutions of H. Rap Brown, Huey Newton, Eldridge Cleaver, Herman Ferguson, William Epton, LeRoi Jones and others. We touch on some of these events in the monthly log which follows.

One trial which would have commanded the attention of the whole nation never took place in 1968. As the year ended, James Earl Ray, a white man and the accused assassin of Dr. Martin Luther King, Jr., remained in a Memphis jail awaiting a trial which was repeatedly postponed at the request of defense lawyers.

In June Justice Thurgood Marshall, the first Black man to sit on the United States Supreme Court, completed his first term as associate justice. Justice Marshall was the author of ten opinions for the Court, including antitrust cases; an obscenity case involving the movie *Viva Maria*; a railroad rate case; the case of a teacher discharged for a letter to an editor; an opinion involving the validity of prosecuting alcoholics for public drunkenness; a case involving the right to be confronted by an accuser; a case about the right to counsel in probation revocation proceedings; a case concerning the right of unions to picket in a shopping center. An unusual feature of Justice Marshall's performance was that he voted in dissent on only one occasion (in a tax case), the lowest rate of dissents of any of the justices. The *Harvard Law Review* calculated that Justice Marshall voted in agreement with Chief Justice Warren in 89 per cent of the cases in which they both participated. The most frequent dissenter was Justice John Harlan, regarded as a conservative on many issues, who dissented seventy-seven times.

The following monthly log, compiled in almanac fashion, should enable the reader to form his own impression of legal events in 1968. I have offered liberal doses of my own opinions, but the main effort has been to cram the log with facts. Obviously, other compilers would have been fascinated by other cases. But I trust you will agree that with regard to the law as it affected Black Americans, 1968 was an exciting year from January to December.

MONTHLY LOG FOR 1968

January

Leading case

January 4: Federal Judge John Butzner, in Richmond, Virginia, ruled in favor of a group of Negro employees of the Philip Morris Tobacco Company, who sued the company and Local 203 of the Tobacco Workers International Union under the fair employment section of the federal Civil Rights Act of 1964. The decision related to the advancement rights of Negro employees trapped in lower paying jobs by seniority arrangements. The court ruled that Black workers could transfer to higher paying jobs in parts of the factory previously closed to them without losing their accrued seniority. The decision was hailed by many persons knowledgeable in the fair employment field because of the difficulty in desegregating seniority systems. A view of the solution to the seniority problem which had been advocated by the NAACP Legal Defense Fund was accepted by the court in this precedent-setting case, which was litigated for several years by a team that included attorneys S. W. Tucker and Henry L. Marsh, III, of Richmond, and several LDF staff lawyers.

Other events

January 4: LeRoi Jones, the Black writer, was sentenced to two-and-a-half to three years in the New Jersey penitentiary and fined $1,000 for possessing two pistols during the 1967 Newark riots. Later in the year Jones won a ruling on appeal giving him a new trial.

January 4: A federal judge ordered a new school board election in Madison Parish, Louisiana, because election officials had made absentee ballots available to whites on a more favored basis than to Blacks.

January 11: Retired federal Judge J. Waties Waring died at the age of eighty-seven. Waring's rulings in favor of Negro rights included a 1947 ruling outlawing the South Carolina white primary, and a 1951 dissent holding school segregation laws unconstitutional (three years before the famous 1954 Supreme Court ruling upheld his viewpoint in the Clarendon County, South Carolina, school case). About two hundred Negroes paid tribute at his funeral in Charleston, which was attended by only about a dozen whites.

January 15: The United States Supreme Court upheld a decision throwing out Louisiana's tuition grants to private school students as a device to preserve school segregation. The Court also agreed to hear arguments in school segregation appeals by Negro parents in Tennessee and Arkansas cases, along with a previously accepted case from Virginia. Once again the Court refused to hear arguments by opponents of a Northern effort to correct racial imbalance in public schools, rejecting the appeal of a white group attacking a Massachusetts integration law in Boston.

January 16: Federal Judge Frank Johnson ruled that police in Autauga County, Alabama, had violated the civil rights of Negro citizens associated with the Student Nonviolent Coordinating Committee and a local group by inflicting summary punishment, interfering with lawful assembly, and failing to provide police protection. The judge also found that the Negroes held meetings at which violent protest was advocated. The court order prohibited unlawful activities by both the police and the Negroes.

January 22: The United States Supreme Court refused to hear the appeal of William Epton, thirty-six-year-old Negro leader of the Progressive Labor Movement, convicted of anarchy and conspiring to riot because of events during the 1964 Harlem riots.

January 24: By a vote of five to two, the Florida supreme court followed a 1967 Supreme Court ruling in a Virginia case and struck down Florida's 136-year-old law prohibiting interracial marriages.

January 29: The United States Supreme Court refused to hear the appeal of a Negro citizens group in Nashville, who complained that a federal highway route arbitrarily discriminated against Negroes by destroying their business community, and that the law's requirement of community hearings had not been obeyed.

February

Various events

February 5: A federal appeals court ruled in favor of a group arrested in the summer of 1964 in the course of integrating a public library in Hattiesburg, Mississippi.

February 7: Ernest Whippler, sentenced to death for murder in Macon, Georgia, in 1960, won a new trial in a federal court of appeals ruling that Negroes were excluded from the county jury lists. Negroes were one-fourth of the county taxpayers, but were only 2 per cent of those on the jury list. Whippler was represented on appeal by LDF lawyer Howard Moore, Jr., of Atlanta.

February 8: The United States Court of Appeals for the Fourth Circuit ruled that several Black schoolteachers in Asheboro, North Carolina, were denied their rights when they were not rehired because their pupils had transferred to white schools under a desegregation plan. The suit was an effort of the North Carolina Teachers Association, the National Education Association and LDF lawyers led by Julius LeVonne Chambers, of Charlotte. LDF cooperating attorney Avon N. Williams, of Nashville, was successful in two similar appeals on behalf of Negro teachers in Lincoln and Franklin Counties in Tennessee; these were decided on *February 19* and *February 20* by the United States Court of Appeals for the Sixth Circuit.

February 19: The supreme court of Nassau County, New York, held that a Black high school student from the South, who was selected under the STEP program to live with a New York family and attend a Northern school, was entitled to attend school free of tuition in a district which had refused to admit the child.

February 23: The Justice Department obtained an integration order from a federal court against an Orangeburg, South Carolina, bowling alley which had been the target of numerous demonstrations. Three Black youths had been killed by shots fired by state policemen in violence following earlier efforts to integrate the bowling alley.

February 28: Harlem Congressman Adam Clayton Powell lost an appeal contesting his exclusion from Congress. He announced plans to seek United States Supreme Court review of the matter.

March

Leading cases

March 7: A decade-long battle to win admission for Negro boys to Girard College in Philadelphia was climaxed when a federal court of appeals ordered the school integrated. Later in the year the United States Supreme Court refused to hear the school's appeal, thus ending the case. The school was established under the early-nineteenth-century will of a wealthy Philadelphian, Stephen Girard, who left money to run a school for "poor white male orphans." William T. Coleman, of Philadelphia, represented the Black students.

March 11: The Supreme Court ruled for the first time that racial segregation in jails and prisons was unconstitutional. The Court in a one-paragraph unanimous ruling rejected Alabama's argument that inmates can be segregated because they forfeit their rights when found guilty of crimes. The court affirmed a lower court order for desegregating all Alabama jails and prisons, which had been won by attorney Charles Morgan, Jr., of the American Civil Liberties Union.

March 18: The Supreme Court interpreted the 1964 Civil Rights Act to require proprietors who discriminate in public accommodations to pay lawyers' fees for Negroes who take their cases to court and win. The suit, against a South Carolina drive-in restaurant chain, was argued by Jack Greenberg, director-counsel of the NAACP Legal Defense and Educational Fund.

Other events

March 1: A federal court held unconstitutional two Illinois laws as restrictions on free speech and assembly in a suit by a group of Negroes arrested in 1967 demonstrations.

March 5: A federal court enjoined Milwaukee officials from submitting to the electorate a proposed resolution to restrict open housing.

March 7: The Department of Justice lost a trial court decision in a suit complaining of discrimination by the Sheet Metal and the Electrical Workers Unions in St. Louis.

March 8: A group of Grambling College students, expelled for campus demonstrations, went to a federal court seeking reinstatement and obtained mixed results. Those found to have blocked college buildings lost their case, but others who had not blocked buildings won reinstatement.

March 11: The United States Court of Appeals for the Fifth Circuit heard arguments in a highly important group of fair employment cases involving procedures under the 1964 Civil Rights Act.

March 12: The fifth appeal involving the Mobile, Alabama, school desegregation plan was won by LDF and Department of Justice lawyers. Southern school desegregation cases are often seemingly endless successions of appeals and rehearings in court after court. Mobile, with the state's largest school system, fits the pattern. The appellate court found only 2 per cent of Black children in integrated schools and ordered a better desegregation plan to be prepared.

March 14: The NAACP Legal Defense and Educational Fund won a summary reversal of a Dougherty County, Georgia, school desegregation order which did not meet current requirements of the United States Court of Appeals for the Fifth Circuit.

March 15: An all-white jury in a state court in Hattiesburg, Mississippi, convicted Cecil Sessum of murdering Negro leader Vernon Dahmer in 1966. Billy Roy Pitts pleaded guilty to the same crime and turned "state's evidence." Later, on *March 27,* a federal grand jury indicted sixteen men for conspiracy in the Dahmer case, including Klan leader Sam H. Bowers.

March 21: An injunction order requiring further school desegregation steps was issued against the Anson County, North Carolina, board of education.

March 26: The Justice Department won an employment discrimination case against the United Papermakers and Paperworkers Union and Crown Zellerbach Corporation.

March 27: The LDF lost an effort in the Fifth Circuit to speed up faculty desegregation in four Louisiana parishes. The cases were sent back to lower courts.

March 27: Two Chicago demonstrators arrested in a "tent-in" lost an effort in a federal court to block state court trials of criminal charges against them.

April

Leading event

April 11: A national open housing law was enacted by Congress and was approved by President Johnson seven days after Dr. Martin Luther King, Jr., was shot to death in Memphis. When Dr. King had risked his life in open housing marches in Chicago two years earlier, he had had his eyes on a national victory for open housing, not just a local campaign. In the days of nationwide grief which followed his death, the Civil Rights Act of 1968 was enacted. The open housing provision prohibits discrimination in the sale or rental of 80 per cent or more of the nation's housing by 1970. It also includes federal criminal penalties ranging up to life imprisonment for violent attacks on persons for exercising civil rights such as voting, attending schools and seeking jobs. The law also contains an anti-riot measure to permit federal crackdown on persons crossing state lines to instigate riots.

Other events

April 1: United States Attorney General Ramsey Clark, in a rare personal court appearance, argued in the Supreme Court that an 1866 civil rights law should be enforced as a federal fair housing law although it had lain dormant for more than a century.

April 1: The Michigan supreme court held that the state's constitution and common law gave Negroes a civil right to fair housing practices.

April 1: A three-judge federal court ordered Alabama's separate athletic associations for white and Black schools merged and operated without racial discrimination.

April 3: A federal court approved a free-choice school desegregation plan for the Elloree, South Carolina, school district over the Justice Department's objections that the plan was inadequate.

April 3: After five years on Alabama's death row, Johnny ("Big Time") Coleman, a thirty-eight-year-old Negro, walked out of court a free man. Michael Meltsner of the LDF won Coleman's case in the United States Supreme Court both times, because Negroes were kept off the jury list in Greene County. On Coleman's second trial before an all-Negro jury, LDF cooperating lawyer Peter Hall won a not guilty verdict for Coleman in the slaying of white mechanic J. D. ("Screwdriver") Johnson. Shortly thereafter, Johnny Coleman died of natural causes.

April 8: The Supreme Court ruled that a Georgia court was wrong in dismissing criminal charges against white hoodlums charged with conspiring to beat up Negroes who patronized a white restaurant.

April 8: The federal court of appeals in Richmond upheld a ruling obtained by LDF attorney J. LeVonne Chambers in a Franklin County, North Carolina, school desegregation case. Chambers won a ruling that the atmosphere of Ku Klux Klan terror surrounding Negroes who sent their children to white schools under a freedom of choice plan required that the whole plan be thrown out in favor of one consolidating white and Black schools.

April 8: LDF attorney Norman C. Amaker won an amusement park discrimination case from an unusual fourteen-judge panel of the United States Court of Appeals for the Fifth Circuit. A nine to five majority enjoined discrimination at the Fun Fair Park in Baton Rouge, after nine-year-old Denise Miller had been turned away from a skating rink in tears because the park excluded Negroes.

April 22: A Mississippi law prohibiting picketing which blocks county courthouse entrances was upheld in a seven to two ruling of the United States Supreme Court. The law was challenged by a group of Negroes arrested in April 1964 for picketing at the Hattiesburg courthouse. Justices Fortas and Douglas dissented.

May

Leading case

May 27: The United States Supreme Court issued one of the few major pronouncements on the subject of school desegregation since the famous May 17, 1954, ruling. Justice Brennan wrote for a unanimous Court that school boards must come forward with a desegregation plan "that promises realistically to work, and promises realistically to work now." The Court ruled that freedom of choice plans which had been adopted in an estimated 1,300 Southern school districts were insufficient unless they actually converted the schools "to a unitary system in which racial discrimination would be eliminated root and branch." The opinion was hailed by Jack Greenberg of the NAACP Legal Defense and Educational Fund, which brought the three cases, from New Kent County, Virginia, Gould, Arkansas, and Jackson, Tennessee. Georgia's segregationist Governor Lester Maddox responded to the above ruling by ordering flags on state property flown at half-mast, and predicted "assaults, rapes, burnings, deaths and violence in our public schools."

Other events

May 3: A federal jury indicted three Detroit policemen on civil rights charges growing out of the killing of three Negro teen-agers in the Algiers Motel during the Detroit riots in July 1967.

May 6: Heavyweight professional boxing champion Muhammad Ali lost an appeal of a five-year federal prison term to which he was sentenced for refusing induction into the Army. A request for United States Supreme Court review was planned by Muhammad Ali's lawyers.

May 8: A federal appeals court affirmed a ruling requiring integration of the Louisiana High School Athletic Association in a suit brought by St. Augustine High School of New Orleans.

May 20: Gary Duncan, a Negro in Plaquemines Parish, Louisiana, was the party in a major

Supreme Court ruling that the Constitution guarantees the right to a jury trial in all criminal cases involving the risk of serious penalties. Duncan's troubles grew out of a school desegregation attempt by two of his cousins, with a resultant alleged altercation in the south Louisiana parish, which is known as the political stronghold of militant segregationist Leander Perez. Duncan's LCDC lawyer, Richard Sobol, got into difficulty with the parish authorities too, but eventually prevailed as reported in our July section.

May 22: H. Rap Brown, twenty-four-year-old Black power advocate and chairman of the Student Nonviolent Coordinating Committee, was sentenced to five years in a federal prison and fined $2,000 for violating a federal firearms law. A jury which included three Negro women returned the verdict, and federal Judge Lansing Mitchell imposed the maximum sentence in New Orleans. Brown was accused of transporting a .30 caliber carbine on an airline trip while under indictment in Maryland. He filed an appeal and was released on bail.

May 24: A court of appeals rejected the appeal of a New Orleans bowling alley operator from an order to admit Negroes.

May 29: A band of demonstrators from the Poor People's Campaign protested a United States Supreme Court decision on Indian fishing rights in the state of Washington. A group shouting "We want justice," banged on the closed bronze doors of the high court, several basement windows were broken by stones and three persons were arrested in a scuffle with police.

May 29: The Illinois supreme court reversed one of its recent decisions and held that the state's Armstrong Act, which requires school boards to eliminate racial imbalance, was valid.

May 30: A court of appeals rejected the challenge of Houston Negroes to their school board's construction plans.

May 31: The LDF won two separate school segregation appeals, involving the Alabama Institute for the Deaf and Blind at Talladega and the public school system of Norfolk, Virginia.

June

Leading events

June 5: Senator Robert F. Kennedy was shot by an assassin in Los Angeles. He died the next day. Sirhan Bishara Sirhan, a Jordanian immigrant, was arrested and charged with the murder. During his career as United States Attorney General, Senator from New York, and, briefly, Presidential candidate, Robert Kennedy had been a vigorous supporter of civil rights laws.

June 8: James Earl Ray, accused assassin of Dr. Martin Luther King, Jr., was arrested at London's Heathrow Airport.

June 17: The United States Supreme Court held that a law passed in 1866, which had been partially dormant for a century, prohibits all discrimination against Negroes in the sale or rental of property. Thus the 1866 law's scope surpassed even the 1968 federal fair housing law enacted in April.

Other events

June 1: Elbert Parr Tuttle, of Atlanta, Georgia, judge (and long-time chief judge) of the United States Court of Appeals for the Fifth Circuit, retired. Judge Tuttle was widely regarded as a jurist who vigorously enforced civil rights laws in the six Deep South states covered by his court.

June 3: The Supreme Court agreed to hear the appeal of Dick Gregory, Negro comedian and civil rights activist, from a Chicago conviction for a demonstration near Mayor Daley's home.

June 3: A federal court of appeals announced a region-wide objective of complete faculty desegregation in all public schools by the 1970–71 school year; the court enforced a speeded program to that end in three Alabama districts.

June 7: The United States Court of Appeals, Fourth Circuit, in an LDF-sponsored suit, held that the Raleigh, North Carolina, YMCA violated the Civil Rights Act of 1964 by excluding Negroes from recreational facilities.

June 7: A federal appeals court held that Black citizens groups in Norwalk, Connecticut, were entitled to a hearing on their claims that a federal urban renewal project violated their rights.

June 10: The Supreme Court agreed to rule on an LDF appeal involving the 1965 Voting Rights Act, in a case arising out of the unsuccessful 1966 Congressional campaign of Black lawyer S. W. Tucker in "southside" Virginia.

June 15: Two Negroes, Herman B. Ferguson, forty-six-year-old suspended public school assistant principal, and twenty-two-year-old Arthur Harris, were convicted in a New York City court of conspiring to kill Roy Wilkins, executive director of the NAACP, and Whitney Young, Jr., executive director of the Urban League.

June 17: The United States Supreme Court sent back to Virginia's courts for reconsideration the case of a Negro Agriculture Department official denied use of a community swimming pool membership which he had leased with his suburban home in northern Virginia.

June 17: The Supreme Court knocked out Alabama's "substitute father" regulation, which had been used to deny welfare aid to children of women with "a man in the house."

June 17: A three-judge district court ruled out Alabama laws denying teacher tenure in counties with large Black populations as racially motivated.

June 21: A three-judge court upheld Alabama's Unlawful Assembly Law, dismissing a suit by a group of Prattville Negroes.

June 24: The Fifth Circuit of the United States Court of Appeals held that Negro physicians must be admitted to practice in the Mobile, Alabama, county hospital.

June 26: The Fifth Circuit held that a case brought by the LDF for low-income tenants in a Talladega, Alabama, public housing project, challenging the eviction of unmarried mothers, should not have been dismissed.

June 27: The Federal Communications Commission ruled (with two dissents) that TV station WLBT in Jackson, Mississippi, was entitled to a license renewal because opponents had failed to prove that the station actively promoted segregationist views and excluded Negro participation.

July

Various events

July 5: The Equal Employment Opportunity Commission won a court of appeals ruling upholding its right to inspect the records of a firm charged with employment discrimination.

July 8: Federal district Judge Julius Hoffman ruled that a suburban school district near Chicago had an affirmative duty to eradicate segregation. The suit, in South Holland, Illinois, was one of the first Northern school desegregation cases brought by the Justice Department.

July 11: The court of appeals in St. Louis rejected the argument of the LDF that there had been racial discrimination in death penalties in Arkansas rape cases against Negro men charged with raping white women.

July 11: A New York appellate court upheld the state law against housing discrimination, which had been challenged as unconstitutional.

July 12: A. W. Richberg tried to sidestep the civil rights laws by calling his cafe, on U.S. Highway 11, in Enterprise, Mississippi, a private club for whites only. The Fifth Circuit Court of Appeals ordered the cafe (called a "rusty spoon" by *Time* magazine) integrated, and dismissed Richberg's private club bylaws as "transparently meretricious."

July 16: In a Lawyers Constitutional Defense Committee-supported suit against the Crown Zellerbach Corporation and two local unions, at Bogalusa, Louisiana, the Fifth Circuit ruled that a lower court had erred in ruling that the case could not be brought as a class suit in behalf of all Negro employees at the plant.

July 19: A federal judge halted construction on a project to enlarge a Negro school in Autauga County, Alabama, saying that the project would work to preserve segregation.

July 22: A three-judge federal court in Louisiana ruled that Plaquemines Parish officials were prosecuting Richard B. Sobol for practicing law without a license only because Sobol was "a civil rights lawyer forcefully representing a Negro." Dick Sobol, a successful Washington, D.C., lawyer, went South to help the civil rights movement. Like other out-of-state lawyers, he handled cases in association with local lawyers, and did so with considerable success. After he had appeared in court four times in defense of Gary Duncan (see May report) Sobol was suddenly arrested. Civil rights lawyers groups and the Justice Department rallied to his defense and successfully blocked the harassment prosecution.

July 23: The LDF won an appeal in the Fifth Circuit establishing the right of Black prisoners to subscribe to Negro magazines and newspapers. The plaintiff, a prisoner in the Florida State Prison, had not been allowed to subscribe to the *Amsterdam News* and the *Pittsburgh Courier*, and *Ebony, Tan* and *Sepia* magazines, and the approved list for the prison contained no Negro publications.

July 23: LDF lawyers representing the Poor People's Campaign won an acquittal for Hosea Williams, city manager of Resurrection City, in a Washington court, where he had been charged with failing to leave the camp grounds when the camp was disbanded by the government.

July 24: Federal Judge Noel Fox temporarily enjoined the city of Lansing, Michigan, from holding a referendum to prevent construction of low-income housing in a white neighborhood. The suit, which was brought by attorneys Michael Davidson of LDF and William Goodman and Paul Rosen of Detroit, complained of discrimination against both Negroes and Mexican Americans.

July 24: The Fifth Circuit ordered the release of L. C. McGarrah from the Georgia State Prison. In 1955 McGarrah had been sentenced, without having had a lawyer, to seventy years in prison. Years later, from his prison cell, he had written the LDF. After numerous hearings and two appeals, McGarrah's release was won by attorney C. B. King of Albany, Georgia, and LDF staff attorney Charles Ralston.

July 24: Federal Judge Frank Johnson held as unlawful a change in voting procedure designed by the Democratic Party in Barbour County, Alabama, to discriminate against Negroes.

July 24: A federal appeals court in Philadelphia rejected an effort by the International Brotherhood of Electrical Workers, Local 5, to stop an investigation by the Equal Employment Opportunities Commission.

July 26: A three-judge federal court held it was sufficient for Alabama state colleges to open their doors to all races and that they had no duty to arrange construction of new colleges so as to maximize desegregation. Later in the year the LDF appealed the case to the United States Supreme Court.

July 26: Chief Judge Keady of the federal court for the northern district of Mississippi ruled that the Quitman County school board's construction plan was designed to promote segregation and therefore violated the Constitutional rights of Negro children.

July 31: The Georgia State Employment Agency and the LDF announced the out-of-court settlement of an employment discrimination suit brought by Robert Anthony against the state agency. The agency agreed to numerous stipulations to promote equal employment opportunities.

August

Various events

August 1: Twelve Negro policemen in St. Petersburg, Florida, won a ruling from the Fifth Circuit Court of Appeals barring the city police department from limiting Black officers to patrolling Negro areas of the city. The case was argued for the policemen by Leroy D. Clark of the LDF.

August 1: A three-judge panel of the Fifth Circuit partially set aside a faculty desegregation order by the district court for the Montgomery County, Alabama, public schools. The court objected to certain minimum racial quotas for integration set by the lower court. Later in the year a petition for rehearing by the full court lost by a tie vote of six to six. The case was then taken to the United States Supreme Court.

August 5: Three federal judges rejected the complaint of Negro citizens about discrimination in selection of jurors and school board members in Taliaferro County, Georgia.

August 5: Rev. Richard Lawrence, Chicago civil rights activist, won a federal court order blocking the Chicago district attorney from prosecuting charges growing out of a demonstration at Chicago's city hall over urban renewal policies.

August 8: Federal Judge E. Gordon West, in Baton Rouge, dismissed a fair employment law case brought by Negroes against the Kaiser Aluminum and Chemical Company.

August 13: Federal Judge Frank Johnson enjoined the Ku Klux Klan from interfering with Negroes attending white schools in Crenshaw County, Alabama. During the trial, G. T. Miller, a former Klansman, stunned the courtroom by admitting to shooting two Negro men and being acquitted by an all-white jury in the 1920's. In recent years Miller, who testified against the Klan, has been working with civil rights leaders and has been helping Negroes to get jobs.

August 16: A federal court blocked an effort by Gaston County, North Carolina, to reinstate literacy tests for voting; the court reasoned that such tests were inherently discriminatory because of educational discrimination against Negroes.

August 20: A federal court ordered further school desegregation in Tangipahoa Parish, Louisiana.

August 23: A federal court in Nashville ruled that the state's higher education officials had a duty to plan desegregation of the higher education system and to take steps beyond a mere open-door policy.

August 29: The Fifth Circuit ruled that a trial court should not have dismissed the fair employment suit of a Texas Negro merely because after he had sued he had obtained a requested promotion; the circuit ruled that the court should have reached a decision on his claim of discrimination against Negro workers as a class.

August 30: Supreme Court Justice Hugo Black set aside a Fourth Circuit order delaying school desegregation in two North Carolina counties, saying that the latest Supreme Court school ruling "requires that the desegregation of schools be completely carried out at the earliest possible moment."

September

Various events

September 5: A federal court of appeals rejected the appeal of New Bern, North Carolina, barbecue restaurant operator John Moore, who objected to a federal court order to serve Negroes. In December, Moore asked for United States Supreme Court review of his case.

September 8: Huey P. Newton, Black Panther leader, was convicted, after an eight-week trial, of voluntary manslaughter in the fatal shooting of an Oakland policeman. His attorneys planned an appeal. He later began a two-to-fifteen-year sentence.

September 10: A federal judge in Little Rock, Arkansas, ruled, in a case brought by LDF cooperating lawyer John W. Walker, that Negroes had been unconstitutionally excluded from county grand juries.

September 12: A federal court in Cincinnati enjoined racial discrimination by an electrical workers local in a suit brought by NAACP general counsel Robert L. Carter.

September 18: A federal court of appeals held invalid a rule, adopted by southern district of Mississippi Judges Cox and Russell, which restricted the right of out-of-state civil rights lawyers to appear in court.

September 19: For perhaps the first time, a white man was sentenced to death for killing a Negro in South Carolina. Wilson Atkinson of Hartsville was found guilty of killing a Black policeman.

September 20: Negro employees of the Duke Power Company in North Carolina lost a fair employment suit challenging tests used for hiring and promotions. The LDF appealed the decision.

September 20: The Justice Department filed a fair employment suit against Parke, Davis and Company, a major pharmaceutical concern in Detroit.

September 26: A federal judge in Little Rock struck down an Arkansas law against interracial marriages.

October

Various events

October 13: The *New York Times Magazine* published an article called "Nine Men in Black Who Think White," written by Lewis M. Steel, a young white lawyer on the staff of NAACP general counsel Robert L. Carter. The article, which criticized the Supreme Court as too conservative in race cases, precipitated a crisis in the organization. On October 14, the NAACP board fired Steel, calling his article an "indefensible rejection" of much of the NAACP's work over the last sixty years. Eventually Carter and his entire staff of eight lawyers resigned in protest. Mathew J. Perry, of Columbia, South Carolina, was named NAACP special counsel. The operations of the NAACP Legal Defense and Educational Fund, Inc., which is entirely separate from the NAACP, were not affected by the resignations.

October 14: The Supreme Court threw out a Louisiana law providing tuition grants for students to attend private segregated schools.

October 15: The Supreme Court heard arguments in a voting rights case from Virginia involving the right of illiterate voters to use gummed stickers to cast write-in votes for Negro candidate S. W. Tucker.

October 23: The Supreme Court for the second time heard arguments in a case centering on whether or not a low-income public housing tenant, Mrs. Joyce Thorpe of Durham, North Carolina, must be told why she was ordered evicted from a project, and must be given a hearing on the reason.

October 24: The Fourth Circuit, in a major employment ruling, held that a Negro need not hold up his suit against the Seaboard Coast Line Railroad to await conciliation efforts by the Equal Employment Opportunity Commission. Robert Belton of the LDF argued the case.

October 29: The Fourth Circuit refused to block a Maryland referendum to approve or reject a state open housing bill.

October 31: An all-white male jury convicted three white men of violating the rights of three Negroes by beating them for eating at a truck stop in Braselton, Georgia.

November

Various events

November 7: At the request of Negro demonstrators, a federal judge threw out a Mississippi law aimed at suppressing civil rights marches.

November 10: A third white man was convicted of arson in the 1966 fire bomb slaying of Vernon Dahmer, NAACP voter registration leader. In separate trials, two other men were convicted of the murder and another pleaded guilty. In December a Forrest County grand jury would indict former Imperial Wizard of the Klan, Sam Bowers, on murder charges. Meanwhile, federal charges were pending against Bowers and fifteen others.

November 13: A federal judge and jury in Vicksburg, Mississippi, returned a judgment of $1,021,500 against the White Knights of the Ku Klux Klan and three Natchez white men charged with killing Ben Chester White, a sixty-seven-year-old Negro caretaker, in 1966. Eight Negroes served on the jury, which was told by Judge William Harold Cox that the three men were responsible for White's death and to fix the amount to be paid to White's estate.

November 13: NAACP general counsel Robert L. Carter argued in the Supreme Court that an Akron, Ohio, referendum violated the Fourteenth Amendment by creating special barriers to open housing laws. The case marked the end of Carter's long career as counsel for the NAACP which had included some two dozen Supreme Court appearances over a period of more than two decades. His resignation from the NAACP was effective from December 1.

November 13: Leon Miller became the first Negro elected to a judgeship in West Virginia.

November 18: The United States Supreme Court agreed to hear arguments in the exclusion of Harlem Congressman Adam Clayton Powell from Congress. Lower federal courts had ruled that the judiciary could do nothing about this action by the 90th Congress. Arguments were scheduled for early 1969. Meanwhile, Powell was reelected to another term

November 18: California's supreme court by a four-to-three vote rejected an LDF challenge to the death penalty in a major decision, although ordering new trials for two death row inmates represented by LDF.

November 18: Rev. Fred L. Shuttlesworth, of Birmingham and Cincinnati, has the most remarkable record in history of being a party in cases in the Supreme Court. The ninth Shuttlesworth case, which involved a 1963 protest march in Birmingham led by the late Dr. Martin Luther King, Jr., was argued by LDF director-counsel Jack Greenberg.

November 19: A major civil liberties victory was won by a Black lawyer for the American Civil Liberties Union who argued before the Supreme Court on behalf of the white supremacist National States Rights Party. Mrs. Eleanor Holmes Norton of New York argued the case, in which the Court held that it was improper for courts to ban a public meeting without hearing evidence from both sides of the dispute.

November 22: Parents and students of an all-Black high school in Nashville won a ruling that suspension of their school from athletic contests was not done in accordance with proper procedures.

November 26: Black poet, playwright and militant leader LeRoi Jones was sentenced to sixty days in jail for using loud and abusive language (he called a policeman a "punk") and resisting arrest in a Newark bank. He appealed the conviction.

November 27: Eldridge Cleaver, minister of

information of the Black Panther Party, best-selling author of *Soul on Ice*, senior editor of *Ramparts* magazine and Presidential candidate of the Peace and Freedom Party, became a fugitive by ignoring his date to return to prison as a parole violator. Cleaver, thirty-three, had served nine years of a thirteen-year sentence for assault to commit rape, assault to commit murder and assault with a deadly weapon. His parole was revoked because of an April 6 shooting incident in which Bobby Hutton, a seventeen-year-old Negro, was killed and Cleaver and two Oakland policemen were wounded.

December

Various events

December 3: Maryland's highest court set aside the order of a lower court judge who had ruled that unwed mothers could be denied custody of their children and found "unfit" if they had had several children out of wedlock.

December 3: The highest court of Massachusetts upheld a complaint against a loan company accused of using a racial code in keeping loan records and of discriminating against Negro and Spanish applicants.

December 5: The Fourth Circuit reversed a lower court order obtained by white parents in Columbia, South Carolina, barring the Department of Health, Education and Welfare from enforcing its desegregation guidelines in the city's school system.

December 5: Georgia's highest court handed down a ruling involving Baconsfield Park in Macon, which had been left to the white women and children of the city by the late Senator A. O. Bacon. In 1966 the United States Supreme Court had ruled that the park could not be operated for whites only. The Georgia courts now ruled that since Bacon, who died in 1919, wanted a white-only park, the land should pass to his heirs. The LDF planned another appeal to the Supreme Court.

December 6: Attorney Conrad Harper of the LDF won a ruling from the Fifth Circuit ordering integration of the Bessemer, Alabama, YMCA and reversing an unfavorable lower court ruling.

December 9: The United States Supreme Court agreed to rule on whether an Arkansas recreational facility called Lake Nixon must admit Negroes.

December 9: The Supreme Court agreed to review the claim of eleven New York Negroes that the state's sixty-six-year-old criminal anarchy law was unconstitutional.

December 9: The Supreme Court affirmed a lower court order striking down South Carolina's law awarding public tuition grants to private school students.

December 13: A federal court struck down a North Carolina law requiring separate tax records for whites, Indians and Negroes.

December 16: A federal judge in San Francisco enjoined any further evictions of residents of a planned urban renewal area until proper plans were made for their relocation. The action was brought by the San Francisco Neighborhood Legal Assistance Foundation, in cooperation with the LDF. During the year, the LDF had opened a San Francisco office to serve the West Coast region.

December 16: The Supreme Court agreed to review challenges to the death penalty urged by the LDF in the case of William Maxwell of Arkansas.

December 20: Attorney George E. C. Hayes died in Washington, D.C. As a Howard University law professor, Hayes had taught several generations of Black lawyers. He was one of the attorneys who participated in the oral arguments of the famous school segregation cases which led to the May 17, 1954, decision barring segregation.

December 20: Nine members of the South Carolina highway patrol were charged by the Justice Department with willfully shooting into a group of Negro students in Orangeburg in February. Three students were killed and many were wounded in the incident. Earlier in the year a grand jury had refused to indict, and the Justice Department action in bringing charges after a grand jury had refused to do so was unusual.

December 21: The United States Supreme Court was asked to review the conviction of Chicago Black leader and former schoolteacher Albert Raby, for staging a sit-down in Chicago streets to protest the treatment of Blacks in Chicago public schools.

Negro marchers staging a protest through downtown Memphis in March 1968.
National Guardsmen with bayonets line the streets.

Black Labor in the American Economy

Herbert Hill

Introduction

THE STATUS of the Black worker in the American economy at the end of 1968 was characterized by a growing crisis of unemployment and underemployment, by large-scale occupational dislocation as a result of technological change, and by the emergence of a new generation of ghetto youth limited to a marginal economic existence.

At the end of 1968, the nationwide unemployment rate for Negroes was more than double the unemployment rate for whites.* The Report of the National Advisory Commission on Civil Disorders issued during March 1968 observed that:

> . . . even during the current unprecedented period of sustained economic growth, unemployment among Negroes has been continuously above the 6.0 per cent "recession" level widely regarded as a sign of serious economic weakness when prevalent for the entire work force.

For nonwhite teen-agers the 1968 national unemployment rate was 25 per cent compared with 11 per cent for white teen-agers. It is necessary to note that broad national statistical data obscures the full extent of Negro unemployment, which can only be understood by examining information on specific major areas of urban Negro population concentration.**

In a series of special studies made by the U.S. Department of Labor of the "sub-employment rate," including unemployment and underemployment in selected Negro ghetto areas, it was found that the unemployment rate of Negroes was really much greater than twice the national rate of unemployment. In the nine ghetto areas surveyed, "the sub-employment rate" was approximately 32.7 per cent or 8.8 times greater than the national unemployment rate.

In the Black ghetto areas of Watts, East St. Louis, the Hough area of Cleveland, as well as in certain all-Negro census tracts in Philadelphia, Oakland and elsewhere, the rate of male Negro unemployment and underemployment now exceeds the general rate of unemployment for the

* The rate of unemployment as determined by the Bureau of Labor Statistics is based upon the number of persons in the labor force actively seeking work. Unfortunately, official figures do not include the significant number of unemployed persons who have been driven out of the labor force as a result of long-term joblessness and who are no longer seeking employment. Thus, many thousands of older Negroes who have exhausted their unemployment insurance benefits, as well as a large but undetermined number of young persons who have never entered the labor market in the first instance, are not included in official unemployment statistics —which are regarded by many economists as a systematic understatement of true unemployment conditions. The problem of the "hidden unemployed" is especially acute in Negro ghettoes.

** The current population surveys of the U.S. government do not include a portion of the nonwhite working-age population. It is generally estimated that from 13 to 15 per cent of Black workers are not counted, compared with an undercount of only 2 per cent for whites. This is especially true in ghetto areas where the undercount among Negro males in the prime working-age group is very high. Given the data on high unemployment rates among this group it may be properly estimated that the actual unemployment rate for Negro working-age males is significantly greater than that given in federal statistical reports.

entire nation during the Great Depression of the 1930's. The Report of the National Advisory Commission on Civil Disorders concludes that "In disadvantaged areas, employment conditions for Negroes are in a chronic state of crisis."

In 1968 the great mass of Negroes, especially in the urban centers, were locked in a permanent condition of poverty. Virtually all cities with large Negro populations had very high Negro poverty rates, varying from over 40 per cent in several communities to 23 per cent in others. Thus, the Report of the National Advisory Commission on Civil Disorders states that:

> . . . the condition of Negroes in the central city remains in a state of crisis. Between 2 and 2.5 million Negroes—16 to 20 per cent of the total Negro population of all central cities—live in squalor and deprivation in ghetto neighborhoods. Employment is a key problem.

During 1968 Negro workers continued to hold a disproportionate number of jobs in declining industries, and the menial and unrewarding work available to most Black workers permitted only a marginal subsistence for families living in the decaying slums of America's racial ghettoes.*

The National Advisory Commission's Report sums up the data on Negro occupational concentration as follows:

> Even more important perhaps than unemployment is the related problem of the undesirable nature of many jobs open to Negroes. Negro workers are concentrated in the lowest skilled and lowest-paying occupations. These jobs often involve substandard wages, great instability and uncertainty of tenure, extremely low status in the eyes of both employer and employee, little or no chance for meaningful advancement and unpleasant or exhausting duties. Negro men in particular are more than twice as likely as whites to be in unskilled or service jobs which pay far less than most. . . .

Violence in the Black ghetto is an expression of the growing alienation of working-class Negroes from the entire society. This is especially true of Black youth, who are potential productive workers but who are kept out of the labor force and thus out of the "opportunity structure" of American life. This alienation is rooted in the most significant source of identity for Western man—work.

As the crisis in the Black ghettoes continues across the country, it becomes evident that in its most significant aspect it is a revolt against the inability to acquire meaningful employment. Related to this is the inability to obtain the rewards not only of wages but also of status: the status that is directly connected to meaningful, productive jobs. The great affluence of American society is visible at every turn, and the disparity between the white American reality and the Black American reality is extremely vivid for the Negro at precisely that moment at which it is most obscure to the white man.

The enactment of federal and state civil rights statutes together with the emergence of a new body of Constitutional law and executive orders prohibiting racial discrimination are important elements of progress. However, despite these developments the Negro's quest for economic justice remains unfulfilled.

Outbreaks of violence in many cities must be understood within the context of a persistent economic crisis in the major urban centers of Negro population concentration. If the traditional patterns of job discrimination are not rapidly elimi-

---

* On July 31, 1968, the U.S. Bureau of the Census and the U.S. Bureau of Labor Statistics released a joint report, *Recent Trends in Social and Economic Conditions of Negroes in the United States.* In this document the following statement appears:

> The data on income for 1967 confirms the sharp increase in the ratio of Negro median family income to white family income first seen last year. It was 59 per cent in 1967 and 58 per cent in 1966—constituting all-time highs compared to 54 per cent in 1965 and 1964.

These percentile statistics imply a movement toward equality of incomes between Negro and white families. However, the Census-Bureau of Labor Statistics Report did not include the fact that the difference between white and nonwhite family income (according to their own data) actually increased from $3,019 in 1964 to $3,158 during 1967.

A close examination of all the available data reveals that the differential in the earnings of Negro and white workers had actually become greater and that the dollar gap between Negro and white workers was growing. It is evident that the income of Negro workers has failed to increase rapidly enough to equal the much greater increase in white income, even in a period of unparalleled prosperity. As Dr. Vivian Henderson has stated:

> People spend and save dollars. It is this dollar difference that counts. Pronouncements regarding economic progress which are confined to acceleration concepts and percentage change obscure the real predicament—*Negroes are losing ground rapidly in gaining dollar parity with whites.*

nated, the continuing crisis of unemployment and poverty among Negroes threatens to plunge Negro communities into further alienation and despair.[1]

The economic well-being of the entire Negro community is adversely affected by the many generations of enforced overconcentration of Negro wage-earners in unskilled and menial job classifications in the industrial economy. As a consequence, Negro workers are more vulnerable to displacement due to technological change than any other group in the labor force. A continuation of this pattern will cause even greater crisis in the years to come, unless fundamental and rapid changes take place in the occupational characteristics and mobility of Negro labor in the United States.

At the end of 1968 many of the programs that promised Black citizens equality, justice and full participation in American economic life were either nullified as a result of non-enforcement, or ended before potentials could be realized. Because the need for hope among Negroes is so great, the promise of FEPC laws, of the so-called "War against Poverty" and of executive orders prohibiting discrimination in employment became all the more vivid. But as the promise and the hope failed to materialize, and as the racial situation deteriorated or remained the same for the majority of Black people, the despair and alienation grew more profound.

But despair and alienation were not the only responses. Black workers engaged in a great variety of local and national efforts in attempts to enter the mainstream of American economic life. Racial injustice in the United States is expressed in the behavior of institutions both public and private. The record of how these institutions responded to the demands of Black workers for the elimination of racist practices tells us much about the nature of American society in 1968.

The Failure of Federal Contract Compliance

During 1968 the United States government gave contracts worth over $54 billion to private industry. More than 23 million people received employment, or approximately one out of every three jobs in the national economy existed as a result of these government contracts.

For the fiscal year 1968–69 (according to the *Budget of the United States Government*, 1969, Appendix, p. 711), there are 225,000 contractor facilities and sites subject to the most recent executive order prohibiting job discrimination by government contractors. A vigorous enforcement of the standard anti-discrimination clause in U.S. government contracts would have had more direct effect in eliminating racial discrimination in employment than all of the lawsuits and complaints filed by Negro workers during 1968 against employers and labor unions with municipal, state and federal civil rights agencies.

Since 1941 the general principle for such enforcement has been established in executive orders, and every President since then has issued successively stronger executive orders intended to prohibit employment discrimination by contractors providing goods and services to the federal government. With the issuance of Executive Order 10925 by President John F. Kennedy on March 6, 1961, the clear and direct power to cancel or withhold government contracts because of employment discrimination was firmly established. Any ambiguity that may have existed in the previous orders on the matter of contract cancellation was now ended, owing to the clarity of the new order. Thus the machinery for genuine enforcement of the contract clause has in fact existed and been available to the government since 1961. At least in the abstraction of the law, the government requirement had moved from passive nondiscrimination to affirmative action.

However, for the past seven years the government has not used that machinery to eliminate the well-documented patterns of employment discrimination. Instead that machinery has become a vehicle of bureaucratic duplicity and delay that has led to bitter frustration for Negro workers and members of other minority groups who have patiently sought those rights their national government has repeatedly told them would be forthcoming if they used proper legal procedures. But instead of utilizing these proper legal procedures, the government has nullified the great potential of these executive orders, has made a mockery of the much vaunted contract compliance program and is directly subsidizing racial discrimination in employment to the extent of billions of dollars of public funds each year.

On March 6, 1961, the President's Committee on Equal Employment Opportunity was established by Executive Order 10925. At that time the President's Committee was the only federal agency existing to enforce the government's antidiscrimination policy in relation to government contracts. The committee possessed the powerful weapons of contract cancellation and debarment of offending contractors from receiving government contracts in the future.

After four years of operation, the President's Committee on Equal Employment Opportunity proved to be a failure. Only a very small percentage of the complaints received were successfully resolved. Broad patterns of employment discrimination in many industries operating with vast government funds were not eliminated. Many of the so-called "settlements" were reopened in 1968 by the Equal Employment Opportunity Commission—the agency established by Title VII of the Civil Rights Act of 1964—which found, upon extensive investigations, that, despite the so-called "settlements," patterns of racial discrimination continued to exist.

The President's Committee never used its power of contract cancellation or debarment of contractors. After four years of non-use these powerful sanctions ceased to exist even as a possible threat to non-complying employers and labor unions, as it became all too clear that they would never be invoked.

Although there were many instances that fully justified either contract cancellation or debarment—which would have had a most desirable effect upon major multi-plant employers dependent on government contracts—in the four years of its operations the committee never took such action.

Unfortunately the possibilities inherent in the order were never realized, as early in the history of the committee the federal government made a political decision to substitute a "voluntary compliance" approach called Plans for Progress, for enforcement through contract cancellation and related procedures. The Plans for Progress program had the dual effect of allowing an employer to publicly proclaim a policy of equal employment opportunity while privately practicing the opposite.

In reality, the Plans for Progress operation functions as a public relations agency for government contractors financed and operated through the U.S. Department of Labor. As of September 1, 1968, 441 major national companies had signed the Plans for Progress pledge.

The record demonstrates that the substitution of voluntarism for enforcement of the executive order brought either no change or only a minimal gain to Negro workers.

In January 1968 the Equal Employment Opportunity Commission held hearings in New York to examine the racial employment practices of one hundred major corporations whose national headquarters were located in that city. These enterprises were among the largest in the United States, contributing 15.8 per cent of the gross national product and having total assets of over $116 billion.

Ninety of the one hundred companies were government contractors and forty-six were Plans for Progress members. On the basis of detailed investigation, the commission found that the one hundred companies' average of Negro employment was only 2.6 per cent.

When the forty-six Plans for Progress companies were compared with the fifty-four non-Plans for Progress companies, it was found that the Plans for Progress companies employed a smaller percentage of Negro managers, supervisors, technicians, professionals and office and clerical workers than the non-Plans for Progress companies. These findings are very significant because they involve key managerial, technical and professional fields of employment where Plans for Progress employers were allegedly making their greatest effort.

The Equal Employment Opportunity Commission report concluded that, on a nationwide basis, non-Plans for Progress employers had made much more progress in the hiring of Negro managers, technicians, professionals and sales and clerical employees than had those contractors in the Plans for Progress program. It should be noted that many of the contractors who were the worst offenders had taken the pledge five years earlier.

In January 1968 the Equal Employment Opportunity Commission released the following statistics regarding Plans for Progress companies:

> Of the first 100 "Plans" signatories, 4 employed less than 1 per cent Negro, 5 employed less than 2 per cent, 16 employed less than 3 per cent, making a total of 25, or one quarter of the first 100 "Plans" members employing less than 3 per cent Negro.
>
> Of all 340 "Plans" companies in 1966, 11 employed less than 1 per cent Negro, 21 employed less than 2 per cent, 40 employed less than 3 per cent, making a total of 72, or more than one-fifth of all "Plans" signers employing less than 3 per cent Negro employees.
>
> One "Plans" company had increased the number of its employees by 915, yet decreased the number of its Negro employees by 163.
>
> Another had increased the number of its employees by 815, while decreasing the number of its Negro employees by 10.
>
> Still another had increased the number of its employees by 693, while decreasing the number of its Negro workers by 11.

A study dated September 1968, prepared for the Colorado Civil Rights Commission and the Equal Employment Opportunity Commission by the Institute of Industrial Relations (University of California, Los Angeles), of minority employment in the four Southwestern states, concludes that the pattern of employment for both Negroes and Mexican Americans is better among employers operating without federal government contracts than it is among prime contractors who have signed contracts with the federal government that contain anti-discrimination provisions. This report is most significant, as it refers to the status of nonwhite workers in California—a state with one of the highest concentrations of U.S. government contracts.

At the end of 1968 there were eighteen lawsuits brought by the U.S. Department of Justice under Title VII of the Civil Rights Act of 1964 against major government contractors, several of whom had signed the Plans for Progress agreement. In addition to the lawsuits initiated by the Department of Justice, many cases initiated by private parties after the Equal Employment Opportunity Commission found "reasonable cause" in their complaints are currently pending in U.S. district courts.

This body of litigation includes pending actions against Bethlehem Steel Corporation; United States Steel Corporation; Timken Roller Bearing Company; Chesapeake and Ohio Railway; American Cast Iron Pipe and Foundry Company; St. Louis-San Francisco Railway Company; Kaiser Aluminum Corporation; Otis Elevator Company; Cone Mills Corporation; P. Lorillard and Company; American Marine Corporation; J. P. Stevens and Company; Avco Corporation; Hughes Tool Company; McClean Trucking Company; Observer Transportation Corporation; American Tobacco Company; American Bakery Company; Seaboard Coast Line Railroad; International Paper Company; and Southwestern Telephone Company, among others.

A finding of "reasonable cause" by the Equal Employment Opportunity Commission should result in an immediate contract disability by all federal contracting agencies. At the very least, the Office of Federal Contract Compliance should delay further contract awards while cases are pending in the federal courts and after the commission has issued a finding of "reasonable cause."

Contracts are not cancelled or withheld by federal agencies in those many cases where the Equal Employment Opportunity Commission, after investigation and after it has exhausted conciliation powers, finds the contractor not complying with Title VII of the Civil Rights Act of 1964. It is known that copies of all such findings are routinely sent by the Equal Employment Opportunity Commission to the Office of Federal Contract Compliance and to the government agencies that have awarded the contracts.

Surely where the U.S. Department of Justice files a lawsuit against a company that is a government contractor yet has been operating in violation of Title VII, the federal contracting agencies should be required to cancel or withhold all government contracts. This has never been done.

As a result of widespread disillusionment and increasing dissatisfaction with the failure of federal contract compliance, an ad hoc committee of the House of Representatives, chaired by representative William F. Ryan (D, N.Y.), held public hearings on the operations of the Office of Federal Contract Compliance on December 4 and 5, 1968, in Washington, D.C.

Martin Sloan, on behalf of the United States Commission on Civil Rights, presented testimony before the Congressional inquiry. In his testimony on the failure of the Office of Federal Contract Compliance to enforce the executive order, Mr. Sloan, who is special assistant to the director of the commission, stated:

> "Voluntarism" has characterized most of the life of contract compliance . . . if any one fact emerges clearly from the history of federal contract compliance, and indeed, from the history of civil rights generally, it is that unless constructed upon a backbone of strict enforcement, voluntarism easily becomes an excuse for inaction.

Mr. Sloan reported to the Congressional committee on the results of its investigations and of the information developed at public hearings held by the U.S. Commission on Civil Rights. He stated that "employment discrimination was one of the main subjects of inquiry" of the commission's investigation of the status of Negro citizens in the San Francisco-Oakland area in California. Mr. Sloan told the committee:

> We took a particularly hard look at one large federally funded construction project, construction of the Bay Area Rapid Transit System. In this construction, the Commission was told, the Bay Area Rapid Transit Authority anticipated grants of up to $80 million in federal funds and employment of 8,000 people at peak construction times. As of May, 1967, we found no Negroes among the electricians, ironworkers, or plumbers engaged on this construction. . . .
>
> We also heard testimony from the federal official responsible for coordinating all construction contract compliance in the San Francisco area. Ample evidence had appeared in the hearings that construction contract compliance was yielding remarkably little increase in the employment of minority workers in the Bay Area. Commissioner Erwin Griswold, who is now Solicitor General of the United States, then asked this federal official, and I quote, "Have the efforts of your office brought about the employment of one minority plumber in the San Francisco Bay area?" And the official replied briefly and frankly, "Not to my knowledge."
>
> Following this hearing, in September, 1967, the Commission addressed to the Office of Federal Contract Compliance a memorandum containing a number of questions and recommendations regarding federal contract compliance in the construction industry in the San Francisco area. Nine months later (May, 1968) we received a reply which candidly summarized the ineffectiveness of the construction compliance program in the area.

The Congressional committee was given detailed information of the commission's findings of blatant violation of the federal executive order by U.S. government contractors in several states, North and South.

On April 27, 1968, the United States Commission on Civil Rights began a series of five-day hearings in Montgomery, Alabama, to establish the facts regarding racial employment patterns in a sixteen-county area, where 60 per cent of the population is Negro and 90 per cent of the population lives well below the poverty line. The Commission on Civil Rights found that broad violation of the executive order and the Civil Rights Act by government contractors existed throughout the area.

The American Can Company, which operates a sawmill in Bellamy, Alabama, is a vast national corporation operating with multi-million-dollar government contracts. As far back as 1962 it took the Plans for Progress pledge.

The American Can Company, in addition to operating the sawmill in Bellamy, also owns and operates a rigidly segregated company town with broken-down shacks and a dilapidated all-Black schoolhouse with an outdoor privy. Both the schoolhouse and the outhouse are owned by the American Can Company. In the all-white residential area, the company-owned houses provided for white workers have indoor bathrooms and running water, but of the twelve company-owned homes for Black workers, only four have such facilities.

In addition, the Commission on Civil Rights found that the company maintains segregated facilities within its sawmill operations together with separate racial job classifications. Out of a total work force of 1,550 employees, 108 are Negroes, all in the lowest paid jobs, and this is an area with over 60 per cent Negro population. The commission noted that exactly two weeks before its hearings in Montgomery began, two Negroes were promoted to hitherto "lily-white" jobs.

Although these conditions have existed since May of 1960, when the American Can Company began operations in Bellamy, the Office of Federal Contract Compliance and the General Services

Administration (which has given substantial contracts to this company) have never initiated a compliance review or enforced the law. In 1968, in addition to its other lucrative government contracts, American Can Company received a $1.7 million contract from the General Services Administration.

The U.S. Commission on Civil Rights also investigated the McGregor Printing Corporation of York, Alabama. This company holds contracts from government agencies and employs Negroes as common laborers exclusively. The McGregor Corporation maintains segregated rest rooms and other facilities, despite the fact that the plant was built after the enactment of the 1964 Civil Rights Act. The commission also found that the Alabama Power Company, which annually receives a $2.5 million contract from the General Services Administration, employs 5,394 people with 472 Negro employees in the lowest job classifications.

In the course of the commission hearings it was established that the Dan River textile mills in Greenville employed exactly three Negroes in the lowest paid menial jobs, while hundreds of whites were employed in a variety of production and skilled occupations. The NAACP filed complaints against Dan River Mills and other major textile producers in 1958 and again in 1962 with federal contract compliance agencies, but the pattern of Negro exclusion in the textile industry in Alabama has not changed—although virtually every major producer operates with federal government contracts.

As a result of the Civil Rights Act of 1964, one Negro was hired by Dan River Mills in the weaver's classification, a traditionally lily-white job category, but in sworn testimony before the Commission on Civil Rights this worker testified as follows: "I was hired as a weaver, but somewhere along the line I got to be a floor sweeper, light-bulb cleaner, and what have you." After it became clear that he would never work as a weaver and that less senior white workers were promoted over him into higher paying production jobs, this veteran of six years of Army service quit and left Greenville. In summing up his experience he told the Commission on Civil Rights, "You know, to be demoted from a staff sergeant down to a boy, that is kind of hard to take." This is the reality for many, many thousands of Negro workers in Southern manufacturing industries.

Upon the conclusion of the commission's hearings in Alabama in April, the Office of Federal Contract Compliance, the Department of Defense, the General Services Administration and other contracting agencies were given a full report of the commission's findings. However, at the end of 1968 no changes had been made in the conditions reported.

Perhaps the most significant testimony presented to the Congressional committee on contract compliance operations was that given by Girard Clark, former director of the Office of Contract Compliance, U.S. Department of Defense. Mr. Clark, who had had extensive experience as a contract compliance officer at the Navy Department and later in the Department of Defense, observed:

> The programs at the Defense Department were largely hamstrung by what General Eisenhower described as the military-industrial complex. The big contractors and high-ranking military had long been wed and the military was not disposed to endanger the marriage over something so alien to both parties as meeting the social needs of the nation. . . .
>
> In September of 1965 President Johnson issued Executive Order 11246, which, on the surface, appeared to strengthen and broaden the program. The immediate effect, however, was the exact reverse. . . . Surveillance of the contractor program was downgraded by assignment to the Secretary of Labor. Surveillance of the government's own hiring practices was assigned to the Civil Service Commission. The agency responsible for creating the problem had been charged with solving it.

Mr. Clark described the Equal Employment Opportunity Program of the Defense Supply Agency as a " 'non-program' which never found fault with any contractor." He also strongly criticized, as a firsthand observer, the operations of the Plans for Progress program:

> The majority of . . . [Plans for Progress signers] were among the worst employers in this respect and signed only because they correctly surmised that this action would make them immune for a time from review by the contracting agencies. This was confirmed by later statistical surveys by the President's Committee on Equal Employment Opportunity.

In a dramatic presentation, Mr. Clark told the Congressional committee of his resignation as director of contract compliance for the Department of Defense in protest against what he called "the military takeover" of the civilian contract compliance operation. He described in detail the resistance and the outrage of major U.S. government contractors when efforts were made to actually enforce the equal employment opportunity clause in their contracts, and he described how the "military takeover" scuttled efforts to establish genuine contract compliance. He concluded by stating that the events in the Defense Department were ". . . also typical of what happened to the program in most other agencies." A simple call from the President could have solved the problem; but no call was ever made. Instead, "President Johnson clung to his long-discredited belief in being able to secure voluntary affirmative action."

Debarment Proceedings against Federal Government Contractors

The racial employment practices of the Timken Roller Bearing Company, another Plans for Progress employer, whose major manufacturing operations are in Ohio, provides further evidence of how the United States government subsidizes racial discrimination in employment.

An examination of the response of the Office of Federal Contract Compliance (OFCC) to the proven charges of racial discrimination practiced by the Timken Roller Bearing Company and the United Steelworkers of America at the company's Columbus, Ohio, plant is most illuminating and reveals the fundamental failure of federal contract compliance. Although federal and state civil rights agencies have repeatedly acknowledged that a clear pattern of racial discrimination exists at the Timken Roller Bearing Company, none of these agencies has exercised its powers to eliminate the discriminatory employment practices, and through 1968 and into 1969 the company continued as a government contractor.

On May 18, 1966, in response to complaints received from Negro workers employed by the Timken Company, the NAACP labor department filed formal complaints against the company and Local 2173 of the United Steelworkers of America, AFL-CIO, with the Equal Employment Opportunity Commission, charging violation of Title VII of the Civil Rights Act of 1964. On the same day complaints were also filed with the OFCC charging violation of Executive Order 11246.

These actions were taken after four months of fruitless negotiations by Negro employees and representatives of the NAACP with both Timken and the union. The aggrieved Negro employees charged in sworn affidavits that the company and the steelworkers' union had conspired to prevent Negroes from holding any jobs other than janitorial and similar menial occupations. The complaints filed with the Equal Employment Opportunity Commission and the OFCC described the operation of a discriminatory seniority system that systematically violated the job rights of Negro workers and limited Negro promotions to certain menial job classifications. The complaints also stated that, in violation of the law, newly hired white workers were promoted to jobs in the "white only" seniority lines, thus by-passing Negro employees with many years of seniority.

On April 22, 1966, as a result of the refusal of the company and the union to eliminate the discriminatory practices, Negro employees staged the first of a series of picket-line demonstrations at the Timken Roller Bearing Company plant in Columbus.

On November 9, 1966, Edward C. Sylvester, director of the OFCC, issued the first of several press releases on the charges against the Timken Company. Page one of the *Wall Street Journal* of that day announced that the company was under close investigation and that the OFCC had initiated procedures that might lead to contract cancellation. On November 15, 1966, the *Wall Street Journal* quoted Mr. Sylvester as stating that "the major bearing producer poses the 'first clear-cut refusal' by a company to supply the government with sufficient information on which to judge equal employment practices."

On December 1, 1966, the Ohio Civil Rights Commission, in a report to the NAACP and to the aggrieved Negro workers, confirmed that a pattern of racial discrimination existed at the Timken plant. Immediately thereafter thirteen additional complaints were filed against the company and the union with the Equal Employment Opportunity Commission.

On January 17, 1967, the NAACP filed thirteen charge forms with the Cincinnati regional office of the National Labor Relations Board. The United Steelworkers of America was charged with violating the National Labor Relations Act because of its refusal to fairly and equitably represent Negro employees. Charges were also filed against the company.

These actions brought about an exhaustive investigation by the regional office of the National Labor Relations Board, the results of which were duly forwarded to Washington on or about July 1, 1967. The report of the regional office sustained and further documented the charges made by Negro workers against the company and the union.

On February 6, 1968, representatives of the Department of Defense met with Negro complainants and with NAACP representatives and requested additional information relative to possible contract cancellation. On May 17, 1968, the Equal Employment Opportunity Commission issued a finding of "reasonable cause" against the Timken Company and the NLRB informed the NAACP that it would "defer" to the commission, thereby abdicating its responsibility under the National Labor Relations Act to intervene.

On August 15, 1968, the NAACP initiated litigation in the U.S. district court in Columbus, Ohio, against the Timken Roller Bearing Company and Local 2173 of the United Steelworkers of America and also against the international union. The suit asked an immediate end to the discriminatory employment practices engaged in by the company and the union, together with $300,000 in back pay and damages for the plaintiffs.

On October 9, 1968, the OFCC recessed hearings on possible cancellation of U.S. government contracts with the Timken Roller Bearing Company pending the conclusion of contract negotiations between the company and the union.

On November 8, 1968, the OFCC completely stopped its proceedings against the company and closed the case with a statement that the new collective bargaining contract settled the question of federal contract compliance violation on the grounds that the new seniority agreement provided job equality. But as Negro plaintiffs charged in court proceedings, the 1968 union contract definitely did not do this. The OFCC distorted the facts to justify its refusal to act against the company and the union.

On November 21, 1968, Negro workers publicly condemned the new bargaining agreement as a fraud, and protested against it in a picket-line demonstration around the plant, during which they distributed a leaflet which stated that *far from providing job equality for all Timken workers, the new bargaining agreement simply perpetuates the old Timken system.*

Immediately thereafter attorneys for the NAACP announced that at the request of the aggrieved Negro workers the NAACP would continue to press the litigation against the company and the union, even though the OFCC had terminated proceedings.

The record of the OFCC in the Timken Company case demonstrates the tragic failure of contract compliance in the North as well as in Southern states, and shows how powerful industrial corporations and labor unions have secured an immunity from the enforcement of a comprehensive body of civil rights laws and executive orders.

The present compliance agency, the OFCC, like its predecessor agencies, has obviously not used the power of contract termination. However, as a result of increasing protests and local dissatisfaction—as in Milwaukee where the NAACP youth organization under the leadership of Father James E. Groppi conducted mass demonstrations at the Allen-Bradley Company plant—the OFCC in May 1968 began to threaten to invoke debarment procedures against several companies that were clearly in violation of the executive order. In two-and-one-half years of its operation, the OFCC has completed only one hearing, has begun a second hearing—which has since been postponed indefinitely—and has announced that five other hearings are pending but without a scheduled date. The status of the seven cases at the end of 1968 was as follows:

1. *Allen-Bradley Manufacturing Company, Milwaukee, Wisconsin.* This company was threatened with debarment on May 24, 1968. Hearings were held August 20, 21 and 28. The company has filed its objections arguing that it should not be denied further government contracts, and the case is currently pending; a decision will probably not be rendered until 1969. When the deci-

sion does eventually come through, it will merely be in the form of a recommendation, which will then be referred to the Secretary of Labor, who has the discretionary power to decide what disposition will be made of the case.

The facts in the Allen-Bradley case are as follows: The company is the largest employer in Milwaukee, which has a Negro population of over ninety thousand. In 1962 the company had 6,383 employees, one of whom was a Negro. In January 1964 the company had 6,500 employees, four of whom were Negroes. As of the date of the hearing—August 20, 1968—the company had thirty-two Negro employees, most of whom were in the less skilled, lower paying job classifications.

The Allen-Bradley Manufacturing Company has been receiving government contracts for several years, although the company employment policy has been to exclude Negroes. On March 25, 1964, the company was informed by the Air Force of its first compliance review. During July 1965 a second inspection was conducted by the compliance officers of the Department of Defense. Two conciliation conferences were held, in September 1967 and January 1968, and the company refused to comply with government requests that it recruit employees from the Milwaukee Negro community, which was suffering from a critical unemployment rate. The record shows that the OFCC found that a clear pattern of employment discrimination had existed at the Allen-Bradley Manufacturing Company since Executive Order 10925 was issued in 1961. Therefore it had taken fully seven years for this case to come to a completed hearing. However, more time will pass before a final decision is made by the Secretary of Labor, and much more time will pass before there is justice for Negro workers in Milwaukee.

2. *Bethlehem Steel Corporation, Sparrows Point, Maryland.* Although the Department of Justice has filed a lawsuit against this company involving its racial employment practices in Buffalo, New York, and the Equal Employment Opportunity Commission has found that discrimination exists at the Sparrows Point, Maryland, manufacturing facility, the OFCC has announced that debarment hearings have been suspended indefinitely.

3. *Timken Roller Bearing Company, Columbus, Ohio.* On November 9, 1966, the director of the OFCC announced that debarment proceedings against this company were under way. A hearing date was set, but the case was dismissed on the basis of an undisclosed stipulation with the company and the union. Attorneys for the NAACP acting on behalf of aggrieved Negro workers have filed suits against both the company and the union in the U.S. District Court in Columbus.

4. *Pullman Company Incorporated, Bessemer, Alabama.* At the end of 1968 this case was in pre-hearing negotiations. No date for a hearing had been set.

5. *B and P Motor Express, Pittsburgh, Pennsylvania.* This case was in pre-hearing negotiations at the close of 1968. No date for a hearing had been set.

6. *Bemis Company, Minneapolis, Minnesota.* This case was in pre-hearing negotiations. No date for a hearing had been set.

7. *Hennis Freight Lines, Winston-Salem, North Carolina.* At the end of 1968, this case was in pre-hearing negotiations. No date for a hearing had been set.

It is only since May of 1968 that the OFCC has finally begun to initiate debarment proceedings. Out of over forty thousand contractors, it had (by December 31, 1968) only threatened seven contractors publicly with debarment proceedings and as of February 1, 1969, the Secretary of Labor had yet to issue a single order that would lead to the actual withholding of further contracts.

It is abundantly clear that the government's policy of voluntary compliance has failed. At the inception of the contract compliance program in 1961 it was argued by government officials that the mere possession of the power of cancellation and debarment would act as a threat and would provide a deterrent to prevent racial discrimination by government contractors. The record of this program proves conclusively that at best there has been paper compliance, but not tangible enforcement of the law.

Only one instance of genuine enforcement, one contract cancelled, would have been real evidence of intent to use the enforcement powers provided by the executive orders. As the history of government contract compliance demonstrates, the deliberate non-use of enforcement powers has so negated their intent that at the end of 1968 they were no longer even functional as a threat. This failure has destroyed not only the real power of governmental authority in this field but the symbolic power as well.

At the final session of the hearings conducted by the ad hoc Congressional committee on federal contract compliance, held on December 5, 1968, the NAACP called upon the incoming Nixon administration to demonstrate that the period of "paper compliance" was over. "But," added a spokesman for the NAACP's labor department, "this can only be done by canceling and withholding government contracts wherever such action is indicated."

The NAACP in its testimony before the committee stated:

> The new Republican administration must also demonstrate that the flagrant violations of contract compliance regulations such as those revealed in Alabama, in Ohio, California, and elsewhere by the U.S. Commission on Civil Rights will not be permitted to continue. It must demonstrate its awareness that the elimination of these outrageous violations of the law will take place not by interminable negotiations but rather by using the full power of federal executive orders. That means contract cancellation.

The NAACP called upon the government to reorganize federal contract compliance procedures and to operate with new criteria. The Association made the following recommendations:

> 1. The Office of Federal Contract Compliance must be immediately removed from the Department of Labor and shifted to the Department of Justice. The Department of Labor has for too long been a captive of institutions that are bitterly resisting changes in their racial practices. Too many high officials of the Department are former functionaries of bigoted labor unions and their original loyalties as well as their attitudes remain unchanged. An investigation of the Solicitor's Office, of the Manpower Policy Operations, of the Bureau of Apprenticeship and Training and of other units in the Department of Labor will reveal that former trade union officials use their high positions as representatives of the United States government to protect the interests of racist labor organizations. If the Office of Federal Contract Compliance is to become a law enforcement agency as it should be, then it properly belongs in that department of the government whose primary function is law enforcement.
>
> 2. Contract compliance agencies must regard violations of the Executive Order as a fundamental breach of contract no different from a failure to comply with any other term or condition of a government contract. Noncompliance must be regarded as non-performance of the contract and sanctions rapidly applied.
>
> 3. Pre-award contract compliance must become a reality. Employers seeking government contracts must demonstrate that they maintain an integrated labor force on all levels before they can be eligible to bid for government contracts. Failure to do so should prevent contract awards. The government has an obligation not to give contracts to discriminatory employers in the first place rather than attempt to "secure compliance" after the contract has been signed.
>
> 4. The Executive Order should be amended to cover labor unions more directly. It has been repeatedly demonstrated that in several industries the racial practices of labor organizations are decisive. Therefore compliance regulations must regard labor unions, especially where there are union controlled referral systems or hiring halls, as being directly covered by the Executive Order. Such coverage by amendment or by administrative interpretation of the Order would bring labor unions under more direct federal pressure to end job discrimination.
>
> 5. As a matter of fundamental policy contract compliance agencies should regard a finding of "reasonable cause" by the Equal Employment Opportunity Commission as grounds for a contract disability. Certainly when a contractor is found to be violating Title VII of the Civil Rights Act of 1964 and the Attorney General initiates a lawsuit after the contractor has failed to comply, the power of contract cancellation should be exercised.
>
> 6. The Office of Federal Contract Compliance should issue new specifications redefining "affirmative action." In the light of new federal court decisions the government can and should issue manpower specifications to prospective contractors requiring the employment of racial minorities. The government, in short, must establish new standards, new manpower requirements that go beyond the empty gestures of the past.

It is evident that prompt and forceful action in the future is necessary to convince employers and labor unions that the United States government is in fact committed to equal employment opportunity as a basic national policy and that the old policy of "voluntary compliance," of interminable delay and futile negotiations without enforcement, has come to an end.

The history of the failure of federal contract compliance provides a classic example of the administrative nullification of civil rights laws and executive orders.

Racial Discrimination in the Construction Industry

The appalling failure of contract compliance in the supply operations of the government is exceeded only by federal complicity in directly subsidizing a nationwide pattern of racial discrimination in the building and construction industry. Jobs in the nation's construction industry are of great importance to Negroes and members of other minority groups. The industry is huge and it is expanding at a rate that will require at least a million more workers by 1975.

In excess of $77.5 billion was spent for new construction during 1968, and public works accounted for almost a third, or $26 billion, of new construction. The Department of Housing and Urban Development (HUD) during the fiscal period 1966–67 was alone responsible, according to its own estimates, for some 465,000 man-years of employment. During this period $5.5 billion in HUD construction projects was involved; because of the Model Cities Program construction scheduled for 1969 and after, this sum will be considerably expanded. In domestic military construction, another example of federal involvement in the industry, the 1968 Congressional appropriation was over $4 billion. On October 18, 1968, the *New York Times*, in a news report headlined "Record Construction Contracts Seen for '69," revealed the results of a study made by the F. W. Dodge Corporation which forecast significant increases in the nation's construction industry.

Despite the vast amount of public funds spent for construction, and despite the growth of the building industry with its ability to provide hundreds of thousands of man-years of employment—together with the fact that acute labor shortages now exist in several skilled occupations—Negroes are permitted to receive what Roy Wilkins, executive director of the NAACP, calls "only the crumbs of expenditures for public construction."

The nation's construction industry is of unique importance to Negro wage earners for many reasons. Among these are the following:

1. It is a huge industry with vast growth potential. State and federal social policies will in the future emphasize massive new urban development programs involving slum clearance, housing, schools, and medical and other public facilities. Typical of these is the program, announced on November 27, 1968, of the Hackensack River Meadowland Development Plan in New Jersey, which will take more than twenty-five years to build at a cost of billions of dollars and will provide many new job opportunities in the building trades in an area of very high Negro population concentration. Many other such programs are planned by federal, state and municipal agencies as well as by private builders. The Report of the National Advisory Commission on Civil Disorders (March 1968) proposed new social programs which, if even partially realized, would create thousands of new job opportunities in the construction industry. The estimate of the U.S. Department of Labor that the construction industry will require one million more workers by 1975 may be most conservative. (According to the *Engineering News-Record* of October 17, 1968, acute labor shortages already exist in twelve building trades in thirty-one cities.)

2. The construction industry, in comparison with other large industries, is highly dependent on public funds. During 1968 public works represented approximately a third of all new construction. However, in the twenty-five major areas of Negro urban population concentration between 50 and 60 per cent of new construction projects were financed by federal, state and local agencies. Given the anticipated new programs, these proportions will be substantially increased.

3. Wages in the construction industry are among the highest in the nation. Wages for the craft occupations in the unionized building trades average about three times the general industrial wage. In 1968 in New York City construction, electrical workers earned $7.70 per hour. Plumbers in several Ohio cities received in excess of $8.00 an hour. There is every indication that these wage levels will be increased during the next round of collective bargaining negotiations, as in Philadelphia, where the new agreement negotiated by Plumbers Local 690 provides that union plumbers will receive over $19,000 a year in wages and fringe benefits. A disproportionately high percentage of employed Negroes work at jobs paying close to the federal minimum wage. These are the working poor, who are limited to the lowest paid menial work and, although they are counted as employed, live in a permanent condition of poverty. The building and construction industry represents a major area of the economy which could provide mobility into higher paying, more desirable occupations.

4. Jobs in the building trades are for men. In the highly important symbolic sense, as well as because of practical considerations, construction jobs are male jobs. These "manly" jobs with their high status implications are especially important for Negro men, who are so frequently either denied employment or permitted to work only in low paying, menial, "dead end" jobs.

5. Jobs in the construction industry are highly visible and are of special significance to low income Black communities. Much of new construction, including urban renewal, model cities, highway and road building and public housing, is in, or very near, large Negro communities. Slum clearance programs are expected to provide employment to slum dwellers, especially as the model cities and other programs specifically require new job opportunities for members of minority groups living in the areas affected.

6. Finally, it should be noted that, throughout the nation, much of the test of what happens to the major recommendations made in the Report of the National Advisory Commission on Civil Disorders will be decided in the construction industry and in the nation's housing and urban development programs. The employment practices of the building and construction trades have unique social implications, especially for Black workers, and if the recommendations of the above-mentioned report have any meaning at all, it will be to a large extent revealed by the future status of Black workers in the construction industry.

During 1963, 1964 and 1965, the nation witnessed demonstrations by Negro workers at public construction sites in many cities across the country. Among these cities were Philadelphia; New York; Cincinnati; Cleveland; Columbus; New Rochelle, New York; and Newark and Elizabeth, New Jersey. These demonstrations had only one purpose: to get the laws against racial discrimination in employment on public works contracts enforced. Although these demonstrations did not succeed in their purpose, they did provoke many official investigations of the pattern of racial exclusion in the building industry and in the construction trade unions.

Among the many groups which conducted such studies were a special committee of the 1965–1967 California general assembly; the Michigan Civil Rights Commission; the New York and New Jersey state advisory committees to the U.S. Commission on Civil Rights; the New York State Commission for Human Rights; the Ohio Civil Rights Commission; and the Philadelphia, Newark, New York City and New Rochelle Commissions on Human Rights. The U.S. Commission on Civil Rights held hearings in San Francisco, Cleveland and other cities which further documented the pattern of discrimination in the building trades. All these studies reached three general conclusions:

1. Negroes are virtually excluded from construction as apprentices and journeymen, except in the lower paid unskilled and semi-skilled jobs, because of union restrictions and widespread racial discrimination by the AFL-CIO building trades unions.

2. Contractors have allowed the unions

to control access to jobs through union hiring halls and illegal closed shops that limit job openings to union members and are unwilling or unable to take corrective action.

3. Government officials at all levels have failed or refused to enforce the laws against discrimination.

In the construction industry, trade union racial practices are the decisive factor in determining the status of Negro workers. The basic operational characteristic of craft unions in the building and construction trades is that they control access to employment by virtue of their rigid control of the hiring process. In this industry labor unions control the assignment of union members to jobs. The refusal to admit Negroes into membership denies Negro workers the opportunity to secure employment. Quite frequently, Negro craftsmen denied union membership are totally excluded from work in white residential neighborhoods, in new commercial construction and in public works projects. This means that skilled Negro workers are restricted to marginal maintenance and repair work within the Negro community and that they are seldom permitted to work on the larger and more desirable public and private construction projects.

There now exists a vast and incontrovertible documentation—consisting of innumerable reports by federal, state and municipal civil rights agencies; scholarly studies sponsored by several universities; decisions and records of lawsuits in state and federal courts involving discrimination in the building trades; a massive collection of reports by private agencies such as the NAACP, the Urban League and other Negro interest groups; and the findings of the Equal Employment Opportunity Commission and of other public agencies—that more than adequately establishes the facts regarding the exclusion of Negroes from the major AFL-CIO building trades craft unions throughout the nation.

Two cases may be cited which reveal much about the status of Negroes in the unionized building trades during 1968. In 1948 the New York State Commission against Discrimination ordered the New York Sheet Metal Workers Union, Local 28, to desist from "executing and/or maintaining constitution or bylaw provisions which exclude Negroes." Yet fifteen years later no progress had been made; not a single Negro had been admitted. Obviously the "Caucasian only" clause was removed from the union's constitution for public relations purposes only.

In 1963 James Ballard, a twenty-two-year-old Negro Air Force veteran, initiated a complaint against Local 28 of the Sheet Metal Workers Union before the New York State Commission for Human Rights, with the assistance of the civil rights bureau of the state attorney general's office. On March 4, 1964, the commission, after an extensive investigation and public hearings, ruled that Local 28 of the Sheet Metal Workers Union had "automatically excluded" Negroes over the entire seventy-eight years of the union's existence. This was held to be a violation of the New York State law against discrimination. The commission announced that it would issue an order for the union to "cease and desist" from such discriminatory practices and would demand affirmative action to guarantee an end to job discrimination.

Local 28 refused to comply with the commission's order, and sixteen years after the original finding against the Sheet Metal Workers Union, the commission was forced to go to court to get the new order enforced. On October 14, 1964, Justice Jacob Markowitz of the state supreme court sustained the action of the state commission and ordered the adoption of a new set of admissions standards. The union publicly announced that it would now admit Negroes to membership as both journeymen and apprentices.

Soon thereafter, Local 28 initiated a testing program ostensibly designed to provide equal treatment; but in fact the new testing procedures were used to screen out Negro applicants. On December 29, 1966, the New York State supreme court issued a restraining order against Local 28 at the request of the State Commission for Human Rights—which was forced to return to court, with the NAACP filing a brief, *amicus curiae*, when the union scrapped the results of a test for admission into the union controlled apprenticeship training program because, according to the union, Negro applicants received "phenomenally" high scores.

For many years the building trades unions had repeatedly stated that Negroes were not qualified and thus were excluded from union membership, but in 1966 it appeared that Negroes were too well qualified to be admitted to union membership. As a result of public protests and pressure from state and municipal civil rights agencies, together with the possibility of further lawsuits, Local 28 again announced that "qualified" Negroes would be admitted. But two years later, on November 23, 1968, the city of New York, which at long last had begun to enforce the municipal contract compliance law, announced that twenty-six city contracts, valued at more than $6 million, were being held up by the city's contract compliance division and the city housing authority because Local 28 of the Sheet Metal Workers Union was unable to supply municipal contractors with a single Negro worker. The *New York Times* of November 24, 1968, in a report headed "Bias Issue Delays 26 City Contracts," stated that "Local 28 of the Sheet Metal Workers International Association has not reported any Negroes qualified as journeymen mechanics among its more than 3,000 members."

Four days later, on November 28, 1968, in a second story, headlined "City Moves To Subpoena Union's Test," the *New York Times* reported that the city's contract compliance division was forced to issue a subpoena to obtain a copy of the test used by Local 28. The *New York Times* reported that "James D. Norton, director of the compliance division, said that Local 28 of the Sheet Metal Workers International Association had refused to supply a copy of the examination on his request. He said the Commission on Human Rights had been asked to initiate legal action to obtain a copy."

Exactly twenty years after the New York State Commission originally ordered Local 28 to eliminate their "Caucasian only" clause and to admit nonwhite members, after two decades of interminable conferences, negotiations, administrative procedures, lawsuits in the state supreme court, investigations, and repeated anti-bias pledges by the union, there was still not a single Negro journeyman in Local 28.

Public relations spokesmen for the AFL-CIO have stated that some Negroes have been admitted to the union's apprenticeship training program, but after twenty long years this represents very dubious progress in a city like New York. At best, it is the triumph of conspicuous tokenism, a device utilized by the labor union bigots to maintain the local's illegal exclusive hiring hall arrangements with the employers and to prevent genuine enforcement of federal, state and municipal civil rights laws and executive orders.

On September 13, 1968, in the U.S. district court in Cincinnati, Judge Timothy S. Hogan ruled that Anderson L. Dobbins, a Negro electrician, must be admitted to Local 212, a lily-white local of the International Brotherhood of Electrical Workers, AFL-CIO. Local 212 has jurisdiction in Cincinnati and in thirteen surrounding counties in Ohio, Kentucky and Indiana. Mr. Dobbins, a veteran of the United States Army, who holds a Bachelor of Science degree from Hampton Institute and who is a fully certified journeyman electrician, had been attempting to gain admission to Local 212 of the Electrical Workers Union since 1949. Because he had repeatedly been denied membership in the union, which maintains an exclusive hiring hall system in the Cincinnati area, Mr. Dobbins had not been able to work in the vast new public and private construction projects in and around Cincinnati.

Spokesmen for organized labor, including George Meany, president of the AFL-CIO, have repeatedly stated, both publicly and privately, that Negroes are not refused admission into the craft unions because of their race and color but because they are "not qualified." But federal Judge Hogan found that in spite of the fact that Anderson L. Dobbins was a college graduate, had successfully passed a journeymen's certifying test and had a wide range of experience as an electrician he was still refused union membership and thereby the right to work in his craft.

In a ninety-page opinion rendered by Judge Hogan in *Dobbins* v. *Local 212, International Brotherhood of Electrical Workers, AFL-CIO*, the court ordered that, because of Mr. Dobbins' extensive training and experience in the electrical field, he must be admitted to union membership immediately; that he must not be required to pass a union qualifying journeyman's admission examination and that he must be placed on the union's referral list as of the time he had last applied for union membership (September 1965).

It should also be noted that in this landmark ruling the court found that the union had committed eleven separate acts of racial discrimination, that there was a clear pattern of racial discrimination under the terms of the Civil Rights Act of 1964 and that there was a violation of an 1866 civil rights statute which prohibits private as well as public discrimination. The federal court noted that Local 212 had limited its membership to white persons only and that it "effectively controls who will work for union contractors within its jurisdiction" through the referral system and its hiring hall arrangements. Of great significance was the fact that the court challenged the union's control of employment through its hiring hall and suspended the union referral system.

The cases of Anderson L. Dobbins and James Ballard are not rare, isolated instances. They represent the position of many thousands of Negroes throughout the country who have looked in vain to the federal contract compliance apparatus of the government to protect their rights.

In 1967 an event occurred which might have been the turning point in the history of federal contract compliance in the nation's construction industry. In a historic decision handed down in the U.S. district court in Columbus, Ohio, on May 17, 1967, in the case of *Ethridge* v. *Rhodes*, a permanent injunction was secured against state officials involved in discrimination in public construction. In this case, brought by the NAACP on behalf of aggrieved Negro construction workers who had been barred from membership in AFL-CIO building trades unions, the court ruled that the state had the "primary responsibility" for ensuring that Negroes had equal job opportunities on all public works contracts.

For the first time a federal court enjoined all state officials from entering into public works contracts until they could provide equal opportunities for Negroes in both journeyman and apprentice job classifications. On June 12, 1967, the *New York Times,* in an editorial comment, noted that "under the circumstances the most likely way to speed integration of the building unions is through lawsuits of the kind the National Association for the Advancement of Colored People has just won in Columbus. It obtained a court order restraining the State of Ohio from entering into a public building contract without a guarantee of nondiscriminatory employment."

As a result of the *Ethridge* v. *Rhodes* decision, construction was halted on a $12.8 million medical science building at Ohio State University because the contractors had entered into agreements with labor unions requiring them to use lily-white union hiring halls as the sole exclusive source of labor supply. As a result of the precedent-setting decision in Columbus, which provided the Office of Federal Contract Compliance with an additional weapon, the government did withhold at one point during 1967 more than $43 million in federal funds earmarked for construction projects in Cleveland and other cities.

These developments gave some reason for hope that now, for the first time, the OFCC would begin regularly to cancel and withhold construction contracts and enforce the law, especially as it was learned that when federal funds had been withheld building contractors had hired a significant number of Negro craftsmen.

But the hope was short-lived as high federal officials responded to pressure from the AFL-CIO. Secretary of Labor W. Willard Wirtz, in a speech to the convention of the Building and Construction Trades Department of the AFL-CIO, on November 29, 1967, promised the building trades unions that the new enforcement procedures and the withholding of federal funds would not become the rule. Mr. Wirtz told the labor leaders:

> . . . I am here to make it perfectly clear in connection with the issues which have been raised before this convention . . . as far as federal contract compliance is concerned I just want to say squarely in the simplest possible way that I think any rule which provides that there must be one or any other number of people or one or any other race on every craft, on every job is wrong, and it won't work. It's a wrong approach to this whole problem . . . in Cleveland and in Philadelphia regulations or rules were issued which were in this pattern; in those two situations the problem had become sufficiently difficult . . . and in those situations I suppose some kind of approach of this sort is the only thing that can be done, and that is what we did.
>
> But I want to make it dead clear that I think it is error to approach this problem, or any other aspect of this problem, in terms that mean a number of people, one or more Negroes or whites or anybody else as being

> required on every single situation . . . as far as I am concerned—and I know I speak for you—that is simply the wrong approach to that problem, and we have got to find a better one.[2]

The Secretary of Labor has kept his promise to the Building and Construction Trades Department of the AFL-CIO. No further funds have been withheld, business continues as usual and Negro workers remain excluded from new job opportunities in the construction industry.

It is necessary to note the influence on and unwarranted power of discriminatory labor unions over the policies and practices of the U.S. Department of Labor. It is perhaps no accident that the OFCC is an agency of the Department of Labor, and perhaps its ineffectiveness is no accident as well.

In addition to the OFCC, the Department of Labor controls the operations of another agency: the Bureau of Apprenticeship and Training (BAT). On June 27, 1963, the *New York Times* reported that Secretary Wirtz had "issued strict new standards . . . designed to prevent racial discrimination in labor-apprenticeship programs." The new regulation (Title 29, Part 30) authorized BAT to de-certify all apprenticeship training programs found to discriminate. The construction unions bitterly protested the new regulation as "unwarranted interference." Yet in the five years following the issuance of the new ruling, not a single apprenticeship training program was deregistered—despite the fact that federal courts, the Fair Employment Practices Commission and other administrative civil rights agencies have found many of these programs to be in violation of anti-discrimination statutes and executive orders.

An example of how governmental power is given to the representatives of traditional anti-Negro institutions can be found in the record of civil rights non-enforcement by BAT.

After widespread public protest in 1965 and 1966 against the failure of BAT and other public agencies to eliminate racial discrimination in the nation's apprenticeship programs, the Secretary of Labor and other government officials had repeatedly announced that new enforcement actions would be forthcoming.

Although there was a plethora of press conferences and press releases pledging new affirmative action programs to end the shameful pattern of Negro exclusion from apprenticeship training, the pattern was not altered. At best there was a shift from total exclusion in certain crafts to tokenism. Craft union officials now permit one or two conspicuous Negroes into a union controlled apprenticeship program as a strategic, minimal adjustment to the requirements of federal civil rights law and executive orders. Unfortunately BAT has used its power not to eliminate fundamentally the pattern of Negro exclusion and white racism, but to assist the discriminators in evading real compliance with the law.

On September 18, 1967, the NAACP revealed the contents of a confidential memorandum, dated April 20, 1967, from Hugh C. Murphy, administrator of the bureau, to all BAT regional directors. The memorandum stated:

> This will confirm our telephone instructions . . . in which we requested that you and your field staff do not take any further action against program sponsors in the BAT states relative to the letters sent them on compliance . . . I repeat, do nothing in the field of compliance follow up until you are given further instructions from the Administrator's office.

In response to an inquiry from a member of Congress, Mr. Murphy confirmed that BAT had never de-certified a single apprenticeship program (*Congressional Record* [House], September 26, 1967, pp. 12495–6). Mr. Murphy is a former official of the Bricklayers Union in New York City. The deputy administrator of BAT, George Sabo, is a former official of the International Association of Machinists, in Nashville, Tennessee.

By March 6, 1967, 636 union controlled apprenticeship training programs had not complied with the anti-discrimination regulation. Among these were the affiliates of the International Typographical Union in New Jersey, Texas, Missouri, Nebraska, Illinois, West Virginia and Arkansas; the Amalgamated Meat Cutters and Butcher Workmen in St. Louis; and more than sixty locals of the Plumbers Union. On March 30, 1967, the *Wall Street Journal* reported that Peter Schoemann, president of the Plumbers Union, had ordered affiliated local unions "to disregard the compliance command until they checked with him."*

During April of 1968, federal Judge Joseph P. Kinneary in the U.S. District Court in Columbus, Ohio, found Local 189, an all-white affiliate of the Plumbers and Pipe Fitters Union, and its Joint Apprenticeship Committee, guilty of racial discrimination and of violating federal law. The plaintiff, Mr. Guillard Locke, a Negro pipe welder, was awarded $10,000 in damages; the union was ordered to admit him immediately to membership, to eliminate their discriminatory hiring hall practices and to cease discriminating in apprentice selection.

But in this case, as in so many others where the federal courts have found discriminatory union apprenticeship control to be a violation of the law and where the Equal Employment Opportunity Commission has found "reasonable cause" in complaints against union apprenticeship programs, not a single apprenticeship program has been de-certified by BAT, nor has the OFCC taken action.

At the end of 1968 there were many lawsuits in U.S. district courts against building trades unions charged with discrimination both in refusing to admit Negro journeymen and in excluding Negroes from union controlled apprenticeship programs. Among these unions were: the Asbestos Workers Union in New Orleans; the Electrical Workers Union in Cleveland, East St. Louis and Las Vegas; the Iron Workers in Cincinnati and Chicago; the Steamfitters Union in Los Angeles; the Sheet Metal Workers Union in St. Louis; the Plumbers and Pipe Fitters in Indianapolis; the Lathers Union in New York City; the Operating Engineers in East St. Louis; and the Plumbers Union in Cleveland. Some of the suits were brought by the U.S. Attorney General; others were brought by Negro workers in private actions.

From its inception in 1965 to the end of 1968, the Equal Employment Opportunity Commission received and processed approximately 250 complaints against building trades unions. And in a majority of these, the commission has found "reasonable cause" to credit the allegations of the complaint. The Justice Department has filed lawsuits charging a pattern of discrimination against sixteen building trades unions and one building trades council of the AFL-CIO, and an additional number of private suits are pending in U.S. district courts in several cities.

Black Workers and Organized Labor

When the American Federation of Labor and the Congress of Industrial Organizations united in 1955, policy resolutions were adopted committing the merged federation to the rapid elimination of racial discrimination and segregation within labor unions. These statements were hailed by Negro workers and civil rights organizations. But in 1968, thirteen years later, the failure to eradicate patterns of discrimination had invalidated the earlier optimism.

From the time of Samuel Gompers, the first president of the American Federation of Labor in 1881, to the current era of sophisticated public relations under George Meany, the profound disparity between the public statements of organized labor on civil rights and the discriminatory practices of many labor unions has continued.[3] Pious resolutions on civil rights are routinely adopted at AFL-CIO conventions, but racial discrimination continues in major labor organizations. The events of 1968 clearly indicate that at best there has been a minimal strategic adjustment, as a result of direct action by the Black protest movement and of litigation in federal and state courts by aggrieved Black workers. The civil rights record of the AFL-CIO since the merger in 1955 can best be described as the triumph of tokenism.

Discriminatory racial practices by trade unions are obviously not isolated or occasional expressions of local bias against Negro workers but are rather, as the record indicates, a continuation of institutionalized patterns of anti-Negro practices.

During 1968 AFL-CIO affiliated unions were engaged in discriminatory racial practices in four primary categories:

* According to *Negroes in Apprenticeship* (U.S. Department of Labor, Manpower Administration: Manpower/Automation Research Monograph No. 6 [Washington, 1967], p. 7), Negro participation on federally supported construction projects was 2.2 per cent. The report significantly notes that "the 1960 census showed only 2,191 Negro apprentices in all trades throughout the country. That figure was one more than had been recorded in the 1950 census."

1. *Exclusion of Black workers from union membership.* Although lily-white exclusion clauses in union constitutions have been removed, Black workers remain excluded from certain craft unions by tacit consent. As a result of orders by state and federal courts several unions have been forced to admit a small number of Negroes, but such tokenism does not change the basic pattern of discrimination. Recent federal court decisions involving the International Brotherhood of Electrical Workers, the United Association of Plumbers and Pipe Fitters, and the Sheet Metal Workers Union, among others, forced several locals to admit Negro workers for the first time.[4]

2. *Segregated locals.* Segregated locals continue to exist in several major AFL-CIO unions. The Brotherhood of Railway Clerks recently eliminated several segregated local lodges by eliminating the jobs of Negro workers. They did so by reclassifying the traditional Negro job categories and declaring them to be within the jurisdiction of the white locals. This meant that the seniority rights of Negro workers were violated as they were dismissed from jobs long held and were replaced by less senior white workers who had been in an all-white seniority line. (Litigation on this issue was pending at the end of 1968.) Segregated locals also continued to exist during 1968 in certain manufacturing plants where all the white workers belong to AFL-CIO craft unions and all the Black workers belong to a separate industrial union. In New York City there is the auxiliary unit known as 60-A which is part of the all-white Local 60 of the International Ladies Garment Workers Union. The auxiliary 60-A consists almost entirely of Negro and Puerto Rican shipping clerks, "pushboys" and delivery men. The auxiliary unit 60-A, with twice the membership of Local 60, has never been chartered by the ILGWU as a separate local, and the manager of Local 60 also functions as the manager of 60-A. Additional examples of segregated local unions are found in other union jurisdictions.

3. *Separate racial seniority and other discriminatory provisions in union contracts.* Many major unions affiliated with the AFL-CIO have negotiated into their collective bargaining agreements separate lines of seniority promotion. These limit Negro workers to unskilled or menial labor classifications which not only deny them equal seniority and other rights but prevent them from developing job skills which permit employment in more desirable classifications.

During 1968 many cases were pending in the courts against labor unions responsible for discriminatory provisions in union contracts. In several recent landmark federal court decisions, involving the Tobacco Workers Union, the Papermakers and Paperworkers Union, the Asbestos Workers, and the Pulp, Sulphite and Paper Mill Workers, among others, the courts have declared that separate racial seniority lines and other provisions in union contracts that lead to job assignments on the basis of race are violations of the law. (On January 14, 1969, in a case against the Brotherhood of Railway Carmen, AFL-CIO, the Supreme Court, by unanimous vote, ruled that Negro workers are not required to exhaust an elaborate series of union and governmental remedies before suing in the federal courts if it can be demonstrated that it would be "futile" to do so in view of traditional union hostility.)

4. *Discrimination in union controlled apprenticeship training programs.* Complaints received by the Equal Employment Opportunity Commission and by municipal and state fair employment practices commissions point to the fact that labor unions controlling admission into apprenticeship training programs continue by and large to exclude Negro youth in the following jurisdictions, among others: the printing industry; the skilled metal crafts; the building trades; and the various railroad craft unions. Some limited progress has been made among the metal crafts and in certain of the building trades as a result of litigation, but such "progress" has involved a limited number of Negro youth, and here, too, the basic patterns of Negro exclusion have not been eliminated.

Both the Amalgamated Clothing Workers and the International Ladies Garment Workers Union have effectively prevented the use of federal funds for training purposes in the industries in which they operate, even though there are acute manpower shortages. In Newark, New Jersey, New York City and elsewhere, action by the ILGWU has destroyed training programs involving unemployed Negro and Puerto Rican ghetto youth. Evans and Novak, in their syndicated column of January 2, 1969, wrote the following:

> What makes this ban so strange is that the apparel industry is the last major unautomated industry with a capacity to hire workers in substantial numbers. It is thus peculiarly fitted for quick, relatively easy training programs to move the uneducated and unemployed poor—including ghetto blacks—into economic self-sufficiency.[5]

In a nationwide survey of union racial practices published by *Look* magazine the following was reported:

> Union control of apprenticeship programs remains a major bar to Black progress—today, there are fewer union Negro plumbers or electricians than Negro Ph.D.'s. . . . In Chicago, where there are a million Negroes, the taxpayers pay for the Washburne Trade School, but the unions decide what student can enter this public school as part of their apprentice training. For years, Negroes made up less than one per cent of the student body because the unions denied them entry. Today after court contests, civil rights protests, newspaper exposés and Herculean efforts by the school board, there are 167 Negro students among the 2,958 pupils, but 37 were brought in under so-called "open enrollment"—they are not part of the union apprenticeship program and get a diploma instead of a union job.
>
> The situation in Massachusetts is typical of what such exclusionary practices achieve: of 137 structural iron worker apprentices in the Bay State, none is Black; of 661 electrician apprentices, eight are Black; of 300 plumber apprentices, eleven are Black; of 353 sheet metal worker apprentices, none is Black; of 256 pipe fitters, one is Black; of 167 newspaper-compositor apprentices, one is Black.[6]

Title VII, the equal employment opportunity section of the Civil Rights Act of 1964, went into effect on July 2, 1965. Between that date and the end of 1968, the Equal Employment Opportunity Commission established by Title VII received over 4,200 complaints against labor unions.The commission has entered a finding of "reasonable cause" in almost 70 per cent of the complaints investigated. But the commission has been unable in many labor union cases involving the job rights of thousands of Negroes to secure compliance through conciliation procedures. As a result, during 1968 there were approximately 170 civil rights cases pending in the federal courts against labor unions.

In some important cases, the courts have already issued decisions in which the unions have been found guilty of discriminatory racial practices. But although now for the first time the federal courts are providing clear legal definitions of what constitutes racial discrimination in employment, administrative remedies are still blocked as many labor unions continue their defiance of the law and attempt to defend their traditional racist practices in complex court challenges. During 1968 the legal departments of many unions were busily engaged in introducing a tangle of procedural legal questions in efforts to maintain the racial status quo.

It is important to note that some labor unions are exceptions to the nationwide discriminatory pattern. Among these are the United Packinghouse Workers of America, Walter Reuther's United Automobile Workers Union and the American Federation of State, County and Municipal Employees, which organized a significant number of Negro workers employed in the public sector of the economy during 1968. District 65 in the distributive trades and Local 1199 of the Hospital Workers Union, both of New York City, as well as some other individual local unions in several cities, have vigorously opposed racial discrimination and have organized thousands of Negro and Puerto Rican workers on the basis of equality within the work-place and within the union. But taken as a whole, organized labor has adamantly resisted Negro demands for a fundamental change in the traditional racist practices of many of its largest and most powerful affiliates, and more than a decade after the merger the AFL-CIO has become increasingly conservative as a social institution.[7]

Black Caucuses and Independent Black Unions

One of the significant developments during 1968 affecting Negro workers was the emergence of Black caucuses in several important labor unions, together with the growth of independent Black labor organizations. The 1968 Chicago convention of the United Steelworkers of America, AFL-CIO, was the occasion for the public emergence of the nationwide Black caucus of steelworkers, operating in one of the largest and most important industrial unions. The Black caucus, known as the Ad Hoc Committee, succeeded in making Negro exclusion from leadership positions within the union and the union's discriminatory collective bargaining agreements a major public issue for the first time. The Ad Hoc Committee placed protest picket lines each day at the entrance to the convention auditorium and distributed a series of handbills.

In a widely distributed leaflet entitled *An Open Letter to President I. W. Abel from a Black Steelworker*, the caucus stated:

> The time has come for black workers to speak and act for ourselves. We make no apologies for the fact that we as black workers and loyal trade unionists now act on our own behalf. Furthermore we are fully prepared to do so.

Part of the demands involved the lack of Black representation in United Steelworkers leadership positions.

> Of more than 1,000 employees of the International, less than 100 are Negroes. Of 14 departments in the International, only 2 have Negro personnel. One of these 2 departments is the Civil Rights Department (obviously). Of more than 30 Districts in the International, there are no Negro directors and only one sub-district director. Blacks were in the forefront during the formation of this Union over 25 years ago. Through the acceptance of crumbs down through the years instead of our just deserts, we now find ourselves hindmost.

An important factor in the development of the Black caucus is that the Steelworkers Union is vigorously defending its traditional discriminatory practices in a series of lawsuits pending in the federal district courts in Birmingham, Alabama, Columbus, Ohio, Lynchburg, Virginia, and elsewhere.

Litigation brought by Negro workers involves charges that the union maintains separate racial seniority lines and other discriminatory job provisions in its contracts with the United States Steel Corporation and other steel manufacturers. This issue was brought to the attention of the international union leadership in 1957 by the NAACP, and there has been a decade of protest by Negro steelworkers, including the filing of complaints with the National Labor Relations Board. But the union continues to defend the discriminatory provisions in its collective bargaining agreements, although the federal courts in several recent decisions have declared such contractual agreements to be illegal.

A study of Negro employment in the basic steel industry of Pittsburgh made for the Equal Employment Opportunity Commision and released during April 1968 observes that:

> Negroes comprise 12.27 per cent of the laborers, 12.93 per cent of the service workers, and 10.86 per cent of the semiskilled operatives, but only 3.21 per cent of the craftsmen. They are, therefore, almost twofold over-represented in the lowest classification and equally disproportionately under-represented in the most skilled blue-collar work.

All of the available data sustains the charge made by the Black caucus that there is a significant connection between the exclusion of Negroes from leadership positions within the union and the status of Negro workers within the steel plants.

The Negro workers also demanded that Steelworkers Union president I. W. Abel (who is both a vice-president and an executive council member of the AFL-CIO, and was recently appointed by George Meany to replace Walter Reuther as head of the industrial union department of the federation) "secure the reorganization of the Civil Rights Department of the AFL-CIO. We insist that a Negro trade unionist be appointed Director of the Civil Rights Department. . . ."

The attack on the civil rights department is at least of equal importance with the demands for reform within the Steelworkers Union itself:

> The present director of the AFL-CIO Civil Rights Department has no involvement with Negro workers and their problems. He does not meet with us. He does not ask our advice. He does not know of our problems. He does not represent us. He does not act in our interests. We believe we speak for many thousands of Negro workers not only in the Steelworkers

> Union but in other AFL-CIO affiliates with large Negro memberships when we demand the replacement of a white paternalist with a Black trade unionist who can honestly represent Negro workers and act on their behalf. . . . For years Negro workers have stopped filing complaints with the AFL-CIO Civil Rights Department because experience has taught us that the department is unable to function on our behalf. *Most often it represents the discriminators in organized labor rather than the Black workers who are the victims of white racism within the house of labor* [my italics].

Factually, the Ad Hoc Committee is correct in citing the federation's civil rights department as a major offender, and as Black militance has grown within the ranks of organized labor so has the discontent against the department.

The failure of the AFL-CIO civil rights department to carry out its designated functions is demonstrated by the fact that, as the Ad Hoc Committee stated, Black workers no longer even try to use the civil rights department to seek redress of their grievances but go directly to the courts and the various public agencies (the National Labor Relations Board, state and municipal FEPC's and, since Title VII of the Civil Rights Act of 1964 went into effect, the Equal Employment Opportunity Commission). The standard response of the federation in the face of repeated documentations of racial discrimination within affiliated unions by public and private agencies is first to deny the existence of such practices and then to mount an intensive public relations campaign to demonstrate labor's devotion to an abstraction called "civil rights."

Black workers are not only attacking the failure of the federation's civil rights department to eliminate racist practices thirteen years after the merger; they are also becoming increasingly critical of the department's activities to maintain the racial status quo by intervening with state and federal agencies on behalf of AFL-CIO affiliates charged with violating fair employment practice laws. In a significant case involving five locals of the Bridge and Structural Iron Workers Union in northern New Jersey, the AFL-CIO civil rights department directly intervened in an unsuccessful effort to prevent the filing of formal charges with the state Commission on Civil Rights.

In another instance, the department intervened with the federal Equal Employment Opportunity Commission, again without success, to prevent the commission from establishing jurisdiction in cases filed by Negro workers against labor unions charging separate racial seniority lines of promotion and other discriminatory provisions affecting job assignment in union contracts.

Black unions and Black caucuses within unions are essentially responses to the adamant resistance of organized labor to Negro demands for fundamental changes in racial policies and practices. The Independent Alliance of Skilled Crafts in Ohio, the Maryland Freedom Labor Union, the United Community Construction Workers of Boston, the United Construction and Trades Union in Detroit, the Allied Workers International Union in Gary, and similar groups in Seattle, Chicago, Boston, Oakland and elsewhere, are examples of independent Black unions.

The growth of these organizations attests to their appeal to two groups of Negro workers: those who live and work in ghetto areas where AFL-CIO unions make no attempt to organize, and those in the building trades who, having been denied admission to the AFL-CIO craft unions, are attracted to Black controlled hiring halls. These hiring halls are now being used by some building contractors, as a result of the 1967 *Ethridge* v. *Rhodes* decision, which ruled that contractors must demonstrate that they have an integrated labor force in order to bid for public construction contracts. The Black unions demonstrate the practical possibilities inherent in this approach and may be increasingly used as legal precedents become more widely established for the enforcement of Title VII. (The decision of the federal court in Cincinnati on September 13, 1968, against Local 212 of the International Brotherhood of Electrical Workers, which had repeatedly refused to admit fully qualified Negro mechanics, established a new legal basis for litigation against discriminatory labor unions. In this case the court suspended the union referral system and ordered the immediate admission of the Negro plaintiff under a civil rights statute of 1866 [a Reconstruction enactment which bars racial discrimination—private as well as public].)

A confrontation of national significance between Black construction workers and the lily-white power structure of the AFL-CIO building trades unions has recently developed in Detroit. The conflict is between a newly formed independent union of Negroes, the United Construction and Trades Union, Local 124, affiliated with the Allied Workers International Union (independent) and the AFL-CIO Laborers Union. The Negro workers belonging to Local 124 are employed by a Negro sub-contractor on a federally financed urban rehabilitation project.

The independent union was formed on June 16, 1968, to help resident Negroes obtain jobs on federally financed construction projects. Calvin Stubbs, president of the new United Construction and Trades Union, stated: "The Black man lives in the ghetto, and the Black man must have equal opportunities for the many jobs now available and which will soon become available as construction goes on."

The two Negro Congressmen from Detroit, John Conyers, Jr. (D), and Charles C. Diggs, Jr. (D), entered the dispute when the AFL-CIO Laborers Union refused to work with the members of the independent Black union. The Detroit AFL-CIO building trades council demanded that all members of the independent union on the project be replaced with members of its own unions. The project involved in this dispute is located in the center of the major Black ghetto area in Detroit, the site of the 1967 riots. Congressman Diggs stated that "the whole rehabilitation program in the Black community is subject to disruption if this issue isn't resolved and this means that the people who are most in need of help will be hurt the most. There are 2,000 rehabilitation programs in the pipeline on the West Side alone, and another 2,000 on the East Side and in other sections of Detroit that could be affected."*

Spokesmen for the independent Black union have argued that their members have a right to jobs on the project because of a government stipulation that up to 90 per cent of the workers in such urban rehabilitation programs be residents of the neighborhood. Mrs. Mildred Rollocks, attorney for the Black union, stated: "We're taking idle men off the streets and teaching them trades. And some Black contractors are getting an opportunity to earn more money through better jobs." The Black union has stated that it has a twofold goal: first, to ensure jobs for Black workers who are denied membership in the AFL-CIO construction unions, and secondly to obtain work for Black contractors and sub-contractors on federal construction projects who will employ the Negro workers who have been traditionally denied construction jobs by virtue of their non-membership in the AFL-CIO. It may be anticipated that similar conflicts will occur in other cities where Black workers form independent construction unions.

In Boston the United Community Construction Workers Union is operating in twenty-two different crafts and is assisting Black-owned construction companies to obtain public works contracts. This union, with an all-Black membership and staff, based in the Roxbury ghetto area, has also had conflicts with the AFL-CIO construction unions, which unsuccessfully attempted to bar members of the Black union from work on public construction.

But Black caucuses which operate within unions are becoming even more significant, and their importance lies in their direct attack upon discriminatory practices together with their threat to established union bureaucracies. Some of the more noteworthy examples of such caucus activity have occurred in the American Federation of Teachers, the Amalgamated Transit Union, the United Automobile Workers and the Interna-

* The Detroit Community Relations Council found that the Iron Workers Union, the Riggers Union, the Glass Workers Union, the Asbestos Workers and Insulators Union, with a combined membership of 2,960, have no Negro journeymen. Only "trowel" trades show a significant number of Negro members. The Plasterers and Cement Masons locals are 50 per cent Negro. In Laborers Local 334, some four thousand out of five thousand members are Negro. These workers do demolition and other rough, hazardous and back-breaking work. Excluding the "trowel" unions, there were 131 Negroes among the 14,166 journeymen—less than 1 per cent. Among carpenters, bricklayers and painters there has been some integration. The 1960 census shows that 11.6 per cent of Detroit building workers were Negro. They were in the Laborers, Carpenters, Plasterers and Cement Workers locals. Eight years later the percentage was about the same.

tional Ladies Garment Workers Union, in addition to the United Steelworkers of America.*

Division 241 of the Amalgamated Transit Union, AFL-CIO, in Chicago, has been controlled for years by an all-white group under the leadership of James J. Hill. This group has perpetuated itself in office by bringing in three thousand retired white drivers to outvote what has now become a Negro majority of working members. The existence of a large Black caucus known as the Concerned Transit Workers came to light during July and August, when this caucus conducted a series of strikes which crippled Chicago bus operations for several weeks. But the strikes were not against the employer, the Chicago Transit Authority, but against the union's leadership. Striking Negro workers placed picket lines around the Transit Authority's garages, defied a court injunction ordering them back to work and forced the international union to place Division 241 in trusteeship.

Nathaniel Howse, attorney for the Concerned Transit Workers, was quoted in the *Chicago Tribune* of August 29, 1968, as saying that the members of the Black caucus were considering withdrawing from the Amalgamated Transit Union and would form their own independent union, after having exhausted all attempts to secure equal representation in the union leadership through reform measures. Howse stated that if such efforts failed the Negro drivers "would become members of a new union if it were to become the bargaining representative for drivers through some election process."

The United Automobile Workers of America, although more sensitive to the "race question" than most other unions, has had a tradition of active Negro caucuses since the early 1940's. Today there are several such caucuses operating in local unions as well as on a district-wide basis. The emergence of a national Negro caucus in the UAW in the late 1950's which openly challenged the Reuther leadership on the issue of Negro participation in policy-making positions led ultimately to the election in 1962 of Nelson ("Jack") Edwards, the first Negro executive board member of the union.

On the recent death of Joseph McCusker, regional director of the UAW's politically important Region 1-A in Detroit, two Negroes ran for the office; Marcellus Ivory was elected and became the first Negro to hold the position of regional director in the UAW—a most influential post in the daily affairs of the union. Because of the dramatic rise in the Black membership of the UAW (over 60 per cent, for example, in Local 7 in Detroit) Black caucuses within the union will continue to grow in power and influence.

One Black nationalist group, DRUM (Dodge Revolutionary Union Movement), crippled auto production through "wildcat strikes" by Negro workers at the Chrysler Corporation's largest Detroit facility, the Hamtramck assembly plant. (A similar disruption of production occurred during October 1968, when the Afro-American Employees Committee staged a sit-down strike at the Hotpoint Electrical plant in Chicago.) At the Chrysler plant, where over half of the seven thousand hourly rated workers are Negroes, the Black caucus not only attacked the Chrysler Corporation for its failure to promote Negroes to supervisory jobs but also attacked the UAW itself for its failure to exert sufficient pressure on the company to eliminate discriminatory employment practices.

The *DRUM Newsletter* suggested that if the UAW did not begin to move decisively against discriminatory practices the Black caucus would call on its members to withhold their union dues. (A major problem for Negro workers in the UAW has been the union's skilled trades department, which is frequently referred to by Black auto workers as "the deep south of the UAW.")

A new nationwide Black caucus has emerged recently within the UAW. This group is called the National Ad Hoc Committee of Concerned Negro UAW Members, and is headed by Robert Battle. Mr. Battle is a vice-president of Local 600, the largest UAW local in the country, at the Ford Motor Company's River Rouge plant in Dearborn, Michigan. For several years Mr. Battle has been a leading figure in the Negro American Labor Council, which has operated in Detroit as the Trade Union Leadership Council.

* A January 31, 1969, dispatch from the Associated Press reported the formation of the Black Workers Alliance in Washington, D.C. Ben Howard, a leader of the new group, called upon Negro workers throughout the nation to form independent Black unions. It is important to note that this group is financed by the National Right to Work Committee, an organization of "open-shop" employers.

On September 29, 1968, at a caucus meeting in Detroit, Mr. Battle reported that a committee of the Negro group had met with Walter Reuther, president of the UAW, on September 18 and that future conferences with the UAW leadership were scheduled. In a written statement the committee warned that unless the problems of Black workers were immediately solved and Negroes received "full equity in the union" it might be anticipated that "chaos would ensue." The National Ad Hoc Committee stated that Negroes constituted one-fourth of the UAW membership but that of the more than one hundred policy-making and key staff positions in the union only seven were held by Negroes. In a memorandum submitted to the UAW president, the Black caucus charged that basic policy decisions that directly affect Negro workers are "determined and dictated by white union officers." This "must be ended now," the caucus declared in its statement.

The American Federation of Teachers, AFL-CIO, has also come under sharp attack from Negroes recently, from both within and without its ranks. The major conflict was over the issue of school decentralization, but coupled with this were increasing charges, especially from the AFT's nationwide caucus of Black teachers (known as the African-American Teachers Association), of growing conservatism on the part of the union leadership and of insensitivity to Negro demands and community interests. The Black caucus, led by Edward Simpkins, a vice-president of the Detroit Federation of Teachers, has repeatedly attacked the AFT's position on educational issues.

In several cities, including Detroit, Philadelphia and Chicago, sharp differences have developed between Negro teachers and the AFT on educational issues vital to the Negro community. Thus Negro teachers have organized both locally and nationally into Black caucuses.

In New York City open warfare developed as a result of bitter opposition by the United Federation of Teachers (UFT), the New York affiliate of the AFT, to a decentralized school system operated by neighborhood school boards. Addressing the 1968 convention of the NAACP, Dr. Kenneth Clark, according to the *New York Times* of June 26, 1968, called for a major effort by Negro interest groups to "break the educational colonialism inflicted on Negro children by a combination of white controlled boards of education, educational bureaucrats and the powerful American Federation of Teachers."

During the 1968 strike of the UFT, which closed the New York City school system, the profound differences between Negroes and organized labor on basic community issues sharply emerged. The American Civil Liberties Union was quite correct in concluding in a report issued on October 10 that "the UFT has used 'due process' as a smokescreen to obscure its real goal, which is to discredit decentralization and sabotage community control."

In the course of the New York school strike, the UFT was joined by other labor unions opposed to local control of public schools in Black communities. This was true especially of the discriminatory building trades craft unions, who feared that Black controlled school boards would insist upon awarding school construction and maintenance contracts to Negro contractors, who employ the majority of Black skilled workers still excluded from the major craft unions.

After the New York AFL-CIO Central Labor Council endorsed the teachers' strike and donated $50,000 to the UFT, a group of Negro and Puerto Rican unionists on November 13 staged a sit-in demonstration at the office of Harry Van Arsdale, head of the Central Labor Council, to protest the council's action in support of the strike, and, according to the *New York Times* of November 14, denounced Albert Shanker, president of the UFT, as "racist." Earlier, on October 25, an influential group of Negro and Puerto Rican labor leaders had publicly attacked the UFT, endorsed the Ocean Hill-Brownsville school district's local governing board, and attacked the Central Labor Council and its affiliated unions for their stand. Cleveland Robinson, president of the Negro-American Labor Council, issued a public statement, signed by one hundred Negro and Spanish-speaking trade unionists from unions with large Negro membership, expressing a refusal to support strikes against the vital interests of the Black community.

One Negro staff member of the UFT resigned during the strike, and Richard Parrish, the Negro assistant treasurer of the UFT, who is also chairman of the Black caucus within the union, publicly criticized the strike.

Inside the AFT, Black caucuses have acted as the agents of the Black community within the teaching profession; now the Black teachers in some cities are considering a separate union.

The new Black caucuses are not merely confronting racial discrimination but are also significantly raising the broad question of internal union democracy and for the first time are resorting to legal action on this front. These challenges may have long-term consequences for the future development of organized labor.

On April 19, 1968, federal Judge Constance Baker Motley handed down a fifty-seven-page decision which voided the election of officers within the National Maritime Union. Judge Motley's decision was upheld by the United States Court of Appeals in a suit brought by the union leadership. In her opinion Judge Motley noted the rigid restrictions written into the NMU's constitution and stated that "it now takes a minimum of ten years to become eligible for national office. No other union studied, except possibly the International Ladies Garment Workers Union, required so much time for its members to qualify for national office."

For the Negro members of the ILGWU this decision had a special relevance. The first public announcement of a Black caucus within the ILGWU occurred on April 16, 1967, when the New York office of CORE held a press conference to protest the 1967 agreements signed by the ILGWU and stated that the "ILGWU has for years permitted conditions to exist which keep the vast majority of black workers in the lowest paying jobs and has denied black workers a policy-making voice in the union through restrictive constitutional provisions."

In announcing that CORE was engaged in the "formation of a black caucus to fight bias and powerlessness in the ILGWU," Roy Innis, chairman of Harlem CORE (now national director) stated:

> The growing number of black workers coming to Harlem CORE to lodge complaints against the ILGWU and the disgraceful contracts signed in 1967 make it imperative that immediate action be taken. CORE is now assisting black garment workers of New York City in organizing for the right of black people to participate in basic policy-making for their own protection. With the help of CORE a black caucus is now being organized to fight for the basic democratic rights of all nonwhite workers and eliminate racial discrimination in one of the richest and most powerful unions in the world.

It is important to note that the membership of the ILGWU is denied the same right to internal political activity that is accepted as commonplace in the United Automobile Workers Union and in certain other labor organizations. Members of the ILGWU are not only not permitted to engage in any internal political activity, but they are specifically forbidden to have clubs, groups or caucuses within their union except for a designated period of three months before conventions every two years. (This is stated on page 52, Article 8, Section 16, of the *ILGWU Constitution.*) This denial of democratic rights of the workers prevents the discussion in an organized fashion of matters vital to every union member and prevents the offering of rank-and-file candidates for union office.

The implications of these restrictions are made more significant by the eligibility requirements for union office within the ILGWU. In order to be eligible to run for president or general secretary-treasurer, a member must be a delegate to the convention—which immediately reduces the number eligible to approximately a thousand out of 450,000 members. The candidate must also have been a union member for ten years and a paid officer for at least five.

In order to run for the general executive board a worker must be a delegate to the convention and must have been a member for five years and a paid officer for three. Page 14, Article 3, Section 6, of the *ILGWU Constitution* reads:

> No member shall be eligible to hold a general office unless he or she has been a member of the ILGWU in continuous good standing, with respect to the office of vice president for at least 5 years prior to the convention, during three years of which he had held a full time, paid elective or appointive office, and with respect to the offices of President and General Secretary-Treasurer, for at least 10 years prior to the convention, during 5 years of which he had held a full time paid elective or appointive office.

An analysis of the composition of the delegates to the last three ILGWU conventions demonstrates that of the 450,000 members the number eligible to run for the general executive board, given the requirements for nomination, is reduced to less than three hundred. Those eligible for the posts of president or general secretary-treasurer are less than two hundred.

Thus of the entire membership of the ILGWU less than $\frac{1}{15}$ of 1 per cent are eligible to run for the general executive board and less than $\frac{1}{20}$ of 1 per cent are eligible for the presidency or general secretary-treasurership.

Under these conditions no more than four or five nonwhite persons would be eligible to run for the general executive board of the union and virtually none at all for the leadership positions. This explains why there is not a single Negro on the twenty-three-member general executive board and not a single Negro vice-president of the union, and why there are no Negro local mangers. (These last are usually hand-picked by the administration.)

These restrictions on political activity within the union and these eligibility requirements for top offices are clearly violations of the Bill of Rights for Members of Labor Organizations, contained in the Labor-Management Reporting and Disclosure Act of 1959 (Section 1010-A2 and Section 401-E).

At its national convention in May of 1968 the ILGWU minimally modified its candidate eligibility requirements, but only after the old leadership had already been elected, and no action was taken to void restrictions on membership participation within the union.

The federal court decision in the National Maritime Union case provided a new legal weapon to be used against the harsh restrictive conditions cited above, and also pointed to the ways in which the issues of racial discrimination and internal union democracy are interlocked. The Black caucus operating within the ILGWU has not been slow to observe the relevance of Judge Motley's decision.

In several cities, white and Black workers in the ILGWU are demanding from union officials copies of the contracts under which they work. Although the right of a union member to obtain a copy of the contract under which he works is guaranteed by federal law, ILGWU leaders refuse such requests virtually as a matter of policy.

In several local unions Negro members, despite harassment by union officials, have recently filed complaints against ILGWU election procedures, thus exhausting the administrative remedies as required by law, with the anticipation that such action will lead to litigation in the federal courts. On November 27, 1968, Negro members of ILGWU Local 155 in New York City filed a complaint with the U.S. Department of Labor protesting the election of local union officers.

Although the procedures established by the Labor-Management Reporting and Disclosure Act of 1959 are time-consuming and cumbersome, and litigation against the offending union must be brought by the Secretary of Labor, Negro workers with increasing frequency will use this new body of law together with other more direct forms of protest.

The Negro caucuses will also avail themselves increasingly of the new protections emerging from court decisions and administrative rulings. However, as the order of priority on social issues becomes vastly different for whites and Negroes, Black caucuses will also engage in independent political action, even if this course brings them into sharp conflict with the political positions of so-called "liberal" labor organizations. This has already occurred several times in Detroit (to take but one example), where the Trade Union Leadership Council, the citywide organization of Black automobile workers' caucuses, turned to an independent political course, breaking sharply with the UAW over local candidates in several Detroit elections and significantly winning over UAW opposition.

Thus the issues and conflicts have now become public. Negro caucuses are operating with increasing visibility, no longer satisfied to carry on their struggles within the confines of "acceptable" procedures. The intransigence and insensitivity of many labor unions to the interests of the Black community and to the increasing radicalization of Negro demands suggest sharp confrontations in the near future.

There is now emerging a new Black working class, concentrated both in heavy industry and in the service occupations, especially in the public sector. Negroes constitute 85 per cent of those teaching in Washington's public schools and 50 per cent of those teaching in Philadelphia's public schools; there are Black majorities in the labor force employed at several major auto-manufacturing plants in and around Detroit; over 90 per cent of the garbage collectors in Memphis are Negro; Black workers constitute 25 per cent of the membership of Local 1014 of the United Steelworkers of America employed at the huge U.S. Steel plant in Gary, Indiana; and in District 8 of the Steelworkers Union in the Baltimore area, Negroes constitute approximately 40 per cent of the membership. A number of the largest ILGWU locals in New York City now have a large majority of nonwhite members. The presence of Black majorities or near-majorities in major industrial plants and labor unions means that Negroes are now strategically concentrated, both geographically and occupationally, to exercise a new leverage within organized labor.

Conclusion

A major factor in the status of Black wage-earners in the American economy both during 1968 and in the decades to come, is the profound change in the demographic characteristics of the Negro people. As of 1968, almost half of the total Negro population was living in the urban North, and more than half of the Southern Negro population was living in the growing urban industrial complexes of the South. According to the 1960 census, 73 per cent of the Negro population lived in cities and the median age of the Negro population was lower than the median age of the white population. The median age for the Negro population was 23.5 years and the median age of the white population was 30.3 years. Furthermore, the Negro population had a significantly larger proportion of members under fifteen years of age. Less than 30 per cent of the white population in 1960 was under fifteen years of age, but 37 per cent of the Negro population was under fifteen years. If the rate of growth since 1950 of the Black population continues, one in eight Americans will be nonwhite before 1972.

An important consequence of the population increase among Negroes is the growth of potential nonwhite participation in the labor force. In 1968 Negroes constituted slightly more than one-tenth of the nation's labor force, but they will account for a much larger proportion of the future increase of the labor force. Based upon population changes that have already occurred, it is estimated that at least one-fifth of the increase in the labor force between 1964 and 1970 will be Negroes. By 1980, according to an authoritative study:

> . . . the total non-white labor force will have risen by 41 per cent compared with only a 28 per cent increase in white workers. This projected difference by growth rates is primarily attributable to the expected greater rate of population growth among non-white youth . . . the number of non-white workers is expected to increase from 8.7 million in 1965 to 12.3 million during the next 15 years.[8]

Projections based upon current economic data indicate that the rate of job expansion will fall seriously behind further increases in the rapid rate of labor force growth. The lag in new job creation for the next several years in conjunction with the continued discriminatory practices of management and certain important sections of organized labor will have the most serious consequences for Negro workers.

Given the deeply entrenched institutionalized patterns of job discrimination, an increase in aggregate demand through an expanding economy by itself does not solve the acute problems of Negro workers. But an expanding economy does at least create the essential context for Negro economic advancement. The combination of an expanding economy *together* with special programs to overcome the generations of racial disadvantage provides the basis for future progress. However, for this to occur extensive economic planning is required, together with the reordering of national priorities.

The failure of federal contract compliance, the demonstrated inability of fair employment practices commissions to alter patterns of employment discrimination, the inadequacy of the private sector in solving the problems of the ghetto, together with the emasculation of the anti-poverty program, clearly suggest that radical departures and new programs are necessary.[9]

Substantive social change is more likely to occur if there has been a change in the distribution and flow of power. Black control of viable institutions such as independent labor unions and business enterprises, among others, can confront the existing white controlled organizations which have exploited Black workers and kept them powerless and lead to the political mobilization of the entire Black community. This will be an essential factor in forcing social change.

It is not possible to confront these issues without establishing new basic priorities in cities and states, and in the nation as a whole. This means a concerted effort through broad social planning together with a new national programmatic agenda involving all the basic institutions of American life. The future of this nation will be decided by the manner and the speed with which the society responds to this crucial challenge.

Reference Notes

[1] See Herbert Hill, "Demographic Change and Racial Ghettos: The Crisis of American Cities," *Journal of Urban Law*, XLIV (Winter 1966), pp. 231–85.

[2] Building and Construction Trades Department of the AFL-CIO, *Proceedings of the Fifty-fourth Convention* [first day] (Bal Harbour, Florida, November 29, 1967), pp. 55–56.

[3] See Herbert Hill, "The Racial Practices of Organized Labor—The Age of Gompers and After," in *Employment, Race and Poverty*, ed. by Ross and Hill (New York, 1967), pp. 365–402.

[4] For additional information, see Herbert Hill, "No End of Pledges," *Commonweal*, XXXVII (March 15, 1968), pp. 709–12.

[5] Rowland Evans and Robert Novak, "Garment Unions Hamper Use of Training Funds," *Washington Post*, January 2, 1969. See also Herbert Hill, "Sewing Machines and Union Machines," *Nation*, CCVI (July 3, 1967), pp. 18–19.

[6] Jack Star, "A National Disgrace: What Unions Do to Blacks," *Look*, XXXII (November 12, 1968), pp. 33–37.

[7] For additional data, see Herbert Hill, "The Racial Practices of Organized Labor: The Contemporary Record," in *The Negro and the American Labor Movement*, ed. by Jacobson (New York, 1968), pp. 286–357.

[8] Cooper and Johnston, "Labor Force Projections by Color, 1970–80," 89, *Monthly Labor Review*, 965 (1966).

[9] See Herbert Hill, "Twenty Years of State Fair Employment Practice Commissions: A Critical Analysis with Recommendations," *Buffalo Law Review*, XIV (Fall 1964), pp. 22–69.

The Harlem River Consumers' Cooperative Supermarket is owned and operated by the Negro community on a profit-sharing basis.

Black Capitalism—1968

Edward D. Irons

OF ALL THE SECTORS of American life, there is none in which the Negro faces more formidable barriers than in the area of business. As a result, nonwhites owned less than 3 per cent of the total number of businesses in the United States at the end of 1968. In manufacturing, which brings the greatest average return on invested capital in the United States, the Negro in 1968 controlled less than 1 per cent.

It is not the purpose of this brief treatise to provide an in-depth assessment of the causal factors regarding this issue. However, it may appear a bit ironic that the intellectual capacity necessary to become a successful businessman is lower than that required by a number of fields in which the Negro has demonstrated the capacity to excel. Notable among these fields are law, engineering, medicine and mathematics. Obviously, then, intellectual capacity is not the most important factor involved in entering and succeeding in business.

If we examine the classical components which are necessary to successfully organize and operate a business enterprise, we conclude that success in business results from the working together of the four "*M*'s": men, money, machines and markets. While these components of business are simple enough, they do not tell the whole story. It is actually the proper interaction of these components that determines the degree of success to be achieved in any given situation. Historically this interaction has been controlled by that group in the business world known euphemistically as the "Establishment." Thus, unless the Establishment has been willing to allow individuals or groups to enter business through the normal channels, there has been little likelihood that such individuals or groups would be able to assemble the whole package necessary for success.

Historically, the most significant victim of the barriers erected by the business Establishment has been the American Negro. As is true of Americans generally, not every Negro aspires to enter business for himself. That portion of the Negro community which has aspired to a business career, however, has developed an attitude of frustration and cynicism over the generations.

Some observers have associated this frustration with the recent riots in America. It would be an overstatement to suggest that the riots which occurred during the last two years were caused by frustrated and cynical Black business aspirants. In my opinion, it would be an understatement, however, to suggest that cynical business aspirants had nothing to do with the riots in any sense. By themselves, this portion of Black America could not have precipitated such fury. Taken along with the frustration of other disillusioned groups, however (e.g., those seeking better health care, those seeking better education, those seeking better jobs—or jobs, period), the result could very well have been the violent explosions which are now a part of contemporary American history.

As a result of these developments, an amalgam of social scientists, philosophers, politicians, educators and businessmen has begun what might be called an agonizing reappraisal of what has gone wrong, and of what should be done to prevent the recurrence of such a debacle.

Thus, 1968 became the year of the "agonizing reappraisal." Each group saw the problem from its own vantage point and advocated an approach compatible with its own philosophy. Perhaps the most thorough and significant of the groups engaged in this reappraisal was the President's National Advisory Commission on Civil Disorders. In February this commission (two members of which were Negroes), headed by Governor Otto Kerner of Illinois and comprising a cross section of liberals and conservatives, of educators and politicians, of business and labor representatives, warned that "the country is drifting toward two societies, one Black, one White, separate and unequal. . . . What white Americans never understood—but what the Negro can never forget—is that the white society is deeply implicated in the ghetto. White institutions created it, white institutions maintain it, and white society condones it."

While this stinging indictment of white America was the subject of considerable controversy within the Establishment, it nevertheless set the stage for a broad spectrum of institutional reassessments and resultant programs designed to provide necessary remedies to problems which, for the first time in American history, were being faced realistically.

Predictably, the most significant of these reassessments and programs were carried out by the business establishment, sometimes independently and sometimes in conjunction with government. For the first time in United States history the commitment of the business Establishment toward the solution of urban problems (used synonymously with ghetto) appeared to be both genuine and forthright.

Some observers raised the question as to whether this new concern on the part of the business community was the result of its newly acquired humanism or whether it was acting out of fear of the system's crumbling. Nobody can answer this question unequivocally. However, no matter what the motivation of the business community is, if the problems are solved, the net result is the same. If one considers the prime motive that drives businessmen in a profit-oriented "free enterprise" system, it is hard to build a strong case for newly found humanity on the part of business. Until the fundamental system is changed (and that is not an issue here) the most significant criterion for measuring business success will be spelled P-R-O-F-I-T and not H-U-M-A-N-I-T-Y. Thus it would seem that the most likely motivation is short-range profit *vs.* long-range profit and, conceivably, maintenance of the system.

Major Industry Business Organization

Within this framework, then, a number of developments have taken place during 1968 that suggest that this year may be looked upon by historians as the beginning of a new era in the field of business as it affects the Black community.

These developments have covered a wide variety of approaches. Among the most significant are: (1) businesses organized in the Black community by major industry; (2) businesses organized in the Black community by Black businessmen; (3) capital and technical assistance by government sources, foundations and church groups. An important adjunct to this activity was the fact that both major Presidential candidates espoused support of Black entrepreneurship.

The business organized in the Black community by major industry took two forms. In one, the industry established a plant in the ghetto, maintaining the control but employing Negroes and other minorities at as many levels as possible, commensurate with their training and experience. In the other, the company, serving as a "mother hen," sponsored the business in cooperation with the Black community with the idea that, at some future date, the control of the firm would be transferred to investors from the Black community complete with management and other personnel.

Several examples of the former approach may serve to illustrate how it is being carried out. During 1968, the International Business Machines Corporation (IBM) built an electrical manufacturing plant in the heart of Brooklyn's Bedford-Stuyvesant slum area. This plant is wholly owned by IBM. However, its policy is to hire Negroes and other minorities on all levels of company operation from janitor to top management. IBM officials, in starting this plant, lowered their traditional hiring standards to a bare minimum. Initially, they were apprehensive about the results of such an operation. According to the latest reports from IBM, however, this plant, which employs some three hundred people, has a lower turnover than, and a productivity rate that compares favorably with, similar operations in which minorities do not predominate. The success of this imaginative venture has demonstrated to IBM and others that profits can be made in plants in which Negroes predominate at all levels.

Another major industry to establish a plant in a ghetto is AVCO, a company that built a $2.3 million printing establishment in the Roxbury section of Boston. Not only did AVCO staff the plant from the area, but they also hired Black firms to construct the building. By the end of 1968 this plant had a total of 189 employees, 80 per cent of whom were Black and 14 per cent of whom were Puerto Rican. By the end of 1968 the management of the plant was turned over to one of the experienced Black printers. While the plant is still very young in terms of operational experience, preliminary results thus far have led AVCO to consider developing another such plant in Los Angeles.

Control Data Corporation, a major electronics firm, was another firm to undertake such a project; they opened a computer parts plant in a Minneapolis ghetto.

Perhaps the most interesting and far-reaching type of business development in the ghetto is that in which a major firm helps to organize, finance and staff a business in cooperation with the Black community. A classic example is an enterprise in Washington, D.C., by the name of Fairmicco. This name is a contraction of the names of the two organizations that participated in the venture. These were MICCO (Model Inner City Community Organization), a conglomerate of community organizations operating in the urban renewal area called Shaw, and Fairchild-Hiller Corporation, a major aircraft and electronics manufacturing firm located just outside Washington. Fairmicco was organized for the purpose of providing employment for the hard-core male population of the ghetto.

To accomplish this, it was decided initially to select products that were relatively simple in their construction and then to progress to more complex products as the employees developed the necessary skills. Specifically, the product line was to begin with a simple woodwork item, then move to sheet metal and, finally, to electronic component assembly. Accordingly, wooden pallets and boxes were the first products which were selected. Through the procurement offices of the Small Business Administration, a major contract approximating $250,000 was negotiated with the Department of Defense. With this contract in hand, the Small Business Administration advanced a loan to the corporation, with which the latter began operations.

To make all this possible, Fairchild-Hiller agreed to provide interim management until a Black successor could be recruited and trained. In adddition, the company agreed to: (1) provide the technical assistance necessary to manufacture the products while skilled labor was being trained; (2) use its own marketing organization to make contacts in the industry for the purpose of facilitating the marketing of the products; (3) take a minority portion of the equity stock; and (4) provide several senior members of the board, one of whom was to be the president of Fairchild-Hiller. To cushion the impact of the excess labor costs stemming from the learning experience in the early phases of the operation, a training grant was awarded the company by the Department of Labor.

The company currently has seventy employees, but plans call for a staff of two hundred when the plant reaches capacity.

This organizational pattern has the obvious advantage of providing Negro employees with substantive experience in all aspects of the manufacturing industry, while hedging their risk during the learning period. Such a development pattern could do much to raise the level of ownership in the manufacturing field within the Black community. The newness of this organization precludes definitive conclusions as to its success level. However, given the level of commitment of Fairchild-Hiller, this project should provide new perspectives to ghetto economic development.

Major Industry Job Creation

One of the significant post-riot developments was the major thrust by big business to find jobs for substantial numbers of hard-core unemployed. As a result of the efforts of President Lyndon B. Johnson, the National Alliance of Business (NAB) was organized in 1968 under the leadership of Henry Ford, II. The specific goal was 100,000 jobs by June 1969 and 500,000 by 1971. By November 1968, NAB had produced 84,000 jobs spread over 12,000 firms. Thus, the NAB was well ahead of the schedule which it had set for itself ten months earlier. A significant factor in the success of this program was the cooperation between government and industry. To make hiring the hard-core unemployed practical from industry's point of view, the federal government subsidized up to one-third of the cost of the program.

It seems clear from the above that there is a genuine commitment on the part of major industry to make its contribution toward the problems of the ghetto.

Government Aid: Project Own

Government, like industry, evidenced considerable concern for the problems of Black entrepreneurship. While a number of agencies, such as the Office of Economic Opportunity (OEO) and the Department of Labor, participated to varying degrees, the most significant impact in this area was made by the Economic Development Administration (EDA) and the Small Business Administration (SBA).

One of the most significant developments on behalf of minority entrepreneurship in recent years has been the Small Business Administration's "Project Own." This program, launched in August 1968 by Howard J. Samuels, Administrator of SBA, was established to facilitate development of minority entrepreneurship and the entrance of minority businessmen into the mainstream of American business. Project Own deals with capital acquisition, managerial training and technical assistance. Obviously, these ideas are not new. What is new, however, is the degree of commitment and energy given them by Mr. Samuels.

A significant feature of Project Own was the coordinated utilization of the various sectors of American society: government, financial institutions, private enterprise and the minority community.

Under Project Own, each of the above was accorded specific responsibilities. For example, the government, through the SBA, provided loan guarantees and served as a liaison with other federal, state and local agencies functioning in this area. The financial institutions were called upon to make loans to minority businesses under SBA guarantee. In addition, they were asked to promote the growth of minority-owned banks, insurance companies, savings and loan associations and similar institutions.

The industrial sector was called upon to provide pilot programs in entrepreneurship through trade associations, franchisers, private foundations and individual firms. In addition, they were asked to assist in the areas of market research, management training programs and procurement assistance.

Perhaps the most vital aspect of this program was the minority community's responsibility to serve as the communications link between the community and the economic forces. The creators of Project Own felt that unless this channel was wide open, little benefit would accrue to the minority businessman.

One of the major innovations of Howard Samuels and Project Own in the area of loan-making was the concept of "compensatory capitalism." Under this concept the lending institutions were encouraged by SBA to lower risk standards for minority entrepreneurs, in an effort to compensate for the past history of social injustices. This concept was based on the premise that it was these social injustices in the course of American history that resulted in the stifling of the minority businessman to the point where he has not been able to develop the necessary qualifications for sound financing. To lead the way to compensatory capitalism, SBA changed its loan policies when dealing with minority entrepreneurs in a number of ways. Among the most important changes were: (1) allowing loans to effect changes in ownership (this was not permissible under previous policy); (2) accepting a lower net worth requirement in granting loans, as long as a business was capable of generating enough cash to meet its obligations.

Despite the fact that by December 1968 Project Own was only six months old, a number of results had begun to manifest themselves. Thus, during the three-month period ending December 31, 1968, the following achievements were in evidence:

1. The number and dollar volume of loans made to minority businesses in the last three months of 1968 as compared with the last three months of 1967 showed an increase of 846 loans, or 224 per cent. Similarly, there was a $19 million or 288 per cent increase in the dollar volume of loans over the same time period of the previous year. This increase was attributable primarily to the expanded participation of the banking industry. The banking industry participation increased from $2 million to $14.1 million, or by 600 per cent, over the previous period.

2. Procedures of processing loans were simplified to make the entrepreneur more comfortable with the process. In addition, the banking community agreed to assist in handling the financial paper work of participation or guaranteed loans.

3. Private industry pitched in and made the management and technical assistance program a reality:

> *a*) "Talent pools," comprising experts from trade and industrial associations, accounting, management and legal firms, and the academic community have been established to assist fledgling entrepreneurs.
>
> *b*) SCORE (Senior Citizens Organization of Retired Executives) volunteers committed themselves in twenty-seven "inner city" target areas to counseling over a thousand Project Own participants.

In addition to the above, Project Own undertook four major steps to improve communications with the minority community. These were: (1) the establishment of the Black National Advisory Council, comprising members from all major Black organizations; (2) the establishment of a Spanish American Advisory Council; (3) the establishment of Minority Entrepreneurship Teams in twenty-eight cities and rural target areas to assist in stimulating existing businesses and in locating worthy businesses and minority entrepreneurs; (4) the development of a program to set up a Black small business advisory council on the community level of each inner city area.

Besides this, Project Own established a long-range program designed to increase the minority business population by an annual growth rate that would bring the minority entrepreneur to parity with the mainstream of business by selected future target dates.

Admittedly these objectives are difficult, and they can only be achieved if they become a part of America's national purpose. It is clear, however, that Project Own has indeed made one of the most significant contributions toward bringing such an objective to the attention of the nation's leaders and toward its ultimate fruition.

Government Aid: Economic Development Administration

Another government agency which exerted considerable effort in 1968 to improve the economic condition of the Black community was the Economic Development Administration of the U.S. Department of Commerce. EDA made a number of "seed money" grants to selected trade associations representing the Black business community. Among the most prominent grantees were the National Bankers Association, the National Insurance Association and the National Business League. While each of these associations has existed for many years (NBA since 1927, NIA since 1919, and NBL since 1900), the "seed money" given them by EDA provided a means for the first substantial programs in their histories.

The grants, totaling over $1 million, supported programs to strengthen existing Black entrepreneurship and served as a catalyst in raising the economic base of the Black communities. A brief explanation of the resultant programs of these three most significant grantees is set forth below.

The National Bankers Association. The NBA was among the first of such associations to receive an EDA grant. The small number of member institutions had until that time prevented the NBA from raising sufficient funds to conduct a meaningful program. By the end of 1968 the association had a membership of twenty (a mere five years earlier the members numbered eleven, although the association had been in operation since 1927). These banks were looked upon by their public as having major responsibility in the economic development of their respective communities. Yet they were hampered by a number of factors from properly carrying out this task.

At the association's fortieth annual convention, in September 1967 in Kansas City, Kansas, Governor Andrew F. Brimmer of the Federal Reserve Board challenged NBA members to seek new ways to increase their effectiveness in the economic development process of the urban centers which they served. Accepting this challenge, the association sought the assistance of Dr. Edward D. Irons, chairman of business administration at Howard University, in Washington, D.C. In cooperation with the executive committee of NBA, Dr. Irons designed a program and sought funding from the Economic Development Administration.

In May 1968 the NBA was awarded $230,000 by the Office of Technical Assistance of EDA to cover a two-year operating period. Dr. Irons then became the first executive director of NBA. The grant was given in support of a technical assistance program designed to help member banks improve their operations and ultimately their competitiveness in the industry. By virtue of their location and the nature of their ownership, EDA felt that these banks provided an excellent vehicle through which additional capital, management assistance, and expertise for economic development could be channeled. The development of viable financial institutions, it was hoped, would measurably improve the economic bases of the communities in which they were located (i.e., the "inner city"). Accordingly, the program was designed to achieve the following objectives: (1) to strengthen NBA member bank management through the provision of timely management information and training programs; (2) to attract deposits from a wider market area and thus provide a larger supply of lendable funds; (3) to develop in the bankers keener insights into the basic economy of the areas which they served; (4) to provide short- and long-range plans for the analysis of each bank's potential growth; (5) to provide technical assistance for worthwhile entrepreneurs' activities which might be suggested by member banks; (6) to assist in a new-bank organization development.

As a result of the increased availability of funds, NBA achieved or initiated the following programs in 1968: (1) the development of a management training program, in conjunction with the American Bankers Association, designed to prepare twenty Black middle management trainees per year for five years for positions in Black banks; (2) the preparation of a ten-year ratio analysis of significant management information of NBA banks in comparison with smaller figures from all insured commercial banks in the country; (3) the establishment of a close working relationship between the NBA and the ABA through the Urban Affairs Committee of the ABA, which has resulted in joint sponsorship of selected programs; (4) the provision of a liaison between Black banks and companies, organizations or foundations desirous of depositing money in these banks; (5) the establishment of an information department which collects and disseminates information which may be of relevance to the member banks; (6) the initiation of computer programs designed to plan and analyze a five-year future growth potential on a continuing basis for NBA member banks.

The National Insurance Association. Another association of Black financial institutions to receive an EDA grant was the NIA. Historically, the NIA has been the most viable of the Black business trade associations. Consisting of forty-six members spread through twenty-five states, NIA had total assets of $417 million and $2.3 billion worth of insurance in force by the end of 1967. By the end of 1968, both total assets and insurance in force had increased by approximately 5 per cent.

As in the case of the NBA grant, EDA hoped that its grant funds would stimulate increased economic activity in the inner city. Upon receipt of its $238,000 grant from EDA in mid-1968, the NIA set certain objectives which it hoped to accomplish on behalf of the inner city. In substance, the program was designed to strengthen members of NIA while devising new ways to invest more funds into the urban centers.

During the months of November and December 1968, the NIA launched a campaign entitled "Security Is Power." Its objective was to increase the economic power in life insurance to approximately 2,000,000 Black people. While it is too soon to assess the results of this program, the NIA members are optimistic about prospects of rendering better service to their communities.

The National Business League. The NBL, currently headed by Mr. Berkley Burrell, was the third Black trade association to receive funds from EDA. Founded in 1900, the NBL has as its basic goal the establishment of a condition of equal participation in business by all citizens, and, more specifically, economic development of the Black community in general and development of entrepreneural activity in particular.

In pursuit of these goals NBL evolved three main programs. The first, "Project Outreach," was funded by both EDA and the Office of Economic Opportunity and was designed to develop pilot programs in twelve cities to provide training and technical assistance for minority businessmen. The second program, "Project Uplift," was designed to provide "tutorial" training to expand the operating capabilities of existing small businesses. The third, "Project Mainstream," was aimed at organizing and upgrading the nation's existing small businesses to the point where they may successfully integrate and become competitive in the mainstream of American economy.

In addition to the above activities, NBL organized in 1968 the Booker T. Washington Foundation. Its purpose is to provide economic assistance to Black businessmen throughout America. The foundation is being funded through private contributions, the first of which was a $1 million grant from the Rosensteil Foundation of New York City.

The primary funding for NBL in 1968 was a combination grant from the Office of Economic Opportunity and EDA in the amount of $413,000. As a result of these increased funds, NBL was able to expand its programs measurably. An example can be seen in the increase in the number of NBL chapters (from thirty-two in 1967 to fifty by December 1968).

Project Outreach has added eight local development companies in different cities throughout the country. These companies have placed most of their emphasis on the establishment of shopping centers. In fact, as a result of Project Outreach a total of 132 businesses were expanded and fifty-eight new businesses were established. Among the most significant of these were Mahalia Jackson Chicken Franchises, a furniture processing plant, and a tool-grinding facility.

While the funds provided by EDA are not intended to finance a program completely, they are designed to provide a nucleus around which sound programs can be planned and executed and to provide a base from which additional sources of funds can be developed. Thus a significant economic impact from the programs set in motion by EDA will be felt in the foreseeable future.

Contributions of Negro Businessmen

One of the principal goals of Black capitalism, if it is to contribute significantly to the economic development of the inner cities, is the generation and retention of wealth inside the ghetto. An effective method of accomplishing this goal is the development of Black-owned and controlled businesses from within the area.

During 1968 there was increasing evidence of this kind of activity. An example was the organization of the Progress Plaza Shopping Center in Philadelphia. This was one of the nation's first Black-owned and operated shopping centers and represents one of 1968's most noteworthy developments.

Organized by Rev. Leon Sullivan, the center was financed by a pledge of $10 monthly for thirty-six months from 650 church members of the Zion Baptist Church, of which Mr. Sullivan was pastor. The Progress Plaza Shopping Center consists of ten stores owned and operated by Negroes and seven stores, including a supermarket, shoe shop and banking offices, which will be managed by Negroes. Also included in the plans is a management entrepreneur school, funded by a Ford Foundation grant and designed to train two hundred Negroes for administrative positions. Additional financing for construction was provided through a $1.3 million bank loan and a $400,000 Ford Foundation grant.

Though the center is not confined solely to Negroes, a company must have not only a Black manager but also a majority of Black employees. This provision serves to keep the dollar from flowing out of the Black community to absentee owners.

In St. Louis, too, a Negro group has purchased and undertaken the development of a seven-acre urban renewal site for a ten-store shopping center. This group, Vanguard Bond and Mortgage

Company, headed by James E. Hurt, Jr., is investing about $689,000 in the project.

In the Watts area in Los Angeles, former basketball star Willie Nauls, with the assistance of A. J. Barnett, chairman of the board of Pacific Mutual Insurance Company, is organizing the development of another shopping center. One of the largest in the area, it will house several chain stores, each with a Black manager. This project provides a good example of the interaction possible between Black and white entrepreneurs in that the insurance company has pledged to supply up to $1.5 million in funds and management expertise.

A further development in the field of Black-owned business includes the hotel industry. In Harlem, a $4.5 million motor hotel is to be built by Harlem investors and the Hotel Corporation of America. Organized by Mr. William Pegg, a Harlem real estate and insurance broker, together with the Interracial Council of Business, the hotel will not only be a first-class facility but will also provide a source of jobs for the community.

Another unique business that was initiated in 1968 by Black businessmen was that of franchising. (Incidentally, franchising is one of the fastest-growing industries in the country.) A prime example of this new development is the above-mentioned Mahalia Jackson Chicken system, which was the first national food franchising system completely under Black management. Opened in December 1968 in Memphis, the system will be offered to Black groups and Black businessmen in major metropolitan areas. This type of business will offer substantial opportunities for businessmen of modest means.

Foundations and Religious Organizations

The fervor generated by the activity of government and industry in the area of Black capitalism had some "fallout" effect on other types of institutions, whose traditional roles did not include economic development. The most significant of these were foundations and religious organizations.

Foundations. The most auspicious beginning in the area of economic development was made by the Ford Foundation. The Foundation announced a $10 million grant in 1968 for the purpose of stimulating economic development among minorities. The fund was used as a source of loans to and investment in minority-owned businesses or businesses that employed substantial numbers of minority employees. Other Ford grants included $350,000 to States Urban Action of Washington, $100,000 to the city of Gary, Indiana, and $520,000 to the Negro Industrial and Economic Union of Cleveland.

Several other organizations were awarded grants totaling over $500,000. These funds were also used to stimulate Negro business ownership and investment. In addition, grants in excess of $3 million were given to improve business administration practices and to broaden education services of predominantly Negro colleges. The Ford Foundation also provided $1,050,000 to research ghetto residents' needs and requests, to help Negroes buy franchises, to help establish Black-owned credit and consumers unions and to organize neighborhood associations. Other grants of $230,000 and $300,000 were awarded to train ministers in the many fields of urban needs, such as business opportunity, education, housing, employment, welfare and political processes—and to help Black contractors compete in the burgeoning construction field.

Although the Ford Foundation was the first to launch its program, other foundations made starts or were in the planning stages of their programs during 1968. Among these were the Taconic and the Rockefeller Foundations.

Religious Organizations. Among the more significant religious organizations to make contributions were the Episcopal and the Presbyterian Churches. These organizations deposited funds in Black financial institutions and bought capital stock in Black business enterprises, and have given aid in other ways as well.

The Episcopal Church, for example, deposited $650,000 in Black financial institutions and circulated letters to all of its dioceses asking them to do likewise on the local level.

The Presbyterian Economic Development Corporation invested money in the central city. They provided $500,000 to be used by the Interracial Council of Business Opportunity to guarantee bank loans made to minority businessmen. And another $500,000 was provided to Freedom National, of New York. Thus the churches began to assert themselves in the crucial battle to bring the opportunities of the mainstream to Black America.

Political Pronouncements on Urban Problems

In politics at this time there existed widespread concern for the condition of the nation's "inner cities" and about possible remedies for these conditions. This was seen in the statements of some of 1968's most prominent political figures. For instance, Richard M. Nixon, when campaigning for the Presidency, advocated what was then (April 1968) a "new approach" to the racial problems of the nation. He called for emphasis on more Black ownership, Black pride, Black jobs, Black opportunity and Black power in its most constructive sense. He then produced the concept of Black capitalism.

He also pointed out the need for the private sector to take the added risks incurred in ghetto development and in training the unemployed in order to help the underdeveloped urban areas. Mr. Nixon suggested that interest on the part of private industry would come about as a result of tax incentives made available through the government.

Vice-President Hubert Humphrey advocated a similar concept which he called the "Marshall Plan." Such a plan was designed to accomplish in the ghettoes what the original Marshall Plan had accomplished in the rehabilitation of post-World War II Europe.

Finally, while it is too soon to see to what extent the programs launched in 1968 will achieve their ends, it seems safe to say that, for the first time in history, all of the major sectors of American society made a definite commitment to use their resources towards the elimination of America's most complex problem—the urban ghetto.

Ralph Matthews, Jr., speaking to a community group on housing problems.

The Urban Scene: Housing and Poverty

Paget L. Alves, Jr.

THE HOTTEST ISSUE in the news in 1968 was the urban crisis. It was a year crammed with confrontations, communication, proposals, ventilation and campaigns—all involving some aspect of the urban crisis.

Early in the year President Johnson laid down a challenge in his "Message on Housing and Cities"; the life insurance industry's $1 billion program rolled into high gear; the savings bank industry announced creation of a special loan committee on urban problems. Urban America and the Urban Coalition stepped up activities; the Civil Rights Act and the Housing Act of 1968 were passed. The Supreme Court upheld an 1866 law banning housing discrimination; three Presidential committees published reports on aspects of the urban crisis; Office of Economic Opportunity (OEO) programs were again attacked; tenants fought landlords; welfare clients demonstrated; model city areas became battlegrounds; income maintenance gained adherents; and it became fashionable to support Black entrepreneurs.

Almost everyone was in search of methods of action relevant to the problems of slums, poverty and the ghetto. Meanwhile, the poor and the disadvantaged were organizing confrontations, battling for community control, and demonstrating, in an attempt to get rid of the day-to-day crunch of poverty, discrimination and powerlessness. Let's take a look at the components that contributed to the urban crisis in 1968.

Migration

At the beginning of the twentieth century over 90 per cent of the Negro population in the United States lived in the South, and most lived on farms. Over the past sixty-eight years the search for a better life has caused Black people to leave the farm and the South, with the majority going to metropolitan centers in the East, Midwest and West. As a result, only 55 per cent of the 21.5 million Black Americans were in the South in 1966. More than half of the Black population in the South now live in cities. A rural Black majority exists in only four states: Arkansas, Mississippi, North Carolina and South Carolina.

The metropolitan Afro-American population was 15.2 million in 1968, an increase of 3.3 million over 1960. In the larger metropolitan areas the nonwhite population was growing faster in gross and in proportion than in smaller areas. Black Americans in rural areas have dropped to 31 per cent. Some 69 per cent of the Black population live in metropolitan areas. About 11.9 million or 45 per cent of the nonwhite population live in the central city—approximately 25 per cent more than in 1960. At the same time, over the years the white population has been decreasing in the central city. In 1968 there were 2.1 million fewer whites in the central city than in 1960, and they were a mere 12.6 per cent of the white population in center city.

The Ghetto

Following a traditional pattern, early Afro-American migrants to the cities settled in the older areas, and as others arrived they moved into the same neighborhoods. As the white immigrants who lived in these areas improved their economic conditions, they moved to new communities with better housing and schools. However, when Black Americans improved their economic, social and cultural levels their access to better areas was effectively blocked.

Discriminatory housing practices—some overt and others subtle—discouraged Black people in their search for a better life for their families. Intimidation, threats, violence and outright refusal were all used to deny Blacks access to improved living conditions. In spite of the existence of laws banning housing discrimination and despite the efforts of various voluntary organizations, exclusionary practices persist. As a result most Afro-Americans are forced to remain in ghetto areas. With continued migration the center city ghetto continues to expand, block by block (see Table 1).

TABLE 1

Population Change by Location inside and outside Metropolitan Areas, 1950–66
(Numbers in millions)

(From the Report of the National Advisory Commission on Civil Disorders)

	Population						Change 1950–66			
	Negro			White			Negro		White	
	'50	'60	'66	'50	'60	'66	#	%	#	%
United States	15.0	18.8	21.5	135.2	158.8	170.8	6.5	43	35.6	26
Metropolitan areas	8.4	12.2	14.8	80.3	99.7	109.0	6.4	77	28.7	36
Central cities	6.5	9.7	12.1	45.5	47.7	46.4	5.6	87	.9	2
Urban fringe	1.9	2.5	2.7	34.8	52.0	62.5	.8	42	27.7	79
Small cities, towns and rural areas	6.7	6.7	6.7	54.8	59.2	61.8	*	1	7.0	13

* Rounds to less than 50,000.

The exodus of white families was aided by the government. In the post-war years, the Federal Housing Administration (FHA) and the Veterans Administration (VA) encouraged and subsidized construction of suburban developments, which assisted some 5 million white families to become home owners. In addition, government subsidies financed construction of highways to connect the expanding suburb to the city, and provided funds to build such community facilities as water supplies, sewer systems and schools.

On the other hand, the government discouraged racial dispersion and thereby helped create and expand the ghetto. Until 1950, FHA and VA manuals set the tone of planning and development by the following language:

> . . . if a neighborhood is to retain stability, it is necessary that properties shall continue to be occupied by the same social and racial group.

Nevertheless, some 300,000 nonwhites moved into the suburbs in the early 1960's, largely in segregated developments. In spite of this, the percentage of Blacks in suburbs between 1960 and 1966 dropped from 8.9 per cent to 4.6 per cent.

The exodus of whites from the central city continued to accelerate. In 1950 some 45.5 million whites lived in central cities. In 1968 the white population of central cities was 45.5 million. If this population had increased in proportion to the nation's white population growth, it would now be 58.3 million. The fact that it is not indicates clearly that almost 13 million whites fled the nation's central cities during these eighteen years. Obviously, white attitudes based on race and color are responsible for housing segregation, which results in Black ghettoes. Unless changed, these are the forces that will continue to determine the future of our cities.

Slums

A recent study (*A Decent Home: Report of the President's Committee on Urban Housing*), based on census data, indicates that there were 6.7 million occupied substandard dwelling units in 1966. The Census Bureau acknowledges that their 1960 figures under-reported substandard units by one-third. We can therefore add another 2.2 million to this estimate, making an adjusted estimate of 8.9 million substandard units. Although Table 2 (p. 187) has not been adjusted, it pinpoints the nature and extent of housing conditions in metropolitan areas and particularly in central cities. When adjusted by one-third, the figures become even more alarming.

In 1960 metropolitan areas had 31.2 million units, or 53.5 per cent of the total supply. Although the poverty areas were some 23 per cent of the land area of central cities, they accounted for some 79 per cent of the units occupied by Blacks as well as about 76 per cent of the substandard and 54 per cent of the overcrowded units. When adjusted for under-count, these figures become even more significant. Obviously, grossly inadequate housing marks the Black slum and constitutes a critical problem for those forced to live in such urban jungles.

TABLE 2

Selected Housing Data for SMSA's* of over 250,000 Population
(Poverty Areas, 1960)

(From *Housing Conditions in Urban Poverty Areas,* National Commission on Urban Problems, Research Report No. 9)

	Central City Units (in thousands)		Poverty Area Percentages	
Item	Total	Poverty Areas	Central City	Outlying Areas
Land area	7.7	1.8	23.3	25.7
All units	16,477	5,481	33.3	10.3
Occupied	15,557	5,067	32.6	9.9
Owner occupied	7,070	1,339	18.9	8.1
Renter occupied	8,487	3,728	43.9	14.8
Vacant	920	414	45.0	14.6
Units occupied by nonwhites	2,522	1,997	79.2	46.7
Substandard nonwhites	1,784	1,352	75.8	32.7
Dilapidated	572	520	90.9	60.6
Overcrowded	1,650	895	54.2	19.2
Nonwhites	581	485	83.5	54.1
Units in multi-family structures	8,283	3,497	42.2	10.5
Nonwhites	1,385	1,152	83.2	37.6
Over 20 years	11,449	4,674	40.8	13.6
Nonwhites	1,953	1,623	83.1	47.8

*SMSA's–Standard Metropolitan Statistical Areas.

Housing Needs

The President's Committee on Urban Housing estimates that 7.8 million families (one in eight) are house poor: they can't afford standard housing if the rent is based on 20 per cent of family income. The report *A Decent Home* indicates that a total of 26.7 million units, 7.5 million for poor families, will have to be provided by 1978 to eliminate substandard housing. Although nonwhite families are expected to be only 30 per cent of the house poor, one in every four Black as against one in twelve white families will need to be subsidized (see Table 3).

TABLE 3

Distribution of Noneffective Demand. Households by White and Nonwhite Head, inside All SMSA's: 1960, 1968, 1978

(From *A Decent Home: Report of the President's Committee on Urban Housing*)

	White Head[1]		Nonwhite Head[2]	
Year	Thousands	%	Thousands	%
1960	3,612	11.8	1,017	29.2
1968	3,374	9.6	989	23.4
1978	3,380	7.7	1,132	18.3

[1] Relative to all white families in SMSA's.
[2] Relative to all nonwhite families in SMSA's.

Of all the house poor families, the large family is the most disadvantaged. In this instance we are talking about families in need of three or more bedrooms and unable to afford adequate housing when spending 25 per cent of their income for rent. Everyone knows that there is a shortage, but few hard facts are available to document the dimensions of the problem.

The staff of the "Douglas Commission" conducted a seven-city survey to pinpoint the magnitude of the shortage (*The Large Poor Family: A Housing Gap*, National Commission on Urban Problems, Research Report No. 4). The report indicated that 103,000 large families were in need. Almost 87 per cent of these families were Black. The available inventory in the cities was from 71 to 85 per cent short of the need. The total need was reduced by the number of existing and planned units, resulting in a net gap of 71,000 units. Some 345,000 children are in the 71,000 house poor large families. Projecting this data to the nation's sixty-one cities of over 200,000 people, the estimated gap is 529,000 units, with 2.5 million disadvantaged children. Assuming that 85 per cent would be Black, there are 450,000 house poor large Black families with 2.1 million children in need of adequate housing.

Poverty

It is generally assumed that most Black people live in slums because of poverty. The table below illustrates the fallacy of this assumption.

TABLE 4

Percentages of White and Negro Families (Total and Poor) Living in the Suburban Ring of the Ten Largest Urban Areas

(From J. F. Kain and J. J. Persky, *Alternatives to the Gilded Ghetto*, Program on Regional and Urban Economics, Harvard University)

	White		Negro	
	All Families	Families with Incomes $3,000	All Families	Families with Incomes $3,000
New York	27.8%	16.3%	9.4%	8.2%
Los Angeles	65.2	61.6	27.3	23.3
Chicago	47.6	37.2	7.7	5.9
Philadelphia	50.8	37.4	15.7	14.2
Detroit	58.9	44.9	12.1	11.3
San Francisco-Oakland	57.8	48.8	29.2	25.8
Boston	74.3	64.0	19.2	13.9
Washington	75.7	59.6	9.8	10.4
Pittsburgh	70.5	63.3	29.4	27.1
Cleveland	59.2	39.3	3.1	2.4

The above table shows that from two to six times more poor whites than Blacks live in suburbs. Obviously many, if not most, Black people are living in slums because of discrimination. Simply stated, poverty is the lack of sufficient money to provide an adequate standard of living. In order to avoid poverty one must have a good job. Although Afro-American unemployment rates have been declining over the past ten years —from 12.6 per cent in 1958 to 8.2 per cent in 1967—the rate for Blacks is double that for whites. Generally, Negro workers are concentrated in lower paid unskilled jobs, marked by substandard wages, unstable tenure, low status and discrimination. Although Black American family incomes have been increasing, about 20 per cent have not improved—despite marked prosperity in our affluent society. The gap between Black and white median family income in metropolitan areas increased from $3,154 in 1959 to $3,323 in 1967. As Daniel P. Moynihan puts it, in the Report of the National Advisory Commission on Civil Disorders (the Kerner Report):

> The principal measure of progress toward equality will be that of employment. It is the primary source of individual or group identity . . . the linkage between problems of employment and the range of social pathology that afflicts the Negro community is unmistakable. Employment not only controls the present for the Negro American but, in a most profound way, it is creating the future as well.

Unemployment and underemployment are chronic conditions in most Black slum areas and are aggravated by a steady flow of unemployed migrants. A Department of Labor survey indicates that some 32.7 per cent of the residents in low income areas of nine cities were unemployed or underemployed in 1966. Table 5 (below) graphically depicts the dimension of the subemployment problem in central city ghettoes.

The most important source of poverty among Afro-Americans is their concentration at the lowest end of the occupational scale. In fact an analysis of the above data showed that upgrading Black men so that their occupational and income distribution would be comparable to that of the total labor force would provide $4.8 billion income to Black families, whereas if unem-

TABLE 5

Nonwhite Subemployment in Disadvantaged Areas of All Central Cities, 1967

(From the Report of the National Advisory Commission on Civil Disorders)

	Unemployment	Under-employ-ment	Total Sub-employ-ment
Adult men	102,000	230,000	332,000
Adult women	118,000	266,000	384,000
Teen-agers	98,000	220,000	318,000
Total	318,000	716,000	1,034,000

ployment were reduced to the white rate and the newly employed were paid the Black median income, it would produce only $1.5 billion more income to Black American families.

Subemployment and discrimination make a disproportionate number of Negro men incapable of supporting a family and send more Negro women into the labor force. A man's inability to support his family causes tensions, ego damage and family disruptions. Statistical evidence documents the close correlation between male unemployment rates, females separated from their husbands and fluctuations in the Aid to Families with Dependent Children rate in the Black community. Twice the number of unemployed Black males are separated and divorced as employed Black men. Fatherlessness becomes endemic, forcing children into crime-ridden, violence-prone, poverty-stricken streets where the model becomes the hustler, dope pusher, number-runner, prostitute and kept woman. The message conveyed is that the system rewards illegal and exploitive activities and frowns on straight or square behavior. The life style in this jungle is marked by escalating illegitimacy rates, narcotics addiction, high rates of truancy, dropouts, juvenile delinquency, venereal disease and crime.

The poor in racial ghettoes are less healthy than the average American, have higher mortality rates, have less money to spend for medical services, find that discrimination restricts access to medical services, and live with an inadequate level of sanitation services on a per capita basis. It is generally conceded that substantial exploitation exists in ghetto areas. The Kerner Report found unfair commercial practices in eleven out of twenty cities studied. The Black poor in cities are less sophisticated than others about choices of stores, are apprehensive about their reception and are not able easily to reach a variety of shopping outlets; they probably have poor credit records and are poorly informed about credit contracts, their legal rights and obligations, and sources of advice. As a result they tend to patronize local retail stores where exploitive practices are the rule; they generally pay higher prices and become further enmeshed in a web of credit purchases which often leads to repossession of merchandise and garnishing of wages—resulting in one more bad mark on the credit record.

Resources for Action

Housing and Urban Development Act. On August 1, 1968, President Johnson signed the new housing act into law. In the next three years, it can make possible the construction and rehabilitation of an estimated 1.5 million units. The most relevant of its programs are provisions that would make home ownership possible for approximately 500,000 families with incomes from $3,000 to $7,000; provide apartments for an estimated 450,000 low and moderate income families; provide family counseling in regard to credit, debt and budget management; make mortgage insurance available in declining neighborhoods; provide interest-free loans and technical advice to non-profit sponsors of low and moderate cost units; increase rehabilitation grants from $1,500 to $3,000; and require training and employment of low income residents. In addition it continues and expands existing programs such as public housing, model cities, rent supplements and urban renewal.

Civil Rights Act of 1968. On April 11, President Johnson signed the Civil Rights Act of 1968 into law. Passage of the law was achieved after a two-year campaign, a dramatic shift by Senator Dirksen (with the explanation that time and reality make you older and wiser) and the assassination of Dr. Martin Luther King. Title VIII of this law prohibits discrimination based on race, color, religion or national origin in the sale, rental, financing or advertising of dwelling units, including vacant land for residential purposes. It also makes "blockbusting" illegal and opens membership on real estate boards and multiple listing services to nonwhites.

Supreme Court decision on 1866 law. On June 17 the U.S. Supreme Court reaffirmed the legality of the 1866 law which provides that:

> All citizens of the United States shall have the same right, in every state and territory, as is enjoyed by white citizens thereof to inherit, purchase, lease, sell, hold and convey real and personal property.

This decision and Title VIII provide the means for eliminating housing discrimination and segregation. Three avenues of redress are now available: complaints to the Department of Housing and Urban Development (HUD) and state agencies, suits in federal courts and requests to the U.S. Attorney General to file suit on behalf of the aggrieved.

At the close of the year, however, the promise implicit in the housing and civil rights laws was shattered by Congress. The same Congress that had approved these measures emasculated implementation of them by denying the necessary moneys. As a result, over the next three years the new housing law will help only thirty-three thousand of low and moderate income families to home ownership; will construct only thirty-three thousand low-cost apartments; will not provide family counseling; will not make available interest-free loans and technical assistance to non-profit sponsors; and other budget cuts will reduce achievements in all other programs. Funds for implementation of the fair housing title of the Civil Rights Act were cut from $11 to $2 million, thereby destroying the potential this measure had of eliminating housing discrimination. The Black American community and others interested in eradicating slums and ghettoes are now challenged to mount the necessary lobbying activities for restoration of adequate funding to achieve the objectives of the recently enacted housing and civil rights laws.

Life insurance program. Although the life insurance industry announced its $1 billion urban investment program in September 1967, the program did not begin to move until 1968. It proposed to provide mortgages, to house low and moderate income families, and to create jobs and services in slum and ghetto areas that would not be financed under normal lending practices.

As of December 1968, over $810.7 million

were committed or loaned, providing funds to projects in 228 cities in forty-two states. Some $622.7 million is going into building or renovating approximately 57,589 housing units. About $188 million is being used to create 26,436 jobs. Under consideration is an additional $127 million for various types of projects.

This effort provided additional dollars for investing in constructing and rehabilitating housing as well as for job producing enterprises. However, initially the program bypassed utilizing the services of Negro real estate brokers, mortgage bankers, banks and other enterprises. Toward the end of the year, however, a number of Afro-American banks and several mortgage bankers were involved. While the additional dollars are significant, these funds represent approximately 6 per cent of the industry's annual investments. Probably more significant is the demonstration of a successful effort which can serve as a model and stimulus to other facets of the private sector. Obviously, the scope of the private sector's response has to be on a larger scale to resolve the crisis in the ghetto.

Savings bank program. On March 6 leaders of this industry announced at a White House meeting a program to increase their financial commitment to help resolve urban housing problems. The co-chairman of the group estimated that from $3 to $5 billion of private credit would be needed for just one program to rebuild the inner city—the model city program. There are some 6,500 banks with resources of over $200 billion in this industry. By the end of the year, industry leaders had decided not to provide comprehensive data documenting the number of project units and dollars financed. They did, however, publish an *Urban Financing Guide*, to stimulate local lending institutions to expand their efforts.

There is a decided lack of enthusiasm in the industry to pick up the challenge of dramatically increasing the flow of mortgage credit to inner city neighborhoods. However, promising efforts were initiated in New York State (where an estimated $125 million was committed for approximately 6,500 units) and in a few cities, notably Boston and New York. One message that persistently comes through is that the industry is watching the pioneer efforts of New York's Bowery and New York Bank for Savings' effort, which is building seven projects to house some five hundred families at an estimated $10 million.

Industry. "If you cats can't do it, it's never going to get done," said Frank Ditto to Detroit's industrial leaders. In less colorful language, many others have pointed to the demonstrated capacity of big business to overcome obstacles once thought to be insurmountable. Appeals to industrial leaders are continually being made by presidents, mayors, humanitarians, civil rights leaders and militants.

Newspapers and magazines report many proposals and plans but few hard accomplishments. Among the more promising of such proposals in 1968 were U.S. Steel and Mayor Hatcher's joint plans to build some three hundred moderate cost units on the fringe of Gary's slum area, and Westinghouse Electric Corporation's creation of a subsidiary to build and rehabilitate housing for low income families. Such reports are widely hailed and tend to give the impression that industry is attacking the problems of the slum with vigor.

The vast majority of big businesses and industries are not involved in programs to build or rehabilitate housing for low and moderate income families. A study of 541 of the largest industrial and business organizations by the President's Committee on Urban Housing found that less than 8 per cent of these organizations are involved in constructing or rehabilitating housing. The major reasons for not being involved were reported as: not interested, not their business and profits too low.

Blacks are building. Afro-American groups around the country are breaking ground building housing, shopping centers and offices. Church groups, individually and in coalitions, fraternal groups from Alpha through the Elks and Masons to Omega, civil rights groups, union groups, poverty and community groups —all are involved in adding to the supply and improving the quality of the existing inventory. Reports from Milwaukee, New Orleans, New York, Boston, Watts and almost every state tell of non-profit as well as profit-motivated groups helping to rebuild urban areas.

Typical of the activities in 1968 were: The first units constructed under Section 235 of the new housing law were completed in Watts by Community Pride, Inc. A $5.5 million development of 264 houses on 175 acres is being constructed in Dayton. Ten development corporations in seven Southern cities are building houses, shopping centers and office buildings in urban renewal areas. A group in Boston is completing a $1 million rehabilitation project. The Masons are building eleven projects in five Southern states and the District of Columbia to provide 1,744 units at a cost of $22.4 million. Afro-Americans in the American Baptist Service Corporation are sponsoring some thirty projects with about four thousand units at an estimated $60 million. Three of an estimated twenty-five Black general contractors were building or rehabilitating some 2,600 units in 1968 at an estimated cost of $45.2 million.

Conclusion

The dialogue today—within the Black community as well as between the Black and white communities—is of tremendous significance. We are really debating the means and ends in regard to the question: What will life in America be like in 1978, and beyond, for Black Americans, other minorities, and Americans as a whole? The dimensions of life in America in the future are being molded by today's debate and decisions.

Analysis of current conditions, generally described as the urban crisis, leads to the conclusion that we are moving with increasing speed toward becoming two separate and unequal societies. Continuation of this trend will certainly heighten frictions and pose the threat of sustained and escalating violence as people try to deal constructively with bankrupt and decaying cities.

Improvement of the ghetto is absolutely necessary. Massive programs and resources need to be applied now to the devastated environment to facilitate escape from poverty and degradation. Tremendous increases are needed in expenditures for programs to improve the quantity as well as quality of employment, for job training and upgrading, for housing, for education and for health and welfare programs. Significant expansion of opportunities and supporting services are needed to foster the establishment and growth of more minority owned and managed business enterprises. More than enrichment of the quality of life in the ghetto is needed if we are to avoid creating two separate, segregated and unequal societies.

At the heart of the dialogue is the question: Can an oppressed minority secure equality of opportunity, self-respect and self-determination in a separate, segregated society composed of some 10 per cent of the total population and literally walled into about 25 per cent of the land area in central cities? Can Black Americans achieve equal employment opportunity and, more important (as was pointed out earlier), significant upgrading in a segregated labor market? In the face of great densities and overcrowding, together with the extreme shortage of land in central cities, is it possible to reduce densities and overcrowding and expand construction of low and moderate cost housing, without dispersion of units and people?

Doesn't the solution to the problems faced by Black Americans lie in both the white and Black communities? Isn't the key to power, self-determination and self-respect the sophisticated use of coalitions or power groups to achieve economic and political power in the pluralistic society that is America? Shouldn't the strategy be a more astute use of the leverages that exist in the diffuse, often fragmented and shifting alliances that constitute power in America? The word "crisis" is written in Chinese by two characters representing "danger" and "opportunity," which aptly describes the alternatives we face as the dialogue is joined.

This Alabama farmer owns three hundred acres of land with eleven other farmers. The Southern Cooperative Development Program helped them purchase the land.

Rural Poverty—1968 Style

Charles Prejean and the staff of the
Federation of Southern Cooperatives

THOMAS PAINE, writing over 150 years ago, described poverty as "a thing created by that which is called civilized life." He added that "the first principle of civilization, ought to be, that the condition of every person born into the world, after a state of civilization commences, ought not to be worse than if he had been born before that period."

The existence of rural poverty in America in 1968 continues to demonstrate the absence of Paine's principle in the United States. For 11 million poor people civilization continues to mean exploitation, hunger, sickness, ignorance, unemployment, no training, no land, and—for Black people—the burden of white racism.

1968 was the year for recognizing "rural poverty." In 1962, with the aid of Michael Harrington, we found poverty amidst affluence. We went to war against the poor in 1964, found maximum feasible participation of the poor in 1965 (learned that one-third of any board was the maximum number of poor any poverty program could stand), learned that "the poor pay more" for everything in 1966 and that urban poverty was too tremendous a rebuilding task to undertake until our destructive task in Vietnam was completed. One of the nation's largest foundations designated 1967 as "the year of the Indian," and set about building better reservations and looking into extremely high rates of suicide, and so forth.

In 1968 rural America took the center of the stage. The Department of Agriculture was accused of having little interest in feeding people. Surplus food and welfare were attacked. Rural poverty was blamed for urban slum conditions, and dozens of organizations designed programs based on self-help for the rural poor.

Hungry children became the grim introduction to this attack on rural poverty. Suddenly there it was. A small child, emaciated, limbs limp, eyes dull, open sores—and it was on TV. The child was dying of hunger in the richest nation in the history of the world, the land of the $850 billion gross (yes, very gross) national product, the 60 million automobiles, the 70 million television sets, the $500 billion worth of common stock. It shocked. But not everyone. It was simply another "discovery" of the type liberals seem everlastingly to be making.

We spend as much for chewing-gum as for model cities.

We spend as much for hair dye as for grants to urban mass transit.

We spend as much or more for tobacco than the government spends at all levels on higher education.

We spend $300 million for jewelry, and quarrel over $10 million for the Teacher Corps.

We spend as much FOR PET FOOD AS ON FOOD STAMPS FOR THE POOR.

The figure for pet food may not be accurate. There are plenty of people eating pet food in the United States.

Hungry children stirred the collective conscience of the country—for about two weeks. Perhaps nothing can hold a well-fed man's attention in this country longer. But for two weeks Americans heard about 256 "hunger counties," so designated by the Citizens' Board of Inquiry into Hunger and Malnutrition in the United States—a private group. And what they heard was not pleasant. "Millions of Americans are being deprived of the food they need," the group's report charged. The hunger counties were principally in the South and Southwest and were largely rural in population. Although the topic lost its news appeal after two weeks, some people didn't forget. The Department of Agriculture was disturbed at being told it was interested chiefly in making crop producers richer and had little interest in feeding people, and that, furthermore, the Department of Health, Education and Welfare should take over USDA's responsibilities in the area of food supplementation. Eventually the Department of Agriculture, OEO and HEW announced a $10 million program to provide emergency food and medical aid to the poor, an interesting amount for the purpose, as the report on hunger had put the number of persons chronically malnourished at ten million. One dollar per person to end hunger.

In fact, only 5.4 million poor persons in the entire country participated in any government food program last year (18.5 per cent of the nation's poor). In rural Alabama, for example, when a woman with no steady income began receiving a $54-a-month welfare check, food stamps, which in the past had been sold to her for $3 per $72 worth of stamps, became worth $22. Where federal commodities are being distributed, a welfare family may actually be too "rich" to qualify, while in food stamp counties they would be too poor to purchase the stamps.

In addition to having the problem of hunger, the poor Black rural dweller in 1968 was expendable in other ways. If in the past he had been a farmer, mechanization, shrinkage of cotton allotments, use of herbicides instead of hoes, retaliatory measures for voting, discriminatory policies of bureaus and organizations intended to aid the small farmer, had combined to see that he was a farmer no more. In 1964 only seven thousand Black farmers who owned their own farms had netted $2,500 or more. In 1968 that number had shrunk. Furthermore, Black farm laborers were no longer needed as cotton fields were sown in soybeans or turned into cattle ranches, or were placed into soil diversion banks. When this last happened, landowners were paid not to plant the specified crop. In some cases, as in Sunflower County, Mississippi, 340 large landowners received $6,809,529 for cutting back their cotton acreage. The Black laborers and tenants got eviction notices.

The primary employer of Black people in rural areas has long been farming. But rarely has the Black man been an employer. Beginning with the Homestead Act in 1862, the government programs designed to encourage family farms have discriminated against the Negro. With the exception of one or two small land distribution efforts in South Carolina by the Freedmen's Bureau (reform measures which were eventually canceled —for the most part—by President Andrew Johnson), and a brief flurry of land reform undertaken by the New Deal, Black people have never been given the opportunity to own land in rural America. Today's Farmers Home Administration policies are not as blatantly anti-Black as policies have been in the past, but a clause demanding "demonstration of a past ability to repay" when applied to a $25,000 farm loan quickly eliminates tenants, sharecroppers and day laborers who have a past history of making $3 a day. A policy such as this, combined with FHA's county loan review committee system, which until recently was all-white throughout the South, has effectively kept the Black man landless, and therefore at the mercy of the white landowner.

It is ironic that agriculture, once the basic reason for the importation of Black men and women into the colonies as slaves, now declares the Black farm laborer and tenant "surplus" labor and the Black farm owner "inefficient." The statistical evidence of this is frightening. In 1964 the number of Negro farm operators (including both owners and renters) had dwindled to 180,000. There are no figures for 1968, but it is reasonable to assume a further decline. Only 1.3 per cent of *all* Black farmers made $2,500 or over in 1960. The Black farmer's average age is over fifty; his average number of years of schooling is around 5.7; and only 7 per cent of adult Negro farm residents have completed high school. Statistics are, as Mark Twain once remarked, "very similar to light poles. They shed light occasionally; it is also possible for them to cast shadows. Nevertheless, they are always there to lean upon." It is possible to say, for instance, that the future of Black men in farm labor capacities is improving. In the Delta over the past few years laborers have increased 62 per cent (24,000 to 39,000). But then, the number of tenants during the same period of time has decreased by 60 per cent (83,000 to 33,000).

What all the figures, facts, memos, papers and statistics point to is that the future of the Black man in agriculture in this country is bleak without a major land reform effort, and, perhaps, a revolution in how we think about efficiency. At present our society prefers to pay the estimated $140,000 a male citizen can cost the public if he lives from seventeen to fifty-seven years of age on public assistance payments, rather than to loan the same man $50,000 to purchase a business, a farm, a recreational area, or to invest in stocks and bonds, for that matter.

In 1968 there was an increase of "surplus" people and a decrease in the number of people receiving "surplus" food. In the rural South it was the year of the squeeze. The Black man was no longer needed. And he was certainly no longer wanted by his former white owners or employers. Without a job, without an education (average of 5.4 years if over twenty-five years old), without training (unless one considers such fiascos as South Carolina's STEP program, which trained maids to be "good" maids), without land and with little hope of getting any, without housing, health or hope, the Black American depends upon whatever job he or she can get, whatever assistance private do-good groups can muster, and upon welfare.

No discussion of rural poverty can be complete without mentioning a great perpetuator of it—welfare policies. In Mississippi, Aid to Families with Dependent Children (AFDC) averages $8.50 a week per family; the maximum is $50 a month regardless of the number of children in the family. Many families are forced to live (or to try to live) on this $50. It must pay for food, shelter, clothing and heat—not to mention health care or recreation or other unnecessary items—at times for eight persons. Mississippi, the same state whose Sunflower County got almost $7 million in crop diversion subsidies, turned down $20.7 million in federal welfare moneys rather than put up $7.9 million in matching funds. While the rich get richer by putting people off their farms, the poor get told they are not worth one county's subsidy payment.

Welfare helps clarify the situation poor people are in. Welfare for rural Black Mississippians is enforced starvation, dislocation, despair and hopelessness. Their situation is not the result of individual backwardness, cultural lag or family breakdown. Government policies and economic strategies have helped create the poor person's dilemma. The same country which pays rich men not to grow food, supplies insufficient and unappetizing surplus foods to its poor men. The same federal agency which gives some companies millions of dollars in price support payments (subsidies) turns back to the Treasury $200 million that could have been used to aid the poor and hungry, because Congress applied "budgetary pressures." In short, the United States has a built-in inadequate welfare system, administered for and by the privileged. It is used to control the poor, not to alleviate their suffering.

Rather than admit to the above, it has been the custom in the United States to put poverty into categories. We have the young poor, the old poor, the "culture of poverty" poor, the rural poor and the urban poor. Instead of land or money, the poor are offered programs to improve their character or their children's education. Not willing or able to say our institutions are incapable of meeting the basic needs of people and therefore need to be radically altered, we look for panaceas and explanations. Recently it has become fashionable to explain urban poverty as being the result of years of neglected rural poverty. The fact that the PEOPLE involved are useless to our high-powered economic machine—whether they are classified as rural or urban—is hidden nicely behind a big finger pointing at rural America saying (in good Blue Meanie fist style): "The problem is there!" The problem of coping with the myriad urban ills, perhaps even an understandable human incapacity to comprehend what it will take to rebuild the worst several blocks of Harlem (where the population density is so high that if all Americans were forced to live in as close quarters all two hundred million could be fitted into three of New York's five boroughs, leaving the rest of the United States unpopulated), makes the thought of building a decent society in rural America seem minor.

And how would this rebuilding of rural America take place? As yet there is no commitment on the part of the federal government to do it. It has sidestepped coping with urban poverty by shifting the blame to supposed rural roots and then deftly placed the burden of rebuilding upon the poor themselves. The irony of the exploitive system in the United States is that its rich create the rural and urban slums and then ask the poor, through "self-help," to change them. Some poor Black people in the urban slums are changing them, but not in an accepted fashion. Poor rural Black people are, on the whole, still receptive to "constructive" methods of change. A number of such efforts have taken place during the past year in the South.

When one attempts to list the various groups attempting to either help poor people or to help poor people help themselves, a feeling of despair begins to gnaw at the soul. With all these groups at work, why has so little been accomplished? Imagine, if you will, all the directors of all the organizations working to end poverty in the rural South sitting on stools on a clean, well-lighted stage. Out in the darkened audience are the poor. The voices begin:

> We in the Welfare Rights Movement succeeded in getting court rulings against the Man in the House clause, prohibiting AFDC payments to children living in a house with a man in it who is capable of work. We fought successfully the AFDC freeze on funds which would have mandatorially limited the number of children receiving welfare to those on the lists as of mid-summer last year. Our aim is to help every poor person eligible for welfare benefits have the opportunity to receive assistance.
>
> * * * * * *
>
> The Southern Rural Research project in Selma, Alabama has interviewed over 1,800 poor black people in the Black Belt of Alabama. We asked you all about living conditions, food and health situations, and how you were assisted by poverty-fighting agencies. Once we passed out free beef to anybody who wanted it in Demopolis, trying to confront the county officials who refused to implement a surplus food program. Using our research we brought suits against several federal agencies for not doing their jobs.
>
> * * * * * *
>
> The Southern Rural Project of the National Sharecroppers' Fund assisted communities in applying for OEO funds and helped other groups of poor people organize co-ops and community organizations.
>
> * * * * * *
>
> Five doctors working for the Southern Regional Council started the Hunger Campaign by issuing a report documenting their findings of a tour of poverty-stricken areas. We also issued Paul Good's article on rural poverty as a special issue of our quarterly magazine, *The New South*. Lastly, we brought to the public's attention the fact that FBI agents "interviewed" a number of the persons who testified at the Congressional Hearings on Hunger in the U.S.A.
>
> * * * * * *
>
> The Southern Christian Leadership Conference sponsored the Poor People's Campaign in Washington, D.C. We hoped to shock America and her elected officials into action. We did. They evicted us from government property. Though not successful, we tried to bring Black, red, brown and white poor people together to pressure our government into doing away with poverty.
>
> * * * * * *
>
> The Voter Education Project of the Southern Regional Council held a conference for all Black elected officials in Southern states at the Downtown Dinkler Hotel in Atlanta. Almost all the 330 elected politicians attended.
>
> * * * * * *
>
> The *Southern Courier* regrets to announce we are going out of business. Our weekly newspaper, reporting the news of rural Alabama, is broke.
>
> * * * * * *
>
> The North Carolina Fund also regrets to tell you we are going out of business. We helped start the OEO program in 1964 and were instrumental in setting up Community Action Programs across North Carolina.

And on and on the program goes, with speaker after speaker. The INC Fund, Rural Advancement Project, New Communities, Panola Land Buyers Association, Southern Conference Educational Fund, Mississippi Research and Development, Center for Social Change, Rural Action Program, SEASHA, West Tennessee Development Corporation, American Friends Service Committee, Civil Rights Commission and many others. The poor people sit and wait, perhaps listening. Surely part of the problem is that the organizations are small groups fighting a huge force which insists hungry babies are good for business.

One group has been saved for last. The reason for this is its potential importance in solving some of the rural South's problems. Also, our own partiality is involved. This group is the forty-five or so cooperative organizations spread over the South. Though self-help oriented, the co-ops rely on "collective" rather than individual self-help, and see themselves as community organizations which are capable of taking advantage (and control) of federal and private moneys in their efforts to offer an alternative other than city migration to rural poor people.

In many ways the cooperatives are simply parallel organizations, doing the jobs of the Extension Service in helping small farmers diversify into vegetable specialty crops cooperatively marketed; doing the job of Farmers Home Administration in helping sharecroppers find and purchase farm land; and doing the jobs of the almost completely impotent rural Community Action Program agencies in helping groups start day-care centers, credit unions, buying clubs, self-help housing groups and the like.

The key to thinking about cooperatives as poor people are using them presently is to consider them as tools—as means rather than ends. As an economic tool cooperatives offer increases in income levels both by adding to a person's wages and by reducing the cost of consumer goods. The fact that cooperatives demand participation of the persons affected by their programs means that they help develop people's potential. Socially, cooperatives offer a power base from which to influence the total community to obtain better schools, better public services and open access to the public resources of the community.

As yet, co-ops have not found a way to solve the critical problem of land. Certainly, none of the co-ops are self-supporting businesses; all require some form of subsidy at present. Their success thus far lies in their ability to keep people, desperate people, together in a variety of community organizations.

An example is SWAFCA. In rural Alabama two thousand poor Black farmers are joined together in the Southwest Alabama Farmers Cooperative Association. SWAFCA has been given a hard time since its organization in the spring of 1967. An OEO grant was vetoed by Governor Wallace, but eventually overridden by the director of OEO. The co-op was hardly in operation when, at the request of Alabama congressmen, the General Accounting Office demanded its books. This delay held up a substantial part of its government grant. Just as the audit was completed, one of the federal audit officers had his briefcase stolen, a theft which held up the audit for another month. When the co-op began marketing its members' cucumbers and okra, trucks carrying the produce were stopped and held long enough to ensure crop damage before they were released. Within a month the FBI was called in to investigate an alleged misuse of funds. At about the same time, Governor Brewer vetoed the second part of the demonstration grant, also overridden by OEO. When the second veto was pushed aside, the Governor and Mayor Smitherman of Selma obtained a circuit court injunction against the co-op, charging mismanagement and misuse of public funds.

What is SWAFCA to merit all this attention? A supplier of guns? A school for training men in guerrilla warfare? No! SWAFCA is a supplier of fertilizer and a marketer of vegetables, a business owned and controlled by two thousand Black men in the heart of racist Alabama. As a business SWAFCA lost money in its first year of operation. As a political force, as a social force, as an organization with the ability to attract over a million dollars worth of federal and private money to be spent by poor people for poor people, it is a qualified success. SWAFCA did a total of $172,000 worth of business, just a shade more than Senator Jim Eastland "earned" last year for not growing cotton. That helps keep SWAFCA in perspective.

There are eight or ten SWAFCA-type cooperatives spread over the South. Three co-ops are leasing land, attempting to buy a hundred or two acres with private money (American congressmen still consider loans to cooperatives for the purchase of land as being "communistic") and trying to reach the poorest of the rural poor. The other agricultural co-ops are presently only reaching the people with a sure hand on their land. In Alabama a Black man farming on white land soon finds his belongings on the side of the road if he joins SWAFCA.

Efforts to begin small industries owned cooperatively by workers are being made across the

South. Handicraft cooperatives, sewing sub-contracting co-ops, bakeries and candy co-ops provide some increase in their owners' incomes. Gasoline stations and bulk suppliers, grocery stores and buying clubs, credit unions and small finance companies, clothing and coal suppliers, fishing wholesalers—almost every type of business is being tried cooperatively. An effort to enable the many co-ops to come together and exercise their collective power is being made through the organization of the Federation of Southern Cooperatives, a service co-op owned by some forty-five different co-ops representing approximately fifteen thousand families.

The co-op movement is weak, small, in many ways ineffectual in the face of hunger, despair and disease. The lack of investment capital constantly hinders it from moving into areas in which it might possibly succeed—areas such as health insurance (with part of the premiums paid through grants from individuals and foundations); life insurance; burial services; land development; low-cost housing integrated with lumber cooperatives owned by small rural landowners; truly specialized farms complete with greenhouses for force-growing, flower production, etc.; community owned recreational facilities; restaurants; civic and social educational programs; day-care centers; small industries in conjunction with small farming operations; large-scale farming operations, fully mechanized, with each member owning a small plot of his own on which to grow specialty crops, and where grazing lands are cooperatively owned and government crop diversion checks pay the overhead and the interest on the loans. You could go on and on—if you had the money.

As 1968 came to an end, talk of a number of methods with which to end poverty—rural and urban—with one or two swift strokes became fashionable. Family allowances and some form of a guaranteed annual income were endorsed by Ford Motor Company, Xerox and IBM presidents. Without some form of organization among the poor people who would receive such an allowance if it ever becomes a reality, any form of subsidy payment will simply mean a greater degree of exploitation. Should the subsidy be made, cooperatives over the next ten years should probably put a great emphasis on consumer efforts among people who would receive these payments. Every co-op which supplements a person's income should build credit and consumer branches into its organization.

Guaranteed annual income was not the only panacea offered in 1968. Talk of "Black capitalism" tended to drown out discussion of hunger and inadequate housing. It is disturbing to see the government once again subsidizing profit-making businesses to do its work. However, there is the feeling among conservatives, as well as among some radicals, that "big government" has failed, and with conservatives in power the resulting belief is that private enterprise could succeed in ending poverty. Inherent in this thinking is the need for nongovernmental and decentralized decision making. The unhappy reality of America is that when government fails all that is left to turn to is private, profit-making business. Therefore, the need for non-profit businesses and organizations, oriented to human needs rather than to money, is critical.

The present infatuation with Black entrepreneurship is just the latest of a number of attempts to involve money-making people in community and social problems. In the past, on-the-job training, with government paying private business to train people, was the thing. Tax incentives to industries if they will locate in a rural or urban slum and hire or train poor people is the new plan. "Turnkey" programs where corporations build plants, enjoy rapid amortization and tax breaks, and eventually turn the plant over to a community corporation, have wide backing. To the extent that such programs, when applied to rural situations, help solve the two most important problems of the rural poor—lack of ownership of land and lack of political power—they are welcomed. However, if Black capitalism is simply an insurance policy that big business is offering to profit-making groups and individuals—5 per cent offered so that 95 per cent will not be burned down—the plan is detrimental.

Summary

The "year of rural poverty" is over. The issues have been raised. Hunger, functional illiteracy, inadequate educational programs, a million dilapidated houses, nonexistence of health care, welfare programs which underwrite suffering (and control), subsidies for the rich but not the poor, discrimination in programs, agencies and departments which are supposed to fight poverty. All the above were raised, discussed, assigned to committees, shelved, testified to and forgotten. Nothing really changed. It is naive to think that because the affluent have learned about the conditions existing in the country things will change. This has never been the case. The only people the poor have been able to trust have been poor people. Some reason for a slight optimism is offered by the several organizations owned and controlled by poor people in the rural South. Otherwise, there is little in which to place one's hope, unless it is the impossible possibility of 1969 being "the year for people" rather than profit.

Saundra Williams: Miss Black America, 1968.

Black Action and White Reaction

Richard Sommerfeld

THE FOLLOWING MATERIAL is based essentially on "sociological studies and white opinion." By sociological studies I mean reports of formal studies published during 1968 and also reports of informal analyses of the social circumstances of Negroes in America. The material on white opinion is much less "scientific." Most of it derives from news reports of the reactions of whites to Negro activities or activities related to Negroes.

An account of current events must of necessity be prepared before the content of those events can be fully evaluated; in other words, it is written while the heat of a presumably significant event or circumstance still warms the intellectual skin of the writer. Dispassionate analysis out of the cool perspective of passed time is neither a possibility for nor a privilege accorded the chronicler. The best of historical writing rarely if ever occurs in the midst of still fluid, developing social situations. Yet contemporary accounts offer something that chronologically removed histories cannot provide: they chronicle the existent heat of situations in which and through which people are still living.

The events recorded here are a one-dimensional chronicle of Negroes in America in 1968. The material was selected because it appeared at the moment to be indicative of the "now-circumstances" of Negroes—and whites—in America in 1968.

Within the plethora of Black studies and white opinion published during 1968, certain circumstances and events stood out: Negro-white relations in daily life; police-citizen conflicts and the charge of "police brutality"; the Kerner Report; the death of Martin Luther King; and—of all things—beauty contests. These topics make up the content of this chapter.

Action and Reaction

In space 1968 was a stellar year for the United States, but back on the ground where most of us still live many of the old discriminatory ways persisted. After a year of negotiation, the Atlanta Community Relations Commission admitted failure in the attempt to break down racial discrimination in area trailer camps. Trailer park operators simply refused to accept Negroes. The 1964 Civil Rights Act did not cover such facilities, and there was uncertainty as to whether they were covered by the 1968 Civil Rights Act. Though many earthbound areas did open up for the Negro in 1968, the fact remains that the development of "openness" across the board for Negroes was not a characteristic of the year.

Negroes continued to be limited to selected areas in choosing a place of residence. For example, the Black People's Topographical Research Center in Chicago reported that Negroes could live in only eighty-one of the 55,930 square miles in the state of Illinois. Of Illinois' 1,176 cities and towns, Negroes are allowed to live in only sixty-five; the pattern in neighboring states was the same. Place of residence was still a matter of Black or white in 1968.

There were some areas in which Negroes and whites "lived" side by side, but they were not typical. Harlem, commonly regarded as a Negro enclave, did continue to have a white population. An estimated 8,500 whites lived out the year in

Harlem, a community with a Negro population that outnumbers whites about thirty to one. The whites who have remained in the area appeared content and willing to stay, but many reported that white friends living outside of Harlem sympathized with their supposed "plight." More than anything else, the accounts of Negroes and whites living together indicated that other whites have difficulty in visualizing such an arrangement as mutually satisfying and harmonious.

The doubt whites manifested about the possibilities of living happily with Negro neighbors was matched by the suspicions of Negroes toward whites who attempted to work in Negro residential areas. A midsummer graduation address before a class of VISTA trainees touched directly on this matter. The speaker, a long-time social worker among Cleveland Negroes, reminded the class that Blacks still tended to regard white social workers as symbols of "white colonialism" and that suburban whites, in turn, still regarded inner city Negro areas as "central city colonies" to which it was appropriate to send social workers in the spirit of a missionary endeavor. The white reaction to the circumstances of Negroes had prompted the rise of Black nationalism in recent months, according to the speaker. The danger lay in nationalism becoming separatism and so preventing any development of Negro-white interaction. After five years of work in Cleveland, particularly among Negroes, this white spokesman saw little evidence of the development of a "one nation" relationship between Negroes and whites in terms of the metropolitan area and the more sensitive social problems of the inner city.

Doubt and suspicion may have characterized the year as regards race relations, but there was also evidence of what might be called uncertain groping.

In the spring of 1968 a group of New York suburbanites journeyed to Harlem to serve as voluntary laborers in painting and generally fixing up the exteriors of tenements. In September many of these people returned to do more painting and to renew social contacts made a few months earlier. When the spring project took place, the *New York Times* editorialized that "last Saturday's happening in New York's slums was not the answer to the urban crisis." The editorial did recognize that the action represented the effort of at least some to stop talking and attempt to do something. The cautious commendation of the enterprise was repeated by Harlem residents during the September effort, though several commented positively on the social contacts that had been made in the spring, nourished during the summer, and increased in the fall.

More than anything else, the spring and fall "paint-up, fix-up" visit—microscopic though it may have been in itself—underscored the uncertainty existing in 1968 between the predominantly white suburbs and the heavily Negro areas of the inner city. Animosity continued, and there was considerable evidence of this, but there were also signs of a desire for greater interpersonal relations in the future. An optimistic view might stress these signs and point to the possibilities they hold. Looking strictly at the year just past, however, the uncertainty of these signs—on both sides—must be noted.

On July 19, *Time* ran a lengthy account of "Black and White Dating." The story included reports of practices and patterns around the country, particularly on college campuses. Interviews quoted in the article indicated that experiences and motivations were mixed. Many young people were willing to try this new form of interpersonal relations, but their words were tinged with uncertainty. Even those most overtly committed to interracial dating showed something of this uncertainty. Parents and middle-aged adults were more skeptical, but the mood of the times could not be denied. We-may-not-know-for-sure-but-we-have-to-try summarized such aspects of Negro-white relations during 1968, instances of antipathy and bitter rejection notwithstanding.

White reaction to the Negro struggle for equality was varied as well as uncertain in 1968. The president of the University of Miami directed that the university band no longer play "Dixie" because the song was racially symbolic and distasteful to Negroes. After some heckling of the band at a football game, the whole matter passed into the dark recesses of history. How significant the president's act will prove to be we cannot know, but it was one effort to smooth interpersonal relations.

Negroes have been active in professional sporting events for some time, and whites have come to accept Negro athletes as a "normal" component of any professional team. In the rarified atmosphere of "society sports," whites have not been as open to Negro participation. Washington's country club circuit suffered a spate of dissension last spring when Mrs. Carl Rowan, wife of the former ambassador to Finland and former director of the USIA, was scheduled as a member of her club's tennis team. Three of the ten members of the local country club tennis league withdrew from the league rather than accept the Negro lady in a tennis match. Mrs. Rowan's club, which is predominantly white in membership, responded by refusing to engage in athletic contests with any club that barred Negroes from participation. The final outcome is not yet known, but it does appear that the controversy may eventually result in opening the historically white grounds of these capital clubs.

In the area of public education in 1968, the 1954 Civil Rights Act had still not been fully implemented by those in positions of influence and control—most often whites. The Southern Regional Council reported that the 1968 rate of integration in public schools in the South did not move appreciably beyond the record for 1967. The council reported that 88 per cent of Negro students in the South had attended all-Negro schools in 1966. In 1967 the figure had dropped slightly to 86 per cent, and 1968 saw little change in the previous year's record. The two earlier annual reports had contained some "guardedly optimistic, some hopeful words" about the future, but the 1968 report indicated "almost no hope, no reason to find optimistic words." The council, a private research agency financed by foundation grants, blamed the general apathy of the nation for the failure to eliminate segregated schools or to move significantly toward that end.

On the other side of the ledger, 1968 saw overt resistance by Blacks toward other Blacks. Negro residents of the Lee-Seville section of the Cleveland area moved to block the entrance of other Negroes into neighborhood houses. A fifty-one-acre tract in the area, owned by Cleveland's Metropolitan Housing Authority, had been chosen as the site for the construction of new homes comparable to the $20,000 houses already in the neighborhood. New residents, mostly from the Hough area from which many current Lee-Seville residents had moved some years back, were to be offered these houses at monthly rentals ranging from $40 to $80. Current residents, who claimed they had worked hard to achieve what they now had, balked at the "giveaway" and quickly acted to block construction of the houses. Cleveland Mayor Carl Stokes asked the Negro residents of Lee-Seville how they expected the suburbs to be integrated if they were unwilling to accept other Negroes into their own neighborhood. Such instances of resistance shown by Blacks to other members of the race paralleled that shown by the Washington country club officers to Negroes.

Long-standing white attitudes toward Negroes surfaced in some unexpected quarters in 1968. On the West Coast a number of women anti-Vietnam war demonstrators were sentenced to jail. All but one of them (each of whom spoke of herself as a liberal on social issues) were white, and the group found itself in the midst of a county jail population that was overwhelmingly Negro. Negro inmates held every position of privilege and prestige; they were the trusties, the guards' helpers and the like. After an initial period of "reciprocity," the white demonstrators attempted to return the Negro inmates to their historic place on the social ladder. This was done by passing candy, cigarettes and personal items to the Negroes in such a way that the whites became the "givers" and the Negroes the "takers." A white demonstrator reported:

> Perhaps the most striking thing about the interaction between white demonstrators and the black inmates was the apparent compulsion on the part of the demonstrators to redress the balance of power between white and black—to restore it to the more familiar patterns of the outside world [*Trans-Action* (September 1968)].

Social scientists such as the woman reporting above may be able to analyze the behavior of others, but such ability does not assure Negroes they will be treated with equality by these same social scientists. Negro sociologists holding membership in the American Sociological Association charged during 1968 that the ASA "substantially excluded" Negroes from the activities of the professional organization. A conference with the

ASA president produced the admission that this was a "reasonably accurate description" of the situation within the overwhelmingly white association.

Economically, Negro action, in many instances supported financially or otherwise by whites, did result in some reported gains during 1968. A University of Michigan Survey Research Center study of Negroes in Detroit's slum area—the area torn by the 1967 riot, which had resulted in forty-three deaths—reported that Detroit Negroes who feel they have moved ahead since the riot significantly outnumber those who feel they are standing still. A number of Detroit corporations, almost all controlled by whites, have been active since the riot in providing jobs and otherwise improving the economic circumstances of slum Negroes. A midsummer study by New Detroit, Inc., indicated that though there are still vast gaps in understanding between the races, the overall racial climate in Detroit has improved considerably since 1967.

A *New York Times* story focusing on Lawnside, a Camden, New Jersey, suburb, reported that average family income has increased to $5,000 a year and that 95 per cent of the residents own their own homes. Much of the economic growth has been due to construction employment opportunities throughout the area and the location near Lawnside of an RCA factory and a Campbell's soup plant. A significant sidelight was that Lawnside, which has always been heavily Negro, still has only four white families in residence, and many Lawnsiders find it convenient to limit their socialization to their own community.

A number of reports cited Negro economic growth during 1968, but there were few reports of economic improvement resulting in racial integration or increased social relations between whites and Blacks. Most often, the economic gains occurred within the framework of existing social relations.

If the trend that began toward the end of World War II and ran through 1968 continues, as some authorities say it will, extensive social contact between large numbers of Negroes and whites will become less likely as cities swell with Negro residents and whites live primarily in the suburbs.

Census Bureau figures released during 1968 stated that 73 per cent of all Negroes live in cities, compared with 70 per cent of all whites. For Negroes this was an almost complete reversal of the situation at the time of World War II. Further, between 1960 and 1966 two million Negroes moved into cities, while one million whites moved out. A report from the University of Chicago Population Research Center predicted that by 1985 the central cities will gain ten million more nonwhites—a 94 per cent increase over present figures—and the suburbs will accommodate fifty-four million more whites—a 104 per cent increase. The geographical distance between residential areas of Negroes and whites will do little to encourage or assist interracial contact. The result may be what the Kerner Report labeled "a splitting into two societies."

At the same time that residential separation was increasing, some major efforts were made during 1968 to counter the trend. The Ford Foundation gave the Chicago Conference on Religion and Race a $3 million grant to promote and assist the movement of Negroes into essentially white suburbs. Growing out of a pilot project that the Ford Foundation regarded as successful, the conference serves primarily as an intermediary between prospective residents and suburban home owners looking for buyers. The grant was considerable, but the task is even larger; during the period of the pilot project, conference officials were able to report only three Negro families directly assisted and forty-two others indirectly helped. As regards population projections, the effort would seem to indicate a white reaction rather than a likelihood of counteracting the trend.

The suburbs are not only the place of residence of whites but are also the seats of power in most metropolitan communities. Two Columbia University professors reported on how whites run the inner cities from the suburbs. And in 1968 a Chicago Urban League study on community decision-making was published, which corroborated the findings of the Columbia University group.

Three years ago the Chicago Urban League initiated this study of the decision-making processes in metropolitan Chicago, with particular attention to the participation of Negroes in community decision-making. The study concluded that "the black community lacks control over decision-making." It examined local, state and federal governmental operations, business corporations, the legal profession, universities, voluntary organizations (business, professional, welfare and religious) and labor unions. Overall, the researchers found that "the number of posts held by Negroes tended to be inversely related to the power vested in these positions—the more powerful the post, the fewer the black policy-makers." Putting it another way, the author of the report stated, "All in all, then, we would suggest the following rule of thumb: The actual power vested in Negro policy-makers is about one-third as great as the percentage of the posts they hold."

In these two reports, as well as in many others, there was documentation of the widely held opinion that though Negro populations are increasing in the cities of America, the power of control over the cities as well as over the rest of the nation continues to reside in white hands. The Cleveland social worker's comments, mentioned earlier, on "central city colonies" might be expanded to say that 1968 saw the continued development of urban colonies populated increasingly by Negroes but administered by white colonials living in the suburbs. In spite of numerous incidents of Negro action and white cooperation, social relations between Blacks and whites in 1968 were couched most significantly within the framework of an ever-widening geographic separation of the races. In response to this growing separation, the executive director of the New York Urban League called for Harlem to have its own police force because "We [Americans] have officially abandoned integration" and so "we must honestly embrace separation."

Police-Community Relations

One of the touchiest areas during 1968 continued to be the relationship between the police and the community, particularly between the police, most of whom are white, and Blacks.

Detroit Negroes may feel that their economic circumstances have improved, as reported above, but there has been no change in the attitude of Negroes toward the police. Immediately following the 1967 riot, area residents cited "police brutality" as the major cause of the riot. More than a year later the feelings toward the police had not changed and complaints about brutality had actually increased. A sampling of brutality charges serves to illustrate the touchiness of police-community relations during 1968.

Off-duty Detroit policemen were charged with attacking and beating Negro youths leaving a church-sponsored dance. Official substantiation of the complaint resulted in the suspension of nine police officers.

One hundred and fifty Negro students gathered outside the Swanquarter, North Carolina, courthouse to protest a cut in welfare payments. Twenty young people marched inside to voice their dissatisfaction. When the delegation moved into one of the meeting-rooms, police lobbed smoke grenades into the room and slammed the only exit door shut. Panic and injury resulted. Arrested for fighting in the street and taken to a hospital for medical examination, a Newark Negro claimed she was "stomped" by a policeman while changing her clothes in the ladies' rest room. The same report cited the case of a Negro arrested for drunkenness and found in his cell the next morning lying in a pool of blood.

In St. Louis two detectives were suspended for scuffling with Black militants in a police station after the militants had been brought in for a minor traffic violation. One of the Negroes was hospitalized. The president of the police board stated: "We believe the officers used greater force than the occasion called for," acknowledging the fact that the altercation had taken place in a police station, where assistance was readily available.

Two Miami policemen were found guilty of dangling a seventeen-year-old Negro by his heels from a bridge eighty feet above a river and threatening to drop him. The president of a Chicago Black detective agency took legal action against two policemen who beat one of his agents to the point that the agent required major surgery and about three weeks' hospitalization.

Most blatant of all was the early September attack by off-duty policemen on members of the Black Panther Party on the sixth floor of the Brooklyn criminal court building, which the *New York Times* called "a mockery of the rule of law and court-decreed justice." The Black Panthers had previously been charged with assaulting policemen. A "thorough grand jury investigation" was promised. A few days later two white policemen directed a barrage of rifle fire into the Black Panther headquarters in Oakland, California. The police chief, in announcing the suspension of the policemen, noted they were on duty, were in uniform and had been drinking.

A Passaic, New Jersey, grand jury formally charged members of the Paterson, New Jersey, police department with vandalism, brutality and intimidation. The jury verdict spoke of "terrorism" and "goon squad" tactics, aimed particularly at Negroes and Puerto Ricans.

Considering the number of substantiated incidents and the national publicity that all incidents regularly receive, it is not difficult to understand the touchiness of police-community relations throughout most of the United States, especially where Blacks or lower class whites are involved. Understanding is one thing, but explaining the basis of police action is quite another. Early in the fall the New York City police commissioner suggested that police thinking and action merely represent what the policemen feel the community wants. This view was expressed in an interview shortly after the Black Panther assault in the Brooklyn courthouse.

Violent, warlike relations between police and community were not limited in 1968 only to the actions of the police. In Pittsburgh the assistant police superintendent was beaten by Black militants during a meeting in city council chambers. A Manhattan grand jury indicted six Negroes who conspired to kill a policeman a week. Reports of anti-police actions—aside from demonstrations and riots—were not as numerous as substantiated charges of police brutality. All these events underlined the fact that for large segments of the American population the police and the community are opposite poles and not complementary components of a single system.

Further signs of this attitude emerged among Washington Negroes during the summer of 1968. After a white policeman was shot to death and his partner seriously wounded in an arrest attempt connected with a family quarrel, the Black United Front passed a resolution which stated in part: "The methods of self-defense by the family charged with the alleged slaying of the honky cop is justifiable homicide, in the same sense that police are allowed to kill black people and call it justifiable homicide." The resolution received considerable attention because the BUF, a loose coalition of Black moderates and militants in the capital, included on its steering committee the vice-chairman of the Washington City Council, the director of the Washington Urban League and a Democratic national committeeman, though the first two were not at the meeting at which the resolution was framed and passed unanimously. Later both of the absent men repudiated the language of the resolution, though one added that "the intention of the resolution is right." A Negro newspaper editorial in Washington termed the resolution "ill-timed" and a "verbal transgression," while noting "that no matter how much cruelty exists in the black community, it has roots in wrongs inflicted by the white community."

In a follow-up to the justifiable homicide resolution, the BUF called for community control over police, and the vice-chairman of the Washington City Council promised to present the BUF plan to the council. The councilman rejected the existing police-community setup as not being reciprocal and as ignoring the problem of putting inner city residents into the mainstream of political power. "We want in on the system," the councilman said.

Complaints about police-community relations frequently cited inadequate protection and a conspicuous absence of Negro policemen, in addition to charges of brutality. Tenants at Manhattanville Houses in Harlem instituted their own twenty-four-hour lobby vigils throughout the six-building project. This came about because requests to the police department for additional security forces brought no results, according to the tenants.

To help improve community relations, many metropolitan police departments made major efforts to recruit Negro and Puerto Rican candidates. The Newark, New Jersey, police department received a $35,000 allocation from the state to help find ninety candidates from minority groups. Prospects would be paid $50 per week for ten weeks while they studied to prepare for the regular department tests for candidates. Boston announced a program aimed at discovering twenty-five Black youths to become police cadets.

Demonstrators in Milwaukee being evicted from the county welfare office on December 6, after a meeting and sit-in at which they requested $25.00 per family member for Christmas purchases.

In mid-1968, Michigan reported on its year-long effort to recruit a thousand policemen from primarily minority groups. The program was funded by a Justice Department grant and used the services of Bill Cosby in much of its state-wide publicity. At the end of the twelve month effort, only 375 applications had been received and only "several dozen" applicants had actually been hired. The civilian chairman of the effort noted that "there was less than real enthusiasm from law enforcement officials throughout the state."

Cleveland invested a $91,000 grant in providing college courses in psychology, chemistry, sociology and other areas for current members of the police department. At the same time the Fraternal Order of Police requested training in "guerrilla warfare" for department members.

An Office of Economic Opportunity study published during 1968 focused directly on the question of how police-community relations might be improved. According to the report, the best hope lies in upgrading the living standards of minority groups so that their basic perceptions and attitudes become more positive toward police action. The researchers offered no plan for accomplishing this end, but they did note that the goal would take years to achieve.

Dallas has been using "storefront" community relations centers to provide civilians with an unofficial but effective avenue of redressing grievances or gaining information about arrested persons. A reporter who toured mid-America investigating police-community relations programs cited the Dallas effort along with similar programs in other communities, but he added, "Many [other cities] are concentrating on riot training instead of community relations programs."

Throughout 1968 community impressions of policemen—especially minority impressions—centered almost exclusively on physical force, publicity and programs to the contrary. In minority neighborhoods almost every arrest elicited a charge of police brutality, and taunting resistance was the regular way of relating to police officers.

Some researchers summarily dismissed brutality charges; others doubtlessly exaggerated any kind of contact into a reign of terror and bloodshed. Frequently conflicting "evidence" mounted, but few researchers studied the problem. One of the most revealing reports, published in 1968 in the July-August issue of *Trans-Action* magazine, involved an extensive study of police action in Boston, Chicago and Washington over a seven-week period in the summer of 1966. The researchers had personally observed many instances of what the report termed "unnecessary force." With regard to the recipient of the force, "the application of force unnecessarily by the police operates without respect to the race of the offender." The report noted that victims were all from the lower class. It also stated that "the use of force by the police is more readily explained by police culture than by the policeman's race." Use of force usually came about when the policeman felt that his authority was threatened, whether this was actually the case or not. The report's author added: "I suspect that policemen are more likely to respond with excessive force when they define the situation as one in which there remains a question as to who is 'in charge.' "

1968 was not a good year for police-community relations, and some of the Presidential campaign statements did little to help the situation. If positive relations are to be established, the recommendations of a September 7 editorial in the *Cleveland Call and Post* bear consideration:

> Reconstitution of the police establishment is essential. Employment of more Negro police officers would help but would not provide the total or permanent answer. The tendency of municipal authorities to regard the police force as a special, privileged category of civil servants not subject to civilian regulation must be abandoned. If the quality of the police force is to be improved, standards must be raised, training augmented, and salaries substantially increased.

Little of what is proposed above characterized 1968, and police community relations continued to flounder.

The Kerner Report

March of 1968 saw the release of the Report of the President's National Advisory Commission on Civil Disorders, commonly labeled the Kerner Report after Governor Otto Kerner of Illinois, the commission's chairman.

Months before the release date rumors floated

freely about the possible content of the report. In the face of these rumors and knowing what the report would likely recommend, the commission chairman felt constrained to call a press conference to prepare the way. He denied rumors that the White House had exerted pressure to "tone down" recommendations that were either too controversial or too costly. He also rejected the idea circulating in some circles that the previous summer's riots were part of a nationwide conspiracy. At the same time he did state that some of the report recommendations may be regarded by some as "abrasive."

What with the experience of the 1967 riots, the report recommendations were eagerly awaited. Much was expected of it, perhaps more than was realistic. Some indication of these expectations was given by its sales when it was made public in March. A Washington store sold ten thousand copies in a few days and stores in other metropolitan centers had similar sales. The publisher estimated a million copies would be sold within a month, far in excess of the sale of the Warren Commission report on the assassination of President Kennedy.

As soon as the report appeared public figures began to react. Mayor Daley of Chicago criticized the report for failing to distinguish between protest and crime, though he termed the document a good report in general. Thirty-six members of the House of Representatives issued a statement saying they were prepared to support the recommendations of the report with their votes in Congress. Other political leaders, on the national and state levels, were more restrained in their appraisals, and some voiced pointed disagreement.

Most of the Presidential candidates, with the exception of George Wallace, took positions of "critical support," favoring the report as a whole while disagreeing with specific parts. President Johnson commended the report to governmental and civic leaders, urging serious consideration of the proposals.

A tabulation might have been made of those supporting and opposing the Kerner Report, but it would be more to the point to record any progress that could be traced to it. At the end of 1968 there was not much to report. Partly this may have been because of the nature of the report itself. The report contained some 160 specific recommendations, some of which were very broad, requiring complicated legislative and administrative action across an extended segment of the political structure of our country. Active implementation—at least of major portions of the report—would understandably require a great deal of time. Then there was the federal government's financial commitment to the Vietnam war. Finally, 1968 was a Presidential election year. The campaign activities and the awareness that a new administration would hold office in 1969 doubtless served to temporarily shelve plans for action. The big question was whether the report would have been forgotten by the time individuals and groups were again prepared for possible action.

Only weeks after the release of the Kerner Report public attention was diverted from it by Mayor Daley's order to Chicago police to "shoot to kill" arsonists and "shoot to maim or cripple" looters in riots. The controversial order elicited two major reactions: "It's about time," and "unbelievable!" Nothing much came of the order directly, but it tended to focus attention on the prospects for the Democratic Party convention scheduled for Chicago in the summer. Millions of words and hours of television time were devoted to the convention and its attendant happenings. The confusion in act and purpose of the Chicago melée only served to detract attention further from the Kerner recommendations.

However, all this did not automatically doom the Kerner recommendations to oblivion. But during 1968 Americans were, by and large, preoccupied with three major concerns: effectively halting rioting, ending the Vietnam war and electing a new President. The summer of 1968 was not as "hot" in the streets as during the previous year, and relief tempered interest in long-range programs of social reconstruction. Late in the year Vietnam did appear to be moving toward some kind of resolution. Later yet, the news of a new set of faces in the federal administration prompted many to take a wait-and-see attitude. At the end of 1968, the Kerner Report had become an historic document. How much of it will ever be translated into action will have to await a later assessment.

Martin Luther King

In April 1968 Martin Luther King was assassinated in Memphis. The news flashed across the country and throughout the world. From almost every quarter came the reaction.

In Minneapolis, signs reading "White Racism Must Go" sold briskly, the proceeds going to a Dr. King Memorial Fund set up by the Minneapolis Commission on Human Relations. Some churches—white as well as Negro—held special memorial services. Newspaper editorials challenged government agencies to heed the warning and act positively to alleviate the causes of such violence. Public figures from politics to show business made the pilgrimage to attend King's funeral.

After the shock of the incident and the pathos of the funeral, attention quickly turned to discovering and apprehending the elusive and personally mysterious killer. James Earl Ray, now formally charged with the murder, was discovered in Britain. Almost as much media space was devoted to examining the history of this unknown assassin as was given to King's death itself. Then the silence of death settled over the entire matter. The charismatic leader was gone, and the Southern Christian Leadership Conference went doggedly about its work under the guidance of another leader, one much less publicly compelling than the deceased King.

Two social scientists conducted a study in Florida of the reaction of school children to King's assassination. The results were not encouraging. About 60 per cent of the white students were either indifferent about or actually pleased by King's death, and 17 per cent felt the assassin should be freed and even congratulated. These were junior and senior high school students, probably reflecting parental attitudes as much as they expressed their own conclusions. The study noted that among white students happiness and indifference increased with grade level. Among Negroes, over 50 per cent desired extra-legal revenge on King's killer. The researchers could find "no basis for optimism in regard to race relations in the South."

Whatever the possible responses to Martin Luther King's death, a physician rejected "communal guilt" as a viable reaction. In an extended article the author argued that national guilt is not only a dubious conception but also self-defeating. The physician took the tack that "we must remember that guilt has little to do with reality situations."

Without passing on the validity of the physician's line of argument, which he developed over several pages of print, the fact does remain that few Americans responded to King's death with any significant sense of guilt, either individual or communal. There was sorrow and there was anger, both of which moderate with the passing of time. But there was no evidence of a guilt which demands redemptive action.

The assassination of Dr. King was a shocking event, but it was only one incident in a year-long parade of incidents clamoring for and receiving attention. What consequences the loss of King will have for the civil rights movement cannot be determined at this point in time, but it is evident that America, though aware of the vacuum left by King's loss—and shocked by the manner of his departure—has moved on, more concerned with today than with a leader that is no longer with them.

Beauty Contests

If there is a lighter side to race relations, beauty contests must represent that side. Judging from some of the exchanges during 1968 over the involvement or exclusion of Blacks, beauty contests in 1968 took on a social significance far beyond the wildest expectations of even their sponsors.

Several Negro girls won the title of queen during 1968. For the first time, "Miss Garden State" (New Jersey) was a Negro. A Negro emerged as national college queen in 1968, and the Empire State boasted a Negro queen. Most often the new queens wore their titles with grace and demonstrated the expected appreciation. In some instances, however, the course of royal life was not smooth. The 1967 homecoming queen at the Univerity of Michigan had been a Negro. By tradition the outgoing queen crowns her successor, but not so in 1968. The outgoing queen simply handed the crown to the new queen and then used the occasion to inform the audience of "experiences of discourtesies because of her race."

The new queen, white, accepted the crown without comment. A Detroit group, promoting its own "Miss Tan Detroit Pageant," sent congratulations and invited the former homecoming queen to participate in its contest.

The "Miss America" contest, grandmother of national and international beauty contests, came in for its own protest and direct competition during 1968. A hundred women, both Black and white, picketed the Atlantic City location of the contest, protesting the "degrading mindless-boob-girlie symbol" represented by the affair, denouncing the contest's "racism" and announcing a boycott of all commercial sponsors of the event. The demonstration did not interfere with the pageant, which went on as scheduled and was climaxed by the selection of a white girl. No Negro girl has ever been a finalist.

A few weeks before the "Miss America" contest, its officials had announced a $1,000 scholarship to the NAACP "to encourage more Negro participation." The announcement came some weeks after Roy Wilkins, the NAACP executive director, characterized the contest as "lily-white."

While the event was taking place in Atlantic City's convention hall, a "Miss Black America" was being selected at the Ritz Carlton auditorium in the same city. Depending on how consequential we consider beauty contests to be, the separate Black and white Miss Americas may have been another 1968 indication of the two societies, one Black and one white, characterized in the Kerner Report.

Conclusion

In the area of interracial social relations, 1968 was an extremely varied year. If a single distinction were to be underscored for the year it would have to be that Negroes, more than ever before, stood up, *as Negroes*, to be recognized and to act. The phrase *as Negroes* covers adequately if not precisely the separatists, the militants, the moderates and those who for the first time harbored the thought that it wasn't inherently bad to be Black. Many of the highlights that marked 1968, some of which have been noted in this chapter, will probably soon pass from public memory. In the years to come, however, those who do recall Black America '68 will probably think of it as pivotal, roughly marking the turning point of Negroes from accommodation within a larger national framework to social distinctiveness within the American scene. A chronicle prepared in the heat of moments and incidents still about us can only speculate; final assessment will have to be left to the historians.

Black Panther Eldridge Cleaver lecturing at American University in Washington, D.C.

The Writer and Black Liberation

John Oliver Killens

"I HAVE SEEN a land right merry with the sun, where children sing, and rolling hills lie like passioned women wanton with harvest. And there in the King's Highway sat and sits a figure veiled and bowed, by which the traveller's footsteps hasten as they go. On the tainted air broods fear. Three centuries' thought has been the raising and the unveiling of that bowed human heart, and now behold a century new for the duty and the deed. The problem of the Twentieth Century is the problem of the color line."

Thus wrote W. E. B. Du Bois in his *The Souls of Black Folk* at the beginning of this century. "The problem of the Twentieth Century is the problem of the color line." The relationship of the Western world with the darker peoples of Africa and Asia and the Americas and the islands of the seas. Some years later the same man wrote, and with even greater certainty: "Most men in the world are colored. A belief in humanity means belief in colored men. The future world will, in all reasonable probability, be what colored men make it." In 1955 George Padmore, writer and Pan-Africanist, wrote, in comment on the Du Bois prophecy: "This is the inescapable challenge of the second part of the Twentieth Century."

Of course, when Du Bois made this prophecy at the beginning of this century it caused very little excitement. Wall Street did no somersaults. Nations called no international congresses to consider the matter, no pompous meetings at the summit. No commissions were established to investigate the question and write interminable reports. It was a time of Monroe Doctrines and Open Door and Big Stick Policies, when there were gunboats in the China Sea and you threw pennies to the grateful "natives." It was an era of good feelings, of noble savages and noblesse oblige, when the relationships of man (white) to non-man (colored) had been ordained by God and settled for eternity. Man and non-man lived with their preordained lots without rancor or hostility. It was a time of Kipling's "White Man's Burden" and "Gunga Din," an age of Great White Fatherism. For centuries colonialism and slavery had become the basis of the relationships between white and colored peoples throughout the earth. On the one hand, the kindly paternalistic master, missionary and bearer of civilization and Christianity; on the other hand, the humble servant, savage, pagan, hardworking, lazy, stupid and cunning, happy and contented in his servile status.

From *The Souls of Black Folk* to *The World and Africa* to *The Ordeal of Mansart*, Du Bois continued to lift his strong clear voice to the Western world, but few men of the Wild West heeded. And now Du Bois is gone, but the drama of his prophecy unfolds before the entire human race. The literary legacy he left us had and has a total relevancy to social change and revolution for the colored peoples of this world. And Rudyard Kipling notwithstanding, the days of Great White Fatherism *are* numbered, and Queen Elizabeth of England *is* the last of the Great White Mothers.

And what is the relationship of the Black writers of today to the "problem" and the "challenge" of the twentieth century? I take the position that, since man is a social animal, his literature should and does have social relevance. And further, that, since the Black Revolt, which is not yet a revolution (rumors to the contrary), is part and parcel of the worldwide revolution of people of color against colonialism and white racism, literature by Black men and women will generally have a social relevance to this worldwide revolution and especially to the Black Revolt presently unfolding in these United States of America. Moreover, any literature worth the designation is social, has social significance, is engaged on one side or the other, for humanity or against. Put another way: all art is propaganda, notwithstanding all propaganda is not art.

If the Black writer has found himself for the most part on the side of the angels fighting with all his might to bring about the kingdom of love and justice and brotherhood right here on this terrible wonderful earth, if much of the literature wrought by Black men has been in the realm of protest, this is because the Black writer, like any other writer, basically reflects his own frame of reference, which is the sum total of his life's experiences. And these experiences have been essentially those of living as Black men in a white racist society. If much of the Black writer's literature is protest, it is because Black culture is in the main a culture of protest. The essential statement of Black culture in this country has come down to us from slavery in the Black folk's music. It can be found in the Negro spirituals, one of which proclaims: "Didn't my Lord deliver Daniel? Why not every man?"

Yet Black writers are continually asked the question: "Why do you insist on writing about Negroes? Why don't you write about people?" It is as if Sean O'Casey had been asked, all the days of his literary life, why he wrote about the Irish, and Dostoevski and Tolstoy why they wrote about the Russians, and so forth. But who will tell the Black man's story if Black writers desert this field? And what experience is richer in drama, in tragedy, and humor? In man's inhumanity to man? Langston Hughes was very clear about this question almost two decades ago when he wrote "You've Taken My Blues and Gone":

You've taken my blues and gone.
You sing 'em on Broadway
And you sing 'em in the Hollywood Bowl
And you mixed them up with symphonies
And you make them so they don't sound like me.
Yep, you've taken my blues and gone.

You've also taken my spirituals and gone.
You put them in *Macbeth* and in *Carmen Jones*
And in all kinds of *Swing Mikadoes*
And in everything but what's about me.

But someday, somebody'll
Stand up and talk about me
And write about me.
And put on plays about me,
Black and beautiful.
And I reckon it'll be me, myself,
Yes, it'll be me.

Even with the best of intentions, most white writers have, historically, found it impossible to create Black people in their literature. For example, let us look briefly at a novel which has probably sold more copies and has been translated into more languages than any other book alive. (Books do live.) I mean Mrs. Stowe's *Uncle Tom's Cabin*. Here were a novelist and a book whose hearts were in the right places. Here was a book that came out unequivocally against the "peculiar institution" of American slavery. The legend goes that when Abe Lincoln first met Harriet Beecher Stowe he remarked: "So you're the little lady who started the Civil War?"

That Mrs. Stowe was antislavery and that her book was an open attack on slavery cannot be intelligently disputed. Nevertheless, *Uncle Tom's Cabin* created more stereotypes about the Negro than any other piece of literature ever written. To mention just a few: "The loyal slave and kindly master." And: "It was the mulatto slaves who were rebellious. Because of their white blood they did not take kindly to enslavement. On the other hand, the black slave was naturally docile and submissive." This concept hardly explains rebellious Nat Turner (William Styron notwithstanding), insurrectionist Denmark Vesey, Underground Railroad conductor Harriet Tubman, or Toussaint L'Ouverture or Gabriel Prosser. And how would Mrs. Stowe explain tall, Black, proud Cinque, who led a mutiny on the slave ship *Amistad*? How explain the thousands of Black folk who dove into the sea on the way over to this Promised Land. And, let's face it, regardless of good intentions, dear old Uncle Tom was an "Uncle Tom" as we use the term today, despite the fact that in the end he gave his life rather than betray some fellow slaves. Indeed, in terms of Tom's very sick love affair with Little angelic Eva, Mrs. Stowe made a faggot out of this gentle figment of her vigorous imagination. Tom was probably the first Black man to be creatively castrated in the annals of American fiction.

And of course there were so many white writers who had no such good intentions. Writers like the author of *The Clansman,* upon which that "great epic film" *The Birth of a Nation* was based. And Margaret Mitchell in *Gone with the Wind*—another monumental best seller glorifying the idyllic happy days of slavery—and authors of scores of other "fictional masterpieces" created out of the urgent need to justify slavery and colonialism. Gunga Din and Uncle Tom and Aunt Jemima became the real authentic "nigger," and Frederick Douglass, Harriet Tubman, Denmark Vesey were the fakes and fictions.

And after a hundred years of "progress and understanding" between the races, we move from Stowe's *Uncle Tom* to William Styron's *Confessions of Nat Turner*, which I choose to fondly think of as *The Confessions of Willie Styron*, meaning that from this book we get a far deeper insight into the psyche of William Styron, the unreconstructed peckerwood, than we do of Nat Turner, the revolutionary slave. Here again, more than a hundred years after Stowe, we get a jazzed up version of Uncle Tom in Styron's fictional characterization of Nat Turner. The title of this sham biographical novel might have been more appropriately *The Reluctant Insurrectionist*. Here again the Black man is castrated. Here again we have "kindly masters" and "loyal slaves." Here again, we have this asexual or homosexual "hero." Here again we have the sick love affair between the "noble savage" (a little less noble and a little more militant?) and the white angelic symbol of purity and virtue (instead of Little Eva we have Miss Margaret Anne). They both die with halos around their golden heads and go swiftly off to heaven.

An important thing to remember is that what white men wrote about Black folk many Black folk believed, and believe unto this very day. Too many Black folk on this earth still believe that they are niggers. Believe in their inherent inferiority. Believe that the more you look like the man the more beautiful you are and the better off you are. Believe that good hair is white folk's hair and that bad hair is the Black man's. Believe in Nadinola and hair straightenings and high yaller. Believe in the universal saying: "A nigger ain't shit!" Oh, yes, brothers, sisters, we have been believers in our own unworthiness. And some of us have always felt the need to act out the roles the white mythmakers scripted for us. Hence the latter-day Uncle Toms and Gunga Dins, even the college educated ones.

What Hemingway and Scott Fitzgerald did for the Lost Generation after the First Worldwide Madness, what Kerouac did for the Beat Generation after the Second Worldwide Madness, what John Steinbeck and his memorable Joad family and their *Grapes of Wrath* did for the Depression Years and the Dust Bowl victims and the Okies, what Richard Wright did for Chicago when he exploded on the scene with his overpowering *Native Son*, we Black writers are challenged to do for the dramatization of the times we find ourselves in at this historic moment. James Baldwin gave us Harlem in his brilliant novel *Go Tell It on the Mountain*, as did Ralph Ellison in his powerful *Invisible Man*. The late Frank London Brown gave us the fighting Black folk of Chicago in his *Trumbull Park*, as did Ronald Fair in his *Hog Butcher*.

The past decade has witnessed the blossoming forth of a group of writers more interested in the posture of *Black Man Speaks* than Richard Wright's *White Man, Listen!* This crop includes Paule Marshall, Julian Mayfield, Ossie Davis, John Clarke, Irving Burgie, John Williams, Loften Mitchell, LeRoi Jones, Ronald Milner, Rosa Guy, Alice Childress, Lerone Bennett, Charles Hamilton, Lonne Elder—to name-drop just a few. For the most part, the Black writer has embarked on a trip from Social Protest to Human Affirmation in the Land of Revolution. He is a man brandishing a literary Molotov cocktail. His art is a hand grenade blasting away at American complacency. He has the sense of urgency that the tide of change for Black people throughout the earth is here and now and that this tide is in the flood, and that we are now afloat on a full sea and so must take the current, or lose our ventures for another hundred years. A hundred years of fraudulent "integration." With no apologies to Shakespeare.

The past few years have seen the advent of a new thing in Black arts which might be called the Era of the Black Poets. People like Margaret

Charles Hamilton

Gwendolyn Brooks

J. Saunders Redding

Margaret Walker

Walker, Arna Bontemps, Gwendolyn Brooks, Margaret Danner, Robert Hayden, Melvin Tolson, Sarah Fabio, Sarah Wright, Lucy Smith, Claude McKay, LeRoi Jones, Ted Joans, Dudley Randall, Countee Cullen and Langston Hughes paid some heavy dues trailblazing for this era which has come to full flower now. Most of the new poets, for example Mari Evans, Don Lee, Donald Graham, Nikki Giovanni, Larry Neal, Askia Muhammed Toure, "The Last Poets," have been tremendously influenced by LeRoi Jones in his post-Village days. Their voices are loud, strong and sometimes strident, and the song they sing is a song of affirmation, affirming the terrible wonderful beauty of their Blackness. It is not a new song. Langston is still the poetic Big Daddy of our Black and Beautiful selves. But more poets are singing today than ever, and to bigger and Blacker audiences. They are singing to Black audiences! Dig it! Writing for Black readers. And these new poets for the most part are writers who know their craft and are continually struggling with the mastery of it. Notwithstanding, for militancy, for love of Black people, for depth of understanding, no new poet has yet reached the heights and depths of Margaret Walker's "For My People" and her "We Have Been Believers." But there is time.

As to the playwrights, the most exciting play about Black life I have seen in the last twelve months was Lonne Elder, III's, *Ceremonies in Dark Old Men*, staged by the Negro Ensemble Company and starred in by Douglas Turner Ward at the St. Mark Playhouse in New York City. Lonne Elder's play is a fine job of thinking, writing, feeling, living. It is a statement of Black life in a white society. A story of love and hate and struggle, of laughter and tears. It is the story of frustration, replete with great humor, which is always on the verge of tears. "Laughing to keep from crying," Langston Hughes once wrote. *Ceremonies* is the epitome of the tragicomic. Tragedy is the dramatic essence of the Black man's frame of reference in this country. Humor has been one of his weapons in his struggle for survival. *Ceremonies* captures all. I laughed, I cried, at *Ceremonies*.

Probably the most important novel on the scene in 1968 was John Williams' *The Man Who Cried I Am*. It was one of the few novels by a Black writer that has encompassed the international scene, and it accomplished this with authority and magnificence. One had the feeling that this was how it was. At the end of it one wished for another chapter, which goes to indicate how much the reader was involved. John Williams reached a peak in creative craftsmanship.

I have just finished reading the galley proofs of a new novel which will be published in the summer of 1969. *This Child's Gonna Live* is about Black folk in a fishing village on the Eastern Shore of Maryland and was written by Sarah Elizabeth Wright, a poet who did not forget her poetry when she moved into the genre of the novel. *This Child* is a powerful prose-poem written out of the pain, struggle and poverty of the people it depicts. Sarah Wright was co-author with Lucy Smith of a beautiful book of poetry, *Give Me a Child*.

Eldridge Cleaver created a tremendous stir in literary and political circles with his *Soul on Ice*. Cleaver has a powerful facility with the written word. His authenticity is undeniable, especially when he is telling us about the he of him. Me, Eldridge Cleaver, "baddest of the baddest niggers." Here is a fine talent, from which great novelists are spawned. It is only when Cleaver begins to generalize about the souls of Black folk, particularly Black men and their sexuality and their obsessive yen for white women, and when he begins to pontificate about the politics of the American dilemma, that he seems to be mouthing the words of white men. He does not sound like my friend Eldridge Cleaver. He begins to sound more like my friend Maxwell Geismar, white liberal-radical literary critic. Geismar is probably one of the most outstanding critics of the American literary scene, anti-Establishment and all that, but, like other whites, he falls on his face when he presumes to deal with the Black blues people. But more about the dire need for Black literary critics a little later. One can only hope, and fervently, that Cleaver quickly realizes that his forte is creative writing, that he has a true gift to give to the world and to the Black Revolt, not yet a revolution, and that that gift is his great pen, which is mightier than his sword. Brother Eldridge, Fred Douglass is still absolutely right: "Who would be free, must themselves strike the blow." Don't lean too heavily on the white "revolutionary" students. They are tomorrow's cop-out liberals.

A most important book in 1968 was *Black Rage*, by William Grier and Price M. Cobbs. Deep are the roots of the Black man's psychological castration according to this penetrating book. To live eternally as a eunuch in a great white harem and still somehow maintain a modicum of manhood is one of the areas explored by these two Black psychiatrists. It is a book of great honesty and tremendous insights. With all the authors' technical knowledge of the problem, the beauty of this book is that it is written with the clarity of everyday expression. For the layman to dig. For the brother and sister to understand.

Now, it must be said that some poets are writing hurriedly these days, as are some novelists, and playwrights, as if they fear that the great Black Beautiful fad might not last long, that the Black Thing might swiftly go out of style like miniskirts or rock 'n' roll, and that they'd better get on board the little Black train before it runs out of steam, or diesel, or Great White Tolerance. Some seem to think it is enough to endow Whitey with a barrel of Oedipus complexes (mother-lovers) and the greatness of their art is guaranteed. There need be no contradiction between artistry and message. The greater and profounder the message, the greater demand on the writer to deliver it with artistry.

There is a tremendous need for the development of a school, or schools, of Black literary criticism. There is a dearth of Black literary critics. Saunders Redding has worked hard and consistently in this vineyard. But who else? Harold Cruse might have been our great bright Black hope in this field, starting with his book *The Crisis of the Negro Intellectual*, had he not allowed his deadly subjectivity and petty peeves to cause him to sink into a quagmire of egotistical self-hatred, self-pity and hatred for his Black colleagues in the world of arts and letters.

So what is it that creates a kind of unity in the Black writers' statements today? A kind of "telling it like it is" and not like the white man wants to hear it. Most Black writers have moved away from the posture: "I'm not a Black writer. I'm a writer who happens to be Black." We are realizing more than ever now that a writer "who happens to be Black" is either terribly naive, lying and bee-essing, or passing literarily. Because the truth of the matter is that all Afro-Americans are Black people who have happened to become ditch diggers, hustlers, preachers, doctors, statesmen, pimps, leaders, writers, or whatever has become their lot. We don't know of any writer who was born hunting and pecking on a typewriter. But every Afro-American writer was born Black in a white society. These are his specificities, his beautiful, terribly important uniqueness. His Afro-Americanese, his rhythm, his idiom which has enriched the American culture and its language in much the same way that blues and jazz and gospel and spirituals and rhythm-and-blues have enriched American music. The Black writer today would have to be out of his mind to divest himself of all these magnificent materials and tools of the trade, which he and only he possesses. He and his club members. I've said it before, and I say it again, that only club members can really sing the blues, because only we have paid the dues. Yes, some Black writers have come to understand the necessity for decolonizing our literature, our language, our craft, our style. Some of us have begun to write in Negritude, in Afro-Americanese. Writing for everyone to dig, but especially for Black folk in our own beautiful Black idiom, in much the same way as Sean O'Casey wrote in the English language, but it was always Irish-English.

The Black writer is an angry man, but his anger is purposeful, positive, constructively destructive, and therefore revolutionary, which is why his anger does not delight the critics, as did that of the "angry young" white men of the cop-out fifties. Who had no wars worth fighting and no worlds worth saving. No white worlds, that is to say, and no white wars. Fascism was dead. Or was it? Had been slain on the bloody battlefields of Europe in the patriotic war of the nineteen forties. But had it? And Black writers, here and now, are warriors, almost one and all, because we have a world to win. To destroy, to change, to reconstruct, to win. A new world to achieve. What was new about that other so-called "new world" for the Black man, except a new kind of slavery, the most vicious in the annals of recorded history? Black writers are Malcolmites and Martinites marching as to war. We have declared war to the death against white racism, which is the enemy of humankind. Black writers are calling to question all those things which have to this very moment been the everlasting never-ever-to-be-questioned truths.

The Black writer's ship is not a *Ship of Fools*. His mood is not *Stop the World, I Want To Get Off*. He wants to ride this old world, kick over all the old dung-heaped corrals, tame this Wild West crazy beast, like the champeen bronco-buster he certainly is. He wants to bring sanity to this madhouse, even if he has to bring the building down, first. Black writers are singing of love: healthy love, requited love. Love and life as opposed to this terrible stench of hate and death that stalks the earth. And now, lest I be misunderstood: As far as this Black writer is concerned, love and hate are total irrelevancies vis-à-vis the Black and white confrontation. I neither need to love the white man nor hate him. But most white men demand that you either love them or hate them, as long as you are so obsessed with them that you don't have time to get your own Black thing together. We will take up the question of love and hate with white America three or four hours *after* liberation. Suffice to say, a slave will never love his master, unless said slave is out of his cotton-picking mind.

And now that Brothers Medgar, Malcolm and Martin have departed, it must be said that Black folk need not look for their Messiahs any longer. They have come, they have fought the good fight and they have been crucified. Black writers must proclaim a new calendar for the disinherited all over this earth. On that calendar, everything Before Martin will be dated "B.M." Everything from these days forward is "A.M." After Medgar, After Malcolm, After Martin. After Messiahs! Now we know for the first time the true significance of A.M. After Martin, and the morning of a new day borning, that Great-Gitting-Up-Morning, the dawn of civilization, when man will just begin to live. Black writers! "Lift every voice and sing, till earth and heaven ring, ring with the harmonies of Liberty!"

Elton C. Fax. *Madonna and Child, Kano, Nigeria*. Drawing.

The American Negro Artist—1968

Elton C. Fax

The Background

TEN YEARS AGO the then newly formed American Society of African Culture was drawing as many American artists, writers, musicians and scholars into its membership as were interested in a cultural exchange with their counterparts in Africa. I was a member of the society. So when John A. Davis, one of the founders, asked me if I would recruit members from among the Black painters, sculptors and printmakers, I knew my response was immediate and enthusiastic. I imagined that the invitation would evoke a favorable response from every quarter. Ha!

My first telephone call was to a well-known New York Afro-American artist and a teacher, a man I had known for more than twenty years. His reply was swift and chilly. No, he would *not* join. Besides, it is high time, he told me, that we Black artists forget about Africa, stop thinking about our Blackness and get down to the serious job of being good American artists. For five uninterrupted minutes he lectured me on the evils inherent in this wild scheme of mine that would separate its followers from the mainstream of the good American life.

Frankly, I was quite exasperated when he finished, though I did manage to thank him and wish him well. One thing helped console me, however. I had the feeling that this same artist and others who felt as he did would soon be singing an entirely different melody. That was in 1958. Today, 1968, the Black American artists who heretofore wanted no part of a "Black label" swallow hard and manipulate phrases in press interviews as they descend to rejoin their more earthbound Black comrades-in-arms. Why? First, and basically, because in a racist social order such as ours there is no other place for them to go if they choose to remain here. Second (and here is one of the paradoxes of American racism), it is quite fashionable now to be Black. Black is "in"—not for *everybody* who happens to be Black, but for that talented, favorably positioned few who happen to get the nod of approval from the white establishment. And when one considers how "out" of things artists traditionally are and how way, *way*, out of everything the average *Black* artist is, one understands why getting "in" is so important to him.

1968 has been an oddly "promising" year for the Black artist, even as it has been an explosive and challenging one for the world in which and of which he draws, paints and carves. So we have the promises, the explosions and the challenges; and that is what this essay is about. It will list what Black artists across the nation did during 1968, but it will not attempt to evaluate the aesthetic merits or demerits of what they did. It will make a *statement* of what the Black artist produced over the past twelve months *in direct relation to significant happenings inside and outside America during the same period*. For everything any artist ever produces is reflective in some way of the world around him.

The buildup to the 1968 art scene that concerns us here began months before the throngs of New Year's Eve celebrants were to jam their way twice into New York's Times Square to reenact a familiarly noisy and drunken ritual. It started toward the end of 1966, when the Museum of Modern Art in New York City began to assemble an exhibit of prints by American painters under the title *Painters as Printmakers*. The show was to circulate among U.S. embassies in Africa.

It soon became apparent that Black artists would not be seen in that show, and when the museum was approached about it their representatives pleaded innocence of the existence of any qualifying American Negro artists. It seemed that the museum knew only Black painters and Black printmakers but none who did both. So it remained for the American Society of African Culture, aided by Romare Bearden and other Black artists, to remind the Museum of Modern Art that its own permanent collection contained prints by Black painters. One of the latter, Norma Morgan, was represented by two engravings, *Granite Tor* and *David in the Wilderness*. Both had entered the museum's collection more than five years previously!

Even more astounding was the case of painter William Majors, who at one time had been employed by the Museum of Modern Art. Mr. Majors had made a series of prints titled *Ecclesiastes* which the Museum of Modern Art had published as a book. A check at the museum just before I wrote this revealed that copies of *Ecclesiastes* are still available. Still the museum authorities who assembled the show claimed no knowledge of Black painters who made prints. So the show went on the road minus Afro-American representation, and as of the first of December 1968, it was being viewed in Abidjan, capital of the Ivory Coast, West Africa. The incident is reminiscent of the project inaugurated by the late Nancy Kefauver involving the placement of American art in American embassies around the world. To the best of our present knowledge no works by Black artists are included.

In the meantime, however, *Topic*, a most attractive monthly magazine published by the press and publications service of the United States Information Agency, produced issue Number 5. This was a special issue subtitled *The Negro in the American Arts*. *Topic* is published for distribution in Africa. The nine contributing writers to this special issue, all Afro-Americans, were Arna Bontemps, Dennis Askey, Luther Jackson, Owen Dodson, John Williams, Samuel Allen, Lucille Roberts, Langston Hughes and Richard Saunders.

Mrs. Roberts' article, "A Gallery of Eight," stressed the freedom of the American artist. It was well written and was illustrated with handsomely printed black-and-white photographs of each artist and full color reproductions of their works. The artists shown were Hughie Lee-Smith, Hale Woodruff, Romare Bearden, Ray Saunders, Norman Lewis, Richard Dempsey, Emilio Cruz and Jacob Lawrence. It was indeed an impressive spread, and African readers unfamiliar with the subtleties of American race prejudice will doubtless feel that claims of discrimination against Black artists are greatly and unfairly exaggerated. But the record stands for what it is. The same *group* of artists has yet to be *similarly* publicized in any of the leading "white" news magazines here at home. Therefore knowledgeable readers of *Topic* will not be overwhelmed and thereby diverted from the basic hard facts of American life as those eight painters and this writer know them.

Time magazine for May 26, 1967, carried a cover story, "The Negro in Vietnam." Featured were the heroic exploits of Alabama-born Sergeant Clide Brown, Jr., leader of a team of five white GI's. In addition, using the quotes of Black soldiers, the article praised General Benjamin O. Davis, Jr., First Lieutenant Dorothy Harris (a nurse), Major James T. Boddie (a bomber pilot), Roy Wilkins and Thurgood Marshall. It criticized armed forces segregation (especially in Saigon's recreational spots), and also criticized Muhammad Ali, the Black Muslims and Dr. Martin Luther King, Jr. The same issue of *Time* carried a news story on page 21 of a "riot" between Black male students on the campus of Texas Southern University and Houston city police. Result: one rookie patrolman died and two patrolmen were wounded; the men's dorm at T.S.U. was completely wrecked; one student was wounded and 488 were arrested. The nation was becoming disturbingly aware of its Black population both overseas and at home.

In the autumn of 1967 the City University of New York with the Harlem Cultural Council and the New York Urban League opened an exhibition titled *The Evolution of Afro-American Artists: 1800–1950*. The show was housed in Great Hall at City College, in New York. Painter Romare Bearden and curator Carroll Greene, Jr., co-directed the organizing of this display; with help from local and outside sources they assembled the paintings, prints and sculptures of some fifty-five American artists along with five carvings and two bronze castings from Africa. Exhibiting artists were catalogued in the following order:

THE NINETEENTH CENTURY

Joshua Johnston, Edward Mitchell Bannister, Edmonia Lewis, Robert Duncanson, William Simpson, Henry O. Tanner, Meta Warrick Fuller.

THE NEGRO RENAISSANCE

Aaron Douglas, Richmond Barthé, Palmer C. Hayden, Hale Woodruff, Archibald Motley, Augusta Savage, William Edouard Scott, Albert A. Smith, James A. Porter, Allan Rohan Crite, Malvin Gray Johnson, William H. Johnson, O. Richard Reid, Laura W. Waring, William E. Braxton, James L. Wells, Edwin A. Harleston, Lois Mailou Jones.

THE DEPRESSION YEARS–WORLD WAR II

Hughie Lee-Smith, Fred Flemister, John Biggers, Jacob Lawrence, Romare Bearden, Charles H. Alston, Charles White, John Wilson, Elizabeth Catlett, William Artis, William Edmonson, Horace Pippin, Earl Richardson, Claude Clark, Ernest Crichlow, Ellis Wilson, Charles Sebree, Robert Blackburn, Robert S. Pious, Norman Lewis, Beauford DeLaney, Joseph Delaney, Selma Burke, Eldzier Cortor, Ronald Joseph.

WORLD WAR II–1950

Humbert L. Howard, Haywood Rivers, Richard Mayhew, Merton D. Simpson, John Farrar.

The selection was an excellent one, though there were omissions that should not have occurred in view of what the show was trying to say. Granting that there were space limitations, the inclusion of additional artists could still have been achieved through the simple process of limiting some of the artists shown to fewer pictures. In that way artists of the Depression Years–World War II, such as the late Henry W. Bannarn, Rex Goreleigh and Sara Murrell (whose works I know were easily available), could have been seen.

The exhibit received excellent public notice and was quite well attended, what with the liberal press, radio and TV announcements of it that circulated throughout the Greater New York area. Large groups of supervised school children filed constantly into Great Hall during its showing. They left with a view of 150 years of art many had never dreamed existed. (*Ebony* magazine covered this show in February 1968, in six inside pages—four in full color.)

Shortly after the show's closing, the Grand Central Galleries in New York opened a significant exhibition on November 16, 1967, which ran until December 2. It was a one-man show of forty-eight paintings by nineteenth-century painter Henry Ossawa Tanner. Tanner was a Pittsburgh-born Negro expatriate who, until his death in 1937, lived for forty-six years in Paris. Excellent as his mystical, Impressionist-inspired canvases are, they did not please all critics. Cedric Dover in his book *American Negro Art* (London, 1960) had flayed Tanner for "forsaking his black roots" and for choosing to paint as any similarly inspired white American might have done.

When the Tanner show opened in New York, however, John Canaday, writing in the *New York Times* (November 19, 1967) and noting the poor condition of the Tanner canvases, decried what he saw as "A Poor Deal for a Good Man." Suggesting that a good cleaning job would have shown Tanner, the painter, to far better advantage, Canaday assailed the projection of Tanner, the Negro, as "the injustice to a proud man" who believed that "an artist should be judged solely on the basis of talent." The opposing views of these two critics met in static deadlock as 1968, young and eager, erupted upon the scene.

1968: The First Quarter

Terry Dintenfass opened a show of paintings by Jacob Lawrence on January 2, 1968, at her East 67th Street gallery in New York City. The twenty gouache paintings on view were illustrations for Mr. Lawrence's book *Harriet Tubman and the Promised Land*, published by Windmill Books, Inc. Critical reviews of the Lawrence paintings included this comment from *Arts* magazine (February 1968):

> Lawrence undeniably understands how illustrations should work—not as a repetition of text but as its natural complement to accelerate the action.

Mr. Lawrence, speaking to a reporter for the New York *Amsterdam News* (January 20, 1968), had this to say about his show:

> I feel very good about it and a challenge to try to portray the character of man and his quest for freedom and man who seeks to better himself . . . not just the Negro thing, but a symbol of man's constant struggle for freedom.

When asked how the Tubman saga relates to the present civil rights movement, he replied:

> It is a continuous struggle. I don't see any separation between then and now—even the mistakes. The civil rights movement today is a very good thing if you look at it as a whole and don't fragment it.

As visitors to the Dintenfass Gallery viewed the paintings of Jacob Lawrence in January, the world at large became acutely conscious of two South Africans. One was twenty-four-year-old Clive Haupt and the other, fifty-eight-year-old Dr. Philip Blaiberg. Haupt was a Cape Colored (a South African of mixed blood) and Blaiberg a white dentist. Each lived in different sections of racially segregated Cape Town. When Haupt died suddenly of a stroke, his heart was swiftly and successfully transplanted into the sick body of Philip Blaiberg, establishing a precedent in modern surgical history. Philip Blaiberg continues to live. Clive Haupt was given one of Cape Town's largest funerals and his remains were buried, quite traditionally, safely away from those of white South Africans.

In a New York revival of Bernard Shaw's *Saint Joan*, Black actress Diana Sands was winning critical praise as Joan of Arc. And across the Hudson River in New Jersey playwright LeRoi Jones drew a two-and-a-half to three-year jail sentence and incurred a fine of $1,000 after his conviction on charges of having possessed firearms during riots in Newark the previous summer.

During January 1968 Charles White was at Fisk University in Nashville, Tennessee, along with thirty-one original drawings from his book *Images of Dignity*. Chicago was host to Jeff Donaldson's one-man show at the Lakeside Gallery, while in Washington, at a White House luncheon, Eartha Kitt told the First Lady and her guests exactly what, in her opinion, was wrong with America. In New York Faith Ringgold displayed a group of her canvases titled *American People* at the midtown Spectrum Gallery, while the Adams School presented drawings and paintings by Frederick R. Noel.

At about this time Judge Waties Waring, a white South Carolina jurist who startled this nation with his 1951 ruling "Segregation is per se inequality," died in a New York hospital. The date was January 18, 1968.

Artist Samuel Countee had died several years earlier. However, on February 7 the Countee Cullen Branch of the New York Public Library opened a memorial showing of Mr. Countee's paintings. Romare Bearden and Bruce Nugent selected the works to be exhibited. Most of the artist's figure studies in this show reflected his awareness of Black America's social problems, while his *Atomic Aftermath* sounded a grim warning against the use of the awesome weapon. Still bombs, shells and napalm continued to rain death and a living horror upon Vietnam military and non-military occupants alike.

From the White House, President Lyndon Johnson issued an indirect plea to Dr. Martin Luther King, Jr., and other civil rights activists to reconsider their plans for a mass demonstration in Washington slated for April. Also in the nation's capital, artist-teacher Leo A. Robinson, a native son, opened an exhibition of his paintings at the Howard University Art Gallery. The date was February 17. On the same day Father James E. Groppi, fiery Roman Catholic priest of Milwaukee, likened a jury of that city to "a Mississippi jury." Moreover, he called its lone Black member "a 'Yes, sir,' Black man." The deliberating body had convicted Father Groppi of resisting arrest during an open housing demonstration the previous summer.

On the West Coast a large collection of the works of Wayne Thiebaud was opened to public view at the Pasadena Art Museum. The exhibition, scheduled to run through March 17, was organized by John Coplans, the museum's art curator. And in Los Angeles, Roderick Sykes displayed his works at Sunset Boulevard's Art Mart on February 25 and 26.

The year's shortest month was over and March stormed on stage, her volatile reputation solidly unchallenged. Much of white America was angrily trying to regain its composure after having read what President Johnson's National Advisory Commission on Civil Disorders had told it. It had no idea, it seemed, that "white racism" was of any consequence here in America—much less that white racism was the cause of our 1967 urban violence. The killing of three unarmed Black students by Orangeburg police at South Carolina State College didn't convince them. Nor did Professor Harry Edwards when, in Seattle, he accused Avery Brundage of lobbying to get South Africa reinstated in the Olympic games booked for Mexico City. Even when blonde Petula Clark affectionately touched the arm of Harry Belafonte at the end of their duet on a national TV show and some racist viewers became incensed —even *then* most of America didn't get the message.

Some did, though. Among them were fifteen young Black artists who put their work together in a show called *New Voices: 15 New York City Artists.* They were Benny Andrews, Betty Blayton, Emilio Cruz, Mel Edwards, Reginald Gammon, Al Hollingsworth, Avel DeKnight, Emma Amos Levine, Tom Lloyd, William Majors, Earl Miller, Mahler Ryder, Ray Saunders, Jack White and Jacky Whitten. Their show hung in the main concourse of New York's Pan Am Building before leaving for a tour of several American cities.

Atlanta University's Trevor Arnett Library, meanwhile, housed a group of Herman Bailey's drawings and paintings, featuring portraits of W. E. B. Du Bois, Denmark Vesey, Harriet Tubman, Frederick Douglass and General Benjamin O. Davis. In Chicago, while David Bradford's work was shown for two days (March 30 and 31) at the Lakeside Gallery, Chicagoans were contemplating the Chicago Art Institute's offer to assist talented students with little or no money of their own. The institute listed its tuition fee for 1968–69 as $1,320, with the footnote that no student who felt he or she might qualify for admission should fail to apply because of inadequate finances.

From March 5 to March 28, a small and arresting retrospective was on view at the Martha Jackson Gallery in New York. It included landscapes with nude figures, an homage to the American Indian and a portrait of LeRoi Jones. These were the paintings of Bob Thompson, who had died less than two years earlier in Rome. Bob Thompson was very young and very talented. Born in Louisville, Kentucky, he studied there before spending a semester at the Boston Museum School. The year 1959 found him in New York, where he formed a close friendship with LeRoi Jones. But Europe magnetized young Thompson, and he made several trips there during his short and somewhat stormy life.

In one of the pastoral landscapes in this retrospective, Thompson had painted a group of Black male nudes playing saxophones—obviously an effort to state strong emotions with implications at once personal and social. It was indeed a poignant note in an exhibition that was, itself, prelude to an American crime that would shortly stun the world.

The Second Quarter

Atlanta University presented its twenty-seventh *Annual Exhibition of Paintings, Sculpture and Prints by Negro Artists* with a formal opening on March 31, 1968. At the same time the all-Black Local 1733 of the American Federation of State, County and Municipal Employees was striking in Memphis. Local 1733 represented that city's garbage collectors. Their strike for what they considered fairer working conditions met with hostile resistance from official Memphis and from the city's white population in general. A strong (and terrifying) link existed between those two seemingly unrelated events taking place in Atlanta and Memphis.

Atlanta University was justly proud of its twenty-seventh successful effort to show the best art of Afro-Americans from all areas of the country. Freddie W. Styles, an Atlantan, had designed the posters for the exhibition, and he had also received an honorable mention for an oil painting in the show. Awards and honorable mentions went to more than twenty exhibitors from fifteen states. Purchase prizes were won by Jewel Simon, Lillie K. Walker, Henry Linton, Arthur L. Britt, Vivian Williams, Jack Jordan, Gregory Ridley, Jr., Calvin Burnett and William C. Henderson. Honorable mention winners were James W. Bridges, Leonard Fields, Raymond L. Floyd, Charles

E. Hayes, Noel Jemison, Howard Mason, Alex McMath, Kermit Oliver, Nazie Lee Strain, Freddie W. Styles, Gerald F. Hooper, Emanuel R. Savage, Calvin Burnett, Robert Glover, Leon M. Hicks, Arthur Parks, Jr., and Hayward L. Oubre.

The Atlanta show remained on view for a month. Within a week of its opening, Dr. Martin Luther King, Jr., an alumnus of Morehouse College, left his home in Atlanta to lend support to the striking garbage collectors in Memphis. There, on April 4, 1968, he was ambushed and fatally shot by an "unknown" gunman. And the civilized world mourned.

From April 16 to April 27, Lois Mailou Jones, painter and teacher, exhibited fourteen oils and thirteen watercolors (depicting aspects of life in Haiti and in Paris) at the Galerie Internationale on New York's Madison Avenue. At the same time, Black artists were liberally publicized by the small but well-edited magazine the *Art Gallery*. Published monthly by the Hollycroft Press in Connecticut, the *Art Gallery*, with a cover design by Samuel Gilliam of Washington, D.C., devoted most of its April issue to Negro artists.

An introductory summary by Carroll Greene, Jr., art historian and curator, was followed by several striking color plates of paintings by David Driskell, Al Hollingsworth, Jacob Lawrence, Richard Mayhew, Raymond Saunders and Hartwell Yeargans. Jay Jacobs, writing of a revealing interview with Romare Bearden and Hughie Lee-Smith, began:

> Although Romare Bearden and Hughie Lee-Smith are both respected artists of the same generation (they are both in their 50's) they have little else but an ethnic heritage in common.

Mr. Jacobs then proceeded to elaborate upon the dissimilarities of the two men, citing surface and visual differences of build, skin tone, mode of dress, speech pattern and degree of public acclaim and "success." But a close study of the interview revealed that, in spite of his opening statement, Mr. Jacobs established *three fundamental areas of agreement* between these two Black men who are artists. The first is that economic pressures within the average Black family (as with whites) engender discouragement to the young member who aspires to be a full-time artist. Second: that while the Black community enthusiastically lends a superficial moral and social support to its artists, it does not provide enough hard financial support to render them independent of white patronage. Third: that success "downtown" within the white establishment depends upon social contact from which the majority of Black artists are excluded.

In addition to the Jacobs interview, Chicago artist Margaret Burroughs reported on her city's Afro-American artists in an essay titled "To Make a Poet Black." Miss Burroughs wrote warmly of two Chicago exhibition places for Black artists, the Lake Meadows Art Fair and the South Side Community Art Center:

> Many of our artists who are prominent today were first seen at street fairs such as these. Some artists—Charles C. Dawson, William Edouard Scott, George E. Neal, and Frank Neal were among them—earned enviable reputations before the advent of the fairs. Marion Perkins and Bernard Goss were among the founders of the Lake Meadows Art Fair and also the South Side Community Art Center, which has been a bulwark of encouragement to black artists.

She concluded with mention of *The Wall of Pride*, a collectively painted mural in the heart of Black Chicago, rising two stories high on the side of a tenement. The uniqueness of *The Wall* is that the heroes and heroines it depicts are selections of the Black community and not those of the white establishment.

This issue of the *Art Gallery* also included a piece by Gordon Hazlitt called "Los Angeles Report," an essay focusing upon the painting of Bernie Casey, who happens to earn his living as a flanker back for the Los Angeles Rams pro football team. Hazlitt borrowed the following quote from Jay Jacobs:

> Bernie Casey's paintings are not simple-minded sea-scapes or cowboys or Indians or sunsets over the Grand Canyon. They are violent explosions of color and protest and integrity which moved even Alfred Frankfurter, San Francisco's crusty old lion of art criticism, to rumbles of approbation.

The fury and frustration which Bernie Casey puts on canvas would be aired in the pages of *Sports Illustrated* in July 1968, in a scalding ex-

David C. Driskell. *The American Chair*. Oil on canvas, 1965.

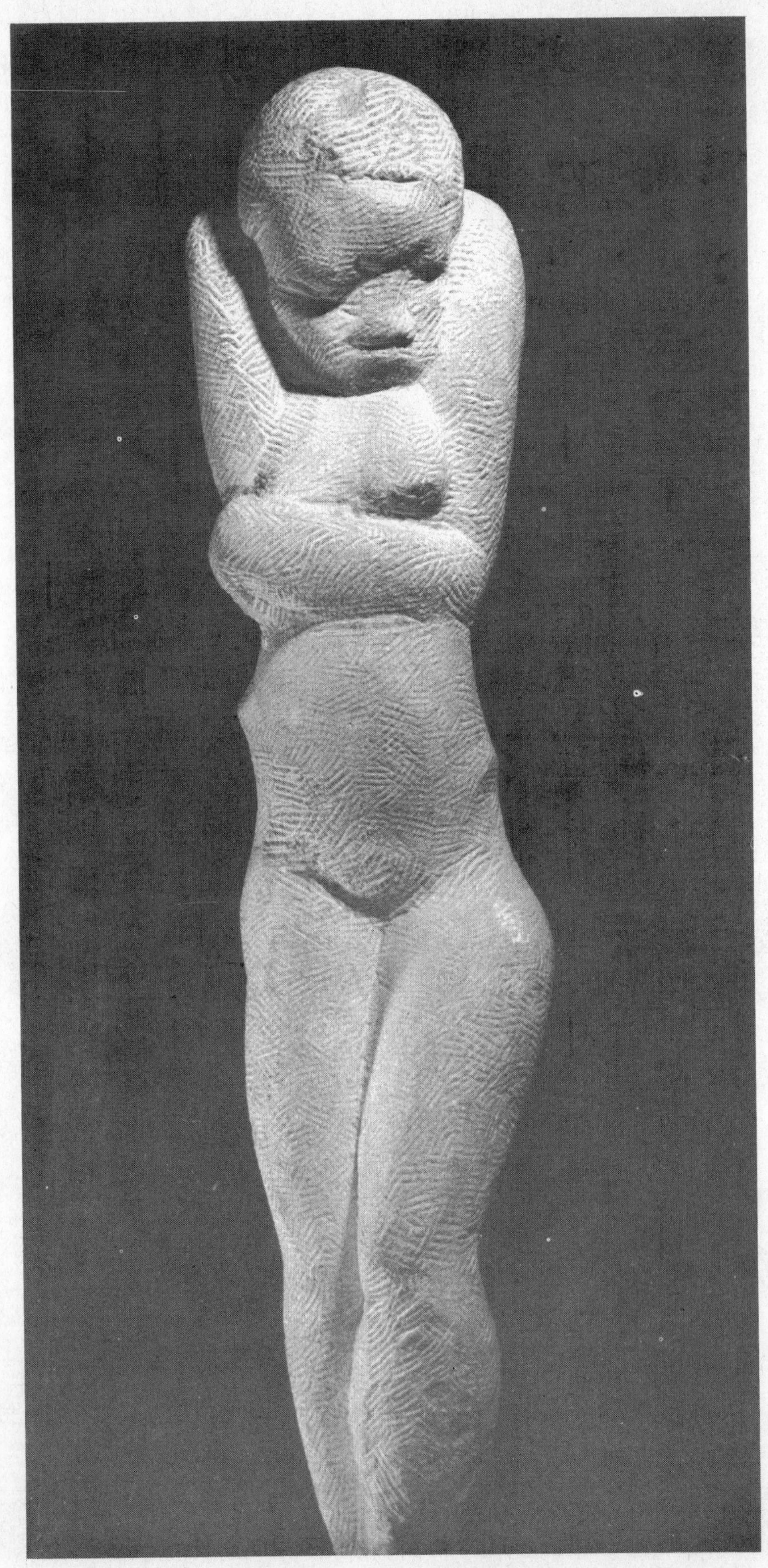

Arnold Prince. *The Virgin*. Limestone.

Norma Morgan. *Dunstanburgh Castle, Northumberland, England*. Intaglio etching. 1968.

Jacob Lawrence. *Street to Mbari*. Gouache. 1964. Private collection.

posé series by Jack Olsen titled "The Black Athlete—A Shameful Story."

The Hazlitt article was followed by Richard A. Long's short essay "The Negro College Museum." Mr. Long cited the excellent African art collection at Hampton Institute, the collections of contemporary art at Howard, Atlanta and Fisk Universities, and those at Tougaloo College and Morgan State College. Nor did he overlook the names of James V. Herring, Hale Woodruff, Aaron Douglas, David Driskell, Donald Schnell and James E. Lewis. Each has had a part in building the collections at the above-mentioned schools.

The *Art Gallery* concluded this issue, appropriately, with three pages of black-and-white reproductions of paintings; this final feature was titled "Afro-American Artists across the Land."

On the last three days of April 1968, the *New York Times* carried a front-page series of three excellent stories on the American Negro in Vietnam. They were done by Thomas C. Johnson, an on-the-spot reporter, who is a Negro. At this time, too, the Council on Interracial Books for Children (New York City) published a front-page feature (with photographs) in its own quarterly, *Interracial Books for Children*, announcing the two winners of $500 cash prizes in a contest for the best juvenile stories by Black writers hitherto unpublished in the children's book field. The recipients were Kristen Hunter and Walter M. Myers who were chosen by a jury of four Black writers. Inside the quarterly was a picture story on nine Negro illustrators of children's books: Tom Feelings, Ernest Crichlow, George Ford, Harold James, Monetta Barnett, Charles White, Alvin Smith, Don Miller and Yvonne Johnson.

Brooklyn painter Vincent D. Smith won a $2,500 grant in art at this time from the National Institute of Arts and Letters. From May 19 through June 30 the Lois Mailou Jones exhibition was on view at Washington's Smith-Mason Gallery. The Washington Gallery of Modern Art presented *66 Signs of Neon*, a macabre group of sixty-six sculptures adapted from charred and twisted metal gathered from the ruins of the 1965 riot in Watts. Noah Purifoy and Judson Powell, who conceived the idea, had this to say about their unusual show:

> The distilled spirit of *66 Signs of Neon* tells us that the world is a confused and fearful place, that God is difficult to find, that our philosophic systems are imperfect, that the only hope is in communication between individuals . . . I Don't Have Anybody But You.

Los Angeles, California, June 5, 1968. The assassin's bullet found its target again. The nation reeled in horror, and Black America was especially shaken, as Robert Francis Kennedy died in yet another act of violence. In Brooklyn's Bedford-Stuyvesant ghetto Dolores Carty and Ernest Crichlow delayed the opening of the Fulton Outdoor Art Fair out of respect for the slain senator. Boys and girls of Harlem's HARYOU Act's after school study program showed their paintings in the Countee Cullen Branch of the New York Public Library. By a stroke of ironic coincidence their show was dedicated to the memory of fifteen-year-old Emmett Till, murdered in Mississippi, and the four Black Sunday-school girls murdered in the infamous church bombing in Birmingham, Alabama.

In art, this quarter year ended with the exhibition, at the Grand Central Galleries in New York, of the drawings, etchings, lithographs and watercolors of Henry O. Tanner. Carroll Greene included these sensitive observations in his introduction to the show:

> A drawing is the first revelation of an artist's imagination. Every line is a note of the melody first conceived. The feeling and emotion of the artist are given spontaneous expression in his drawings at the moment of creation. . . . Although not a part of the abstract revolution that overtook so many of his colleagues, Henry O. Tanner reaffirmed the values he felt were essential to the human experience. That quiet strength appears through these master drawings.

The Third Quarter

The summer of 1968, unexpectedly quiet in the nation's Black ghettoes, was quite traditionally quiet in the nation's art circles. Early in July the Black community of San Francisco announced that it had received $45,000 from the San Francisco Foundation for the establishment of ten arts workshops. Randall Horton, a musician and teacher, was appointed coordinator of the project called "The Black Madonna." The site was the San Francisco College for Women, and the grant covered expenses for the first six months. Painting, sculpture, photography and silk-screen classes were planned.

Jordan Davies' paintings were on view in the Chicago State College's temporary office building, and Frieda High had her first one-man show in mid-July at the Chicago South Side Community Art Center. Joyce E. Widoff wrote a sympathetic commentary (with pictures) on *66 Signs of Neon* for Chicago's *Tuesday* magazine: "Out of the Ashes—Art and Understanding." *Black Heritage*, an exhibition of African sculpture, was seen at the South Side Center from August 8 to September 15. Lenders to the show included Etta Moten Barnett and the Chicago Art Institute.

Time readers saw a different kind of painting on its August 23 cover. The unusual portrait of Biafra's Colonel Ojukwu was painted by Jacob Lawrence. Meanwhile, the *New York Times* for August 28 ran a news story by Donal Henahan headlined: NEGROES SOUGHT FOR ART BOARDS. Mr. Henahan reported that "around the board tables of the nation's art museums and symphony orchestras, by tradition the impregnable strongholds of white Anglo-Saxon wealth and social position, there are few black faces." He further stated that in a dozen leading museums surveyed, two Negroes serve on the board of the Philadelphia Museum of Art and one on that of the Detroit Art Institute. The Museum of Modern Art in New York employs Kynaston L. McShine, a Trinidadian educated at Princeton and Yale, as an associate curator; and the Boston Museum of Fine Arts recently put painter John Wilson in charge of its Operation Outbreak program in Roxbury. Mr. Henahan concluded by asserting that since museum trustees and board members usually come from the ranks of moneyed art collectors, the Negro is virtually eliminated from consideration in this area.

Vermont Academy, a private school at Saxtons River, Vermont, was host to a unique summer art program. Initiated by Black sculptor John Torres and aided by the Ford Foundation and Stewart Klonis, director of the Art Students League of New York, the program was designed to help gifted and economically deprived students. Most of the eighty-five carefully picked participants came from New York City's High School of Music and Art and High School of Art and Design. A few were from rural Vermont, and there were American Indians from the West Coast as well as Puerto Rican young people from New York City. Most were nonwhite. Their five instructors were professional artists, each of whom had been faced with the problems of the minority group member. Three of them, Joseph Delaney, Earl Miller and Hughie Lee-Smith, have been mentioned earlier.

A handsome quarterly, the *Humble Way*, published by the Humble Oil and Refining Company, provided another showcase for Black artists in its 1968 summer issue. Taking its material from the aforementioned show *The Evolution of Afro-American Artists: 1800–1950*, the *Humble Way* did well by the twenty-five color plates it reproduced on the cover and inside the magazine. Carroll Greene's informed comments accompanied the pictures. But it was the editor's brief foreword, "Afro-American Artists: Yesterday and Today," that seemed especially to the point:

> *The Yellow Hat*, on the cover of this issue, was painted by Norman Lewis, a New York artist whose work has been exhibited in many galleries in the U.S. and in Africa, Europe, and South America.
>
> This painting and the examples shown on pages 10 to 15 were done by 25 artists and sculptors whose lives span 200 years—from the 18th Century to the present. Styles range from primitive to sophisticated. There are examples of landscapes and portraiture, academic realism, social commentary, abstract expressionism. In addition to their high level of quality they have only one thing in common. All are the work of American Negroes.
>
> The examples shown here were gathered from many galleries and private collections from New York to Los Angeles. They make it clear that Negro artists have never belonged to one school, but have responded to all the currents moving through American and European art history. Many Negro artists have naturally been concerned with Negro subject matter, but today they are in the international mainstream. Whether they choose to call themselves Negro, black or Afro-American, these talented individuals ask to be judged only on their merits—in other words, as artists.

The Studio Museum in Harlem opened on September 26, 1968. Its initial exhibition, a one-man show by thirty-nine-year-old Brooklynite Tom Lloyd, presented *Electronic Refractions 2*, a series of compositions of blinking colored lights. The new upper Fifth Avenue museum (near 125th Street) was two years in the making. Its attractively remodeled second floor loft was not, however, designed to become a mausoleum for an art collection. Director Charles Innis and his associate Randy Abbott have planned workshop and exhibition programs that will give artists opportunities to create and show new works. The planned artist-in-residence program will give resident artists the chance to share their skills while creating works for exhibition.

A social worker, Frank Donnelly, conceived the idea of the Studio Museum in Harlem. Along with attorney Carter Burden, he began to form a director's board which included publisher Charles Cowles, art collector Frederick Byers, III, Kynaston McShine and Harlemite Theodore Gunn, a self-taught artist. Thomas Hoving and Bates Lowry, directors of the Metropolitan and Modern Museums respectively, serve on the advisory board. Control in such hands has prompted the criticism that the new museum is nothing more than "an establishment-oriented institution in Harlem." The response is that such will not *remain* true as more residents of Harlem are recruited to serve on the board. Meanwhile, the full-time staff of four (including a guard), a reported $150,000 a year, and the eagerness of Black artists to show their works, keep the Studio Museum in Harlem going.

In Washington, D.C., the USIA, ever alert to the advantages and the propaganda value of presenting Black Americans favorably to Africans, brought out its thirty-second volume of *Topic* with a four-page spread on art. Under the heading "African Gallery," the editors purported to show how "a growing body of work by U.S. artists owes its inspiration to the African scene." Nine artists and samples of their works were presented, and, of the nine, seven were Black. These latter were sculptor John Rhoden and painters Jacob Lawrence, Hale Woodruff, William H. Johnson, James A. Porter, John Biggers and Elton C. Fax.

Controversy sprang to life in Brooklyn at the end of September. Henri Ghent and a group of local Black artists confronted the staid Brooklyn Museum with the charge that color discrimination was keeping the works of Negro artists out of the museum's shows. The museum's denials were rebuffed by the community's artists, and the museum turned to Mayor John V. Lindsay and Walter Hoving for a ruling. The latter decided that the Brooklyn Museum, a tax-supported institution, should have an exhibition of contemporary art by the artists of the Bedford-Stuyvesant community. Thus the Community Gallery of the Brooklyn Museum was formed, and, with Mr. Ghent as its director, presented a show on September 29, 1968, of non-prejudged works by neighborhood Black artists.

The Final Quarter

From Mexico City's Olympic Stadium the world saw Black American sprinters Tommie Smith and John Carlos defy tradition with an angry gesture of protest during their victors' ritual. It also saw Black heavyweight boxer George Foreman wave an American flag after winning the Olympic championship from his Soviet opponent.

But no two young people could have been less concerned with racism or nationalism than were twenty-two-year-old Stephen Pollack and twenty-one-year-old Elizabeth Vambe, students at England's University of Sussex, when they announced plans to be married within a month. Mr. Pollack, heir to the title of Viscount Hanworth, is white. His fiancée is a slender Black beauty from Rhodesia.

From Chicago came word that thirty-two-year-old sculptor Richard C. Hunt had been appointed by President Johnson to a six-year term on the National Council on the Arts. And the Chicago Art Institute announced that it was sending three Black recruiters into predominantly Black Chicago high schools in search of talented students who might hesitate to apply for admission to the institute because of lack of funds.

On October 4, 1968, Fisk University opened an exhibition of African and Afro-American Art, to commemorate the inauguration of Fisk's eighth president, Dr. James R. Lawson. The twenty-two traditional and contemporary African works of art were assembled by David C. Driskell and Earl J. Hooks of the Fisk art department. Exhibiting Afro-Americans, in addition to Driskell and Hooks, were Richmond Barthé, Sargent

Johnson, William Artis, William Taylor, Gregory Ridley, Jr., Marion Perkins, William H. Johnson, Malvin Gray Johnson, Claude Clark, Ellis Wilson, Keith Morrison, Walter Williams, Jacob Lawrence, Stephanie Pogue, Aaron Douglas and Charles White.

Thirty Contemporary Black Artists was seen at the Minneapolis Art Institute, while farther west, at Oakland, California, *New Perspectives in Black Art* was shown for three weeks (beginning October 5) at the Oakland Museum's Art Division, Kaiser Center Gallery. Exhibitors were: Cleveland Bellows, David P. Bradford, Harrison Branch, Arthur Carraway, Frances D. Catlett, Charlotte J. Chambers, Claude Clark, Sr., Claude Clark, Jr., Irene Clark, Richard L. Collins, Marva Cremer, Urania Cummings, Jonathan Eubanks, Lawrence Fisher, Doyle Foreman, Ibibio Fundi, Kenneth Green, Ben Hazard, Elvoys Hooper, Margo Humphrey, Janice Jefferson, Herbert Johnson, Marie E. Johnson, Lawrence McGaugh, Barrington McLean, William E. Smith, Evangeline J. Montgomery, Robert Newsome, George Smith, Carlton Taylor, Roberta Thompson, Royce Vaughan, Ruth G. Waddy, Mary B. Washington and Laura G. Williams.

A new organization, Black Pride Arts Unlimited, was launched in San Francisco by artist Earl Scarborough; and Huey Newton, convicted leader of the Black Panthers, was sentenced to from two to fifteen years by a California judge in connection with the killing of a policeman.

Time magazine's cover for November 1, 1968 (a collage depicting New York Mayor John Lindsay as the besieged and harried focal point of a city in turmoil), was the work of Romare Bearden. And the NAACP was in an uproar following the resignation of Robert Carter who, after twenty-four years as the association's legal counsel, quit in anger because the association had fired white associate attorney Lewis Steele. Mr. Steele's essay "Nine Men in Black Who Think White," published in the *New York Times Magazine*, provoked the firing.

The November issue of *Ebony* gave enthusiastic support to artist Lois Mailou Jones Pierre-Noel in a colorful five-page picture story. Meanwhile, the nation elected Richard M. Nixon to its highest public office in a close popular vote, with minimal support from Black voters. On November 3, an exhibition of thirty-three *Contemporary Drawings of Africa*, by Elton C. Fax, opened at Fisk University.

Grace Glueck, writing in the *New York Times* for November 18, described the picketing of a show that had opened a month earlier at the Whitney Museum. Some thirty Black artists, led by Henri Ghent, carried signs in front of the Whitney protesting the "lily-whiteness" of its show called *The 1930's: Painting and Sculpture in America*. Branding the title a misnomer, Mr. Ghent organized a countershow, *Invisible Americans: Black Artists of the '30's*, which opened at the New Studio Museum in Harlem. Artists included were those of the same period who had been seen in the show *The Evolution of Afro-American Artists: 1800–1950*.

Hilton Kramer, writing in the *New York Times* for Sunday, November 24, in defense of the Whitney, insisted that the Black artists of the 1930's showing at the Harlem museum (with four possible exceptions) did not measure up to the standards set by the artists in the Whitney show. He was hotly contradicted by Henri Ghent in a letter published on Sunday, December 8, to the "Art Mailbag" editor of the *Times*.

If the Whitney deliberately discriminated against the Black artists of the 1930's, the Houston Museum of Fine Arts went all out to show her Yankee sister how a Black artist should be treated as it showed and publicized the Africa-inspired drawings and paintings of John Biggers. The Biggers exhibition, paired with a collection of Benin sculptures, was given excellent press coverage in the *Houston Post* of Sunday, November 17. Charlotte Phelan did a splendid two-page story (with pictures) of Dr. Biggers and his work, presenting the winner of the elusive Harbison Award for Distinguished Teaching with a dignity befitting his talents.

Johnson C. Smith University in Charlotte, North Carolina, was host during November to an exhibition celebrating the Charlotte-Mecklenburg Bi-Centennial. Selma Burke, James T. Diggs, Walker Foster, J. Eugene Grigsby, Ethel Guest, Ethel Hill, Harvey Johnson, Paul Keene, Jr., Kermit Oliver, Oliver Parsons, B. D. Roberts, Carroll Sockwell, Alma W. Thomas, Theodore

Wells, Otis Williams, Rip Woods and Kenneth V. Young were among the exhibitors.

Norman Lewis, Richard Mayhew and Charles Alston were among those artists participating in a show at the Museum of Modern Art (New York), honoring the late Dr. Martin Luther King, Jr.; and Beauford DeLaney was one of thirty artists working in the New York area to receive $5,000 grants each from the National Council on the Arts. Paintings by Reginald Gammon were shown at the Greenwich Mews Theatre in New York in conjunction with Vinnie Burrows' one-woman show, *Walk Together, Children.*

As the year ended, Fisk University held a showing of the thirty-year-old but still fresh and exciting Toussaint L'Ouverture series of tempera paintings by Jacob Lawrence. New York's Gallery of Modern Art held a semi-retrospective show of paintings and sculpture by Charles Alston from December 3 through January 19, 1969. The exhibition received special mention in the *New York Times* "Art Notes" for December 8, 1968, in an article by Grace Glueck titled "The Best Painter I Can Possibly Be."

Several Black artists who may or may not have had fancy one-man shows or participated in important group shows made noteworthy contributions nonetheless; and they deserve brief special mention here. Sterling V. Hykes is one. A former dishwasher and presently artist-in-residence at Cleveland's Karamu House, Mr. Hykes was cited in the December 4 issue of the *Cleveland Plain Dealer* for his successful three-dimensional paintings in sand and acrylics.

In Chicago, two artists, Jan Wittenber and William McBride, combined efforts to get drawings, paintings and prints into the drab, seventy-year-old building, Dixon State School for mentally handicapped children. One hundred works were quickly assembled, and the school's officials enthusiastically published a brochure advertising the project. They chose one of Mr. McBride's paintings, *Mother and Child,* to use on the brochure's cover. Mr. McBride is Black. His partner Jan Wittenber, who initiated the project, is white.

Arnold Prince, a brilliantly gifted sculptor from the West Indies who makes his home in the New York area, had this to say of his art:

> In spite of the "isms" which crowd the art world I consider the human form the most direct medium with which to communicate human experience through sculpture; and direct carving from a block the most powerful sculptural method in that it is devoid of pretense.

A small group of artists in New York donated their drawings to *Freedomways* magazine for use as greeting-cards. They were Joan C. Bacchus, John Biggers, Brumsic Brandon, Margaret Burroughs, Leo Carty, Ernest Crichlow, Roy DeCarava (photographer), Jack Devine, Elton C. Fax, Tom Feelings, Oliver Harrington, Jacob Lawrence, Jack Lee Morton and Charles White. Painter Don Miller did likewise for CORE.

Archie Jefferson, a fine young painter, illustrated a juvenile book, *The Frightful Nobody,* published by Shelley Graphics, Ltd. Inge Hardison's sculpture portraits of Black heroes of the past were seen along with Carl Owens' drawings in the Old Taylor Distillery series appearing regularly in the Black press. And sports fans who are readers of *Ring* magazine saw Ted Carroll's black-and-white drawings in its pages frequently during 1968.

The end of December brought with it a spectacular space success for our country as we dramatically completed the Apollo 8 mission. At this time, too, the appellate division of the New Jersey supreme court suddenly reversed the convictions of playwright LeRoi Jones on charges of possessing guns during the Newark riot and of court contempt at his trial. So it would seem, coming full circle on two positive notes, that the nation could at last breathe a bit more easily. But not quite.

Ours was still a nation that could place three astronauts in the moon's orbit while its demoralized Indians decayed on reservations. Poor whites continued to suffer deprivations in Appalachia; outraged Blacks and Puerto Ricans rebelled in their slums; and artists at large languished in the doldrums of official indifference.

A great deal of art was both produced and shown in America in 1968, and Black artists shared in both functions. Of the dozens of Black artists whose activities made this essay possible, it is no exaggeration to say that not more than two have really "made it"—and that, only in a relative sense. The same generally applies to white artists, though any existing odds do favor them. In either case, "making it" means that along with talent and hard work one must also have first-rate professional gallery representation. The artist without it is practically out of the running.

So in this context I continue to be haunted by that interview I mentioned earlier, the one that Jay Jacobs held with Romare Bearden and Hughie Lee-Smith. He asked each whether he had encountered much in the way of prejudice in trying to show and sell his work to a white market. Said Mr. Bearden:

> That's a difficult question and one that every artist would answer differently. To me, so much of the gallery scene has to do with social things. For instance, a lot of artists used to go to the Cedar Bar, you know, to meet Kline or De Kooning, and a lot of them were helped in that way. If the Negro artist isn't helped in that sort of thing . . .

Here, according to interviewer Jacobs, Bearden's voice trailed off.

Said Mr. Lee-Smith:

> The mere fact that Negroes are increasingly forming their own galleries speaks for itself. They form them because they say they have no opportunities in the white established galleries.

One learns, in seeking information, to listen long and hard to what the experienced experts have to say.

Miles Davis

Black Music and Musicians—1968

Orde Coombs and Barry Beckham

Jazz

THE YEAR in jazz was marked by a number of successful concerts, benefit shows, new experiments and, unfortunately, some unexpected deaths. These deaths came as a shock to a musical world that was still mourning the loss of John Coltrane, who had died in July 1967. Coltrane's playing had become a symbol of a kind of ordered freedom that is so much a part of jazz composition, and had lately grown increasingly religious. His roaring, free-wheeling "sheets of sound" technique, heard on such classics as "My Favorite Things," "Summertime" and "Africa Brass," had established him as one of the giants of jazz, whose future experiments were eagerly awaited.

In June 1968 Wes Montgomery died at the age of forty-two. Montgomery, who had been described as the best thing to happen to the guitar since Charlie Christian, died at a time when his commercial appeal and success were very high. Noted for using his thumb instead of a pick, Montgomery had attacked his instrument with fire and verve. He was voted the best jazz guitarist of the year by *Downbeat*.

Before Montgomery died, he had been preparing for an international tour of sixty-seven performances that would have brought him $10,000 a week. His album *A Day in the Life* became his eighth in a row to make the sales charts. He had never learned to read music.

Hilton Jefferson, who used to play alto sax for Fletcher Henderson, Cab Calloway and Duke Ellington, died at sixty-five.

Jazz festivals offered major opportunities for jazz buffs to see their favorite musicians on one stage. At the third annual *Boston Globe* Jazz Festival, the two-day bill featured Count Basie, Carmen McRae, Wes Montgomery and Miriam Makeba.

A new concept in festivals came to light at Hampton Institute. Before its weekend of concerts (two afternoons and three evenings), there was a week of study of historical and sociological aspects of jazz. Lecturers included Earl (Fatha) Hines, Ken McIntyre and Cannonball Adderley.

At Philharmonic Hall, Lou Rawls, Duke Ellington, Clark Terry and others gathered for a concert to raise funds for the Billy Strayhorn Scholarship Fund of the Juilliard School of Music. Mr. Strayhorn, who died a year ago, was the composer of "Take the 'A' Train" and "Passion Flower."

The third annual New York Jazz Festival attracted 37,000 aficionados for a two-day series of concerts. Featured performers included Miriam Makeba, Hugh Masekela, Mongo Santamaria, Ray Charles, Miles Davis, Ahmad Jamal and Dizzy Gillespie.

Edward Kennedy Ellington, better known as Duke Ellington, forever forging new ground, gave a concert of sacred music in January at Manhattan's Cathedral of St. John the Divine, America's largest church. Ellington, who was sixty-eight, performed his new composition,

"Praise God and Dance," for the first time. It is based on the 150th Psalm.

The late W. C. Handy was honored at the New York City Town Hall concert for the benefit of the W. C. Handy Scholarship for the Blind Fund. Participants included Arthur Prysock and James Earl Jones.

Miles Davis continued to be a leading jazz experimenter on the trumpet. He has reshuffled his group but still has his driving, piercing trademark.

Twenty-nine-year-old Herbie Hancock, pianist for five years with the Miles Davis Quartet, left to form his own group and began with a three-week engagement at Manhattan's Village Vanguard. His new sextet is headed by Clifford Jordan and Ron Carter.

The basic innovators of jazz remained Black. Their work was led by the avant-garde explorations of Albert Ayler, Pharaoh Sanders, Sun Ra and Cecil Taylor.

Jimmy Smith remained the top performer on the organ, and he continued to meet its challenge with characteristic vigor and innovation.

Oliver Nelson, arranger-composer-conductor-saxophonist, became one of the handful of Black composers ever to have the American Wind Symphony play three of his works during the symphony's Ohio River Valley concerts.

Ornette Coleman, composer, altoist and the first jazz musician to receive a Guggenheim Fellowship, was chosen as the subject of a ninety-minute documentary film being made by Shirley Clarke, known for *The Connection* and *The Cool World*.

Oscar Brown, Jr., best known for his sociological songs, was in the vanguard of the movement to get youth interested in Black music and theatre. During the summer, Brown put on musical programs and revues for young people with the aid of grants from the Office of Economic Opportunity.

The Craig Hundley Trio caused the biggest surprise among old jazz standbys. Their ages are fourteen, fourteen and twelve, and apparently they earned the respect of critics and almost $10,000 during a six-month period. They showed they were a serious group to be reckoned with after appearances on Jonathan Winters' and Johnny Carson's TV shows. Their instruments are piano, drums and bass.

More jazz albums were waxed than in any previous year, and more AM as well as the dependable FM stations programmed jazz for their audiences.

Some critics noted a disappearance of the lines between jazz and pop music, and suggested that soon the two disciplines will be indistinguishable. This was noted to an even greater degree with jazz and rock. One example of this fusion could be seen in the engagement of Chico Hamilton's octet at the Rainbow Grill in the RCA Building, Manhattan. Never before associated with dance music, Mr. Hamilton found many of his customers dancing to his music at the grill.

Popular Music

Dionne Warwick, best known for her hit "Alfie," is basically a pop singer, but frequently her renditions take on a jazzed-up atmosphere—as in her singing of "Summertime"—and her first hit was a rock 'n' roll song, "Don't Make Me Over." Burt Bacharach and Hal David still do her songs, and Miss Warwick still records for the same label. She says that her musical taste is open-minded but she prefers what she likes to call "gentle" tunes. Miss Warwick left recently for a six-month break from work to prepare for the stork's arrival.

The same kind of mixture of jazz and popular music can be seen in the delivery of Lou Rawls, who was chosen by the readers of *Downbeat* as their favorite vocalist. Rawls' delivery is keynoted by introductory monologues and progressions from standard tunes such as "Old Man River" to upbeat numbers such as "Tobacco Road."

Among the solid pop singers, Sammy Davis, Jr., as in previous years, contributed more than his share to encourage young talent. He received an award from the American Musical and Dramatic Academy in New York for these efforts. Davis continued to bolster his reputation as an international singer and as an actor as well, appearing in the London production of *Golden Boy*.

Ella Fitzgerald showed no sings of slowing down—either as a singer or as a recipient of awards. She received New York City's Cultural Award for her "exceptional achievement in the performing or creative arts." Alpha Kappa Alpha, the oldest and largest predominantly Negro sorority, made her an honorary member. The great lady of swing, honorary chairman of the Martin Luther King Foundation, wrote and recorded a song dedicated to the slain civil rights leader.

Pearl Bailey, with a similarly long career behind her, also gave no indications of easing her pace, although the nightclub circuit was not graced by her presence. Her performance in *Hello Dolly* brought her talents to even larger audiences. Her role in the Broadway production, considered by many to be the apex of her career, was the principal reason for her being named Entertainer of the Year by the editors of *Cue* magazine. Another tribute came from the City of New York, naming her official 1968 hostess for the New York Summer Festival.

Eartha Kitt, however, did play the supper-club circuit. Her personality has remained as arresting as it seemed to be in her Broadway debut, *New Faces of 1952*. She still maintains the exotic and sexy air that singles her style out from that of others. Miss Kitt probably became the most newsworthy singer of the year when her criticism of the Vietnam war at a White House luncheon hit the nation's headlines.

Joining the vanguard of singers who take time out to help others, Nancy Wilson accepted an appointment to the President's Advisory Board on Youth Opportunities. In this capacity, she combined many of her high school concerts—where she sang in her usual mellow, fair-pitched voice—with talks to young people about staying in school.

More than a few critics seemed to think that Sarah Vaughan, who has been singing professionally for a quarter of a century, had finally taken full advantage of the flexible qualities of her voice. She made obvious attempts to cut down the displays of highs and lows her voice can achieve and began to concentrate instead on more subtle voice shadings. In addition to this refocusing of her attack, Miss Vaughan made it clear that she was interested in exploring new musical horizons—such as opera.

Billy Daniels continued in the nightclub circuit, where he was constantly asked to sing "That Old Black Magic."

Lena Horne, after a long absence from the screen, returned to Hollywood to make a film, *Patch*, with Richard Widmark.

Rhythm and Blues

In rhythm and blues, 1968 was the year of a new, wild, electric sound and the acceptance of soul as the dominant force in rock. Twenty-three-year-old Jimi Hendrix, originally from Seattle, went to England, formed his group and returned to America to rave acceptance. He had played with Little Richard, Ike and Tina Turner, King Curtis and the Isley Brothers among others, and he presented a piercing blend of guitar and drum he terms the Experience. Frequently that experience includes Hendrix' smashing his loudspeaker in frenzy.

Wilson Pickett, twenty-seven-year-old soul singer, was rated with James Brown as the boss of soul by many observers of the rhythm and blues circuit. His style has a kind of gospel melody with funky, mean lines that are sometimes more suggestive than believable.

Fans were enthusiastic about Little Richard's return to show business after a retirement to study and practice theology. The style that pushed him and "Tutti Frutti" to the head of the charts during his heyday has been changed. He has become more sedate and stylish, abandoning a zoot suit for a Nehru.

Frankie Lymon, twenty-seven-year-old singer who at the age of fifteen had made it big with over a million copies sold of "Why Do Fools Fall in Love?" was found dead in an apartment from an apparent overdose of heroin. In recent years Mr. Lymon had tried to make a comeback after his career had declined.

Another top moneymaker was out to make a comeback, and most music followers were betting that it wouldn't be difficult, considering that Brook Benton's records have sold more than fifteen million copies. Mr. Benton, whose most memorable ballads include "Just a Matter of Time" and "Thank You Pretty Baby," is best remembered for his smooth, cool-as-ice delivery. Before leaving for England, he made one record which, it is hoped, will be one of many more during the future.

Among the new groups, the Chambers Brothers received some of their biggest acceptances in clubs and on the college and concert-hall circuit. Experienced critics foresaw a lucrative career for the group. The best example of their approach

—a combination of gospel, rock and blues—is demonstrated on their hit single "Time Has Come Today."

Another example of a group with an entirely new successful approach is the Fifth Dimension. The three males and two females usually dress in psychedelic outfits and perform with perfect melody and harmony, with a free-wheeling choreography.

Not many young groups were from California. The Watts 103rd Street Rhythm Band, a group of musicians in their twenties with a full-band, yet relaxed, sound, was discovered by actor Bill Cosby and given their first recording contract with Warner Brothers-Seven Arts.

Probably the youngest of the stars, Stevie Wonder, in his mid-teens, remained at the top of the list in popularity. He plays the piano, organ, drums and harmonica, in addition to singing.

The Raelets, the three back-up singers for many of Ray Charles' recordings, left the blind blues king, added another girl to their ranks and formed their own quartet, the Sisters Love.

In Manhattan, the Scene continued to be a top location for the best rhythm and blues talent, even booking Slim Harpo, who had the top-ten hit, "Scratch My Back." Harpo rarely appears in non-Black clubs or in the North.

James Cotton was the recipient of more attention and dates during the year as a result of the resurgence of interest in real, funky blues. Singing and blowing through his harmonica, Cotton brought the Chicago Blues School to its greatest acclaim with his playing.

The quest for the origins of rhythm and blues —certainly the most dominant music of the sixties in terms of acceptance by the young—became a vogue during the year. Many record companies attempted to trace the history of rock through albums, and some attempts are sure to be notable contributions to discography. A four-record collection issued by Atlantic, *History of Rhythm and Blues*, includes selections by the Ravens, Ray Charles and the Coasters.

The Comers

There is always a group of very talented people waiting in the wings for the signal that will tell them when it is time to come out on the stage. Once they get there—if the vibrators are working—if they are lucky—they are catapulted into the limelight. Four young ladies to watch are: Dorothy Ramsey, Clydie King, Lyn Roman and Marilyn Thomson. In 1968 they showed signs of being more than just singers. Their stage personalities had begun to take shape.

Dorothy Ramsey is making her stand in Cleveland, her hometown. And although she realizes that Cleveland is really little league if one expects to "make it" in the entertainment field, she has opted for that city. Like so many other artists, she started as a gospel singer, and one can detect the subtle shadings, the triumphant shouts in a voice that has mellowed on the gospel bag. Today she sings anything. She is dedicated to the sounds of today, but she loves the dreamy standards that tell of love, moonlight and faraway places. She is the modern girl who weaves the spell onstage, but knows that when she leaves that stage, the magic must be left behind. The realities of Cleveland and New York and Los Angeles tend to destroy magic. She knows this. But she is determined that we share her magic for a while.

Clydie King is young and pretty, and sings beautifully. She now has a contract with Minit Records. Clydie grew up in southern California, and she has been singing "from ever since I can remember." When she was twelve she made her first record, "Written on the Wind." It didn't sell. But she was on her way. We will hear more from her.

Lyn Roman, like Dorothy Ramsey, knows the gospel scene. She calls Washington, D.C., home, and she first came to public attention there. Last March she appeared at the Frontier in Las Vegas, and this is what Joy Hamann, Las Vegas critic for the *Hollywood Reporter* and United Press International, had to say about her: "Dot Records star Lyn Roman made a very creditable Las Vegas bow in the Frontier's Post Time Theatre, she . . . socks over a song with gusto." No one is going to dare to rain on her parade.

Marilyn Thomson is a triple-treat: singer, dancer and actress. She has made numerous nightclub appearances and has recently been booked by the Americana chain of hotels.

Two promising young men were observed in 1968 who had that quality called "star presence," in combination with a great deal of talent. One of these young men is Charley Pride, who was born in Mississippi and now lives in Canada. His bag is not blues, not jazz, not soul, not opera. He is a country and western singer with a style all his own. He is being touted as the successor to the legendary Hank Williams. But he is his own man. Pride recognizes influences, but he wants to be Charley Pride, not the "Second Hank Williams." His new album, *Charley Pride in Person* (RCA Victor LSP 4094), is very good indeed.

The other is a man with a very improbable name: Lovelace Watkins. In December he made his debut on the Ed Sullivan show and received —it can be called nothing less—tumultuous applause. Since then everything has been happening to this man with the booming baritone voice. He has records coming up, more appearances on the Sullivan show, talk about movies and Broadway. It looks as if it is another of those "overnight successes," but Watkins has paid his dues. He was born in New Brunswick, New Jersey, and graduated from Rutgers with a B.S. His mother was a registered nurse and wanted her son to be a physician. The Army called him, and Lovelace was stationed in Stuttgart, Germany. There he appeared with Mahalia Jackson. That concert convinced him that his would be a life of music. He has made the rounds of the New York clubs: the old Birdland, the Living Room, the Latin Quarter—and has even filled in twice for Sammy Davis at Club Harlem in Atlantic City. After some disappointing attempts at overnight fame, he is now steadily on the circuit. He has a record contract with UNI, and he is booked into the Americana hotel chain. His unusual name is going to be a big one.

Motown

There was mild dissension in the ranks of the Motown Record Corporation during 1968. David Ruffin of the Temptations left the group to become a single. He was replaced by Dennis Edwards, a young tenor who made his first appearance with the group at the Valley Forge Music Fair in Pennsylvania. Florence Ballard of the Supremes left that group when it became Diana Ross and the Supremes. She was replaced by Cindy Birdsong, a former member of Patti and the Bluebelles.

These changes did not cause any deterioration in the quality of the music of these groups, and their songs consistently appeared on the best-seller charts. Martha Reeves and the Vandellas, Gladys Knight and the Pips, Smokey Robinson and the Miracles, Marvin Gaye and Tammi Terrell helped make 1968 a bounty one for Motown. In association with George Schlatter-Ed Friendly Productions, Motown presented "TCB." "Taking Care of Business" was the first television special of the multi-talented Diana Ross and the Supremes. They were joined in this superb hour of entertainment by their fellow Motown artists, the Temptations.

Otis Redding

In February 1968, two months after his death, the Georgia state senate unanimously passed a resolution honoring Otis Redding for contributions to the state and to the music world. He had received no such commendations when he was alive. The senators praised Redding's rise from "poverty and obscurity to become one of the most famous entertainers in the United States." They then expressed their condolences to Redding's widow and presented her with a copy of the resolution.

Redding, who recorded for Stax/Volt Records, died after his private plane crashed in Lake Monana, Wisconsin, on December 10, 1967. *Billboard* announced that "Sitting on the Dock of the Bay," Redding's last Volt recording, was the best-selling record during that week.

Many songs sung by Redding, for example, "Sweet Soul Music" by Arthur Conley, and "Respect," by Aretha Franklin, had become million dollar records and had held the number one spot in the country. But Redding as a singer of his own songs had not been so successful. Three months after his death, however, his last record —and his own song—was the double success that had eluded him.

Personalities of 1968

Aretha Franklin and James Brown are perhaps the most popular Black singers in the United States. During 1968 so much was written about these artists that it is superfluous to recount their series of successes on records and on the concert stage. What is important, however, is an evaluation of where they are likely to go with their music and what may be their future possibilities.

Miss Franklin began 1968 with her fifth million-selling single: "Since You've Been Gone." She became the first female singer to earn five certified gold records when the Record Industry Association of America presented her with a gold trophy. She was on the cover of the June 28 issue of *Time*, and was hailed as the epitome of soul. She had successful concerts in Europe and New York.

Towards the end of 1968, one noticed a slackening off of the number of records Miss Franklin produced. Perhaps this was a time for reflection, for exploring intonations even more subtle than those heard in "Ain't No Way" or "Natural Woman." Whatever the reason for this respite, it must have been welcomed. Since February 1967, with her first Atlantic single, "I've Never Loved a Man the Way I Love You," Lady Soul had been singing continuously as if to reaffirm emphatically her brilliance and to confound her critics and Columbia Records—where she had spent six years in relative obscurity.

What of the future? Miss Franklin has kept her faith, her truth. Her insistence on the nitty-gritty has been responsible for her success. It is no longer necessary to dilute one's hard vision of reality to make it more palatable to the squares who never buy records anyway. It is hard to think of her ever changing her style. The mood may change. New vocal and background experiments may be tried. But Aretha Franklin could not possibly fake any other reality than her own.

The year 1968 was a controversial one for James Brown. It was also a very successful one. He received a citation from Vice-President Hubert Humphrey for his work with the Stay in School Campaign. He was President Johnson's guest at a White House dinner on May 8, and his dinner card, autographed by Mr. Johnson, read: "Thank you for everything you are doing for your country."

During the riots that followed the death of Dr. Martin Luther King, Jr., the mayors of Boston and Washington welcomed him as a new commissioner of peace. He starred in a TV special, "James Brown: Man to Man," which was taped at the Apollo Theatre in Harlem. He recorded "I'm Black and I'm Proud," which was rapturously received by many Blacks. When he recorded "America Is My Home" he brought upon himself the ire of the same Blacks who had previously applauded him.

His interest in the youth of the ghetto is immense. His "Stay in School" bag has become an obsession, and so he always manages to shout "Don't be a dropout!" to his teen-age audience. What of the future? What will be Papa's brand-new bag? James Brown stands at the top of the rhythm and blues pantheon. The gaudy clothes, the excessively styled hair, the conspicuous display of wealth are now muted. This is an era of Black seriousness, and James Brown has always been well aware of the moods of the struggling Black man. In a country in which entertainers often wind up as politicians, the speculation on this man's future has begun.

Spotlight

Tom Wilson is a tall, slim Black man from Waco, Texas. He is also an independent producer of rock groups. He controls fourteen of them and owns three production companies, two publishing companies and a management company with an annual budget of half-a-million dollars. Wilson has worked with Odetta, Coltrane, Bob Dylan, Simon and Garfunkel, the Animals and the Mothers of Invention. Over the past ten years he has worked with five record companies, and in 1968 he left MGM Records to set up the Tom Wilson Organization with headquarters in Brooklyn, New York. He graduated with honors in economics from Harvard, and he is in the record business because his is the only profession he knows in which it is legally possible to make a million in a relatively short time.

Gospel

In *The Fire Next Time* James Baldwin speaks of the gospel music that was so much a part of his childhood: "There is no music like that music, no drama like the drama of the saints rejoicing, the sinners moaning, . . . all those voices coming together crying holy unto the Lord."

He knows the power of that music. He knows

the passion that a line of gospel music can evoke. He knows the subtleties and changes of meaning in the intonations, the shouts, the murmured prayers, the voices raised in rejoicing. And if anything in 1968 had great significance for gospel, it was that year's triumph of soul music. The root of all soul is gospel. Al Rutledge of the Baltimore *Afro-American* states: "It is the gourd from which it all flows. . . . Black people shouting and singing praises to the Lord. An emotion transformed to music. But even that isn't the whole of it for in its purest sense a Gospel song is a sermon; a conversation between man and God; a prayer."

Among the more interesting developments in the area of Gospel music was the installation of Rev. Harold A. Salmon as pastor of St. Charles Borremeo Roman Catholic Church in Harlem. The thirty-eight-year-old priest, who is now the pastor of Harlem's largest parish, was named by Archbishop Terence J. Cooke in July 1968. He is the first Black man to hold a pastorate in a New York archdiocese, and he will serve as the Archbishop's Vicar Delegate in the area. He will plan activities for all of Harlem's seven parishes.

In September 1968 his investiture was conducted by the Archbishop in the traditional manner, with certain exceptions. The new music for this ancient ceremony had been written by Eddie Bonnemère, a jazz pianist, and was played by his eight-piece band. And when the Archbishop intoned: "Receive these keys, receive these Holy Gospels, receive these holy oils," the congregation replied after each petition: "Let My People Go." This service was an example of the new fusion of Roman Catholic rites with the shouts and music and feeling of gospel music.

After twenty years of "slaving," gospel musician James Cleveland has finally come into his own; he has finally begun to get the attention that his talent warrants. As a singer, pianist, arranger, composer, recording artist, Cleveland must rank as the most versatile man in gospel. He is certainly the richest. It has not been easy. He now lives in a Spanish-style house on Garthwaite Avenue in Los Angeles, and that house is a far cry from the one in which he grew up on Chicago's South Side. His influences are Mahalia Jackson, Roberta Martin and Thomas A. Dorsey. But he has refined what he learned, and has made his own sound. The foghorn quality of his singing today may be the result of straining an adolescent voice, but it has given him his distinctive sound.

Cleveland is the highest-paid star of Savoy Records, and has, in fact, worked out an unusual contract with this record company. He receives a guaranteed annual salary for making four albums a year. There is no talk of advances against sales. His records sell well, and "Peace Be Still," which started it all for him five years ago, is still Savoy's biggest seller.

A liberation of sorts came about in 1968. When Gertrude Ward first took her Ward Gospel Singers into the nightclubs of Las Vegas, many exponents of gospel denounced the move as sacrilegious. Today the noise has stopped. Not that it would have mattered to Gertrude Ward. She knew exactly what she was about when she signed her first contract to appear at a nightclub. Of her critics she has stated: "They thought that when we went into clubs we'd be singing blues and jazz and rock 'n' roll. But we sing the same songs in the clubs that we sing in the church. And it's wonderful how they accept Gospel singing sometimes even more than people do in church." She firmly believes that "we have reached out and touched as many souls in nightclubs as we have in churches." The controversy about whether or not gospel should be carried to the nightclubs is over. Gertrude Ward has proved her point.

The Classical Scene

For the Black composer, conductor and opera singer 1968 was not a spectacular year. The New Jersey Symphony named Henry Lewis its musical director. The thirty-six-year-old conductor became the first Black man to head a major symphony orchestra in the United States. There has always been a dearth of Black symphony musicians, mainly because they have not had the opportunities or encouragement. Mr. Lewis feels that the doors are open now. He feels that the last hurdle in symphonic music was the conductor barrier and that now that barrier is down. It remains to be seen, however, whether his prediction is in fact correct.

In the South, thirty-three-year-old Paul Freeman was appointed associate conductor of the

Dallas Symphony. Mr. Freeman was born in Richmond, Virginia. He attended Virginia State College before going on to the Eastman School of Music in Rochester where he received his Bachelor's and Master's degrees in 1956 and 1957. In 1963 he earned his Ph.D. from Eastman.

Four years later, Mr. Freeman achieved national acclaim when he won a $2,500 second prize in the Dimitri Mitropoulos conducting competition at Carnegie Hall. During the summer of 1968 he conducted Wagner's *Tristan und Isolde* at the Festival of Two Worlds in Spoleto, Italy.

Walter F. Anderson, professor of music at Antioch College, was named director of music programs for the National Endowment for the Arts. The goals of the Endowment (which is a major branch of the National Foundation on the Arts and the Humanities, established by Congress in 1965) are to provide opportunities, stimulate interest and give grants to individuals and organizations throughout the country. With the federal funds at his disposal, Mr. Anderson will evaluate requests for moneys.

Mr. Anderson was a Rosenwald Fellow from 1948 to 1949, and a Hazen Foundation Associate from 1948 to 1953. He is a graduate of the Oberlin Conservatory of Music and has studied at the Cleveland Institute of Music and the Berkshire Music Center.

Composers

Black composers were working steadily during 1968. If their publicity had not yet begun to match their talent, at least they were beginning to come together, to get to know and hear and appreciate each other. In May the Harlem School of the Arts, in a concert entitled "Music by Black Composers," presented the works of Noel da Costa, Hale Smith, Carman Moore, Ulysses Kay, Dorothy Rudd Moore, William Fischer and Stephen Chambers. The performers included Sanford Allen, a violinist with the New York Philharmonic, and Kermit Moore, the cellist. The composers, from Mr. Chambers, aged twenty-eight, to Mr. Kay, aged fifty, presented a broad range of styles. Among the notable compositions were Dorothy Rudd Moore's "Modes for String Quartet," Mr. Kay's "Chamber Music for Violin, Voice, Cello and Piano," Hale Smith's "Evocation," Mr. da Costa's "Statement and Response" and William Fischer's "Predilections for Solo Viola."

In November the Society of Black Composers presented its first concert of the season at Harlem's Public School 201. The program included works by Howard Swanson, Hale Smith, Hank Johnson and William Fischer.

Singers

The Chicago Symphony Orchestra, the third oldest in the United States, established in 1891, presented for the first time a series of public open-air concerts in the Windy City. Carolyn Smith-Meyer—a soloist with the symphony—sang selections from Puccini, Gershwin and Verdi. A graduate of the University of Kansas, Miss Smith-Meyer began vocal studies in 1963 with Thomas Peck of Chicago, later winning the Society of American Musicians Award, and making her concert debut at De Paul University in April 1966.

Wilma Shakesnider, a soprano from Washington, D.C., won a $1,000 Distinguished Performance Award from the Minna Kaufmann-Rudd Foundation. Miss Shakesnider, one of five recipients of the award, was among fifty entrants for the contest. She is a student at the Juilliard School of Music.

In the world of opera, perhaps the year's most exciting event was Shirley Verrett's debut as Princess Eboli in Verdi's opera *Don Carlos* at the Metropolitan. Miss Verrett described her debut as "the whipped cream on the cake." In Moscow, earlier, when she had sung Carmen, she had received nine encores. A rhythmic handclapping, and shouts of "Verrett! Verrett! Verrett!" from the usually phlegmatic British had greeted her after her performance as Princess Eboli at Covent Garden. But, understandably, it was New York and the Metropolitan that she wanted to conquer. And the New York audiences and critics raved. Mary Campbell of Associated Press said, "Another Metropolitan star has been born."

Leontyne Price was awarded an honorary Doctorate in music at the reunion of her class of 1948 at Central State University, in Wilberforce, Ohio. Among her many concerts in 1968, one was in Birmingham, Alabama, on October 18. She donated her fee to Mrs. Martin Luther King, Jr., in memory of the deceased civil rights leader who, she said, "made it possible for me to perform there."

Coloratura soprano Mattiwilda Dobbs returned from Sweden to sing opera in her hometown of Atlanta for the first time. She sang Musetta in an updated version of Puccini's *La Bohème* with the Atlanta Opera Company. Miss Dobbs, who has sung at La Scala and at the Metropolitan in New York, commented to an Atlanta reporter, Molly Sinclair: "Atlanta is a completely different city from the one I grew up in . . . in such simple ways that you all take for granted . . . like being able to eat in a downtown restaurant. . . ." She was happy, she said, "to really come home now."

Douglas Turner Ward and Rosalind Cash of the Negro Ensemble Group in *Ceremonies in Dark Old Men,* by Lonne Elder, III.

The Negro in the Performing Arts

Lindsay Patterson

THE BLACK PERFORMER, during 1968, was more visible to the American public than at any time since the 1920's, but his visibility had a double edge. It was still tokenism and fell far short of what it could have been. It had the appearance of hastily contrived window dressing, and Black performers themselves were well aware that the millennium was not just around the corner but some light years away. A question that plagued many performers was: Should we work for our own theatre or continue to try and crack Broadway? Barbara Ann Teer, actress and director of the successful Off-Broadway musical play *The Believers,* writing in the Sunday *New York Times* sums it up this way:

> Up to now, the Negro artist has been totally concerned with integration, with finding a place for his creative talents in the existing theatre. He has spent thousands of dollars on classes and training, and countless years of pain and frustration, to compete in an already established, highly competitive industry. Clearly he feels that if he can just make it to Broadway, he will have reached the pinnacle of success, he will have arrived! For years this has been his dream.
>
> In the process of trying to realize this dream, he has had to picket, sit-in, march and, even in the various theatrical unions, negotiate new rules to provide more employment. The situation for the Negro in the theatre and other mass media remains frighteningly depressing.
>
> How long will it take the Negro artist to understand fully what his status in show business really is? How long will it take him to wake up, see, realize, grasp, comprehend, how he is being used—or how he has allowed himself to be used—by the white establishment? Until he can answer these questions honestly, he will naturally see no need for a Black cultural art form. I believe the need for such an art form is far more critical even than the issue of white racism. And the Negro artist must examine the need for a Black cultural art form before he can take any next step forward.

The issue of color also emerged in 1968. In an elegant letter, also to the *Times,* actress Ellen Holly stated:

> Black is not a color of the skin or a bangle. It is a state of mind. The time has come for someone to make this very clear as the *Times* Drama Section makes its contribution to the pernicious idea that the only kind of Negro actor that should be hired is one whose skin is black and whose features are 100 per cent African, and that any other choice represents a compromise, "copout," or tokenism on the part of those doing the hiring. In his article about the new TV season, "Will the Blacks Say, 'Too Little, Too Late'?" Robert Dallos supports the view with a quote from *Variety* as follows: "A touch of black has come to 'Peyton Place,' but upon close examination the hue turns out to be a magic color designed not to offend the most sensitive white eye. The new hue is cast by Percy Rodriguez, a dark actor with definitely un-African features. . . . [He] has the facial structure that makes him look like a white man in black face. . . . The result is that A.B.C. has injected a Negro into the cast of 'Peyton Place' without integrating the show. White viewers can identify with any number of the different levels of white society portrayed on the show, but the Negro watchers are going to find it hard."
>
> For *Variety* to write this in the first place and the *Times* to reprint it in the second place is appalling because it permits two white writers

> with pseudo-liberal concerns to further obscure, rather than illuminate, an issue that they do not understand—namely, what "black" is about.
>
> Let's examine the quote and all its ugly implications, but first let's look at a basic reality: While the African Negro has had the good fortune to exist in circumstances that have allowed him to retain his purity, the American Negro has become so diluted and bastardized —after wholesale miscegenation during slavery times and partial assimilation into a predominantly white society in the generations that followed—that an American Negro of 100 per cent African appearance is rare.

Miss Holly goes on to say that "if African criteria are to be the yardstick by which American blacks are hired few Americans will qualify, and we must consider importing actors from Uganda."

Another problem facing Black actors in an integrated theatre is, what kind of roles can and should they play? While there are few stereotyped roles in the tradition of Amos 'n' Andy today, the Black actor seems to be concerned about the relevance of a role to the Black experience. James Earl Jones, in an interview after his triumph in *The Great White Hope* on Broadway, said:

> I don't believe in integrated casting unless the parts can be played psychologically and physically by Negroes. Otherwise, it's employment, not art. The day will come when black actors will enter the psyche of white characters and vice versa and we'll play the hell out of it until your hair stands on end. But you can't integrate a Tennessee Williams play by having a black Blanche and a white Stella. That's not the way to do it. To play Hal as a black man in *Picnic*—the play would cave in. I'd like to play it in workshops, but I don't want to see it as a definitive statement of me as an actor. My father and I played in *Of Mice and Men.* I was Lenny. He's a character in any country, any color; he goes beyond a social theme. I thought Diana Sands probably knew more about the psyche of a French peasant girl in *Saint Joan* than any white actress, and it worked. It was good for the audience because it allowed their imaginations to stretch. Integrated casting is fine as long as it doesn't distort the scope of the play, but I'm not out to prove anything and I don't want to be used to further causes because I'm black.

Contrary to Jones' opinion are those of some actors who think that if the performer is proficient enough it doesn't matter what color he is, since we live in a multiracial society and must get used to the idea of seeing people of all colors in all situations. Of all the Black actors in the theatre in 1968, Jones had the most resounding success, as Jack Jefferson (Jack Johnson) in *The Great White Hope,* a play by Howard Sackler, a white author. The role made Jones a star. Almost all of his previous work in the theatre had been done Off-Broadway.

The most interesting feature of the 1968 scene was the roaring success and development of Black theatre itself. Two companies, the New Lafayette Theatre and the Negro Ensemble Company, proved to be the best theatre groups in America today, both in terms of quality of acting and choice of material.

The Negro Ensemble Company opened their season with an announcement of four works by Black writers. The group had been severely criticized the previous year for not performing any plays by Black authors. Douglas Turner Ward, artistic director of the company, answered his critics thus:

> Being criticized, even severely, was to be expected. The NEC couldn't possibly please everyone. A theatre reflects the standards, tastes, values, predilections, and even the personalities of its creators. It would be idiotic to expect that this profile could meet everybody's approval. In addition [the group was funded by the Ford Foundation], six-figure money has a way of inflaming six-figure antagonisms.
>
> What we had not expected was the outraged tone and virulent nature of these condemnations which so ignored our statements of purpose and distorted our motives that it was difficult to recognize either our program or presences.

Mr. Ward went on to cite the ratio of Black actors (100 per cent), technicians and other workers employed by the Ensemble. In every case over 90 per cent. Black audience attendance he said rose from 25 to 70 per cent. The NEC had also been criticized for not being located in a Black neighborhood, but Mr. Ward defended the location as central to all the ghetto areas in the city. "Even more significant," he states, "they [the audience] comprise all age groups and stations of life, from elderly Delaware migrant workers to youths of every black ghetto community in the surrounding metropolitan area. In essence, a mass audience of free choice, not a coterie of committed followers. The measure of any theatre of black identity, no matter where located, is winning the adherence of such an audience."

The NEC's second season was its most successful to date. Indeed, all of its plays by Black writers—*God Is (Guess What?),* by Ray McIver, *Ceremonies in Dark Old men,* by Lonne Elder, III, *Man Better Man,* by Erroll Hill—received good critical receptions. Critics have been especially ecstatic about *Ceremonies in Dark Old Men.* The company, which had received $434,000 from the Ford Foundation initially, received another $750,000 in 1968 to be used over a two-year period for various programs. Other NEC productions, such as *Song of the Lusitanian Bogey* and *Daddy Goodness,* have gone on tour to Karamu House in Cleveland and Spelman College in Atlanta.

More important to the Black community is the New Lafayette Theatre, located in Harlem and founded and directed by Robert Macbeth. In January of 1968 the company's original home was gutted by fire, and with the help of foundations and other groups it was able to convert a movie house on Seventh Avenue near 137th Street into a theatre. The first production in its new home was *In the Wine Time,* by Ed Bullins, a stunning play about ghetto dwellers. Bullins is probably the most gifted young Black playwright today. Among other things, he is a superb craftsman.

But 1968 belonged even more to the Black actor. It was the year that Moses Gunn was rediscovered for the hundredth time by New York theatre critics, the year that Butterfly McQueen came to town, both in the revival of the movie *Gone with the Wind* and in the Off-Broadway play *Curley McDimple,* as a lamebrained cook. Miss McQueen defended her role as Prissy in *GWTW* and challenged the dedication of white actors. "I found it disappointing when I began working with white people," she said in an interview with Guy Flatley of the *New York Times.* "There was no hunger for perfection, no hunger for elegance that you find in so many Negroes. And I discovered that the white people had what I call their three B's: the bar, the bed, and the battlefield. . . ."

It was also the year that Diana Sands portrayed a magnificent Saint Joan at New York's Lincoln Center Repertory Theatre. Later in the year Miss Sands appeared on Broadway as the female lead of *We Bombed in New Haven.* There were also Josephine Premice as Madame Fleur in an Off-Broadway revival of *House of Flowers;* Kenneth Frett in *Walk Down Mah Street;* Richard Ward in a short-lived play at the Martinique, *The Firebugs;* Jane White in another non-success, *The Cuban Thing;* Leslie Uggams as Cleopatra in *Her First Roman,* a musical version of Shaw's *Caesar and Cleopatra,* which co-starred Claudia McNeil; Vinie Burrows in a limited engagement of her one-woman show *Walk Together, Children,* at the Off-Broadway Greenwich Mews Theatre; Marcella Lowery in *Americana Pastoral; Christophe,* with J. A. Preston and Marion Berry, at the Chelsea Theatre Center; Leon Bibb in a revival of the musical play *Carnival!* at the City Center.

One of the most controversial plays of the year was *Big Time Buck White.* It was reported as evolving out of a Watts workshop, from an idea supplied by a white author. It received splendid reviews from some white critics, but Black critics generally considered it stereotyped. Clive Barnes of the *New York Times* thought that "the brilliance is partly in its awareness of the stereotype, the ability to carry the stereotype through to a kind of reality, and, also, in the seriousness beyond the comic routines." Many Black critics, however, didn't buy that interpretation.

As for the question of a separate Black theatre—many whites seemed appalled that Black actors by 1968 were losing interest in Broadway as an ultimate goal. The Drama Desk, an organization of stage reporters and editors which meets regularly at Sardi's in New York City, at one of their sessions discussed "The American Theatre: Integration or Separation?" Among the panelists were Godfrey Cambridge, Diana Sands, Josephine Premice and Robert Macbeth. Cambridge was quoted as saying, "We need a black theatre for black playwrights to emerge. It will give black actors a sense of pride, a home and continuum."

Cab Calloway and Pearl Bailey invite Louis Armstrong and Jane Russell (far left) to join them on stage after a performance of *Hello Dolly*.

Diana Sands added, "Until such time as we can have a totally integrated theatre, we must have a Negro theatre." Robert Macbeth felt that the Drama Desk's topic was not a fit subject for debate.

There were also a number of Black cultural conferences, held by groups throughout the States, which debated the role of the Black artist. In Harlem at one such conference, sponsored by Onyx Publications and billed as the first Black cultural conference, the dominant theme was that the arts must help Negroes win their revolution. The poet Larry Neal, supporting that theme, said, "I began with the assumption that we are at war. The first function of art and culture is to liberate my people. The function of art for us as a people is to liberate us."

With the rise of Black cultural awareness and Black theatre, there has also come the belated emergence of Black playwrights. Previously, the Black playwright has not had a suitable arena in which to experiment or even to show his wares, and it seems certain that if the American theatre is going to be saved Black playwrights may well do it. Africa was also represented in the American theatre in 1968 by Wole Soyinka, the imprisoned Nigerian playwright, with two plays, *The Trials of Brother Jero* and *The Strong Breed,* both of which received warm critical notices. Soyinka had a third production at the Negro Ensemble Company Theatre, *Kongi's Harvest.* But it is the American Black playwright who seems well on his way to new dimensions in drama and the musical form.

In addition to Ed Bullins, Ray McIver, Lonne Elder, III, and Erroll Hill, there were such writers as Clifford Mason, whose *Sister Sadie and the Sons of Ham* was staged at the New Dramatists Committee Theatre, Philip Deane, whose *This Bird of Dawning Singeth All Night Long* was seen at the American Place Theatre, and Gordon Watkins, whose *A Lion Roams the Streets* played at the Hudson Guild Theatre. At Princeton University's McCarter Theatre, Charles Fuller's play about racial integration, *The Village: A Party,* was staged. Fuller is one of the founders of the Afro-American Arts Theatre in Philadelphia. Ed Bullins was further represented by *The Electronic Nigger* and *Clara's Ole Man,* at the American Place Theatre. The Ashby Players, a group in Detroit, had great success with their first venture, *Games,* a musical which spoofs both whites and Blacks. The play was authored by John Ashby; music and lyrics were by his wife, Dorothy. And finally, there was *The Believers,* a panoramic musical depicting Negro history. It opened May 5, at the Garrick Theatre in New York, and has been running ever since. A compilation, it was co-produced by Jesse de Vore.

Other theatre groups and cultural arts centers to surface in 1968 included the Elma Lewis School of Fine Arts, in Boston, the Nat Turner Theatre Group in New Orleans and the Cooperative Theatre Club in New York.

Perhaps the single most important event in the theatre in 1968 was the hearing conducted by the New York State Commission for Human Rights on discrimination in the theatre. The commission revealed that out of a total of 523 performers on Broadway in the 1967–68 season, only fifty-seven were Black, and that number included the forty-five cast members of the all-Black company of *Hello Dolly!*

Movies

Sidney Poitier's first directorial effort on Broadway, *Carry Me Back to Morningside Heights,* bombed, but it really didn't matter because it was his year in films. He was named by the theatre exhibitors as the number one box-office attraction of the year. But as Poitier's star has risen, he has come under increasing attack from Black critics. They claim that his roles are of a neuter gender and that he is more imitation white man than anything else. There was sharp criticism for *Guess Who's Coming to Dinner?* in which, as a prospective suitor, he doesn't really get to kiss his white fiancée. Poitier seemingly set out to answer his critics with an original story idea by him of a Black man and Black woman romantic involvement. It was *For Love of Ivy,* co-starring Abbey Lincoln with Poitier, and many critics were even more sharply critical of it, for they contended that it was Rock Hudson and Doris Day in blackface. Abbey Lincoln was criticized for wearing a pressed wig in the movies when she ordinarily wears her hair au naturel.

Most critics, however, don't remember Poitier's earliest movies, which do show him more racially involved. James Baldwin, writing in *Look* magazine about Poitier, does:

> I must state candidly that I think most Hollywood movies are a thunderous waste of time, talent and money, and I rarely see them. For example, I didn't think *Blackboard Jungle* was much of a movie—I know much more than that about the public-school system of New York—but I thought that Sidney was beautiful, vivid and truthful in it. He somehow escaped the film's framework, so much so that until today, his is the only performance I remember. Nor was I overwhelmed by *Cry, the Beloved Country,* but Sidney's portrait, brief as it was, of the young priest, was a moving miracle of indignation. That was the young Sidney, and I sensed that I was going to miss him, in exactly the same way I will always miss the young Marlon [Brando] of *Truckline Cafe* and *Streetcar Named Desire*. But then, I miss the young Jimmy Baldwin, too.

In the same article, Baldwin had some very important things to say about the appearance of the Black image on both the Hollywood and television screens:

> It is of the utmost importance that a Black child see on that screen someone who looks like him. Our children have been suffering from lack of identifiable images for as long as our children have been born.
>
> Yes, there's a difficulty, there's a rub, and it's precisely the nature of this difficulty that has brought Sidney under attack. The industry is compelled, given the way it is built, to present to the American people a self-perpetuating fantasy of American life. It considers that its job is to entertain the American people. Their concept of entertainment is difficult to distinguish from the use of narcotics, and to watch the TV screen for any length of time is to learn some really frightening things about the American sense of reality. And the black face, truthfully reflected, is not only no part of this dream, it is antithetical to it. And this puts the black performer in a rather grim bind. He knows, on the one hand, that if the reality of a black man's life were on that screen, it would destroy the fantasy totally. And on the other hand, he really has no right not to appear, not only because he must work, but also for all those people who need to see him. By the use of his own person, he must smuggle in reality that he knows is not in the script. A celebrated black TV actor once told me that he did an entire show for the sake of one line. He felt that he could convey something very important with that one line. Black people have no power in this industry at all. Furthermore, the actor may be offered dozens of scripts before anything even remotely viable comes along.

Poitier, who once decried his role as *the* Black film actor, is not alone anymore. Jim Brown and Raymond St. Jacques are fast becoming top box-office attractions. Brown, a former football star with the Cleveland Browns, started out in Hollywood with one supporting role, in *Rio Conchos,* and then jumped into starring parts. Since his appearance in *The Dirty Dozen,* his career has moved into high gear. Brown says that he doesn't want to become strictly a Negro actor. "None of my parts has specified a black man," he says. Two movies released in 1968, starring Brown, *The Split* and *Riot,* were moderate box-office successes. He also co-starred with Rock Hudson in *Ice Station Zebra.* Brown is noted more for his physical appearance than his acting ability. He refuses to take acting lessons, claiming, "I'm scared some teacher will rip my ego to pieces."

Raymond St. Jacques, on the other hand, is a thoroughly trained professional actor who is a product of the Yale Drama School and the Broadway stage. But Hollywood has given St. Jacques only one role that has come close to tapping his considerable talent. That was in *The Comedians* of two years ago. In 1968 he starred in a dismal film about racial tensions in the South called *If He Hollers, Let Him Go!* In this, St. Jacques seemed, on screen at least, to have had no respect for the part and to have merely walked through it. He showed his power as an actor in *Up Tight!*, a film about Black militants, but his role in that movie was too brief and did not have the emotional range that St. Jacques is capable of.

However, *Up Tight!* was the most notable film of the year, and the one that many Black stars hoped would make a major breakthrough for them in Hollywood. But this was not the case. The film was almost unanimously panned by reviewers. It was based on the novel *The Informer*, about the Irish Rebellion in the twenties, and that was unfortunate since the Irish Rebellion and Black militancy in the American ghetto had distinct and separate tones. *Up Tight!* was notable for the fact that some of the best acting talent in America appeared in it: Roscoe Lee Browne, Ruby Dee, Frank Silvera, Juanita Moore and Max Julien. They were all superb. Julian Mayfield, who played the central role, and Ruby Dee, along with director Jules Dassin, wrote the screenplay.

For the first time in Hollywood history a Black man was signed to direct a film. Gordon Parks, the *Life* photographer, directed a screen version of his novel *The Learning Tree*. The film is scheduled for release in 1969. Another Black director to emerge in 1968 was Melvin Van Peebles, who lives in France, where he directed *The Story of a Three-Day Pass*. Van Peebles had tried some years earlier to break into Hollywood as a director; the only job offered to him was that of an elevator operator.

For the most part Hollywood films are still lily-white, though now crowd scenes almost always include Black people. Behind the scenes, however, Hollywood is still almost exclusively lily-white. Black technicians are getting work only because some Black actors and white directors are demanding that they be employed on films they are involved with.

Some of the more outstanding films of 1968 that gave Blacks substantial roles were: *Joanna,* with Calvin Lockhart; *The Detective,* with Al Freeman, Jr.; *Dr. Doolittle,* with Geoffrey Holder; *Decline and Fall,* with Clifton Jones; *Planet of the Apes,* with Jeff Burton.

One of the most pleasant and surprising announcements by Hollywood in 1968 was the return of Lena Horne to the screen in a straight dramatic part. Miss Horne from the outset of her career refused to play any part in movies that she felt degraded Black people. After appearing in *Stormy Weather* and *Cabin in the Sky,* she refused to accept any more parts in that vein, and Hollywood virtually banned her from the screen. The only roles she was offered were those of a singer in a nightclub sequence, or something similar—which could be easily cut out for Southern audiences. Her new movie is *Patch,* in which she co-stars with Richard Widmark, whom she marries at the end of the film.

Hollywood also announced in 1968 that it was filming the autobiographies of Ethel Waters and Malcolm X. The Malcolm X autobiography script is being written by James Baldwin. Another version, it was also announced, was being written by Louis Lomax.

Also, in 1968, the State Division of the Commission on Human Rights held hearings on discrimination in the movie industry. Hilda Simms, director of the State Division's Creative Arts Program, criticized the hearings for not calling in casting directors to testify. "This is the gut issue," she said. "Negro actors are not being hired because they aren't being sent." She also scored the hearings because no agents or producers testified. "These are the people we have to put the pressure on," she declared.

Radio-TV

The most eagerly awaited program of the 1968 television season was "Julia," starring Diahann Carroll. Almost everyone except the mass audience was disappointed. More militant Blacks saw it as just another comedy program. Others applauded it for just that fact, for they said that the agonies of the ghetto in a program week after week would become exhausting. All agreed that Miss Carroll as a nurse widowed through the Vietnam war looked beautiful, and that her son, Marc Copage, was delightful. Since the program's premiere on September 17, it has been constantly rated in the top ten.

Despite the fact that "Julia" disappointed some viewers, this was the year in which television discovered that Black people do exist in America in all kinds of circumstances. Every major network seemingly concerned itself with the Black man's history in this country. C.B.S. started the year off with a seven-part series called "Of Black America," which included programs on Black history, the Black soldier and slavery. The Westinghouse Broadcasting Company's Group W presented "One Nation, Indivisible," a three-and-a-half-hour examination of America's racial crisis. "Color Us Black," a one-hour documentary on the student uprising at Howard University, was produced by the National Educational Television network. One of the most stunning documentaries was "Still a Brother: Inside the Negro Middle Class." A series on racism in America was presented by A.B.C. Its first program was

"Bias in the Mass Media." Television's finest and most poignant moments came during April of 1968, when it covered the entire funeral of Dr. Martin Luther King, Jr.

Other notable productions included "Black Letters," a series dealing with Black literature, and "Black Journal," a monthly magazine devoted to Negro culture and affairs, designed for a Black audience and to bridge the gap between the white and the Black communities.

This year, too, Black faces became more visible on continuing series: Robert Hooks in "N.Y.P.D."; Don Mitchel in "Ironside"; Ena Hartman in "It Takes a Thief"; Peter DeAnda and Ellen Holly in the soap opera "One Life To Live"; Don Marshall in "Land of the Giants"; Nichelle Nichols in "Star Trek"; Darlene Cotton in "Love of Life"; Otis Young in "The Outcasts"; Clarence Williams, III, in "Mod Squad"; Gregg Morris in "Mission Impossible"; Hari Rhodes in "Daktari."

It was also the year in which Black comedians like Flip Wilson were seen often and became popular with television audiences. Pigmeat Markham got back into the action with appearances on "Laugh In" after Sammy Davis, Jr., made his "Here Come the Judge" routine famous on the "Tonight Show."

And on the "Tonight Show," too, some of the most entertaining and pertinent television time was provided when Harry Belafonte did a week's substitution for vacationing host Johnny Carson. Belafonte elevated the show from one of mindless entertainment to discussions of some of the most pressing issues confronting the world today. Belafonte's presence was felt forcefully again on a Petula Clark special. What became known as "the touch" occurred during the taping of that special when Miss Clark lightly placed her hands on Belafonte's arm during their singing of a duet together. The advertising representative for the Chrysler Corporation, which sponsored the show, stalked off the set after the show's producer refused to do another take of the scene. Belafonte exploded and the segment was televised with touch and all.

During 1968 even the kiddy shows became aware of Black culture. "Captain Kangaroo," for example, brought jazz pianist Billy Taylor and his trio on for a series to illustrate Black history and culture. Another television breakthrough was specials by Diana Ross and the Supremes, Leslie Uggams, and Jesse Owens.

The Commission on Human Rights also sponsored hearings on discrimination in television programming. A number of Black actors testified, and William Booth, chairman of the commission, opened the hearings with these remarks:

> They [Negroes and other minority group members] are still not reflected in the everyday content of general programming and commercials. This is harmful because the public then sees the Negro and Puerto Rican solely as a rioter, a social problem, and not as a human being. For the most part Negroes are still limited to the stereotyped supporting and servant roles. The few programs which feature Negro performers treat them in such a nervous and unnatural manner as to make them seem hardly credible as human beings.

Radio, that nearly forgotten medium, discovered in 1968 that it is a very potent force in the ghetto. Stations found that ghetto residents were willing to express their opinions on every issue concerning them, oftentimes most eloquently, and subsequently many stations started audience participation shows in which callers could express their grievances over the air. One of the most successful of such shows is "Night Call," broadcast over WRVR-FM in New York and syndicated to more than twenty-eight other stations throughout the nation.

Businessmen have become increasingly aware that Blacks in this country spend $35 billion and that a prime way to reach them is through radio stations with Black programming. There are 528 radio stations in America that beam to Black audiences, and only a handful of these are owned by Negroes. Nevertheless, these stations are becoming more community minded. Many stations are credited by civic groups and city legislators with having kept their communities "cool" during the rioting that broke out after the murder of Dr. Martin Luther King. But some critics maintain that these "white-owned" stations are only interested in presenting "safe" public-service programs and are not concerned with ferreting out the root cause of ills that plague the Black community.

Dance

Dancers, seemingly, more than any other members of the performing arts, are involved with the youth of the ghetto. Arthur Mitchell, Eleo Pomare, Pearl Primus, Alvin Ailey and others conduct classes in their own studios or in community centers. In addition, many of the creations of these artists reflect Black culture and history.

Some of the more interesting dance programs in 1968 included Al Minns and Leon James in a concert at Town Hall in New York, in which they traced the history of jazz dancing from the cakewalk to rock 'n' roll. Arthur Mitchell of the New York City Ballet won top notices for his work in a revival of *Slaughter on Tenth Avenue*. Alvin Ailey proved again that his masterpiece *Revelations,* which is set to Negro spirituals, is one of the great dance works. His company performed that work and others at Hunter College in New York, and Donald McKayle's dance company also had a New York showcase in 1968. The Negro Ensemble Dance Company Workshop premiered its progress to date. The most moving dance program of the year was the New York City Ballet Company's *Requiem Canticles,* performed at Lincoln Center in New York, as a tribute to Dr. Martin Luther King, Jr. Arthur Mitchell was soloist.

A SENGSTACKE NEWSPAPER

Pittsburgh NEW Courier

America's Best Weekly

VOL. 61 — NO. 16

NATIONAL EDITION

MEMBER OF AUDIT BUREAU OF CIRCULATION

Two Sections 16 — Pages 20 cents

The Sacramento Observer

"the paper with an eye for the news"

VOL 6 NO. 19

10¢ PER COPY

LARGEST WEEKLY

NEW YORK Amsterdam News

Vol. 58 — No. 13

Entered as Second Class Matter, New York City

Jamaica Church Bombing Remains A Mystery
See Story Page 25

2340 Eighth Ave. New York, N. Y.

15c — Outside NYC 20c

THREE STAR FINAL EDITION

CHICAGO Daily Defender

America's Only ABC Negro Daily

WEATHER
Tuesday is expected to be cloudy and warmer, high in the mid 60s. Wednesday: Partly cloudy and mild, chance of showers.

Price 10 cents

VOL. XIV — No. 39

CITY EDITION

Call and Post

VOL. 56 - NO. 16

SATURDAY

40 PAGES

Atlanta Daily World

CITY EDITION
"NEWS WHILE IT'S NEWS"

Published Every Morning Except Monday

PRICE 7 CENTS

ATLANTA, GEORGIA, 30303

VOLUME 41, NUMBER Tel.: 521-1459

(See Washington Sidelights)

BLUE STAR EDITION

Washington Afro-American

AND THE WASHINGTON TRIBUNE

77th Year, No. 80

Copyright 1969 by the AFRO-AMERICAN Co. for all material previously printed in the current National Edition

WASHINGTON, D.C.

(See Col. 1)

24 PAGES

15 CENTS

The Sound of a Different Drum

Race in the News

Luther P. Jackson, Jr.

Say that I was a drum major for justice.

Martin Luther King (1929–1968)

AS TIME is measured in the rush of news events, it now seems like aeons since March 1965, when the career of the drum major for justice, the latter-day prince of peace, reached its apogee during the parade from Selma, Alabama, to the first capital of the Confederacy at Montgomery. That March the Nobel Peace Prize winner's nonviolence earned him a third portrait on the cover of *Time* magazine. And it was five months before the violence of Watts.

In 1968 newsmen focused on wars and rumors of wars, bloody clashes in the nation's streets and universities, a turbulent Presidential campaign and the assassinations of Robert F. Kennedy and Dr. King himself, on April 4 on the balcony of a Memphis motel room. The latter slaying touched off another round of looting and burning; this time in 125 cities, leaving 46 killed, 2,600 injured, 21,000 arrested. Then when Dr. King's tape-recorded voice, *I want you to say I tried to love and serve humanity*, sounded above the hot crush of mourners and TV lights in Atlanta's tiny Ebenezer Baptist Church, it was as though nonviolence had been long consigned to the American past. For in 1968 the news media—if not the nation—marched to the sound of a different drum.

In a pre-Watts year, the 1968 Civil Rights Act's open housing provisions, buttressed by a Supreme Court decision upholding a long-ignored 1866 act outlawing *all* racial discrimination in sale and rental of property, could have very well been the number one "hard" news story in the area of race relations. Or, if one were to look for trends, one might note that Black political power was surfacing through Georgia legislator Julian Bond's bid for the Democratic vice-presidential nomination, through the addition of three Black congressmen, from Brooklyn, St. Louis and Cleveland, and through an increase in Southern Negro political officeholders to nearly four hundred. Surveys by *Fortune* magazine and C.B.S.-TV showed that Negroes favored integration more than whites; that Negroes felt their lot had steadily improved since 1960, when nonviolence had received its biggest impetus through peaceful Southern student demonstrations. This feeling was substantiated by employment and education figures, and, if further proof were needed, nearly nine out of ten Negro voters endorsed eight years of Democratic rule by backing the candidacy of Hubert H. Humphrey. Yet the Negro mood, as reflected by the media, was one of militancy and separatism, as though Blacks, en masse, had supported the Peace and Freedom candidacy of Black Panther Eldridge Cleaver and comedian Dick Gregory.

For all the publicized clamor for Black pride, Black capitalism, Black this and Black that, it was whites, not Blacks, who stemmed the tide of Great Society legislation. And the majority of whites—demanding law and order while safely ensconced in their suburban and exurban abodes—were frightened not so much by crime in *their* streets as by newspaper headlines and angry voices emitting from radio and TV sets. Thus 1968 seemed to prove that reality is what the media depict as real.

This is not to deny the reality of Black rage; for such gains that were made only served to remind Negroes how far so many of them have to go to gain economic, political and social parity.

Negroes were still three times as likely to die in childbirth and infancy; three times as likely to be in poverty and twice as likely to be jobless. Black disenchantment may well have stemmed from the evidence, mounting since World War II, that whites may well desert the cities; that despite the passage of scores of open housing laws, whites will not stand still long enough to be integrated. It was in the face of white intransigence that the Black mystique—aided by the media—emerged.

It is not likely that the press willed it so, for in theory most media men have shared the nation's commitment to racial togetherness. But the media were faced with a dual and contradictory role of (1) reporting what they conceived as news—no matter how unsettling—and (2) helping the Establishment preserve the domestic tranquillity. Apostles of social change, whether headed by King, Cleaver or Columbia University's Mark Rudd, forced their way into news columns and video tubes by making themselves dramatically visible through the Poor People's Campaign, through student and street rebellions and by exotic hippie attire and pseudo-African garb. Thus CORE's Roy Innis, wearing a dashiki, was a better subject for color TV than the NAACP's Roy Wilkins in a business suit. And a demonstration, the livelier the better, would surely win out over a voter education campaign unless some gimmick were used to catch an editor's eye—such as a four-page comic book called *The Adventures of Voteman*, in which the Black hero destroys a slum tenement with a swing of his fist. "Voteman" was good for a six-column spread on the front page of the second section of the *New York Times*. Thus the most enlightened media were the captives of their own predilections for what makes news.

By any news standard, the death of Dr. King and the ensuing riots was the top racial story of the year—demanding about as much space and attention as the assassination of another Kennedy, the Presidential election and man's first flight to the moon. For six days in April, from the Thursday at dusk when Dr. King was shot down until the Tuesday afternoon when he was lowered in his grave, Black America had the eyes and ears of white America as never before. It was estimated by an N.B.C. spokesman that 120 million in the United States watched some part of Dr. King's funeral services on one of the three major networks. But more significant was the fact that Dr. King's death and the resulting Black anger underscored the validity of these now famous words from the March 3 Report of the National Advisory Commission on Civil Disorders: *What white Americans have never fully understood—but what the Negro can never forget—is that white society is deeply implicated in the ghetto. White institutions created it, white institutions maintain it and white society condones it.*

Better known as the Kerner Commission Report—for its chairman, ex-Governor Otto Kerner of Illinois—the report's confession of guilt was described by *New York Post* columnist Murray Kempton as white America's "finest hour." The report also ominously noted the separatist trend: "Our nation is moving toward two societies, one black, one white—separate and unequal." But while the latter statement had the ring of prophecy, the first had the ring of truth. Yet in cataloguing the causes of riots, the report's findings (as psychologist Kenneth B. Clark noted) were about the same as those recorded in similar studies, dating back to the classic 1922 Chicago report on the riot of 1919. Further, the Kerner Report prompted little official action—indeed, President Johnson was miffed by the findings because he felt they did not give sufficient attention to the civil rights accomplishments of his administration. And future President Nixon, then priming himself for the campaign, criticized the report for its "undue emphasis" on the role of "white racists" and its failure to indict the "perpetrators" of the riots themselves.

Nixon's pre-campaign oratory perhaps was attuned to white American opinion. Of the whites polled by C.B.S., 55 per cent disagreed with the finding of white racism, while only 31 per cent supported it. The poll also showed that 65 per cent of the whites had never heard of the report, despite what *Times* critic Jack Gould called "an exceedingly rare demonstration of concentration of coverage by TV on a social issue." It took Dr. King's death and the ensuing riots to jar the white media, if not the white public and its government, into frenzied action towards the mission of saving the nation's cities.

The juxtaposition of the Kerner Commission

finding of white racism and Dr. King's death a month later set the style, rather than the substance, for the media's news policies and coverage throughout the year. Rather than trying to fully explore the need and possibility of social change, the media focused on symbols of change—new faces, or old faces like Nixon's in new places; mod and Afro fashions; Black history and local control; soul music and soul food—leaving the profit system inviolate.

At year's end, it appeared as though the media were most sensitive to the commission's charge that they "report and write from the white man's world." Many media executives sought to change this all-white image by following these guidelines from Chapter XV of the report:

> The media have not communicated to whites a feeling for the difficulties and frustrations of being a Negro in the United States. They have not shown understanding or appreciation of —and thus have not communicated a sense of—Negro culture, thought or history.
>
> When the white press does refer to Negroes and Negro problems it frequently does so as if Negroes were not part of the audience . . . such attitudes, in an area as sensitive and inflammatory as this, feed Negro alienation and intensify white prejudices.
>
> News organizations must employ enough Negroes in significant responsibility to establish an effective link to Negro actions and ideas and to meet legitimate expectations. Tokenism —the hiring of one Negro reporter, or even two or three—is no longer enough.
>
> It would be a contribution of inestimable importance to race relations in the United States to treat ordinary news about Negroes as news of other groups is now treated. Specifically, newspapers should integrate Negroes and Negro activities into all parts of the paper, from the news, society and club pages to the comic strips. Television should develop programming which integrates Negroes into all aspects of televised presentations . . . . For example, Negro reporters and performers should appear more frequently—and at prime time—in news broadcasts, on weather shows, in documentaries, and in advertisements.

Those and other Kerner Commission recommendations told media men little that they did not already know. Some had previously begun to implement many of the ideas later contained in the report. But the fact that the commission functioned under the President's mantle of authority gave the media the mandate they needed to stand on principle or at least counteract nasty letters and phone calls from white viewers and readers.

Predictably, though, the media were most responsive to changes affecting image rather than substance. The mere substitution, for instance, of a Negro newscaster for a white one did not alter the fact that almost all radio and TV news stories amounted to little more than an audio account of information contained in the first paragraphs of articles in the next morning's newspaper. More often than not, both the broadcast and print media obtained their information from the same wire service or the same publicity agent rather than through the intelligence and perseverance of their own reporters. Regardless of whether the faces on the screen were white, Black or both, TV commercials were as silly and as unrelated to the Black experience as ever.

Again, it was infinitely easier for the *New York Times* to run feature stories about Negroes in its business, fashion and magazine sections than to interpret the social implications of the school decentralization dispute in the Ocean Hill-Brownsville section of Brooklyn and the ensuing teacher strike and power struggle between Negroes and Jews. Although the fact that the *Washington Post* had some fifty Negroes on its editorial staff, including columnist William Raspberry and editorial writer Jesse W. Lewis, Jr., gave that newspaper an advantage in reporting and interpreting racial news, it would be farcical to expect that the presence of Black reporters would help relieve the manifold problems of Black poverty in the nation's capital.

And no matter how many Negroes were hired, or how well the news columns were integrated, the media were almost totally white-owned and Establishment dominated. Except for a few radio stations, Negro ownership was nonexistent in the broadcast field. Of 150 Negro newspapers listed in the 1968 *Editor and Publisher Year Book*, only two—the *Chicago Defender* and the *Atlanta World*—were listed as dailies. While the broadcast media had sharply narrowed the gap between an event and the reporting of it, Negro weeklies and semi-weeklies were days behind the times. Nor did Negro newspapers have the money and manpower to explore fully new "angles" or prepare "in depth" reports of any given story. As the race issued continued to be the number one domestic story in 1968, Negro newspapers relied on social and club news, which were generally ignored by the white media. Yet the axiom that in the white press "Negroes are never born, educated, married, and never die" was less true than ever before.

The Kerner Commission reported that most Negroes distrust the "white press," and it was certain that this alienation—developed over so many years—could not be dissipated in a few months. "Distrust and dislike of the media among Negroes," the report said, "encompass all the media, though in general, newspapers are mistrusted more than television. This is not because television is thought to be more sensitive or responsive to Negro needs and aspirations, but because ghetto residents believe that television at least lets them see the actual events for themselves."

Broadcast: Through a Prism of Commercials, Ratings, Profits

What the Kerner Commission did not fully take into account is that purveying news is only a minor function of commercial television. Through its endless display of situation comedies, game shows, Westerns, adventure tales, dramas, movies, variety shows and commercials, television presents a false image not only of the Black world but of the white one as well. The act of integrating Negro performers into some of its Westerns and soap operas did not improve the product. One can only speculate as to the product's impact on the nation's morals, goals and behavior, but, as the *Nation*'s John Horn insisted, "Affluent whites who have control of televison employ it to their own ends, not for human communication."

It is through the prism of commercials, ratings and profits that one must view the steps that TV took in 1968 to right social wrongs. By its own terms commercial TV did quantitatively better by Negroes than ever before, but in human terms, not nearly enough. Nor were the under-financed education stations equipped for the task; their shows, by and large, were pale carbon copies of their affluent competition's.

Perhaps the most significant development among the broadcast media in 1968 was the greater use of the air waves as a means of direct social communication. Audience participation shows, both on radio and TV, were nothing new; but seldom before had they been used to allay fears and relieve tensions. Following Dr. King's death, for instance, two Negro-oriented, white-owned radio stations, WLIB and WWRL, and the FM station WRVR, in New York, aired phone calls from aggrieved persons, Black and white. WLIB even brought in Mayor John V. Lindsay and Percy Sutton, the Negro borough president of Manhattan, to take calls at its microphones. In the wake of looting and burning in Washington, D.C., rock singer James Brown was summoned by station WTTG-TV. "Please go off the streets," Brown urged. "From one brother to another, go home." In Bangor, Maine, some six hundred NAACP demonstrators protesting Dr. King's assassination came into the WEMT-TV station and joined a call-in show.

Television magazine, in its August issue, listed the programs of ninety-five commercial stations dealing with "urban unrest, civil disturbance and lawlessness"—all euphemisms for the race issue. The survey showed that the most widespread format aimed at Negroes was the job opportunity program. The first of these was aired in June 1967, on WBBM-TV, Chicago, in cooperation with the state employment service and the Chicago Urban League. The "Opportunity Line" program offered jobs and discussed job counseling and training on the air. The series eventually spread to fifteen C.B.S. owned and affiliated stations.

Of the ninety-five stations, seventeen carried job programs on a regular basis. Job opportunity was the subject for "special" programs on several other stations. In Sacramento, for instance, all three commercial stations and a nearby Redding, California, educational TV station joined in a twelve-hour "Work-a-Thon," aimed at generating jobs and financial pledges to help provide summer employment for youngsters. Other cities with job opportunity stations included San Diego, Los Angeles, San Francisco, Indianapolis, Detroit, Pittsburgh, Zanesville (Ohio) and San Antonio.

Additional evidence that television was attempting to alter, however slightly, its white middle class image was shown by other public service programs beamed directly at the ghetto. Chicago's WBBM followed up its pioneer job program with "The Paycheck Line," which assisted victims of consumer and contract frauds and money mismanagement. Another consumer education program was launched in April by Philadelphia's KYW. The sixty-five-week series was titled "The Thing about Money."

Skeptics could point out that most of these programs were presented during the early morning or midday weekend hours when relatively few people watch TV. Some programs were substitutes for the normal run of low-budget talk programs that constitute a major portion of TV's "public affairs" commitment to the Federal Communications Commission for their use of the public air waves. Others sprang up as summer substitutes for the dreary re-runs which are normal TV fare during the vacation season. The summer lull also coincided with a time when stations had an obvious interest in keeping their cities "cool," or, as Lou Potter, Black TV producer, was quoted by the *New York Times* as saying: "The networks discover the Negro every summer. The Negro in the ghetto knows he's being hyped. . . . He knows that the race problem is a great deal more than a summer problem and that's why there is a summer problem."

In the South, local discussion programs about such topics as housing and employment were no longer uncommon, but opportunity type programs were scarce in Dixie. Exceptions included Jacksonville's WJXT "Opportunity Line" and Orlando's WFTV program report on the employment of nonprofessional Negroes in central Florida. WQXI presented "Atlanta Responds," a summary of reports seen on newscasts dealing with the city's actions relating to suggestions made by the Kerner Commission, and WAGA interviewed Atlantans who had known Dr. King. The Central Virginia Educational Television Corporation presented Edgar Allan Toppin, professor of history at Virginia State College, in a series of thirty lectures titled "Americans from Africa: A History." The lectures were described in July by the *Richmond Times-Dispatch* as "the first instructional television series in the nation on the role of the Negro in American History."

But if the Virginia series was the first, it was far from the last "Black heritage" offering during 1968. C.B.S.-TV's seven-part summer series "On Black America" was a mixed bag of history, culture and topical comment. It began with a narration by comedian Bill Cosby on how Black history had been ignored or distorted. Then the series traced the role of the Black soldier through all American wars, conducted an intercontinental dialogue between Black American and Black African leaders, and presented a discussion of Negro contributions in sports and entertainment. Next came the heritage of slavery; then an odyssey of American Negro youth to Africa "in search of a past," and finally a report on the findings of the C.B.S. poll.

By and large, the series was neither good history nor good television, yet the Bill Cosby episode and the Negro soldier story, co-authored by the *New York Times*' Thomas A. Johnson, had their perceptive moments. The series established a precedent for network television by extensively employing Negroes in the production side of the business. In addition to Cosby and Johnson, writer-producer Perry Wolff and narrators Hal Walker and George Foster all had a hand in the series. In December, a Negro production staff joined C.B.S. and Columbia University in launching a daily series in which the lecturers, headed by Spelman College's Vincent Harding, were Black historians and scholars. Even so, C.B.S. was faulted for scheduling the lectures at 9:00 A.M.—a time when wage earners are due at work and children at school, leaving less busy housewives as the only possible viewing audience. The series also was attacked by Dr. Harding and others for not giving Blacks enough of a voice in making decisions.

In 1968 television often acquiesced in letting Negroes—or Blacks, as many preferred to be called—"do their own thing." A.B.C.'s New York outlet featured a weekly 4:00 P.M. Sunday documentary program, "Like It Is," which had the misfortune of directly competing with professional football on C.B.S. and N.B.C. Yet its all-Black staff, headed by producer Charles Hobson and commentator Gil Noble, was permitted—because of its coloration—to film a class at a junior high school in Ocean Hill-Brownsville as part of a documentary on the teacher strikes. Discussing the legacy of Malcolm X was a bearded dashiki-

Paul Delaney (front center), of the Washington, D.C., *Star,* winner of one of the ten Washington-Baltimore Newspaper Guild Front Page Awards for 1969, covers a hearing on rebuilding in the ghetto areas of the District of Columbia.

clad Leslie Campbell, who was later to gain city-wide notice for his reading of an anti-Semitic poem on radio station WBAI. The all-Black staff's documentary, according to the *New York Post*, "seems to have been the only report of the school crisis that both Albert Shanker (president of the striking United Federation of Teachers) and Rhody McCoy (Ocean Hill-Brownsville administrator) agreed was fair to both sides." Another notable program was a media critique by five Black New York reporters: Johnson and Nancy Hicks of the *Times*, Hugh Wyatt of the *Daily News*, Ed Cumberbatch of *Newsweek* and George Barner of the *Amsterdam News*.

The *Post* also described "Like It Is" as WABC-TV's answer to National Education Television's "Black Journal" series. "Journal" was conceived by N.E.T. as a cultural program "by, for and of" the Black community. Hobson and ten other Negroes quit "Black Journal" with the protest that they were being exploited as a promotional "front" and that most of the film segments were being produced by whites. Another Black-oriented program was introduced by the *Times* in the condescending "hipster" vein often adopted in 1968 by white media men. Under the headline "Dig It or Forget It," Robert Berkvist wrote:

> Channel 13, with $631,000 worth of white power from the Ford Foundation, is trying to find out whether black can be beautiful on a television screen. Last Thursday at 9 P.M., the noncommercial station launched "Soul!" a 39-week series in color that, according to its originators, is "devoted entirely to and aimed at the Metropolitan area's two-million black population." And if you don't dig the title, baby, forget it, because in that case nobody connected with the show cares whether you tune in or walk the dog.

Also in 1968, programs were produced which purported to have their "roots" in Black communities. These included Brooklyn's "Inside Bedford-Stuyvesant" and Southern California's "From the Inside Out." The latter program, produced by KTTV in Los Angeles, ran from May through mid-September for a total of ninety shows. According to *Television* magazine, one program devoted forty-seven minutes to Negro hair styling, "with the emphasis on how it aped white standards in the past and now has become a symbol for a new breed, a black badge of identity." Other features included fashion shows and "Black Profiles in History." The program was co-produced by two Blacks, Vantile E. Whitfield and Jackie Gober, with a white camera crew, but it was planned "to phase out the whites and make it exclusively a production created by members of the Black community."

Whereas the Kerner Report's assessment of media performance during the 1967 riots noted that "moderate" Negro leaders were given more exposure on television than more militant types, the trend in 1968 seemed to be reversed. This may have been partly due to aggressiveness on the part of younger, more militant, Blacks, but it also reflected reluctance by veteran leaders to expose themselves to the old panel show format in which the David Susskinds and Mike Wallaces vie with their guests for the camera's attention. Television interviewing was described by Kenneth B. Clark—according to his research editor Jeannette Hopkins—"as part of a degrading 'charade,' an intellectual 'soft-shoe' that entertains or titillates the white audience without stimulating it to action. . . ." For the most part, documentaries, too, continued to be dominated by TV personalities, as seen in N.B.C.'s two-hour Boston show which featured commentator Frank McGee and relegated political scientists Charles V. Hamilton and Daniel P. Moynihan to supporting roles.

There were some programs, however, which rose to the Kerner Report's challenge to tell racial stories "honestly, realistically and imaginatively." The experimental Public Broadcast Laboratory by chance followed Dr. King throughout the last three months of his life; this resulted not only in a stunning obituary but also in a report on the yearnings of poor Blacks in the Deep South for a better life. Most innovative was the Los Angeles KNXT production "Black on Black," culled from four hundred interviews of what life is like among Negroes in the south central section of that city. According to *Television* magazine, the show "had no reporters, no script, no white faces or voices." Perhaps the best network documentary was the Westinghouse Broadcasting Company's "One Nation Indivisible," a title alluding to the separatist trend noted by the Kerner Report. By midsummer, the prime-time program had been shown by sixty-three stations. W.B.C. provided the first two hours of programming, and in a detailed booklet suggested how stations might localize an additional sixty- or ninety-minute segment. In New York the program first presented ninety minutes of individual opinions among a wide assortment of Blacks and whites in several cities. Then the participants—including a police officer, clergymen, a national guardsman, a labor leader and several teachers—were brought into a studio for a face-to-face confrontation. "The ensuing colloquy," the *Times*' Gould reported, "covered the innumerable issues involved in the racial problem and elicited a fascinating diversity of opinions on housing, employment, self-respect, union discrimination and the Black dream of economic well-being."

But such oases in the TV desert were too few and far between. Rare moments of enlightenment were hardly enough to compensate for the medium's neglect of its major role as arbiter of the nation's morals and behavior and stimulator of desires and expectations. With the *Nation*'s John Horn, one might pessimistically conclude: "The frightful thing is that we have institutionalized white American prejudice by entrusting television to commercial interests which are committed to the majority (white) audience on a limited, materialistic basis. We have in effect given away the instrument that could save us."

Newspapers: Running Faster yet Standing Still

In 1968 daily newspapers gave little cause for optimism. They were, by and large, hidebound in their ancient tradition of reporting who, what, when, where and how, without seriously addressing themselves to the one question—why?—that they should be infinitely better prepared to answer than radio or television. Newspaper reporters were still the captives of the city room clock, scrambling to inject immediacy into their "big" stories as though the broadcast media did not exist. It might be argued that stories not covered by radio-TV would twice again fill an issue of the Sunday *New York Times*, but if newspapers cannot redefine their concepts of news and find better ways of reporting, writing and presenting it, the debate could well be waged over a newspaper corpse. Meanwhile, the evidence mounted on newsstands and in city rooms and journalism schools across the nation that people—especially young people who had not yet become creatures of habit—were being "turned off" by U.S. daily newspapers, despite their total circulation of 61.5 million, up 9 million since 1950. Given the tremendous increase in the nation's literate population, the upsurge in the reading of books and magazines, the likelihood is that newspaper circulation figures deceive; that the dailies, like the Queen in Wonderland, are running faster yet standing still.

Among no group was there greater disenchantment with newspapers than among Negroes. For example, a two-year-old survey of the residents of Gum Springs, Virginia, a poor Black enclave near Washington, D.C., showed that for local news, readership of the *Gum Springs News*, a one-sheet mimeographed weekly, exceeded by five to one that of the only Washington paper, the *Star,* which covered the community. At that time the *Gum Springs News* cost ten cents per copy (the same as the *Star*) or $5 a year and was read by 94 per cent of the community's families. Again, from a percentage standpoint, the fastest-growing newspaper in New York City was the Negro weekly *Amsterdam News,* not the *Times* or the *Post,* whose circulation gains might be mainly attributed to the simultaneous demise of three competing dailies. The massive 2.1 million circulation of the *Daily News* was on the decline. But, more ominous for metropolitan newspapers, neighborhood and "underground" newspapers—paced by the weekly *Village Voice*—sprouted like weeds all over Manhattan. They included at least three in Harlem. These publications mainly were a ragtail lot and far more subjective than the conventional journalistic wisdom would allow, but Black and white youngsters were reading them.

The irony was that daily newspapers throughout the nation were making an unprecedented effort to capture Negro reporters, if not readers. A survey by the Southern Education Reporting Service of 108 newspapers located thirty-seven Negroes working alongside whites as reporters and copy-desk editors on newspapers in eleven Southern states. On the staffs of forty dailies that had desegregated their newsrooms were fifty-eight other Negroes who were employed in such editorial capacities as reporting interns, librarians and copy boys. These figures, released in September, were impressive when compared with a two-year-old American Newspaper Guild survey which located only sixty Negroes working on editorial staffs throughout the United States. None were identified as working in the South.

By 1968 the *Washington Post* alone reported fifty Negro editorial employees in response to a joint survey by the *Columbia Journalism Review* and the Anti-Defamation League. The *Post* also reported the largest percentage of Black employees: 388 out of 1,850, or 20.9 per cent. And in the *Post* staff's book *Ten Blocks from the White House: Anatomy of the Washington Riots of 1968,* deputy managing editor Ben W. Gilbert wrote that the *Post*'s riot squad of one hundred included "fourteen Negro reporters and photographers, who helped correct the kinds of misjudgment that coverage of the black community by whites and for whites sometimes produces."

There was no evidence that any other news organization, broadcast or print, could mount as much Black power as the *Post*, but it was evident that superior Black reporters could carefully select the cities and newspapers, and often the media, of their choice. Thus, in a few years, the *Newark News* lost Rudy Johnson to the *Times,* Tony Somerville to Washington's *Star* and John L. Dotson, Jr., to the *Detroit Free Press* and finally to *Newsweek*. N.B.C.-TV's Bob Teague was a former *New York Times* man. So was Layhmond Robinson, Jr., who worked at A.B.C.-TV before becoming public relations director for the National Urban League. Even the *Washington Post* lost Wallace H. Terry, II, to *Time* magazine. As an example of how the media were raiding each other's staffs for Blacks, the *New York Post*'s Ted Poston, the "dean" of Negro reporters on white dailies, told the probably apocryphal story that when he left on his summer vacation his paper had four other Negro reporters, and by the time of his return he was the only one left.

Thus the Kerner Report's assessment that "the journalistic profession has been shockingly backward in seeking out, hiring, training and promoting Negroes" was probably far less true at year's end than it was in March. Since Kerner, scarcely an issue of *Editor and Publisher* has appeared that did not report on a new training or employment program launched by organizations ranging from the Sigma Delta Chi Journalism Fraternity, to the Columbia School of Journalism, to the Urban Coalition, to the Washington Journalism Center, to the New York Governor's Employment Committee.

This flurry of training and hiring was prompted partly by the realization that no city editor wanted to be caught with a riot on his hands without at least one Black reporter to help cover it. This is precisely what happened to the *Los Angeles Times* during the Watts conflagration, when the only Black man it could muster was one working as a messenger. And Black militants, such as those attending the third annual Black Power conference in Philadelphia and the CORE convention in Columbus, Ohio, were making the race "beat" more difficult by barring white reporters and even verbally abusing Black ones. Another consideration was that metropolitan newspapers, plagued by the cost and time of delivering their wares through clogged streets and highways to white suburbia, were turning a covetous eye to the Negro sections of the inner cities. But all such practical considerations aside, most newsmen perhaps felt that Negro reporters would help do the reporting job better.

Yet newspapers were captives, not only of the city room clock and of their archaic writing style, but also of their dearth of experience in effectively examining not just the race problem, but any social problem. Traditionally, analyses of social illnesses—beyond the purview of the criminal and the divorce courts—were scorned by most city editors as "sociology," and a good many of these fire and ambulance chasers still occupied editorial desks. Newsmen also doted on keeping stories short and simple, so it would follow that they would seek simplistic solutions to the most complicated of problems by hiring Negroes as "instant" experts on the ghetto. With the increase of Negro staffers, one would think that the quality of ghetto coverage would automatically improve, right?

Perhaps.

At year's end, it was too soon to evaluate the coverage of newspapers—and also that of Negro reporters—because of the unprecedented number of articles that had been written on race and related subjects. John Hohenberg, secretary to the advisory board on the Pulitzer Prizes, commented that the number of entries on the "urban crisis" for journalism's top awards far exceeded those in any other field; in fact, he added, never before had the board received so many entries on a single issue.

Of the relatively few articles that came to the attention of this writer, a series by the Charlotte, North Carolina, *Observer* certainly met the Kerner Commission's standard of "imaginative" reporting by first examining rural poverty among Blacks and whites in North Carolina and then tracing the migration of white Appalachians to Chicago and Negroes to Washington, D.C. Thus the *Observer*'s Dwayne Walls and James K. Batten, both white, demonstrated that many urban problems are rooted on the farm; that the problems are national, not regional. This was done by perceptive reporting rather than through the glib assumptions that characterize most articles on migration to the cities. The reportage, however, was far better in North Carolina than it was in Chicago and Washington. This suggests another fresh approach. Why shouldn't Southern papers like the *Observer* combine forces, say, with the *Washington Post* and the *Chicago Daily News* and pinpoint the travails of specific families in both their Southern and Northern habitats?

Of the major news syndicates, the Associated Press compiled a report titled "In Black and White," which listed some of the articles published by eighty of its member newspapers and comments by many editors. Among the features commissioned by the AP was a summary statement on Negro history by Prince E. Wilson, executive secretary of the Atlanta University Center Corporation and a board member of the Association for the Study of Negro Life and History. The *Kansas City Star,* not especially noted for its liberalism, freed nine staff members for several weeks to prepare a special section on the Negro's role in history, and—according to the AP report—scores of other papers ran "The Last American," a twenty-four-part Negro history series. United Press International issued a series of twelve articles based on major recommendations of the Kerner Report. UPI also assigned H. D. Quigg and a Black Chicagoan, John Taylor, to a story on "A Day in the Life of a Ghetto Family." Taylor spent three days, in fact, in a New York home as part of his research.

Whether Taylor or any other Black reporter brought fresh insights into race coverage obviously depended upon whether he possessed the qualities of *any* good reporter: knowledge, intelligence, enterprise. One story not likely obtainable by a white reporter was Jesse Lewis' interview, for the *Washington Post*, with hooded Black arsonists. Yet if being Black had some advantages, it also had handicaps, particularly in the newsroom. When the Kerner Commission spoke of the pervasiveness of white racism in this country, newsmen were not excluded. By and large, Negroes were seen as Blacks first—reporters second. The white astigmatism which presumes Black ignorance of nonracial subjects was illustrated in Bob Teague's book *Letters to a Black Boy*. Teague recalled that some years ago he was asked by the moderator of a popular panel show to come to Washington to interview James Farmer, then national director of CORE. Teague said he had no objection, but he was determined not to be confined to Negro news. Then he asked if he would be called at another time to interview somebody not connected with civil rights. The moderator, in all innocence, replied: "What else do you know anything about?"

Too often in 1968 were Black reporters ghettoized. Day after day, many were assigned to Black community activities or to problems associated with the ghetto, i.e., slum housing, welfare, crime-in-the-streets. Some reporters, consumed by the Black mystique, welcomed these assignments, even though their middle class backgrounds and white-oriented educations had left them no more prepared for the task than were the blondest of their colleagues. Others saw the ghetto as a short route to by-lines and pay hikes, even though overspecialization might later deter their progression into the higher ranks of the profession. Again, Black awareness might also compromise their effectiveness as reporters. In other words, a Black reporter often felt obliged to serve two masters—the Black community and his white employer; and in this ambivalence, it might be presumed that neither could be served well.

The qualified response to the question of a Black reporter's ambivalence was prompted by the view that newsmen should no longer kneel to the false god of objectivity. By 1968, the city room view that "objectivity is a myth" had become a cliché, but seldom were reporters permitted to abandon their posture of infallibility: that they could tell the "facts" or "all sides" of a story in six inches of type. But newspapers were generally bereft or wary of the rare talent which enables some few reporters to expose their biases and still retain a reasonable measure of credibility. Almost all reporters who demonstrated this talent—such as the *New York Post*'s Jimmy Breslin and the *Washington Post*'s Nicholas von Hoffman—eventually became columnists or wrote for the *Village Voice* and for the growing number of magazines which encouraged the "new" journalism of subjectivity and advocacy.

The Negro Press: What Price Freedom?

If Black journalists sought advocacy, why did they not join the staffs of Black newspapers or start publications of their own? The easy answer to both questions is "money." Negro newspapers could not offer comparable salaries or prestige. Negroes also lacked sufficient talent and expertise—especially in the vital advertising, production and distribution sides of the business—to compete in a high-cost, low-profit industry. Another less tangible factor was that few of the established Negro publications had a sense of mission. At a time when Black journalists wanted to be socially relevant, the Negro press was increasingly out of touch. Editorial policies were often to the right of the more liberal white publications. In Atlanta, for instance, C. A. Scott's *Daily World* was perhaps more conservative than the late Ralph McGill's *Constitution*.

The combined circulation (126,452) of the five *Afro-American* newspapers still topped the Negro field, but the numbers of *Afro* readers, along with those of the *Pittsburgh Courier*, the *Chicago Defender* and the *Norfolk Journal and Guide*, were far below the heights reached during World War II. According to the *Editor and Publisher Year Book*, the circulation of 150 newspapers was only 1,200,000, scarcely more than that of Johnson Publications' *Ebony* magazine. At year's end, the New York *Amsterdam News* claimed the highest single edition circulation at 85,000, but its success was attributed by publisher C. B. Powell to its being run as a business and not for its advocacy of racial causes.

The only publishing enterprise in the history of Negro journalism that can be compared commercially to the more successful white publications is the magazine empire (*Ebony, Jet, Tan, Negro Digest*) of Chicago's John H. Johnson. In 1968 Johnson ran a series of full-page advertisements in the *New York Times* proclaiming the advantages to white companies of buying space in *Ebony*. In late November the *Ebony* ad showed a picture of a Black Santa Claus. Under the blurb "We're dreaming of a Black Christmas," the ad stated that only through *Ebony* could advertisers reach "2,500,000 households every month of which 34.1 per cent of the male heads earn $10,000 a year."

"One of these days," the ad continued, "more advertisers will realize that the American Negro's Blackness goes deeper than his skin; that the Negro finds white-oriented advertising colorless, unrealistic, unbelievable; that the Negro responds to advertising in which he can see himself—advertising that makes use of his hunger for status and recognition."

Thus Johnson used the Black mystique as a way of attracting advertisers, which are as important to his magazine's success as his Black circulation base. In the promotion campaign and in the magazine's articles on parties and cotillions, eligible bachelors and fashionable women, Johnson told advertisers that many Negroes have money to spend—even to waste—and told less affluent Blacks that they also might aspire to the comfortable life. That this way of life was being at least philosophically rejected by young Black and white militants seemed commercially irrelevant. Yet Johnson struck a militant note through *Negro Digest*, which contains almost no advertising, and historical articles by *Ebony* senior editor Lerone Bennett, Jr. Few white commercial publications would ask, as Bennett did, "Was Abe Lincoln a White Supremacist?" and answer in the affirmative. No matter what the historical case for or against Lincoln, the fact that the article was published (prompting an outraged response from Herbert Mitgang in the *New York Times Magazine*) certainly indicated the potential for the Negro press as being a provocateur in behalf of its people.

Another way in which the Negro press might better serve its constituency is by trying to keep its white counterpart honest. The Richmond *Afro-American*'s Preston M. Yancy, for instance, attacked the *Times-Dispatch* and the *News-Leader* for condemning "preferential treatment" in federal employment for Negroes in Washington, D.C., as well as a proposal to elevate Negro lawyers to judgeships in Richmond. "They [the Richmond dailies] ignore discrimination under their noses," Yancy wrote. "Their lily-white news and editorial staff is evidence that they practice discrimination themselves. Yet if they hear a reason that colored people are being shown preferential treatment off in west hell they scream bloody murder."

Again, the bi-weekly *Detroit Tribune* spearheaded a movement against the *Detroit News* for the latter's daily publication of a "crime blotter" with racial identification of assailants. When the *News* explained that it wanted to expose muggers, rapists and gun-carrying robbers who were "strangling urban life," the *Tribune* replied: "The *News*' 'Crime in Detroit' column is not being published in a social vacuum. To the contrary, the *News* has elected to publish this column in a period both in this city and in the nation where the issue of 'crime in the streets' and of 'law and order' has become an issue of national controversy of hysterical proportions."

Yet most criticisms of the white press and the Establishment were expressions of opinion, rarely supported by thorough reporting. Johnson was the sole Black publisher who seemed competitive with the white press for talent and articles, but his bread was buttered by white advertisers. Thus the Black press cannot be free until Black business and industry are developed to the point where Johnson does not feel obliged to run full-page ads in the *Times*. In 1968 the prospect of a free Black press, unfettered by white controls, seemed as far away as the possibility of Negro journalists becoming an effective voice in decisions reached by the white media.

One of the more hopeful signs was that Black youngsters increasingly recognized the potential power of communications and began publishing newspapers and magazines of their own. That they often had to seek funds for training and printing from white volunteers, donors and foundations did not deter them. *Forty Acres and a Mule* was published by students engaged in the New York Urban League's Street Academy Program; *Dig This*, by a street gang in North Philadelphia; *The Voice*, by a group of Plainfield, New Jerseyans; and *What's Happening?* by young New Yorkers. Although these and other publications were of varying quality, their display of young talents intent on doing "their own thing" augured well for the future of the press—Black, white or integrated.

Forecast: The Prospects for "Telling It like It Is"

Of the white media, magazines offered the greatest hope for "telling it like it is." Perhaps the best reporting on any subject was done for *Harper's* by the novelist Norman Mailer in articles on the anti-Vietnam demonstration at the Pentagon and on the Republican and Democratic conventions. These later appeared in book form as *Armies of the Night* and *Miami and the Siege of Chicago*. In a five-part series *Sports Illustrated*'s Jack Olsen shattered the illusion that sport is one area in which Negroes are fully emancipated. All year long, *Saturday Review* carried reflective articles on ways of improving urban education. *Newsweek* twice focused on ways in which the urban crisis can be solved, with particular emphasis on the need for jobs, lending support to the movement for a guaranteed income. Magazines also outshone newspapers and television in their versions of Black life and history, even though sensational cover stories on ghetto unrest by the late *Saturday Evening Post, Newsweek* and especially *Esquire*, may have served to inflame passions rather than cool them. But magazines were still the vehicle in 1968 for stirring public interest and concern.

Metropolitan newspapers seemed headed toward dire commercial trouble, hastened by their compulsion to appear to be all things to all people while actually bound to the Establishment. This contradiction reduces their ability to fully report race news or any other aspect of the urban crisis. Further, metropolitan newspapers cannot match the immediacy of broadcast, the interpretive capacity of magazines or the potential ability, at least, of community, neighborhood and

Negro newspapers to reflect the views of smaller audiences. Some metropolitan newspapers are needed to the extent that they can provide in-depth reports and supplement the skimpy news content of radio-TV, but those which are commercially redundant and socially irrelevant could very well pass unmissed off the American scene. The surviving large papers might assume more of a regional tone as smaller ones focused more on local issues. By such a rationale, there should always be a *New York Times*, but aside from a few reporters and columnists like Murray Kempton, are the *New York Post* and *Daily News* really necessary?

But the big question is what to do about television—that McLuhanesque monster which has a grip on the eyes, ears and minds of the society. Surely television is as much a public utility as water, gas and electricity and should be more responsive to public needs. The medium with the greatest potential for educating the society away from avarice and violence stood in 1968, as in previous years, as the chief perpetrator of the media's disposition to fill the air waves and news columns with copious tears when its heroes die and its failure to stem the forces of prejudice and hate which killed them. No sooner than Dr. King, free at last, was buried, the media were in search of a new drum major. Who, the *Times*' Claude Sitton asked, "will fire the faithful's hopes with recitations of their unfulfilled dream? Who will stand for the Negro, as Black and white Americans wrestle with a racial crisis of increasing immensity and complexity?" At year's end there was no heir apparent in sight, for with the 1968 assassinations of Dr. King and Robert F. Kennedy, the myth of a new messiah—Black or white—was dying, if not dead.

Salvation, voices in the ghettoes and on the campuses were trumpeting, lies not in a change of the guard but a change in the system: a system which perpetuates division by class and caste; a system whose selfish factions immobilize its government; a system which tolerates any vice—from war to narcotics to starvation—as long as profits can be made therefrom. As a C.B.S. documentary, "Hunger in America," fluttered briefly among the standard TV fare of soap operas and cigarette commercials, the nation harked back to the Depression days when novelist John Steinbeck (dead in December of natural causes) wrote that "children dying of pellagra must die because a profit cannot be taken from an orange."

Mrs. Dorothy Porter with a collection of books from the Moorland Room, Howard University.

Public, University and Private American Library Holdings on the Negro

Ernest Kaiser

Surveys of and Conferences on United States Negro Collections

As EARLY as 1936 Dorothy Porter, long-time curator of the Moorland-Spingarn Collection at Howard University, published "Library Resources for the Study of Negro Life and History" in the then recently started *Journal of Negro Education* (April 1936), a Howard University publication. In March 1940 the American Council of Learned Societies held an important conference on the problems of research and scholarship in the field of Negro studies. At this conference L. D. Reddick, in a paper entitled "Bibliographical Problems in Negro Research" (*ACLS Bulletin No. 32,* September 1941), stated (as he had in his article "Library Facilities for Research in Negro Colleges," *Quarterly Review of Higher Education among Negroes,* July 1940) that there were then about a half dozen important Negro collections in the United States, and that they were all suffering from rather indifferent support. Reddick, then curator of the Schomburg Collection, emphasized the necessity of building up a few great collections of Negro literature in the country and called for much greater effort in the area of Negro studies. He appealed to all sections of the country, including the then largely uninterested states of the Far West. He also pointed to the need for three guides to the sources on the Negro, to cover the sources in Europe, in Latin America and in the United States. Reddick later supplied (and it was probably the first of its kind) a summary—but quite good—nonexhaustive roundup of library holdings on the Negro in these three areas in his essay "Library Resources for Negro Studies in the United States and Abroad," included in *Encyclopedia of the Negro: Preparatory Volume* (1945; 1946). This publication was edited by W. E. B. Du Bois and Guy B. Johnson.

Since 1945 there has been very little in the way of resource or holdings guides on the Negro in the United States. Paul Lewinson, author of *Race, Class and Party: A History of Negro Suffrage and White Politics in the South* (1932; 1963), compiled in 1947 *A Guide to Documents in the National Archives: For Negro Studies,* for the Committee on Negro Studies of the American Council of Learned Societies. Since 1947 the only valuable published material of this sort has been in bibliographical essays found in books such as Gilbert Osofsky's *Harlem: The Making of a Ghetto* (1966) and August Meier's *Negro Thought in America, 1880–1915* (1963; 1968) and occasional periodical pieces on individual libraries such as the Schomburg Collection or the Moorland-Spingarn Library. If any papers on Negro sources in the United States were read at the annual meetings of the Association for the Study of Negro Life and History or at the occasional Atlanta University School of Library Science conferences, they were never published. Collections on the Negro are listed in general and special library directories, but the descriptions of the holdings are brief, inadequate and usually out of date.

Eighteen years after Lewinson's *Guide* was published, the Atlanta University School of Library Science and Trevor Arnett Library convened in October 1965 an institute to discuss the role of United States Negro and African collections in libraries. This was, as the call stated, because of the increased and unprecedented interest in the Negro in America, in Africa and throughout the world. It was further pointed out that A. A. Schomburg, Henry P. Slaughter, Arthur B. Spingarn and Carter G. Woodson had labored in relative obscurity to document the Negro's contributions and that their cumulations are the nuclei respectively of the Schomburg Collection (New York Public Library), and the Atlanta University, Howard University and Library of Congress Negro collections. But now, said the conference call, new Negro collections are being developed and large sums of money are being spent in this field.

Lorenzo J. Greene started a series titled "Negro Manuscript Collections in Libraries" in the *Negro History Bulletin* in March 1967, but to date only three articles in the series have appeared. August Meier described the recent growth and development of great interest in American Negro history in his article "Black America as a Research Field: Some Comments" (*American Historical Association Newsletter*, April 1968). He also pointed up what remains to be done in the field of Negro studies. It should be added here that of the 14,285 biographical sketches in the twenty-two-volume *Dictionary of American Biography* (including the first supplementary volume; the second supplement was not counted) only eighty-nine are about Negroes. Wilhelmena S. Robinson's *Historical Negro Biographies* (1967; 1968), Sylvia G. L. Dannett's *Profiles of Negro Womanhood, 1619–1900; Twentieth Century* (2 vols.: 1964; 1966) and Walter Christmas' *Negroes in Public Affairs and Government* (1966) are attempts to make up for the DAB's exclusion of many Negroes.

Walter Schatz, librarian of the Southern Education Reporting Service (Nashville, Tennessee), is compiling a sorely needed handbook or directory of the holdings of Negro materials (African and art holdings excluded) in all of the libraries in the United States. It will be published by R. R. Bowker in 1970.

Finally, Congressman James Scheuer of New York City, William D. Hathaway of Maine and Augustus F. Hawkins (Negro) of California, of the Select Subcommittee on Labor of the House Committee on Education and Labor, held hearings on March 18, 1968, in New York City, on a bill to establish a national commission on Negro history and culture. (These hearings and documents are now published and are available from the U.S. Government Printing Office, Washington, D.C.) This commission will (1) study the steps necessary to unearth, preserve, collect and catalogue historical materials dealing with Negro history and culture, (2) consider the possibilities of establishing a museum or center of Negro history and culture and (3) work out methods of disseminating Negro history and culture materials so that the information can be best integrated into the mainstream of American education and life. There have also been similar Senate hearings.

Surveys of and Conferences on African Collections in the United States

In the field of African resources in the United States the record is much better, although the period of considerable interest in African materials is much shorter than that for North American Negro materials. The early, pioneering and continual lecturing, writing and publishing on Africa by W. E. B. Du Bois, W. Leo Hansberry and Carter G. Woodson—along with the books of the late anthropologist Melville J. Herskovits and his building of the African library at Northwestern University—helped to develop African studies over the last four or five decades.

The predominantly white African Studies Association, formed in 1957, has been one of the two organizations largely responsible for the increased interest in this field; this it has helped stimulate through its annual conferences and its scholarly quarterly *African Studies Bulletin*, which published its eleventh volume in 1968. The other organization which has furthered American scholarly interest in Africa is the all-Negro American Society of African Culture. Organized in 1958 as an affiliate of the older, Paris-based Society of African Culture, it brought out in the same year (with the help of the parent organization, which had been publishing books and the periodical *Présence Africaine* since 1947) the very important book *Africa Seen by American Negroes*, edited by John A. Davis. The scholarly papers read at AMSAC's annual conferences have always been available (mimeographed) to the conferees, and two of its sets of annual conference papers, *Pan-Africanism Reconsidered* (1959) and *Southern Africa in Transition* (1966), as well as Leopold S. Senghor's *On African Socialism* (1965), have been published as books.

Dorothy Porter again pioneered in 1960, with her "Research Centers and Sources for the Study of African History" (*Journal of Human Relations*). Two bibliographical essays of great value to librarians and scholars in developing useful, nonexhaustive collections on Africa are Adelaide C. Hill's "Developing a Collection on Africa, South of the Sahara" (*College and Research Libraries*, November 1961) and Robert I. Rotberg's more limited "The Teaching of African History" (*American Historical Review*, October 1963). The Library of Congress has published three editions of *African Newspapers in Selected American Libraries* (1956; 1962; 1965). The first had sixteen pages; the third has 135 pages. *A Catalogue of the African Collection in the Moorland Collection* (at Howard University, Washington, D.C.) was published in 1958. In the early 1960's, G. K. Hall of Boston published dictionary catalogues of the African libraries at Boston University, Northwestern University and the Schomburg Collection of the New York Public Library.

The African Department of Northwestern University libraries has published six times a year a *Joint Acquisitions List of Africana*, beginning in January 1962. The *List* consists of items published in the current year and the five preceding years which have been received after June 1961. Many libraries of Africana contribute to this list. The U.S. Department of State's considerable interest in Africa goes back to the 1950's. It has published two editions of the useful *African Programs of U.S. Organizations: A Select Directory* (1961; 1965).

The Hoover Institution on War, Revolution and Peace, of Stanford University, has published many important and useful bibliographies of and guides to Africa over the past decade—with an occasional deplorable volume on Africa and communism or a defense of European imperialism in Africa. Its *Africana Newsletter* (1962–1964) merged with the *African Studies Bulletin*. In 1963 the Hoover Institution published Robert Collins and Peter Duignan's *Americans in Africa: A Preliminary Guide to American Missionary Archives and Library Manuscript Collections on Africa*, which described fifty-two Protestant and Catholic missionary archives and forty-seven private and public library manuscript collections and cited only records and papers of Americans who went to Africa. In 1967 the Institution published Peter Duignan's extremely valuable 234-page *Handbook of American Resources for African Studies*, which, though incomplete, attempts to describe all materials relevant to African studies. Descriptions are given of the holdings of ninety-five library and manuscript collections, mostly in colleges, universities and historical societies; 108 church and missionary libraries and archives; ninety-five art and ethnographic collections (mostly in museums and private collections); and four business archives. The Institution's project to make a survey of the Africa-related materials in the National Archives has been merged with a larger, more scientific survey than Duignan's *Handbook*; this new survey is already under way.

The African Studies Association received a grant from the Ford Foundation in 1963 to prepare a descriptive *National African Guide* to African-related archival and manuscript sources in the United States covering the entire continent of Africa and the coastal islands, and having no chronological limits. The Association and the Archivist of the United States, at the National Archives and Records Services, are responsible for this project, which will cover materials in American government agencies, commercial concerns, religious and missionary groups and other noncommercial agencies. Materials of private individuals will be covered if they are in a depository. Morris Rieger of the National Archives will prepare the guide, which will also serve as the United States national volume of the projected *Guide to the Sources of African History* (outside of Africa) sponsored by the International Council of Archives.

Warren M. Robbins, founder and director of the Museum of African Art in Washington, D.C., brought out in 1966 his very useful survey *African Art in American Collections*, with the assistance of Robert H. Simmons. This big book, with text and 347 photographs, covers the African

A reading class at the Anacostia Neighborhood Museum of the Smithsonian Institution, which specializes in Black history and culture.

tribal sculpture in American museums and private collections.

The African Studies Association's *African Studies Bulletin*, over its eleven years of publication, has carried articles from time to time on the special collections of African materials in the Africana Section of the Library of Congress, in the many universities such as Northwestern, Boston University and Howard, in the National Archives and the U.S. Department of State, in the Schomburg Collection of the New York Public Library and in the theological seminaries. The *Bulletin* has also carried an annual listing and description of all the academic African studies centers, with their programs, in the many American universities. The latest listing by Norman R. Bennett in the April 1968 number covers forty-five pages.

American Public Library Holdings on the United States Negro

We now turn to American library holdings on the United States Negro, discussing, first of all, the public libraries.

There are many Negro collections in libraries open to the public. The Schomburg Collection of Negro Literature and History, a branch of the New York Public Library, consists of forty-five to fifty thousand volumes (with some 50 per cent about Africa), art objects, musical recordings, photographs, prints, sheet music, manuscripts, scrapbooks, pamphlets, playbills, programs, newspaper clippings, magazine articles, Negro newspaper files (mostly on microfilm) and Negro periodicals. The basis of the Schomburg Collection was the large, important private library on the Negro collected by Arthur A. Schomburg (1874–1938), a Puerto Rican of African descent who lived in New York City. A Harlem citizens' committee persuaded the Carnegie Corporation in 1926 to buy Schomburg's library for the New York Public Library and place it in a branch in the heart of Harlem.

The Schomburg Collection contains rare books and pamphlets; manuscripts of slavery; manuscripts on the West Indies; manuscripts of Alexander Crummell, John E. Bruce and the Citizens' Protective League; the Booker T. Washington correspondence with F. S. Garrison; some Leigh Whipper material; the Hiram Revels papers; the John B. Rayner papers (on microfilm); the papers of Christian Abraham Fleetwood, a free Negro Civil War major and worker in the Freedmen's Bureau and the Freedmen's Savings and Trust Company; some letters of Ira Aldridge, William Stanley Braithwaite and Richard T. Greener; many Civil War papers; some Paul Laurence Dunbar manuscripts; the William Pickens papers; files of the Civil Rights Congress and the National Negro Congress; the Paul Robeson papers (restricted); about half of the files of Friendship House, a long-time, now defunct, Catholic settlement house in Harlem; the papers of Bessye J. Bearden, a former Harlem community leader; the papers of the musical Spiller family; the eighty-one volumes of manuscripts and field notes that Gunnar Myrdal's *An American Dilemma* is based on; the Francis L. Broderick notes on the W. E. B. Du Bois papers; the Harry A. Williamson Collection of Negro Masonry; the Lyons family papers (Williamson's family); Pauli Murray's family papers (mostly on microfilm); some letters and unpublished manuscripts of Langston Hughes (second depository); Yale Professor R. W. Winks' research notes and documents on the Negro in Canada; the manuscripts of Claude McKay and others; galleys of many books; the National Association of Colored Graduate Nurses material; the Bert Williams scrapbooks; the Rose McClendon scrapbooks; Earl Conrad's Harriet Tubman collection; Stetson Kennedy's Ku Klux Klan material; and the Federal Writers' Project's Negroes of New York material. There is a *Calendar of the Manuscripts in the Schomburg Collection*, done in 1942 by the Historical Records Survey of the Works Projects Administration, which is an old, incomplete listing of the manuscripts there. The big, nine-volume *Dictionary Catalog of the Schomburg Collection of Negro Literature and History* was published by G. K. Hall in Boston in 1962; a two-volume supplement was added in 1967. Mrs. Jean Blackwell Hutson has been curator of the Schomburg Collection for twenty years.

The New York Public Library's Library of the Performing Arts has material on the Negro in music, theatre, dance and the films, and its Reference Department contains a huge amount of United States Negro material in its special collections. Mrs. Aubrey Bowser's T. Thomas Fortune scrapbook (1879–1914), microfilmed by the New York Public Library, has not been located recently. Other materials in the Reference Department are those on slavery and antislavery and the Manuscript Division's several thousand letters of Pierre Toussaint (the Santo Domingo free Negro who became famous in New York City), as well as the scrapbooks of the late New York City African model Maurice Hunter.

The Library of Congress also has a tremendous amount of United States Negro material scattered through its special collections. It also has a Folk Archives of Negro folk songs and tales, the Daniel Murray Collection of Negro authors, and the Federal Writers' Project's material, which includes thousands of slave narratives and much state and city material. (B. A. Botkin's *Lay My Burden Down: A Folk History of Slavery* [1945] and Julius Lester's *To Be a Slave* [1968] are drawn from this slave narrative material.) In the Manuscript Division there are the papers of Booker T. Washington (see E. Franklin Frazier's "The Booker T. Washington Papers," *Quarterly Journal*, February 1945); the NAACP papers; the papers of Carter G. Woodson, Mary Church Terrell and Robert H. Terrell, James G. Birney, and Matthew C. Perry; Rev. Daniel Coker's *Journal*; the papers of the American Colonization Society; the Robert Todd Lincoln collection of the Abraham Lincoln papers (1790–1916: 194 vols.); the papers of Moorfield Storey, one of the white founders of the NAACP; the Lewis Tappan antislavery letters; the Fulham and Lambeth Palace collections; the papers of the Society for the Propagation of the Gospel in Foreign Parts; the papers of Dr. Bray's Associates; and the proceedings of various British antislavery societies.

There is important historical material on the United States Negro in the National Archives, such as: material on the suppression of the African slave trade; War Records Office material on the Negro in the military service of the United States, including Congressional Medal of Honor files; Freedmen's Bureau files; full records of the U.S. Senate; material on Ku Klux Klan investigations and the Negro press. (See also Harold T. Pinkett's "Recent Federal Archives as Sources for Negro History," *Negro History Bulletin*, December 1967.)

The papers of the Harmon Foundation of New York City, an organization that helped and promoted American Negro and African artists from the 1920's until the 1960's when it terminated its activities, went to the Smithsonian Institution in Washington. The very important Frederick Douglass papers, which were originally in the Frederick Douglass Memorial Home in Anacostia, D.C., are now stored by the National Park Service in Washington.

The Detroit Public Library has the E. Azalia Hackley Memorial Collection of Negro Music, Dance and Drama. This collection was presented to the Detroit Public Library by the Detroit Musicians Association in 1943, as a memorial to Mme. E. Azalia Hackley, a pioneer Negro music educator and concert singer who died in Detroit in 1923. The George Cleveland Hall Branch of the Chicago Public Library has a special collection by and about Negroes which is now thirty-five or forty years old. The Paul Cuffe papers are now deteriorating in boxes in the New Bedford (Massachusetts) Library. The papers of the Congress of Racial Equality are in the library of the State Historical Society of Wisconsin, in Madison, as are the papers (1954–1964) of Rev. Milton A. Galamison, the civil rights and education leader of New York City. The Benjamin "Pap" Singleton scrapbook is in the library of the Kansas State Historical Society, in Topeka. John Brown letters and manuscripts are in many libraries and state historical societies' collections.

There is material on Negro pioneers and explorers and similar subjects in several of the libraries of the state historical societies and state archives of the Western and Far Western states —and also at the New York Historical Society. The Paul Laurence Dunbar papers are at the Ohio Historical Society Library in Columbus. There is Negro material in the Boston Athenaeum. The William Monroe Trotter papers are at the Congregational Library in Boston. The Boston Public Library has the papers of the abolitionists Parker, Garrison, Child, May and Phelps, and others. The Charles Sumner papers are at the Chicago Historical Society. The minutes of meetings of the Freedmen's Aid and Southern Education Society of the Methodist Church, North, are at the Methodist Board of Education in Nashville. The A. Philip Randolph papers are at the

A. Philip Randolph Institute, headed by Bayard Rustin, in New York City. A small Carter G. Woodson Memorial Library is in the Queensboro Public Library central building in Jamaica, New York City. The George Edmund Haynes Memorial Library is in the Mount Vernon Public Library, Mount Vernon, New York.

United States University Library Holdings on the American Negro

The universities also have many holdings in this field. The Moorland-Spingarn Collection at Howard University, Washington, D.C., is the largest. It is basically the extensive Lewis Tappan antislavery collection, given to Howard University in 1873, plus former Howard trustee Jesse Edward Moorland's gifts in 1914 and 1940 of his large private Negro collection of books, pamphlets, engravings, portraits, manuscripts, curios, pictures and clippings. Organized as a research library in 1930, this collection has been augmented by purchases and gifts and has been greatly expanded (especially in the field of African materials). The Works Projects Administration brought out in 1939 "A Catalogue of Books in the Moorland Foundation" (mimeographed).

The over-seven-thousand-item Arthur B. Spingarn collections of Negro authors and Negro music were purchased and added to the Moorland Collection in 1946. Spingarn has explained how he assembled the collection of Negro authors in a valuable 1937 Negro History Week address, "Collecting a Library of Negro Literature" (*Journal of Negro Education*, January 1938). He has also published an annual annotated bibliography of Negro authors all over the world in the NAACP's *Crisis* magazine over the last thirty-two years. Spingarn has continued to add new and old works (about a thousand annually) to his collection since 1946. Howard University published a descriptive brochure of the Spingarn Collection of Negro authors in the 1940's, soon after it was purchased.

The Moorland Collection also contains the papers of the following: James T. and John Rapier; Kelly Miller; Alain Locke; George L. Ruffin; Blanche K. Bruce; P. B. S. Pinchback; Joel E. Spingarn, an early chairman of the NAACP board of directors; Dr. Louis T. Wright; the Grimké family; Mordecai Johnson; E. Franklin Frazier; Marian Anderson. Judge J. Waties Waring's collection of albums on civil rights is in the collection, as are some Leigh Whipper papers and the four volumes of John Mercer Langston clippings. Holdings now are more than 95,000 catalogued and recorded items, including: books, pamphlets, periodicals, newspapers, manuscripts, photographs, clippings, musical compositions, phonograph records and microfilm.

The Negro Collection of Fisk University in Nashville absorbed the collection of the defunct Y.M.C.A. graduate school in Nashville many years ago and became, with additional gifts and purchases, one of the strongest libraries in the South for the study of the Negro. Some of its outstanding holdings are the John Mercer Langston papers; the George Gershwin music collection; the Charles S. Johnson papers (1893–1956: 13 vols.); the Charles W. Chesnutt papers; the John Hope papers; the J. C. Napier papers; the W. E. B. Du Bois library (over two thousand volumes), together with some rare manuscripts and files acquired in the fall of 1961 by the then librarian of Fisk University, Arna Bontemps, when Dr. Du Bois went to Ghana to work on the multi-volume *Encyclopedia Africana*. The rest of Dr. Du Bois' library, along with some of his papers, is in Ghana. About thirty thousand pieces of the manuscript material of Negro novelist and poet Jean Toomer have been deposited in the Fisk Negro Collection under the terms of Toomer's will (he died in 1967). A part of the Alfred Stieglitz Collection of paintings, sculpture and other works of art is at Fisk. A catalogue of the Stieglitz collection was published many years ago. The American Missionary Association Archives (1839–1879), with more than 250,000 manuscripts and containing Negro material, are also at Fisk.

The Negro Collection of the Trevor-Arnett Library at Atlanta University, Atlanta, Georgia, has been built up over the last twenty-three years. After the death of the Negro writer Countee Cullen in 1946, the late Harold Jackman started the Countee Cullen Memorial Collection at Atlanta University; it consists largely of materials on the Negro in writing, drama, painting and music and includes some Leigh Whipper material, which was added later. A committee in New York City has continued to add to this collection since the death of Harold Jackman some years ago. In 1946 Atlanta University purchased the private collection of Henry P. Slaughter of Washington, D.C. This collection, consisting of fifteen thousand items, contains many pamphlets and prints. It was at this time that the Negro Collection was established as a separate department. The Atlanta University Library also has some papers of Thomas Clarkson, a leading British abolitionist.

Yale University Library has the James Weldon Johnson Memorial Collection of Negro Arts and Letters donated by Carl Van Vechten in the early 1940's. Opened in 1950, it consists largely of manuscripts, typescripts, letters, photographs and autographed copies of works by contemporary American Negro authors. It was the first depository of the letters and manuscripts of the late Langston Hughes. It contains the papers of James Weldon Johnson; New York businessman John B. Nail; Carl Van Vechten (white); and many other Negro authors. This is the country's largest collection of Negro arts and letters of the twentieth century.

Morris A. Soper, who was a trustee of Morgan State College, Baltimore, left a grant for the purchase of books for a Negro collection at the college. The result is the large Morris A. Soper Library or Negro Collection at Morgan State College, which has, among other things, the Emmett J. Scott Collection of papers (about three thousand pieces on the history of the Negro from 1900 to 1951) and the Matthew Henson Collection donated by Herbert Frisby of Baltimore.

There is an old, sizable Negro collection in the library at Tuskegee Institute in Alabama. Tuskegee also has the material in the Department of Records and Research, founded in 1908 by Monroe N. Work, who compiled and published nine editions of the *Negro Year Book* from 1912 to 1938. Work died in 1945, and Jessie P. Guzman brought out two more editions of the *Negro Year Book*, in 1947 and in 1952. The George Washington Carver Museum, set up in 1938 and containing Dr. Carver's scientific discoveries and art productions, is also at Tuskegee. This museum was damaged by fire some years ago.

The George Foster Peabody Collection on the Negro, in the Huntington Memorial Library at Hampton Institute, Hampton, Virginia, is also a large, old library. It contains a magnificent collection of several hundred scrapbooks of clippings on almost every conceivable subject for the years 1898–1920.

Columbia University, in New York, has the Alexander Gumby Collection on the Negro. This consists of valuable scrapbooks compiled by the New York Negro Gumby over many decades and sold to Columbia some years ago. Columbia University also has the J. G. Phelps Stokes Collection. Texas Southern University, Houston, has the Charles F. Heartman Negro Collection. A catalogue of the Heartman Collection was published a few years ago. The Mary McLeod Bethune documents and private papers are at Bethune-Cookman College, Daytona Beach, Florida, an institution which Mrs. Bethune founded. Joseph Charles Price, the founder of Livingstone College, Salisbury, North Carolina, has his papers there. Delaware State College, near Dover, has a Negro collection in its library. Harvard University, the University of Chicago, the University of Michigan and other white universities also have good collections on the Negro.

Half of the files of the now closed Friendship House, a Harlem settlement house, are at Roosevelt University, Chicago, or the University of Chicago. Bishop Reverdy C. Ransom's papers are at Wilberforce University, Wilberforce, Ohio. The Hallie Q. Brown Negro Collection, named for the outstanding Negro teacher and elocutionist at Wilberforce University, is at Central State University, Wilberforce, Ohio.

The Richard Wright papers are at Kent State University, Kent, Ohio (see *Richard Wright: Letters to Joe C. Brown,* Occasional Paper No. 1, Kent State University Libraries). The Martin Luther King, Jr., papers are at Boston University, in Boston, but will be moved to the Martin Luther King, Jr., Memorial, to be constructed on the Morehouse College campus in Atlanta.

Materials on the Negro in the Far West are found in the Henry E. Huntington Library and Art Gallery, San Marino, California, and in the libraries of the University of California at Berkeley, and of Stanford University, as well as in other university libraries in the area.

American Private Library Holdings on the United States Negro

There are many private holdings of the papers of important figures in Negro history. There are also good private Negro collections. The John C. Dancy papers are in the possession of John C. Dancy, Jr., of Detroit, and Mrs. Lillian Dancy Reid of Salisbury, North Carolina. Mrs. Mae Miller Sullivan of Washington, D.C., has some papers of her father Kelly Miller. Dr. Otelia Cromwell of Washington, D.C., has some papers of John W. Cromwell.

Mrs. Ida Cullen Cooper, the poet's widow, has the Countee Cullen papers in New York City. The W. C. Handy papers are in the possession of Mrs. W. C. Handy and of Handy's brother, in New Rochelle, New York, and Mount Vernon, New York, respectively.

Some George Edmund Haynes papers are held by Mrs. Olyve Jeter Haynes at her home in Mount Vernon, New York. They are being prepared for the Negro Collection at Fisk. Most of Dr. Haynes' papers are already in the James Weldon Johnson Memorial Collection of Negro Arts and Letters in the Yale University Library. The W. E. B. Du Bois papers are in the basement of Herbert Aptheker's home in Brooklyn, New York. Some Du Bois papers are also in Ghana and at Fisk University, as stated earlier. Aptheker's "The W. E. B. Du Bois Papers" (*Political Affairs*, March 1966) describes the papers as consisting of letters; manuscripts of his writings and speeches; his organizational manuscripts, and memoranda on movements and on periodicals he edited; book reviews; newspaper and periodical clippings; diaries; travel notes; memorabilia; photographs and other items.

The valuable Hall Johnson manuscripts and papers are at Hall Johnson's home in Harlem. The late New York African model Maurice Hunter's papers are in the hands of his son, who lives in Queens, New York. The Lewis H. Latimer papers are held by his descendants the Gerald Norman family in New York. Fred R. Moore's papers are in the possession of his daughter, in New York City. Some papers of Victoria Earle Matthews are held by her relative Mrs. Carolyne Williams of Queens, New York. The papers of George T. Downing, a pioneer Negro fighter for Civil War Negro troop equality and for school integration, and of Negro physician John V. DeGrasse, who served in the Civil War, are held by Rev. Howard Asbury in Jamaica, New York. Middleton A. Harris, author of *A Negro History Tour of Manhattan* (1968), has a large collection of old documents, manuscripts, photographs and other things on the Negro in New York and over the United States. Franklin D. Brower of New York City, a Negro and a former newspaper reporter, has a tremendous collection of basically newspaper clippings (over a million) and magazine articles on virtually all subjects relating to the Negro. Brower, the brother of reporter William Brower of the *Toledo Blade*, has files of the Brotherhood of Sleeping Car Porters (including many A. Philip Randolph papers) and of the American Negro Theatre in New York City during the 1940's.

Glen Carrington, a Negro social worker and long-time New York City connoisseur and devotee of the fine arts, whose knowledge is broad and deep, has a large, invaluable Negro collection that includes rare books, letters, old record albums and many other things. Clarence L. Holte, another New Yorker and an executive in the advertising firm of Batten, Barton, Durstine and Osborn, has a tremendous six-thousand-volume Negro collection with many rare books. He sells duplicates, and Johnson Reprint Corporation in New York City is reprinting a series of old volumes from the Holte collection. A catalogue of this collection was recently published.

Clarence S. Gee of Lockport, New York, and Boyd B. Stutler have good collections of John Brown manuscripts and materials. There are papers and records in the possession of the living descendants of Barzillai Lew, who fought in the Revolutionary War, Cyrus Bustill, Paul Robeson's great-great-grandfather, who supplied bread to the Revolutionary Army, Nat Turner, R. R. Wright, Sr., and R. R. Wright, Jr., Robert Smalls and many others. *Ebony*, the *Journal of Negro History* and, especially, the *Negro History Bulletin* have carried many articles about the outstanding Negro families, which have been based on family records held by the descendants.

Two children respond to the signs on a Harlem storefront church.

Black Religion—1968

Clifton F. Brown

I

THE DEATH of Dr. Martin Luther King and the publication of *The Black Messiah* (Sheed and Ward, Inc., 1968) by Rev. Albert B. Cleage, Jr.—the former representing the end of a dream, the latter heralding a new hope: these two events, more than any others in 1968, represented points of departure for Black religion in the United States. Dr. King, the apostle of nonviolence and the symbol of the Negro's struggle for admittance to the mainstream of the American experience, had held firm to his vision that Black and white Americans could and must live in harmony. Once again, Dr. King was planning to demonstrate that nonviolence could successfully attack structural racism and provide a valid alternative to violence. During December 1967, King's energies were directed toward another march on Washington. The Poor People's Campaign, as the projected march was designated, would either represent the reaffirmation of nonviolence as the vehicle of change or it would represent the swan song of nonviolence as a means and of total integration as the goal of the civil rights movement. April was chosen as the month in which the march was to take place, and the preparations included the involvement of not only Blacks but also other ethnic minorities, as well as poor whites.

In March 1968, King's attention was diverted from the planned march to the more immediate problem of a garbage strike in Memphis, Tennessee. On March 28, Dr. King, in support of the strike, led his last march. Ironically this march, led by the champion of nonviolence, ended as a full-scale riot. Looting and the smashing of windows, death and injury, all followed. Shaken and depressed, King flew to Atlanta, but he returned to Memphis on April 3 to lead a second march. On the following day, Thursday, April 4, in the late afternoon, Martin Luther King was shot. Dr. King died a few hours later. He was thirty-nine years old. The senseless assassination of Dr. King was tragic—as is the death of any man. Yet for Blacks and all other Americans the real tragedy was just beginning. The violent death of Dr. King prompted more violence, and in over one hundred American cities the Black ghettoes erupted in a convulsion of rioting, arson and looting. It was the end of the dream—and the dream was not to be recaptured when the Poor People's Campaign finally arrived in Washington.

Young Black militants were demanding more direct and forceful means to ameliorate the Black man's plight in America. New concepts, often diametrically opposed to King's concepts of Christian love, nonviolence and integration, surfaced in the Black community. "We shall overcome" was being replaced as a slogan with such phrases as "Black is beautiful" and "We are not the Black minority but the chosen few." A social movement was turning into a holy cause. With the publication of Cleage's *The Black Messiah*, the "religiocification" of the revolution began in earnest. The religious slave mentality attitude of "pie in the sky someday" was being ousted, or at least challenged, by a new religious orientation that, among other things, emphasized a Black Messiah, the concept of a Black Nation as a chosen people and the recapture of the revolutionary imperative in Christianity. The demand for integration into white society, including the white church, was giving way to the demand for separation. Two concepts, one symbolized by Dr. King's unfailing belief in universal brotherhood and redemptive suffering and the other symbolized by Cleage's annunciation of a Black theology; two peoples, Black and white; two worlds, the ghetto and suburbia—against this background the events in Black religion unfolded in 1968.

II

The foundation of Black religion in America, conceived as it was against a background of slavery and segregation, provided the Black man with the opportunity to be free while still in chains. Black religion produced a gospel of future hope and a theology of the suffering servant. Yet Black religion was also a protest movement —a protest against a system and a society that were deliberately designed to demean the dignity of a segment of God's creation.

In the Negro spirituals one can see both the qualities of a gospel of a future hope and the expression of protest against the evils of slavery. No other spiritual illustrated both of these tendencies better than the familiar "When Israel Was in Egypt's Land." The expression of protest is sounded in the first few lines:

> When Israel was in Egypt's land,
> Let my people go,
> Oppressed so hard they could not stand,
> Let my people go.
>
> Go down, Moses,
> 'Way down in Egypt's land,
> Tell old Pharaoh
> To let my people go.

Several lines later, a future hope of freedom is expressed. Although this is couched in physical or political terms, it was no more than a symbol of the hope of a complete union with God in a blissful Kingdom of Heaven:

> No more shall they in bondage toil,
> Let my people go,
> Let them come out with Egypt's spoil,
> Let my people go.

The theme of future hope was even more pronounced in the spiritual "Heaven":

> I got a robe,
> You got a robe,
> All God's children got a robe.
> When we get to heaven
> Goin' to put on our robe
> And goin' to walk all over God's heaven.

The expression of protest and future hope became institutionalized with the formation of the Negro churches. The first independent Negro church, the African Methodist Episcopal Church, was formed as a result of a meeting called by Richard Allen in 1816. In 1820 the African Methodist Episcopal Zion Church severed all connections with the white Methodist Church and became a separate church.

The Negro Baptist Church did not become an active force in Black religious life until after the Civil War. Within all of these churches, the slave heritage of future hope and of protest had been carried on. However, as memories of slavery faded and as the Negro churches increasingly reflected their white counterparts, the protest tradition receded into the background. In the 1950's, however, with the emergence of Dr. Martin Luther King and with the growing prominence of the Southern Christian Leadership Conference, much of the protest tradition was recovered. And the form it now took was that of nonviolent protest. The freedom that had been voiced in the spirituals was identified with integration—with equality. When integration failed to become a reality, the protest began to take on more revolutionary dimensions. Essentially, the Negro church was faced with the question of whether the church would maintain a more traditional approach to the protest movement or whether it would attempt to remold its position in the light of the Black power movement.

Within the traditional Negro churches (the African Methodist Episcopal Church; the African Methodist Episcopal Zion Church; the Christian Methodist Church; the National Baptist Convention of America; the National Baptist Convention, U.S.A., Inc.; the Progressive Baptist Convention of America), 1968 seemed to be the year that crystallized the question of how these denominations could best relate to and identify with the plight of the Black man in America. Though the final solution was, and is, elusive, the alternatives seemed relatively clear. The first was the pursuit of the traditional modes of theological and liturgical expression and the continued advocacy of integration and nonviolence. The second was the creation of a Black theology and the support of radical or even revolutionary methods of achieving social change. Needless to say, various positions representing a combination of these two were also found. But these first two alternatives have represented the two extremes around which the great debate has centered.

Speaking before an audience of some fifteen thousand delegates at the eighty-eighth annual session of the National Baptist Convention, Inc., in Atlanta, Dr. J. H. Jackson, president of the convention, defended the traditional approach of Negro churches to the civil rights problem. Comparing Black militants to the Ku Klux Klan, Dr. Jackson lamented the rejection of integration by many Blacks as the most tragic loss in the history of the civil rights struggle. Dr. Jackson, an opponent of the principle of civil disobedience, further observed that because of the rejection of the concept of complete integration, the Negro is now viewed as "one of the most dangerous threats to the orderly conduct and growth of American life."

Dr. Gardner C. Taylor, retiring president of the Progressive Baptist Convention, during the closing session of their convention in Washington, D.C., in September, challenged the delegates to search for the kernel of reality or truth in the separatist movement in the Black community. Dr. Taylor raised the question of whether there might not be some validity in the separatist tendencies of young Blacks, and suggested that the separatist movement might "provide an awareness of the Black man's particular and peculiar spiritual genius." In the course of his address Taylor linked the United States' involvement in Vietnam with the problems of poverty and racism in America. Throughout his speech Taylor questioned the comfortable concepts, outdated attitudes and ineffective practices of American Christians and challenged his audience to seek new and creative responses to the many social, economic and spiritual problems facing the Black American.

Bishop Herbert B. Shaw of the African Methodist Episcopal Zion Church, speaking at one of the sessions of the National Committee of Black Churchmen, in St. Louis in November 1968, dramatically and eloquently stated that the Negro church must seek new directions in the future if it is to remain relevant to the Black community and true to its God. One of the suggestions made by Bishop Shaw was that the Black church identify itself more closely with its African heritage. The Bishop stated, "We must emphasize more about Egypt than that the Hebrews stayed there. We must seek out our brothers in all of Asia and Africa. We must rediscover the truth concerning the descendants of Hagar's son Ishmael as well as those of Sarah's son Isaac for both are sons of Abraham."

Somewhere between the position of Dr. Jackson on the one hand and the positions of Dr. Taylor and Bishop Shaw on the other, were the majority of the members of the Negro church. For them 1968 was a year of uncertainty. The untimely death of Dr. King raised many doubts, not only about the efficacy of nonviolence as a strategy and integration as an end, but also about the function and ethos of the Negro church. Regretfully, a fear was present that to articulate doubt of the effectiveness of traditional Black religion would lead to the complete radicalization of the church and the rejection of all familiar and time-honored practices. This often resulted in an increased, if sporadic, involvement in social action without a critical and meaningful re-evaluation of the role the Negro church was to play in the future of the Black revolution.

The year also saw a growing interest in what might be called the underground, or forgotten, Black church—the storefront church. Whatever their denomination (Pentecostal, Holiness, Baptist, etc.), these churches have been found in ghettoes in all American cities, are usually identified with the socio-economic background of their membership. These religious bodies have been a stabilizing influence in the ghettoes. This influence probably stems from the fact that these churches were organized entirely by Blacks and have been close enough to their communicants to be able to minister to their personal needs. Generally, storefront churches have a membership of perhaps fifty or less, and more often than not their pastor has been self-ordained.

These churches also often serve the social needs of their members. Many storefront churches have established impromptu day-care centers for children and have collected food and clothing for anyone in need in the community. One pastor of a storefront church in Washington, D.C., summed up the role of such churches in this way: "Many of the people in the community feel they have been forsaken. Many tell you, 'What's the use, nobody cares about me.' Lots of times the smaller churches can reach them when the larger churches can't because the smaller churches are more down-to-earth in a way the people understand."

III

If the traditional Negro churches have had doubts as to how to respond to the growing militancy and separatism in the Black community, such hesitancy was apparently lacking for the Black communicants of the so-called "white" churches. Perhaps this difference of attitude lies in the fact that in the traditional Negro churches the power structure has always been Black, and if their modes of worship, their theology and attitude toward social action reflected traditional Christianity, it has been at least through their own choice. In the case of Black communicants of white churches, however, their mode of worship and their theology have reflected a system imposed on them by a hierarchy in which their race has often not been represented, and by a laity of which they have constituted a minority. For the Black clergy in predominantly white denominations, the problem of racism has been most obvious. Often Black clergymen have a second-class status. They often earn less than their white colleagues, and generally they are kept with Black congregations, and in the hierarchies they are relegated, if included at all, to token positions. Perhaps most significant is the charge raised by Black clergymen that the white church has been more concerned with protecting the interests of the middle class than with its ministry to the poor.

Partly because of inability to accomplish much within the regular channels of these churches and partly in response to a growing sense of Black identity, "Black power" began to emerge in white churches in 1967. By early 1968 an unofficial Black caucus had even been formed in the Roman Catholic Church.

The real significance and potential resulting from the formation of these Black caucuses did not really become obvious until the meeting of the Second Annual Committee of Black (formerly Negro) Churchmen in St. Louis, October 29 through November 1, 1968. Present were leaders of all the traditional Negro churches as well as the various Black caucuses: the Black Catholic Clergy Caucus, representing fifty-seven of the nation's 130 Black Catholic priests; Black Churchmen of the American Baptist Convention; the Coordinating Committee of Black Lutheran Clergymen, formed in May by fifty-six of the eighty-two Black ministers in America's major Lutheran branches; the Black Caucus of the Unitarian-Universalist Association; Black Methodists for Church Renewal, representing three hundred Black ministers, laymen and bishops; members of the United Presbyterian Church and the interdenominational Association for Black Seminarians.

The radicalization within the membership of the committee was evident in the topics and tones of the three hundred or so delegates as they discussed many issues in denominational caucuses, workshops and general sessions. St. Louis alderman Joseph W. B. Clark seemed to capture the mood of the delegates when he said, "We must now reverse this machinery and become Black missionaries to the white community, because the Negro problem is not the problem; the problem is the white community."

The separatist tendencies manifested at the St. Louis meeting were the result of the growing cynicism of the delegates toward white Christian response to the needs and aspirations of the Black churchmen. Many delegates expressed the opinion that there was no justification for Black churchmen participating in predominately white churches if those churches were not willing to involve themselves in the plight of Black people. Hayward Henry, president of the Black Unitarian Caucus, clearly indicated the possibility of a separatist movement: "Black churchmen are putting white churches on notice that old paternalistic relationships will not continue. Black people can't stay in mainly white denominations if those groups can't begin to deal with racism and distribution of power. Yes, it is still an open question, but if whites don't answer positively, it could look pretty bad."

Pressures brought by the caucuses within their denominations met with varying degrees of success. The general assembly of the Unitarian-Universalist Association, meeting in late May in Cleveland, voted its Black Affairs Council a budget of $1 million for the next four years. The caucus will receive $250,000 each year and will decide how the money is to be spent. The Methodist Church in October set aside $46,000 for Negro church aid. In May 1968 the Protestant Episcopal Church approved grants totaling $553,497 to twenty-eight community organizations that represented the interests of minority peoples.

Dr. Cleage's church, the Shrine of the Black Madonna, a congregation of the United Church of Christ, has illustrated two growing tendencies of Black congregations in predominately white denominations. The Shrine has shown an almost complete freedom in adapting the traditional symbols of worship to its own needs. For example, above the altar a Black Madonna and child are depicted in a thirty-foot-high mural. Perhaps more significantly, the Shrine has actively engaged itself in the concerns of the community. The congregation has opened a cooperative supermarket, a clothing center catering to Afro-American clothing, and a gasoline station.

The year not only witnessed the mushrooming of the Black caucus movement, but also saw Black caucus strategy move beyond national and denominational dimensions. The formation of the Association of Black Seminarians and the caucus of the Fourth Assembly of the World Council of Churches had broad implications for Blacks within predominantly white religious structures. Black seminarian caucuses, beginning at Princeton Seminary, quickly spread to many Northeastern theological schools. One such caucus, the Black Seminarians of Greater Boston, sponsored the Consultation on the Black Church which was held at Boston University School of Theology on November 6–9, 1968. The consultation, which was national in scope, gave Black seminarians at predominantly white schools an opportunity to examine in depth some of the presuppositions that undergird theology in the Black church and to discuss how curricula at predominantly white seminaries could better relate to Black institutions—historically, theologically and sociologically.

On July 17, 1968, at the fourth assembly of the World Council of Churches, meeting in Uppsala, Sweden, Bishop Joseph H. Johnson, speaking for the Black caucus, rose to protest that only two Blacks were among the twenty-one Americans nominated to the council's policy-making central committee. Four Black clergymen chosen by the caucus were proposed as substitutes for whites on the list.

The climate for such a move by Bishop Johnson had been set the preceding day, when Black novelist James Baldwin addressed the 2,200 delegates and visitors attending the council. Indicting the Church for its racist tendencies and perversion of the teachings of Christ, Baldwin warned, "If you are born under the circumstances in which Black people are born, the destruction of the Christian churches, as presently constituted, may not only be desirable but necessary." Though Baldwin's remarks offended some delegates, others, at the conclusion of his speech, gave him a standing ovation.

Determined not to be overtaken by the events occurring in Black Protestant circles and feeling that their Church had failed to deal adequately with the needs, particularly in ghetto areas, of Black people, the Black Catholic Clergy Caucus, composed of priests attending the unofficial Catholic clergy conference on the interracial apostolate in Detroit in mid-April of 1968, denounced the Catholic Church in the United States as "primarily a white racist institution." The caucus, in a list of demands, asked that efforts be increased to recruit Negroes for the priesthood and that a department be established to deal with the Church's role in the Black people's struggle for freedom. This type of militant stance by Black Catholic clergy was not an isolated incident but in fact represented a trend. As early as February, seven Black priests in the Roman Catholic Archdiocese of Chicago had charged that the Church had followed rather than led the demands for the fulfillment of legitimate Black aspirations. In the paper stating their position, the priests made recommendations which were similar to the demands of the Black priests attending the Detroit conference.

Even within the Roman Catholic religious orders, generally the last organs of the Catholic Church to feel the impact of social change, Black consciousness made itself felt. Indicative of this new spirit was the First National Black Sisters' Conference held at Mt. Mercy College in Pittsburgh. The week-long conclave was attended by some 150 Black nuns from seventy-six religious communities. The nuns, often wearing "I am proud to be Black" buttons, sought to determine their responsibility to their fellow Blacks, to their church and to their individual religious communities.

IV

Among the most ominous developments in race relations in 1968 were the charges and countercharges of anti-Semitism and white racism that were hurled by Black militants and Jews at each other. New York City became the focal point of the growing tensions between Black militants and Jews, although such tensions existed in practically every major American city. Many reasons have been given for this. Fear resulting from competition between Jews and Blacks for dominance in local neighborhoods has been viewed as one cause. Another possible factor has been the growing presence of Blacks in such fields as social work and teaching, fields which have attracted large numbers of Jews. Because of the practice of compensatory hiring to benefit Blacks, Jews have found themselves threatened economically.

Another important consideration is the fact that many Southern Blacks, like many conservative white Protestants, have had a Fundamentalist Christian background. Indicative of this type of background was the concept of the Jews as a people guilty of deicide. Supplementing this heritage has been the fact of economic resentment. In ghetto after ghetto, the storekeeper, the welfare worker and the landlord have been Jewish. In some instances, the Jewish merchant and landlord have been guilty of overpricing merchandise and of rent exploitation. For many Blacks, these men have not been viewed as merely individuals but often as "Jew landlord" and "Jew merchant." The obvious consequence is that the hatred of an individual has been transformed into a hatred of a race.

Finally, as more Black militants identified with the Muslim religion, there came the traditional Muslim hostility toward the Jew. This tendency was seen when many militants supported the Arabs in their war with Israel.

The tension between Blacks and Jews broke into the open over the decentralization of the Ocean Hill-Brownsville school district in New York. After several Jewish teachers were transferred from their local school, the United Federation of Teachers, comprised largely of Jewish teachers, called a strike. The result was a thirty-six day boycott of classes in three separate city-wide walkouts. Negro parents of school children reacted vigorously, denouncing the striking teachers as "Jew pigs" and carrying signs calling Hitler the "Messiah."

These tensions have troubled both Jewish and Black leaders. Black clergymen have been particularly active in the attempt to heal the breach between their community and the Jewish community. In December 1968, in New York, thirteen Black ministers issued a statement in which they said: "We decry and denounce any statements emanating from the black community that bear the slightest hint of anti-Semitism. Any word of this kind in no way reflects the attitude of our people. Any person who has concluded that a tide of anti-Semitism is sweeping the Black community is terribly naive." They went on to say that such statements were the product of "exploiters of a minute, minority point of view. . . ."

Later in the same week about two hundred rabbis and over twenty Black ministers from New York City met in an effort to establish an open dialogue between the two groups. In a joint statement issued after the meeting, Rev. Calvin O. Pressly, chairman of the Interfaith City-Wide Coordinating Committee against Poverty, and Rabbi Henry Siegman, executive vice-president of the Synagogue Council of America, observed that although the two communities often had diverse interests, such differences are "no cause for pain or alarm as long as we retain the ability to discuss these differences with one another and to work towards compromises which do not deny the fundamental hopes and aspirations of our respective communities."

V

The trends in Black religion in 1968 have indicated, by their nature, by their complexity and by the manner in which they have found expression, the problem areas or weaknesses of the Black religious experience in America. The most crucial of these areas has been denominationalism. This problem existed in both of the chief divisions of the Black church—the traditional Negro church and the Black membership of predominantly white churches.

The bulk of the Black laity belongs to the traditional Negro church bodies. The membership of these denominations comes from every economic, social and educational level of society. The broad spectrum from which the traditional Negro church draws its membership indicates both its ability to accommodate the diverse elements of Black society and its potential to act as spokesman for the Black community. Yet because of the nature of the Negro church, it speaks with many voices and, as with the tower of Babel, confusion and chaos everywhere abound. The Negro church will only be able to assume a forceful and meaningful leadership role in the Black community when it is able to speak with one voice.

It was among the Black membership (particularly the clergy) of mainly white churches that the most vocal element of Black religion was found in 1968. The Black caucuses were the agents of this. Yet these caucuses represented only two million of the twenty-two million Black church members in the United States. Consequently the indictments, the challenges and the innovative schemes of the Black caucuses lacked the broad power base by which they could have assumed a leadership role in Black religion. Furthermore, the Black caucuses, too, have often spoken in different voices, reflecting the sad fact that, as in the traditional Negro churches, denominationalism has created barriers which prevent concerted action on common problems.

The social and economic status of the Black membership of predominantly white denominations also prevents the caucuses from assuming a leadership role in the Black church. With the possible exception of the Roman Catholic Church, Black membership in these churches comes from the middle class, a minority group in the Black community. And although the middle class Black is interested in and concerned about the economic and social plight of his less fortunate Black brother, he is not always able to empathize completely with him. Even when he is able to empathize and to act constructively, the programs initiated often fail because the ghetto Black resents aid from someone he considers a deserter—the Black middle class person living in suburbia.

The significance of this, and the great challenge for 1969 and succeeding years, is that until the fragmentation in the Black church ceases, duplication of projects, competition between ingroups, misunderstanding, and confusion relating to methods and goals will continue. A unified leadership with the general backing of the Black community is the greatest need and the only hope for the survival of the Black church as a meaningful expression of the Black experience in America.

U.S. soldiers in Vietnam climb aboard air cushion vehicles as they set out to patrol an area in the Mekong Delta.

The Military and the Negro

Theodore D. Harris

THE MILITARY SERVICE rendered by Negroes in the armed forces of the United States during 1968 represented the continuing fulfillment of four goals sought by Black Americans since the first shot of the Revolutionary War. Over the years these goals encompassed the right to full participation in America's wars, opportunity for permanent careers in the armed forces, the chance to qualify for leadership positions, and racial integration within all the services.

The right to serve was more difficult to attain than one might realize today, when some young men, particularly affluent and educated whites, are trying to avoid military service. From as early as 1775, Negroes sought to illustrate their manhood and prove their loyalty to America by fighting in the nation's wars. In a sense, this urge was fulfilled when Black men were permitted to fight and die for their country in every war in America's history. However, considerable persuasion had to be exerted by Negro leaders and white progressive supporters to gain combat eligibility instead of hard labor status for Black troops in both the Civil War and World War I. During World War II, even more pressure was necessary to secure for Negroes the hazardous duty of fighter pilots. Another battle had to be waged in both World War II and the Korean War with the Navy. This was to ensure opportunity for dangerous combat and seamanship assignments, as well as skilled trades training, in place of blanket relegation to mess-boy duties.

Two racist myths made these struggles necessary. The first held the Black man—first as slave but later as citizen—to be so racially savage and culturally backward as to turn upon his white countryman the moment arms were placed in his inherently treacherous Black hands. The second myth portrayed this supposedly ferocious Black warrior as so inherent a coward as to break ranks and flee in panic whenever faced in combat by an enemy of his country. Both of these contradictory myths were proven false from the Battle of Bunker Hill to the most recent fire fight in Vietnam.

As to the second goal, it should be realized that a permanent career in the ranks of the military has always been sought by economically and culturally disadvantaged persons since ancient times throughout the world. This is still true in America today, despite the efforts of some economically and educationally privileged young whites to discredit the advantages of military service for anyone. Sometimes these young men do this in mere hope of avoiding the military experience themselves. Often they combine their rhetorical, and occasionally violent, attacks on the military with claims to be the white saviors of Black people from the evils of white racism. Throughout American history, however, the Negro has had to be more realistic about the advantages and disadvantages of military service whether temporary or permanent.

Military career opportunities for Black men are commonplace today. But until after the Civil War, the only Negroes accepted for enlistment in the regular peace-time Army were apparently light-skinned individuals who presented themselves at times and places where white recruits were lacking in sufficient number. The Navy accepted many Negro seamen until 1850. After that, however, their number was reduced under pressure from Southern congressmen who feared the seafaring life was an escape hatch for runaway slaves. During the manpower crisis of the Civil War, both the Union Navy and Army enlisted thousands of Negro seamen and soldiers. However, neither service envisioned a permanent place for them. After the war it would be many decades before the Navy permitted their few Negro (or Filipino, for that matter) enlistees to advance beyond menial duties aboard ship. It was in the post-Civil War Army that Black men finally achieved a recognized status as professional military men.

In 1867 Congress authorized the establishment of four regular Army regiments to be manned by Negro troops. These units compiled distinguished combat records throughout the Indian and Spanish-American Wars and the Philippine insurrection. Nineteen Congressional Medals of Honor were won by these Black professional soldiers. Although Army life in these regiments was racially segregated, and often arduous and hazardous, it afforded Black men a permanent career of equal pay for equal work with white men, including free medical care and retirement benefits. Such opportunities were not available to Negroes in other walks of American life for over half a century after the Civil War. Thus, until the turn of the century, the Army—sometimes maligned as a reactionary social institution—was still decades ahead of the rest of America in having to confront the nation's racial dilemma. In addition to providing economic security to thousands of Black men, it offered them the sense of masculine identity and pride which comes with performance of manly duties and with facing and achieving manly goals, regardless of skin coloration.

The successive shocks of World War II and the Korean War did much to improve the career status of Negroes in all the services. Manpower shortages, combined with justifiable demands for racial integration, especially shook the policies of the Navy, the Army Air Corps and the Marines. All of them not only made broader provisions for Negro enlistment on a career basis but also increased professional opportunities by opening all phases of their operations to Black personnel instead of restricting them to purely supportive functions.

Because of such progress, an increasingly large number of Negroes are now choosing enlisted careers in the professional military, despite the possibility of combat duty in Vietnam. The prospect of economic security is doubtless a major factor in such choices. But the chance for upward social mobility in a racially integrated environment is also of great importance. Even with a limited formal education a Negro can gain promotion as readily as a white man by demonstrating strength of character and mastery of practical military skills. With promotion, the Black man gains the rare opportunity of supervising other men, including white men. With all this comes the psychological satisfaction of performing a challenging masculine job, and a certain sense of belonging which is peculiar to military esprit de corps.

The third goal, leadership opportunity, presented an obviously delicate problem. It meant the possibility of Black men commanding white men. Today this problem is resolving itself under pressure from combat realities in Vietnam and from continued insistence by many Black and white Americans on equal advancement opportunities for individuals, irrespective of racial origins. Regretfully, attainment of such ethnic objectivity has required a near century of struggle, even in the pragmatically-oriented armed services.

The Army led the other services in the evolution of Black leadership. The noncommissioned officers in the segregated units, from 1867 to integration after World War II, were all Negroes. In those cases they commanded only fellow Blacks. But in Vietnam today, ebony sergeants command both Black and white in combat, and their invaluable leadership performances are praised by all races. The reality of combat needs has moved the Marine Corps to a position similar to that of the Army in the effective use of Negro noncommissioned officers.

Appointment of Black commissioned officers posed an even more difficult social problem historically for all the services than did the noncommissioned officer status. It meant not only white obedience to Black officers, but also the rendering of outward rituals of respect and deference required by military regulations, customs and etiquette—such as saluting and use of the term "Sir" as a form of address. One Negro officer did serve on a temporary basis in the Army as early as the Revolutionary War, as did several more during the Civil War. Officer candidate training and commissioning was more extensive in World War I, but only after insistence by civil rights groups. Somewhat less resistance to commissioning Negroes as officers was encountered by the time of World War II.

Permanent Army commissions on a regular career basis were made available to Negroes shortly after the Civil War. Naturally, the generally poor educational opportunities for Negroes made preparation for West Point an exceedingly arduous task. Added to this were the hurdles of the politically-oriented Congressional appointment process, and frequent social ostracism by white cadets after appointment to West Point had been achieved. However, a few young Negroes succeeded in overcoming all these handicaps. Beginning with Henry O. Flipper, five young Black men graduated from West Point during the racially bitter years from 1877 through 1941. Since 1943, however, Negro West Point graduates are no longer a rarity.

As the result of distinguished performances by Black soldiers in the Spanish-American War, several Negroes were commissioned in the regular Army without West Point attendance, beginning in 1901. Among these career officers raised from the ranks was Benjamin O. Davis, Sr., who, by 1940, had become the Army's first Negro brigadier general. In today's Army the number of Black commissioned officers is steadily increasing. The year 1968 saw Frederic E. Davison become the second Negro brigadier general in Army history. Furthermore, he was exercising the full combat command authority and responsibility of that high rank in Vietnam, rather than serving as a mere token of racial progress for public relations purposes.

At the start of World War II, commissions in the Army Air Corps for Negroes were severely limited because of certain traditional racialist beliefs. It was feared that Negroes lacked the aptitudes necessary for combat aircraft pilots. After some prodding from Black and white humanitarians, the Air Corps proffered its challenge to young Negroes. They responded by compiling an admirable record in aerial combat against their nation's enemies. When a separate Air Force emerged after the war, Negroes were able to qualify for leadership status with a minimum of racial barriers. From the rigors of World War II air combat came a fighter pilot who holds the highest rank of any Negro in American military history. He was the fourth Negro to graduate from West Point, and the first one to achieve that goal in this century. He is Lieutenant General Benjamin O. Davis, Jr., of the Air Force—the son of that first Black brigadier general of the Army.

Some Negroes won temporary commissions in the Navy during World War II. In 1949 Wesley A. Brown became the first Negro graduate of Annapolis. Today the Navy and the Marine Corps are expanding the number of their Black officers in both permanent and temporary categories.

The fourth goal, that of complete racial integration in all the services, has at last been attained. There had actually been considerable integration of Black and white troops in combat units during the Revolutionary War. But from the end of that first American war until the latter part of World War II, racial segregation was the general pattern in the ground, sea and air services. Only further historical research can tell us whether this segregationist trend was temporarily reversed in the Army and Navy from 1783 to 1861. During that period Negroes were apparently accepted for peacetime enlistment in either service, but on a somewhat undercover basis—partly because of the existence of slavery in America.

Toward the close of World War II, the Army experimented successfully with limited integration among some combat units. In 1948 President Harry Truman ordered total integration in all the armed forces. The effective performances of integrated fighting men in Korea proved to even the most skeptical minds that racial integration improved America's strength in defending herself. The same lesson is being proved daily now in Vietnam.

There are many possible explanations for the length of time before these four military goals of Black people were finally attained. Obviously, the perpetuation of Negro slavery through half of American history presented a hurdle for Black men that was surmountable only occasionally and on an individual basis. Even after emancipation, the low quality of education available to

Marine Corporal Kenneth W. Miller passes out candy to Vietnamese children.

Lieutenant General Benjamin O. Davis, Jr. (right), confers with (from left to right) Senior Master Sergeant John W. Johnson, Lieutenant Colonel John W. Daniels and Colonel Norman P. Phillips, in a recent visit to Southeast Asia.

most Negroes worked against their qualifying for either admission or advancement in the armed forces—just as it did in all other fields of endeavor. Added to this is the fact that historically the armed services have usually simply mirrored the state of racial discrimination prevalent in American society as a whole—except for the notable period of comparative Army progressiveness from 1867 to about 1901. (Perhaps one of the reasons for the Army's relative liberalism in such matters throughout the years grew from its greater need for manpower in comparison with the other services.) Finally, the influence of white Southerners in all the regular services has been quite potent historically. In the Army, for instance, fully one-third of all the career officers who reached the rank of brigadier general or above from 1898 through 1940 were natives of the eleven former Confederate states. In the enlisted ranks, the armed forces had always attracted a high proportion of their career recruits from Southern whites of limited economic, social and educational background. Fortunately, prejudices of geographical origin are rapidly diminishing today in all levels of rank in the services as the nation's educational standards advance and as more white Americans gain understanding of the Black man's problems.

During the year 1968, the entire military establishment accelerated its efforts to provide broader opportunities for Negroes and to improve its image in the eyes of the Black people of America.

Concerted efforts were made to recruit more Negro enlisted and officer personnel for the state National Guard units and the Organized Reserve components of all the services. In doing this, the military had to face the reality of growing hostility toward the National Guard on the part of some Black ghetto youths because of recent Guard participation in riot control actions. Balancing this hostility, however, were several practical factors. National Guard, or Reserve component membership, affords deferment from selective service. This fact is particularly meaningful for the future of those Black young men who may not desire a permanent career in the military. Most of them still lack the money and necessary educational preparation for college attendance, with its resulting student draft deferment privileges which are enjoyed by so many affluent and educationally fortunate white youths. Furthermore, there appears to be little likelihood that many Guard or Reserve units will be mobilized for Vietnam combat duty. Finally, participation provides badly needed supplemental income to disadvantaged young men.

Draft boards themselves drew the attention of civil rights leaders who agreed that Negroes had a moral and legal obligation to defend their country but who felt that too few Black citizens were represented on these potentially fatal tribunals. This was in support of President Johnson's 1967 appeal that all draft boards be more racially representative. By the middle of 1968, all the states except Mississippi had some Negroes on their draft boards. But even though the number of Negro members had tripled since the beginning of 1967, they still equaled only 4.6 percent of the nation's total draft board personnel. And young Black men have, admittedly, been heavily hit by draft calls. Lack of college deferment opportunities is, again, a factor here. Statistics for 1967, the latest figures available, indicate that the approximately 37,000 Negroes conscripted that year were 16.3 per cent of all men drafted, whereas Black men comprised only about 12 per cent of all draft-age males.

In 1968 the armed forces continued to place emphasis on expanding the career opportunities for Black men and also, now, for Black women. As to the latter, all the women's service branches hoped to attract a greater number of Negro young women for both enlisted and commissioned categories. The need was apparent in the Navy's WAVES, for instance, where only 4 per cent of the personnel were Negro. However, the women Marines could boast of 328 Black women out of 2,651 members, or approximately 12.4 per cent.

Despite some draft inequities, and despite the risks of combat in Vietnam, the military was continuing to prove a career choice for a great many Black men. By 1968 the reenlistment rate for Negroes was exceptionally high in all the services. In the Army Negroes reenlisted at a ratio three times that of white soldiers, while the Navy, Air Force and Marines reported a two-to-one "re-up" margin of Blacks over whites.

In 1968, too, the war in Vietnam triggered much discussion about the advantages and disadvantages of a volunteer professional Army in place of the somewhat discriminatory system of selective service. Richard Nixon advocated a volunteer Army during his successful campaign for the Unites States Presidency. Much of the support for the idea came from white critics of the draft, even though it was the Negro who was being drafted rather disproportionately. Critics of the plan among both races contended that the Negro's low economic status would result in a practically all-Black mercenary Army, while relieving more prosperous whites of the obligation of serving their country.

During the same year the armed forces did not neglect their obligation to provide means for Negroes to qualify as commissioned officers. All the services moved toward the establishment of additional Reserve Officers' Training Corps units at predominantly Negro colleges, while Black students at mostly white colleges were encouraged to apply for enrollment in their schools' R.O.T.C. programs. At Prairie View A. and M. College in Texas, the Navy formed the first N.R.O.T.C. unit ever located at a Black institution. Protests against R.O.T.C. accreditation by anti-military white students at many schools across the nation threatened to rob their fellow Black students of hard-earned military leadership opportunities, since R.O.T.C. programs are at present the largest single source of Negro officers.

The national service academies also took action in 1968 to broaden racial representation in their cadet corps by active recruitment of potential Negro appointees from the nation's high schools, including schools in Black neighborhoods. The Navy and Marines were especially anxious to erase their old reputations for racial conservatism. They both hoped to lessen feelings of discouragement about career futures as Navy or Marine officers held by many American Negroes. Despite much progress in racial matters, some old images of the Navy and Marines were still current in Black communities. Although in 1968 only 5 per cent of the Navy's Black personnel were mess stewards in contrast with 95 per cent in 1949, the old memories still lingered. Even some Negro college presidents remembered being limited to mess-boy duties while in the Navy years ago. Critics of the Navy often pointed out that it was not until after the Korean War that Samuel L. Gravely, Jr., became the first Negro to command a naval warship and, with his promotion to captain, the first Black four-striper of the line in American naval history. However, despite the Navy's declining racial traditionalism, the fact remains that Navy officers must possess advanced mathematical and technological skills. It is therefore unfortunate for young Black Americans, as well as for the Navy and the country, that Negro educational disadvantages still make it so difficult to obtain the knowledge requisite for naval commissions.

The Marine Corps, which draws some of its officers from Annapolis, also faced image problems during the year. The Corps' pre-World War II policy of refusing to accept Negroes for enlistment came back to haunt it in 1968 by cooling the passion of some Black youths for commissioned Marine careers. The old policy may have been a mistake in more ways than one. In the years before 1941 the Marines, on their far-flung battle lines, could have used the splendid fighting qualities of Black men as displayed earlier in the regular Army.

Service academy recruitment efforts have borne fruit, and the sparse Negro enrollment records of past decades are disappearing. West Point had thirty-one Black cadets in 1968 and hoped to triple that number as quickly as possible. During the year, Major Raymond C. Baugh, himself a West Point graduate, became the first Negro ever appointed to the faculty of the United States Military Academy. Annapolis expected to have thirty-one Negro midshipmen in 1968, in contrast to only four in 1964. The Air Force Academy had fifty-five Black cadets in comparison to the six enrolled in 1964.

Black Americans could take pride in the growing numbers and increasing ratios of Negro commissioned officers on active duty in all the services in 1968. Nevertheless, many a Black GI at home and in Vietnam longed to see more of his own Black brothers in positions of authority and responsibility. In July of 1968 the Defense Department released official figures showing the increase in Negro officers after twenty years of racial integration in the armed forces. The Army had more than quadrupled its number of Black officers, from 1,306 in 1948 to 5,637 in 1968. They included one brigadier general and twenty-seven full colonels, compared with a single colonel in 1948. The Navy had only four Black officers in 1948, but a total of 330 in 1968, with three of them captains. The Air Force in 1948 could claim but 330 Black officers, only one of whom had risen to the rank of colonel. By 1968 there were 2,417 Negro officers, a great many of whom were combat pilots. Wearing the Air Force blue was one Black lieutenant general, along with nineteen full colonels. The Marine Corps had only one Negro officer twenty years ago, but 180 of them in 1968, and was striving to double that number.

Even with the growing proportion of Black careerists who remained in the military, thousands of other Negroes were preparing to return to civilian status in 1968 as their terms of service expired. It was estimated that 41,000 Black veterans would be discharged, 5,000 of whom had served in Vietnam. Government agencies and civic organizations took steps to aid the development of their future civilian careers beyond the conventional services and benefits provided by the Veterans Administration. It was felt that the Black veteran should never have to face second-class citizenship again after having defended his country in a war that is so unpopular with many first-class white citizens. The Defense Department administered a training and placement project at many military installations, which was dubbed Operation Transition. Open to all servicemen preparing for discharge, it was particularly concerned with the Black man's future. One of its objectives was the recruitment of more Negro veterans for careers with the nation's urban police forces. With impetus from Whitney Young, who had recently talked with many young Negro soldiers in Vietnam, the National Urban League operated a highly active information, job placement and housing bureau program specifically for the Black veteran of Vietnam.

For all their concern with race relations, the armed forces did not remain immune in 1968 from dissent and charges of lingering racism.

In August, several Negro soldiers at Fort Hood, Texas, refused to be sent to Chicago with their units for possible riot control duty during the Democratic national convention. They objected on the grounds that they might be called upon to quell disturbances involving other Black people. Some of them faced courtsmartial for their actions.

A note of discord was sounded in Vietnam by Negro Major Lavell Merritt. After being passed over twice for promotion, he issued a rather embittered press release. In it he denounced the Army for alleged racial discrimination in officer promotion policies and charged that most Black military officers were Uncle Toms. His attack came only one month after Negro Colonel Frederic Davison had been promoted to brigadier general in Vietnam. A few weeks prior to Major Merritt's statement, General Davison, while readily admitting that the Army was not yet absolutely perfect in racial matters, publicly praised it for its rapid progress in integration and equalization of opportunities.

Successful integration during combat and garrison duty was not always carried over into social relations behind the front lines or during after-duty hours. Some Negro servicemen complained of social discrimination by white comrades in Vietnam, Germany and Japan. A trend seemed to be developing among Black and white to seek their off-duty entertainment and recreation in voluntarily segregated places of amusement, away from the integrated military facilities. Younger men of both races overseas seemed increasingly prone to react defensively toward one another as news spread of racial troubles in America. In Vietnam several interracial brawls occurred in rear areas during the year which involved men from all branches of the service and included a serious military prison riot. The unfortunate fact remained that some individuals of both races still suffered from ingrained prejudices which they had brought with them into the service and which military regulations, and even the comradeship of combat duty, had not yet completely erased.

The realities of Vietnam overshadowed all the thinking of the Negro about the military in 1968, just as they did for the rest of America. A growing feeling of skepticism about the war began to be evident among some young people of the Black ghetto. Balancing this, however, was a genuine sense of pride in Black military accomplishments and contributions on the part of most American Negroes. This positive attitude was reflected rather generally throughout the nation's

Negro press. A special issue of *Ebony* magazine in August 1968 was devoted entirely to the subject of Negroes in the military. Although some of its articles were critical of the armed forces, the overall tone of the issue was one of pride in the Black combat record in Vietnam and of hope for increased racial justice in the military services.

Dissent against the Vietnam war was less prevalent among Black leaders than among prominent whites. But a few militant Black spokesmen did protest the war and Negro participation in it. Their views ranged from those of the martyred Reverend Dr. Martin Luther King, Jr., through the diverse perspectives of such figures as Black Panther Eldridge Cleaver, Black power advocates Stokely Carmichael and H. Rap Brown, Black Muslim spokesman and former boxing champion Muhammad Ali, former CORE director Floyd B. McKissick, comedian Dick Gregory and youthful political aspirant Julian Bond of Georgia.

The vast majority of Negro servicemen appeared to be unimpressed by Black or white dissent at home. As of August 1968, only fourteen Black deserters were numbered among the American military personnel who had taken refuge in Sweden. In Vietnam, Black troops seemed to have no difficulties resisting the blandishments of constant Vietcong propaganda aimed at the American Negro's racial frustrations.

There was one conclusion, however, that all Negroes could agree upon. This was that the Black soldier in Vietnam was determined to realize the full promise of American citizenship when he returned home from the war. The Black veteran had fought for his country in a conflict avoided by many white Americans and he deserved better from his country than a return to a racist society. Black militant extremists spoke darkly of luring mythical demolition experts from the ranks of returning veterans into urban guerrilla warfare activities. Of more concrete danger was the simple fact that total disillusionment could set in if effective steps were not taken immediately to build a better America for all Negroes.

In the Vietnam conflict itself, the year 1968 witnessed a continuing parade of Black military glory along with a heavy flowing of Black men's blood. Four Negro servicemen received the Congressional Medal of Honor, the nation's highest military award, in 1968. Only Specialist 5 Dwight H. Johnson remained alive to wear his medal; the three other awards were made posthumously. They went to Captain Riley L. Pitts, the first Negro officer to win the Medal of Honor; Private First Class James Anderson, Jr., the first Negro Marine to be so honored; and Sergeant Russel Long. During earlier years of the Vietnam war, two other Black fighters had won the Medal of Honor. They were Private First Class Milton L. Olive, III, who received the award posthumously, and Specialist 6 Lawrence Joel, who survived. In the case of all awards, the medals were presented personally by President Lyndon Johnson to the men or to members of their families. During 1968, too, several Silver Star medals were won by Negroes for gallantry in combat.

The latest Pentagon figures on Negro involvement in Vietnam date from June 30, 1968. They reveal that of the 627,729 American servicemen in the Vietnam area at that time, 10.5 per cent, or approximately 66,000, were Black. This compares, for instance, with a little over 25,000 Negro personnel stationed in Germany. The ratio of Blacks serving in Vietnam was 1.5 per cent higher than the 9 per cent total of Negroes in the whole American military establishment. Total American battle deaths in Vietnam from 1961 to June 30, 1968, were 25,616. Of these, 13.7 per cent, or approximately 3,500, were Negro. Thus Black combat fatalities were 4.7 per cent higher than the ratio of total Negro personnel serving in all the armed forces.

These higher ratios for Negroes serving and dying in the "Nam," as the GI's call it, can be attributed to several factors. In some instances, low educational attainments disqualify Negroes for safer administrative duties and increase the chances of assignment to combat rifleman status. On the other hand, an exceptionally large number of Black servicemen volunteer for overseas duty even if it means combat in Vietnam. The preference for overseas assignment has much to do with the hope that men and women of other lands will prove more accepting of men with dark skins than has been customary in America. The readiness to accept combat duty also has its rationales in Negro thinking. To the career soldier, the risks of combat considerably increase the odds in favor of rapid promotion if he is fortunate in gambling with his life. To the young man from the ghetto, perhaps helping to support a mother and brothers and sisters at home, the extra pay for hazardous duty is either very tempting or downright essential. Furthermore, to any young Black man in uniform there is available the ego satisfaction of testing one's courage combined with the rare opportunity of venting one's pent-up aggressions against an adversary in a legally sanctioned altercation. American society permits the Negro few such opportunities. On a less lethal scale, athletic competition perhaps serves a similar function.

In 1968 many a young white American viewed the Vietnam war as an abrasive intrusion upon an otherwise secure future. But for many young Black Americans the war, with all its harshness, seemed an opportunity to grasp at a future better than the life they had known in the past. Even amid the horrors of war, something racially beneficial may perhaps be emerging. Black Americans and white Americans on the firing line are being forced by the conditions of war to face the holocaust in a position of mutual dependency and in a spirit of mutual trust. Perhaps some of the foundations for future racial brotherhood in America are being forged today in the storm of steel in Vietnam.

Mrs. Mary Ghorm of Newark, New Jersey, and her daughter Mrs. Daisy Kaple, sign up for Social Security and Medicare. Mrs. Ghorm, who is 107 yeas old, was born a plantation slave when Abraham Lincoln was President.

Medicine and Health

Herbert M. Morais

THE YEAR 1968 saw the more than $50-billion-a-year health industry in the midst of a profound crisis. This was reflected in medical manpower shortages; soaring medical costs; inadequate systems of health care delivery; government agencies with overlapping jurisdictions; federal budgetary cutbacks occasioned by an ever-escalating and costly war in Vietnam; and the lack of any clear-cut plan of operation.

Such was the framework within which Black Americans carried on their continuing fight to eliminate racial discrimination in medicine and to achieve a greater measure of adequate health care for the residents of the ghettoes. No longer content with tokenism and gradualism, Afro-Americans insisted on genuine representation in and responsibility for the decision-making policies of medical societies, hospitals, and schools for the training of medical and auxiliary personnel. At the same time, they pressed for an active role in the planning and servicing of medical centers and health care units in Black communities.

Increased pressure on the part of the predominantly Black National Medical Association (NMA), the biracial Medical Committee for Human Rights and a number of Black activist organizations (particularly of students) produced some encouraging results. Definite advances were made in talent recruitment, compensatory education, increased admission to medical schools, equal rights in professional bodies, hospital desegregation and the delivery of urgently needed health care services. Yet in terms of the overall picture progress was exceedingly slow, and it varied from one community to another.

Racial Imbalance in Medical Personnel

In 1968 the medical manpower shortage was nowhere more glaringly revealed than in the scarcity of Black doctors, dentists and nurses. Although Negroes constituted more than 11 per cent of the total population of the United States, only 2 per cent of physicians, less than 2 per cent of dentists and fewer than 5 per cent of nurses were Black.

There were more than 300,000 doctors in the United States in 1968. The number of Black physicians was estimated to be between 5,800 and 7,000. With an average of roughly 6,400 and a Black population of about 22,000,000, this represented a ratio of one Black physician to 3,500 Black people, as against one doctor to 670 people for the country as a whole. Although the number of Black practitioners was decreasing in some parts of the United States and remaining stationary in others, on the West Coast a marked increase was taking place. According to the *Medical Tribune* of October 21, 1968, the number of Negro physicians in Los Angeles rose from 50 in 1963 to about 400 five years later and in San Francisco from approximately 100 to between 150 and 200.

Valuable information concerning the number of Black dentists in the United States appeared in the Washington *Afro-American* of September 28, 1968. Citing Dr. Joseph L. Henry, dean of the Howard University College of Dentistry, as its source, the newspaper stated: "In the last 30 years the number of black dentists has been decreasing to the point that today there is only one black dentist per 11,500 black people." To make matters worse, fewer and fewer Black students were turning to dentistry—a situation which also prevailed in nursing.

Talent Recruitment Program

To meet the need for more medical and allied personnel and to correct the racial imbalance in the health field, special efforts were made to recruit Black students for careers in medicine. Accordingly, the talent recruitment program projected years earlier by the National Medical Association under the leadership of its then president, Dr. W. Montague Cobb, assumed newer and broader dimensions.

Designed to search out and direct gifted Black students in elementary school, high school and college to careers in medicine and health, the program gathered momentum as support was enlisted from the main centers of organized medicine in the country. Following liaison talks during the early part of 1968, the American Medical Association (AMA) and the National Medical Association issued a joint statement in which both "agreed that special emphasis should be exerted in recruiting more Negro students" aspiring to careers in medicine and health. The statement recommended that medical schools and other related groups "expand their careers programming with students, parents and guidance counselors at schools of all levels. . . ."

A similar appeal was made by the Association of American Medical Colleges. This produced some positive results and a survey conducted by the association in May 1968 showed twenty-four medical colleges having special recruiting programs for minority groups at four-year colleges and twenty at senior high, junior high and grade schools.

Meanwhile, the National Medical Association and the Medical Committee for Human Rights continued their efforts to attract Black and other minority group students to medicine. Local affiliates of both organizations arranged visits to medical schools and hospitals in the hope of stimulating interest in the field. The Detroit Medical Society, an NMA unit, worked with the International Afro-American Museum, of Detroit, on a film called *You Can Be a Doctor*, which was shown at the seventy-ninth annual convention of the Association of American Medical Colleges, held at Houston from October 31 to November 4, 1968. Neighborhood health care centers, sponsored by the Office of Economic Opportunity, undertook to recruit and train nurses' aides, technicians, dieticians, medical clerks and social workers, but sharp reductions in appropriations caused by the war in Vietnam hampered the program.

Although the high cost of a medical education was still a deterrent to many Black students, scholarships and fellowships had become so plentiful that it was no longer as decisive a factor as it once had been. In fact, in 1968 there were more financial grants available for tuition and other needs than there were Black applicants for them. In addition to the federal government, such voluntary bodies as the National Medical Fellowships and the National Medical Association gave qualified needy students monetary assistance. For the academic year of 1968–69, the National Medical Fellowships alone awarded a total of $190,000 to 134 Black students for study in fifty-five of the country's medical schools. This was the largest number of grants in the history of the twenty-two-year-old organization. In commenting on scholarship awards to seven young women by the Woods Charitable Fund of Chicago, Dr. John C. Troxel, president of the National Medical Fellowships, said, "I am very pleased that increased attention is being given to opportunities for Negro women in medicine. . . . The country would benefit greatly by fully exploring the potential of Negro women for medicine."

Yet, despite everything, the drive to tap the greatest source of unused and wasted talent in the country failed to attract more than a sprinkling of Black youth to medical careers. The fact was that medicine was becoming far less attractive to gifted Black students than other professions where the training period was not as long and arduous. Furthermore, "the sins of the past"—the persistence of discriminatory practices in medicine—did not help matters.

Medical Education

Handicapped by a "Jim Crow" system of inferior schooling, and by a home life circumscribed by material and cultural deprivation stemming from traditional patterns of discrimination in American life, few Black students were able to qualify for admission to medical schools. A three-day conference, called in February 1968 by the Josiah Macy, Jr., Foundation and co-sponsored by the Association of American Medical Colleges and the Southern Regional Board, focused attention on the problems besetting Negroes applying for entrance to medical schools. One such problem was the Medical College Admission Test (MCAT) which, while presumably "objective" and not the only criterion for admission, clearly favored white urban middle class students with precise language skills and a solid educational background. The conference recommended that further research be undertaken in regard to these tests and that Black and white students who did poorly on them be given instruction at training centers set up by medical schools "to the end that, upon re-examination, their MCAT score would indicate that these students have become qualified candidates for admission. . . ." The growing acceptance of the idea that until the same kind of instruction was available to all, compensatory education for disadvantaged Black students was both desirable and necessary, was a step in the right direction.

Compensatory education was vigorously championed by Black student leaders and medical civil rights organizations. In Philadelphia, where it was charged that less than 1 per cent of the students in six of the city's medical schools were nonwhite, the Committee for Black Admissions of the Philadelphia Student Health Organization proposed that the number of Black students be increased to one-third of the next freshman class. In September 1968 the deans of these six medical colleges agreed to seek means of recruiting more nonwhite students. At Stanford University's School of Medicine, the Black Student Union welcomed the unanimous approval by the faculty senate of a program to increase the enrollment of minority group students starting in September 1969. In New York, pressure on the part of civil rights groups led most of the city's medical schools to turn to the recruitment of Black and Puerto Rican students.

These and similar developments were summarized in an article in the *Medical World News* of December 27, 1968. Entitled "Med Schools Now Seek More Black Freshmen," the article reported that the medical faculty at Boston University had asked the trustees to raise sufficient funds so that the school could take in more than the two Negro students originally planned for, and so that by 1970 special help could be given disadvantaged students. Medical school administrators at Johns Hopkins and at the University of Maryland were being prodded by several organizations to increase the number of Black students to at least one-third of the freshman class. In San Francisco, at the University of California Medical Center, Black students and employees demanded a minority group quota of 20 per cent.

These pressures on the part of student activists and civil rights organizations combined with the spirit of the times to produce some concrete results. According to a report released on June 26, 1968, by the Association of American Medical Colleges, about three hundred Negro students were expected to enter the country's medical schools in September, an increase over previous years. These students would represent 3.1 per cent of the anticipated first-year class of 9,653. As a result of this increase in admissions, the total enrollment of Black students for the academic year 1968–69 was expected to rise, but not enough to significantly alter the overall picture of the previous year. Of the approximately 33,000 students who attended the nation's medical schools in 1967–68, less than eight hundred, or fewer than 2.5 per cent were estimated to be Black. During that year, there were only fifty-one nonwhite students in twenty-seven medical schools in the South. According to *Time* magazine (August 23, 1968), most Southern medical colleges accepted "only token admissions to stay within the law governing federal support funds."

More than two-thirds of the estimated two hundred Negroes who graduated from the country's medical schools in June 1968 came from Howard and Meharry—eighty-eight and forty-nine respectively. Because of the physician shortage, these 137 graduates had no difficulty in obtaining internships at sixty-four different hospitals. Similarly, Black doctors were finding no trouble in obtaining residencies, for here, too, there were more posts available than applicants for them.

Medical Civil Rights: Professional Bodies

Some significant advances were made in 1968 to eliminate racial barriers and prejudices in professional organizations. Unrelenting pressure on the part of civil rights groups and Black activists accounted for most—if not all—of the gains.

Probably the outstanding breakthrough of the year took place at the 117th annual convention of the American Medical Association, held at the Hotel Fairmont in San Francisco from June 16 to 20, 1968. On the opening day, fifty to a hundred supporters of the Medical Committee for Human Rights and the Poor People's Campaign marched in protest outside the Fairmont. Inside, pandemonium reigned as two young men—one a medical student and the other a leader of the Poor People's Campaign delegation—seized microphones on the podium while other demonstrators circulated a statement, issued by the Medical Committee for Human Rights, which denounced the AMA's record on racial discrimination and health services.

The following day Dr. T. G. G. Wilson, national chairman of the Medical Committee for Human Rights, appeared before the AMA's reference committee on constitutional bylaws to urge the passage of a resolution outlawing racial discrimination in the organization's constitutent medical societies. Such a resolution had already been presented to the committee by the Massachusetts delegation. In a move obviously designed to sidetrack the Massachusetts proposal, the committee recommended the passage of a motion reiterating the older anti-bias statements of the AMA. A floor fight ensued, and by a voice vote the Massachusetts resolution was adopted. It called for the drafting of new bylaws which would permit the organization's judicial council "to admonish, censure or, in the event of repeated violations," recommend the expulsion of state medical societies practicing racial, religious or ethnic discrimination.

The new bylaws were formally adopted by the AMA's house of delegates at the organization's twenty-second clinical convention in Miami Beach in December 1968. The vote for adoption was 170 in favor and sixty-nine against. It was estimated that the new bylaws would open the way for admission to the AMA of nearly a thousand Black physicians hitherto barred by local affiliates in the states of Alabama, Mississippi, Florida, Georgia, South Carolina and Louisiana.

While the AMA was moving forward nationally, progress on the local level left much to be desired. As the *Medical Tribune* of October 24, 1968, put it in its survey "The Negro in Medicine Today," Black physicians in county medical societies were aggrieved that their "views [were] not sought in policy making and little effort [was] made to advance them to responsible posts." The same periodical indicated that Negro doctors, especially in a number of Southern local medical units, felt that they were being accepted only in a limited and formal sense and not as members of a team.

In the meantime, other professional organizations in the health field were pushing ahead in an effort to remove racial prejudices. On May 17, 1968, the American Nurses' Association, meeting in Dallas, adopted a resolution calling upon all nurses to intensify their efforts to eliminate discriminatory practices within and outside of the health field.

The American Public Health Association, at its ninety-sixth annual meeting in Detroit in November 1968, made history when it named Dr. Paul B. Cornely—head of the Department of Preventive Medicine at Howard University—president-elect, the first Black man to be so honored by a major, predominantly white, medical body. The association's executive board went on record as calling for an end in such states as Louisiana and Arkansas of the practice of segregating blood prior to transfusion according to race. During the convention, the organization's Black members formed a caucus to work for specific objectives within the body.

Similarly, at the seventieth annual meeting of the American Hospital Association, in Atlantic City in September 1968, a group of some thirty Black hospital administrators formed their own unit within the organization. Back of the move was a desire to improve educational facilities for health workers of minority groups and to study the problems involved in supplying health care to impoverished communities. In a statement on the formation of the group, Dr. George W. Graham, president of the AHA, reiterated the organiza-

DO THEY "GIVE A DAMN?"

tion's 1964 Statement on Human Rights, including the point, "Equality of opportunity is an equal right."

Hospital Desegregation

There was ample evidence in 1968 that racial discrimination with regard to hospital staffs and to patients was still very much in evidence. The widespread practice of excluding Black physicians from hospital staffs was commented on in the press and in popular periodicals. Dr. Howard A. Rusk, in the *New York Times* of April 7, 1968, pointed out that "of the 23,000 physicians in New York City, 7,000 [had] no hospital affiliation and more than half of these [were] Negro physicians." A *Time* magazine article, "The Plight of the Black Doctor" (August 23, 1968), observed that "in Chicago and other major cities, it is still far more difficult for a Negro doctor to get into a good hospital than it is for a white."

At the seventy-third annual convention of the National Medical Association, held in Houston from August 11 to 15, 1968, Dr. James M. Whittico, Jr., observed in his inaugural address that "the number of Negro physicians admitted on hospital medical staffs, particularly in large cities, remains relatively small." The new president and the delegates welcomed an AMA offer to work closely with the NMA to investigate cases of racial discrimination, including those involving hospital staffs. In a report to the convention, the NMA Council on Medical Education and Hospitals urged the adoption of a resolution strongly endorsing "the universal system of open staffs for all hospitals."

Black doctors condemned not only the exclusion of nonwhite practitioners from hospital staffs, but also the treatment often accorded Black hospital patients. Discrimination and segregation were still all too common. Often, Black patients were consigned to basements, attics and deteriorating older wings of hospitals. In the South Negro patients were not infrequently relegated to segregrated quarters, while in the North they were at times ingeniously placed in separate wards and semi-private rooms. And if they were poor—as many of them were—they were treated by an overworked staff in cramped, dilapidated wards devoid of some of the most elementary sanitary safeguards.

Although some progress was made in this area in 1968, it fell far short of the high expectations engendered by the passage of the Civil Rights Act of 1964. Under Title VI of the act, government agencies were directed to withhold federal funds from hospitals practicing discrimination. Medical civil rights leaders viewed with alarm the token enforcement of Title VI. From 1966 to the early part of 1968 the Department of Health, Education and Welfare instituted enforcement proceedings against no more than thirty-five hospitals. And only twelve of these, according to an official summary, lost federal financial assistance because of non-compliance with the law.

Civil rights leaders in the medical field were also alarmed by the passage of the Talmadge Amendment to Title VI of the Civil Rights Act, which paved the way for non-complying hospitals to be paid by Medicare and Medicaid for "emergency" treatment of patients. *Medical World News* of December 13, 1968, reported that of the 21,000 emergency Medicare claims filed nationally in one fiscal year, as many as 17,700 came from the South—more than half of them from Alabama and Mississippi. In Mississippi two hospitals which did not meet the civil rights standards for Medicare submitted 2,700 or more claims. In November 1968 the Department of Health, Education and Welfare attempted to close the loophole through a proposed new regulation to the effect that a non-complying hospital would be paid only if it was nearest to the patient involved or the nearest one equipped to take care of his particular emergency.

Health Status Problems

The unfavorable health and medical position of the Negro was of great concern to Black physicians. One aspect of this concern was seen in the controversy surrounding one of the major medical achievements of 1968: transplants of human organs. According to the *Chicago Daily Defender* of October 14, 1968, the issue involved was "a new concept of judging when life has ceased and the threat which this poses to the wholesale use of organs from black bodies to give extended life to white persons." The issue arose as a result of action taken by the American College of Chest Physicians at its meeting in Washington, D.C., in October 1968. In a secret session, from which the Black delegates (three out of a total of approximately fifteen hundred) were excluded, the group adopted a five-point set of recommendations with regard to organ transplants. Among these recommendations was one on press relations which suggested that the names of donors be withheld. Dr. James M. Whittico, Jr., president of the National Medical Association, and Dr. W. Montague Cobb, editor of the association's journal, issued statements highly critical of the "anonymity" recommendation, Dr. Cobb characterizing it as "premature, superficial and fraught with dangers to the poor, particularly the black poor."

Shortly before this, three Black physicians, together with the project director for the Watts (Los Angeles) Health and Family Planning Group, had voiced serious misgivings concerning a federally planned birth control program. Alarmed by white racist attitudes in the country, the four had issued a letter expressing the fear that such a program administered from outside the community might be used to reduce the nation's Black population. The letter, calling for proper safeguards with regard to the administration of the program, was quoted in the *Los Angeles Times* of August 30, 1968, as follows: "It is because we feel we are uniquely qualified as black men first, and doctors second, that we can take this step forward to keep watchful vigil over the sanctity of procreation among black people."

Poverty and Poor Health

Socio-economic patterns have played a significant role in undermining the health of Black Americans. For large numbers of nonwhites living in the inner cities and in the rural slums of the South, poverty is a stark reality. To the mass of Black workers, unemployment and underemployment are no strangers. Last year roughly four out of ten (or 1,871,000) nonwhite families had cash incomes below the poverty level of approximately $3,000 a year set by the government. Victimized by joblessness, part-time employment and low wages, very few Black families earned the estimated $9,789 a year needed in June 1968 to maintain an urban family of four in what the Bureau of Labor Statistics described as "a moderate living standard."

The latest statistical data on mortality and morbidity rates indicate that in 1968 Black Americans were more apt to die in infancy or to lose their mothers at childbirth than were their white counterparts. They had a shorter life expectancy and were also more likely to suffer from chronic illnesses, spend more time disabled and bedridden and lose more days of work per year than whites.

The National Advisory Commission on Civil Disorders, in its report to President Johnson in March 1968, summarized the situation as follows:

> The residents of the racial ghetto are significantly less healthy than most other Americans. They suffer higher mortality rates, higher incidence of major diseases, and lower availability and utilization of medical services. They also experience higher admission rates to mental hospitals.

The report went on to give the following statistical comparison between the health of Black Americans and that of whites:

> Maternal mortality rates for nonwhite mothers are four times as high as those for white mothers. . . . Infant mortality rates among nonwhite babies are 58 per cent higher than among whites for those under one month old, and almost three times as high among those from one month to one year old. . . . To some extent because of infant mortality rates, life expectancy at birth was 6.9 years longer for whites (71.0 years) than for nonwhites (64.1 years) in 1965. Even in the prime working ages, life expectancy is significantly lower among nonwhites than among whites.

The report also stated:

> Environmental conditions in disadvantaged Negro neighborhoods create . . . reasons for poor health conditions there. The level of sanitation is strikingly below that which is prevalent in most higher income areas. One simple reason is that residents lack proper storage facilities for food—adequate refrigerators, freezers, even garbage cans. . . . In many areas . . . rats proliferate. It is estimated that in 1965, there were over 14,000 cases of ratbite in the United States, mostly in such areas.

Poverty and poor health went hand in hand not only because of insanitary living conditions but also because of inadequate diet. In the Black Belt of the Deep South, as well as in other parts of the country, hunger and malnutrition were facts of life. In a study covering 1,250 pre-school children in Mississippi, the University of Mississippi Medical Center and the State Board of Health found that 25 per cent of the nonwhite children were anemic, as against 10 per cent of the white. In addition, the study showed that the Black children had an average of 20 to 25 per cent less proteins and calories a day than their white counterparts. The dull faces and stunted growth of starving children, Black and white, were vividly portrayed in a Columbia Broadcasting System report on television entitled "Hunger in America." In a very perceptive article, "Poverty, Illness and the Negro Child," inserted in the *Congressional Record* for March 25, 1968, Dr. Max Seham, emeritus clinical professor of pediatrics, University of Minnesota, estimated that 11 million or more American children were suffering from a "deprivation syndrome" which included poor nutrition as well as poor housing and poor education.

The Poor People's Campaign of 1968, organized by the Southern Christian Leadership Conference, sought to dramatize the presence of poverty and hunger in the world's most affluent country. Early in May hundreds of indigent demonstrators from all parts of the nation gathered in Washington, D.C. There, in the very shadow of the Lincoln Memorial, they built a shantytown called Resurrection City. The first to provide medical services for this community's residents was the Medical Committee for Human Rights, whose experience in such matters went back to Selma in 1965 and the Mississippi Freedom March in 1966. As other organizations began their programs, a health services coordinating committee was formed and an executive board established under the chairmanship of Dr. Edward C. Mazique, a past president of the National Medical Association. More than three hundred doctors, dentists and nurses worked around the clock to provide health services to hundreds of poverty-stricken demonstrators many of whom were experiencing such attention for the first time in their lives.

In 1968, as in previous years, poverty prevented a large number of Black Americans from receiving much-needed medical care. Without financial resources of any kind, they were forced to use the outpatient clinics of hospitals, where they were generally treated without compassion or concern for their dignity as individuals. In cases of serious accidents and illnesses, they were taken to hospitals usually located outside their own neighborhoods because of the unsatisfactory distribution of such facilities "geographically and in relation to the poor, particularly the nonwhite poor," as Secretary Wilbur J. Cohen of the Department of Health, Education and Welfare put it, in a report to President Johnson in June 1968.

The relatively few Black Americans who were covered by existing health insurance programs found such plans insufficient for the purchase of even a minimum of health services, because of rising medical costs, which in 1968 continued to climb at a rate far in excess of the general cost of living. And there was no end in sight; President Johnson predicted in his health message to Congress in March that by 1975 payments for general hospital services would increase 250 per cent, doctors' bills 160 per cent, dental fees 100 per cent and drugs 65 per cent.

Another problem facing Black Americans was the shortage of doctors—particularly in the Deep South, where many doctors had moved to the Northern cities. In Georgia there was a decrease in the number of Black physicians from some 150 in 1958 to about a hundred ten years later, the drop being felt most severely in the rural areas. In Mississippi, too, the number of Black doctors had decreased—to such an extent that by 1968 they comprised less than 5 per cent of all physicians in the state, despite the fact that 42 per cent of Mississippi's population was Black. The Black doctors who left the rural South were not replaced by white physicians, and this fact added to the shortage experienced in this part of the country.

Health Care for the Poor

Medicare and Medicaid played an important role in bringing urgently needed health services to the poor of the racial slums. Under these programs many elderly persons received badly needed medical assistance which previously they could not have had. In mid-1968, nearly 20 million persons age sixty-five or over were covered under the law. About a third were impoverished, and they included a disproportionate number of Black people. In the two years prior to July 1, 1968, Medicare funds to the amount of $8.4 billion had been spent to pay for the medical and hospital bills of persons sixty-five or over. More than a million elderly citizens received post-hospital care in nursing institutions and at home, while another million and a half were treated in outpatient diagnostic clinics attached to hospitals. Spiraling medical costs, however, were slowing down the Medicare and Medicaid programs. In December 1968 the Advisory Commission on Intergovernmental Relations in its 125-page report expressed great concern about the situation, particularly in respect to Medicaid, but said that the cost spiral should not prevent the federal government from realizing its goal of providing health care to "substantially all" of the country's poor by 1975.

During the year, the Office of Economic Opportunity stepped up its program to establish comprehensive health care centers in poor neighborhoods. Designed to provide services which would include medical and dental care, immunization, diagnostic tests, rehabilitation and care of drug problems, the program was directed by OEO's Office for Health Affairs, headed by Dr. Joseph T. English. Though government financed, these health care centers were administered by university medical schools, county medical societies, health departments, hospitals and associations formed by the community itself. In Brooklyn, New York, the Provident Clinical Society, an affiliate of the NMA, received a grant to provide comprehensive medical care for some thirty thousand people in the poverty-stricken Bedford-Stuyvesant area, while in Nashville, Tennessee, Meharry Medical College was given funds to construct a permanent health care center to service a neighborhood of thirty-seven thousand needy people. Black physicians took an active part in the development of these health centers and were appointed to top administrative posts in a number of them. Among these appointees were: Dr. Rodney Powell, director of the South Central Multi-purpose Health Center in Watts, Los Angeles; Dr. Calvin A. Brown, Jr., co-director of the Price Neighborhood Health Center in Atlanta, Georgia; and Dr. Samuel U. Rodgers, director of the Neighborhood Health Center in Kansas City, Missouri.

By the end of April, the OEO was reported as having funded forty-two neighborhood health centers at a cost of almost $90 million. Sixteen units were fully operational, eleven were functioning on a limited basis and four more were scheduled to open in May. Later in the year, additional projects were added to the program; according to a July 1, 1968 status report prepared by the Health Services Office of the Department of Health, Education and Welfare, some fifty centers were listed. When all these units should become fully operational, they were expected to serve about a million poor people—a very small percentage of the conservatively estimated number of "less than 29 million" poor Americans which President Johnson gave in his budget message to Congress in January 1968. The vast majority of the OEO health centers were located in large urban areas across the nation. Of the few that were established outside of the big cities, the most notable was the Tufts Delta Medical Center in Bolivar County, Mississippi, whose seven physicians and eighty auxiliary medical personnel were serving about three hundred persons a week.

Although the NMA fully accepted the concept of the comprehensive health care program of OEO as "a logical means of bringing good medical care to the poor of our country," it nevertheless had certain reservations about the way in which the idea was being implemented. These reservations appeared in an official policy statement published in the January 1968 issue of the organization's journal. The NMA was critical in particular of the taking over of neighborhood health units by medical schools, of workers soliciting patients for particular clinics, and of proposals concerning transportation and housekeeping services. After making concrete suggestions for improvement, the NMA concluded by noting that "only if the community residents and their physicians [were] part of the planning and made a part of the governing body of the facility" could the program succeed.

The NMA recommendations, by focusing attention on ghetto residents and their doctors, helped further the cause of both. On March 8, 1968, the *Medical World News*, in an article on these health centers, noted the formation of "health councils" or "associations" composed of local residents to assure community participation in the program. On November 14, 1968, the *New York Times* quoted Dr. Paul B. Cornely, president-elect of the American Public Health Association, as saying that as a result of the NMA initiative Black physicians, previously ignored under the program, were now "getting part of the action."

In the meantime, the NMA, working through a new organization, the NMA Foundation, embarked on a health care project of its own. In January 1968 the Department of Health, Education and Welfare granted the NMA Foundation $60,550 to plan a program that would provide health and housing facilities for the urban poor, with particular emphasis on the elderly. By the summer of 1968, members of the NMA had contributed more than $175,000 to the foundation's equity fund. In August 1968, during its annual convention in Houston, the NMA announced that the foundation's first project would be a two-hundred-bed nursing home and health care complex in one of the low-income areas of Washington, D.C. According to the announcement, preliminary discussions were under way with local affiliates to establish programs along similar lines in Atlanta, Chicago, Detroit, Newark, Oakland and Tuskegee.

The right of every citizen to good health care was implicit in the movement to deliver comprehensive medical assistance to the poor. That health care was a fundamental right and not a privilege was the keynote of President Johnson's address to 2,800 delegates and guests attending the NMA convention in Houston in August 1968. After listing the basic rights of employment, decent housing, education and freedom from discrimination, the President added the "right of every American to as healthy a life as modern medicine can provide." Along these lines the President urged Congress to extend the Medicare program to include young children.

Other concerned Americans went even further. In March 1968 Dr. Quentin D. Young, national chairman of the Medical Committee for Human Rights, after asserting that some 47 million Americans were medically indigent, called for the establishment of a system of universal health insurance to cover everyone regardless of age. In December 1968 Dr. Malcolm L. Peterson, national chairman of the Physicians Forum, an organization dedicated to the principle of high quality medical care for all, stated that one of the best ways to attract doctors to disadvantaged areas was to implement current proposals for comprehensive national health insurance.

Health Legislation

The second session of the 90th Congress adopted no new major health legislation. Marking time, it contented itself with the passage of laws extending the life of existing programs.

The only new major proposal—the child health bill of 1968, introduced by Senator Russell B. Long (D, Louisiana) and Representative Cecil R. King (D, California)—was not even given the benefit of Congressional hearings. The proposal, which advocated extended comprehensive medical care to low-income mothers and young children, embodied the request made by President Johnson in his health message of 1968.

In retrospect, the year was marked by much activity but little progress in bringing genuine racial equality to organized medicine and adequate health care to impoverished Black communities. While advances were made in medical civil rights, the gains registered were few and far between, especially in the vital area of participation in decision making. And at the end of the year, it was still a matter of speculation whether the American Medical Association would enforce its most recent antidiscrimination resolution or would allow it to remain on the statute books as one more in a long line of rhetorical flourishes.

As in the field of medical civil rights, so in the organization and delivery of high quality health care for all, the year 1968 produced a bumper crop of words and promises rather than deeds and performance. The crises in the health industry—not enough doctors and allied personnel to meet increased needs, skyrocketing medical costs, a disorganized, jerry-built and obsolete system of health care—were the subject of much discussion. The solutions suggested—group practice, incentives to reduce costs, greater utilization of doctors' aides—sounded like a worn-out record. Congressional stand-patism, with its emphasis on the warfare state as against the welfare state (more money was spent to prosecute the war in Vietnam in one month than to fight the war on poverty at home in one full year), relegated to limbo any serious discussion (let alone action) on a constructive and imaginative program of universal, tax-supported health insurance which would bring the United States abreast of the twentieth century in health legislation. Even the modest proposal to extend Medicare to poverty-stricken mothers and young children was scuttled, an action not calculated to raise the most affluent and technologically advanced country in the world from its low standing among the nations in infant mortality rates, a standing that has fluctuated from thirteenth to fifteenth place in recent years.

In short, there was still much work to be done before meaningful racial equality in medicine and adequate health care in Black ghettoes could be realized.

Walter Washington

Rev. Ralph Abernathy

William Clay

Louis Stokes

Biographies in Black America, 1968

Wilhelmena S. Robinson

IN THE COURSE OF 1968 a great number of Black personalities hit the spotlight—through the news media, on television, in movies, in magazines and in commercial advertising. The viewing of Black Americans through these media has given an overly optimistic picture of the scene as it was in 1968. There have been some setbacks, and many apparent gains are in fact fairly superficial. The loss of a dynamic civil rights leader in April 1968 was a serious blow and created a vacuum which has not been filled.

A number of new personalities appeared on the scene, however, and a sampling of them is given here, together with certain well-known men and women who were in the news in 1968.

Individuals in the fields of sports, entertainment and the arts are not covered in this section but appear elsewhere under those categories.

Abernathy, Ralph David

The "New Thrust," a five year plan to organize the nation's poor, is one of the Reverend Ralph Abernathy's plans for the Southern Christian Leadership Conference in 1969. Rev. Ralph Abernathy took over the leadership of the SCLC after Dr. Martin Luther King's assassination on April 4, 1968. Dr. King had named Abernathy as his successor two years ago. The two had been friends for more than a decade. They first worked together in 1955 on the successful 382-day bus boycott, which began when Mrs. Rosa Parks, a Black seamstress, refused to move to the rear of a Montgomery, Alabama, bus. Since then, Dr. King and Abernathy had been jailed together on nineteen occasions.

Pledging nonviolence and at the same time warning that the rights organization would be more militant than ever, Ralph Abernathy led the Poor People's Campaign (planned by Dr. King) in their march on Washington in May and June 1968. Early in this campaign, Abernathy called the bluff of officials in Selma, Alabama, who threatened to stop his marching caravan of poor Blacks, by telling them to get a few hundred jail cells ready because the marchers were going ahead.

As pastor of the West Hunter Street Baptist Church in Atlanta, Rev. Ralph Abernathy adheres to the philosophy that "if everything is moving smoothly in your life you aren't doing anything."

Ralph Abernathy was born on a farm in Marengo County, Alabama, in 1926. He served overseas during World War II, and afterwards went to Alabama State College on the GI Bill, graduating with honors in sociology. He helped found the SCLC with Dr. King in 1957.

Bond, Horace Julian

Paving streets, picking up garbage, putting in new street lights—actions to placate ghetto residents? "Not at all," says Julian Bond, often described as a quiet, but angry, young rebel. Instead Bond sees such acts as part of a vital attempt to free Blacks from the troubles and inadequacies of ghetto life and absorb them into the greater problems of the Black community. Through such functional means as these, Bond strives for a broader goal of racial progress and equality.

He is a member of the Georgia house of representatives, filling a seat created by reapportionment. Bond had to fight for his seat, as the legislature had refused to seat him because of his endorsement of a Vietnam policy statement issued by SNCC, of which he was once information director. By bringing his case before the United States Supreme Court, Bond was able to sit in the legislature.

The Supreme Court case put Bond in the national spotlight, as did the Democratic national convention in Chicago, when his name was placed in nomination as running mate to Presidential candidate Hubert Humphrey. "It may be symbolic now, but it may not be four years from now," Ted Warshafsky of Wisconsin said of the motion. Bond, who was too young to hold the office of Vice-President, withdrew his name from the nomination.

Born in Nashville, Tennessee, in January 1940, Julian Bond is the son of Dr. Horace Mann Bond, head of the Department of Education and Research at Atlanta University. Julian Bond attended Morehouse College in Atlanta. An early activist in the field of civil rights, Bond was a founder of the Committee on Appeal for Human Rights, the Atlanta University Center student organization which was a forerunner of SNCC.

Brown, H. Rap

It was a rough year for H. Rap Brown, militant Black power advocate and former chairman of the Student Nonviolent Coordinating Committee. In 1968 SNCC seemed on the decline. An unsuccessful attempt to merge with the Black Panther Party fell through. Brown, who had become the Panthers' minister of justice, later left the Panthers because of disagreements.

In 1968 Rap Brown was involved in a series of legal entanglements. He was charged with inciting a riot and counseling to burn the Black section of Cambridge, Maryland, during the July 1967 racial disturbances. He awaited a court review of a federal conviction in New Orleans on a charge of carrying a gun across state lines while under indictment in Maryland. He was also under bond in Richmond, Virginia, and had been arrested in New York in February for violating the conditions of his bail in New Orleans by making a trip to California to appear at Black power rallies in Los Angeles and Oakland. At one point Brown sought refuge in a Cuban mission in New York after a scuffle with police who allegedly demanded to know the contents of packages Brown was carrying. Brown's defense attorney is the famous civil rights lawyer William Kunstler.

Rap Brown, twenty-four years old in 1968, sees 1969 as a period of further oppression for Blacks.

Cahn, Jean Camper

Activist lawyer Jean Camper Cahn sent dozens of law students into all the police precincts to aid and advise citizens arrested during the April riots in Washington, D.C. Mrs. Cahn is committed to making the law work for the poor and the Black.

In the early years of their marriage Mrs. Cahn and her husband Edgar could not afford public housing in New Haven, Connecticut. In 1964, their final year at Yale Law School, the Cahns wrote an article together for the *Yale Law Journal* which proposed a national system of legal services for the poor. The article inspired the federal government's Neighborhood Legal Services Program and Washington's unique Citizens Complaint Bureau.

In July 1968 Mrs. Cahn was appointed head of George Washington University's new Urban Law Institute. Her job is to train graduate lawyers in community organization techniques for service in VISTA.

Jean Camper Cahn is a graduate of Swarthmore College and Yale Law School. She had a year's study at Cambridge University in England.

Carmichael, Stokely

As marchers, mostly Negroes, moved along in the Mississippi sun, Stokely Carmichael raised his voice and cried "What do we want?" The marchers shouted back "BLACK POWER!"—the cry that made Carmichael the herald of the Black power movement.

After that cry was heard, during the Meredith march in 1966, Carmichael strove to make a Black power structure a reality. At the time of the march, and until 1968, Carmichael was chairman of SNCC and an undisputed leader in the field of civil rights. He formulated a strategy aimed at welding a broad range of Negro organizations into a union that could be a powerful political factor in American life. Since Carmichael stepped down as chairman, SNCC has leaned more towards a revolution-oriented militancy rather than political unity to achieve its aims. Not that Carmichael is against revolution, but "before you create revolution, you have to heighten contradiction. As long as there is hope, people are not going to fight. They won't fight unless you push. . . . You create disturbances, you keep pushing the system until they have to hit back." In August 1968 the SNCC-Carmichael relationship was terminated, and Carmichael concentrated his efforts on his post as prime minister of the Black Panthers.

Born in Port of Spain, Trinidad, Carmichael came to the United States at the age of eleven and is now a naturalized citizen. He graduated from Howard University in 1964 and has been working in the field of civil rights ever since. He is married to the talented singer Miriam Makeba.

Chisholm, Shirley Anita St. Hill

Campaigning as "Fighting Shirley Chisholm" in the predominantly Black Bedford-Stuyvesant district of Brooklyn, Shirley Chisholm defeated Republican James Farmer, former head of CORE, to become the first Negro congresswoman.

Compelled to enter politics by the people she worked for and fought for on the local level, Mrs. Chisholm considers herself representative of a new breed of politician. Outspoken and independent, Shirley Chisholm is confident of her own ability and is afraid of no one. While campaigning on street corners she shouted back to male hecklers who argued that Congress is a place for men, "It doesn't matter what you think; I'm going to win because I'm tough, baby."

Mrs. Chisholm has lived in Brooklyn most of her life. When she walks around her district, which is 30 per cent white and 70 per cent Black and Puerto Rican, she says, "I get discouraged when I see I'm just one person and can't cure the ills of three hundred years. But I'm going to fight for my people. It's a tremendous challenge and I accept it." She is opposed to the Vietnam war because she believes we have a more urgent domestic war going on in this country.

Shirley Chisholm was born in 1924. An honors graduate of Brooklyn College, she was named alumna of the year in 1957. She took her M.A. at Columbia University. She had been a member of the New York state assembly since 1964, and had also served as an educational consultant with the Bureau of Child Welfare. She speaks fluent Spanish, which enables her to communicate with her Puerto Rican constituents.

Clay, William

William Clay, newly elected U.S. representative from St. Louis, believes in rocking the system from within.

"The name of the game is power," he says—and now that he has it, he plans to make the most of it. One of his main objectives is to become a vocal leader, creating a general attitude within Congress that will be responsive to liberal causes and push through more progressive social legislation. In this way, he can effect on a national level the kinds of changes that he has made in his own community.

Clay's credentials for representing what he terms "the little people" of the urban areas are sound. On the local level, he was the author of a fair employment law—in which he sought the elimination of testing procedures, arrest records, diploma requirements and periods of unemployment as barriers to getting a job—and of a report entitled *Anatomy of an Economic Murder*. He was sponsor of a bill restricting police release of records, was the chief exponent of the Public Accommodations Bill and is a 112-day veteran of the St. Louis jails because of his civil rights activities. As race relations coordinator for the Steamfitters Union Local 562, Clay has opened the field for Negro apprentices, trainees and journeymen. He has advanced job opportunities for Negroes in retail sales, public utilities, the aircraft industry, bakeries, breweries and banks. Clay feels that "Black people must stop assessing progress in terms of individual attainment. Until all Blacks are free, none are free, and as long as one Black man is not free, then all men in America are potentially enslaved."

Clay, who was thirty-seven in 1968, grew up in a St. Louis tenement complex. At thirteen he worked as a janitor in a clothing store, where he stayed for ten years. One of his sisters taught him to sew, and he took over the tailoring department at fifteen. At eighteen he was one of the clothing salesmen. He saved enough to pay his tuition to St. Louis University, where he took a degree in history and political science. He was one of four Negroes in a class of eleven hundred. After serving in the Army, where he became involved in protest activities and organized other Negro GI's to challenge Jim Crow at his base in Anniston, Alabama, he returned to St. Louis. Here he held a variety of jobs, ranging from making aeronautical charts, driving a city bus, setting up business interests, selling insurance and representing the Municipal Employees Union, to working with the NAACP, being on the board of aldermen, and then serving as ward committeeman.

Cleaver, Eldridge

In 1968 Eldridge Cleaver, then thirty-three years old, had spent nineteen years on probation and parole or inside California institutions including San Quentin, Folsom and Soledad Prisons. First arrested at the age of eighteen on marijuana charges, Cleaver was returned to prison again and again by an outside world which failed to offer him a relevant alternative to crime. In Soledad Prison, however, Cleaver was converted by Muslims and was encouraged to spend time studying and learning to write. In 1968 Cleaver rose from obscurity to become the leading intellectual light of Black militancy. The author of *Soul on Ice,* Cleaver was released from prison to become senior editor of *Ramparts* magazine. Although in 1968 Cleaver could have settled down to a comfortable life among the literary avant-garde, this was not the year for him to abandon his conscience. He used his position to publicize the changes he believes are necessary for both Black and white America. He has been a leader in instilling racial pride in Black students and ghetto youth. He became minister of information for the Black Panther Party and was chosen as Presidential candidate by the Peace and Freedom Party. Since his release Cleaver has been the object of constant controversy. One notable example of this was the dispute which occurred when Governor Ronald Reagan intervened in the Berkeley students' choice of Eldridge Cleaver as lecturer for their Black studies course.

Eldridge Cleaver was born in Wabbeseka, Arkansas. He is a graduate of Bay View High School in San Quentin Prison.

Edelman, Marian

"People cannot be left with the option of giving up or committing violence. Regardless of allegations of disorganization—and why should the poor be organized?—that has nothing to do with the fact that babies die, people are hungry, and jobs are needed; that the houses the poor live in are often inferior to those the country saw in Resurrection City."

As SCLC Congressional liaison, Marian Edelman attacked the legal roots of the problems she mentions above by pushing, in 1968, for "a jobs bill, a repeal of repressive welfare legislation, and a major resolution of the hunger issue." Reared and educated in the South, with extensive experience in the civil rights movement, and with "a fine grasp of that complicated web of legislation, the welfare and public assistance laws," in the words of Senator Fred Harris of Oklahoma, Mrs. Edelman came to Capitol Hill highly qualified to represent the Black Southern poor.

With the end of the 90th Congress the twenty-eight-year-old attorney left her post with SCLC, feeling that the crucial laws were already on the books, that the incoming administration would not be amenable to new poverty legislation and that emphasis should now be placed on implementation of the existing laws. Supported by a Field Foundation Fellowship, and working as director of the Washington Research Project, she began a study of the responsiveness of federal agencies to poor people.

Formerly Marian Wright, she was born in Bennettsville, South Carolina, and was educated at Spelman College and at the Yale Law School. In 1964 she opened her first law office in Jackson, Mississippi, and in 1966 she became the first Negro woman admitted to the Mississippi bar. Working with the NAACP Legal Defense and

Educational Fund, she gained the expertise in welfare law that brought her to Washington. In 1968 she married Peter Edelman, former aide of Robert Kennedy.

Edwards, Harry

"For years we have participated in the Olympic Games, carrying the U.S. on our backs with our victories, and race relations are now worse than ever. Now they are even shooting people in the streets. We're not trying to lose the Olympics for the Americans. What happens to them is immaterial. . . . But it's time for Black people to stand up as men and women and refuse to be . . . performing animals for a little extra dog food."

Harry Edwards led the boycott of the Olympics from his office at San Jose State College in California, where he is a sociology instructor. His classes in Racial and Cultural Minorities and Youth Problems Today attract hundreds of students, white and Black, and stimulate vehement discussions. Though his tendency to make his point via overkill provokes a great deal of controversy, his basic premise remains: "Now that so many brothers have awakened, there is nothing we can't accomplish."

After graduating from San Jose State, Edwards went to Cornell on a Woodrow Wilson Fellowship. Then, in 1966, after receiving his M.A., he returned to San Jose, where he soon set to work, demanding changes and following through on ideas that he had formulated in graduate school. As a result, such policies as prohibiting white coaches from demoting Black athletes without the confirmation of a Black council have gone into effect at San Jose State, whose administration thus far has been extremely responsive to Harry Edwards' ideas.

Galamison, Milton Arthur

"I thought I could roll up my sleeves and spin around a few times and it would be done—and, look, it's turned into a lifetime project."

Milton Galamison, pastor of a Presbyterian church in the Bedford-Stuyvesant section of Brooklyn, has been committed to ending de facto segregation in New York schools since his first involvement in 1956, when he unsuccessfully attempted to work out a plan to "desegregate" an all-Negro junior high school in Brooklyn. Since then, he has led two massive boycotts and has been arrested at least nine times in futile efforts toward integration. The struggle has been a long and frustrating one and has finally led Galamison, along with many other Black leaders, to decide to de-emphasize the goal of integration and concentrate instead on obtaining Black control of Black institutions.

The racial crisis that 1968 brought to the New York educational system focused attention on Galamison's activities and on his special concern for quality education for ghetto residents in the form of community controlled schools. While December 1966 saw Galamison installed in the school board president's chair after angry Black parents had taken over the board's office for three days and declared him president of a "People's Board of Education," December 1968 saw him as actual vice-president of New York City's board of education. He was appointed to this post by Mayor John Lindsay.

Born in Philadelphia on January 25, 1923, Mr. Galamison received a Bachelor of Divinity degree from Lincoln University in Pennsylvania in 1947 and a Master's degree from the Princeton Theological Seminary in 1949. Once chairman of the Citywide Committee for School Integration, Galamison served as its director when it became the School and Community Organized for Partnership in Education (SCOPE), which received a one-year grant of $160,000 from the Ford Foundation to finance its program "to enhance communications and cooperation among teachers, parents, and other community residents and organizations."

Gregory, Dick

Dick Gregory dramatically climaxed his emergence from the entertainment world into politics by running for President in 1968. Feeling that the available candidates were products of antiquated and unresponsive machinery, the thirty-six-year-old comedian offered voters his own commitment to the struggle for a "Clean Society."

Gregory had already demonstrated that commitment. In 1968 he had protested the war in

Vietnam by severe and repeated hunger strikes; in June he had been jailed for participation in a Nisqually Indian protest over a broken treaty; in September he had met with North Vietnamese officials in Paris in hopes of promoting peace; and in December he had raised enough money to send ten thousand pounds of navy beans to the poor people of Marks, Mississippi. Upon Gregory's return from Paris, the Peace and Freedom Alternative Party of New Jersey had endorsed him as its Presidential candidate.

His perspective on various political and social issues has always been a broad one and not a purely racial one. He has argued that the draft is not (as is alleged by some Black leaders) a plot against Black people, but is against the interests of all the nation's young people. Gandhi's response to injustice is, in Gregory's mind, the ideal one, "militant towards the system, humble towards everybody." But he takes his protest seriously. Thus, Gregory, feeling that negotiations alone would be of little value, was ready to participate in the late Dr. Martin Luther King's planned April demonstrations only if "Dr. King really means to paralyze the town."

Hatcher, Richard G.

Richard Hatcher, Gary, Indiana's, first Black mayor, opposed his own Democratic Party in the mayoral contest by challenging the incumbent, A. Martin Katz. He found himself victorious, but with no political allies by his side. On his council were four Negroes, two of whom were holdovers from the Katz administration and one of whom was a political competitor, and five whites, three of whom he can count on to vote in opposition to him. George Coker, executive director of the Urban League, is quoted as saying that Hatcher has "all the problems of New York, Chicago, and Los Angeles multiplied by three."

But Hatcher has been anxious to meet the challenge. "You just have to deal with these problems one at a time," he feels. And dealing with two problems at a time is twice as good, so Hatcher, acutely aware of the fact that crime is a manifestation of a more deeply rooted problem, attempts to work simultaneously at both the cause and the effect of his city's difficulties.

Born in 1923, Hatcher was the twelfth of thirteen children, six of whom failed to reach adulthood because of indifferent medical care in the rural Georgia community where the family then lived. With the help of his brothers and sisters, an athletic scholarship for sprinting and a part-time job waiting on tables, Hatcher attended Indiana University. After graduating he entered the Valparaiso University Law School. At this time he worked full-time as a psychiatric aide at a nearby state mental hospital. In 1959 he moved to Gary to live with an older brother and practice law, and by 1963 he had come into the limelight by being voted president of the city council when a freshman member—a success that would lead him to the mayor's seat.

Higginbotham, A. Leon

Added to the Ten Most Outstanding Men in America awards roster, which includes such notables as John Kennedy, Richard Nixon, Leonard Bernstein, Orson Welles and Dr. Tom Dooley, was Judge A. Leon Higginbotham, Jr., a 1963 selection.

The youngest person to be appointed a federal district judge in the last thirty years, A. Leon Higginbotham, Jr., is judge of the U.S. District Court for the Eastern District of Pennsylvania. He was sworn into office January 7, 1964. In 1968 Judge Higginbotham was appointed to the National Commission on the Causes and Prevention of Violence, by Lyndon Johnson. Before that, he had been nominated by President Kennedy for a seven-year term as a commissioner for the Federal Trade Commission. Not only was he the first Black man to be a member at the commission level of any federal regulatory agency, but he was the youngest person ever to be named a commissioner for the Federal Trade Commission.

Born on February 25, 1928, in Trenton, New Jersey, Judge Higginbotham began to study engineering at Purdue University, but changed to liberal arts and to Antioch College from which he graduated in 1949. He then went to the Yale Law School, from which he got his degree in 1952. He also holds an honorary LL.D. from North Carolina College at Durham.

Dick Gregory

Innis, Roy

"Integration is as dead as a doornail. In fact it never came alive," says Roy Innis. He thinks that Americans must come to understand that there are two distinct peoples in this country—Black and white—and that they must "try to work out a social contract between them for co-existence." He also suggests that the white power structure return tax money to the Black community so that public institutions can function for Black people. In this way community control would be economically feasible at several levels.

The depth of his belief in community control is evident in his vociferous support of a Congressional bill put together by CORE (of which he is acting executive director). Called the Community Self-Determination Act, this bill offers a plan to establish community business corporations that would create new community enterprises and regenerate old ones. Mr. Innis believes this is a much better way to approach urban problems than are the "Mickey Mouse" programs sponsored by the federal government since the 1930's.

Born in the Virgin Islands in 1934, Mr. Innis came to Harlem at the age of twelve. He joined the Army at sixteen and later attended City College, New York, where he majored in chemistry. Before becoming director of CORE in 1968, he was chairman of Harlem CORE for three years. He has long been an advocate of Black separatism, even in the early 1960's when most of the civil rights movement, including CORE, was geared towards integration.

Jackson, Jesse Louis

"America worked us for 350 years without paying us. Now we deserve a job or an income." The life that Jesse Louis Jackson leads makes it clear that he is willing to fight to make those jobs and that income a reality. As early as his student days at North Carolina Agricultural and Technical College, he was involved in the struggle for Black rights. It was there that he led the student sit-ins in Greensboro restaurants.

At the personal request of the late Dr. Martin Luther King, Jesse Jackson was made the nationwide head of SCLC's Operation Breadbasket. Jackson was also the city manager for SCLC-sponsored Resurrection City.

The Reverend Jesse Jackson is convinced of the need for Black-owned businesses. "We would rather own A & P than burn it." But his concept of Black capitalism far exceeds the addition of a few more Black entrepreneurs. He is hoping to develop an Inner City Transit Authority which would be an "authentic public company" responsive to the needs of Black and poor communities in Chicago.

Jesse Jackson was born in Greensville, South Carolina, on October 8, 1941. He was ordained a Baptist minister on June 30, 1968, after studying at the Chicago Theological Seminary. He is married and has three children.

Jordan, Barbara C.

Above and beyond her assaults upon unjust legal barriers from her post as Texas state senator, Barbara Jordan has broken several barriers simply by achieving that post. She was the first Black woman ever elected to the Texas senate, the first Negro to serve in the Texas senate since 1883, the first Negro to preside over the Texas senate, the first Black woman to preside over a state senate in the United States, the first freshman senator ever named to the Texas Legislative Council since its inception in 1949, and the first Negro ever named chairman of a major committee in the Texas senate. Other honors include being named by UPI in 1967 as one of the top ten most influential women in Texas, and, in 1968, being named by President Johnson to the Commission on Income Maintenance Programs.

After her reelection to the Texas senate in January 1969, she sponsored, from her new post as chairman of the Labor-Management Relations Committee, the first piece of major legislation to pass the Texas senate in 1969, which was also the first legislation originating from the Texas legislature in twelve years to increase workers' compensation. Her plans for 1969 include investigation of Texas reform schools and raising of the minimum wage in Texas. She is also a member of a committee on medical programs for the poor and of a committee to encourage the performing arts.

Senator Jordan was born in Houston in 1936. She graduated from Texas Southern University *magna cum laude* in 1956, and from the Boston University School of Law in 1959.

Karenga, Ron Ndabezitha Everett

The year 1969 will be the year for reconstruction; 1970 will be the year of separation; 1971 will be the year of guerrillas—of defense rather than development. So says Ron Karenga, Los Angeles-based Black power leader. Karenga, who is twenty-seven, is the founder and the leader of a militant organization called US, whose primary goal is the unity of Black Americans.

To Karenga, who promotes a program of self-determination, self-respect, self-security and self-defense, being Black means commitment. Karenga's revolutionary philosophy was cemented shortly after the Watts riots in 1965, which he terms "the revolt." The riots meant the end of nonviolence as the dominant philosophy in the Negro movement. Mr. Karenga is credited with having prevented riots in Los Angeles after the assassination of Dr. Martin Luther King. Speaking about his role in preventing riots, Karenga says, "The capacity to use power often eliminates the need to use it."

Urging Negroes to create a distinctive Afro-American culture, Karenga insists he is not for isolation but for interdependence. Once Black people have power they can live interdependently with whites.

Descriptions of Karenga (whose Swahili name means "keeper of the tradition") range from "charming" and "humorous" to "nasty." His shaved head, Ghengis Khan style mustache and his sunglasses create a striking, if not intimidating, appearance.

The fourteenth child of a Baptist minister, Ron Karenga was born in Maryland in 1941. He graduated from the University of California at Los Angeles *cum laude*, has a Master's degree in languages and has credits towards a Doctorate in political science. He speaks fluent Swahili, reads French and Spanish and is learning Zulu. Academic accomplishments, however, as well as personal life, are secondary to his dedication to Black unity.

King, Coretta

Formerly an unassuming supporter of the civil rights movement and of its champion, Mrs. Martin Luther King was forced into poignant visibility by the events of April 4, 1968. Despite her grief, Coretta King immersed herself in her husband's unfinished tasks with all the commitment and determination that was his. The day before his burial she led the Memphis march for the sanitation workers whose cause her husband had championed. With classic forbearance, she reminded them of her husband's words: "With every Good Friday comes an Easter."

With his hopes and his promises as her guide and her goal, Coretta King immersed herself in plans and activities for future programs. Urging that the organization of the Poor People's Campaign continue, she became deeply involved in its activities. When it reached its climax on Solidarity Day, she told the tens of thousands of people there that "the problems of racism, poverty and war can all be summarized in one word, 'violence,' which seems to be fashionable in our society. If we do not stop this madness, we will certainly destroy ourselves and the whole world."

In addition to espousing her husband's ideas, Mrs. King has taken on the responsibility of formulating an ideology of her own—one whose particular emphasis is on women and their role in modern society. Challenging them to join in a "campaign of conscience," she has alerted women to the essential need for participation and commitment, saying, "Women, if the soul of this nation is to be saved, I believe you must become its soul. You must speak out against the evils of our time as you see them. Those of us women who have been blessed with the privilege of bearing children have the sacred task of rearing them with a knowledge and understanding of our democratic heritage and the eternal values of love, justice, mercy and peace."

Martin, Louis Emanuel

As vital to the Johnson Administration as he was to John Kennedy's, Louis Martin is optimistic about the political gains made by Blacks in the past eight years. He singles out the 1965 Voting Rights Bill as the most significant of these.

Mr. Martin played an important part in the desegregation of the Democratic Party, which culminated in the 1968 convention with the seating of integrated delegations from Mississippi and Georgia. There were 387 Black delegates and alternates at the convention.

In December 1968 Louis Martin retired as deputy chairman and director of minorities for the Democratic National Committee, to return to an executive post in the Sengstacke newspaper chain, which he had left in 1960. Through his knowledge of the power groups in Washington and his promotion of civil rights and support of the Democratic Party, Mr. Martin is acknowledged to be responsible for some four hundred Black appointments.

Louis Martin was born in 1912 in Shelbyville, Tennessee. He took his degree at the University of Michigan, where he also did his postgraduate work. In 1934–35 Mr. Martin was a freelance writer in Havana, Cuba. He helped establish the *Michigan Chronicle* and was its first editor and publisher. Wilberforce University gave Louis Martin an LL.D. in 1951. Martin has served two terms as president of the National Newspaper Association, and for a year was editorial adviser to the *Amalgamated Press* in Lagos, Nigeria. He has also been editor-in-chief of the *Chicago Daily Defender*, and has been instrumental in establishing Black-owned life insurance companies.

Matthew, Dr. Thomas W.

"I decided I wasn't making a contribution unless I followed the patient out of the hospital and tried to change his environment." With this in mind, Dr. Thomas Matthew gave up a $100,000-a-year practice as a neurosurgeon to found NEGRO, a non-profit corporation dedicated to Black self-help. Starting with only $50 capital, the National Economic Growth and Reconstruction Organization today has assets of over $3 million. It is financed by bond sales and accepts no charitable contributions. All its enterprises are Black-run, and include 140-bed Interfaith Hospital, Domco Chemical Company (with $700,000 in government and private contracts), a textile company, a paint plant, two one-hundred-family apartment buildings rehabilitated by NEGRO, and a thirty-vehicle bus line—all in and around New York City. In Pittsburgh, NEGRO runs a clothing manufacturing plant, and in Watts it runs two bus lines. Dr. Matthew has fought more than one battle with city governments and creditors to keep his operation running.

Thomas Matthew was born in Brooklyn forty-four years ago and was one of eleven children of a janitor to an all-white apartment building. "I was eighteen before I lived outside a basement," he says. His sisters all became teachers or librarians and his only brother is a dentist. Thomas, the first Black graduate of the Bronx High School of Science and of Manhattan College, took his medical degree at Meharry Medical College. He was an intern at Harvard Medical School. He has been an instructor at Albert Einstein Medical College, at Harvard Medical School and at Boston University Medical School. At the present time, he is staff neurosurgeon for four New York City hospitals. Dr. Matthew was the first Negro to be trained as a neurosurgeon in the United States.

Newton, Huey

"The Panther's nature is not to strike first, but when he is attacked and backed into a corner he will respond viciously and wipe out the aggressor, thoroughly, wholly, absolutely and completely."

Huey Newton, the leader and founder of the Black Panther Party, is in prison serving a two-to-fifteen-year voluntary manslaughter sentence for the 1967 killing of an Oakland policeman. At Los Padres, California, Men's Colony Newton was put in solitary confinement because he refused to work in the mess hall at what he considered menial tasks. He said that he would take another job under the institution's industrial training program.

In 1966, with Bobby Seale, Huey Newton began the Black Panther Party for Self-Defense. It was formed to keep police in Black neighborhoods under surveillance. Armed with loaded shotguns and cameras, the Panthers patrolled ghetto streets to avert "suspicious police activity."

During his trial in July, 2,500 demonstrators ringed the courthouse; 250 of them were uniformed members of the Black Panther Party.

Newton, who quotes from Dryden, didn't learn to read until he was about sixteen. He explains this by saying, "I was one of the top ten bad guys in school and the teachers passed me on because they wanted to hurry and get me out of there. Knowing how to read was irrelevant to me then, but one day I decided I didn't want to be ignorant any longer."

The youngest of seven children, Huey Newton was born in Monroe, Louisiana, on February 17, 1942. He attended Oakland City College (now Merritt College), where he founded the Afro American Society, and San Francisco Law School.

Phillips, Channing E.

"Having seen the party, I'm rather glad I lost," were the sentiments of the Reverend Channing E. Phillips, the first Black man ever to be put up for nomination as President by either major political party. Reverend Phillips received sixty-seven and a half votes at the Democratic national convention in Chicago in 1968. The forty-year-old pastor of Washington, D.C.'s, Lincoln's Temple Church of Christ considers his own engagement in politics as an outgrowth of participation in peace projects. Dr. Phillips was elected a national committeeman in April on the Robert Kennedy ticket. He ran Kennedy's campaign in Washington. According to Phillips, Kennedy's death left the Black man with no candidate.

Though disappointed with events at the Democratic convention, militant Dr. Phillips is still willing to give his party one more chance. When asked if Black delegates intended to walk out at the convention he answered, "We are just getting into the Democratic Party. No, we are not going to walk out."

Born in Brooklyn in 1928, Channing Phillips attended public schools in Brooklyn, New York, and in Pittsburgh. He received a scholarship in painting and sculpture to Carnegie Tech. He has a B.A. degree in sociology from Virginia Union University and a B.D. in biblical studies from Colgate-Rochester Divinity School. He went to Drew University graduate school. Three of his brothers and a brother-in-law are also ministers. His father was a Baptist minister.

Robinson, Peter H.

Peter H. Robinson (1879–), retired railway mail clerk and real estate dealer, quietly donated $50,000 to Bethune-Cookman College of Daytona Beach, Florida, in February of 1966. This philanthropic gift was the largest amount of money ever given by a single Negro donor to a Negro college in the state of Florida. Mr. Robinson specified that the gift was to be used toward the construction of a $250,000 music building as a tribute to his deceased wife. He requested that the building be named the Julia E. Robinson Memorial Music Hall.

His acquaintances had been unaware of the financial ability of Peter Robinson and of the extent of his fortune until the gift was publicized by the Associated Press. Many had considered him a mere "dabbler" in real estate. (As a railway mail clerk he had invested his savings in real estate in the city of Jacksonville, Florida.)

Born in Pensacola, Florida, in 1879, Peter Robinson was trained for a career in carpentry at Tuskegee Institute, where the philosophy of thrift of Booker T. Washington deeply influenced his life. After working two years as a carpenter in Memphis, he decided to take the United States Civil Service examination for the position of a railway mail clerk. His first assignment was from Dothan, Alabama, to Panama City, Florida, where he encountered threats and discrimination. Through dogged determination he remained in the service for thirty-three years.

A great humanitarian, Peter Robinson helps people who are having difficulty in holding onto their property. Over the years he has concerned himself with the financial situation of Edward Waters College in Jacksonville and the Florida Normal College in St. Augustine. The Negro Nursing Home in Jacksonville has been another recipient of contributions from this philanthropist.

Stokes, Carl

In 1967 the great-grandson of a slave defeated the grandson of a U.S. President to become the first Negro mayor of a major United States city. When Carl Stokes assumed office, Cleveland,

Ohio, offered all the grim problems of a large urban center in the midst of a racial and economic crisis. The task of quelling disorder and at the same time attracting new business and industry was a considerable challenge.

Stokes began with a barrage of imaginative programs, including a series of Town Hall meetings in which he and his cabinet discussed neighborhood problems on a person-to-person basis with residents, thus bringing the government as close as possible to the people and assuring its responsiveness to their needs. Stokes utilized this alliance with all of Cleveland's citizens, and had confidence in the community's willingness and ability to assist him, more than once—particularly in the summer of 1968. After the tragic incident involving a bloody gun battle between Black militants and white policemen, Stokes removed all white officials from the scene of the conflict and called upon five hundred ghetto leaders to assist a hundred Black policemen and a few Black sheriff's deputies to restore order to the area. Though the idea behind this handling of the incident provoked a great deal of controversy, it proved to be a thoroughly effective method of preventing further disorders and of winning the confidence of Cleveland's Negroes.

Carl Stokes and his brother Louis began working at an early age to augment the income of their widowed mother. Dropping out of high school, Carl worked until he was eighteen, then joined the Army, where he was with the army of occupation in Germany. Returning to Cleveland after his honorable discharge as a corporal, he resumed his studies at East Tech High School and received his diploma in June 1947. He then went on to West Virginia State College and to Western Reserve University. He took his first law degree at the University of Minnesota Law School and an LL.B. from the Cleveland-Marshall Law School. After completing his education, he joined his brother in the law firm of Stokes and Stokes.

In 1968 Mayor Stokes received honorary degrees from Central State and Wilberforce Universities, the Cleveland-Marshall Law School, St. Francis College and Tufts University. In May he delivered the Sidney Hillman memorial lecture at Brandeis University.

Stokes, Louis

Louis Stokes is giving the voters "a hot line to a greater Cleveland." The first Black man to be elected to Congress from Ohio, brother of the first Black man to be elected mayor of a major U.S. city, Louis Stokes works jointly with his brother Carl towards the progress of their city.

Once a shoe-shine boy, Louis also worked selling newspapers and various mail-order items, and also sold clothes in an Army-Navy surplus store. The GI Bill put him through Western Reserve University in 1948. From there, he went on to receive his Doctor of Jurisprudence degree from Cleveland-Marshall Law School. Since 1954 Louis Stokes has been a practicing attorney in Cleveland. The events of 1965 brought Stokes his greatest legal challenge. The Ohio legislature had redrawn the boundaries of the Twenty-first District so that Black wards were dispersed and Black voter strength so diluted that no Black Congressional candidate could possibly win. When Black Republican leader Charles P. Lucas (who was Stokes' opponent in the race for Congress) brought suit, Stokes was appointed the attorney. On appeal to the United States Supreme Court, Stokes won the case and forced the legislature to create a new and acceptable redistricting plan.

Stokes has always taken on the cases of poor people, has always defended civil rights marchers and has assisted Black militants whose rights have been violated. He has also fought local "stop and frisk" procedures. It is said of him: "If a 'brother' needed a lawyer, all he had to do was ask Louis."

Washington, Bennetta Bullock

An expert at working with disadvantaged youth, Bennetta Washington is director of women's centers of the Job Corps at the Office of Economic Opportunity. The program is designed to create positive attitudes and confidence in women regarded as unemployable. Training and education are provided towards careers as nurses' aides, medical technicians, saleswomen, teachers' aides, stenographers and work at other skilled and semi-skilled jobs.

Mrs. Washington, the wife of the District of Columbia's Mayor Walter E. Washington, began her own education in the D.C. public schools. Later she became a teacher in the same system. She later became a counselor and then the principal of three high schools. At Cardozo High School, Dr. Washington directed the Cardozo Project in Urban Teaching, a pilot project using Peace Corps returnees, which served as a model for the National Teacher Training Program.

In 1968 Dr. Washington was the first Martin Luther King Scholar-in-Residence at Rutgers University.

Dr. Washington was born in 1918 in Winston-Salem, North Carolina. She is a graduate of Howard University with a B.A. in liberal arts and an M.A. in counseling. She took her Ph.D. at Catholic University. She is the author of *Background Factors and Adjustment* (1951), *Youth in Conflict* (1963) and *Color by Prejudice* (1964).

Washington, Walter E.

Walter Washington makes no apologies for concerning himself equally with both the white and the Black communities in Washington, D.C. As a result, the District's Mayor-Commissioner has been criticized by both. Despite his critics, Walter Washington has been popular with both Blacks and whites during his term in office as top administrator in the nation's capital. Mayor Washington was appointed in 1967 by President Lyndon Johnson to head the reorganized D.C. government. He has attempted to form a community out of the city. His desire is to strengthen the links between citizens and their government. Acknowledged by many as the best administrator in city government, Mayor Washington has worked tirelessly to make contact with his city.

There was some fear that Richard Nixon would not reappoint Democratic Mayor Washington. President Nixon, however, conformed with community sentiment and reappointed Mayor Washington for another term.

Born April 15, 1915, in Dawson, Georgia, Walter Washington has an A.B. and an LL.B. from Howard University. He took graduate courses in public administration at American University and has an honorary degree from Fisk University. He is married to Bennetta Bullock Washington. They have one daughter, Bennetta Jules-Rossette, a graduate student at Harvard.

Watson, Barbara

Tall, attractive, and most of all competent, Miss Barbara Watson stands at the head of what has often been described as the "crisis bureau," the Bureau for Security and Consular Affairs of the State Department.

As the first woman and the first Negro to serve in that position and to hold the title of assistant secretary of state, Miss Watson is charged with the full-time responsibility of "protecting American citizens in other countries, whether they become sick and die, get into jail or become pawns of war." In addition, she supervises a worldwide operation that issues two million passports and nearly as many visas each year and looks after 280 consular posts throughout the world—ranging from the large embassies in London and Paris to the small consulates of small countries.

"If you stop to think of the enormity of the job," she says, "you collapse. So I don't stop and think. I just plunge on and hope I don't make any mistakes. You also might say that I'm just the sort of person who likes a challenge."

Born in 1918, the daughter of New York City's first Negro judge, the late James S. Watson, Miss Watson at one time established a model agency and charm school in response to a growing Black advertising market. But her family's legal tradition lured her back to law school and a series of jobs within the New York City legal system. Then, after two years on the international scene, in which one of her tasks was to chair a conference in Manila involving 1,261 American merchant ships carrying supplies to Vietnam, Miss Watson accepted President Johnson's 1966 offer to come to Washington to the State Department.

Olympic heavyweight champion George Foreman displays his gold medal to admirers at the Parks Job Corps Center in Pleasanton, California, where he is a staff instructor.

Heisman Trophy winner O. J. Simpson receives the Men of Tomorrow outstanding achievement award from Dr. Edward H. Ballard, M.D. (left), chairman of the board, and Al Patton, special events chairman, of Men of Tomorrow, Inc., on December 21. This was the first time Simpson had been honored by a Black community group.

The Black Athlete—1968

Dave Sendler

College Basketball

FOR ALL THE pomp (like the flashy sharpshooting of Niagara's little Calvin Murphy) and circumstance (like the thundering rebounding and scoring of Louisville's Wes Unseld), the '67–'68 season came down to a single confrontation: Elvin Hayes *vs.* Lew Alcindor.

The experts had said before the season that Alcindor's UCLA team, the reigning national champion, would doubtless repeat as titlist—and would just as unquestionably go undefeated again. First, there was the 7 ft. 1⅜ in. Alcindor, a graceful shooter, dominating rebounder and towering shot-blocker. And then there was some talented help from two swift, versatile guards, Mike Warren and Lucius Allen—among others.

As the season developed, counter pressure began building up in Houston, where a big team, starring the 6 ft. 9 in. Hayes, rolled up victory after victory. Hayes' fans felt he might be equal to —or better than—Alcindor, and they pointed to Elvin's feathery shooting touch, his agility and his great leaping ability.

The two teams and their stars clashed in a dramatic extravaganza on January 20. The site was the Houston Astrodome, and a record 52,693 people turned out to see which team would fall from the ranks of the undefeated. UCLA's winning streak was at 47.

The night belonged to Hayes. He moved away from the basket—where Alcindor wouldn't chase him—and tossed in shot after shot. He rebounded and defended. In all, he hit on 68 per cent of his shots, scored 39 points, got 15 rebounds and sank two free throws in the final seconds to win the game for Houston, 71–69. Alcindor, plagued by an eye injury that impaired his vision, made only four of fourteen shots, managed just 14 points and seemed to play timidly.

Leaving Texas, the dejected UCLA team, unused to being number two, vowed revenge if it could meet Houston in the NCAA tournament.

Neither team lost a game the rest of the regular season, and so into the tournament they went, Houston undefeated and number one, and UCLA one-time loser to the Cougars. When Houston beat Texas Christian 103–68, and UCLA whipped Santa Clara 87–66 in regional finals, the stage was set for their showdown. It came in the NCAA semifinals in Los Angeles. And it proved to be awesome and conclusive. UCLA sped up the court, zipped its passes smartly and shot with precision. Back on defense, the Bruins pressed Houston's ballhandlers, smothered Hayes with harassing attention (Elvin scored 10 points in the game) and rebounded vigorously. The Bruins, sizzling for revenge, poured it on. The final score was 101–69, and no one doubted that Alcindor—with 19 points and 19 rebounds—and UCLA were number one.

The next night, almost anticlimactically, UCLA beat North Carolina 78–55, as Alcindor scored 34 points and blocked nine shots. The 23-point margin of victory was the largest ever in an NCAA title game. Said North Carolina coach Dean Smith, "UCLA has got to be the greatest college basketball team ever assembled." Alcindor, Warren and Allen all made the all-tournament team.

Alcindor and Hayes were on both the AP and

UPI All-America teams. And so was Unseld, another great frontcourt man, who had been the heart of the Louisville squad. In the UPI poll—with the coaches making the selections—the 5 ft. 10 in. Murphy, a sophomore, was picked as a guard. Murphy averaged 38.2 points a game, the fourth highest mark ever recorded for a season of college play, and he was second in the country in scoring to Pete Maravich of Louisiana State.

When it came time for the Olympic trials—and with plenty of talk around about boycotts, missing schoolwork and spoiling pro chances either through injury or by reporting late—Alcindor, Hayes and Unseld were among the Black players who declined invitations. Murphy tried out, but didn't make the squad. The U.S. team, considered second-rate by many, nonetheless won all its games in Mexico City to take the gold medal for the U.S. Spencer Haywood, a youngster just going into his sophomore season at the University of Detroit, was the team's sensation with his rebounding, defense and scoring. Jo-Jo White of Kansas did much of the quarterbacking from backcourt and contributed some strong outside shooting.

As the '68–'69 season got under way, Alcindor and UCLA seemed destined for number one honors again, while North Carolina, led by Charlie Scott, appeared to be one of the major challengers.

Pro Basketball

In the pro ranks, fans were treated to the instant success of flashy rookie Earl Monroe and the emergence of young Dave Bing as a rising superstar. But when it came time for championships and climaxes, the drama was supplied by supposedly dimming superstar Bill Russell and his aging Boston Celtics.

Long dominant in the National Basketball Association, Boston had lost its title to the Philadelphia 76ers in '66–'67 and appeared to be headed for also-ran status in '67–'68 as well. For Wilt Chamberlain and Hal Greer had Philadelphia on the move. The 76ers had won the Eastern Division crown and seemed strong enough to roll on through the Eastern playoffs and the finals that would follow.

Philadelphia got unexpectedly stiff resistance from third-place New York in the Eastern semifinals, but finally prevailed, four games to two. Meanwhile, second-place Boston fell behind, two to one, to fourth-place Detroit, before rallying to eliminate the Pistons in six games.

And so it was Boston *vs.* Philadelphia, Chamberlain *vs.* Russell, in the Eastern finals. With Russell going to the boards and playing his usual intimidating defense, Boston got a fast start against Philadelphia, winning 127–118. But then the 76ers came on—with Chamberlain, Greer, Chet Walker, Luke Jackson and Wally Jones among others. They swept three straight and the series appeared about over. Except that the Celtics weren't quitting. Back they fought, driving to 122–104 and 114–106 victories, and now there would be a seventh and decisive game. It was nip-and-tuck all the way, and one of the compelling sights was that of Russell's work in blocking shots and forcing errors. Chamberlain took just one shot in the second half, and when it was over the game was Boston's, 100–96.

From there, Boston went on to the finals against Los Angeles, the winner in the West. The Lakers, with superstar Elgin Baylor having one of his best seasons ever, had eliminated Chicago four to one and San Francisco four to nothing. Boston, though, was equally hot now and simply defied the critics who said that veterans like Russell, Sam Jones and Satch Sanders couldn't keep up a fast pace throughout the playoffs. The Celtics wasted relatively little time in disposing of Los Angeles, four games to two. It was their ninth NBA title in the last ten years and it was the tenth championship for Russell in his twelve seasons of play.

Overall, the season was exciting because players like Bing and Monroe had come on to challenge the experienced standouts like Baylor, Russell, Chamberlain, Oscar Robertson and others. In his second year, Detroit's Bing led the league in scoring with 2,142 points and coolly directed the Piston offense from backcourt. Baltimore's Monroe, also a guard, shot spectacularly (he was fourth in the NBA in scoring), passed with flair and won the league's Rookie-of-the-Year award. Another young guard, Walt Hazzard of Seattle, had a fine year, averaging 23.9 points a game.

Baylor, afflicted in recent years with serious injuries, played with all his former firepower, scoring 2,002 points (second best in the NBA) with his stunning assortment of jump shots, drives and follow-ups. Cincinnati's Robertson, considered by most the best all-round player in the game, played in only sixty-five games because of injuries, but still managed the best per game average with 29.2. Other top scorers in the league included Chamberlain (24.3), Greer (24.1), Zelmo Beaty of St. Louis (21.1), Bob Boozer of Chicago (21.5), Willis Reed of New York (20.8) and Lenny Wilkens of St. Louis (20.0).

In the American Basketball League, Connie Hawkins paced Pittsburgh to the championship with his league-leading 26.8 points per game. Pittsburgh beat Minnesota four to one in the final series.

Before the '68–'69 season started, a major trade sent Wilt Chamberlain to Los Angeles to join Baylor and Jerry West, and, as the season moved into its '69 phase, the three stars had the Lakers out front in the Western Division. Baltimore was a surprising power in the East during the early going, and a lot of the success could be attributed to the rebounding and scoring of rookie Wes Unseld. Despite the loss of Chamberlain, Philadelphia was getting sufficient production from Walker, Greer and others to stay in the fight for first place, and player-coach Russell of Boston had his team not far off the pace. The New York Knicks, after trading center Walt Bellamy to Detroit, started to come on strongly with Willis Reed at center. The best new player in the league had to be Elvin Hayes of San Diego, who stepped right in and started scoring points faster than anyone else in the NBA.

The ABA shifted around a bit—sending the Pittsburgh team to Minnesota and the Minnesota club to Miami—and through it all, Connie Hawkins' scoring kept his squad atop the Eastern Division while seemingly awaiting a showdown with Oakland and Rick Barry in the West.

Baseball

Baseball's regular season in 1968 had all the suspense of a movie rerun you've seen time and again on television. Which is to say that you knew early on that the heroes—in this case the St. Louis Cardinals and the Detroit Tigers—were the good guys and that they would naturally win in the end.

Fine, because they did. But baseball 1968 managed some extra dimension, too, some bold drama that kept fans buzzing and, in the end, inspired. For first, it turned out to be the Year of the Pitcher. And second, the clash of the good guys in the World Series spun this way and that with the great play and the unexpected, and whirled to as tense a climax as any fan would have a right to expect.

The larger-than-life figure in the National League was the Cardinals' Bob Gibson, a tall, strong right-handed pitcher with a fastball that seems to explode as it whizzes into a batter's strike zone. How tall he looked as he poured it on, pitching 13 shutouts (five of them in a row), running up a string of 47 straight scoreless innings at one point, setting a league record with his 1.12 earned-run average, striking out 268 batters, winning 22 games (against nine losses) and leading his team to a first-place finish, nine games ahead of second-place San Francisco.

Though winner of his league's Most Valuable Player Award and Cy Young Award (for being the best pitcher), Gibson was hardly the only star of the St. Louis show. There was centerfielder Curt Flood, stylish both afield, with his grace and range, and at bat, with his controlled, if not entirely powerful, stroke. Flood hit only five home runs, but his .301 average was fifth in the league. And flanking him in left field was dashing Lou Brock, swift and flashy. Brock, also not a noted power hitter, nonetheless generated plenty of offense, leading the league in such departments as stolen bases (62), doubles (46) and triples (14), while hitting a respectable .279.

St. Louis' pick up—Gibson—and go—Flood and Brock—notwithstanding, the Tigers had an even easier time clinching their pennant. Detroit shot home twelve games in front of second-place Baltimore and the man supplying the booster power was heavyset outfielder Willie Horton. He socked the ball for distance (his 36 homers put him second in the league), drove in 85 runs and maintained consistency (his .285 average was fifth best in the American League). Another important force was pinchbatter Gates Brown, a deadly effective man coming off the bench in the late innings. Brown averaged .370 and hit 6 homers, though he had only 92 official at-bats.

Seasoned right-handed pitcher Earl Wilson, though bothered by injuries, went 13–12 for the Tigers with a 2.85 ERA, and young John Hiller, going mostly in relief, was 9–6 with a 2.39 ERA.

When it came down to Detroit *vs.* St. Louis, the experts inclined to the Cardinals, winners of the '67 Series. But the atmosphere was charged for opening day, because Gibson was matched against the Tigers' thirty-one-game winner Denny McLain. It was a fitting way to climax the Year of the Pitcher, and Gibson, at least, rose to the occasion. He drove his live fastball at the Tiger hitters relentlessly, boring it in on them high and hard. He won in a breeze—a breeze created by a lot of wild swinging and missing. Gibson fanned a record seventeen men, allowing just five hits, and won 4–0. In the fourth game, the giants, Gibson and McLain, again faced each other. This time Gibson took it 10–1, giving up five hits and striking out ten.

Gibson had staked his club to a 3–1 lead in the Series, but the Tigers fought back. They took two straight, and with momentum going for them, sent Mickey Lolich against Gibson in the seventh and decisive game. Gibson threw manfully but with less oomph than previously, and what might have been the sweetest ending to a magnificent season went slightly sour. It was Lolich and Detroit, 4–1.

For the Tigers, Horton had come through nicely with a .304 average, while Flood and Brock had had some outstanding moments for St. Louis. Flood batted .286, while Brock collected the most hits in the Series (thirteen) and had the best batting average—.464. Though Brock was thrown out on the bases a couple of crucial times, he nonetheless tied his own record of seven stolen bases for a Series and needs just one more to break the career Series mark of fourteen.

While all the struggling beneath the Cards and Tigers produced less-than-noteworthy results on a team basis, there were still some fine individual performances throughout both leagues.

Though it was not really the hitters' year, a mixture of fine veterans and upcoming youngsters did well enough to keep the pitchers from getting too complacent. In the National League, the big three of Willie McCovey, Willie Mays and Jim Ray Hart clubbed the Giants to a second-place finish. McCovey, particularly, excelled, leading the league with 36 home runs and 105 runs-batted-in and placing eighth with his .293 average. Mays, yielding ever so slightly to age, still managed 23 homers, 79 RBI and a .289 average, while Hart contributed 23 home runs and 78 RBI. Mays now has 587 homers—setting him above any other National Leaguer and any other right-handed batter in history (and leaving him second only to Babe Ruth's career total of 714).

The wallop behind the Chicago Cub attack—the team placed third—got much of its zing from steady Billy Williams (30 homers, 98 RBI) and seemingly ageless veteran Ernie Banks (32 homers, 83 RBI). The Cubs' best pitcher was Ferguson Jenkins, who ran up a 20–15 record, struck out 260 men and had a 2.63 ERA.

Over in Cincinnati, three of the younger men, Alex Johnson (with a .312 average), Lee May (.290 average, 22 homers, 80 RBI) and Tommy Helms (.288 average) furnished the punch that aided the Reds' push to fourth place. Two big swingers, Will Stargell (24 homers, 67 RBI) and Donn Clendenon (17 home runs, 87 RBI), gave some authority to the Pittsburgh offense.

Elsewhere in the National League there was the encouraging rise of the New York Mets' Cleon Jones (whose .297 average was sixth best in the league) and the expected excellence of superhitters Hank Aaron of Atlanta (.287, 29 homers, 86 RBI) and Richie Allen of Philadelphia (.263, 33 homers, 90 RBI).

One of the bright stories in the American League was that of Don Buford, who shuttled from journeyman status at Chicago to the old reliable at Baltimore. Given his chance to play, Buford hustled as he always had and hit the way he never could. The result was a team-leading .282 average, which was sixth highest in the league.

Lee Maye of Cleveland and Tommy Davis of Chicago, both seasoned men, were tops on their squads, Maye with a .281 mark and Davis with a .268. Kansas City got some fine offense from Reggie Jackson (29 homers) and Bert Campaneris (.276 average) and strong pitching from Blue Moon Odom (16–10, 2.49 ERA). Boston, slipping to fourth from its '67 pennant year, was heartened by the development of young Reggie Smith, while the New York Yankees, coming on late in the season, got much of their spark from the running, hitting and fielding of young outfielders Roy White (.267, 17 homers, 62 RBI) and Bill Robinson (.240, 40 RBI). Infielder Rod Carew had another strong year with Minnesota, batting .273.

Off the field, baseball recognized the contributions of two Black athletes with a pair of front-office announcements. In Atlanta the Braves, part-way through the season, put pitching immortal Leroy (Satchel) Paige on its active roster—this in spite of the fact that he is probably in his sixties. The reason? To help him qualify for pension, and definitely not to pitch. In New York, at season's end, the Yankees got catcher Elston Howard back from the Boston Red Sox and announced that he would retire as a player and serve as a coach.

Golf

Lee Elder, a thirty-three-year-old former caddy, gave golf one of its most dramatic moments in '68 when he challenged the renowned Jack Nicklaus for top prize money in the American Classic at Akron, Ohio. Nicklaus, one of the sport's superstars, and Elder, in his first full year on the tour under official sanction, had finished the regulation seventy-two holes tied at 280. And with a national television audience watching, the two went at it in a sudden-death playoff for the first-prize money of $25,000. Through one, two, three, four holes they went, still deadlocked. With darkness gathering, they went onto the fifth hole and finally Elder cracked, missing the putt he needed to tie Nicklaus. It had been a valiant try—and the longest sudden-death ever in a major tournament. Still, Elder collected $12,187.50 and by year's end finished the tour with earnings of $31,690.00. That put him in fifty-fourth place among all golfers on the tour.

Top Negro golfer was Charlie Sifford, in fiftieth place with $33,180.83. Sifford, who had won the Greater Hartford, Connecticut, Open in 1967, did not place first in any 1968 tourney, but did play steadily enough to compile a solid record of achievement. With the turn of the new year, however, he got off spectacularly, winning the Los Angeles Open and its $20,000 first prize. He clinched it by shooting a birdie three on the first hole of a sudden-death playoff against Harold Henning of South Africa. Afterward Sifford answered a reporter's question about why he—as a Black man—had struggled against the odds to become a professional golfer. Said Sifford: "I wanted to prove to myself that I could play and that a Negro could play. I caddied and used to give a golfer the right club to hit the ball, so if I could do that, I thought I could use the right club myself."

Pete Brown finished as the third-leading Black moneywinner in 1968 with $8,356.00 (120th place overall), while Ray Botts was fourth with $3,431.13 (165th place overall).

In women's play, Ethel Funches won her second straight national women's golf championship. Her victory—at Langston Golf Course in Washington, D.C.—was her fifth national title in the last ten years and seemed to indicate that she is the most consistent lady golfer on the United Golfers' Association tour. In her '68 title triumph, she wound up thirteen strokes ahead of her nearest competitor.

Tennis

Lieutenant Arthur Ashe made tennis history in 1968 and yet ended up the year in tears. For despite his victory in the U.S. Open at Forest Hills and his ranking as the United States' top amateur, Ashe slipped once in a match that meant more to him than it could have to anyone else.

It came in Davis Cup play, the competition that determines the number one nation in the world in amateur tennis. Through eight months of Cup preliminaries, Ashe had won every match. He had been superb in the interzone final against a strong India team. First he disposed of Premjit Lall, and then, with America ahead 2–1, faced Ramathan Krishnan in a crucial pairing. Ashe boomed his serve, ran Krishnan from side to side chasing his powerful strokes, and broke the Indian's service five times in the first two sets. It was Ashe's match, 6–1, 6–3, 6–2, and it clinched the victory for America and sent the U.S. on to Australia for the Davis Cup challenge round. The Australians had won the Cup for eleven of the last thirteen years, and the United States hadn't taken it since 1963.

Though he had been bothered by a tennis el-

Leroy Kelly, Cleveland Brown running back, became the third player in NFL history to rush for over 1,000 yards in three consecutive seasons. He led the NFL with 1,239 yards gained and 120 points.

St. Louis hurler Bob Gibson, winner of the National League's Most Valuable Player Award and Cy Young Award (best pitcher).

Despite the intense pressure, the NBA's two supercenters, Los Angeles' Wilt Chamberlain (top) and Boston's Bill Russell (bottom), find time for a little laughter during two regular season games.

Lieutenant Arthur Ashe, winner of the U. S. Open at Forest Hills, was ranked top amateur tennis player in the United States.

Bob Beamon is caught in the middle of his record-breaking leap in the Olympic long jump. Beamon's jump, 29 feet, 2½ inches, broke the previous record by almost 2 feet.

Bob Foster delivers a hard right to the face of champion Dick Tiger in their May 24 title bout. Foster's fourth round kayo earned him the light-heavyweight crown.

bow for more than a month, Ashe went out and defeated Ray Ruffels, 6–8, 7–5, 6–3, 6–3, on a cold and windy day in Adelaide. By the time Ashe played again, the U.S. had an insurmountable 4–0 lead. So there was nothing more than pride involved, and Ashe—the U.S. mainstay all these months—lost to Bill Bowery, 2–6, 6–3, 11–9, 8–6, to ruin America's bid for a sweep. "Arthur cried like everything," said Donald Dell, the U.S. captain. "He really wanted to win and make it a sweep. Some of the other guys choked up, too. I did myself."

But the Bowery match notwithstanding, Ashe had put together a sensational year for himself. The crowning achievement, of course, had to be his winning the first U.S. Open Tennis tournament against the best players—pros and amateurs—in the world. In the final against Tom Okker of Holland, Ashe whipped his service in for twenty-six aces and smashed his way to a 14–12, 5–7, 6–3, 3–6, 6–3 triumph. It was a most notable accomplishment in men's tennis, and yet Okker carried off the top prize money of $14,000. Ashe, an amateur, was ineligible. Not long afterward, though, a New York stockbroker called Ashe to tell him that he was about to receive a gift of a hundred shares of General Motors stock—worth $8,900. "The broker told me," said Ashe, "that one of his clients didn't think it was fair for Tom Okker to receive the $14,000 even though I beat him in the final of the tournament."

Among the other tournaments Ashe won in 1968 were the U.S. amateur title, the Personna tournament in Puerto Rico, and the West of England Open. But the U.S. Open triumph was the big one. Within ten days of his victory there, he appeared on the cover of *Life* magazine, became the first athlete to be interviewed on the C.B.S. "Face the Nation" show, and appeared on A.B.C.-TV's "Dating Game" and the Joey Bishop show.

He had almost decided to quit the Davis Cup team early in the year because of his sympathies with the Black athletes who were considering the possibility of boycotting the Olympic Games. "But I decided my situation was different," Ashe said. "In tennis, I'm the only one. I can make my protest heard by winning. If I chose not to play, who'd miss me?

"I know I'm not the favorite person of a lot of people in the Black community. I'll be the first to admit I arrived late. I've got a backlog of unpaid dues." And he plans to start paying off by doing volunteer work with the Urban League when he finishes his active service with the Army in early '69.

In late December another Black champion surprised the tennis world. Althea Gibson (now Althea Gibson Darben), forty-one and the winner of both the Wimbledon and U.S. championships in 1957 and 1958, announced she was attempting a tennis comeback. The first Negro ever to win a major tennis title, she said she wanted to get a pro contract and have at least one more try at a Wimbledon title. She had done indifferently in five years as a golf pro (in '68 she won $2,764.50 in nineteen tournaments). "Tennis is my first love," she said, "and that's where the money is."

Track and Field

There were, in this tumultuous Olympic year, principles, boycotts, symbolic gestures, angry rhetoric, and, oh yes, some surpassing running and leaping. When it was all over, everyone seemed much the wiser for having lived it—both socially and athletically.

The social issues involved (1) the threatened boycott by Afro-Asian nations if South Africa, with its discriminatory racial policies, would be allowed to compete in the Olympic Games in Mexico City, and (2) the repeated hints by American Blacks of a boycott or demonstration to express resentment at the injustices in U.S. race relations.

South Africa, finally, was not allowed to compete, and though America's Black athletes approved of that, many still bridled at the thought of running nobly for a nation they felt would not accept them as first class citizens.

So they dramatized their feelings. They called a boycott of the New York Athletic Club meet in New York in February—an organization, they said, that excluded Blacks from membership. Said Harry Edwards, a sociology instructor at San Jose College in California at the time and a spokesman for those considering a boycott of the Olympics: "We deplore the use of black Americans in the NYAC track meet for the same fundamental reasons that we deplore the exploitation of black Americans in the Olympic Games and in Vietnam. If we're good enough to make $15,000, $20,000, and $30,000 on one track meet for the New York AC, then we should be good enough to do anything that the New York Athletic Club has to offer."

Most Black athletes declined to compete in the meet; only nine participated in an overall field of four hundred.

In April, eight Black members of the track team at the University of Texas at El Paso refused to take part in a triangular meet at Brigham Young. Bob Beamon, holder of the world indoor record for the long jump, was among those who signed a statement protesting the Mormon belief "that blacks are inferior and that we are disciples of the devil."

This was the atmosphere, and Harry Edwards had world-class runners like Tommie Smith and Lee Evans sympathetic to his movement for an Olympic boycott. But in the last instance it was canceled. In track and field, the athletes decided they would go to Mexico City to compete but hinted they might make their protest in some way.

The Blacks' record in Mexico City was astonishing. Jim Hines set an Olympic record and equaled the world mark by dashing the 100 meters in 9.9. With about fifty yards to go in the 200, America's John Carlos had the lead when he turned around to check the competition. As he did, Tommie Smith, heavily taped because of a groin injury, roared by him and finished first in world-record time of 19.8. Australia's Peter Norman also passed Carlos to get second place.

Smith and Carlos then made what was the only substantial protest of the Games. As they stood on the victory stand, Smith and Carlos bowed their heads during the playing of the "Star-Spangled Banner" and raised black-gloved fists aloft, symbols of Black power. The international Olympic committee forced the U.S. Olympic committee to suspend the two runners from the team. "What we did," explained Carlos when he returned to the United States, "was an individual action against . . . the racist United States." Their action touched off a heated controversy.

Meanwhile, Lee Evans was establishing another world record by running the 400 meters in 43.8, while teammate Larry James was a close second in 43.9 and Ron Freeman took third for a U.S. sweep. Willie Davenport won the 110-meter high hurdles in 13.3, an Olympic record, and both of the U.S. relay teams—the 400 (Charlie Greene, Mel Pender, Ronnie Ray Smith and Jim Hines ran it in 38.2) and the 1,600 (Vince Matthews, Ron Freeman, Larry James and Lee Evans ran it in 2:56.1)—set new world marks.

Perhaps the most remarkable record achieved in the Games came in the long jump. Never before had anyone leaped farther than 27 ft. 4¾ in. when the 6 ft. 3 in., 160-pound Bob Beamon soared off the board in his first jump. He landed an amazing 29 ft. 2½ in. away—and was so overwhelmed by his effort that he put his forehead to the ground and cried.

In the women's track events, Wyomia Tyus won a gold medal and set a world mark with her 11.0 clocking in the 100. Madeline Manning did a 2:00.9 in the 800 to win first place and break the existing Olympic standard, and the 400-meter relay team of Barbara Ferrell, Margaret Bailes, Mildrette Netter and Wyomia Tyus won in the world-record time of 42.8.

Boxing

Never whipped professionally in the ring, Cassius Clay-Muhammad Ali, dethroned heavyweight champion of the world, spent an embattled 1968 trying to outmaneuver various courts of justice. He wasn't entirely successful. For in December he served seven days of a ten-day jail sentence in the Dade (Miami, Florida) County jail for having driven without a proper driver's license.

His stay was a mere preliminary, however, to what might be in store for him, because he faces a five-year term in federal prison for refusing to be drafted into the armed forces. The case is scheduled for hearing by the U.S. Supreme Court. From jail, where he did mostly kitchen chores with good cheer, Ali sounded anything but chastened: "They have made my armor stronger," he said. "I'm right on the doorstep of the federal jail now and all my money is gone and I'm talking stronger than ever."

With the dazzle—of Ali's dancing feet and

swift, jabbing fists—out of the heavyweight picture, bullish Joe Frazier and earnest Jimmy Ellis became caretaker champions.

Frazier won title recognition of five states (including New York), Mexico and part of the Orient after his March 4 bout with 243½-pound Buster Mathis. Both Black and both undefeated, Frazier and Mathis had had more than a passing relationship, for when they were amateurs Mathis had twice beaten Frazier in the 1964 Olympic trials (though Frazier subsequently won the gold medal when an injury sidelined Mathis).

Enormous Buster, surprisingly more stylish than Frazier, started strongly in their title fight in New York. Mathis moved quickly and punched crisply but couldn't sustain his advantage. Frazier relentlessly pursued, swinging away, and a worn-down Mathis grew ever more passive behind his gloves. Finally, in the eleventh round, Frazier landed his money punch, a left hook over Mathis' right eye that spilled Buster to the canvas. Though over-ample Mathis struggled to his feet, the referee ruled that he was finished.

Frazier went on to defend his part of the title two more times. He chopped down 6 ft. 4 in. Manuel Ramos, knocking the Mexican out in two rounds. And then he took a unanimous decision from Oscar Bonavena. Frazier mauled Bonavena, slicing and battering him with strong left hooks and right hands—as well as with a new weapon, an uppercut—but he was frustrated in his efforts to knock Bonavena out.

Ellis, meanwhile, was also becoming a heavyweight champion—and was also running into his disappointments. Jimmy, Ali's former sparring partner, emerged the victor of the World Boxing Association's eight-man tournament. He fought a clever fight to win the final by decision over Jerry Quarry in Oakland, California, on April 27. Ellis, fast and free-swinging, showed surprising endurance in going fifteen rounds. In Stockholm on September 14, Ellis made the only defense of his title in a punchout with former champion Floyd Patterson. Both landed rattling blows in a rock-em-sock-em duel, and Ellis suffered some downgrading in the press for not handling Patterson with more dispatch.

Away from the main headlines, former champion Charles (Sonny) Liston worked at a comeback by knocking out a series of undistinguished fighters—men like Bill McMurray, Bill Joiner, Henry Clark and Amos Lincoln.

The light heavyweight division got a new champion when Bobby Foster came on and knocked out Dick Tiger in four rounds. It was the first time in seventy-seven fights that Tiger, the champion, had been knocked out. Foster, 6 ft. 3½ in. and 173 pounds to Tiger's 5 ft. 8 in. and 168 pounds, forced Tiger to fight him at long range—where he had the advantage in reach, 79 inches to 71. In the fourth round, Foster snapped off a left hook, two uppercuts, and a jolting left hook to the side of the head that sent Tiger down for the full count. "I would hate to think where I'd be if that hook hadn't done the job," Foster said much later. "I was broke going into that fight and I came out with only three or four bucks. But I had the title and a new lease on life." In his next fight he defeated Roger Rouse and collected a purse of $15,000.

Emile Griffith, powerful but erratic, fought his third fight with Nino Benvenuti of Italy and lost his middleweight crown to Nino on a fifteen-round decision. The fight was part of a doubleheader on March 4 to start off the boxing program at New York's new Madison Square Garden (the Frazier-Mathis match was the other bout of the evening) and the 18,096 fans had paid a world indoor record $658,503 to view the proceedings.

Welterweight champion Curtis Cokes held onto his title in 1968 by knocking out Willie Ludick in five rounds on April 16 in Dallas.

In the Olympics, young George Foreman created a stir both as a fighter and as a Black athlete. Against the background of Black protests and disenchantment with conditions in America, Foreman won the gold medal for the U.S. in the heavyweight division and then kissed the American flag. "I felt I should do it, and I did it," he said. "I hope I was respected for it." Foreman said he respected the Black athletes who gave the Black power salutes. Ronnie Harris was the only other gold medalist for the U.S. in boxing, as he won the lightweight competition. Al Robinson, questionably disqualified in the featherweight finals by a Russian referee, was later reinstated as the silver medalist. Robinson, who accepted the ups and downs with great restraint, subsequently received an award in New York for showing the best example of sportsmanship at the Olympic Games.

College Football

Week in and week out, O. J. Simpson of the University of Southern California had exhausted the nation's sports writers. After they had finished describing him as superfast, durable, agile, powerful, instinctive, competitive, etc., they moved on to compare him to Jim Brown and Gale Sayers—probably the two best ballcarriers who ever lived. After that, the sports writers tried sensational, smashing and incredible, until they ran out of superlatives with which to capture the sense of what O. J. Simpson did for USC in 1968.

Simpson merely rushed for 1,709 yards in ten regular-season games (for an NCAA record), scored twenty-two touchdowns and carried the Trojans into the Rose Bowl with nine victories and one tie. Only twice in the regular season did he gain less than 163 yards on the ground. In the Rose Bowl, with second-ranked USC against Ohio State, the nation's number one team, Simpson rushed for 171 yards in twenty-eight carries, caught eight passes for 85 yards, but couldn't do it all. USC bowed, 27–16. On one play, particularly, Simpson showed off many of the skills that pro scouts have been raving about. In the second quarter, Simpson drove off left tackle, cut sharply to the middle to escape heavy traffic, broke two tackles and then turned on that sprinter speed of his (9.4 for the 100-yard dash) to beat everyone up the sideline and into the end zone. The run was good for 80 yards, second-longest dash from scrimmage in Rose Bowl history.

Simpson, 6 ft. 1 in. and 207 pounds, was a landslide choice as the Heisman Trophy winner for '68, an award given annually to the best player in college ranks.

In a more normal year (one in which a player of Simpson's overwhelming talent wasn't playing), Leroy Keyes of Purdue would certainly have been number one. The 6 ft. 3 in. 205-pounder was runner-up for the Heisman Trophy and might well have been the most versatile player in the country. Take Purdue's 37–22 upset of powerful Notre Dame early in the season. Keyes passed for one score, ran for two touchdowns, caught passes, and played defense at crucial times so he could cover Notre Dame's All-America end Jim Seymour. Seymour did not catch a pass while Keyes was defending against him. There have been other times when Keyes has kicked off and returned punts and kickoffs. With his size, speed (9.8 in the 100) and hands, Keyes is likely to settle into a flanker spot in the pros, though he was designated as a running back on '68 All-America teams.

It was a year for running backs. There were also Paul Gipson of Houston, a tough, fast ballcarrier who, for example, ripped through a grudging Georgia defense for 230 yards one afternoon; Mercury Morris, a swift, shifty halfback out of West Texas State; Ron Johnson, a strong gainer for Michigan; and Calvin Hill, a big, versatile halfback for Yale. Among the best receivers were Jerry Levias, a little flanker from Southern Methodist University who caught eighty passes for 1,131 yards, Gene Washington of Stanford and Eddie Hinton of Oklahoma. John Tatum of Ohio State and Jim Marsalis of Tennessee State were two of the best defensive backs in the nation, and offensive lineman Rufus Mayes of Ohio State, defensive tackle Joe Greene of North Texas State, and linebacker Emory Hicks of Kansas, were among the best men up front.

Besides Ohio State and USC, Penn State (10–0 in the regular season) showed that it deserved high national ranking when it beat formidable Kansas (9–1), 15–14, in the Orange Bowl. Charlie Pittman, who scored fourteen touchdowns and averaged 5.2 yards a carry during the season, scored one of the Penn State touchdowns and ran well all through the game. Breakaway runner Don Shanklin of Kansas was voted the game's most valuable player.

Pro Football

The '68 season turned out to be a year of upsets—both on and off the field. On the field both Green Bay and Oakland, supposedly the super teams of their respective leagues, failed to make the Super Bowl. Gale Sayers, reputed to be the game's best ballcarrier, wasn't—but mostly because a knee injury sidelined him part-way through the season. And off the field there was some evidence of racial dissension that threatened to tear apart the Cleveland Browns and the St. Louis Cardinals early in the year. The season, of course, was climaxed by THE upset, the New York Jets' 16–7 win over the Baltimore Colts, and while Jet quarterback Joe Namath deservedly got most credit for the win, he could not have penetrated the great Colt defense without the turned-on performance of his fullback, Matt Snell. Snell was the leading runner in the Super Bowl, with 121 yards in thirty carries, and also caught four passes for 40 yards, blocked for Namath and scored his team's only touchdown on a four-yard plunge. Defensively, cornerbacks Randy Beverly and Johnny Sample shared the headlines. Beverly intercepted two passes and Sample one to break the back of Baltimore drives.

Before the season had really got under way, it appeared as if the white *vs.* Black friction on the Cleveland Browns and St. Louis Cardinals would compromise the teamwork on both squads. In Cleveland, whites and Blacks got into a dispute over a celebrity golf tournament at the Ashland Country Club—a competition promoted by white defensive back Ross Fichtner. Black athletes, present in the past, were not invited in '68 and Fichtner said it was because the Blacks hadn't socialized with whites at previous tournaments. Before the dispute was over, Fichtner and Black offensive guard John Wooten were put on waivers. Said Negro defensive tackle Walter Johnson, gloomily looking ahead to the season: "The togetherness won't be there." He was, as it happened, wrong. Meanwhile, in St. Louis, the Cardinals revamped half of their defensive team after a national magazine printed reports about racial discord on the squad in 1967.

Ironically, it was Cleveland and St. Louis ultimately fighting it out for first place in the Century Division. Cleveland did get together, took eight straight games at one point, and wound up with the division title. Perhaps the key to the Browns' success was their explosive offense, which ate up yardage both on the ground and through the air. For running, Cleveland had Leroy Kelly, fast, strong, slippery, durable, and the number one rusher in the league (1,239 yards on 5.0 yards per carry). Kelly also led the league in scoring with 120 points on twenty touchdowns. For the passing game, the Browns had quarterback Bill Nelsen throwing to the exceptional Paul Warfield, among others. Warfield caught fifty passes for 1,067 yards and twelve touchdowns.

In the NFL playoff sequence, Century champion Cleveland had to meet the winner in the Capitol Division, the Dallas Cowboys. Dallas, too, had a superb runner-receiver tandem in fullback Don Perkins (who rushed for 836 yards) and split end Bob Hayes (who caught fifty-three passes for 909 yards and ten touchdowns and also led the NFL in punt returns with an average of 20.8 yards per runback). Cleveland's finely tuned attack and timely defense prevailed, 31–20.

In the other preliminary to the NFL title game, Baltimore, the Coastal Division champ, played Minnesota, winner in the Central Division. Most experts conceded that Baltimore had the strongest team in the NFL—the Colts had lost just once—and two of the reasons were All-Pro tight end John Mackey (forty-five catches for 644 yards) and 295-pound defensive end Bubba Smith. Minnesota had been a surprise winner in its division, and it was the Viking defensive platoon, featuring All-Pro defensive end Carl Eller, that had most to do with the Minnesota success. The Colt-Viking match-up turned into a bruising affair, and the superior balance of the Colts tipped the game to Baltimore, 24–14. Colt receiver Willie Richardson caught six passes for 148 yards and Mackey grabbed three for 92 yards and one touchdown.

So it came down to Baltimore *vs.* Cleveland for the NFL championship, and the Colts rose up to humiliate the Browns, 34–0. The experts hailed Baltimore's magnificent defense and grinding offense and considered the Colts an overwhelming favorite in the Super Bowl.

Over in the AFL it was a case of the defending champs, the Oakland Raiders, trying to beat back the challenge of an aggressive New York Jet squad. Oakland was loaded with good ballplayers —men like fullback Hewritt Dixon (third-best rusher in the AFL with 865 yards), receiver Warren Wells (sixth in the league with fifty-three catches for 1,137 yards and eleven touchdowns), defensive end Ike Lassiter and defensive backs Willie Brown and Dave Grayson. But before taking on the Jets, the Raiders had to contend with Kansas City in a Western Division playoff. And the Chiefs, too, had plenty of talent, in Robert

Holms (second in the AFL in rushing with 866 yards), Mike Garrett (tenth in rushing with 564 yards), receiver Otis Taylor and All-Pro defenders Buck Buchanan (tackle), Bobby Bell (linebacker) and Willie Lanier (linebacker). The teams appeared evenly matched—they had split two games during the season—but in the big one the Raiders took control. It was Oakland 41, Kansas City 6, as Wells caught two touchdown passes and rookie halfback Charlie Smith led the ground-gainers with 74 yards in thirteen carries.

The Jets had won easily in the Eastern Division and were well rested for the title game with Oakland in New York's Shea Stadium. In a dramatic struggle on a raw, windy day, the Jets rallied to win, 27–23, on Joe Namath's clutch passing.

People were saying the Jets would lose by two to three touchdowns in the Super Bowl. The AFL teams had lost in the two previous Super Bowls, and this year the NFL was represented, many said, by one of its best teams ever. So the results were all rather shocking for the football world. There, for example, was the Jet offensive line protecting Namath for his passes (tackle Winston Hill had an especially fine afternoon in checking Baltimore's outstanding defensive end Ordell Braase) and opening up holes for backs Snell and Bob Boozer. And there was that defense and the cornerbacks the experts had laughed at—Beverly and Sample—holding Baltimore off. Many called the Jets' 16–7 win the greatest upset in sports history.

It had been a rather special season for fascinating ups and downs anyway. The ups? Marlin Briscoe, a sturdy little man, became the first Negro quarterback in the AFL when he took over the job for the Denver Broncos part way through the season. He finished seventh among the league passers in overall efficiency ratings. Halfback Paul Robinson of Cincinnati won the AFL rushing title with 1,023 yards gained, and became the league's Rookie of the Year. Clifton McNeil, traded from Cleveland to San Francisco, led the NFL in pass receiving with seventy-one catches. New York Giant defensive back Willie Williams, who went from the NFL to the AFL and back to the NFL, was tops in the latter with ten interceptions. And flanker Earl McCulloch of the Detroit Lions (forty pass receptions for 680 yards and five touchdowns) became the NFL Offensive Rookie of the Year, while 6 ft. 5 in., 225-pound defensive end Claude Humphrey of Atlanta was the NFL Defensive Rookie of the Year.

The downs? Gale Sayers of the Chicago Bears was headed possibly for the NFL rushing championship—he had picked up 856 yards with an extraordinary 6.2 yards per carry—when an injured knee forced him out for the season. He had to undergo surgery and missed the Bears' stretch drive to beat out Minnesota in the Central Division. Perhaps the most bitter disappointment in pro football was in Green Bay, where the champion Packers and men like Willie Davis, Dave Robinson, Herb Adderley, Willie Wood, Lionel Aldridge, Marv Fleming, Travis Williams, Elijah Pitts, Bob Jeter and others fell from grace with a thud, winning six, losing seven, and tying one. Inevitably, it seemed, 1968 would be the year of the reversal, and the New York Jets crowned it with the most stunning turnabout of them all.

FACES 1968

abc

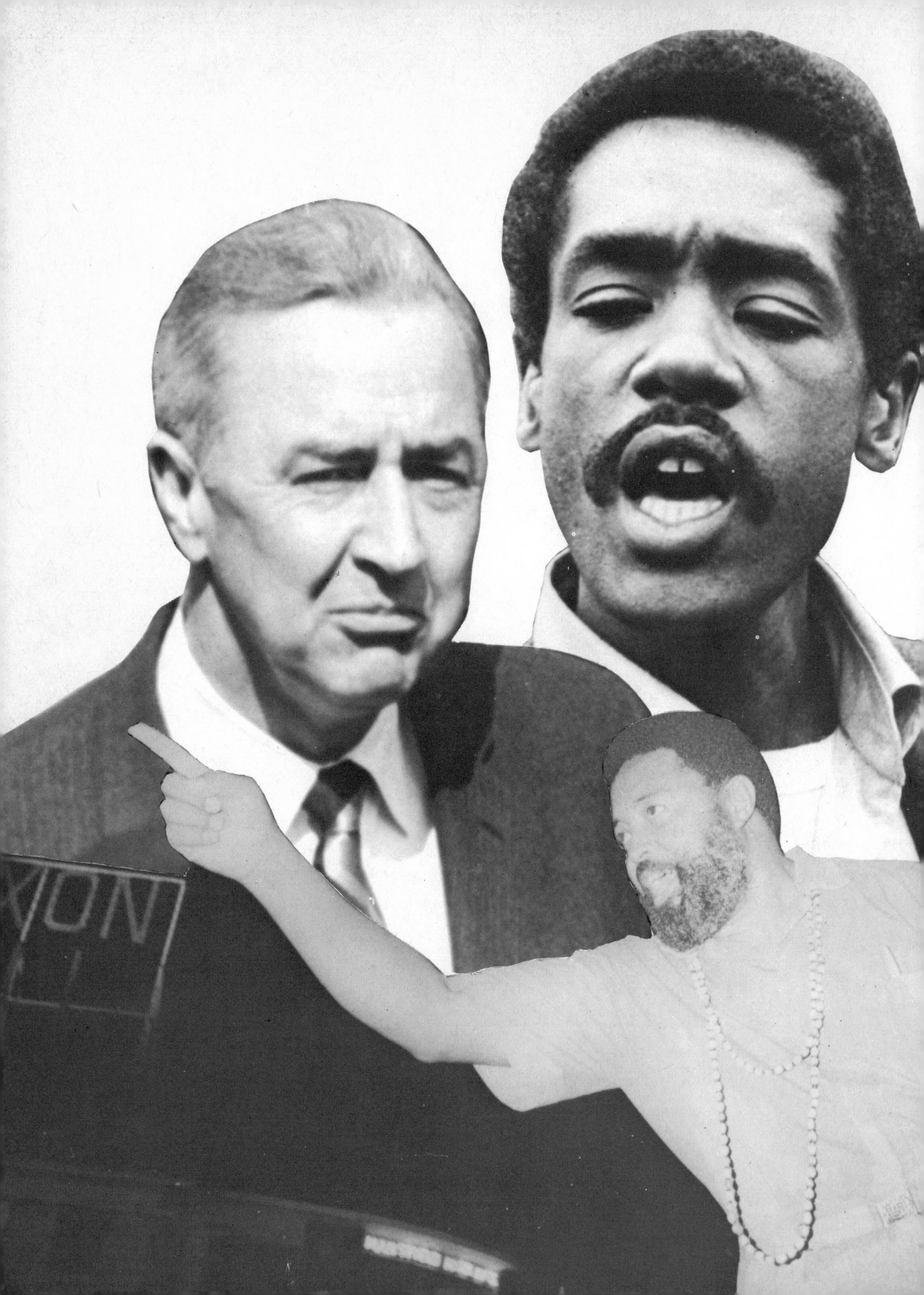
XON

NBC

MAU MAU

2
3

FOI

CHILDRENS
HOSPITAL DC

JOSEPH AND CLARA FORD HALL

WE MARCH FOR JOBS FOR ALL NOW!
WE MARCH FOR JOBS FOR ALL NOW!
WE DEMAND VOTING RIGHTS NOW!
WE DEMAND AN FEPC LAW NOW!
UAW SAYS: END SEGREGATED RULES IN PUBLIC SCHOOLS
REV MARTIN LUTHER KING JR
1929 —— 1968
"FREE AT LAST, FREE AT LAST,
THANK GOD ALMIGHTY I'M FREE AT LAST."

Captions to Faces 1968

Page	
339	Richard Nixon at Dr. Martin Luther King's funeral.
340	Mulana Karenga (bl) and James Farmer (br); "Thunder" Stevens, of the Blackstone Four Corners Rangers, is behind James Farmer.
341	tl: Ronald Reagan; tr: Rhody McCoy; br: Omar Abu Ahmed.
342	l: Eugene McCarthy; tr: Bobby Seale; br: Rev. Hosea Williams.
343	t: Robert Kennedy (l) and Eugene McCarthy at the funeral of Dr. Martin Luther King, Jr.; b: Robert Kennedy and Rev. Walter Fauntroy inspecting riot damage in Washington, D.C.
344	l: Albert Shanker, tr: James Earl Ray; br: Richard Daley.
345	bl: Member of the Harlem Mau Mau Society; c: Rev. James Bevel; tl: Julian Bond; tr: H. Rap Brown.
346	tl: Andrew Young; tr: Eartha Kitt: bl: Floyd McKissick; br: Stokely Carmichael.
347	tl: Lyndon B. Johnson: tc: Marian Edelman; tr: Edward Brooke; bl: Coretta King; br: Barbara Watson.
348	tl: John Conyers, Jr.; tr: Katherine Cleaver; bl: Carl B. Stokes; br: Adam Clayton Powell.
349	John Carlos (center) and Tommie Smith (right) giving the Black power salute at the 1968 Olympic Games in Mexico City.
350	tl: Shirley Chisholm; tr: Muhammad Ali; bl: Elijah Muhammad; br: Hubert H. Humphrey.
351	t: Roy Innis (l) and Clyde DeBerry.
352	bl: Peggy Lipton; bc: Michael Cole; br: Clarence Williams, III.
354	t: Mark Rudd (in plaid shirt) and other students demonstrating at Columbia University; b: Father James Groppi and members of the Youth Council of the Milwaukee NAACP.
355	t: Demonstrators at a Wallace rally; b: Students and police at San Francisco State College.
356	t: Students at Brandeis University; b: John Carlos speaking at Howard University.
357	t: Thomas Hayden (l) and Julius Hobson; b: Nathan Hare (l) and students, with Acting President S. I. Hayakawa, at San Francisco State College.
358	t: Police at San Francisco State College; b: Highway patrolmen and demonstrators in front of the county courthouse in Swanquarter, North Carolina.

SECTION II

Personalities

THE YEAR 1968 was one of achievement and reward for many Black Americans. Listed below is a selection of personalities who either merited attention for outstanding achievement in their own fields or received national recognition for their contributions to society.

Sadie T. M. Alexander, the first Negro woman in the nation to receive a Doctorate (from the University of Pennsylvania), retired as chairman of Philadelphia's Commission on Human Relations. She had earlier been a member of President Truman's Commission on Civil Rights.

Walter F. Anderson was named director of music programs for the National Endowment for the Arts. He is also a professor of music at Antioch College.

Arthur Ashe, Jr., of Richmond, Va., was the number one singles tennis player in the U.S. championship for 1968. He has been a member of the Davis Cup Team since 1963 and has received many other awards in tennis.

Victor J. Ashe, attorney, of Norfolk, Va., was named to the State Board of Welfare and Institutions by Governor Mills E. Godwin on July 18, 1968.

Pearl Bailey was honored with several awards for 1968: a Tony "Special" Award; Entertainer of the Year (*Cue* magazine); and official "'68 Hostess of the New York Summer Festival."

William W. Ban became deputy director of youth services for the District of Columbia's Welfare Department. He had previously headed Cedar Knoll, a center for delinquent teen-agers.

Harry Belafonte received a special award "for continuing commitment to the cause of interracial justice and brotherhood" from the Catholic Interracial Council.

Robert B. Blackwell, at the age of forty-five, became the first Negro mayor of Highland Park, Mich.

James H. Blair, of Montclair, N.J., was named director of the Civil Rights Division of the state Department of Law and Public Safety.

Charles H. Boone, of Atlanta, was elected president of the National Association of Market Developers.

Clothilde Dent Bowen was promoted to the rank of colonel in the Army, in July. She is the first Negro woman to attain this rank. Colonel Bowen holds advanced degrees in psychiatry and medicine.

Dr. Dorothy L. Brown was named by the Democratic National Committee as one of nine "Women Doers of 1968." She is a Nashville physician and a member of the state legislature.

Juliette B. Buford was appointed director of NABOHR, the North American Baha'i Office for Human Rights. She is also a trustee of Bennett College, Columbia, S.C.

Calvin E. Burton was appointed to the Equal Opportunity Program of the Personnel Department of N.B.C. Before joining the network, he was administrator for R.C.A.'s Direct Hire Program.

John Carter, of St. Louis, was chosen "composer in residence" in 1968 for the Washington National Symphony. He studied at the Oberlin Conservatory.

Robert L. Carter, former general counsel for the NAACP, has been appointed a Center fellow at the Urban Center of Columbia University. While at the Center he plans to write a book which he has tentatively titled *Law and the Black Community*. He holds an LL.M. from Columbia's School of Law.

Yolande Johnson Cheatham, of Chicago, is the new president of the Girl Friends, an organization for participation in cultural, social and civic activities.

Kenneth B. Clark, psychologist and civil rights leader, was named by Governor Rockefeller to the Urban Development Corporation's board of directors. He is currently a professor of psychology at New York's City College.

Robert G. Clark took his seat in the Mississippi state house of representatives on January 3, 1968. He is the first Negro legislator in Mississippi in seventy-four years.

Eliza M. Coleman, of Natchez, Miss., is the new head of the Imperial Court, Daughters of Isis (a charitable organization).

David C. Collington joined the Florida Public Relations Association. He is director of university relations at Florida A. and M. and is the first Negro to be admitted to the FPRA.

Dr. Paul B. Cornely, chief of the Howard University Department of Community Health Practices, was named president-elect of the American Public Health Association and will take office in November 1969. He is the first Negro to hold this position.

Alfred D. Cowles was appointed press aide to Senator Charles E. Goodell of New York. He was the executive director of the Washington State Board against Discrimination.

Wardell C. Croft, of Detroit, became president of the National Insurance Association. He is president of Wright Mutual Insurance and is the recipient of various business citations.

Rupert G. Currey became the first Negro to be elected to the Rockville, Md., city council.

Sammy Davis, Jr., was the recipient in 1968 of the Spingarn Medal, which is awarded for the highest achievement of an American Negro by the NAACP. He was also given an award by the American Musical and Dramatic Academy in New York, for encouraging young talent.

John B. Duncan resigned as assistant to the Secretary of the Interior for Urban Relations to join a new private housing development firm. Mr. Duncan has held leading posts with some sixty civic organizations.

Robert M. Duncan, of Urbana, Ohio, was appointed to the state supreme court by Governor Rhodes. He is the first Negro to sit on the court. He had been a member of the Columbus municipal court.

Samuel B. Ethridge was appointed chief of the National Education Association Center for Human Relations. He received his B.A. from Howard University and his M.A. from the University of Cincinnati.

Myrlie Beasley Evers, wife of the slain civil rights leader Medgar Evers, was appointed assistant director of the Center for Educational Opportunity, at Claremont College.

Clarence H. Featherson was appointed deputy contracts compliance officer for the Post Office Department. He has served as an attorney with the Equal Employment Opportunity Commission.

Austin L. Fickling was appointed by President Johnson to the District of Columbia court of appeals. He is the first Negro to be a member of the court. He is currently a general sessions judge.

Carl A. Fields, a guidance counselor, social worker and former director of student aid at Princeton University, has been appointed assistant dean. He is the first Black man in the school's 221-year history to be appointed to a major administrative post.

Ella Fitzgerald received New York City's Cultural Award for exceptional achievement in the performing arts.

Paul Freeman was appointed associate conductor of the Dallas Symphony after receiving second prize in the Dimitri Mitropolous conducting competition at Carnegie Hall. The thirty-three-year-old conductor received his B.A. and M.A. from the Eastman School of Music.

Stewart B. Fulbright has been named to the five-man advisory board of the Commodity Credit Corporation. He is dean of the undergraduate school at North Carolina College at Durham.

Paul Stewart Green has been promoted to the rank of captain in the U.S. Navy. A native of Manson, N.C., Dr. Green is the third Negro captain in the Navy.

William J. Hamilton, of Cleveland, is the newly elected president of the National Association of Real Estate Brokers.

James T. Harris became executive director of the National Catholic Conference for Interracial Justice on January 1, 1969. He had been vice-president of the African American Institution, in New York, since 1966. He has an M.A. from Princeton University.

Jerome H. Holland, president of Hampton Institute, was elected chairman of Planned Parenthood-World Population. He has a Ph.D. in sociology from the University of Pennsylvania and is the recipient of many honorary degrees and awards.

Levi A. Jackson, of Bradford, Conn., is the new manager of retail personnel services for the Ford Motor Company's marketing staff. He was also named "Ford Citizen of the Year" for 1968, for his county.

Eugene H. Johns was named chief administrative officer for the Department of Labor's Manpower Division in Maryland and Virginia. He was a civil rights specialist for HEW and worked with OEO as a supervisory psychologist for VISTA. He received his Doctorate in counseling psychology at Boston University.

Spec. 5 Dwight H. Johnson won the Congressional Medal of Honor in 1968 for accumulated acts of valor in Vietnam. Johnson, who was twenty-one in 1968, is from Detroit.

Jesse Johnson was appointed administrative officer to the District Recreation Department of Washington, D.C. He was previously administrative assistant to the President's Committee on Government Contracts.

Joe Lang Kershaw is the first Negro elected to the state legislature in Florida. He was a junior high school civics teacher in Miami and had worked as a janitor while attending college.

Elizabeth D. Koontz was installed as president of the National Education Association. She is the first Negro to hold this office.

Cornell T. Lewis, of Silver Spring, Md., was appointed to the county Board of Social Services by the Montgomery County council. He is the first Negro to serve on the council.

H. Carl McCall resigned as deputy administrator for operations of New York City's Human Resources Administration to take a fellowship to study Negro-Jewish conflict in urban areas and to develop means of greater understanding. He is a Congregational minister.

Will McIntosh, of Birmingham, became one of the first two Negroes to serve on an Alabama draft board.

B. Bartin McIntyre has been promoted to second in command of the Salvation Army's Metropolitan New York Division. He was the founder of the Harlem String Band and has been in charge of the Harlem Temple Corps for the last twelve years.

Anita Mack was appointed to the newly created position of regional management training officer for the U.S. Department of Labor Work-Training Programs. She is responsible for programming in seven Midwestern states.

Ruby Martin, a lawyer, was named chief of the federal school desegregation program. She was also appointed director of civil rights for the Department of Health, Education and Welfare.

Dr. Gilbert Mason, of Biloxi, Miss., long active in civil rights organizations on the Gulf Coast, became the first Negro delegate from Mississippi to the Democratic Party nominating convention since Reconstruction.

Ernest N. Morial is the newly elected general president of Alpha Phi Alpha fraternity.

Paul Murray became the first Negro county commissioner for Williamsburg County, S.C.

Major Owens, a Brownsville antipoverty leader, was appointed commissioner for New York City's Community Development Agency by Mayor John Lindsay.

Bill Passmore has been selected "Handicapped American of 1968" by the President's Committee on Employment of the Handicapped. He will be presented the award by President Nixon.

J. Saunders Redding assumed the professorship of American History and Civilization at George Washington University. Dr. Redding is one of the nation's leading scholars and is well known as a writer.

Harry V. Richardson, founder and president of the Interdenominational Theological Center in Atlanta, Ga., retired in August. He will continue as president emeritus of the institution which he helped found in 1958.

Bill Robinson was named head of the welfare department of Charles City County, Va. He was director of the Richmond Urban League. He is a Baptist minister and holds a Master's degree in social work.

Gertrude J. Rogers, of Gilmer, Tex., is the newly elected president of the National Housewives League of America.

Emory R. Searcy, of Atlanta, is the new presiding officer of the Progressive National Baptist Convention.

Arthur Shores, an attorney and early civil rights activist, whose home was bombed twice in 1963, was named to the Birmingham city council by unanimous vote of the all-white government body. He is a graduate of Talladega College and the University of Kansas.

B. Winford Smith was named director of Washington, D.C.'s, Small Business Administration office. He is the first Negro to ever head one of the agency's sixty-two regional offices.

Julian D. Steele, of West Newbury, Mass., was named commissioner of the Department of Community Affairs of Massachusetts by former Governor John Volpe. This new department was established at the end of the 1968 legislature.

Harold Arnoldus Stevens, of the New York supreme court, became presiding justice of the appellate division, first department, on January 1, 1969. He is the first Negro to be appointed presiding judge and also the first to be successively a judge on the city's court of general sessions and a justice of the state supreme court.

Harrison Taylor became the first Negro city councilman in Wichita Falls, Tex.

Edward B. Toles was appointed federal bankruptcy referee of the bankruptcy court. He will be the second Black man appointed to this post. A native of Columbus, Ga., he took his degrees at the University of Illinois and Loyola University Law School.

Luska J. Twyman is the first Negro mayor of a Kentucky city, Glasgow. He was unanimously appointed by the Glasgow common council.

Leslie Uggams received the twenty-second annual Tony Award for the 1967–68 season, for her role in *Hallelujah Baby*.

Preston Valien was appointed acting associate commissioner for higher education in the U.S. Office of Education. He is from Beaumont, Tex., and took his M.A. and Ph.D. at the University of Wisconsin.

James C. Wallace, Jr., of Chicago, was elected president of the National Dental Association.

Booker Robinson Warren received the Barton Kyle Young Award, the top award of the American Institute of Foreign Trade, near Phoenix, Ariz. The third Negro to have attended the school in its twenty-two-year history, he was cited for "scholarship, accomplishment and character."

Dr. James M. Whittico, of St. Louis, was elected president of the National Medical Association for 1968–69.

Roger Wilkins was appointed program officer in charge of the Social Development Section of the National Affairs Division of the Ford Foundation. Since 1966 he has directed the Justice Department's community relations service as assistant attorney general for New York City.

Capt. E. D. Williams, of Newark, assumed command of the police precinct in mainly Negro Central Ward. He is the first Black man to hold command.

Agnes Wilson, of Sumter County, S.C., was cited as "Teacher of the Year" by the state. It is the first time in South Carolina's history that a Negro has won the award. Mrs. Wilson, who has been teaching for thirty-two years, has a B.A. from Allen University in Columbia, and an M.A. from Temple University in Philadelphia.

Nancy Wilson, the well-known popular singer, was appointed to the President's Advisory Board on Youth Opportunities.

Green T. Wood was named group coordinator for the United Planning Organization Housing Component. He is a former manpower development specialist for the UPO, and was chief NAACP housing advocate in Chicago and Cleveland. He took his B.S. at Morehouse College and his LL.B. at Howard University.

Herman C. Wrice, at twenty-eight, was named "Outstanding Young Man of the Year" by the Philadelphia Junior Chamber of Commerce for his work in organizing the Young Great Society—an organization which works with street gangs. Wrice himself had been a gang leader in West Philadelphia.

Grant Wright was named chief of the U.S. Park Police in Washington after twenty-one years of service on the three-hundred-man force. He holds a B.S. from Virginia Union University in Richmond, Va.

Dr. Jane Cooke Wright was honored by the Jewish women's organization Hadassah as one of four recipients of the Myrtle Wreath Award for "far-reaching contributions to cancer research." She also became the first Negro associate dean of a medical school—New York Medical College—last year.

Wayman Scott Wright, an Atlanta public relations man, was elected president of the Georgia Young Democrats. It is the first time that the post has been filled by a Black man.

Whitney M. Young, Jr., was named a co-winner of the annual Golden Key Award which promotes the teaching of citizenship. It is given by the National Congress of Parents and Teachers, the National Education Association, the National School Boards Association, the American Association of School Administrators, the Council of Chief State School Officers and the National Council of State Education Associations. He is executive director of the National Urban League.

Obituaries

THE PASSING from the American scene of distinguished Black men and women in 1968 is recorded in the following list. Those selected for inclusion had enjoyed prominence during their lifetimes in their own fields.

Nanine Champney Alba, 53, member of Tuskegee Institute faculty and poet. Her poems appeared in *Negro Digest*, *Pittsburgh Courier*, etc. She died in Tuskegee.

Pfc. James Anderson, of Los Angeles, was awarded the Congressional Medal of Honor posthumously for "conspicuous gallantry and intrepidity in action at the risk of his life above and beyond the call of duty" on August 21, 1968. He was killed in action in Vietnam at the age of twenty-one. He was the first Negro Marine to receive the Medal of Honor.

Jessie Banks, 103, widow of Civil War veteran, died in Chicago.

James N. Bradby, 38, first Negro sheriff in Virginia. Died of carbon monoxide poisoning three months after taking office.

Rev. T. E. Brown, 79, pastor of Chicago's Progressive Baptist Church, died in Rochester, Minnesota.

Theodore W. Coggs, 51, Milwaukee attorney and former state president of the NAACP, died of a heart attack.

Warren R. Coleman, 67, radio, stage and film actor (played Kingfish on the "Amos 'n' Andy" radio program), died in Massachusetts.

Robert P. Daniel, 65, president of Virginia State College, died in Virginia.

Joseph E. Davis, 58, former shoe-shine boy, was, at the time of his death, president of Carver Federal Savings and Loan Association (the first such institution established by Negroes).

J. Daniel Diggs, 74, one of the two Negro members of the New York City council (Brooklyn, Democrat), was chairman of the council's Health and Education Committee. A native of South Carolina, he graduated from South Carolina State College in 1921.

Eugene Henry Duckrey, 69, retired head of Cheyney State College (Pennsylvania), had served on the state's council on education.

Paul B. Dunbar, 86, former Food and Drug Administration commissioner, died in Rockledge, Florida.

Daniel W. Edmonds, 81, Howard University treasurer for thirty-one years, died after a long illness.

Meta Warrick Fuller, 90, sculptor, died in Framingham, Massachusetts.

Christopher (Happy) Goldstone, 74, retired New Orleans jazz drummer who had played with the Eureka Marching Band and other groups, died in New Orleans.

Juanita Hall, 66, who had played Bloody Mary in the stage and screen versions of *South Pacific*, died on Long Island, New York.

Samuel Hammond, 18, of Fort Lauderdale, Florida, was killed in a battle between police and students in Orangeburg, South Carolina.

Willie Gertrude Haugh, 67, Republican committeewoman in Kansas City, Missouri, died in Kansas City.

George E. C. Hayes, 74, pioneer of civil rights, lawyer, professor and Washington community leader, died of pneumonia. He was the first Negro chairman of the old D.C. Public Utilities Commission, and the first Negro elected to the board of directors of the Metropolitan Board of Trade. He fought for the abolition of segregation in the District's school system and was a member of the school board from 1945 to 1949. A native of Richmond, Virginia, he graduated from Brown University and Howard Law School.

Roy Innis, Jr., 13, son of CORE's associate national director Roy Innis, was shot and killed while playing near his New York City home.

Little Willie Johnson (real name William Edward John), 51, singer, who sold over a million copies of "Fever" in the late 1950's, died of complications resulting from an attack of influenza.

"Ziggy" Johnson, 54, news columnist, nightclub entertainer and dance instructor. She died of a heart attack.

Lulu Knight, the only Negro Christian Science teacher in the United States, died in Los Angeles.

Clyde A. Lawlah, 64, civil rights leader, died in Pine Bluff, Arkansas.

Maj. Robert H. Lawrence, 33, the first Negro astronaut, died in the crash of an F-104 D starfighter jet at Edwards Air Force Base, California.

Frankie Lymon, 27, popular singer, died of an apparent overdose of drugs.

Nunn McClinton, 62, executive director of the Toledo Metropolitan Housing Authority (commended by President John F. Kennedy for running the best public housing authority in the nation), died in Toledo, Ohio, of complications following surgery.

Merle M. McCurdy, 56, general counsel to the National Advisory Commission on Civil Disorders and recently named consumer counsel in the Justice Department, died in Cleveland. He was the second Negro to be a U.S. district attorney.

Garland L. Mackey, 74, retired court officer and former newspaperman, died of a heart attack.

George W. McLaurin, 75, the first Negro to attend the University of Oklahoma (in 1948), died in Los Angeles.

Elder Solomon Lightfoot Michaux, 84, founder of a religious movement that attracted many followers during the 1930's and 1940's, died in Washington, D.C., of a heart attack. A leading radio evangelist and a friend of President Franklin D. Roosevelt, Elder Michaux founded, in Washington, the Good Neighbor League, as a means of feeding, housing and clothing victims of the Depression.

Delano Middleton, 17, a high school student, was killed in a battle between police and students in Orangeburg, South Carolina.

Norman S. Minor, 67, one of the nation's leading criminal lawyers, died in Cleveland. He trained many attorneys, including Mayor Carl B. Stokes.

Susie Monroe, 89, Pennsylvania state representative for the last twenty years of her life, died in Philadelphia.

Wes Montgomery, 42, jazz guitarist, died in Indianapolis of a heart attack.

Allan Morrison, 51, former New York editor for *Jet* and *Ebony*, died in New York.

Kenneth M. Phipps, 51, New York criminal court judge, died of a heart attack.

Rev. Otis Redding, 55, father of the late Otis Redding, rhythm and blues singer, died of a heart attack in Macon, Georgia.

Ira D. Augustine Reid, 67, sociologist and head of Haverford College's sociology department from 1947 to 1966, died in Bryn Mawr, Pennsylvania.

Johnny Richards (real name Johnny Cascales), 56, "progressive" jazz band leader, died in New York.

Ruth Logan Roberts, 76, a leader in many Negro and welfare groups, died in a nursing home in New York City.

Mallie Robinson, 78, mother of Jackie Robinson, died in Pasadena, California. She had been chairman of the George Washington Carver Memorial Institute for ten years.

Walter C. Robinson, Sr., 75, publisher of the *Chattanooga Observer*, which he had founded, died after a long illness.

Willard Robison, 73, bandleader and composer of spirituals, died in Peekskill, New York.

Guido St. Laurent, 42, head of a civil rights group known as the New England Grass Roots Organization, was shot, along with two co-workers, by robbers at his Boston headquarters.

Calvin L. Smith, 61, Illinois state representative, former deputy coroner of Cook County, chief pharmacist at Cook County Jail and president of the Chicago Pharmacists Association, died in Chicago of a heart attack.

Henry Smith, 18, was killed in a battle between police and students in Orangeburg, South Carolina.

Maceo Turner, 51, president of the Atlantic City NAACP from 1963 to 1965, died in Atlantic City, New Jersey.

Waters E. Turpin, 58, novelist and professor of English at Morgan State College, died after an operation. He was co-author of *Better Skills for Better Writing* with Aaron Ford, and author of the novels *These Low Grounds, The Rootless* and *Canaan.*

Walter (real name Marion Walter Jacobs), 38, who played harmonica with the Muddy Waters Blues Band, died in Chicago.

Dr. Ralph J. Young, 75, the first Negro appointed to the Maryland board of health and to the Johns Hopkins Hospital clinical staff, died in Baltimore of a heart attack.

Greek Social and Professional Organizations

AS A GOOD DEAL of attention within Black society has traditionally been focused on Greek letter societies—professional as well as social—the following list of organizations and their memberships is included.

Name	National Officer	Membership (1968)	Founded
Alpha Kappa Alpha Sorority Social sorority	Dr. Larzette G. Hale	45,000	1908
Alpha Kappa Mu National Honor Society Scholastic honor society	Dr. E. K. Williams	10,593	1937
Alpha Phi Alpha Fraternity Social fraternity	Ernest N. Morial	50,000	1906
Chi Delta Mu Fraternity Medical fraternity	Nolan N. Atkinson, M.D.	600	1913
Chi Eta Phi Sorority Nursing sorority	Leota P. Brown	1,200	1932
Delta Sigma Theta Sorority Social sorority	Frankee M. Freeman	50,000	1913
Eta Phi Beta Sorority Business women's sorority	Annette Clardy	——	1942
Iota Phi Lambda Sorority Social sorority	Mrs. Mahala S. Evans	3,000	——
Kappa Alpha Psi Fraternity Social fraternity	William Davenport	31,000	1911
Lambda Kappa Mu Sorority Social sorority	Mrs. Marie G. Leatherman	500	1927
Omega Psi Phi Fraternity Social fraternity	Ellis F. Corbett	35,000	1911
Phi Beta Sigma Fraternity Social fraternity	Dr. Alvin J. McNeil	13,124	1914
Sigma Gamma Rho Sorority Community service sorority	Lorraine Williams	6,000	1922
Tau Gamma Delta Sorority Business and professional women's sorority	Agnes Fischer	325	1948
Zeta Phi Beta Sorority Social sorority	Mildred Bradham	20,000	1920

Elected Negro Officials

THE THEME "1968: The Year of Awakening" could well be illustrated by the list provided below, of the many Blacks who were either elected to office in 1968 or who held office in that year. The breakdown by states makes it possible to see the shifting political trends as reflected on the local level.

Alabama

William C. Allen
Justice of Peace
Tuskegee

Lucius Amerson
Sheriff
Tuskegee

A. R. Ashley
Justice of Peace
Tuskegee

C. R. Atkinson
City Council
Hobson City

David Barnes
Councilman
Triana

Hillie Belcher
Justice of Peace
Faunsdale

Mrs. Alice Belle
Constable
Coatopa

Frank H. Bentley, Jr.
Councilman
Tuskegee

John S. Billingsley
Councilman
Roosevelt City

Dr. Prosanto K. Biswas
Member, School Board
Tuskegee

Albert C. Bulls, Jr.
Councilman
Tuskegee

William J. Childs
Justice of Peace
Tuskegee

Jerry D. Coleman
Councilman
Fairfield

Robert Conley
Councilman
Hobson City

Joe L. DuBose
Councilman
Fairfield

Rev. V. A. Edwards
Board of Revenue
Tuskegee

Jesse Favor
Justice of Peace
Hayneville

Joe L. Fletcher
Councilman
Triana

Clyde Foster
Mayor
Madison

Theodore Fox
Councilman
Jacksonville

Davie Frazier
Justice of Peace
Troy

T. M. Gilchrist
Justice of Peace
Hayneville

Dr. C. G. Gomillion
Member, School Board
Tuskegee

William Griffin
Councilman
Triana

James M. Harper
Justice of Peace
Thomasville

A. M. Hayden
Councilman
Uniontown

Isaiah Hayes, III
Justice of Peace
Attalla

R. T. Hayes
Justice of Peace
Magnolia

Dr. J. H. M. Henderson
Member, School Board
Tuskegee

Elias Hendricks
Constable
Birmingham

Oscar Hildreth
Justice of Peace
Thomasville

John Hoard
Justice of Peace
Livingston

James Johnson
Constable
Birmingham

Earl Jerome King
Justice of Peace
Gadsden

Rev. Peter Kirksey
Member, County School Board
Boligee

McKinley Kolb
Member, City Council
Fairfield

Afton M. Lee, Sr.
Member, City Council
Homewood

Samuel Little
School Board Chairman
Eppes

L. A. Locklair
Tax Collector
Tuskegee

Miss Patricia McAlpin
Justice of Peace
Gadsden

Ernest McLin, Sr.
Councilman
Fairfield

John L. Mason
Councilman
Roosevelt City

Wilbur Miller
Councilman
Roosevelt City

Lorenzo S. Mitchell
Councilman
Bessemer

Aris Morris
Justice of Peace
West Attalla

Virgie Lee Pearson
Councilman
Fairfield

William T. Peterson
Councilman
Tuskegee

Freddie C. Rogers
Mayor
Roosevelt City

Richard Rowe
Constable
Witfield

Calvin Smith
Councilman
Roosevelt City

A. Snow
Councilman
Hobson City

James M. Snow
Councilman
Hobson City

Mrs. Willie Maud Snow
Councilman
Hobson City

Moses Springer
Councilman
Hobson City

Charles Stanton
Councilman
Hobson City

J. R. Striplin
Mayor
Hobson City

Lewis Thomas
Constable
Panola

Mrs. Tessie Thomas
Justice of Peace
Panola

Frank J. Toland
Councilman
Tuskegee

James R. Weatherly
Coroner
Livingston

Harold Webb
Board of Revenue
Tuskegee

Rev. Herbert Wheeler
Constable
Birmingham

Mrs. Annie B. Williams
Justice of Peace
Panola

Jimmie Lee Williams
Councilman
Fairfield

Mrs. Bettie Wimbley
Justice of Peace
Witfield

Arthur Woods
Justice of Peace
Faunsdale

Lee D. Young
Councilman
Hobson City

Arizona

Clovis Campbell
State Senator
Phoenix

Johnny Green
Constable
Phoenix

Mrs. Ethel Maynard
State Representative
Tucson

Leon Thompson
State Representative
Phoenix

Arkansas

Mrs. Mabel Allen
Member, School Board
Eudora

Earl Austin
Member, School Board
Lockesburg

D. B. Bell
Member, School Board
Lockesburg

Mervin Bell
Member, School Board
Lockesburg

James Boone
Town Council
Dumas

Alex Brown
Member, School Board
Tucker

Charles Bussey
City Manager's Board
Little Rock

R. C. Cravens
Member, School Board
Lockesburg

Sammie S. Criswell
Member, School Board
Springfield

Cain Crockran
Member, School Board
Solgohachia

Dennis Curry
Member, School Board
Pine Bluff

Mrs. Syble Dockery
Member, School Board
Bucker

Jethro Fair
Member, School Board
Pine Bluff

Johnnie E. Gay
Mayor
Humnoke

A. L. Grant
Alderman
Dumas

DeArthur Grice
Member, School Board
Moscow

J. C. Hamilton
Member, School Board
Pine Bluff

J. D. Hammond
Member, School Board
Menifee

R. E. Hemphill
Member, School Board
Center Ridge

John Holmes
Member, School Board
Magnolia

Frank Hunter
Member, School Board
Sheridan

Moses Johnson
Mayor
Reed

Oscar Johnson
School Director
Stephens

Rev. Lorenzo Jones
Alderman
Earle

D. W. Jordan, Sr.
Alderman
West Helena

Frank Jordan
Member, School Board
Helena

Charles Kelley
Mayor
Dumas

Shuley Lovett
Member, School Board
Banks

Miss Minnie Macklin
Member, School Board
Sherrill

Rev. G. R. Mazique
Alderman
Helena

Abraham McCarrell
Alderman
Dumas

Arthur H. Miller
Member, School Board
Pine Bluff

Donald Mills
Member, School Board
Ashdown

Ladell Morris
Alderman and Member, School Board
Menifee

Ivory Murphy
Member, School Board
Chidester

C. W. Olloway
Member, School Board
Pine Bluff

T. E. Patterson
Member, School Board
Little Rock

Charles Portis
Member, Town Council
Dumas

James Sims
Member, School Board
Wabbaseka

Frank Smith
Mayor
Menifee

John W. Smith
Member, School Board
North Little Rock

T. L. Story
Member, School Board
Emerson

Frank E. Taylor
Recording Treasurer (Norall, Ark.)
Earle

Aaron Thompson
Member, School Board
Rosston

Ira J. Tidwell
Member, School Board
Rosston

Andrew Walker
Member, School Board
Altheimer

Joe Walls
Member, School Board
Lockesburg

Rev. G. Edward West
City Board of Directors
Fort Smith

California

Horace C. Anderson
Member, Palo Alto Unified School District
Palo Alto

Orville Anderson
Member, Willowbrook Elementary School District
Compton

Tom Bradley
Councilman
Los Angeles

Mrs. Yvonne Brathwaite
State Representative
Los Angeles

Harry Bremond
Member, Ravenswood City Elementary School District
Palo Alto

Gilbert Brooks
Member, School Board Elementary School District
Milpitas

Lewis F. Brown
Councilman
Vallejo

Willie L. Brown, Jr.
State Assemblyman
San Francisco

Lionel B. Cade
Councilman
Compton

Mary Carr
Member, Enterprise Elementary School District
Compton

Mrs. Doris A. Davis
Compton City Clerk
Compton

Ron Dellums
Councilman
Berkeley

Carrie L. Dobie
Member, Enterprise Elementary School District
Compton

Douglas Dollarhide
Councilman
Compton

Mervyn M. Dymally
State Senator
Los Angeles

Bernard Evans
Councilman
Richmond

Morris Ewing
Member, Willowbrook Elementary School District
Los Angeles

William (Bill) Green
State Assemblyman
Los Angeles

Norris Gregory
Councilman
San Bernardino

Ben E. Gross
Mayor
Milpitas

Wendel Handy
Member, School Board Elementary School District
Compton

Terry T. Hatter
Member, Richmond Board of Education
Richmond

Hon. Augustus Hawkins
U.S. Congressman
Washington, D.C.

Melvin L. Hester
Member, Compton Elementary School District
Compton

Barney Hilborn
Member, Board of Education
Oakland

Mrs. Mary Joe Howell
Member, School Board Elementary School District
San Mateo

Dr. Matthew Jenkins
Member, School Board Junior College District
Compton

James Jones
Member, Board of Education
Los Angeles

John O. Lewis
Member, Enterprise Elementary School District
Los Angeles

Gilbert Lindsay
Councilman
Los Angeles

George L. Livingston
Councilman
Richmond

Dubois McGee
Mayor
El Centro

John J. Miller
State Assemblyman
Berkeley

Dr. Ross Miller
Member, Union High School District
Compton

Billy Mills
Councilman
Los Angeles

Preston A. O'Neill
Member, Enterprise Elementary School District
Compton

Dr. William K. Payne
Member, Elementary School District School Board
Compton

Leon Ralph
State Assemblyman
Los Angeles

Lewis Roach
Member, Willowbrook Elementary School District
Compton

Jessie L. Robinson
Member, Compton Elementary School District
Compton

Joshua R. Rose
Councilman
Oakland

Stephen E. Ross
Councilman
Seaside

S. Del Rucker
Councilman
Bakersfield

Lillie Lee Sherman
Member, Willowbrook Elementary School District
Los Angeles

George Smith
Member, San Diego Board of Education
San Diego

Roscoe Steverson
Member, Enterprise Elementary School District
Compton

Dr. George Stewart
Member, School Board Los Rios Jr. College District
Sacramento

James Stratten
Member, San Francisco Board of Education
San Francisco

Wilmont Sweeney
Councilman
Berkeley

Alzue A. Thompson
Member, Willowbrook Elementary School District
Compton

Dr. Walter Tucker
Member, School Board High School District
Compton

Jules Weldon
Councilman
Ridgecrest

Andrew B. White
Member, Ravenswood City Elementary School District
Menlo Park

Rev. W. H. Williams, Jr.
Member, Board of Education
Oakland

Jardine Wilson
Member, School Board Elementary School District
Compton

Thomas R. Yarborough
Mayor
Elsinore

Colorado

George L. Brown
State Senator
Denver

James Flanigan
Judge, District Court
Denver

Paul Hamilton
State Representative
Denver

Jerry Rose
State Representative
Denver

Connecticut

Boce W. Barlow, Jr.
State Senator
Hartford

Mrs. Augusta M. Bishop
Councilwoman
New Haven

Otha Brown, Jr.
State Representative
South Norwalk

Rev. Jeremiah Covington
Councilman
New Haven

Walter Edwards
Alderman
Bridgeport

Leonard Frazier
State Representative
Hartford

Leander Gray
Alderman
New Haven

William Gray
Alderman
New Haven

Donald Harris
Member, Board of Education
Bloomfield

Gerald Lamb
State Treasurer
Waterbury

Ralph Lockhard
Councilman
Stamford

Charles Marshall
City Clerk
South Norwalk

Mrs. Rita Miller
Selectman
Bridgeport

Charles R. Mitchell
Councilman
Stamford

Lorenzo Morgan
State Representative
Hartford

Bruce Morris
State Representative
New Haven

Ray Neal
Councilman
Meriden

Noah Perry
Councilman
New Haven

Sherman Robinson
Constable
New Haven

Alfred Rogers
Member, Board of Education
Hartford

Mrs. Ella Scantlebury
City Treasurer
New Haven

George C. Scott
Alderman
Bridgeport

Louis Skinner
Selectman
New Haven

E. Eugene Spear
Member, School Board
Bridgeport

Jerry F. Walden
Councilman
Stamford

Alvin Wood
Councilman
Bloomfield

Alonzo Woods
Constable
Waterbury

Delaware

Napoleon Cupton
Councilman
Wilmington

Oliver Fonville
State Representative
Wilmington

Reese L. Hammond
State Representative
Wilmington

Wade Hampton
Councilman
Wilmington

Herman N. Holloway
State Senator
Wilmington

Howard Moore
Councilman
Wilmington

Florida

Bobby E. Brooks
City Commission
Riviera Beach

Earl J. Carroll
County Commission
Miami

Jackie Caynon
City Council
Fort Pierce

F. M. Cunningham
City Council
West Palm Beach

George H. Gause
City Commission
Bartow

James Huger
City Council
Daytona Beach

Earl Johnson
City Council
Jacksonville

Joe Lang Kershaw
State House
Miami

Mrs. Sallye B. Mathis
City Council
Jacksonville

Mrs. Athalee Range
City Commission
Miami

Robert Scott
City Council
Lawtey

William Shellman
Constable
Jacksonville

Charles E. Simmons, Jr.
Civil Service Commission
Jacksonville

Mrs. Mary L. Singleton
City Council
Jacksonville

Oscar N. Taylor
City Council
Jacksonville

Rudolph Von Slaughter
City Commission
Melbourne

Boisy Waiters
City Commission
Dania

Ozie F. Youngblood
City Commission
Del Ray Beach

Georgia

David C. Albert
Councilman
Augusta

William H. Alexander
State House
Atlanta

Earl Baggs
City Commission
Riceboro

Julian Bond
State House
Atlanta

Benjamin D. Brown
State House
Atlanta

Mose Cooper
Councilman
Sylvania

Henry Curry
County Commission
Townsend

J. C. Daugherty
State House
Atlanta

James E. Dean
State House
Atlanta

B. L. Dent
Councilman
Augusta

Richard L. Dent
State House
Augusta

Clarence G. Ezzard
State House
Atlanta

Rev. C. S. Hamilton
Councilman
Augusta

Mrs. Grace T. Hamilton
State House
Atlanta

Bobby L. Hill
State House
Savannah

Richmond D. Hill
City Council
Greenville

John Hood
State House
Atlanta

Miss Edith J. Ingram
Ordinary
Sparta

Robert Ingram
School Board
Sparta

Leroy Johnson
State Senate
Atlanta

John McCown
County Commission
Sparta

E. J. Shepherd
State House
Atlanta

James H. Smith
County Commission
Sparta

Rev. L. Scott Stell, Jr.
County Commission
Savannah

Dr. Horace E. Tate
City School Board
Atlanta

Albert Thompson
State House
Columbus

Horace T. Ward
State Senate
Atlanta

Q. V. Williamson
Board of Aldermen
Atlanta

Asa G. Yancey
City School Board
Atlanta

Rev. N. B. Young
School Board
Augusta

Illinois

George Blakey
Magistrate
Chicago

Lewis A. G. Caldwell
State Representative
Chicago

Kenneth B. Campbell
Councilman
Chicago

Archibald J. Carey, Jr.
Judge, Cook County
Circuit Court
Chicago

James Carter
State Representative
Chicago

Lloyd Carter, Jr.
Alderman
Urbana

George W. Collins
Councilman
Chicago

Otis Collins
State Representative
Chicago

Cyrus Coulter
Board of Commissioners
Chicago

William Cousins, Jr.
Councilman
Chicago

James Crosson
Judge
Chicago

Corneal A. Davis
State Representative
Chicago

Hon. William L. Dawson
U.S. Congressman
Washington, D.C.

Richard R. Edwards
Member, Champaign
Board of Education
Champaign

Raymond W. Ewell
State Representative
Chicago

William Frost
Councilman
Chicago

Ernest Green
Magistrate
Chicago

Richard Gumbel
Magistrate
Chicago

Kenneth Hall
State Representative
East St. Louis

William W. Harvey
Councilman
Chicago

Edwin Hatfield
Judge
Chicago

Claude W. B. Holman
Councilman
Chicago

Glenn T. Johnson
Associate Judge, Circuit
Court
Chicago

Mark E. Jones
Judge
Chicago

Sidney Jones
Associate Judge, Circuit
Court, Cook County
Chicago

George N. Leighton
Magistrate, Circuit Court
Chicago

James McLendon
State Representative
Chicago

Ralph Metcalf
Councilman
Chicago

Robert Miller
Councilman
Chicago

Earl Neal
Magistrate
Chicago

Richard Newhouse
State Senator
Chicago

Maurice Pompey
Magistrate
Chicago

A. A. Rayner
Councilman
Chicago

Mrs. Edith Sampson
Judge
Chicago

Ester Saverson
Councilman
East St. Louis

William Shannon
Councilman
Chicago

Isaac Sims
State Representative
Chicago

Mrs. Josephine B. Sneed
Member, Board of Commissioners
Chicago

Earl Strayhorn
Judge, Circuit Court, Cook County
Chicago

Myrtle Stryker
Judge, Circuit Court
Chicago

Alvin Turner
Judge
Chicago

Frederick Walden
Alderman
Urbana

Harold Washington
State Representative
Chicago

William S. White
Judge, Circuit Court
Chicago

Willie Whiting
Judge
Chicago

Kenneth E. Wilson
Board of Commissioners
Chicago

Indiana

Dozier Allen
Councilman
Gary

Patrick Chavis, Jr.
State Senator
Indianapolis

James Dent
Councilman
East Chicago

Mrs. Henry Gibson
Marion County Recorder
Indianapolis

Hon. Richard Hatcher
Mayor
Gary

Mrs. Jesse Mitchell
Councilwoman
Gary

John Nuchlos
Councilman
Fort Wayne

Thomas Sleat
Councilman
Indianapolis

Quentin Smith
Councilman
Gary

James L. Thomas
Councilman
E. Chicago

John Todd
Councilman
Lawrence

Mrs. Cleo Wesson
Councilwoman
Gary

Alexander Williams
Coroner
Lake County

Iowa

Mrs. A. June Franklin
State Representative
Des Moines

Hon. Luther Glanton
Judge, Municipal Court
Des Moines

Kansas

James P. Davis
State Representative
Kansas City

Clarence C. Love
Assemblyman
Kansas City

Billy McCray
Assemblyman
Wichita

Cordell D. Meeks
County Commissioner
Kansas City

Kentucky

Mrs. Georgia M. Davis
State Senator
Louisville

Dr. Albert B. Harris
Councilman
Louisville

Mrs. Mae Street Kidd
State Representative
Louisville

Hughes E. McGill
State Representative
Louisville

Louisiana

Roland Adams
County Constable
Vacherie

Wesley Albert, Sr.
Justice of Peace
New Roads

F. J. Atlas
School Board
Lake Providence

Larry Balthazar
Ward Constable
Natchez

Morris Barnes
Constable
Palmetto

John Bobb, Jr.
City Council
Grand Coteau

Joseph J. Borne
Constable
Edgard

Dr. Ruth D. Bradford
Alderman
Grambling

Anderson Broussard
Justice of Peace
Franklin

J. Woodrow Calvey
School Board
Welcome

Felton C. Ceasar
Justice of Peace
Welcome

Oliver Cooper
Police Jury
Welcome

Eddie Davis
Police Jury
Weyanoke

Joseph M. Davis
Police Jury
Jeanerette

Joseph Delphin
Justice of Peace
Natchez

Joseph A. Delpit
City Council
Baton Rouge

Harry Lee Fusilier
City Council
Crowley

Isaac Garritt, Jr.
Police Jury
Vacherie

Whitmore Gordon
Town Council
Edgard

Reed Green
Town Council
Maringouin

Charlie Harris
Justice of Peace
New Roads

Jake W. Holmes
School Board
Bayou Gaula

Levis T. Jackson
Marshal
Grambling

Rev. C. P. Jenson
Alderman
Grambling

Stanley Johnson
Justice of Peace
Franklin

Raymond Julien
Police Jury
Donaldsonville

Milton Kelly
Alderman
Grambling

L. D. Land
Alderman
Grambling

Ledell Mackie
Police Jury
St. Francisville

Mrs. Helena McClinton
School Board
Tallulah

Ernest Metz
Constable
Franklin

Raymond A. Minor
School Board
St. Francisville

Anatole Monconduit
County Constable
Welcome

Henry A. Montgomery
Alderman
Ferriday

Ernest Morial
State House
New Orleans

Thomas Nelson
Constable
New Roads

Jesse Paul
Marshal
Patterson

Joseph A. (Joe) Pete
City Council
Crowley

Joseph R. Richard, Sr.
Town Council
Grand Coteau

Watson Sanders
Police Jury
Sondheimer

Harvey Schexnayder
Justice of Peace
Vacherie

Arthur D. Smith
Alderman
Grambling

Nathaniel Smith, Sr.
Police Jury
St. Francisville

Peter Smith
City Council & Mayor
Pro Tem
Grand Coteau

Rudolph Sorapuru
Police Jury
Lucy

Leonard Tardy
Constable
Franklin

James A. Thomas
School Board
Tallulah

Rev. O. L. Virgil
Police Jury
Lake Providence

Alvin White, Jr.
School Board
St. Francisville

John Williams
School Board
Weyanoke

B. T. Woodard
Mayor
Grambling

Anderson Yancy
Police Jury
Franklin

Maryland

Floyd B. Adams
State Representative
Baltimore

Mrs. Victorine Q. Adams
State Representative
Baltimore

Troy Brailey
State Representative
Baltimore

Joseph A. Chester
State Representative
Baltimore

Isaiah Dixon
State Representative
Baltimore

Walter Dixon
Councilman
Baltimore

Calvin A. Douglas
State Representative
Baltimore

Robert L. Douglass
Councilman
Baltimore

Dr. Emerson R. Julian
Councilman
Baltimore

Arthur King
State Representative
Mt. Rainier

Mrs. Lena K. Lee
State Representative
Baltimore

Clarence Mitchell, III
State Senator
Baltimore

Henry G. Parks
Councilman
Baltimore

Robert B. Watts
Judge, Municipal Court
Baltimore

Mrs. Verda Welcome
State Senator
Baltimore

Massachusetts

Tom Atkins
Councilman
Roxbury

Rev. Michael Haynes
State Representative
Boston

Franklin Holgate
State Representative
Boston

Michigan

Richard Austin
Wayne County Auditor
Detroit

James Bradley
State Representative
Detroit

John Burton
Mayor
Ypsilanti

Augustus Calloway
Board of Governors
Detroit

Hon. John Conyers, Jr.
U.S. Congress
Detroit

George Crockett
Magistrate, Recorder's Court
Detroit

Elvin Davenport
Judge, Recorder's Court
Detroit

James del Rio
State Representative
Lansing

Hon. Charles Diggs, Jr.
U.S. Congress
Detroit

George H. Edwards
State Representative
Highland Park

Mrs. Daisy Elliott
State Representative
Detroit

Robert Evans
Judge, Recorder's Court
Detroit

Joel Ferguson
Councilman
Lansing

Mrs. Rosetta Ferguson
State Representative
Detroit

Mrs. Geraldine B. Ford
Magistrate
Detroit

Marcus Gray
Calhoun County Clerk
Battle Creek

David S. Holmes, Jr.
State Representative
Detroit

Rev. Nicholas Hood
Councilman
Detroit

Raymond W. Hood
State Representative
Detroit

Kenneth Hylton
Vice Chairman, State Central Committee
Detroit

Henry Marsh
Mayor
Saginaw

Floyd J. McCree
Mayor
Flint

Hon. Wade McCree, Jr.
Judge, U.S. Circuit Court
Detroit

Matthew McNeeley
State Representative
Detroit

Dr. Charles Morton
Member, State Board of Education
Detroit

Dr. Remus Robinson
Member, School Board
Detroit

Nelis J. Saunders
State Representative
Detroit

Mrs. Ethel Terrell
Councilwoman
Detroit

Robert Tindal
Clerk, Common Court
Detroit

Jackie Vaughn, III
State Representative
Detroit

Mrs. Nancy Waters
Corresponding Secretary, State Central Committee
Detroit

L. C. Williams
Councilman
Mt. Clemens

Mississippi

Howard T. Bailey
Election Commission
Lexington

Miss Julia Banks
Election Commission
Fayette

Osborne Bell
Coroner
Holly Springs

Ellis Braxton
Election Commission
Lorman

Robert G. Clark
State House
Lexington

Rogers Clark
Election Commission
Port Gibson

Alexander Collins
Justice of Peace
Port Gibson

Mrs. Geneva Collins
Chancery Clerk
Port Gibson

John Daugherty
Election Commission
Lamar

Mrs. Gladys Davis
Election Commission
Woodville

Rev. Dan Ferguson
Justice of Peace
Clarksdale

Sylvester Gaines
Board of Supervisors
Lorman

W. E. Garrett
Election Commission
Canton

Mrs. Flonzie B. Goodloe
Election Commission
Canton

Matthew Gray
Election Commission
Port Gibson

Robert Dean Gray
Board of Aldermen
Shelby

John Green
County School Board
Woodville

Mrs. Marie Green
County School Board
Woodville

Mrs. Sallye W. Griffin
Board of Aldermen
Mound Bayou

Sol Jackson
Election Commission
Fayette

Everett Jennings
Election Commission
Hermansville

Elra Johnson
Election Commission
Durant

Hermon Johnson
Board of Aldermen
Mound Bayou

James Jolliff, Jr.
Board of Supervisors
Woodville

Charlie Jones
Justice of Peace
Coahoma

Marshall Jones
Election Commission
Holly Springs

R. W. Jones
City Council
Mound Bayou

Mrs. Martha Lee
Justice of Peace
Lorman

Wesley Liddell
Mayor
Mound Bayou

Horace Lightfoot
County School Board
Port Gibson

Earlie Lott
Constable
Fayette

Mrs. Arenia C. Mallory
County School Board
Lexington

James Malone
Justice of Peace
Waterford

Griffin McLaurin
Constable
Tchula

Leander Monroe
Constable
Port Gibson

Sandy Nealey
Constable
Natchez

Mrs. Legora A. Reed
City Council
Mound Bayou

U. S. Rimmer
Justice of Peace
Camden

Leroy Robinson, Jr.
Election Commission
Lorman

Floyd Rollins
Election Commission
Port Gibson

William Matt Ross
Board of Supervisors
Port Gibson

Rev. W. S. Scott
Justice of Peace
Natchez

Melvin Smith
Constable
Mayersville

Kermit Stanton
Board of Supervisors
Shelby

Burrell Tate
Election Commission
Pickens

Willie Thompson
Justice of Peace
Fayette

Matthew Walker
Justice of Peace
Rolling Fork

McEwen Walker
Constable
Waterford

Robert Lee Williams
School Board
Lorman

Rev. C. C. Woodley
City Council
Mound Bayou

Missouri

Johnnie S. Aikens
State Representative
St. Louis

J. B. Jett Banks
State Representative
St. Louis

Frank S. Bledsoe
Magistrate
St. Louis

Edna Brown
Councilwoman
St. Louis

Mrs. DeVerne Calloway
State Representative
St. Louis

Joseph W. B. Clark
Councilman
St. Louis

Hon. William Clay
U.S. Congress
Washington, D.C.

Louis Cluner
Judge, Municipal Court
Kansas City

John Conley
Committeeman
St. Louis

Russell Goward
Committeeman
St. Louis

John W. Harvey
Magistrate
St. Louis

Mrs. Ernestine Hinton
Councilwoman
St. Louis

Raymond Howard
State Senator
St. Louis

DeWitte Lawson
Councilman
St. Louis

Clarence W. Lee
Mayor
Kinloch

T. D. McNeil
State Senator
St. Louis

Franklin Oayne
State Representative
St. Louis

Dr. John E. Ramos
Member, School Board
Kansas City

Nathaniel Rivers
Councilman
St. Louis

Nathaniel K. Rivers
State Representative
St. Louis

Richard T. Singleton
Alderman
St. Louis

Waymen Smith
Councilman
St. Louis

Earl D. Thomas
Councilman
Kansas City

James P. Troup, Sr.
State Representative
St. Louis

Bruce R. Watkins
Judge, Circuit Court
Kansas City

Fred Williams
State Representative
St. Louis

Lawrence Woodson
Councilman
St. Louis

Nebraska

Ed Denner
State Senator
Omaha

New Jersey

James Abrams
Essex County Surrogate
Newark

Alfred W. Brown
Councilman
East Orange

Foster Burnett
Councilman
Somerset

Matthew G. Carter
Mayor
Montclair

Albert T. Collier
Member, Board of Freeholders
East Orange

Thomas Cook
Councilman
East Orange

William C. Holt
Councilman
East Orange

William R. Jenkins
Councilman
Camden

William Kline
Councilman
Paterson

Rev. Everett Lattimore
Councilman
Plainfield

Karlos R. Lesane
Member, City Commission
Atlantic City

Mrs. Wynona Littman
Office of Freeholder
Montclair

Fred W. Martin
Councilman
Jersey City

Charles Matthews
Director of Freeholders
Newark

Dr. Adam McDaniels
Councilman
Rahway

Addison M. McLeon
State Representative
Jersey City

Ronald Owens
State Representative
Newark

George C. Richardson
State Representative
Newark

Harold J. Smith
Councilman
East Orange

Vincent Tibbs
Councilman
Englewood

Irwin Turner
Councilman
Newark

Calvin West
Councilman
Newark

S. Howard Woodson
State Representative
Trenton

New Mexico

Ray Hardwick
Councilman
Carlsbad

Albert Johnson
Councilman
Las Cruces

New York

Edrie F. Archibald
District Leader
New York

Bertram Baker
State Assemblyman
Brooklyn

Mrs. Josephine Bravo
District Leader
Brooklyn

Guy Brewer
Director of Community Planning Board
Jamaica, L. I.

Mrs. Henrietta Brown
District Leader
New York

Kenneth W. Brown
State Assemblyman
Jamaica, L. I.

Bernard Charles
Councilman
Spring Valley

Hon. Shirley Chisholm
U.S. Congresswoman
Washington, D.C.

Mrs. Margaret Cox
District Leader
New York

Mrs. Geraldine Daniels
District Leader
New York

J. Daniel Diggs
Councilman
Brooklyn

Herbert B. Evans
Judge
New York

Arthur O. Eve
State Assemblyman
Buffalo

Thomas Fortune
State Assemblyman
Brooklyn

Hulan E. Jack
State Assemblyman
New York

Archie Long
District Leader
New York

Delmar Mitchell
Councilman
Buffalo

Miss Eva S. Neil
District Leader
New York

Miss Jannie Norfleet
District Leader
New York

Basil A. Paterson
State Senator
New York

Hon. Adam C. Powell
U.S. Member of Congress
Washington, D.C.

Charles B. Rangel
State Assemblyman
New York

Mrs. Isadora Rogers
District Leader
Jamaica, L. I.

James H. Shaw
Judge, Civil Court
Brooklyn

Mark T. Southall
State Assemblyman
New York

Edward A. Stevenson
State Assemblyman
Bronx

Wadabla Stewart
State Senator
Brooklyn

Miss Hilda Stokely
District Leader
New York

Percy E. Sutton
President, Borough of Manhattan
New York

Andrew R. Tyler
Judge, Civil Court
New York

Mrs. Lillian Upshur
District Leader
New York

Ivan W. Warner
State Senator
Bronx

Samuel D. Wright
State Assemblyman
Brooklyn

Judicial Appointive Winners

Amos E. Bowman
Supreme Court
Manhattan & Bronx

Kenneth N. Browne
Civil Court
Queens

George Fleary
Civil Court
Brooklyn

Thomas R. Jones
Supreme Court
Brooklyn

Franklin R. Morton
Supreme Court
Brooklyn

Jawn A. Sandifer
Supreme Court
Manhattan & Bronx

Clifford A. Scott
Civil Court
Manhattan

Ivan Warner
Supreme Court
Manhattan & Bronx

Samuel Welcome
Civil Court
Brooklyn

North Carolina

Mrs. Elreta M. Alexander
District Court Judge
Guilford County
Greensboro

Fred Alexander
City Council
Charlotte

Thurman Anderson
County School Board
Lumberton

C. E. Boulware
City Council
Durham

Felton J. Capel
Mayor Pro Tem
Southern Pines

Dr. Joseph S. Colson
City Commission
Oxford

Henry Fry
State House
Greensboro

Howard Hunter
County School Board
Ahoskie

Dr. Lillian B. Lewis
School Board
Winston-Salem

Clarence E. Lightner
City Council
Raleigh

Rev. Cecil Marcellus, Jr.
City Council
Reidsville

Fred D. McNeill, Jr.
County School Board
Durham

J. Ely Reid
City Council
Winton

Charles C. Ross, Sr.
Board of Aldermen
Winston-Salem

Carl H. Russell
City Council
Winston-Salem

Asa T. Spaulding
County Commission
Durham

John S. Stewart
City Council
Durham

Dr. E. B. Turner
City Council
Lumberton

Ohio

John C. Armstrong
Councilman
Cleveland

James H. Bell
Councilman
Cleveland

William F. Bowen
State Representative
Cincinnati

Lloyd Brown
Judge
Cleveland

Myron B. Bush
Councilman
Cincinnati

Charles V. Carr
Councilman
Cleveland

Craft C. Carter, Jr.
Councilman
Cleveland

Calvin Conliff
Member, School Board
Cincinnati

Edward Davis
Councilman
Akron

Phillip Delaine
State Representative
Columbus

Arthur O. Fisher
Judge, Municipal Court
Dayton

George Forbes
Councilman
Cleveland

Dr. Robert Ford
Member, Jefferson Township School Board
Dayton

Jack B. Franklin
Judge, Police Court
Ottawa Hills

Robert V. Franklin
Judge, Municipal Court
Toledo

Warren Gilliam
Councilman
Cleveland

Samuel Glover
Board of Education
Lincoln Heights

Rev. Phale D. Hale
State Representative
Columbus

Hon. W. E. Harrison
Jefferson Township Trustee
Dayton

James T. Henry
Councilman
Xenia

Ozie Hill
Councilman
Mansfield

Thomas E. Hill
State Representative
Cleveland

Leo Jackson
Councilman
Cleveland

Troy L. James
State Representative
Cleveland

Casey Jones
State Representative
Toledo

Avora Knight
Board of Education
Lincoln Heights

C. J. McLin, Jr.
State Representative
Dayton

Larry G. Smith
State Representative
Cleveland

P. Peter Starks
Councilman
Youngstown

Hon. Carl B. Stokes
Mayor
Cleveland

Hon. Louis Stokes
U.S. Congressman
Washington, D.C.

Dr. Watson H. Walker
Member, School Board
Columbus

George White
Judge, Common Pleas Court
Cleveland

Theodore Williams
Judge, Municipal Court
Cleveland

Oklahoma

Mrs. Hanna Atkins
State Representative
Oklahoma City

Archibald B. Hill, Jr.
State Representative
Oklahoma City

Rev. Ben Hill
State Representative
Tulsa

A. Visanio Johnson
State Representative
Oklahoma City

Pennsylvania

Mrs. Sarah A. Anderson
State Representative
Philadelphia

Herbert Arlene
State Senator
Philadelphia

James Barber
State Representative
Philadelphia

Andrew Bradley
Treasurer, Democratic State Committee
Harrisburg

Hon. Homer Brown
Magistrate, Common Pleas Court
Pittsburgh

Edgar Campbell
Councilman-at-large
Philadelphia

Charles Durham
Councilman
Philadelphia

Freeman P. Hankins
State Senator
Philadelphia

K. Leroy Irvis
State Representative
Pittsburgh

Joel J. Johnson
State Representative
Philadelphia

Paul N. Lawson
State Representative
Philadelphia

Louis Mason, Jr.
Councilman
Pittsburgh

Tom McIntosh
Councilman
Philadelphia

Mitchell Melton
State Representative
Philadelphia

Robert N. C. Nix
U.S. Member of Congress
Washington, D.C.

Rev. Marshall Shephard
Councilman
Philadelphia

Hon. Juanita Kidd Stout
Judge, Municipal Court
Philadelphia

Earl Vann
State Representative
Philadelphia

Hon. Warren Watson
Judge, Allegheny County Court
Pittsburgh

Rhode Island

Peter J. Coelho
State Representative
Providence

South Carolina

Leroy E. Browne
County Board of Directors
Frogmore

Freddie Campbell
City Council
Eastover

W. Cook
Town Council
Summerville

St. Julian Devine
City Council
Charleston

Franklin DeWitt
City Council
Conway

Anthony Eddings
Magistrate
Frogmore

Herman H. Felix
City Council
Lynchburg

Bennie Hopkins
Town Council
Sellers

George Jacobs
Town Council
Summerville

William Jefferson
City Council
Mayesville

Richard Johnson
City Council
Eastover

David Jones
County Board of Directors
Hilton Head

Eddie Kline
Magistrate
Dale

J. O. Wendell Martin
County Council
Jenkensville

Jessie McClellan
Town Council
Sellers

John L. McCoy
City Council
Great Falls

Mrs. Frieda R. Mitchell
Board of Education
Sheldon

Charles H. Ross
Mayor
Summerville

Mrs. Agnes Sherman
School Board
Frogmore

Mrs. Hattie Sims
Magistrate
Hopkins

Joseph Stroy
Magistrate
Hopkins

Arnic Washington
Town Council
Summerville

Booker T. Washington
County Council
Lobesco

Charlie Bell Williams
Town Council
Sellers

Joseph Wright
City Council
Beaufort

Tennessee

Mrs. Gladys Allen
Magistrate
Oakland

Dennis Bank
Constable
Knoxville

M. G. Blakemore
State House
Nashville

Robert J. Booker
State House
Knoxville

Lawrence Curry
Constable
Chattanooga

Fred L. Davis
City Council
Memphis

Mansfield Douglas
City Council
Nashville

John Driver
City Council
Nashville

William Hazlett
County Court
Collierville

Blair T. Hunt
School Board
Memphis

Mrs. Geraldine Johnson
County Court
Mason

Alvin King
State House
Memphis

Robert Lilliard
City Council
Nashville

Albert Lockard
School Board
Ripley

Z. Alexander Looby
City Council
Nashville
Nashville

Charlie Minon
County Court
Somerville

Ira H. Murphy
State House
Memphis

Harold M. Love
State House

Rev. James L. Netters
City Council
Memphis

Dan Nixon
Magistrate
Brownsville

Cooper Parks
County Court
Collierville

J. O. Patterson, Jr.
State Senate
Memphis

Sherman Perry
Magistrate
Oakland

A. D. Powell
Magistrate
Brownsville

Rev. Robert Richards
Justice of Peace
Chattanooga

Robert Scales
City Council
Murfreesboro

James Staples
Constable
Knoxville

James I. Taylor
State House
Memphis

Jesse Turner
County Court
Memphis

Avon N. Williams, Jr.
State Senate
Nashville

Texas

Harmon Bell
City Council
Bryan

I. W. Brown
Board of Aldermen
Malakoff

Asberry Butler
School Board
Houston

Dr. Emmett J. Conrad
School Board
Dallas

Mrs. Exalton A. Delco, Jr.
School Board
Austin

Wilbert Lee Eagleton
School Board
Crosby

Dr. Marion G. Ford
School Board
Houston

Curtis M. Graves
State House
Houston

Arthur J. Guidry
Mayor Pro Tem
Port Arthur

Dr. E. W. Gwinn
City Council
Fort Worth

Zan Wesley Holmes, Jr.
State House
Dallas

Rev. S. H. James
City Council
San Antonio

Scott E. Johnson
City Council
Huntsville

Miss Barbara Jordan
State Senate
Houston

Alfred Zack McElroy
President, School Board
Port Arthur

John Miles, Jr.
City Council
Hearne

Dr. G. H. Radford
City Council
Waco

William H. Taft
School Board
Beaumont

Harrison E. Taylor
Board of Aldermen
Wichita Falls

Mrs. Artie Mae White
School Board
Houston

Virginia

Mrs. Iona W. Adkins
County Clerk
Charles City

Embria Byrd
City Council
Port Royal

Rev. Lawrence Davis
City Council
Fredericksburg

Garland Faison
Justice of the Peace
Greensville

H. E. Fauntleroy
City Council
Petersburg

Oliver Fortune
City Council
Port Royal

Ernest A. Gaines
City Council
Tappahannock

Charles H. Harris
City Council
Danville

William D. Hobson
City Council
Martinsville

Dr. James W. Holley, III
City Council
Portsmouth

Kenneth L. Jones
City Council
Staunton

Joseph A. Jordan, Jr.
City Council
Norfolk

Henry L. Marsh, III
City Council
Richmond

Henry A. Minor
City Council
Fairfax

Joseph Owens
Justice of Peace
Petersburg

John William Porter
City Council
Dumfries

W. Ferguson Reid
State House
Richmond

Moses Riddick
Board of Supervisors
Suffolk

Basham Sims
City Council
Purcellville

Richard Thomas Spinner
City Council
Buena Vista

S. O. Sykes
Board of Supervisors
Southampton

Charles R. Turner
City Council
Middleburg

Raymond Turner
City Council
Portsmouth

Washington

George T. Fleming
State Representative
Seattle

Wisconsin

Lloyd Barbee
State Representative
Milwaukee

Isaac Coggs
County Board of Supervisors
Milwaukee

Cornelius L. Golightly
Member, School Board
Milwaukee

Calvin Moody
County Board of Supervisors
Milwaukee

Mrs. Vel R. Phillips
Councilwoman
Milwaukee

Orville E. Pitts
Councilman
Milwaukee

Courtesy of the Democratic National Committee

Selected Appointed Black Officials

THIS SELECTION of people appointed to major government positions during the Johnson Administration forms a basis of continuity in a year of political change. The following list, though not all-inclusive, gives some idea of the unparalleled number of Black appointments to positions carrying high levels of official responsibility.

Robert Weaver, Secretary of Housing and Urban Development

Thurgood Marshall, Associate Justice, United States Supreme Court

William H. Hastie, Judge, United States Court of Appeals, Third Circuit

Wade H. McCree, Jr., Judge, United States Court of Appeals, Sixth Circuit

Constance Baker Motley, United States Judge, Southern District of New York

James Benton Parsons, United States Judge, Northern District of Illinois

Scovel Richardson, Presiding Judge, Third Division, United States Customs Court

Robert K. Shoecraft, Chief Justice, High Court in Guam, United States Trust Territory

Joseph C. Waddy, Judge, District of Columbia Court of General Sessions

James L. Watson, Judge, United States Customs Court

Homer Benson, Member, United States Board of Parole

Andrew Felton Brimmer, Member, Federal Reserve Board

John Hope Franklin, Member, Board of Foreign Scholarships, Bureau of Educational and Cultural Affairs, Department of State

Frankie Muse Freeman, Member, United States Commission on Civil Rights

Samuel Charles Jackson, Commissioner, Equal Employment Opportunity Commission

Howard Jenkins, Jr., Member, National Labor Relations Board

Samuel Nabrit, Member, Atomic Energy Commission

Hobart Taylor, Jr., Member, Board of Directors, Export-Import Bank

Walter E. Washington, Mayor, Washington, D.C.

Samuel Clifford Adams, Jr., Overseas Director, Agency for International Development

Clifford L. Alexander, Jr., Deputy Special Counsel to the President

Samuel W. Allen, Chief Counsel, Community Relations Service, Department of Commerce

Kermit G. Bailer, Director, Office of Community Programs, Department of Housing and Urban Development

Mark Battle, Deputy Administrator, Neighborhood Youth Corps

Theodore Moody Berry, Director, Community Action Program, Office of Economic Opportunity

Edward W. Brice, Director, Adult Education Branch, Office of Education, Department of Health, Education and Welfare

George Carter, Regional Director for North Africa, Near East and South Asia, Peace Corps

Lisle C. Carter, Jr., Assistant Secretary, Department of Health, Education and Welfare

Arthur Christopher, Jr., Trial Examiner, National Labor Relations Board

Lieutenant Commander Ben Cloud, White House Presidential Social Aide

Roy K. Davenport, Deputy Undersecretary, Department of the Army

Frederic E. Davison, Brigadier General, United States Army

Joseph H. Douglass, Chief, Office of Interagency Liaison, National Institute of Mental Health

George William Draper, II, Chief Counsel, Office of Metropolitan Development, Department of Housing and Urban Development

Alfred Leroy Edwards, Deputy Assistant Secretary of Agriculture

William E. Fowler, Jr., Member, Appeals Council, Social Security Administration, Bureau of Hearings and Appeals, Department of Health, Education and Welfare

Robert T. Freeman, Associate Director for Management, Peace Corps

Francis Gregory, Assistant Director for Manpower Development, Department of Labor

Laura Harris, Executive Secretary, Incentive Awards Program, Department of Labor

Stanley P. Hebert, Deputy General Counsel, Department of the Navy

George Holland, Area Field Director, Veterans Administration

John Hope, Assistant Executive Director for Federal Employment, Department of Labor

Ruth Jones, Collector of Customs, United States Virgin Islands

Robert W. Kitchen, Director, Office for International Training, Agency for International Development

Clifton P. Lander, Program Planning Officer, Office of Territories, Department of the Interior

Jean Lightfoot, Liaison Officer, Bureau of Public Affairs, Department of State

Merle M. McCurdy, United States Attorney for the Northern District of Ohio

Henry McGee, Regional Personnel Director, Post Office Department

Ivan C. McLeod, Regional Director, Second Region, National Labor Relations Board

Robert J. Mangum, Regional Director, Office of Economic Opportunity

Ernest N. Morial, Assistant United States Attorney for the Eastern District of Louisiana

Jeanne Noble, Member, President's Task Force on Poverty

Cecil F. Poole, United States Attorney for the Northern District of California

Thomas E. Posey, Chief of Labor and Industry Division, Agency for International Development

Lawrence Prattis, Regional Counsel, Department of Housing and Urban Development

Samuel D. Proctor, Associate Director for Peace Corps Volunteers

Anne B. Roberts, Deputy Regional Administrator, Housing and Home Finance Agency

Cecil E. Robertson, Assistant United States Attorney for the Eastern District of Oklahoma

Major Hugh C. Robinson, White House Presidential Military Aide

Christopher C. Scott, Deputy Postmaster General for Transportation

Leslie Shaw, Postmaster, City of Los Angeles

Leroy A. Smith, Director, Intergroup Relations Branch, Federal Housing Administration

Laura Lee Spencer, Standards and Procedures Officer, Opportunity Standards and Regulations Staff, Department of Housing and Urban Development

Clifford M. Spottsville, Assistant United States Attorney for the Western District of Missouri

Edward Sylvester, Deputy Administrator for International Affairs, Department of Labor

Barbara M. Watson, Administrator, Bureau of Security and Consular Affairs, Department of State

George Leon-Paul Weaver, Assistant Secretary of Labor for International Affairs

Samuel Z. Westerfield, Deputy Assistant Secretary for Economic Affairs, Bureau of African Affairs, Department of State

Roger Wilkins, Director, Community Relations Service, Department of Commerce

Howard B. Woods, Associate Director, United States Information Agency

Courtesy of Professor J. Erroll Miller

Black Press

EVER SINCE John B. Russwurm established *Freedom's Journal* in 1827, the Black press has been an important factor in Negro life and history. The following list of Black owned and operated newspapers in the United States in 1968 is illustrative of Black capitalism at work and points to its continuing growth over the past one hundred and forty-one years. This list also serves as a research tool for those interested in pursuing studies in Black history or in contemporary race relations.

Alabama

Birmingham World
Emory O. Jackson
312 17th Street North
Birmingham, 35203

Mobile Beacon
Frank P. Thomas
415 S. Cedar Street
P.O. Box 1407
Mobile, 36603

Arizona

Arizona Tribune
Edward Banks
2137 East Broadway Road
Phoenix, 85040

California

The Post
Edith M. Austin
2999 Shattuck Avenue
Berkeley, 94705

Star News—The Voice
Rowland K. Reblee
Star News Pub. Co.
Chula Vista, 92010

Los Angeles Sentinel
Leon Washington
1112 E. 43rd Street
Los Angeles, 90011

California Voice
E. A. Daly
814 27th Street
Oakland, 94607

Sacramento Observer
William H. Lee
Box 209
Sacramento, 95801

San Diego Lighthouse
N. M. Young
2652 Imperial Avenue
San Diego, 92102

San Francisco Sun Reporter
Carlton V. Goodlett
1599 Post Street
San Francisco, 94109

Colorado

Denver Blade
Joe Brown
3224 Downing Street
Denver, 80205

Florida

Fort Pierce Chronicle
C. E. Bolen
1527 Avenue D
Fort Pierce, 33450

Florida Star
E. O. Simpson
2323 Moncrief Road
Jacksonville, 32209

Jacksonville Advocate
M. J. Greens
7326 Richardson Road
Jacksonville, 32209

Miami Times
Garth Reeves
6740 N.W. 15th Street
Miami, 33126

Florida Sentinel Bulletin
G. Blytha Andrews
2207 N. 21st Street
Tampa, 33605

News Reporter
James Jackson
1610 N. Howard Avenue
Tampa, 33607

Photo News
A. A. Williams
2108½ N. Tamarind Ave.
West Palm Beach, 33407

Georgia

Southwest Georgian
A. C. Searless
517 Gordon Avenue
Albany, 31701

Atlanta Daily World
C. A. Scott
210 Auburn Avenue, N.E.
Atlanta, 30303

Atlanta Inquirer
Earnest Pharr
787 Parsons Street, S.W.
Atlanta, 30314

Columbus News
Vernon Mitchell
500 9th Street
Columbus, 31901

Illinois

Chicago Crusader
Balm L. Leavell, Jr.
7121 E. 45th Street
Chicago, 60637

Chicago Defender
John Sengstacke
2400 So. Michigan Ave.
Chicago, 60616

Johnson Publishing Co.
John Johnson
1820 So. Michigan Ave.
Chicago, 60616

Muhammad Speaks
Herbert Muhammad
634 East 79th Street
Chicago, 60619

New Crusader
Balm L. Leavell, Jr.
6429 S. Park Avenue
Chicago, 60637

East St. Louis Crusader
John Kirkpatrick
1600 Missouri Avenue
East St. Louis, 62205

The Monitor
Clyde C. Jordan
413 St. Louis Avenue
East St. Louis, 62201

Voice
Dr. L. H. Holman
168 S. Chicago Street
Joliet, 60436

Rockford Crusader
Joseph S. Saunders
821 S. Winnebago
Rockford, 61103

Indiana

Indiana Herald
Opal Tandy
225 W. 30th Street
Indianapolis, 46208

Indianapolis Recorder
Marcus Stewart
518 Indiana Avenue
Indianapolis, 46202

Iowa

Iowa Bystander
James Morris
223½ E. Locust Street
Des Moines, 50309

Kansas

Wichita Enlightener
Edwin T. Saxon
2226 Mossman
Wichita, 67214

Kentucky

Louisville Defender
Frank L. Stanley
1503 S.W. Broadway
Louisville, 40203

Louisiana

News Leader
J. L. Land
156 S. 15th Street
Baton Rouge, 70802

News Leader
Samuel Douglas
P.O. Box 1217
Monroe, 71201

Louisiana Weekly
C. C. Dajois, Jr.
640 S. Rampart Street
New Orleans, 70113

Shreveport Sun
W. L. Collins
1030 Texas Avenue
Shreveport, 71101

Maryland

Afro-American
John and Howard Murphy
628 N. Eutaw
Baltimore, 21201

Massachusetts

Boston Roxbury City News
Nelson Noble
719 Boylston
Boston, 02116

Bay State Banner
Melvin Miller
25 Ruggles Street
Roxbury, 02119

Michigan

Michigan Chronicle
Longworth Quinn
479 Ledyard Street
Detroit, 48201

Jackson Blazer
Rollins Greens
1124 Page Avenue
Jackson, 49203

Minnesota

Minneapolis Spokesman
Cecil Newman
2722 4th Street
Minneapolis, 55422

Twin Cities Courier
Frank C. Kant
322 W. 48th Street
Minneapolis, 55409

Mississippi

Jackson Advocate
Percy Greens
406½ N. Farish
Jackson, 39202

Mississippi Free Press
Charles Butt
538½ N. Farish Street
Jackson, 39202

Missouri

Kansas City Call
Lucille Bluford
1715 E. 18th Street
Kansas City, 64108

People's Guide
J. Vaughn Chapman
5927 Easton Avenue
St. Louis, 63112

St. Louis American
N. A. Sweets
3608 Cozens Avenue
St. Louis, 63113

St. Louis Argus
Frank Mitchell
4595 Easton Avenue
St. Louis, 63113

St. Louis Sentinel
Howard B. Woods
3000 Easton Avenue
St. Louis, 63106

Nebraska

Omaha Star
Mildred Brown
2216 N. 24th Street
Omaha, 68110

Nevada

Las Vegas Voice
Charles I. West
902 W. Bonanza
Las Vegas, 89106

New Jersey

New Jersey Herald News
Oliver Brown
188 Belmont Avenue
Newark, 07108

New York

Westchester County Press
Algar Adams
61 Pinecrest Drive
Hastings-on-Hudson, 10706

Queen's Voice
Kenneth Drew
170-11 Hillside Avenue
Jamaica, 11432

The Voice
Kenneth Drew
171-18 Liberty Avenue
Jamaica, 11433

Amsterdam News
Jimmy Hicks
2340 8th Avenue
New York, 10027

North Carolina

Charlotte Post
J. S. Nathaniel Tross
219 North McDowell
Charlotte, 28204

Queen City Gazette
Bill Johnson
2224 Beatties Ford Road
Charlotte, 28208

Carolina Times
L. E. Austin
436 East Pettigrew Street
Durham, 27701

The Carolinian
R. P. Jarvey
518 E. Martin
Raleigh, 27601

Wilmington Journal
T. C. Jarvey
412 S. 7th Street
Wilmington, 28401

Ohio

Cincinnati Herald
N. B. Porter
313 Opera Place
Cincinnati, 45202

Cleveland Call and Post
William D. Walker
1949 E. 105th Street
Cleveland, 44106

Dayton Express
Joseph S. Saunders
P.O. Box 911
Dayton, 45401

Oklahoma

Black Dispatch
John Dungee
P.O. Box 1254
Oklahoma City, 73101

Oklahoma Eagle
Edwin Goodwin
123 N. Greenwood Ave.
Tulsa, 74120

Pennsylvania

Philadelphia Independent
Robert Williams
1708 Lombard
Philadelphia, 19146

Philadelphia Tribune
E. Washington Rhodes
526 S. 16th Street
Philadelphia, 19146

The New Pittsburgh Courier
Eleanor Lofton
315 E. Carson
Pittsburgh, 15219

South Carolina

Palmetto Times
E. Cedric Hart
2022 Taylor Street
Columbia, 29204

Tennessee

Chattanooga Observer
W. C. Robinson
124½ 9th Street
Chattanooga, 37403

The Knox County Observer
William J. Robinson
236 New Avenue, S.E.
Knoxville, 37915

Tri-State Defender
Whittier Sengstacke
124 Calhoun Avenue East
Memphis, 38103

Texas

"In Sepia Dallas"
Tony Davis
2700 Grand Avenue
Dallas, 75215

Fort Worth Mind
R. L. Milton
805 Bryan
Fort Worth, 76104

Forward Times
Julius Carter
4411 Almeda Road
Houston, 77004

Houston Informer
Doris Wesley
2418 Leeland Avenue
Houston, 77003

San Antonio Register
W. K. Andrews
207 N. Center Street
San Antonio, 78202

Virginia

Norfolk Journal and Guide
Thomas Young
719 E. Olney Road
Norfolk, 23504

Roanoke Tribune
F. E. Alexander
312 First Street, N.W.
Roanoke, 24016

Wisconsin

Milwaukee Star
Kenneth Coulter
2334 N. Third Street
Milwaukee, 53212

Annotated Bibliography of Articles Published In 1968

THE FOLLOWING source materials are articles written on various topics dealing with Black America in 1968. Each article selected for inclusion was thoroughly researched and is briefly analyzed for its relevance to the scope of this volume.

"As Another Riot Season Nears: Findings of White House Study," *U.S. News and World Report*, LXIV (March 11, 1968).

A summary of the Kerner Commission's final report on civil disorders (summer 1967).

BEARDWOOD, ROGER. "The Southern Roots of Urban Crisis," *Fortune*, LXXVIII (August 1968).

> . . . The malaise of the rural South and the resulting migration are inexorable results of policies and programs devised by the agricultural committees of Congress in which white Southerners have long had the dominant voice. . . . This collision with agricultural economics has been disastrous for all farm workers. But it has been catastrophic for Negroes . . . .

A look at the Northern movement of the Southern Negro: its causes and patterns; the ways in which the Southern Negro farmer is trying to solve his dilemma, i.e., through cooperatives.

"Black Power: A Discussion," *Partisan Review*, XXXV (Spring 1968).

Statements on Black power by Robert Coles, Ivanhoe Donaldson, Paul Feldman, Charles V. Hamilton, Abbie Hoffman, Tom Kahn, William Melvin Kelley, Norman Mailer, Jack Newfield, Fred Powledge, Stephan Thernstrom and Dr. Nathan Wright, Jr.

"The Black Soldier: A Special Issue," *Ebony*, XXIII (August 1968).

> Black GI's . . . in Vietnam are more than twice as likely as whites to reenlist for a second term of military service. The statistics have been used to show racial progress in the armed forces, but critics insist that the high black reenlistment rates reflect the persistence of inequality in American civilian society.

Nineteen articles cover the Black soldier in Vietnam, his lot as an officer, his opinions on the draft and desertion, and other subjects.

BOND, JULIAN. "The Negro and Politics," *Motive*, XXVIII (May 1968).

A brief historical account of Negro participation in (or exclusion from) American politics, concluding with an outline for a new politics and a new equality.

BOOKER, SIMEON. "Black Politics at the Crossroads," *Ebony*, XXIII (October 1968).

> As the spirit of Julian Bond revitalized elements of the party, other blacks seemed to carry the ball in what probably could be called the most constructive, yet disillusioning, convention in modern times.

A study of the 1968 political conventions, with emphasis on the Democratic convention and the emergence of a new breed of Black politician.

CANZONERI, ROBERT. "Charles Evers: Mississippi's Representative Man," *Harper's*, CCXXXVII (July 1968).

An account of Charles Evers' campaign for Congress in March 1968, which gives his philosophy and tactics.

CHAMBERS, ERNEST W. "We Have Marched, We Have Cried, We Have Prayed," *Ebony*, XXIII (April 1968).

The testimony of a thirty-year-old Black militant before President Johnson's Commission on Civil Disorders.

"Civil Disorders Panel Blames 'White Racism' for Riots," *Congressional Quarterly Weekly Report*, XXVI (March 8, 1968).

> Our nation is moving toward two societies, one black, one white—separate and unequal.

A categorical breakdown of the findings of the Kerner Commission; reaction to the commission's findings by members of the Executive branch, members of Congress, labor and civil rights leaders and state and local officials; the complete text of the Summary of the Report of the National Advisory Commission on Civil Disorders.

"The Cycle of Despair: The Negro and the City," *Life*, LXIV (March 8, 1968).

A special section composed of five articles: (1) A photographic essay of life in a New York ghetto, by Gordon Parks; (2) A story on Chicago's West Side, by Gerald Moore; (3) Business experiments in Bedford-Stuyvesant, described by Jack Newfield; (4) An analysis of the Kerner Commission's Report, by Donald Jackson; (5) A plea to all Americans, by John W. Gardner.

DONADIO, STEPHEN. "Black Power at Columbia," *Commentary*, XLVI (September 1968).

A case study of the spring 1968 crisis at Columbia University.

———. "Columbia: Seven Interviews," *Partisan Review*, XXXV (Summer 1968).

Columbia students and professors comment on the spring 1968 crisis (Ray Brown, Bill Sales, Eric Bentley, Peter Gay, Charles Parsons, Mark Rudd, Lewis Cole, Lionel Trilling and Immanuel Wallerstein).

DUBERMAN, MARTIN. "Black Power in America," *Partisan Review*, XXXV (Winter 1968).

An attempt to define Black power by historical analogy with the abolitionists and the anarchists.

"Eldridge Cleaver: An Interview," *Playboy*, XV (December 1968).

> If we don't get justice in the courts, we'll get it in the streets. If atrocities against us continue unpunished, if police aggression is not stopped, more and more blacks may have to fight gunfire with gunfire.

A candid conversation with the revolutionary Black Panther leader.

FRAZIER, THOMAS R. "An Analysis of Nonviolent Coercion as Used by the Sit-In Movement," *Phylon*, XXIX (Spring 1968).

An analysis favoring the tactics of nonviolent coercion employed by Gandhi in India and by members of the civil rights movement in the United States.

FRIEDRICHS, ROBERT W. "Interpretation of Black Aggression," *Yale Review*, LVII (Spring 1968).

> The phenomenon of black power . . . comes to be seen for what it functionally is: not primarily an effective political movement *per se* . . . but rather a necessary stage on the long trek back to psychic and social health.

A criticism of the sociological approach toward Black power, with emphasis on the need for a psychologically-oriented approach.

GARLAND, PHYL. "I've Been to the Mountaintop," *Ebony*, XXIII (May 1968).

A pictorial and textual biography of Martin Luther King, Jr.

GERGEN, DAVID R. "Renewal in the Ghetto: A Study of Residential Rehabilitation in Boston's Washington Park," *Harvard Civil Rights-Civil Liberties Law Review*, III (Spring 1968).

An exploration of "the major social and technical issues in residential rehabilitation through an examination of one of the nation's most widely acclaimed rehabilitation efforts, the Washington Park project in the Roxbury section of Boston."

GIBSON, DONALD B. "The Negro: An Essay on Definition," *Yale Review*, LVII (Spring 1968).

A discussion of the myth of "the Negro" as a monolithic type with a discrete culture.

GILMAN, RICHARD. "Nat Turner Revisited," *New Republic*, CLVIII (April 27, 1968).

A detailed critique of William Styron's *The Confessions of Nat Turner.*

GOODMAN, WALTER. "Ebony: Biggest Negro Magazine," *Dissent*, XV (September–October 1968).

> *Ebony* speaks a language that both Negroes and whites can understand and act upon, and that is no little thing in a troubled territory whose *lingua franca* seems to be deteriorating into yawps of hatred and yowls of apocalypse.

A look at *Ebony*'s editorial stance, audience appeal and role in the Black community.

HUBBARD, HOWARD. "Five Long Hot Summers and How They Grew," *Public Interest* (Summer 1968).

A re-examination of the tactics and of the events which have contributed to the present climate of racial conflict: Birmingham, 1963; Mississippi, 1964; Watts, 1965; Spring, 1966; Summer, 1966; Summer, 1967.

"Jim Brown: An Interview," *Playboy*, XV (February 1968).

An interview with the football legend, now an actor and a civil rights activist.

"King Is the Man, Oh Lord," *Newsweek*, LXXI (April 15, 1968).

A detailed look at the life of Martin Luther King, Jr.

KORNBERG, ALLAN, TEPPER, ELLIOT L., and WATSON, GEORGE L. "The National Elections and Comparative Positions of Negroes and Whites on Policy," *South Atlantic Quarterly*, LXVII (Summer 1968).

A comparison of Negro and white positions on selected domestic and foreign issues. Domestic policy questions to determine attitudes towards the scope and efficacy of governmental activity in the welfare and electric power fields. Foreign policy questions to determine attitudes towards the extension of foreign aid, interactions with communist countries, intervention in Cuba and in Vietnam. Data derived from a national study in 1964.

LASCH, CHRISTOPHER. "The Trouble with Black Power," *New York Review of Books*, X (February 29, 1968).

A discussion of: *Black Power: The Politics of Liberation in America,* by Stokely Carmichael and Charles V. Hamilton; *Black Power and Urban Unrest,* by Nathan Wright, Jr.; *Black Power/White Resistance: Notes on the New Civil War,* by Fred Powledge; *White Reflections on Black Power,* by Charles E. Fager; *The Crisis of the Negro Intellectual,* by Harold Cruse.

A probing analysis of the strategy of Black power —its genesis, inconsistencies and shortcomings. Exciting material; excellent reading.

LEE, ULYSSES. "The Draft and the Negro," *Current History*, LV (July 1968).

> In a more nearly perfect democracy, there would be little reason to discuss Negroes and the draft. . . . But . . . no one can seriously argue in 1968 that Negroes do not constitute a special still "unfinished business" for the American democracy. . . .

An historical discussion of discrimination in the draft from the Civil War to the present.

LLORENS, DAVID. "Black Separatism in Perspective," *Ebony*, XXIII (September 1968).

The failure of integration reflected in the separatist movement.

MCCARTY, L. THORNE, and STEVENSON, RUSSELL B., JR. "The Voting Rights Act of 1965: An Evaluation," *Harvard Civil Rights-Civil Liberties Law Review*, III (Spring 1968).

The tension between change and the control of change, between the movement toward equality and the inevitable reaction, has been the central theme in the recent history of Negro voting rights.

MAGNUSON, WARREN G. "How the Ghetto Gets Gypped," *Ebony*, XXIII (September 1968).

The indignities, terror, violence, despair and helplessness the poor suffer from deception in the marketplace should weigh heavily on the conscience of America. . . . Running through the cacophony of deception is a recurring, disturbing theme: the complicity of the law, either seeming or real, in supporting fraudulent business practices, while oppressing the poor and the innocent.

A discussion of the economic exploitation of the poor, with specific instances cited.

MILLS, NICOLAUS C. "Black Power," *Yale Review*, LVII (Spring 1968).

. . . "black power" is less a single definable plan of action than a series of choices by which Negroes have come to distinguish between color consciousness and color blindness, power blocs and ineffective alliances, equality and pseudo-integration.

A discussion of the effects of Black power and of its future implications.

OLSEN, JACK. "The Black Athlete" [A special five-part series], *Sports Illustrated*, XXIX.

Part 1: "The Cruel Deception" (July 1, 1968).

Certain truths about the Negro college athlete have been carefully concealed in the groves of academe. Some of the truths are painful, some are embarrassing, some show too clearly the heavy hand of White America.

Part 2: "Pride and Prejudice" (July 8, 1968).

The typical Negro athlete discovers an immense gap between himself and the college community.

Part 3: "In an Alien World" (July 15, 1968).

The harsh and perhaps inescapable consequences when status-conscious universities seek fame by importing Negro athletes: a case study of the University of Texas at El Paso.

Part 4: "In the Back of the Bus" (July 22, 1968).

The world of professional sport has offered great opportunity to the Negro in recent years —but it has not offered him equality.

Interviews with ten retired athletes.

Part 5: "The Anguish of a Team Divided" (July 25, 1968).

The St. Louis Cardinals of the NFL provide a disturbing and poignant example of the chaos that can result from racism on professional athletic teams in the United States.

"The Olympic Jolt: 'Hell No, Don't Go!'" *Life*, LXIV (March 15, 1968).

Black athletes and talk of an Olympic boycott. Close-ups on San Jose State College, University of Washington, Niagara University, Berkeley and UCLA.

OSOFSKY, GILBERT. "The Enduring Ghetto," *Journal of American History*, LV (September 1968).

Despite continuing efforts to effect racial reform, little has been accomplished that [has] permanently improved the fundamental conditions of life of most Negroes in New York, nor has any ideology or program radically bettered the tone of race relations in the North.

An historical comparison of New York's Negro community of the mid-1800's with that of the present day.

PEASE, JANE H., and PEASE, WILLIAM H. "Black Power: The Debate in 1840," *Phylon*, XXIX (Spring 1968).

What began as an effort by Negroes to gain basic civil rights through independent conventions [in 1840] became as well an appeal for direct action against the hard core of slavery. Not dissimilar is the contemporary channeling of civil rights action into the greater militancy of black power and open challenge to the established institutions of the 1960's.

PIVEN, FRANCES FOX, and CLOWARD, RICHARD A. "What Chance for Black Power?" *New Republic*, CLVIII (March 30, 1968).

A discussion of the economic and political impotency of the unorganized Black poor.

RASMUSSEN, KARL R. "The Multi-Ordered Urban Area: A Ghetto," *Phylon*, XXIX (Fall 1968).

An attempt to clarify the term "ghetto": its misuse, confusion and implications; the distinction between "ghetto" and "slum."

ROBERTS, WALLACE. "The Battle for Urban Schools," *Saturday Review*, LI (November 16, 1968).

A discussion of the social and political issues involved in the struggle for community control of inner city schools.

"Roots of Riot: Call to Battle," *Newsweek*, LXXI (March 11, 1968).

A discussion of the Report of the Kerner Commission.

ROSHCO, BERNARD. "The Negro Press Views the Riots," *Interplay*, I (February 1968).

Examples from the predominantly conservative Negro newspapers reflect a perspective lacking in the coverage of Black America by the white American press.

SCHRAG, PETER. "Why Our Schools Have Failed," *Commentary*, XLV (March 1968).

An interesting look at integration and the built-in prejudices of the American school system, beginning with criticism of the government's report *Equality of Educational Opportunity*.

SCHWARTZ, ROBERT, PETTIGREW, THOMAS, and SMITH, MARSHALL. "Is Desegregation Impractical?" *New Republic*, CLVIII (January 6, 1968).

Until the United States is willing to undertake some form of substantial income redistribution, "standard" educational attainment remains the Negro's best hope for breaking out of poverty.

A strong case made for school integration.

SCOBLE, HARRY M. "The McCone Commission and Social Science," *Phylon,* XXIX (Summer 1968).

Criticism of the McCone Commission's study of Watts, 1965: its point of view, findings and omissions; emphasis on the commission's failure to employ the techniques of social science.

"The Search for a Black Past" [A special four-part series on Black history], *Life,* LXV.

Part 1: "The Bitter Years of Slavery" (November 22, 1968).

Part 2: "The Hard Reality of Freedom" (November 29, 1968).

Negroes were lost during the years of Reconstruction and repression.

"Shaped by a Dream: A Town Called Boley," by Luther P. Jackson, Jr. The story of Boley, Oklahoma, one of the twenty-six all-Black towns founded in Oklahoma between 1889 and 1910.

Part 3: "Mobilization of Black Strength" (December 6, 1968).

The past half-century in Negro history: wars, Depression, struggle, a renaissance and progress.

Part 4: "A Separate Path to Equality" (December 13, 1968).

The spokesmen shift from moderate to militant—and eloquent voices from the past are heard. Excerpts from interviews with Jesse Jackson, Roy Innis, Albert Cleage, Jr., Dick Gregory, LeRoi Jones, Harry Edwards, Eldridge Cleaver, Thomas Matthew and Julian Bond.

SEGAL, DAVID R., and SCHAFFNER, RICHARD. "Status, Party and Negro Americans," *Phylon,* XXIX (Fall 1968).

The conclusions of a study analyzing political differentiation among Negro Americans. Based on the 1964 elections.

"Seven Days in April," *Newsweek,* LXXI (April 15, 1968).

A look at the disruptions in Washington, D.C., Chicago, Detroit and Toledo after the assassination of Martin Luther King, Jr.

SHASKOLSKY, LEON. "The Negro Protest Movement: Revolt or Reform?" *Phylon,* XXIX (Summer 1968).

An analysis of the relationship between American society as a whole and the socio-economic development of the Negro community. Argues that the course of Negro action might paradoxically depend upon the responsiveness of the "white power structure."

STROUT, CUSHING. *"Uncle Tom's Cabin* and the Portent of Millennium," *Yale Review,* LVII (Spring 1968).

A reply to James Baldwin's criticism of *Uncle Tom's Cabin.*

STURDIVANT, FREDERICK D. "Better Deal for Ghetto Shoppers," *Harvard Business Review,* XLVI (March–April 1968).

> *The most direct contact between the poor and the business community is at the retail level.* The greatest opportunity to assist and to revolutionize the daily lives of the poor rests in the retailing communities serving poverty areas.

A study of retailer-consumer relationships in a ghetto (Watts) and a proposal for a workable solution.

WHEELER, HARVEY. "A Moral Equivalent for Riots," *Saturday Review,* LI (May 11, 1968).

> What the Negro—and the society in general—needs is the moral equivalent of riots: officially provided self-strengthening institutions.

An international study of violence: theories, conclusions and alternatives.

WILDAVSKY, AARON. "The Empty-Head Blues: Black Rebellion and White Reaction," *Public Interest* (Spring 1968).

A discussion of various social theories and their application to the racial problem in America.

Bibliography of Non-fiction Books by or about Negroes Published in 1968

THE YEAR of the Black American, 1968, witnessed a tremendous surge of non-fiction works on Black topics. The days of fiction as the vehicle for acting out racial hostilities, for envisioning a better America in fantasy and for relaying the message of Black America to white America, have passed. In 1968 more books by Negroes who "told it like it was" were published than in any previous year. There were also a number of attempts by both Black and white writers to analyze and present the current state of race relations. For the most part, however, 1968 was the year chronicling a voice crying from the wilderness, the answer to which historians of the future will evaluate from the literature cited below.

Biography

**Also suitable for juvenile readers*

Bailey, Pearl. *The Raw Pearl.* New York.

*Borland, Kathryn K., and Speicher, Helen R. *Phillis Wheatley: Young Colonial Poet.* Indianapolis.

*Douty, Esther M. *Forten the Sailmaker: Pioneer Champion of Negro Rights.* Chicago.

*Epstein, Sam, and Epstein, Beryl. *Harriet Tubman: Guide to Freedom.* Champaign, Ill.

Forman, James. *Sammy Younge, Jr.: The First Black College Student To Die in the Black Liberation Movement.* New York.

*Lawrence, Jacob (illus.). *Harriet and the Promised Land.* New York.

*Meltzer, Milton. *Langston Hughes: A Biography.* New York.

*Metcalf, George R. *Black Profiles.* New York.

*Montgomery, Elizabeth R. *William C. Handy: Father of the Blues.* Champaign, Ill.

Moody, Anne. *Coming of Age in Mississippi: An Autobiography.* New York.

Parks, David. *GI Diary.* New York.

Parks, Gordon. *A Poet and His Camera.* New York.

*Peterson, John (ed.). *Portfolio of Pictures of Famous Negroes in American Life.* New York.

*Sterne, Emma Gelders. *They Took Their Stand.* New York.

Webb, Constance. *Richard Wright: A Biography.* New York.

*Young, Margaret B. *The Picture Life of Ralph J. Bunche.* New York.

Black Athletes

*Aaron, Henry (with Bisher, Furman). *Aaron, r.f.* Cleveland.

*Cepeda, Orlando (with Einstein, Charles). *My Ups and Downs in Baseball.* New York.

*Gibson, Bob (with Pepe, Phil). *From Ghetto to Glory.* Englewood Cliffs, N.J.

Henderson, Edwin B., and Sport Magazine. *The Black Athlete: Emergence and Arrival.* Washington.

Olsen, Jack. *The Black Athlete, a Shameful Story: The Myth of Integration in American Sport.* New York.

Robinson, Frank (with Silverman, Al). *My Life Is Baseball.* Garden City, N.Y.

Black Literature

Adoff, Arnold (ed.). *Black on Black: Commentaries by Negro Americans.* New York.

Baldwin, James. *The Amen Corner.* New York.

———. *Tell Me How Long the Train's Been Gone.* New York.

Bennett, Hal. *The Black Wine.* Garden City, N.Y.

Boles, Robert. *Curling.* Boston.

*Bristow, Robert O'Neil. *Time for Glory.* New York.

Brooks, Gwendolyn. *In the Mecca.* New York.

*Burchard, Peter. *Bimby.* New York.

*Chapman, Abraham (ed.). *Black Voices: An Anthology of Afro-American Literature.* New York.

Clarke, John Henrik (ed.). *William Styron's Nat Turner: Ten Black Writers Respond.* Boston.

Couch, William, Jr. (ed.). *New Black Playwrights: An Anthology.* Baton Rouge.

Drake, St. Clair. *Negro History and Literature: A Selected Annotated Bibliography.* New York.

Emanuel, James A., and Gross, Theodore L. (eds.). *Dark Symphony: Negro Literature in America.* New York.

Gaines, Ernest J. *Bloodline.* New York.

Heard, Nathan C. *Howard Street.* New York.

Heckert, Eleanor. *Muscavado.* Garden City, N.Y.

Heifetz, Harold. *Jeremiah Thunder.* Garden City, N.Y.

*Hunter, Kristin. *The Soul Brothers and Sister Lou.* New York.

*Jackson, Jesse. *Tessie.* New York.

Jones, LeRoi, and Neal, Larry. *Black Fire: An Anthology of Afro-American Writing.* New York.

LEE, AUDREY. *The Clarion People*. New York.
*MCWHIRTER, MARY ESTHER (ed.). *Books for Friendship: A List of Books Recommended for Children*. New York.
*MADIAN, JON. *Beautiful Junk: A Story of the Watts Towers*. Boston.
MARGOLIES, EDWARD. *Native Sons: A Critical Study of Twentieth-Century Negro American Authors*. Philadelphia.
PATTERSON, LINDSAY (ed.). *An Introduction to Black Literature in America: From 1746 to the Present*. Washington.
*STERNE, EMMA GELDERS. *The Long Black Schooner*. Chicago.
WALKER, ALICE. *Once*. New York.
WEATHERBY, WILLIAM J. *One of Our Priests Is Missing*. Garden City, N.Y.
*WEINER, SANDRA. *It's Wings That Make Birds Fly: The Story of a Boy*. New York.

Black Music and Dance

CARAWAN, GUY, and CARAWAN, CANDIE (eds.). *Freedom Is a Constant Struggle: Songs of the Freedom Movement*. New York.
JACKSON, CLYDE OWEN. *The Songs of Our Years: A Study of Negro Folk Music*. New York.
JONES, LEROI. *Black Music*. New York.
SCHOENER, ALLON (ed.). *Harlem on My Mind: Cultural Capital of Black America, 1900–1968*. New York.
SCHULLER, GUNTHER. *Early Jazz: Its Root and Musical Development*. New York.
STEARNS, MARSHALL, and STEARNS, JEAN. *Jazz Dance: The Story of American Vernacular Dance*. New York.

Black Power

BARBOUR, FLOYD B. (ed.). *The Black Power Revolt*. Boston.
BELL, INGE P. *CORE and the Strategy of Nonviolence*. New York.
*BENNETT, LERONE, JR. *Pioneers in Protest*. Chicago.
CLEAGE, ALBERT B., JR. *The Black Messiah*. New York.
CLEAVER, ELDRIDGE. *Soul on Ice*. New York.
CRUSE, HAROLD. *Rebellion or Revolution?* New York.
*DOUGLASS, FREDERICK. *The Mind and Heart of Frederick Douglass: Excerpts from Speeches of the Great Negro Orator*, ed. BARBARA RITCHIE. New York.
DU BOIS, W. E. B. *The Autobiography of W. E. B. Du Bois*. New York.
EPPS, ARCHIE (ed.). *The Speeches of Malcolm X at Harvard*. New York.
GREGORY, DICK. *The Shadow That Scares Me*, ed. JAMES R. MCGRAW. Garden City, N.Y.
———. *Write Me In!* New York.
*HARRISON, DELORIS (ed.). *We Shall Live in Peace: The Teachings of Martin Luther King, Jr*. New York.
KILLIAN, LEWIS M. *The Impossible Revolution? Black Power and the American Dream*. New York.
KING, MARTIN LUTHER, JR. *The Trumpet of Conscience*. New York.
LESTER, JULIUS. *Look Out, Whitey! Black Power's Gon' Get Your Mama!* New York.
LIGHTFOOT, CLAUDE M. *Ghetto Rebellion to Black Liberation*. New York.
LOKOS, LIONEL. *House Divided: The Life and Legacy of Martin Luther King*. New York.
LOMAX, LOUIS E. *To Kill a Black Man*. Los Angeles.
MEMMI, ALBERT. *Dominated Man: Notes towards a Portrait*. New York.
MILLER, WILLIAM ROBERT. *Martin Luther King, Jr.: His Life, Martyrdom and Meaning for the World*. New York.
MUSE, BENJAMIN. *The American Negro Revolution: From Nonviolence to Black Power, 1963–1967*. Bloomington, Ind.
NELSON, TRUMAN. *The Right of Revolution*. Boston.
*PRESTON, EDWARD. *Martin Luther King: Fighter for Freedom*. Garden City, N.Y.
STONE, CHUCK. *Black Political Power in America*. Indianapolis.
———. *Tell It like It Is*. New York.

Civil Rights

BLACK, ALGERNON D. *The People and the Police*. New York.
BLAUSTEIN, ALBERT P., and ZANGRANDO, ROBERT L. (eds.). *Civil Rights and the American Negro: A Documentary History*. New York.
CRAIN, ROBERT L. *The Politics of School Desegregation*. Chicago.
DAMERELL, REGINALD G. *Triumph in a White Suburb*. New York.
DORSEN, NORMAN. *Frontiers of Civil Liberties*. New York.
HERSEY, JOHN. *The Algiers Motel Incident*. New York.
MACK, RAYMOND W. (ed.). *Our Children's Burden: Studies of Desegregation in Nine American Communities*. New York.
MAYHEW, LEON H. *Law and Equal Opportunity: A Study of the Massachusetts Commission against Discrimination*. Cambridge, Mass.
STRONG, DONALD S. *Negroes, Ballots and Judges: National Voting Rights Legislation in the Federal Courts*. Tuscaloosa, Ala.
U.S. COMMISSION ON CIVIL RIGHTS. *Political Participation*. Washington.
WEINBERG, MEYER. *Desegregation Research: An Appraisal*. Bloomington, Ind.
——— (ed.). *Integrated Education: A Reader*. Beverly Hills, Calif.

Culture and Art of Africa

BODROGI, TIBOR. *Art in Africa*. New York.
FAGG, WILLIAM. *African Tribal Images*. Cleveland.
LEIRIS, MICHEL, and DELANGE, JACQUELINE. *African Art*. London.
MOORE, CLARK D., and DUNBAR, ANN (eds.). *Africa Yesterday and Today*. New York.
WASSING, RENÉ S. *African Art: Its Background and Traditions*. New York.

Economic and Urban Issues

Aukofer, Frank A. *City with a Chance.* Milwaukee.

Barnwell, William H. *In Richard's World: The Battle of Charleston, 1966.* Boston.

Bradford, Amory. *Oakland's Not for Burning.* New York.

Citizens Board of Inquiry into Hunger and Malnutrition in the United States. *Hunger, U.S.A.* Boston.

Eley, Lynn W., and Casstevens, Thomas W. (eds.). *The Politics of Fair Housing Legislation: State and Local Case Studies.* San Francisco.

Endleman, Shalom (ed.). *Violence in the Streets.* Chicago.

Ferman, Louis A. *The Negro and Equal Employment Opportunities: A Review of Management Experiences in Twenty Companies.* New York.

———, Kornbluh, Joyce L., and Miller, J. S. (eds.). *Negroes and Jobs: A Book of Readings.* Ann Arbor.

Foley, Eugene P. *The Achieving Ghetto.* Washington.

Fortune Magazine. *The Negro and the City.* New York.

Gilbert, Ben W., and the Staff of the Washington Post. *Ten Blocks from the White House: Anatomy of the Washington Riots of 1968.* Washington.

Ginzberg, Eli (ed.). *Business Leadership and the Negro Crisis.* New York.

Good, Paul. *The American Serfs.* New York.

Jones, Thomas B. *How the Negro Can Start His Own Business.* New York.

Lincoln, James H. *The Anatomy of a Riot: A Detroit Judge's Report.* New York.

Masotti, Louis H., and Bowen, Don R. (eds.). *Riots and Rebellion: Civil Violence in the Urban Community.* Beverly Hills, Calif.

Millea, Thomas V. *Ghetto Fever.* Milwaukee.

Randall, Dudley. *Cities Burning.* Detroit.

Riessman, Frank, and Popper, Hermine I. (eds.). *Up from Poverty: New Career Ladders for Non-Professionals.* New York.

Sauter, Van Gorden, and Hines, Burleigh. *Nightmare in Detroit: A Rebellion and Its Victims.* Chicago.

Schuchter, Arnold. *White Power/Black Freedom: Planning the Future of Urban America.* Boston.

Tucker, Sterling. *Beyond the Burning: Life and Death of the Ghetto.* New York.

U.S. National Advisory Commission on Civil Disorders. *Report of the National Advisory Commission on Civil Disorders.* Washington.

U.S. National Advisory Council on Economic Opportunity. *Focus on Community Action.* Washington.

U.S. National Commission on Urban Problems. *Hearings before the National Commission on Urban Problems.* Vol. II. Washington.

Vadakin, James C. *Children, Poverty and Family Allowances.* New York.

Waxman, Chaim I. (ed.). *Poverty: Power and Politics.* New York.

Weinberg, Kenneth G. *Black Victory: Carl Stokes and the Winning of Cleveland.* Chicago.

Wright, Nathan, Jr., *Ready to Riot.* New York.

Education

Dawson, Helaine S. *On the Outskirts of Hope: Educating Youth from Poverty Areas.* New York.

Fantini, Mario D., and Weinstein, Gerald. *The Disadvantaged: Challenge to Education.* New York.

Herndon, James. *The Way It Spozed To Be: A Report on the Classroom War behind the Crisis in Our Schools.* New York.

Jaffe, A. J., Adams, Walter, and Meyers, Sandra G. *Negro Higher Education in the 1960's.* New York.

Rosenthal, Robert, and Jacobson, Lenore. *Pygmalion in the Classroom: Teacher Expectation and Pupils' Intellectual Development.* New York.

Trubowitz, Sidney. *A Handbook for Teaching in the Ghetto School.* Chicago.

History

*Chambers, Bradford. *Chronicles of Negro Protest: A Background Book for Young People.* New York.

Drimmer, Melvin (ed.). *Black History: A Reappraisal.* Garden City, N.Y.

Drotning, Philip T. *A Guide to Negro History in America.* Garden City, N.Y.

Dulles, Foster Rhea. *Civil Rights Commission: 1957–1965.* East Lansing, Mich.

Goldston, Robert. *The Negro Revolution.* New York.

Grant, Joanne (ed.). *Black Protest: History, Documents and Analyses, 1619 to the Present.* New York.

Harris, Middleton A. (Uncle Spike). *A Negro History Tour of Manhattan.* New York.

Hoover, Dwight W. (ed.). *Understanding Negro History.* Chicago.

Ingraham, Leonard W. *Slavery in the United States.* New York.

Jacobson, Julius (ed.). *The Negro and the American Labor Movement.* Garden City, N.Y.

Jordan, Winthrop D. *White over Black: American Attitudes toward the Negro, 1550–1812.* Chapel Hill, N.C.

Katz, William Loren. *Teachers' Guide to American Negro History.* Chicago.

Kay, F. George. *The Shameful Trade.* New York.

Kellogg, Charles F. *NAACP: A History of the National Association for the Advancement of Colored People.* Vol. I, 1909–1920. Baltimore.

*Lester, Julius. *To Be a Slave.* New York.

Lutz, Alma. *Crusade for Freedom: Women of the Anti-Slavery Movement.* Boston.

McCague, James. *The Second Rebellion: The Story of the New York City Draft Riots of 1863.* New York.

*Patrick, John J. *The Progress of the Afro-American.* Westchester, Ill.

Phillips, Ulrich B. *Slave Economy of the Old South: Selected Essays in Economic and Social History.* Baton Rouge.

Pope-Hennessy, James. *Sins of the Fathers: A Study of the Atlantic Slave Traders.* New York.

Ratner, Lorman. *Powder Keg: Northern Opposition to the Antislavery Movement, 1831-1840.* New York.

ROMERO, PATRICIA W. (ed.). *I Too Am America: Documents from 1619 to the Present*. Washington.

STERLING, DOROTHY. *Tear Down the Walls! A History of the American Civil Rights Movement*. Garden City, N.Y.

WEINSTEIN, ALLEN, and GATELL, FRANK O. (eds.). *American Negro Slavery: A Modern Reader*. New York.

WESLEY, CHARLES H. *In Freedom's Footsteps: From the African Background to the Civil War*. Washington.

———. *The Quest for Equality: From Civil War to Civil Rights*. Washington.

WOOD, FORREST G. *Black Scare: The Racist Response to Emancipation and Reconstruction*. Berkeley, Calif.

Military

McCONNELL, ROLAND C. *Negro Troops of Antebellum Louisiana*. Baton Rouge.

McPHERSON, JAMES M. *Marching toward Freedom: The Negro in the Civil War, 1861–1865*. New York.

*PLACE, MARIAN T. *Rifles and War Bonnets: Negro Cavalry of the West*. New York.

STILLMAN, RICHARD J., II. *Integration of the Negro in the U.S. Armed Forces*. New York.

Race and Race Relations

BAUGHMAN, EMMETT EARL, and DAHLSTROM, GRANT W. *Negro and White Children: A Psychological Study in the Rural South*. New York.

BILLINGSLEY, ANDREW. *Black Families in White America*. Englewood Cliffs, N.J.

*BOYD, MALCOLM, ROBERTS, BRUCE, and SEVAREID, ERIC. *You Can't Kill the Dream*. Richmond, Va.

COHEN, HENRY. *Justice, Justice: A Jewish View of the Negro Revolt*. New York.

COHEN, ROBERT, and HEYMAN, KEN. *The Color of Man*. New York.

DAVID, JAY (ed.). *Growing Up Black*. New York.

DUNBAR, ERNEST. *The Black Expatriates*. New York.

FRANKLIN, JOHN HOPE (ed.). *Color and Race*. Boston.

FRAZIER, EDWARD FRANKLIN. *On Race Relations: Selected Writings*, ed. GILBERT FRANKLIN EDWARDS. Chicago.

FREED, LEONARD. *Black in White America*. New York.

GRIER, WILLIAM H., and COBBS, PRICE M. *Black Rage*. New York.

HESSLINK, GEORGE K. *Black Neighbors: Negroes in a Northern Rural Community*. Indianapolis.

HOUGH, JOSEPH C., JR. *Black Power and White Protestants*. New York.

LEVY, CHARLES. *Voluntary Servitude: Whites in the Civil Rights Movement*. New York.

LINCOLN, C. ERIC (ed.). *Is Anybody Listening to Black America?* New York.

LYLE, JACK (ed.). *The Black American and the Press*. Los Angeles.

MEAD, MARGARET, DOBZHANSKY, THEODOSIUS, TOBACH, ETHEL, and LIGHT, ROBERT. *Science and the Concept of Race*. New York.

NEWBY, I. A. *Development of Segregationist Thought*. Homewood, Ill.

NEWMAN, JEREMIAH. *Race: Migration and Integration*. Baltimore.

OTIS, JOHNNY. *Listen to the Lambs*. New York.

WILLS, GARRY. *The Second Civil War: Arming for Armageddon*. New York.

WRIGHT, NATHAN, JR. *Let's Work Together*. New York.

SECTION III

Statistics

THIS SECTION contains brief statistical information in the areas of politics, education, labor, poverty, population, business and sports. The use of statistics for research purposes has been kept to a minimum in most of the interpretive articles in this book; therefore this section is intended to supplement the analysis in the first section, as well as to record achievements and/or inequities. Since the most up-to-date figures are not always available in all the areas mentioned above, those materials included here (with the exception of the sports information) have been chosen to illustrate trends. For further statistical information in these areas, students and interested readers may contact the sources cited below in each category. In the sports section, the coverage is completely up-to-date.

TABLE 1

Per Cent Distribution of Negro Population by Region,* 1960 and 1968

	1960	1968
United States	100	100
South	60	53
North	34	40
Northeast	16	18
North Central	18	22
West	6	8

* The standard census definition for each region is used. In that definition the South includes the states of the old Confederacy, as well as Delaware, the District of Columbia, Kentucky, Maryland, Oklahoma and West Virginia.

(**Credit:** Bureau of Labor Statistics, Bureau of the Census)

TABLE 2

Per Cent of Nonwhite Families Living in Poverty Areas of Large Cities with Incomes below the Poverty Level,* 1960, 1966 and 1968

	1960	1966	1968**
All large cities***	38	36	30
Central cities in metropolitan areas of—			
1,000,000 or more	34	34	30
250,000 to 1,000,000	45	40	30
New York City	28	35	31
Chicago	33	37	35
Los Angeles	32	29	33

* The poverty level relates to the previous year. The poverty definition (as developed by the Social Security Administration) is based on the minimum food and other needs of families, taking account of family size, number of children and farm-nonfarm residence. As applied to 1967 incomes, the poverty threshold for a nonfarm family of four was $3,335.

** Based on revised methodology.

*** In metropolitan areas of 250,000 or more in 1960.

(**Credit:** U.S. Department of Commerce, Bureau of the Census)

TABLE 3

Numbers and Per Cent of Nonwhite Families in Poverty Areas* of Large Cities, 1960, 1966 and 1968

(Numbers in Thousands)

	Nonwhite families			Families in poverty areas* as a per cent of nonwhite families		
	1960	1966	1968	1960	1966	1968
All large cities **	2,024	2,558	2,543	77	62	56
Central cities in metropolitan areas of—						
1,000,000 or more	1,392	1,770	1,816	76	59	53
250,000 to 1,000,000	633	788	728	79	69	63
New York City	260	388	406	77	62	59
Chicago	187	239	247	80	54	48
Los Angeles	100	128	150	61	47	40

* Poverty areas were determined by ranking census tracts in metropolitan areas of 250,000 or more in 1960, according to the relative presence of each of the following equally weighted poverty-linked characteristics: (1) family income below $3,000, (2) children in broken homes, (3) persons with low educational attainment, (4) males in unskilled jobs, (5) substandard housing. It includes an adjustment for changes brought about since 1960 by urban renewal. In general, the lowest 25 per cent of census tracts are included.

** In metropolitan areas of 250,000 or more in 1960.

(**Credit:** U.S. Department of Commerce, Bureau of the Census)

TABLE 4

Number and Per Cent of Persons below the Poverty Level and of Persons Receiving Welfare, 1967 and 1968

(Numbers in Millions)

	Nonwhite		White	
	1967	1968	1967	1968
Total population	23.2	23.7	170.2	172.0
Below poverty level*	9.3	8.3	19.5	17.6
Per cent of total population	40	35	12	10
Receiving welfare	3.2	3.4	4.5	5.0
Per cent of total population	14	14	3	3

* Based on revised methodology. The poverty level refers to the previous year.

(**Credit:** U.S. Department of Commerce, Bureau of the Census, and U.S. Department of Health, Education and Welfare)

TABLE 5

The Geographic Distribution of Hunger in the United States
(Similar data for subdivisions in Hawaii and Alaska was not available)

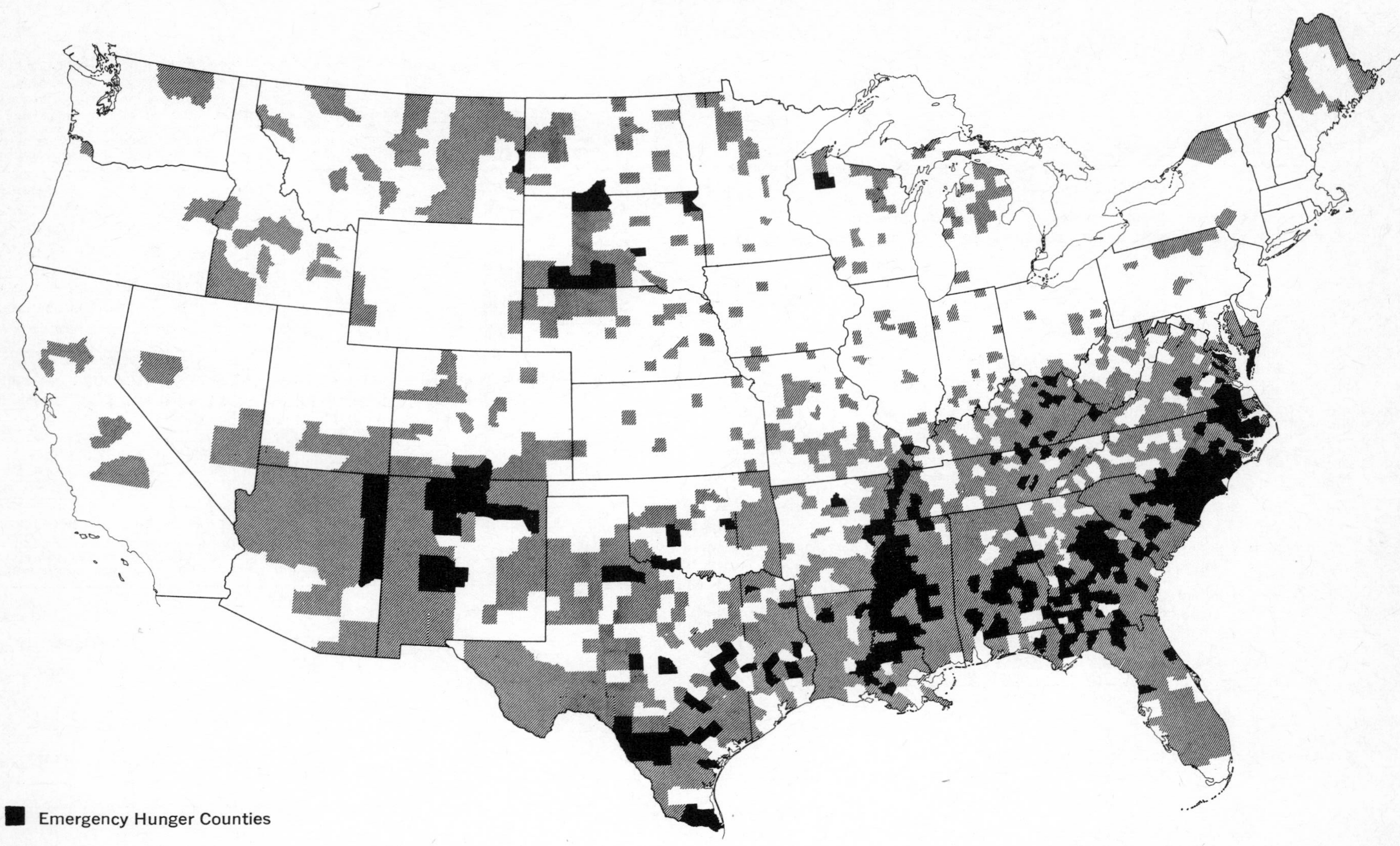

(**Credit:** New Community Press, Washington, D.C., Copyright © 1968)

TABLE 6

Growth of Segregation in 40 School Systems in Southern, Border and Northern States, in Elementary Schools

State and city	Total elementary students	Total white students in elementary schools		Total Negro students in elementary schools		Negro students in schools 90 to 100 per cent Negro		Increase or decrease in Negro students in schools 90 to 100 per cent Negro; earliest year to latest year		Negro students in majority Negro schools		White students in schools 90 to 100 per cent white		Increase or decrease in white students in schools 90 to 100 per cent white; earliest year to latest year	
		Number	Per cent of total elementary students	Number	Per cent of total elementary students	Number	Per cent of total Negro elementary students	Number	Per cent increase or decrease	Number	Per cent of total Negro elementary students	Number	Per cent of total white elementary students	Number	Per cent increase or decrease
Southern															
Florida—Miami:															
1965–66 ..	11,300	81,410	73.1	29,890	26.8	27,321	91.4	19,423	245.9	28,213	94.4	77,572	95.3	39,823	105.5
1960–61 ..	93,440	72,348	77.4	21,092	22.6	21,066	99.9	....	....	21,066	99.9	72,348	100.0	....	......
1950–51 ..	45,647	37,749	82.7	7,898	17.3	7,898	100.0	....	....	7,898	100.0	37,749	100.0	....	......
North Carolina—Charlotte:															
1965–66 ..	43,300	30,205	69.8	13,095	30.2	12,533	95.7	5,346	74.4	12,533	95.7	28,622	94.7	10,411	57.2
1960–61 ..	40,218	27,814	69.2	12,404	30.3	12,403	99.9	....	....	12,403	99.9	27,814	100.0	....	......
1955–56 ..	32,076	22,408	69.9	9,668	30.1	9,668	100.0	....	....	9,668	100.0	22,408	100.0	....	......
1950–51 ..	25,398	18,211	71.7	7,187	28.3	7,187	100.0	....	....	7,187	100.0	18,211	100.0	....	......
Oklahoma—Oklahoma City:															
1965–66 ..	44,924	35,389	78.8	9,535	21.2	8,628	90.5	6,175	251.7	9,231	96.8	34,010	96.1	10,308	43.5
1950–51 ..	26,155	23,702	90.6	2,453	9.4	2,453	100.0	....	....	2,453	100.0	23,702	100.0	....	......
Texas—Dallas:															
1965–66 ..	95,935	69,504	72.4	26,431	27.5	21,840	82.6	12,558	135.3	23,883	90.3	62,633	90.1	21,818	53.5
1960–61 ..	89,528	69,787	77.9	19,741	22.1	19,741	100.0	....	....	19,741	100.0	69,787	100.0	....	......
1955–56 ..	74,951	60,633	80.9	14,318	19.1	14,318	100.0	....	....	14,318	100.0	60,633	100.0	....	......
1950–51 ..	50.097	40,815	81.5	9,282	18.5	9,282	100.0	....	....	9,282	100.0	40,815	100.0	....	......
Virginia—Richmond:															
1965–66 ..	28,622	10,108	35.3	18,514	64.7	18,228	98.5	1,541	9.2	18,288	98.5	9,637	95.3	–1,435	–13.0
1960–61 ..	27,759	11,072	39.9	16,687	60.1	16,687	100.0	....	....	16,687	100.0	11,072	100.0	....	......
Border															
Delaware—Wilmington:															
1965–66 ..	7,847	2,412	30.7	5,435	69.3	2,704	49.7	1,004	59.1	5,034	92.5	659	27.3	–3,600	–84.5
1960–61 ..	6,959	3,114	44.7	3,845	55.2	1,487	38.6	....	....	3,449	89.7	1,545	49.6	....	......
1957–58 ..	6,866	3,993	58.2	2,873	41.8	1,563	54.4	....	....	1,766	61.5	1,581	39.6	....	......
1950–51 ..	5,959	4,259	71.5	1,700	28.5	1,700	100.0	....	....	1,700	100.0	4,259	100.0	....	......
District of Columbia—Washington:															
1965–66 ..	91,994	8,308	9.0	83,686	90.9	75,688	90.4	44,817	145.2	83,142	99.3	2,853	34.3	–25,674	–90.0
1960–61 ..	80,279	13,498	16.8	66,781	83.2	55,806	83.6	....	....	66,001	98.8	6,902	51.2	....	......
1955–56 ..	67,384	22,415	33.3	44,969	66.7	33,055	73.5	....	....	42,972	95.6	14,804	66.0	....	......
1950–51 ..	59,398	28,527	48.0	30,871	52.0	30,871	100.0	....	....	30,871	100.0	28,527	100.0	....	......

TABLE 6—(Continued)

State and city	Total elementary students	Total white students in elementary schools		Total Negro students in elementary schools		Negro students in schools 90 to 100 per cent Negro		Increase or decrease in Negro students in schools 90 to 100 per cent Negro; earliest year to latest year		Negro students in majority Negro schools		White students in schools 90 to 100 per cent white		Increase or decrease in white students in schools 90 to 100 per cent white; earliest year to latest year	
		Number	Per cent of total elementary students	Number	Per cent of total elementary students	Number	Per cent of total Negro elementary students	Number	Per cent increase or decrease	Number	Per cent of total Negro elementary students	Number	Per cent of total white elementary students	Number	Per cent increase or decrease
Border (Cont.)															
Kansas—															
Wichita:															
1965–66 ..	41,938	36,381	86.7	5,557	13.3	3,531	63.5	575	19.5	4,955	89.1	34,509	94.8	6,218	22.0
1960–61 ..	33,903	29,900	88.2	4,003	11.8	2,956	73.8	....	....	3,593	89.8	28,291	94.6	....	......
Maryland—															
Baltimore:															
1965–66 ..	118,759	42,382	35.7	76,377	64.3	64,308	84.2	25,996	67.9	70,540	92.4	28,395	67.0	–24,123	–45.9
1960–61 ..	105,989	45,684	43.1	60,305	56.9	50,673	84.0	....	....	56,416	93.6	34,025	74.5	....	......
1955–56 ..	97,418	54,358	55.8	43,060	44.2	39,418	91.5	....	....	41,060	95.4	45,903	84.4	....	......
1954–55 ..	94,627	54,914	58.0	39,713	42.0	38,312	96.5	....	....	38,672	97.4	52,518	95.6	....	......
Missouri—															
Kansas City:															
1965–66 ..	47,991	27,647	57.6	20,344	42.4	14,068	69.1	7,670	119.9	17,426	85.7	18,027	65.2	–12,360	–40.7
1960–61 ..	45,877	31,775	69.2	14,102	30.7	9,453	67.0	....	....	12,271	87.0	25,831	81.3	....	......
1955–56 ..	42,401	33,525	79.1	8,876	20.9	6,500	73.2	....	....	7,666	86.3	29,414	87.7	....	......
1950–51 ..	36,785	30,387	82.6	6,398	17.4	6,398	100.0	....	....	6,398	100.0	30,387	100.0	....	......
Northern															
California—															
Oakland:															
1965–66 ..	35,639	15,033	42.2	18,570	52.1	9,043	48.7	9,043	....	15,455	83.2	7,547	50.2	–13,466	–64.1
1959–60* ..	37,214	21,548	57.9	14,453	38.8	1,110	7.7	....	....	10,274	71.1	12,190	56.5	....	......
1949–50* ..	30,466	25,628	84.1	4,305	14.1	......	.....	....	....	2,632	61.1	21,013	82.0	....	......
Pasadena:															
1965–66 ..	17,680	11,286	63.8	4,538	25.7	......	.....	....	....	3,240	71.4	9,270	82.1	–314	–3.3
1963–64 ..	17,114	11,682	68.3	3,746	21.9	......	.....	....	....	2,785	74.3	9,966	85.3	....	......
1961–62 ..	16,543	12,047	72.8	3,001	18.1	......	.....	....	....	1,816	60.5	10,937	90.7	....	......
1955–56 ..	13,793	11,536	83.6	1,374	10.0	......	.....	....	....	706	51.4	10,457	90.6	....	......
1950–51 ..	11,687	10,317	88.3	747	6.4	......	.....	....	....	196	26.2	9,584	93.0	....	......
Sacramento:															
1965–66 ..	28,743	19,387	67.4	3,869	13.5	......	.....	–295	–100.0	1,689	43.6	15,920	82.1	181	1.2
1963–64 ..	27,424	19,131	69.8	3,218	11.7	295	9.2	....	....	1,459	45.4	15,739	82.3	....	......
San Francisco:															
1965–66 ..	49,813	21,331	42.8	14,337	28.8	3,031	21.1	1,452	92.0	10,369	72.3	13,879	65.1	–9,093	–39.6
1962–63 ..	52,959	31,782	60.0	13,639	25.8	1,579	11.6	....	....	10,334	75.8	22,972	72.2	....	......
Connecticut—															
New Haven:															
1965–66 ..	12,951	6,470	49.9	5,903	45.6	2,171	36.8	975	81.5	4,329	73.4	3,048	47.1	–367	–10.7
1964–65 ..	12,851	6,786	52.8	5,515	42.9	2,023	36.7	....	....	3,812	69.1	2,624	38.7	....	......
1963–64 ..	13,429	7,643	56.9	5,305	39.5	1,196	22.5	....	....	3,769	71.0	3,415	44.7	....	......

TABLE 6—(Continued)

State and city	Total elementary students	Total white students in elementary schools: Number	Total white students in elementary schools: Per cent of total elementary students	Total Negro students in elementary schools: Number	Total Negro students in elementary schools: Per cent of total elementary students	Negro students in schools 90 to 100 per cent Negro: Number	Negro students in schools 90 to 100 per cent Negro: Per cent of total Negro elementary students	Increase or decrease in Negro students in schools 90 to 100 per cent Negro; earliest year to latest year: Number	Increase or decrease in Negro students in schools 90 to 100 per cent Negro; earliest year to latest year: Per cent increase or decrease	Negro students in majority Negro schools: Number	Negro students in majority Negro schools: Per cent of total Negro elementary students	White students in schools 90 to 100 per cent white: Number	White students in schools 90 to 100 per cent white: Per cent of total white elementary students	Increase or decrease in white students in schools 90 to 100 per cent white; earliest year to latest year: Number	Increase or decrease in white students in schools 90 to 100 per cent white; earliest year to latest year: Per cent increase or decrease
Northern (Cont.)															
Illinois—															
East St. Louis:															
1965–66	14,657	5,366	36.6	9,291	63.4	7,467	80.4	2,941	65.0	8,585	92.4	3,678	68.6	–673	–15.5
1962–63	13,242	6,026	45.5	7,216	54.5	6,434	89.2	...	...	6,899	95.6	5,184	86.0	...	...
1954–55	9,714	4,864	50.1	4,850	49.9	4,526	93.3	...	...	4,526	93.3	4,351	89.4	...	...
Peoria:															
1965–66	17,092	14,256	83.4	2,824	16.5	592	21.0	592	...	2,454	86.9	12,779	89.6	4,604	56.4
1950–51	10,163	9,340	91.9	821	8.1	...	...	...	...	308	37.5	8,173	87.5	...	...
Indiana—															
Fort Wayne:															
1965–66	22,963	19,597	85.3	3,250	14.2	1,977	60.8	1,977	...	2,694	82.9	17,183	87.7	1,138	7.1
1960–61	20,636	18,107	87.7	2,474	12.0	...	...	...	...	1,783	72.1	16,045	88.6	...	...
Indianapolis:															
1965–66	71,102	49,236	69.2	21,866	30.8	15,426	70.5	7,789	102.0	18,423	84.2	39,715	80.7	6,537	19.7
1960–61	59,547	42,699	71.7	16,848	28.3	11,945	70.9	...	...	13,356	79.2	34,461	80.7	...	...
1951–52	45,362	36,181	79.8	9,181	20.2	7,637	83.2	...	...	8,101	88.2	33,178	91.6	...	...
South Bend:															
1965–66	20,852	16,787	80.5	4,065	19.5	1,064	26.2	529	98.9	2,077	51.1	12,773	76.0	961	8.1
1963–64	21,032	17,206	81.8	3,826	18.2	588	15.4	...	...	2,627	68.7	14,090	81.9	...	...
1960–61	17,740	14,664	82.7	3,076	17.3	535	17.4	...	...	1,859	60.4	11,812	80.6	...	...
Massachusetts—															
Springfield:															
1965–66	19,061	14,830	77.8	3,689	19.4	567	15.4	567	...	2,651	71.9	12,272	82.8	–489	–3.8
1963–64	19,417	15,588	80.3	3,386	17.4	...	...	...	...	1,989	58.8	12,761	81.8	...	...
Michigan—															
Ann Arbor:															
1965–66	9,748	9,046	92.8	702	7.2	...	...	...	...	...	...	7,477	82.7	290	4.0
1963–64	8,669	8,123	93.6	546	6.3	...	...	...	...	153	28.0	7,187	88.5	...	...
1965–66	194,338	85,226	43.9	107,461	55.3	77,654	72.3								
1960–61	201,257	106,836	53.1	93,192	46.3	62,391	66.9								
Detroit:															
1965–66	194,338	85,226	43.9	107,461	55.3	77,654	72.3	15,263	24.5	98,274	91.5	55,395	65.0	–25,220	–31.3
1960–61	201,257	106,836	53.1	93,192	46.3	62,391	66.9	...	...	84,939	91.1	80,615	75.4	...	...
Flint:															
1965–66	28,493	19,054	66.9	9,439	33.1	6,410	67.9	5,631	722.8	8,103	85.9	15,234	80.0	2,703	21.6
1959–60	24,751	18,261	73.8	6,490	26.2	2,711	41.8	...	...	6,156	94.9	16,309	89.3	...	...
1955–56	21,557	17,215	79.9	4,342	20.1	2,260	52.1	...	...	3,360	77.4	15,219	88.4	...	...
1950–51	15,398	13,456	87.4	1,942	12.6	779	40.1	...	...	1,681	86.5	12,531	93.1	...	...

TABLE 6—(Continued)

State and city	Total elementary students	Total white students in elementary schools: Number	Total white students in elementary schools: Per cent of total elementary students	Total Negro students in elementary schools: Number	Total Negro students in elementary schools: Per cent of total elementary students	Negro students in schools 90 to 100 per cent Negro: Number	Negro students in schools 90 to 100 per cent Negro: Per cent of total Negro elementary students	Increase or decrease in Negro students in schools 90 to 100 per cent Negro; earliest year to latest year: Number	Increase or decrease in Negro students in schools 90 to 100 per cent Negro; earliest year to latest year: Per cent increase or decrease	Negro students in majority Negro schools: Number	Negro students in majority Negro schools: Per cent of total Negro elementary students	White students in schools 90 to 100 per cent white: Number	White students in schools 90 to 100 per cent white: Per cent of total white elementary students	Increase or decrease in white students in schools 90 to 100 per cent white; earliest year to latest year: Number	Increase or decrease in white students in schools 90 to 100 per cent white; earliest year to latest year: Per cent increase or decrease
Northern (Cont.)															
New Jersey—															
Newark:															
1965–66 ..	53,266	12,404	23.3	36,805	69.1	18,881	51.3	6,528	52.8	33,238	90.3	4,604	37.1	−1,159	−20.1
1963–64 ..	48,012	14,323	29.8	30,844	64.2	18,880	61.2	....	....	24,661	79.9	4,759	33.2	....	......
1961–62 ..	43,460	16,057	36.9	25,353	58.3	12,353	48.7	....	....	21,503	84.8	5,763	35.9	....	......
New York—															
Albany:															
1965–66 ..	8,744	6,217	71.1	2,527	28.9	......	.....	....	....	1,869	74.0	4,134	66.5	−235	−5.4
1962–63 ..	8,891	6,927	77.9	1,964	22.1	......	.....	....	....	1,354	68.9	4,369	63.1	....	......
Buffalo:															
1965–66 ..	49,219	31,007	63.0	17,016	34.6	13,106	77.0	3,907	42.5	15,097	88.7	25,131	81.1	5,930	30.9
1961–62 ..	34,485	22,471	65.2	11,422	33.1	9,199	80.5	....	....	10,212	89.4	19,201	85.4	....	......
Syracuse:															
1965–66 ..	17,611	14,263	81.0	3,348	19.0	......	.....	−667	−100.0	1,679	50.2	9,937	69.7	−312	−3.0
1964–65 ..	17,672	14,577	82.5	3,095	17.5	......	.....	....	....	1,499	48.4	11,178	76.7	....	......
1962–63 ..	14,974	12,785	85.4	2,189	14.6	667	30.5	....	....	1,258	57.5	10,249	80.2	....	......
Ohio—															
Akron:															
1963–64 ..	33,797	25,570	75.6	8,174	24.2	3,347	40.9	1,954	140.3	5,568	68.1	6,801	26.6	−12,163	−64.1
1960–61 ..	32,940	25,574	77.6	7,366	22.4	1,393	18.9	....	....	5,440	73.8	18,964	74.2	....	......
Cincinnati:															
1965–66 ..	55,922	33,363	59.7	22,559	40.3	11,155	49.4	7,174	180.2	19,868	88.0	21,141	63.3	−1,422	−6.3
1960–61 ..	51,030	33,597	65.8	17,433	34.2	10,935	62.7	....	....	13,605	78.0	24,520	73.0	....	......
1955–56 ..	52,351	39,547	75.5	12,804	24.5	4,922	38.4	....	....	9,566	74.7	31,648	80.1	....	......
1950–51 ..	40,038	30,973	77.3	9,110	22.7	3,981	43.7	....	....	6,442	70.7	22,563	72.8	....	......
Cleveland:															
1962–63 ..	92,395	42,564	46.1	49,831	53.9	41,034	82.3	28,665	231.7	47,160	94.6	34,175	80.2	−5,501	−13.9
1952–53 ..	70,614	49,075	69.5	21,539	30.5	12,369	57.4	....	....	18,174	84.4	39,676	80.9	....	......
Columbus:															
1965–66 ..	66,215	48,913	73.9	17,302	26.1	5,933	34.3	4,267	256.1	13,986	80.8	37,651	77.0	18,032	91.9
1960–61 ..	56,624	42,511	75.1	14,113	24.9	3,235	22.9	....	....	10,841	76.8	31,508	74.1	....	......
1955–56 ..	39,341	32,189	81.8	7,152	18.2	2,677	37.4	....	....	4,720	65.9	26,369	82.0	....	......
1950–51 ..	29,839	25,005	83.8	4,834	16.2	1,666	34.5	....	....	3,391	70.2	19,619	78.5	....	......
Oregon—															
Portland:															
1965–66 ..	54,717	50,235	91.8	4,482	8.2	2,085	46.5	858	69.9	2,653	59.2	46,223	92.0	−688	−1.5
1964–65 ..	55,246	51,012	92.3	4,234	7.7	1,548	36.6	....	....	2,635	62.3	46,701	93.3	....	....
1963–64 ..	54,747	50,902	93.0	3,845	7.0	1,227	31.9	....	....	2,532	65.8	46,911	92.2	....	....

TABLE 6—(Continued)

State and city	Total elementary Students	Total white students in elementary schools		Total Negro students in elementary schools		Negro students in schools 90 to 100 per cent Negro		Increase or decrease in Negro students in schools 90 to 100 per cent Negro; earliest year to latest year		Negro students in majority Negro schools		White students in schools 90 to 100 per cent white		Increase or decrease in white students in schools 90 to 100 per cent white; earliest year to latest year	
		Number	Per cent of total elementary Students	Number	Per cent of total elementary students	Number	Per cent of total Negro elementary students	Number	Per cent increase or decrease	Number	Per cent of total Negro elementary students	Number	Per cent of total white elementary students	Number	Per cent increase or decrease
Northern (Cont.)															
Pennsylvania—															
Chester:															
1965–66 ..	6,482	1,990	30.7	4,492	69.3	3,499	77.9	538	18.2	4,001	89.1	755	37.9	356	89.2
1963–64 ..	6,311	2,148	34.0	4,163	66.0	2,961	77.1	....	......	3,573	85.8	399	18.6	....	......
Harrisburg:															
1965–66 ..	8,208	4,456	54.3	3,752	45.7	2,025	54.0	–78	–3.7	3,048	81.3	2,505	56.2	–109	–4.2
1963–64 ..	8,320	4,702	56.5	3,618	43.5	2,103	58.1	....	......	2,994	82.7	2,614	55.6	....	......
Philadelphia:															
1965–66 ..	156,523	64,829	41.4	91,694	58.6	66,052	72.0	36,497	123.5	82,704	90.2	37,370	57.7	–34,356	–47.9
1960–61 ..	148,464	71,246	48.0	77,218	52.0	60,636	78.6	....	......	53,820	75.5	70,619	91.5	....	......
1950–51 ..	139,060	92,324	66.4	46,736	33.6	29,555	63.2	....	......	39,633	84.8	71,726	77.5	....	......
Pittsburgh:															
1965–66 ..	47,363	28,717	60.6	18,646	39.4	9,226	49.5	6,000	186.0	15,428	82.8	17,883	62.3	–1,560	–8.0
1957–58 ..	44,855	30,244	67.4	14,611	32.6	4,996	34.2	....	......	10,736	73.5	19,924	65.9	....	......
1955–56 ..	43,699	30,693	70.2	13,006	29.8	4,204	32.3	....	......	9,338	72.1	19,387	63.1	....	......
1950–51 ..	43,078	32,449	75.3	10,629	24.7	3,226	30.4	....	......	5,408	51.0	19,443	59.9	....	......
Utah—															
Salt Lake City:															
1965–66 ..	22,066	19,893	90.2	361	1.6	......	....	....	......	......	....	19,212	96.6	–3,708	–16.2
1960–61 ..	25,324	23,557	93.0	268	1.1	......	....	....	......	......	....	22,920	97.3	....	......
Washington—															
Seattle:															
1964–65 ..	50,628	42,053	83.0	5,318	10.5	525	9.9	525	......	3,212	60.4	37,751	89.8	–10,295	–21.4
1962–63 ..	54,455	46,407	85.2	4,960	9.1	576	11.6	....	......	3,207	64.6	43,128	92.9	....	......
1957–58 ..	57,915	51,861	89.5	3,569	6.2	......	0.0	....	......	2,110	59.1	48,046	92.6	....	......
Wisconsin—															
Milwaukee:															
1965–66 ..	75,033	55,230	73.6	19,803	26.4	14,344	72.4	13,028	990.0	17,204	86.8	47,648	86.3	9,752	25.7
1960–61* ..	66,423	53,716	80.9	12,707	19.1	8,559	67.4	....	......	10,990	86.5	49,743	92.6	....	......
1950–51* ..	43,487	40,916	94.1	2,571	5.9	1,316	51.2	....	......	1,716	66.8	37,896	92.6	....	......

* Estimated figures based on census and school enrollment data.

TABLE 7

Extent of Teacher Segregation in 75 School Systems in Southern, Border and Northern States, in Elementary Schools in 1965–66

State and city	Total elementary teachers	Total white teachers in elementary schools		Total Negro teachers in elementary schools		Negro teachers in schools 90-100% Negro		Negro teachers in majority-Negro schools		White teachers in schools 90-100% white	
		Number	Per cent of total elementary teachers	Number	Per cent of total elementary teachers	Number	Per cent of total Negro elementary teachers	Number	Per cent of total Negro elementary teachers	Number	Per cent of total white elementary teachers
Southern											
Alabama:											
Anniston	151	89	58.9	62	41.1	62	100.0	62	100.0	89	100.0
Tuscaloosa	248	133	53.6	115	46.4	115	100.0	115	100.0	133	100.0
Arkansas:											
Fayetteville	90	90	100.0	.....	....	.....	.....	.....	.....	90	100.0
Forrest City	94	45	47.9	49	52.1	49	100.0	49	100.0	45	100.0
Helena	126	54	42.9	72	57.1	72	100.0	72	100.0	54	100.0
Hot Springs	111.5	92	82.5	19.5	17.5	19.5	100.0	19.5	100.0	92	100.0
Jonesboro	106	96	90.6	10	9.4	10	100.0	10	100.0	96	100.0
Little Rock	519	346	66.7	173	33.3	171	98.8	171	98.8	327	94.5
Pine Bluff	195	115.9	59.4	79.1	40.6	78.5	99.2	78.5	99.2	113	97.5
Florida:											
Miami	4,392	3,420	77.9	972	22.1	908	93.4	929	95.5	3,021	88.3
Tallahassee	366	191	52.2	175	47.8	175	100.0	175	100.0	191	100.0
Georgia: Atlanta	2,784	1,411	50.7	1,373	49.3	1,362	99.2	1,370	99.8	1,285	91.1
Mississippi:											
Hattiesburg	159	96	60.4	63	39.6	63	100.0	63	100.0	96	100.0
Vicksburg	118.6	55.6	46.9	63	53.1	63	100.0	63	100.0	55.6	100.0
North Carolina:											
Charlotte	1,688	1,208	71.6	480	28.4	469	97.7	469	97.7	1,102	91.2
Raleigh	413	287	69.5	126	30.5	126	100.0	126	100.0	287	100.0
Rocky-Mount	150.9	89.9	59.6	61	40.4	61	100.0	61	100.0	80.2	89.2
Winston-Salem	962	725	75.4	237	24.6	224	94.5	231	97.5	655	90.4
Oklahoma:											
Muskogee	169.1	132.1	78.1	37	21.9	37	100.0	37	100.0	120.4	91.1
Oklahoma City	1,396	1,138	81.5	258	18.5	246	95.3	252	97.6	1,040	91.4
South Carolina:											
Anderson	219	171	78.1	48	21.9	48	100.0	48	100.0	171	100.0
Columbia	612	355	58.0	257	42.0	257	100.0	257	100.0	355	100.0
Florence	267.7	152.7	57.0	115	43.0	115	100.0	115	100.0	152.7	100.0
Sumter	190.5	99	52.0	91.5	48.0	91.5	100.0	91.5	100.0	99	100.0
Tennessee:											
Knoxville	932.8	825.2	88.5	107.6	11.5	102.6	95.4	102.6	95.4	767.7	93.0
Nashville	1,934	1,497	77.4	438	22.6	433	98.9	434	99.1	1,279	85.5
Texas:											
Amarillo	724.5	675	93.2	49.5	6.8	49.5	100.0	49.5	100.0	658.25	97.5
Austin	1,022.7	849.2	83.0	174.5	17.0	164.5	94.3	164.5	94.3	766.7	90.3
Corpus Christi	887.5	861.5	97.1	26	2.9	16	61.5	19	73.0	758.5	88.0
Houston	4,994	3,441	68.9	1,553	31.1	1,548	99.7	1,551	99.9	3,255	94.5
Lubbock	762	702	92.1	60	7.9	53	88.3	55	91.6	625	89.1
Marshall	170	93	54.7	77	45.3	77	100.0	77	100.0	93	100.0
Texarkana	125	91	72.8	34	27.2	34	100.0	34	100.0	91	100.0
Wichita Falls	367	319	86.9	48	13.1	40	83.3	42	87.5	285	89.3
Virginia: Richmond	952	360	37.8	592	62.2	590	99.7	590	99.7	318	88.4
Border											
Delaware: Wilmington	357	182	51.0	175	49.0	99	56.6	166	94.9	28	15.4
District of Columbia: Washington	3,138	523	16.7	2,615	83.3	2,390	91.4	2,610	99.8	104	19.9
Kentucky:											
Lexington	209	141	67.5	68	32.5	38	55.9	52	76.5	58	41.1
Louisville	957	632	66.0	325	34.0	270	83.1	310	95.4	319	50.4
Maryland: Baltimore	3,691	1,639	44.4	2,052	55.6	1,753	85.4	1,890	92.1	814	49.6
Missouri:											
Kansas City	1,617	1,142	70.6	475	29.4	392	82.5	433	91.1	609	53.3
St. Joseph	399	386	96.7	13	3.3	6	46.2	......	....	336	87.1
St. Louis	2,633.9	1,147.5	43.6	1,486.4	56.4	1,413.9	95.1	1,439.9	96.8	613.5	53.4
New Mexico: Albuquerque*	1,567	1,531	97.7	23	1.5	.....	....	6	26.1	1.493	97.5

TABLE 7—(Continued)

State and city	Total elementary teachers	Total white teachers in elementary schools		Total Negro teachers in elementary schools		Negro teachers in schools 90-100% Negro		Negro teachers in majority-Negro schools		White teachers in schools 90-100% white	
		Number	Per cent of total elementary teachers	Number	Per cent of Total elementary teachers	Number	Per cent of total Negro elementary teachers	Number	Per cent of total Negro elementary teachers	Number	Per cent of total white elementary teachers
Northern											
California:											
Pittsburg*	449	401	89.3	22	4.9	2	9.1	2	9.1	52	13.0
San Diego	2,178	2,086	95.8	74	3.4	6	8.1	38	51.3	1,638	78.5
San Francisco**	1,676	1,353	80.7	114	6.8	20	17.5	57	50.0	736	54.4
Colorado: Denver	2,047	1,818	88.8	183	8.9	41	22.4	81	44.2	1,498	82.4
Connecticut:											
Hartford	1,158	1,003	86.6	150	13.0	15	10.0	99	66.0	390	38.9
New London	113	108	95.6	5	4.4	....	....	1	20.0	39	36.1
Illinois:											
Chicago	14,294	9,036	63.2	5,181	36.2	4,744	91.6	4,970	95.9	5,695	63.0
East St. Louis	461	204	44.3	257	55.7	222	86.4	238	92.6	122	59.8
Peoria	624	599	96.0	24	3.8	4	16.7	17	70.8	452	75.5
Indiana:											
Gary	996	349	35.2	623	62.4	501	80.4	523	83.9	232	66.4
Indianapolis	2,647	1,987	75.1	660	24.9	535	81.0	608	92.1	1,436	72.2
Massachusetts: Springfield	650	596	91.7	54	8.3	2	3.7	20	37.1	393	66.0
Michigan:											
Detroit	6,615	4,484	67.8	2,115	32.0	1,410	66.7	1,707	80.7	1,801	40.1
Flint	1,042	812	77.9	230	22.1	155	67.4	185	80.4	504	62.0
New Jersey: Camden	434	225	51.8	207	47.7	56	27.1	160	77.3	96	42.7
New York:											
Buffalo	1,922.8	1,720.1	89.5	202.7	10.5	162.6	80.2	171.7	84.7	963.4	56.0
Jamestown	195.5	193.5	99.0	2	1.0	......	.....	.....	....	152.5	78.8
Rochester	1,041	954	91.6	87	8.4	38	43.7	60	68.9	465	48.7
Schenectady	237	232	97.9	5	2.1	....	....	.....	....	192	82.7
Syracuse	618	563.5	91.2	54.5	8.8	......	....	22	40.4	335.5	59.5
Ohio:											
Akron***	1,145.9	1,057	92.2	87.9	7.6	40.7	46.3	66.7	75.8	570	53.9
Cincinnati	1,778	1,327	74.6	451	25.4	223	49.4	361	80.0	615	46.4
Columbus	2,508	2,206	88.0	302	12.0	117	38.7	214	70.8	1,194	54.2
Oregon: Portland	2,548	2,411	98.1	47	1.9	13	27.7	17	36.2	2,039	84.6
Pennsylvania:											
Chester	227	115	50.7	112	49.3	101	90.2	105	93.8	26	22.6
Harrisburg	285	221	77.5	64	22.5	34	53.1	50	78.1	88	39.8
Philadelphia	4,357	2,529	58.0	1,828	42.0	1,437	78.6	1,679	91.8	767	30.3
Pittsburgh	1,556	1,373.3	88.2	182.7	11.8	109	59.7	160	87.6	553	40.3
Scranton	298	294	98.7	4	1.3	......	.....	.....	....	287	97.7
Washington: Seattle**	1,895	1,760	92.9	83	4.4	4	4.8	23	27.7	1,399	79.5
Wisconsin: Milwaukee	1,810	1,470	81.2	340	18.8	248	72.9	281	82.7	1,097	74.6

* Figures for 1966–67.
** Figures for 1964–65.
*** Figures for 1963–64.

TABLE 8

Pupil Desegregation in Eleven Southern States

Desegregation Percentages

	Fall 1967	Fall 1968		Fall 1967	Fall 1968
Alabama	5.4	7.4	South Carolina	6.4	14.9
Arkansas	16.8	23.3	Tennessee	18.4	24.3
Florida	18.0	24.1	Texas	26.1	38.9
Georgia	9.5	14.2	Virginia	20.4	25.7
Louisiana	6.7	8.8			
Mississippi	3.9	7.1	11-State Percentage	13.9	20.3
North Carolina	16.5	27.8			

(**Credit:** U.S. Department of Health, Education and Welfare)

TABLE 9

Labor Force by Age, Sex and Color

Age, sex and color	Total labor force				Civilian labor force			
	Thousands of persons		Participation rate		Thousands of persons		Participation rate	
	Dec. 1968	Dec. 1967	Dec. 1968	Dec. 1967	Dec. 1968	Dec. 1967	Dec. 1968	Dec. 1967
Total Male								
16 years and over	52,745	52,155	80.1	80.5	49,283	48,721	79.0	79.4
16 to 19 years	3,825	3,854	52.7	54.0	3,402	3,193	49.7	49.3
16 and 17 years	1,517	1,502	40.8	41.7	1,491	1,472	49.7	49.3
18 and 19 years	2,309	2,353	65.1	66.5	1,911	1,721	60.6	59.3
20 to 24 years	6,813	6,514	85.1	84.9	5,037	4,981	80.8	81.1
25 to 54 years	32,973	32,690	96.4	96.5	31,714	31,457	96.2	96.4
25 to 34 years	11,515	11,156	96.8	97.2	10,743	10,420	96.6	97.0
35 to 44 years	11,043	11,239	97.2	97.5	10,649	10,843	97.1	97.4
45 to 54 years	10,415	10,294	95.0	94.8	10,322	10,193	95.0	94.7
55 to 64 years	7,030	6,991	83.7	84.4	7,026	6,985	83.7	84.4
55 to 59 years	4,109	4,102	89.1	90.4	4,105	4,096	89.1	90.4
60 to 64 years	2,921	2,889	77.2	77.2	2,921	2,889	77.2	77.2
65 years and over	2,103	2,105	26.5	26.8	2,103	2,105	26.5	26.8
White Male								
16 years and over	47,465	46,945	80.4	80.7	44,358	43,818	79.4	79.6
16 to 19 years	3,370	3,394	53.4	54.6	2,984	2,782	50.4	49.6
16 and 17 years	1,353	1,321	42.0	42.2	1,329	1,293	41.5	41.7
18 and 19 years	2,017	2,073	65.4	67.1	1,655	1,489	60.8	59.4
20 to 24 years	6,016	5,752	85.0	84.7	4,408	4,352	80.6	80.7
25 to 54 years	29,694	29,467	96.8	97.0	28,583	28,356	96.6	96.8
25 to 34 years	10,279	9,966	97.1	97.5	9,603	9,310	96.9	97.4
35 to 44 years	9,940	10,127	97.6	98.0	9,590	9,768	97.5	97.9
45 to 54 years	9,476	9,373	95.5	95.3	9,390	9,278	95.5	95.3
55 to 64 years	6,451	6,389	84.4	84.8	6,447	6,384	84.4	84.8
55 to 59 years	3,767	3,754	89.9	91.0	3,764	3,749	89.9	91.0
60 to 64 years	2,684	2,635	77.8	77.3	2,684	2,635	77.8	77.3
65 years and over	1,934	1,942	26.6	26.9	1,934	1,942	26.6	26.9
Nonwhite Male								
16 years and over	5,280	5,210	77.3	78.0	4,926	4,903	76.1	76.9
16 to 19 years	455	460	47.8	49.8	418	411	45.7	46.9
16 and 17 years	164	181	33.5	37.9	162	178	33.3	37.5
18 and 19 years	291	279	63.0	62.5	256	232	59.9	58.1
20 to 24 years	798	762	85.4	86.7	629	629	82.2	84.3
25 to 54 years	3,279	3,223	93.0	92.7	3,130	3,100	92.7	92.4
25 to 34 years	1,237	1,190	94.7	94.3	1,140	1,110	94.3	94.0
35 to 44 years	1,103	1,112	93.7	93.8	1,059	1,075	93.5	93.6
45 to 54 years	939	921	90.2	89.4	932	915	90.2	89.4
55 to 64 years	579	601	76.7	80.3	579	601	76.7	80.3
55 to 59 years	342	348	81.0	84.2	342	348	81.0	84.2
60 to 64 years	237	254	71.3	75.6	237	254	71.3	75.6
65 years and over	169	163	25.5	25.1	169	163	25.5	25.1
Female								
16 years and over	29,873	29,372	42.2	42.2	29,835	29,337	42.2	42.2
16 to 19 years	2,821	2,851	39.8	40.9	2,811	2,840	39.7	40.8
16 and 17 years	1,121	1,068	31.0	30.4	1,121	1,068	31.0	30.4
18 and 19 years	1,700	1,782	49.0	51.5	1,691	1,772	48.9	51.4
20 to 24 years	4,414	4,240	55.6	55.7	4,397	4,226	55.5	55.6

TABLE 9—(Continued)

Age, sex and color	Total labor force				Civilian labor force			
	Thousands of persons		Participation rate		Thousands of persons		Participation rate	
	Dec. 1968	Dec. 1967	Dec. 1968	Dec. 1967	Dec. 1968	Dec. 1967	Dec. 1968	Dec. 1967
Female (Continued)—								
25 to 54 years	17,575	17,360	49.0	48.9	17,565	17,349	49.0	48.9
25 to 34 years	5,303	5,141	43.6	43.8	5,297	5,135	43.6	43.7
35 to 44 years	5,987	6,044	50.2	50.0	5,983	6,040	50.2	49.9
45 to 54 years	6,286	6,175	53.3	53.1	6,284	6,173	53.3	53.1
55 to 64 years	3,992	3,905	42.6	42.5	3,991	3,905	42.6	42.5
55 to 59 years	2,458	2,363	48.6	47.7	2,457	2,363	48.6	47.7
60 to 64 years	1,534	1,542	35.6	36.4	1,534	1,542	35.6	36.4
65 years and over	1,071	1,016	10.1	9.8	1,071	1,016	10.1	9.8
White Female								
16 years and over	26,070	25,554	41.4	41.2	26,036	25,522	41.3	41.2
16 to 19 years	2,522	2,514	41.3	41.7	2,513	2,505	41.2	41.7
16 and 17 years	1,016	958	32.6	31.7	1,016	958	32.6	31.7
18 and 19 years	1,505	1,556	50.3	51.9	1,497	1,547	50.1	51.7
20 to 24 years	3,830	3,710	55.1	55.4	3,816	3,697	55.0	55.4
25 to 54 years	15,165	14,901	47.8	47.4	15,155	14,891	47.8	47.4
25 to 34 years	4,482	4,268	42.1	41.5	4,476	4,263	42.0	41.4
35 to 44 years	5,114	5,168	48.7	48.4	5,111	5,165	48.7	48.4
45 to 54 years	5,569	5,465	52.6	52.3	5,568	5,464	52.6	52.3
55 to 64 years	3,576	3,509	42.0	42.0	3,576	3,509	42.0	42.0
55 to 59 years	2,188	2,108	47.8	47.0	2,188	2,108	47.8	47.0
60 to 64 years	1,388	1,401	35.3	36.3	1,388	1,401	35.3	36.3
65 years and over	976	920	10.0	9.7	976	920	10.0	9.7
Nonwhite Female								
16 years and over	3,803	3,818	49.0	50.4	3,799	3,815	49.0	50.4
16 to 19 years	299	336	30.6	35.5	298	335	30.6	35.4
16 and 17 years	105	110	20.9	22.6	105	110	20.9	22.6
18 and 19 years	195	226	40.8	49.1	194	225	40.7	49.0
20 to 24 years	584	530	59.3	57.2	582	529	59.2	57.2
25 to 54 years	2,410	2,459	58.5	60.5	2,409	2,458	58.5	60.5
25 to 34 years	821	873	55.0	60.0	821	873	55.0	60.0
35 to 44 years	872	876	61.3	61.5	872	876	61.3	61.4
45 to 54 years	716	710	59.4	59.9	716	710	59.4	59.9
55 to 64 years	415	396	48.6	47.5	415	396	48.6	47.5
55 to 59 years	270	255	56.2	55.0	270	255	56.2	55.0
60 to 64 years	145	141	38.8	38.0	145	141	38.8	38.0
65 years and over	95	96	11.5	12.1	95	96	11.5	12.1

TABLE 10

Employed Persons by Major Occupation Group, Color and Sex

(Per Cent Distribution)

Occupation group and color	Total		Male		Female	
	Dec. 1968	Dec. 1967	Dec. 1968	Dec. 1967	Dec. 1968	Dec. 1967
Total						
Total employed (thousands)	76,700	75,338	48,000	47,250	28,699	28,088
Per cent	100.0	100.0	100.0	100.0	100.0	100.0
White-collar workers	47.7	47.1	40.4	39.8	59.9	59.5
Professional and technical	14.0	13.7	13.8	13.4	14.4	14.2
Managers, officials and proprietors	10.2	10.0	13.6	13.4	4.4	4.3
Clerical workers	17.0	16.9	7.1	7.2	33.4	33.1
Sales workers	6.5	6.5	5.8	5.8	7.8	7.8
Blue-collar workers	36.2	36.1	47.6	47.4	17.1	16.9
Craftsmen and foremen	13.3	13.0	20.5	20.1	1.1	1.0
Operatives	18.4	18.6	20.2	20.5	15.5	15.5
Nonfarm laborers	4.5	4.4	6.8	6.8	.5	.4
Service workers	12.4	12.5	6.9	7.0	21.4	21.8
Private household workers	2.2	2.4	.1	.1	5.9	6.4
Other service workers	10.1	10.1	6.9	6.9	15.6	15.4
Farm workers	3.8	4.3	5.1	5.8	1.5	1.8
Farmers and farm managers	2.3	2.5	3.6	3.8	.2	.3
Farm laborers and foremen	1.5	1.8	1.6	1.9	1.3	1.5
White						
Total employed (thousands)	68,476	67,193	43,307	42,587	25,169	24,606
Per cent	100.0	100.0	100.0	100.0	100.0	100.0
White-collar workers	50.4	49.9	42.6	42.1	63.8	63.4
Professional and technical	14.8	14.4	14.6	14.2	15.1	14.9
Managers, officials and proprietors	11.1	11.0	14.7	14.6	4.8	4.7
Clerical workers	17.5	17.4	7.1	7.2	35.4	35.2
Sales workers	7.0	7.1	6.2	6.2	8.4	8.6
Blue-collar workers	35.3	35.4	46.2	46.2	16.6	16.7
Craftsmen and foremen	13.8	13.7	21.2	21.0	1.1	1.1
Operatives	17.8	18.1	19.4	19.6	15.0	15.3
Nonfarm laborers	3.7	3.7	5.6	5.6	.5	.4
Service workers	10.5	10.4	6.1	6.0	18.0	18.1
Private household workers	1.4	1.5	*	*	3.7	4.0
Other service workers	9.1	8.9	6.0	6.0	14.3	14.1
Farm workers	3.8	4.3	5.1	5.7	1.6	1.8
Farmers and farm managers	2.5	2.7	3.8	4.1	.3	.4
Farm laborers and foremen	1.3	1.5	1.3	1.6	1.3	1.4
Nonwhite						
Total employed (thousands)	8,223	8,145	4,693	4,663	3,530	3,482
Per cent	100.0	100.0	100.0	100.0	100.0	100.0
White-collar workers	25.4	24.2	19.8	18.6	32.9	31.7
Professional and technical	8.0	7.7	7.0	6.2	9.3	9.6
Managers, officials and proprietors	2.4	2.3	3.0	3.0	1.5	1.4
Clerical workers	12.8	12.2	7.9	7.8	19.3	18.2
Sales workers	2.3	2.0	1.9	1.6	2.9	2.5
Blue-collar workers	43.2	41.6	60.3	59.0	20.4	18.3
Craftsmen and foremen	8.4	7.4	14.0	12.4	.9	.7
Operatives	24.0	23.5	28.1	28.5	18.6	16.7
Nonfarm laborers	10.8	10.8	18.3	18.1	.9	.9

TABLE 10—(Continued)

Occupation group and color	Total		Male		Female	
	Dec. 1968	Dec. 1967	Dec. 1968	Dec. 1967	Dec. 1968	Dec. 1967
Nonwhite (Continued)						
Service workers	28.0	29.7	14.8	16.1	45.6	47.7
Private household workers	9.3	9.9	.3	.4	21.2	22.6
Other service workers	18.7	19.8	14.5	15.8	24.4	25.1
Farm workers	3.4	4.5	5.1	6.2	1.1	2.4
Farmers and farm managers	.9	1.0	1.4	1.7	.1	.2
Farm laborers and foremen	2.5	3.5	3.7	4.5	1.0	2.2

* Less than 0.05 per cent.

TABLE 11

Employment Status of Persons in Urban Neighborhoods,* by Color, Sex and Age, in 1967–68

(In Thousands)

Employment status, sex and age	Total		White		Nonwhite	
	1968	1967	1968	1967	1968	1967
Males, 20 years and over						
Urban poverty neighborhoods						
Civilian labor force	3,597	3,714	2,213	2,281	1,385	1,433
Employment	3,446	3,539	2,127	2,189	1,318	1,351
Unemployment	151	176	86	93	66	82
Unemployment rate	4.2	4.7	3.9	4.1	4.8	5.7
Other urban neighborhoods						
Civilian labor force	22,218	21,794	20,633	20,308	1,584	1,487
Employment	21,811	21,355	20,274	19,916	1,537	1.439
Unemployment	407	439	359	391	47	47
Unemployment rate	1.8	2.0	1.7	1.9	3.0	3.2
Females, 20 years and over						
Urban poverty neighborhoods						
Civilian labor force	2,337	2,382	1,258	1,296	1,078	1,086
Employment	2,208	2,238	1,198	1,230	1,010	1,008
Unemployment	128	145	60	65	67	80
Unemployment rate	5.5	6.1	4.8	5.0	6.2	7.4
Other urban neighborhoods						
Civilian labor force	12,466	11,976	11,277	10,882	1,189	1,094
Employment	12,050	11,522	10,925	10,496	1,125	1,027
Unemployment	417	454	352	387	64	67
Unemployment rate	3.3	3.8	3.1	3.6	5.4	6.1
Teen-agers, 16–19 years						
Urban poverty neighborhoods						
Civilian labor force	537	568	303	314	234	253
Employment	430	434	260	267	170	167
Unemployment	107	133	43	47	64	86
Unemployment rate	20.0	23.5	14.3	15.0	27.3	34.0
Other urban neighborhoods						
Civilian labor force	3,012	2,951	2,771	2,749	241	202
Employment	2,645	2,587	2,463	2,440	182	148
Unemployment	367	363	308	309	59	54
Unemployment rate	12.2	12.3	11.1	11.2	24.5	26.9

* Pertains only to Standard Metropolitan Statistical Areas with populations of 250,000 or more.

TABLE 12

Employment by Month (Seasonally Adjusted) from December 1967 through December 1968

(In Thousands)

Characteristics	1968												1967
	Dec.	Nov.	Oct.	Sept.	Aug.	July	June	May	Apr.	Mar.	Feb.	Jan.	Dec.
White													
Total:													
Civilian labor force	70,769	70,457	70,000	70,123	69,871	69,995	70,105	69,609	69,560	69,892	69,959	69,355	69,686
Employed	68,695	68,369	67,789	67,848	67,630	67,655	67,761	67,415	67,437	67,654	67,655	67,154	67,391
Unemployed	2,074	2,088	2,211	2,275	2,241	2,340	2,344	2,194	2,123	2,238	2,304	2,201	2,295
Unemployment rate	2.9	3.0	3.2	3.2	3.2	3.3	3.3	3.2	3.1	3.2	3.3	3.2	3.3
Males, 20 years and over:													
Civilian labor force	41,652	41,345	41,261	41,322	41,385	41,369	41,350	41,042	41,137	41,268	41,419	41,260	41,295
Employed	40,984	40,575	40,434	40,497	40,566	40,517	40,454	40,238	40,364	40,441	40,548	40,425	40,448
Unemployed	668	770	827	825	819	852	896	804	773	827	871	835	847
Unemployment rate	1.6	1.9	2.0	2.0	2.0	2.1	2.2	2.0	1.9	2.0	2.1	2.0	2.1
Females, 20 years and over:													
Civilian labor force	23,299	23,313	22,979	22,976	22,691	22,831	22,785	22,672	22,531	22,652	22,616	22,467	22,812
Employed	22,565	22,591	22,205	22,151	21,887	22,046	22,026	21,943	21,797	21,908	21,821	21,669	21,997
Unemployed	734	722	774	825	804	785	759	729	734	744	795	798	815
Unemployment rate	3.2	3.1	3.4	3.6	3.5	3.4	3.3	3.2	3.3	3.3	3.5	3.6	3.6
Both sexes, 16 to 19 years:													
Civilian labor force	5,818	5,799	5,760	5,825	5,795	5,795	5,970	5,895	5,892	5,971	5,924	5,628	5,579
Employed	5,146	5,203	5,150	5,200	5,177	5,092	5,281	5,234	5,276	5,304	5,286	5,060	4,946
Unemployed	672	596	610	625	618	703	689	661	616	667	638	568	633
Unemployment rate	11.6	10.3	10.6	10.7	10.7	12.1	11.5	11.2	10.5	11.2	10.8	10.1	11.3
Nonwhite													
Total:													
Civilian labor force	8,894	8,674	8,601	8,509	8,728	8,859	8,802	8,837	8,815	8,919	8,819	8,639	8,892
Employed	8,361	8,110	7,963	7,937	8,190	8,245	8,164	8,272	8,227	8,301	8,187	8,085	8,281
Unemployed	533	564	638	572	538	614	638	565	588	618	632	554	611
Unemployment rate	6.0	6.5	7.4	6.7	6.2	6.9	7.2	6.4	6.7	6.9	7.2	6.4	6.9
Males, 20 years and over:													
Civilian labor force	4,562	4,500	4,458	4,485	4,523	4,532	4,554	4,567	4,569	4,591	4,565	4,504	4,547
Employed	4,409	4,332	4,249	4,302	4,355	4,373	4,384	4,399	4,386	4,400	4,369	4,312	4,391
Unemployed	153	168	209	183	168	159	170	168	183	191	196	192	156
Unemployment rate	3.4	3.7	4.7	4.1	3.7	3.5	3.7	3.7	4.0	4.2	4.3	4.3	3.4
Females, 20 years and over:													
Civilian labor force	3,547	3,443	3,417	3,346	3,397	3,479	3,460	3,484	3,427	3,478	3,486	3,386	3,527
Employed	3,336	3,242	3,203	3,141	3,200	3,230	3,229	3,281	3,212	3,261	3,251	3,167	3,273
Unemployed	211	201	214	205	197	249	231	203	215	217	235	219	254
Unemployment rate	5.9	5.8	6.3	6.1	5.8	7.2	6.7	5.8	6.3	6.2	6.7	6.5	7.2
Both sexes, 16 to 19 years:													
Civilian labor force	785	731	726	678	808	848	788	786	819	850	768	749	818
Employed	616	536	511	494	635	642	551	492	629	640	567	606	617
Unemployed	169	195	215	184	173	206	237	194	190	210	201	143	201
Unemployment rate	21.5	26.7	29.6	27.1	21.4	24.3	30.1	24.7	23.2	24.7	26.2	19.1	24.6

TABLE 13

Unemployed Persons by Duration of Unemployment, Sex, Age, Color and Marital Status for December 1968

Sex, age, color and marital status	Thousands of persons					Less than 5 weeks as a per cent of unemployed in group		15 weeks and over as a per cent of unemployed in group	
	Total	Less than 5 weeks	5 to 14 weeks	15 to 26 weeks	27 weeks and over	Dec. 1968	Dec. 1967	Dec. 1968	Dec. 1967
Total	2,419	1,303	814	165	137	53.9	50.3	12.5	15.3
16 to 21 years	932	564	282	55	31	60.5	52.6	9.2	12.5
16 to 19 years	728	429	236	44	20	58.9	54.0	8.7	12.8
20 to 24 years	435	277	123	21	14	63.7	53.1	8.1	11.6
25 to 44 years	678	326	240	59	51	48.1	48.9	16.2	14.9
45 years and over	579	272	215	40	53	46.9	46.0	16.1	21.0
Male	1,283	671	454	77	81	52.3	52.8	12.3	14.4
16 to 21 years	503	286	176	31	11	56.7	56.4	8.4	9.8
16 to 19 years	410	225	149	25	11	54.9	57.4	8.7	9.3
20 to 24 years	211	136	62	10	3	64.2	60.1	6.4	8.1
25 to 44 years	314	157	114	15	27	50.0	53.3	13.4	14.0
45 years and over	347	154	129	26	39	44.2	44.1	18.6	23.3
Female	1,136	632	360	88	56	55.6	47.3	12.7	16.2
16 to 21 years	428	278	107	24	20	65.0	48.2	10.2	15.7
16 to 19 years	317	203	87	18	9	64.1	49.7	8.6	17.1
20 to 24 years	223	141	60	11	11	63.2	45.4	9.7	15.3
25 to 44 years	363	170	127	44	23	46.8	45.5	18.5	15.2
45 years and over	232	118	86	15	14	50.8	49.2	12.2	17.3
White: Total	1,917	1,050	644	116	107	54.8	51.2	11.6	15.2
Male	1,051	556	374	56	64	52.9	53.2	11.5	15.0
Female	866	495	269	60	43	57.1	48.5	11.8	15.5
Nonwhite: Total	501	253	170	49	29	50.4	46.9	15.6	15.6
Male	232	116	80	21	16	49.8	51.1	15.8	11.7
Female	269	137	90	28	13	51.0	43.9	15.4	18.4
Male: Married, wife present	562	272	211	34	45	48.5	51.3	14.0	17.3
Widowed, divorced or separated	105	55	34	7	10	52.2	45.8	15.8	18.6
Single (never married)	616	344	210	36	26	55.9	55.6	10.1	10.7
Female: Married, husband present	559	308	185	39	27	55.1	49.8	11.9	12.8
Widowed, divorced or separated	194	105	67	15	6	54.1	43.4	11.1	19.0
Single (never married)	383	219	108	33	23	57.3	45.4	14.6	20.3

TABLE 14

Voting Choices in Selected Cities in the 1968 Senatorial Elections

City	Democrat		Percentages		Republican		Percentages	
	City	Negro Areas	City	Negro Areas	City	Negro Areas	City	Negro Areas
Atlanta, Ga.	112,665	28,836	66%	71%	58,086	11,903	34%	29%
Charlotte, N.C.	42,418	7,359	63%	95%	24,817	359	37%	5%
Chicago, Ill.	881,848	271,955	64%	88%	491,104	36,202	36%	12%
Columbus, Ohio	74,007	13,751	45%	74%	89,436	4,776	55%	26%
Denver, Colo.	101,924	17,420	50%	75%	101,697	5,943	50%	25%
Kansas City, Mo.	86,549	28,339	59%	80%	60,303	7,098	41%	20%
Los Angeles, Calif.	593,795	85,990	60%	92%	393,433	7,887	40%	8%
Philadelphia, Pa.	499,800	149,557	62%	85%	305,597	2,563	35%	15%
Pittsburgh, Pa.	128,953	24,756	62%	86%	80,700	4,172	38%	14%
Raleigh, N.C.	36,226	3,371	62%	94%	21,887	215	38%	6%
St. Louis, Mo.	147,841	44,975	70%	93%	64,541	3,368	30%	7%

(Courtesy of J. Erroll Miller)

TABLE 15

Voting Choices in Selected Cities in the 1968 Congressional Elections

City	Congressional District	Democrat				Republican			
		City	Negro Areas	Percentages		City	Negro Areas	Percentages	
				City	Negro Areas			City	Negro Areas
Atlanta, Ga.	4th	17,543	7,082	58%	91%	12,741	672	42%	9%
Atlanta, Ga.	5th	63,183	34,293	44%	95%	79,258	1,775	56%	5%
Columbus, Ohio	12th	32,032	8,271	37%	70%	53,412	3,555	63%	30%
Columbus, Ohio	15th	20,986	3,579	33%	70%	42,836	1,520	67%	30%
Denver, Colo.	1st	91,199	14,855	52%	76%	82,677	4,651	48%	24%
Detroit, Mich.	13th	81,951	71,023	86%	87%	12,873	10,833	14%	13%
Detroit, Mich.	16th	30,987	12,161	88%	91%	4,340	1,211	12%	9%
Detroit, Mich.	17th	123,376	41,368	75%	86%	40,906	6,925	25%	14%
Kansas City, Mo.	4th	86,618	25,227	65%	86%	45,951	4,160	35%	14%
Kansas City, Mo.	5th	9,719	4,457	64%	74%	5,409	1,579	36%	26%
Los Angeles, Calif.	21st	63,875	63,875	91%	91%	6,143	6,143	9%	9%
Memphis, Tenn.	7th	13,132	10,924	87%	95%	1,910	598	13%	5%
Memphis, Tenn.	9th	43,797	18,689	39%	91%	67,142	1,822	61%	9%
Minneapolis, Minn.	5th	108,588	15,129	58%	65%	78,819	8,008	42%	35%
Pittsburgh, Pa.	14th	96,117	21,300	71%	73%	39,671	8,017	29%	27%
Raleigh, N.C.	4th	30,718	3,546	51%	97%	30,056	115	49%	3%
St. Louis, Mo.	1st	65,723	42,178	74%	89%	22,790	5,381	26%	11%

(Courtesy of J. Erroll Miller)

TABLE 16

Voting Participation in Selected Cities in the 1968 Presidential Election

City	Total Number of Persons Registered		Total Number of Persons Voting		Percentages	
	City	Negro Areas	City	Negro Areas	City	Negro Areas
Atlanta, Ga.	273,339	77,538	178,164	48,167	65%	62%
Charlotte, N.C.	104,434	14,363	74,139	8,833	71%	61%
Chicago, Ill.	1,722,618	416,683	1,471,355	330,628	85%	79%
Columbus, Ohio	200,009	31,048	177,513	24,999	89%	81%
Detroit, Mich.	774,288	350,447	610,687	270,118	79%	77%
East Chicago, Ind.	27,018	6,269	19,516	4,336	72%	69%
Gary, Ind.	103,516	47,756	72,193	33,546	70%	70%
Hammond, Ind.	61,040	1,741	43,798	1,164	72%	67%
Kansas City, Mo.	183,842	47,793	139,896	35,469	76%	74%
Los Angeles, Calif.	1,260,278	137,799	1,095,821	105,895	87%	77%
Memphis, Tenn.	252,815	81,493	184,102	53,703	73%	60%
Minneapolis, Minn.	258,087	34,185	193,192	24,108	75%	71%
Philadelphia, Pa.	1,004,091	231,833	843,427	179,426	84%	77%
Pittsburgh, Pa.	277,502	41,210	227,308	32,313	82%	78%
Raleigh, N.C.	88,902	7,620	67,157	5,281	76%	69%
St. Louis, Mo.	262,531	73,557	220,830	57,396	84%	78%

(Courtesy of J. Erroll Miller)

TABLE 17

Voting Choices in Selected Cities in the 1968 Presidential Election

City	Nixon				Humphrey				Wallace			
	City	Negro Areas	Percentages City	Percentages Negro Areas	City	Negro Areas	Percentages City	Percentages Negro Areas	City	Negro Areas	Percentages City	Percentages Negro Areas
Atlanta, Ga.	63,705	1,888	36%	4%	77,646	47,599	44%	94%	36,813	1,017	21%	2%
Charlotte, N.C.	38,081	270	51%	3%	24,323	8,459	33%	96%	11,735	104	16%	1%
Chicago, Ill.	452,914	32,935	31%	10%	874,113	281,615	59%	85%	.....	....	....	....
Columbus, Ohio	80,848	3,152	46%	13%	74,264	21,085	42%	84%	22,401	762	12%	3%
Denver, Colo.	92,013	4,864	44%	20%	106,081	19,088	51%	78%	11,404	608	6%	2%
Detroit, Mich.	119,829	29,401	18%	11%	427,396	223,252	70%	83%	50,369	9,916	8%	4%
East Chicago, Ind.	3,750	357	20%	8%	12,737	3,706	69%	88%	2,054	151	11%	4%
Gary, Ind.	17,475	2,081	25%	6%	44,043	29,488	63%	91%	8,917	904	13%	3%
Hammond, Ind.	3,944	60	42%	5%	3,657	1,030	39%	90%	1,697	52	18%	5%
Kansas City, Mo.	56,963	6,136	36%	17%	82,933	29,327	53%	77%	16,485	2,440	11%	6%
Los Angeles, Calif.	444,919	6,714	42%	7%	579,588	93,829	54%	92%	44,036	1,092	4%	1%
Memphis, Tenn.	56,127	2,077	30%	4%	71,290	47,873	39%	92%	56,885	2,297	31%	4%
Minneapolis, Minn.	70,016	6,862	36%	28%	114,721	16,091	59%	67%	8,455	1,155	4%	5%
Philadelphia, Pa.	254,153	22,044	30%	12%	525,768	153,990	62%	86%	63,506	3,452	8%	2%
Pittsburgh, Pa.	57,681	2,923	26%	9%	138,877	27,066	63%	87%	24,931	1,257	11%	4%
Raleigh, N.C.	28,928	130	43%	3%	20,979	4,731	31%	96%	17,250	38	26%	1%
St. Louis, Mo.	58,252	2,679	26%	5%	143,010	47,326	65%	94%	19,674	272	9%	1%

(Courtesy of J. Erroll Miller)

TABLE 18

Negro-White Voter Registration in the South, Spring–Summer 1968

(Voting Age Population Figures Are from the 1960 Census)

State	White voting-age pop.	Negro voting-age pop.	White reg.	Negro reg.	Per cent White reg.	Per cent Negro reg.
Alabama	1,353,058	481,320	1,117,000*	273,000*	82.5	56.7
Arkansas	850,643	192,626	640,000	130,000	75.2	67.5
Florida	2,617,438	470,261	2,195,000	292,000	83.8	62.1
Georgia	1,797,062	612,910	1,524,000	344,000	84.7	56.1
Louisiana	1,289,216	514,589	1,133,000	305,000	87.9	59.3
Mississippi	748,266	422,256	691,000	251,000	92.4	59.4
North Carolina	2,005,955	550,929	1,579,000	305,000	78.7	55.3
South Carolina	895,147	371,873	587,000	189,000	65.6	50.8
Tennessee	1,779,018	313,873	1,448,000	228,000	81.3	72.6
Texas	4,884,765	649,512	3,532,000	540,000	72.3	83.1
Virginia	1,876,167	436,720	1,256,000	255,000	67.0	58.4
TOTALS	20,096,735	5,016,100	15,702,000	3,112,000	78.1	62.0

* Reflects estimates more recent than figures in county-by-county table.

Credit: Voter Registration in the South
Summer 1968
Voter Education Project
Southern Regional Council, 5 Forsyth Street, Atlanta, Ga., 30303

TABLE 19

Negro Participation on Local Draft Boards in Southern States in 1967 and 1968

	1967	1968		1967	1968
Alabama	0	3	Mississippi	0	0
Arkansas	0	35	Missouri	1	28
Florida	3	29	North Carolina	7	16
Georgia	2	17	South Carolina	1	12
Kansas	0	9	Tennessee	11	20
Kentucky	2	7	Texas	8	26
Louisiana	0	40	Virginia	12	27

As of August 1968, a total of 822 Negroes served on local boards across the country as compared to 278 at the start of 1967. In the calendar year 1967, 345 Negroes were added to local boards.

The 18-month study reflects nearly a 300 per cent increase in the number of Negroes serving on local boards and the number continues to grow.

TABLE 20

Negro Participation in the Armed Forces, 1968

Over 300,000 Negroes were on active duty with the armed forces as of September 30, 1968; they represent 8.8 per cent of the total active forces. Negro participation by service, by number and per cent, was as follows:

	Officer	Enlisted	Total
Army	5,646 (3.4)	153,516 (11.4)	159,162 (10.5)
Navy	352 (0.4)	31,809 (4.8)	32,161 (4.3)
Marine Corps	196 (0.8)	32,055 (11.3)	32,251 (10.5)
Air Force	2,461 (1.8)	78,422 (10.3)	80,883 (9.0)
Defense Dept. Total	8,655 (2.1)	295,802 (9.7)	304,457 (8.8)

TABLE 21
Negro Participation in Southeast Asia, 1966–68
(Vietnam, Thailand and Nearby Off-Shore Waters)

	December 31, 1966*		December 31, 1967		September 30, 1968	
	Total	Negro (%)	Total	Negro (%)	Total	Negro (%)
Army	242,043	30,603 (12.6)	337,234	37,456 (11.1)	382,493	45,121 (11.8)
Navy	57,840	3,108 (5.4)	69,336	3,228 (4.7)	82,435	3,956 (4.8)
Marine Corps	67,601	5,461 (8.0)	78,374	6,462 (8.2)	80,164	8,554 (10.7)
Air Force	52,006	5,379 (10.3)	83,188	8,758 (10.5)	90,241	9,582 (10.6)
Defense Dept. Total	419,490	44,551 (10.6)	568,132	55,904 (9.8)	635,333	67,213 (10.6)

* Excluding personnel in Thailand

TABLE 22
Deaths of Negro Personnel by Hostile Action in Connection with the Conflict in Vietnam, 1961–68

	1961–1966		1967		Jan. through Sept. 1968		Total	
	Total	Negro (%)	Total	Negro (%)	Total	Negro (%)	Total	Negro (%)
Army	4,156	832 (20.0)	5,443	733 (13.5)	7,941	1,057 (13.3)	17,540	2,622 (14.9)
Navy	199	1 (0.5)	311	9 (2.9)	390	10 (2.6)	900	20 (2.2)
Marine Corps	2,027	223 (11.0)	3,452	441 (12.8)	4,055	576 (14.2)	9,534	1,240 (13.0)
Air Force	262	4 (1.5)	172	9 (5.2)	153	2 (1.3)	587	15 (2.6)
Defense Dept. Total	6,644	1,060 (16.0)	9,378	1,192 (12.7)	12,540*	1,645 (13.1)	28,562	3,897 (13.6)

* Coast Guard: 1

TABLE 23
Small Business Administration Loans
(Dollars in Millions)

	Fiscal Year 1968 [1]		Fiscal Year to Date 1968 [2]		Fiscal Year to Date 1969 [3]	
	Number	Amount	Number	Amount	Number	Amount
Total loans	13,157	623.2	8,555	405.9	9,499	437.2
Minority loans	1,676	29.9	981	16.9	2,580	55.2
Per cent	13	5.0	11	4.0	27	13.0

[1] July 1, 1967—June 30, 1968

[2] July 1, 1967—February 29, 1968

[3] July 1, 1968—February 28, 1969

Total SBA plans include Regular Business Loans, Equal Opportunity Loans, Development Company Loans and Displaced Business Loans.

Total Loans Approved: Fiscal year 1969 activity surpassed fiscal year 1968 for comparable periods.

Current month and fiscal year to date actual is below plan.

Minority Loans Approved: Fiscal year 1969 actual exceeds fiscal year 1968 for comparable periods. Plans have not been attained.

Total Private Sector Participation: Fiscal year 1969 actual is greater than fiscal year 1968. Plans have not been achieved.

Total Private Sector Participation: Actual for the current month and fiscal year to date is below plan.

Number of Banks Participating: 719 banks participated in 911 total private sector loans. 180 banks participated in 257 minority private sector loans.

TABLE 24

Major League Baseball, Selected Individual Leaders †

American League Rank	Name and Team		National League Rank	Name and Team	
	Batting				
4.	Willie Horton, Det.	.285	4.	Alex Johnson, Cin.	.312
13.	Frank Robinson, Bal.	.268	5.	Curt Flood, St. L.	.301
14.	Roy White, N.Y.	.267	6.	Cleon Jones, N.Y.	.297
15.	Reggie Smith, Bos.	.265	8.	Willie McCovey, S.F.	.293
25.	Reggie Jackson, Oak.	.250	11t.	Lee May, Cin.	.290
	Runs Batted In				
4t.	Willie Horton, Det.	85	1.	Willie McCovey, S.F.	105*
8t.	Reggie Jackson, Oak.	74	2t.	Billy Williams, Chi.	98
10.	Reggie Smith, Bos.	69	5.	Richie Allen, Phil.	90
14t.	Roy White, N.Y.	62	6.	Donn Clendenon, Pitt.	87
17t.	Joe Foy, Bos.	60	7.	Hank Aaron, Atl.	86
	Hits				
6t.	Roy White, N.Y.	154	4.	Alex Johnson, Cin.	188
13.	Reggie Smith, Bos.	148	5.	Curt Flood, St. L.	186
21t.	Reggie Jackson, Oak.	138	6t.	Billy Williams, Chi.	185
27.	Horace Clarke, N.Y.	133	8.	Lou Brock, St. L.	184
33t.	Joe Foy, Bos.	116	10t.	Hank Aaron, Atl.	174
			10t.	Maury Wills, Pitt.	174
	Doubles				
1t.	Reggie Smith, Bos.	37*	1.	Lou Brock, St. L.	46*
9.	Frank Robinson, Bal.	27	6.	Hank Aaron, Atl.	33
24t.	Willie Horton, Det.	20	7t.	Alex Johnson, Cin.	32
24t.	Roy White, N.Y.	20	7t.	Lee May, Cin.	32
28t.	Joe Foy, Bos.	18	9.	Billy Williams, Chi.	30
	Triples				
7t.	Roy White, N.Y.	7	1.	Lou Brock, St. L.	14*
13t.	Reggie Jackson, Oak	6	3.	Willie Davis, L.A.	10
17t.	Reggie Smith, Bos.	5	4.	Richie Allen, Phil.	9
32t.	Willie Horton, Det.	2	5.	Billy Williams, Chi.	8
32t.	Joe Foy, Bos.	2	8t.	Donn Clendenon, Pitt.	6
			8t.	Alex Johnson, Cin.	6
			8t.	Vada Pinson, Cin.	6
			8t.	Maury Wills, Pitt.	6

American League Rank	Name and Team		National League Rank	Name and Team	
	Home Runs				
2.	Willie Horton, Det.	36	1.	Willie McCovey, S.F.	36*
4.	Reggie Jackson, Oak.	29	2.	Richie Allen, Phil.	33
15t.	Roy White, N.Y.	17	3.	Ernie Banks, Chi.	32
18t.	Frank Robinson, Bal.	15	4.	Billy Williams, Chi.	30
18t.	Reggie Smith, Bos.	15	5.	Hank Aaron, Atl.	29
	Runs Scored				
3t.	Roy White, N.Y.	89	4.	Lou Brock, St. L.	92
7.	Reggie Jackson, Oak.	82	5.	Billy Williams, Chi.	91
10t.	Reggie Smith, Bos.	78	6.	Richie Allen, Phil.	87
16.	Frank Robinson, Bal.	69	7t.	Willie Davis, L.A.	86
17.	Willie Horton, Det.	68	9.	Jim Wynn, Hou.	85
	Slugging				
2.	Willie Horton, Det.	.543	1.	Willie McCovey, S.F.	.545*
8.	Reggie Jackson, Oak.	.452	2.	Richie Allen, Phil.	.520
10.	Frank Robinson, Bal.	.444	3.	Billy Williams, Chi.	.500
11.	Reggie Smith, Bos.	.430	4.	Hank Aaron, Atl.	.498
14.	Roy White, N.Y.	.414	5.	Willie Mays, S.F.	.488
	Stolen Bases				
5.	Joe Foy, Bos.	26	1.	Lou Brock, St. L.	62*
7.	Reggie Smith, Bos.	22	2.	Maury Wills, Pitt.	52
8t.	Horace Clarke, N.Y.	20	3.	Willie Davis, L.A.	36
8t.	Roy White, N.Y.	20	4.	Hank Aaron, Atl.	28
13t.	Reggie Jackson, Oak.	14	5.	Cleon Jones, N.Y.	23
	Strikeouts				
12t.	Earl Wilson, Det.	168	1.	Bob Gibson, St. L.	268*
15.	John Odom, Oak.	143	2.	Ferguson Jenkins, Chi.	260
	Most Valuable Player (First place votes in parentheses)				
4.	Willie Horton, Det.	102	1.	Bob Gibson, St. L. (14)	242
12.	Roy White, N.Y.	17	3.	Willie McCovey, S.F.	135
17t.	Reggie Jackson, Oak.	8	4.	Curt Flood, St. L.	116

* League leader
† To qualify, batters must have a minimum of 502 plate appearances and pitchers a minimum of 162 innings pitched
t: Tied for that position in the standings

TABLE 25

Major League Baseball, Awards and Honors

Major League All-Star team as compiled by the Associated Press and United Press International: Willie McCovey, San Francisco (NL), 1B; Curt Flood, St. Louis (NL), OF; Bob Gibson, St. (NL), P

Major League Rookie All-Star team as compiled by Topps Chewing Gum Company: Bobby Bonds, San Francisco (NL), OF

Cy Young Award to the National League Pitcher of the Year: Bob Gibson, St. Louis

Sporting News Award to the National League Pitcher of the Year: Bob Gibson, St. Louis

TABLE 26

Major League Baseball, Record Performances

Major League Records Set by National League Players

Most Home Runs, Right-Handed Batter (lifetime): 587, Willie Mays, San Francisco*

Most Years Leading League, Double Plays by a First Baseman: 5, Donn Clendenon, Pittsburgh

Most Years, Consecutive, Leading League in Fewest Errors by an Outfielder: 5, Lou Brock, St. Louis*

Major League Records Tied by National League Players

Most Years, 150 or more Games: 13, Hank Aaron, Atlanta

Most Years, 300 or more Total Bases: 13, Hank Aaron, Atlanta

Most Years, 20 or more Home Runs: 16, Willie Mays, San Francisco

Most Home Runs, 2 Consecutive Games: 5, Billy Williams, Chicago (September 8–10)

Most Base on Balls, Intentional (game): 3, Richie Allen, Philadelphia (August 16)

Most Home Runs, Consecutive At Bats by a Pinch-Hitter: 2, Ed Charles, New York (June 1–2)

Most Years Leading League in Fewest Errors by an Outfielder: 5, Lou Brock, St. Louis

Most Years, Consecutive, Leading League, Double Plays by a First Baseman: 4, Donn Clendenon, Pittsburgh

Major League Record Set by American League Player

Most Major League Parks, one or more Home Runs: 26, Frank Robinson, Baltimore

TABLE 26—(Continued)

National League Records Set

Most Years, 600 or more At Bats: 10, Hank Aaron, Atlanta*

Most Home Runs (lifetime): 587, Willie Mays, San Francisco*

Most Home Runs (lifetime), Outfielder: 587, Willie Mays, San Francisco

Most Years, Consecutive, 20 or more Home Runs: 15, Willie Mays, San Francisco*

Most Games, 2 or more Home Runs (lifetime): 58, Willie Mays, San Francisco*

Lowest Earned Run Average (season): 1.12, Bob Gibson, St. Louis (305 innings)

National League Records Tied

Most Years, 100 or more Extra Bases on Long Hits: 14, Hank Aaron, Atlanta

Most Years, 200 or more Strikeouts by a Pitcher: 6, Bob Gibson, St. Louis

Most Shutout Games Won (month): 5, Bob Gibson, St. Louis (June)

Most Base on Balls (game): 5, Richie Allen, Philadelphia (August 16)

Miscellaneous Records (1968) by National League Players

Most Total Bases: 321, Billy Williams, Chicago

Fewest Double Plays Grounded into: 3, Willie Davis, Los Angeles

Longest Winning Streak: 15 games, Bob Gibson, St. Louis, June 2 through August 19

Most Shutouts: 13, Bob Gibson, St. Louis

Most Games Started: 40, Ferguson Jenkins, Chicago

* Extended own Major League Record

(American League records courtesy the American League of Professional Baseball Clubs, Howe News Bureau, Statisticians; National League records courtesy the National League of Professional Baseball Clubs, Elias Sports Bureau, Statisticians)

TABLE 27

1967–68 Major-College Basketball, Selected Individual Leaders †

Scoring

Name and Team	Rank	Games	FG	FT	Pts.	Avg.
Calvin Murphy, Niagara	2	24	337	242	916	38.2
Elvin Hayes, Houston	3	33	519*	176	1214*	36.8
Rich Travis, Okla. City	4	27	324	160	808	29.9
Simmie Hill, W. Tex. St.	7	21	237	99	573	27.3
Shaler Halimon, Utah St.	8	25	256	159	671	26.8

*Led nation

TABLE 27—(Continued)

Field-Goal Percentage**

Name and Team	Rank	Games	FGA	FG	Pct.
Joe Allen, Bradley	1	28	394	258	.655*
Lew Alcindor, UCLA	3t	28	480	294	.613
Westley Unseld, Louisville	3t	28	382	234	.613
Don Sidle, Oklahoma	6	26	321	189	.589
Elnardo Webster, St. Peter's	7	28	477	279	.585

*Led nation
**Minimum 130 field goals scored

Rebounds

Name and Team	Rank	Games	No.	Avg.
Garfield Smith, E. Ky.	2	24	472	19.7
Elvin Hayes, Houston	3	33	624*	18.9
Westley Unseld, Louisville	4	28	513	18.3
Larry Lewis, St. Francis	6	25	443	17.7
Ed Wilson, Idaho St.	7	24	420	17.5

*Led nation

† Approximately 190 college basketball teams, which play most of their games against each other, are classified as "Major-College" or University Division teams. They represent the field of so-called "big time" college basketball as judged by class of competition rather than seasonal strength. The basketball teams of all other four-year, accredited NCAA-member colleges comprise the College Division field.

TABLE 28

1967–68 Major-College Basketball, Awards and Honors

Consensus All-America Team

(Compiled from the first and second All-America teams of Associated Press, United Press International, NBA Coaches and the Basketball Writers Association)

Lew Alcindor, UCLA	Calvin Murphy, Niagara
Lucius Allen, UCLA	Don Smith, Iowa State
Elvin Hayes, Houston	Westley Unseld, Louisville
Merv Jackson, Utah	Mike Warren, UCLA
Bob Lanier, St. Bonaventure	Jo Jo White, Kansas

Other Honors

Player of the Year (Helms Foundation): Lew Alcindor, UCLA
Player of the year (AP and UPI): Elvin Hayes, Houston

TABLE 29

1967–68 National Basketball Association, Selected Individual Leaders

Scoring

Name and Team	Rank	Games	FG	FT	Pts.	Avg.
Dave Bing, Det.	1	79	835	472	2142*	27.1
Elgin Baylor, L.A.	2	77	757	488	2002	26.0
Wilt Chamberlain, Phil.	3	82	819	354	1992	24.3
Earl Monroe, Balt.	4	82	742	507	1991	24.3
Hal Greer, Phil.	5	82	777	422	1976	24.1

* League leader
Best performance (game): 68 points, Wilt Chamberlain, Philadelphia vs. Chicago, 12/16/67
Highest average (season): 29.2, Oscar Robertson, Cincinnati

Field-Goal Percentage**

Name and Team	Rank	FG	Att.	Pct.
Wilt Chamberlain, Phil.	1	819	1377*	.595*
Walt Bellamy, N.Y.	2	511	944	.541
Oscar Robertson, Cin.	6	660	1321	.500
Tom Hawkins, L.A.	7	389	779	.499
Bob Boozer, Chi.	10t	622	1265	.492

* League leader
** Minimum 220 field goals scored
Most field goals (season): 835, Dave Bing, Detroit
Most field goals (game): 30 (40 attempts), Wilt Chamberlain, Philadelphia vs. Chicago, 12/16/67

Free-Throw Percentage**

Name and Team	Rank	FT	Att.	Pct.
Oscar Robertson, Cin.	1	567*	660	.873*
Adrian Smith, Cin.	5	320	386	.829
Sam Jones, Bos.	6	311	376	.827
Flynn Robinson, Chi.	7	288	352	.818
Cazzie Russell, N.Y.	10	282	349	.808

* League leader
** Minimum of 220 free throws
Most attempts (season): 932, Wilt Chamberlain, Philadelphia
Most attempts (game): 20, Zelmo Beaty, St. Louis vs. Seattle, 12/3/67

TABLE 29—(Continued)

Rebounds

Name and Team	Rank	Games	No.	Avg.
Wilt Chamberlain, Phil.	1	82	1952*	23.8*
Bill Russell, Bos.	3	78	1451	18.6
Nate Thurmond, S.F.	5	51	1121	22.0
Ray Scott, Balt.	6	81	1111	13.7
Bill Bridges, St. L.	7	82	1102	13.4

* League leader
Best performance (game): 38, Wilt Chamberlain, Philadelphia vs. Seattle, 12/20/67

Assists

Name and Team	Rank	Games	No.	Avg.
Wilt Chamberlain, Phil.	1	82	702*	8.6
Len Wilkens, St. L.	2	82	679	8.3
Oscar Robertson, Cin.	3	65	633	9.7*
Dave Bing, Det.	4	79	509	6.4
Walt Hazzard, Sea.	5	79	493	6.2

* League leader
Best performance (game): 21, Wilt Chamberlain, Philadelphia vs. Detroit, 2/2/68

TABLE 30

1967–68 National Basketball Association, Awards and Honors

Official NBA All-Star Team

First Team	Second Team
Wilt Chamberlain, Philadelphia (C)	Bill Russell, Boston (C)
Dave Bing, Detroit (G)	Hal Greer, Philadelphia (G)
Oscar Robertson, Cincinnati (G)	Willis Reed, New York (F)
Elgin Baylor, Los Angeles (F)	

Most Valuable Player (Podoloff Cup): Wilt Chamberlain, Philadelphia

Official NBA All-Rookie Team

Rob Rule, Seattle (C)
Walt Frazier, New York (G)
Earl Monroe, Baltimore (G)
Al Tucker, Seattle (F)

Rookie of the Year: Earl Monroe, Baltimore

TABLE 31

1967–68 National Basketball Association, Record Performances

Records Set

Most Consecutive Games without Disqualification on Personals: 706, Wilt Chamberlain, Philadelphia

Most Points Scored (lifetime): 25,434, Wilt Chamberlain, Philadelphia (9 seasons)

Most Assists by a Center: 702, Wilt Chamberlain, Philadelphia (the first time a center has led the NBA in this category)

TABLE 32

1967–68 American Basketball Association, Selected Individual Leaders

Scoring

Name and Team	Rank	Games	2-Pt. FG	3-Pt. FG	FT	Pts.	Avg.
Connie Hawkins, Pitt.	1	70	633	2	603	1875*	26.79*
Levern Tart, Oak.-N.J.	3	73	632	1	451	1718	23.53
Larry Jones, Den.	5	76	594	8	530	1742	22.92
Mel Daniels, Minn.	6	78	668	1	390	1729	22.17
Willie Somerset, Hou.	7	61	434	33	359	1326	21.74

* League leader

2-Point Field Goals

Name and Team	Rank	FG	Att.	Pct.
Tom Washington, Pitt.	1	310	594	.522*
Connie Hawkins, Pitt.	2	633	1214	.521
Cincy Powell, Dal.	8	532	1085	.490
Julian Hammond, Den.	9	224	458	.489
James Jones, N.O.	13	549	1172	.468

* League leader
Most field goals attempted (season): 1635, Mel Daniels, Minnesota
Most field goals scored (season): 668, Mel Daniels, Minnesota
Most field goals scored (game): 19, Larry Jones, Denver vs. Oakland, 11/28/67

TABLE 32—(Continued)

3-Point Field Goals

Name and Team	Rank	FG	Att.	Pct.
Charles Vaughn, Pitt.	3	137	410	.344
Les Selvage, Ana.	5	147*	461*	.320
Ben Warley, Ana.	6	52	166	.313
Tony Jackson, N.J.	8	91	302	.301
Charlie Williams, Pitt.	9	51	178	.287

* League leader
Most field goals attempted (game): 26, Les Selvage, Anaheim vs. Denver, 2/15/68
Most field goals scored (game): 10, Les Selvage, Anaheim vs. Denver, 2/15/68

Free Throws

Name and Team	Rank	FT	Att.	Pct.
Tony Jackson, N.J.	4	450	543	.829
Mel Nowell, N.J.	5	176	213	.826
Ben Warley, Ana.	12	313	389	.804
Steve Jones, Oak.	15	186	233	.798
Fred Lewis, Ind.	16	465	583	.797

Most free throws attempted (season): 789, Connie Hawkins, Pittsburgh
Most free throws made (season): 603, Connie Hawkins, Pittsburgh
Most free throws attempted (game): 29, Tony Jackson, New Jersey vs. Kentucky, 11/27/67
Most free throws made (game): 24, Tony Jackson, New Jersey vs. Kentucky, 11/27/67

Rebounds

Name and Team	Rank	Games	Off.	Def.	Tot.	Avg.
Mel Daniels, Minn.	1	78	502*	711*	1213*	15.6*
Connie Hawkins, Pitt.	2	70	368	577	945	13.5
Ira Harge, Pitt.-Oak.	4	82	357	681	1038	12.7
Jim Hadnot, Oak.	6	77	303	633	936	12.2
Jim Ligon, Ky.	7	78	370	559	929	12.2

* League leader
Most offensive rebounds (game): 16, Mel Daniels, Minnesota vs. New Orleans, 12/28/67
16, Mel Daniels, Minnesota vs. Pittsburgh, 1/30/ 68
Most defensive rebounds (game): 23, Reggie Harding, Indiana vs. New Jersey, 2/8/68
Most rebounds (game): 32, Ira Harge, Oakland vs. Pittsburgh, 2/9/68

TABLE 32—(Continued)

Assists

Name and Team	Rank	Games	No.	Avg.
Connie Hawkins, Pitt.	4	70	320	4.6
Roger Brown, Ind.	5	76	327	4.3
Maurice McHartley, Dal.	6	58	230	4.0
Willie Somerset, Hou.	8	61	225	3.7
Larry Jones, Den.	11	76	270	3.6

TABLE 33

1967–68 American Basketball Association, Awards and Honors

Official ABA All-Star Team

First Team	Second Team
Mel Daniels, Minnesota (C)	Roger Brown, Indiana (F)
Larry Jones, Denver (G)	Cincy Powell, Dallas (F)
Charlie Williams, Pittsburgh (G)	
Connie Hawkins, Pittsburgh (F)	

Most Valuable Player: Connie Hawkins, Pittsburgh

Official ABA All-Rookie Team

Mel Daniels, Minnesota (C)
James Jones, New Orleans (G)
Tom Washington, Pittsburgh (F)

Rookie of the Year: Mel Daniels, Minnesota

TABLE 34

1967–68 American Basketball Association, Record Performances

Records Set (season)

Best Percentage, 2-Point Field Goals Made (minimum 10 attempts): .92 (12 for 13), Tom Washington, Pittsburgh vs. Anaheim, 3/5/68

Best Percentage, 2-Point Field Goals Made (no minimum): 1.00 (8 for 8), Julian Hammond, Denver vs. Indiana, 11/12/67 and Willis Thomas, Anaheim vs. Oakland, 12/23/67

TABLE 34—(Continued)

Records Set (season)—Continued

Most Points Scored (quarter): 24, Les Selvage, Anaheim vs. Denver, 2/15/68
Most Points Scored (half): 41, Larry Jones, Denver vs. Oakland, 11/28/67
Most 2-Point Field Goals (consecutive): 16, Ben Warley, Anaheim vs. Houston, 2/12/68

Records Set (individual playoff games)

Most Points Scored: 47, Connie Hawkins, Pittsburgh vs. New Orleans, 4/25/68
Most 2-Point Field Goals Attempted: 34, Connie Hawkins, Pittsburgh vs. New Orleans, 4/25/68
Most 2-Point Field Goals Made: 17, Connie Hawkins, Pittsburgh vs. New Orleans, 4/25/68
Most 3-Point Field Goals Attempted: 15, Charles Vaughn, Pittsburgh vs. New Orleans, 4/20/68
Most Free Throws Attempted: 21, Les Hunter, Minnesota vs. Pittsburgh, 4/10/68
Most Offensive Rebounds: 17, Tom Washington, Pittsburgh vs. Minnesota, 4/6/68
Most Defensive Rebounds: 18, Tom Washington, Pittsburgh vs. Minnesota, 4/6/68
Most Rebounds: 35, Tom Washington, Pittsburgh vs. Minnesota, 4/6/68
Most Assists: 11, Don Freeman, Minnesota vs. Pittsburgh, 4/13/68

TABLE 35

Professional Boxing, Ring Magazine World Ratings

(As of December 31, 1968)

Heavyweights (over 175 pounds)
Champion: Cassius Clay, Houston, Tex.

1. Joe Frazier, Philadelphia, Pa.
2. Jimmy Ellis, Louisville, Ky.
5. Sonny Liston, Las Vegas, Nev.
7. Leotis Martin, Philadelphia, Pa.
9. Alvin Lewis, Detroit, Mich.
10. Floyd Patterson, New York, N.Y.

Light Heavyweights (not over 175 pounds)
Champion: Bob Foster, Washington, D.C.

1. Dick Tiger, Biafra
9. Eddie Jones, Los Angeles, Calif.
10. Harold Johnson, Philadelphia, Pa.

Middleweights (not over 160 pounds)

3. Stan Hayward, Philadelphia, Pa.
4. Emile Griffith, New York, N.Y.
10. Freddie Little, Las Vegas, Nev.

Welterweights (not over 147 pounds)
Champion: Curtis Cokes, Dallas, Tex.

2. Percy Pugh, New Orleans, La.

Junior Welterweights (not over 140 pounds)

3. Adolph Pruitt, St. Louis, Mo.

Lightweights (not over 135 pounds)

1. Ismael Laguna, Panama

Junior Lightweights (not over 130 pounds

2. Ruben Navarro, Los Angeles, Calif.
8. Don Johnson, Los Angeles, Calif.

Featherweights (not over 126 pounds)
Champion: Title vacant

1. Jose Legra, Spain
5. Dwight Hawkins, Los Angeles, Calif.

Bantamweights (not over 118 pounds)
Champion: Lionel Rose, Australia

Flyweights (not over 112 pounds)

5. Raton Mojica, Nicaragua

(Courtesy of *Ring* magazine)

TABLE 36

Professional Boxing, Selected Championship Fights

Light Heavyweights

May 24—Bob Foster, Washington, D.C., knocked out Dick Tiger, Biafra, 2:05 of the fourth round, to win the crown. The fight was held in Madison Square Garden and the referee was Mark Conn.

Middleweights

March 4—Nino Benvenuti, Italy, defeated Emile Griffith, Weehawken, N.J., in 15 rounds, unanimous decision. The fight was held in Madison Square Garden and the referee was John Lo Bianco.

Welterweights

April 16—Curtis Cokes, Dallas, Texas, knocked out Willie Ludick, South Africa, 0:34 of the fifth round, to retain the crown. The fight was held in Dallas and the referee was Lee Eskin.
October 21—Curtis Cokes, Dallas, Texas, defeated Ramon La Cruz, Argentina, in 15 rounds, unanimous decision, to retain the crown. The fight was held in New Orleans and the referee was Lucien Jubert.

Bantamweights

February 26—Lionel Rose, Australia, defeated Fighting Harada, Japan, in 15 rounds, unanimous decision, to retain the crown. The fight was held in Tokyo and the referee was Ko Toyama.
July 2—Lionel Rose, Australia, defeated Takeo Sakurai, Japan, 15 rounds, to retain the crown. The fight was held in Tokyo and the referee was Nike Pope.
December 2—Lionel Rose, Australia, defeated Chucho Castillo, Mexico, 15 rounds, split decision, to retain the crown. The fight was held in the Forum, Inglewood, California, and the referee was Dick Young.

(Courtesy of *Ring* magazine)

TABLE 37

Boxing: Awards, Honors and Records

Professional

Ring Title Belts: Lionel Rose (Featherweight Champion)
Bob Foster (Light Heavyweight Champion)
Edward J. Neil Trophy: Bob Foster
Ring's "Round of the Year": May 24, Dick Tiger vs. Bob Foster, 4th round
Ring's "Most Controversial Contest": September 14, Ellis decision over Floyd Patterson in Göteborg, Sweden
Ring's "Fight of the Year": October 25, Dick Tiger vs. Frank De Paula

Amateur

Gustavus Town Kirby Sportsmanship Award: Albert Robinson, silver medalist in the featherweight division, 1968 Olympics

(See Table 44, page 427, for Olympic boxing performances)

TABLE 38

Major-College Football, Selected Individual Leaders †

Rushing**

Name and Team	Rank	Games	Plays	Yards	TDs
O. J. Simpson, So. Cal.	1	10	355	1709*	22*
Eugene Morris, W. Tex. St.	2	10	262	1571	17
Paul Gipson, Houston	3	10	242	1550	13
Art Malone, Arizona St.	5	10	235	1431	15
Ron Johnson, Michigan	6	10	255	1391	19
Ron Poe James, New Mex. St. ..	8	10	225	1291	12
Roland Moss, Toledo	11	10	267	1145	13
Leo Taylor, N. Tex. St.	15	10	246	1017	9
Leroy Keyes, Purdue	16	10	193	1003	14

* Led nation
** Those with over 1,000 yards

Passing

Name and Team	Rank	Games	Att.	Comp.	Int.	Pct.	Yards	TDs
Mike Stripling, Tulsa	8	10	347	164	15	.473	1968	8
Fred Summers, Wake For. ..	21	10	250	125	25	.500	1664	9

Pass Receiving

Name and Team	Rank	Games	Cght	Yards	TDs
Jerry Levias, SMU	2t	10	80	1131	8
Gene Washington, Stanford	4	10	71	1117	8
Louis Thomas, Utah	11t	10	60	1006	7
Eddie Hinton, Oklahoma	11t	10	60	967	6
Oscar Patrick, W. Va.	19t	10	50	770	5
Ron Gardin, Arizona	27t	10	48	892	4
Ron Shanklin, N. Tex. St.	31t	10	47	724	8*

* Led nation in 1967 with 13 TD receptions for a two-year total of 21. He needs 12 in 1969 to set a major-college record
t: Tied for that position in the standings

TABLE 38—(Continued)

Scoring

Name and Team	Rank	Games	TDs	XPT	PTs
O. J. Simpson, So. Cal. ..	2	10	22*	0	132
Ron Johnson, Michigan ..	4	10	19	2	116
Eugene Morris, W. Tex. St.	5t	10	19	0	114
Art Malone, Arizona St. ..	8t	10	16	0	96
Leroy Keyes, Purdue	12	10	15	0	90

* Led nation

Total Offense

Name and Team	Rank	Games	Plays	Yards	TDR*
Mike Stripling, Tulsa	8	10	465	2275	13
Cleve Bryant, Ohio U.	9	10	372	2258	22
Fred Summers, Wake For. .	13	10	409	2103	16
O. J. Simpson, So. Cal. ...	28	10	358	1724	22

* Touchdowns-responsible-for are player's TDs rushed and passed for

† Approximately 115 college football teams, which play most of their games against each other, are classified as "Major-College" or University Division teams. They represent the field of so-called "big-time" college football as judged by class competition rather than seasonal strength. The football teams of all other four-year, accredited NCAA-member colleges comprise the College Division field.

TABLE 39

Major-College Football, Awards and Honors

The consensus All-America team as compiled from the first and second All-America teams of the American Football Coaches Association, the Football Writers Association of America, the Associated Press, United Press International and the Newspaper Enterprise Association: Paul Gipson (HB), Houston; Joe Greene (DT), North Texas State; Ron Johnson (HB), Michigan; Leroy Keyes (HB-CB), Purdue and Jerry Levias (E-FL), Southern Methodist University.

Player of the Year Awards won by O. J. Simpson, Southern California halfback: Heisman Trophy, Maxwell Trophy, Sporting News, American Football Coaches Association, National Sportscasters and Sportswriters Association, United Press International (Back of the Year) and the Helms Foundation.

TABLE 40

National Football League, Selected Individual Leaders

Rushing

Name and Team	Rank	Att.	Yards	Avg.	Long	TDs
Leroy Kelly, Cleve.	1	248*	1239*	5.0	65	16*
Gale Sayers, Chi.	5	138	856	6.2*	63	2
Don Perkins, Dall.	6	191	836	4.4	28	4
Willis Crenshaw, St. L.	7	203	813	4.0	66	6
Don McCall, N.O.	11	155	637	4.1	48	4

* League leader
Best performance: 205 yards in 24 attempts, Gale Sayers, Chicago vs. Green Bay, 11/3

Pass Receiving

Name and Team	Rank	No.	Yards	Avg.	Long	TDs
Clifton McNeil, S.F.	1	71*	994	14.0	65	7
Roy Jefferson, Pitt.	2	58	1074*	18.5	62	11
Bob Hayes, Dall.	5	53	909	17.2	54	10
Paul Warfield, Cleve.	6	50	1067	21.3	65	12*
Charlie Taylor, Wash.	8	48	650	13.5	47	5

* League leader
Best performance: 11 for 199 yards, 4 TDs, Roy Jefferson, Pittsburgh vs. Atlanta, 11/3
Longest: 99 yards, TD, Gerry Allen, Washington vs. Chicago, 9/15
Highest average gain: 23.5, Homer Jones, New York

Scoring

Name and Team	Rank	TD R	TD P	Tot.	Points
Leroy Kelly, Cleve.	1	16*	4	20*	120*
Bob Hayes, Dall.	13t	2	10	12	72
Roy Jefferson, Pitt.	13t	1	11	12	72
Paul Warfield, Cleve.	13t	0	12*	12	72
Willie Richardson, Balt.	22	0	8	8	48

* League leader
t: Tied for that position in the standings
Best performance: 24 points (4 TDs), Roy Jefferson, Pittsburgh vs. Atlanta, 11/3
24 points (4 TDs), Leroy Kelly, Cleveland vs. New York, 12/1

Punt Returns

Name and Team	Rank	No.	Yards	Avg.	Long	TDs
Bob Hayes, Dall.	1	15	312	20.8*	90	2*
Alvin Haymond, Phil.	2	15	201	13.4	54	1
Charlie West, Minn.	4	20	201	10.1	98*	1
Roy Jefferson, Pitt.	5	28*	274	9.8	80	1
Timmy Brown, Balt.	8	16	125	7.8	25	0

* League leader
Longest: 98 yards, TD, Charlie West, Minnesota vs. Washington, 11/3

Kickoff Returns

Name and Team	Rank	No.	Yards	Avg.	Long	TDs
Preston Pearson, Balt.	1	15	527	35.1*	102*	2*
Ron Smith, L.A.	2	26	718	27.6	94	1
Gale Sayers, Chi.	3	17	461	27.1	46	0
Lem Barney, Det.	5	25	670	26.8	98	1
Charlie West, Minn.	6	22	576	26.2	82	0

* League leader
Longest: 102 yards, TD, Preston Pearson, Baltimore vs. Detroit, 11/10

Interceptions

Name and Team	Rank	No.	Yards	Long	TDs
Willie Williams, N.Y.	1	10*	103	24	0
Kermit Alexander, S.F.	2	9	155	66	1
Ben Davis, Cleve.	3t	8	162*	44	0
Carl Lockhart, N.Y.	3t	8	130	72	2*
Brig Owens, Wash.	3t	8	109	38	0

* League leader
t: Tied for that position in the standings
Longest: 96 yards, TD, Rosey Taylor, Chicago vs. Philadelphia, 10/20

TABLE 41

American Football League, Selected Individual Leaders

Rushing

Name and Team	Rank	Att.	Yards	Avg.	Long	TDs
Paul Robinson, Cin.	1	238*	1023*	4.3	87*	8*
Robert Holmes, K.C.	2	174	866	5.0	76	7
Hewritt Dixon, Oak.	3	206	865	4.2	28	2
Matt Snell, N.Y.	6	179	747	4.2	60	6
Jim Nance, Bos.	8	177	593	3.4	30	4

* League leader
Best performance: 187 yards in 28 attempts, Hewritt Dixon, Oakland vs. Houston, 9/29

Passing

Name and Team	Rank	Att.	Comp.	% Comp.	Yds.	TDs	LP	Int.	% Int.	Av. Gain
Marlin Briscoe, Den.	7	224	93	41.5	1589	14	66	13	5.8	7.09

Pass Receiving

Name and Team	Rank	No.	Yards	Avg.	Long	TDs
Warren Wells, Oak.	6	53	1137	21.5	94*	11*
Alvin Reed, Hou.	9	46	747	16.2	60	5
Haven Moses, Buff.	11	42	633	15.1	55	2
Hewritt Dixon, Oak.	13	38	360	9.5	41	2
Eric Crabtree, Den.	15	35	601	17.2	72	5

* League leader
Best performance: 10 for 163 yards, 1 TD, Warren Wells, Oakland vs. Denver, 12/8

Scoring

Name and Team	Rank	TD R	TD P	Tot.	Points
Warren Wells, Oak.	6	1	11*	12*	72
Paul Robinson, Cin.	14	8*	1	9	54
Robert Holmes, K.C.	18t	7	0	7	42
Matt Snell, N.Y.	18t	6	1	7	42
Mike Garrett, K.C.	27	3	3	6	36

* League leader
t: Tied for that position in the standings

Punt Returns

Name and Team	Rank	No.	Yards	Avg.	Long	TDs
Noland Smith, K.C.	1	18	270	15.0*	80	1
George Atkinson, Oak.	2	36*	490*	13.6	86	2*
Les Duncan, S.D.	3	18	206	11.4	95*	1
Floyd Little, Den.	4	24	261	10.9	67	1
Larry Carwell, Hou.	5	27	227	8.4	32	0

* League leader

Kickoff Returns

Name and Team	Rank	No.	Yards	Avg.	Long	TDs
George Atkinson, Oak.	1	32	802	25.1*	60	0
Floyd Little, Den.	2	26	649	25.0	89	0
Zeke Moore, Hou.	4	32	787	24.6	45	0
Noland Smith, K.C.	6	23	549	23.9	37	0
Les Duncan, S.D.	7	25	586	23.4	53	0

* League leader

Interceptions

Name and Team	Rank	No.	Yards	Long	TDs
Dave Grayson, Oak.	1	10*	195	54	1
Johnny Sample, N.Y.	3t	7	88	39	1
Leroy Mitchell, Bos.	3t	7	41	20	0
George Byrd, Buff.	5t	6	76	53	1
Ken Houston, Hou.	7t	5	160	66	2*
Joe Beauchamp, S.D.	7t	5	114	35	2*
Bobby Bell, K.C.	7t	5	95	50	0
Kenny Graham, S.D.	7t	5	87	42	0
Willie Mitchell, K.C.	7t	5	46	46	0

* League leader
t: Tied for that position in the standings

TABLE 42

Professional Football, Awards and Honors

Consensus All-Star Teams*

Pos.	National Football League Name and Team	American Football League Name and Team
	Offense	
SE	Bob Hayes, Dallas Paul Warfield, Cleveland	
TE	John Mackey, Baltimore	Alvin Reed, Houston
OT	Charlie Cowen, Los Angeles Bob Brown, Philadelphia Ernie McMillan, St. Louis	Winston Hill, New York
OG	George Seals, Chicago	Gene Upshaw, Oakland
OB	Leroy Kelly, Cleveland Don Perkins, Dallas Gale Sayers, Chicago	Hewritt Dixon, Oakland Robert Holmes, Kansas City Paul Robinson, Cincinnati
FL	Roy Jefferson, Pittsburgh Clifton McNeil, San Francisco Willie Richardson, Baltimore	
	Defense	
DE	Carl Eller, Minnesota Deacon Jones, Los Angeles Bubba Smith, Baltimore	Rich Jackson, Denver Ike Lassiter, Oakland Jerry Mays, Kansas City
DT	Walter Johnson, Cleveland Alan Page, Minnesota Jethro Pugh, Dallas	Houston Antwine, Boston Buck Buchanan, Kansas City Dan Birdwell, Oakland
MLB		Willie Lanier, Kansas City
OLB	Dave Robinson, Green Bay	Bobby Bell, Kansas City Frank Buncom, Cincinnati George Webster, Houston
CB	Kermit Alexander, San Francisco Lem Barney, Detroit Ben Davis, Cleveland Cornell Green, Dallas Bob Jeter, Green Bay Jim Johnson, San Francisco	Willie Brown, Oakland George Byrd, Buffalo Miller Farr, Houston Leroy Mitchell, Boston Johnny Sample, New York
S	Willie Wood, Green Bay	Dave Grayson, Oakland

* Based on the first and second all-star teams selected by Associated Press, United Press International, Newspaper Enterprise Association (Players' Poll) and the Professional Football Writers Association of America.

TABLE 42—(Continued)

Awards

Bert Bell Memorial Award by the Maxwell Club of Philadelphia to the NFL Player of the Year: Leroy Kelly, Cleveland Halfback

Newspaper Enterprise Association Award to the NFL Defensive Player of the Year: Deacon Jones, Los Angeles End

United Press International NFL Rookie of the Year: Earl McCullouch, Detroit Flanker

Newspaper Enterprise Association NFL Rookie of the Year: Earl McCullouch, Detroit Flanker

Associated Press NFL Offensive Rookie of the Year: Earl McCullouch, Detroit Flanker

Associated Press NFL Defensive Rookie of the Year: Claude Humphrey, Atlanta End

United Press International AFL Rookie of the Year: Paul Robinson, Cincinnati Halfback

AFL Coaches Rookie of the Year: Paul Robinson, Cincinnati Halfback (unanimous)

Sporting News AFL Rookie of the Year: Paul Robinson, Cincinnati Halfback

Associated Press AFL Offensive Rookie of the Year: Paul Robinson, Cincinnati Halfback

Associated Press AFL Defensive Rookie of the Year: George Atkinson, Oakland Cornerback

TABLE 43

Professional Football, Record Performances

Record Set by American League Football Player

More than 1000 Yards Rushing in a Rookie Season: 1023, Paul Robinson, Cincinnati

Records Tied by National League Football Players

Most Years Leading League in Touchdowns Scored by Rushing: 3, Leroy Kelly, Cleveland

Longest Pass Reception: 99 yards, Gerry Allen, Washington vs. Chicago, 9/15/68

Longest Punt Return: 98 yards, TD, Charlie West, Minnesota vs. Washington, 10/3/68

TABLE 44

1968 United States Olympic Team Personnel*

(Alphabetically by sport)

Name	Team	Event	Medal
	Men's Track and Field		
Robert Beamon	Houston Striders	Long Jump	Gold
Ralph H. Boston	So. Calif. Striders	Long Jump	Bronze
Reynaldo Brown	Compton H.S.	High Jump	——
John Carlos	Santa Clara V.Y.V.	200 Meters	Bronze
Edward J. Caruthers	Pacific Coast Club	High Jump	Silver
Leon Coleman	So. Calif. Striders	110 Meters High Hurdles	——
Willie Davenport	Southern Univ.	110 Meters High Hurdles	Gold
Lee Edward Evans	Santa Clara V.Y.V.	400 Meters 4 x 400 Relay	Gold Gold
Ronald Freeman	Arizona State	400 Meters 4 x 400 Relay	Bronze Gold
Charles Edward Greene	Cornhusker T.C.	100 Meters 4 x 400 Relay	Bronze Gold
Ervin Hall	Phila. Pioneer Club	110 Meters Hurdles	Silver
James Hines	Houston Striders	100 Meters 4 x 100 Relay	Gold Gold
George Larry James	Villanova Univ.	400 Meters 4 x 400 Relay	Silver Gold
Vincent Matthews	New York Pioneer Club	4 x 400 Relay	Gold
Charles Mays	Grand Street Boys Club	Long Jump	——
Captain Melvin Pender	U.S. Army	100 Meters 4 x 100 Relay	—— Gold
Louis Scott	Motor City Striders	5000 Meters	——
Ronnie Ray Smith	So. Calif. Striders	4 x 100 Relay	Gold
Thomas Smith	Santa Clara V.Y.V.	200 Meters	Gold
Norman Tate	New Jersey Astros	Triple Jump	——
Arthur Walker	Moorehouse Univ.	Triple Jump	——
Stanley V. Wright	Western Illinois Univ.	Assistant Coach	
Mrs. Margaret Johnson Bailes	Oregon Track Club	100 Meters 200 Meters 4 x 100 Relay	—— —— Gold
Estelle Baskerville	Tennessee St.	High Jump	——
Iris Davis	Tennessee St.	4 x 100 Relay	——
Julia Mae Dyer	Texas Southern	80 Meters Hurdles	——
Barbara Ferrell	Los Angeles Mercurettes	100 Meters 200 Meters 4 x 100 Relay	Silver —— Gold
Madeline Manning	Tennessee St.	800 Meters	Gold
Eleanor Inez Montgomery	Tennessee St.	High Jump	——
Mildrette Netter	Alcorn A&M	4 x 100 Relay	Gold
Mamie Rallins	Mayor Daley Youth Foundation	80 Meters Hurdles	——
Jarvis Scott	Los Angeles Mercurettes	400 Meters	——
Esther Stroy	Sports International	400 Meters	——
Wyomia Tyus	Tennessee St.	100 Meters 200 Meters 4 x 100 Relay	Gold —— Gold
Martha Rae Watson	Tennessee St.	Long Jump	——
Willye B. White	Mayor Daley Youth Foundation	Long Jump 4 x 100 Relay	——
Conrad A. Ford	New York City	Head Coach	——
	Basketball		
Spencer Haywood	Univ. of Detroit	Forward	Gold
Charles Scott	Univ. of No. Carolina	Forward	Gold
Joseph (Jo Jo) White	Kansas Univ.	Guard	Gold

TABLE 44—(Continued)

Boxing

Name	Team	Event	Medal
John Baldwin	Detroit, Mich.	Light Middleweight	Bronze
George Foreman	Pleasanton, Calif.	Heavyweight	Gold
Sam Goss	Trenton, N.J.	Bantamweight	——
Ronnie Harris	Kent State	Lightweight	Gold
Alfred Jones	E. Michigan Inst.	Middleweight	Bronze
Harland Marbley	Washington, D.C.	Light Flyweight	Bronze
Arthur Redden	U.S. Marine Corps	Light Heavyweight	——
Albert Robinson	U.S. Navy	Featherweight	Silver
James Wallington, Jr.	U.S. Army	Light Welterweight	Bronze
Robert Gault	Washington, D.C.	Head Coach	——
Fencing			
Uriah Jones	Santelli Salle	Foil	——

* In supporting their position that the 1968 Olympic Team was a single non-racially oriented unit representing the United States, the Olympic Committee would not identity, even for this publication, the Black athletes. This list, therefore, was compiled with the assistance of individuals present at the games. Any omissions, although unavoidable, are deeply regretted.

TABLE 45

AAU All-America Track Team

Event	Name	Team
60-yard dash	John Carlos	Santa Clara Valley Youth Village
	Bill Gaines	Santa Clara V.Y.V.
	Mel Pender	U.S. Army
100-meter dash	Charlie Greene	Husker A.A.
	Jim Hines	Houston Striders
	Mel Pender	U.S. Army
200-meter dash	John Carlos	Santa Clara V.Y.V.
	Tommie Smith	Santa Clara V.Y.V.
400-meter dash	Lee Evans	Santa Clara V.Y.V.
	Ron Freeman	Arizona State
	Larry James	Villanova
600-yard run	Lee Evans	Santa Clara V.Y.V.
	Jim Kemp	U.S. Army
	Martin McGrady	Santa Clara V.Y.V.
60-yard hurdles	Willie Davenport	Southern University
	Earl McCullouch	Southern California
110-meter high hurdles	Willie Davenport	Southern University
	Erv Hall	Villanova
	Earl McCullouch	Southern California
400-meter hurdles	Russ Rogers	Grand Street Boys
High jump	Ed Caruthers	Pacific Coast Club
Long jump	Bob Beamon	Houston Striders
	Ralph Boston	So. Calif. Striders
	Charlie Mays	Grand Street Boys
Triple jump	Charles Craig	Pacific Coast Club
	Dave Smith	Athens A.C.
	Art Walker	So. Calif. Striders

Picture Credits

The editor is grateful to the following for their aid in the search for unusual and interesting photographs with which to illustrate the text:

Key: T: Top; B: Bottom; L: Left; R: Right; C: Center

Anacostia Neighborhood Museum, Smithsonian Institution, Washington: 274

Ankers, Del, Washington: 353TL

Atlanta Daily World: 303

Chicago Daily Defender: 130

Department of Defense, Washington: 288, 292

Di Joseph, John, Washington: 120, 216TL, 310TR, 346TL, TR

Dintenfass, Terry, Inc., New York: 229B

Driskell, David C., Nashville, Tennessee: 227

Fax, Elton C., New York: 220

Gray, Vernard R., Washington: 236, 280, 345C, 357

Morgan, Norma, New York: 229T

Office of Economic Opportunity, Washington: 353 BL, R

Office of Economic Opportunity, Washington—Fletcher Drake: 351BR, 352T

Office of Economic Opportunity, Washington—Ralph Matthews, Jr.: 184

Office of Economic Opportunity, Washington—Michael D. Sullivan: 351BL

Prince, Arnold, New York: 228

Southern Cooperative Development Program, Lafayette, Louisiana—Keith McNeill: 192

United Press International: 2, 32, 38, 52, 62, 72, 108, 114, 144, 174, 200, 207, 212, 246, 250, 298, 317, 324, 330–32, 339–44, 345TL, TR, B, 346B, 347TL, TR, BL, 348–49, 350TR, BL, BR, 351T, 352B, 354–56, 357B, 358–59

Washington *Evening Star*: 216BL, BR, 262, 270, 310TL, 347TC, BR

Zetterstrom, Tom, Washington: frontispiece

Index

Numbers in *italics* refer to picture pages.